READING

THE

ENEMY'S

MIND

READING THE ENEMY'S MIND

Inside Star Gate— America's Psychic Espionage Program

Paul H. Smith

Foreword by Jack Anderson

A TOM DOHERTY ASSOCIATES BOOK | NEW YORK

Book design by Mary A. Wirth

A Forge Book
Published by Tom Doherty Associates, LLC
175 Fifth Avenue
New York, NY 10010

www.tor.com

Forge® is a registered trademark of Tom Doherty Associates, LLC.

Library of Congress Cataloging-in-Publication Data

Smith, Paul H., 1952–
    Reading the enemy's mind : inside Star Gate—America's psychic espionage
program / Paul H. Smith.—1st ed.
        p. cm.
    "A Forge book"—T.p. verso.
    Includes index.
    ISBN 0-312-87515-0
    EAN 978-0312-87515-2
    1. Remote viewing (Parapsychology) 2. Parapsychology—Military aspects—United
States. 3. Military intelligence. 4. Espionage, American. I. Title.
    BF1389.R45S65 2004
    133.8—dc22   2004047211

First Edition: January 2005

Printed in the United States of America

0 9 8 7 6 5 4 3 2 1

To Mabel Mitchell,
my English Forum teacher for four years
and my seminary teacher for two, and her husband,
Andrew J. Mitchell,
my elementary school principal,
who are living proof that teachers really *do* make a difference

Contents

Acknowledgments

Memory is a peculiar thing. We are all sure we can trust it, but it often lets us down right when we need it most. The so-called "witness effect," where several eyewitnesses sometimes remember the same event in vastly different ways, is only one example of memory's flightiness. Many memoirs and first-person accounts of history, whether related to the field of remote viewing or not, have often stumbled because of too much reliance on the author's memories and not enough on the memories of others or on further research.

I owe a debt of gratitude to all those who have helped my own sometimes-poor memory, and they are many. My most heartfelt thanks go to those who spent many hours in allowing me to interview them numerous times. Among these are Harold E. Puthoff, Ph.D., F. Holmes "Skip" Atwater, Col. William P. Johnson, U.S. Army (Ret.), Mel Riley, Gabrielle Pettingell, Jeannie Betters, Gene Lessman, but most especially (and profusely), Dale Graff and Ingo Swann—appropriately so since Dale, with his nineteen-year involvement in nearly every facet of the remote-viewing program, possesses probably the greatest institutional memory (and some of the most thorough contemporaneous notes) of anyone in the field. And Ingo, not just for the many hours he spent with me, but because, in a very literal way, he was the one most responsible for making the story of remote viewing possible.

Of great additional assistance were Col. John B. Alexander, U.S. Army (Ret.), Lieut. Col. Brian Buzby U.S. Army (Ret.), Maj. Gen. Albert N. Stubblebine III, U.S. Army (Ret.), Lieut. Col. Ken Bell, U.S. Army (Ret.), Maj. William G. Ray, U.S. Army (Ret.), Linda Anderson, Fernand Gauvin, Angela Dellafiora Ford, Arthur Hebard, Ph.D., Gregory Seward, Charlene Shufelt, and army psychologist "Jared Schoonover," as well as the still-active operative "John Koda," both of whom requested I use pseudonymns instead of their real names.

The following people aided my project greatly by answering questions, responding to my queries, granting interviews, providing me papers they wrote, and so forth. Russell Targ, Jessica Utts, Ph.D., Bob Andraka, Lyn Buchanan, Jack Houck, Dale Van Atta, Kenneth Kress, Dr. Ed May, Joe McMoneagle, Nancy McMoneagle, Dean Radin, Ph.D., Tom McNear, John Nolan, Ed Dames, Col. Bill Caniano, Dennis Roeding, former U.S. Rep. Charlie Rose (Democrat-North Carolina), Dr. Bill Schul, Stephan Schwartz, Brig. Gen. James Shufelt, U.S. Army (Ret.), and Lieut. Col. Kent Johnson, USAF (Ret.).

I appreciate Juan Salinas, Ph.D., of the psychology department, and Fred Kronz, Ph.D., of the department of philosophy at the University of Texas at Austin for their advice in handling certain technical points in my book, and the late Marcello Truzzi, Ph.D., who provided insights into the skeptical side of the story and guidance with some thorny philosophical issues that arose. Mr. John Taylor, at the National Archives, who at over eighty years of age must be one of the oldest federal employees still working, also deserves recognition for the patient way he fielded all my phone calls about access to Star Gate documents.

Then there were my helpers—people who lent their time, reading, editing skills, and other abilities without which this book would be much less polished than it even is now. Most importantly, my wife and first-line editor, Daryl Gibson. Without her patience, assistance, and merciless pencil this would be a far more bloated book than it has turned out to be. Also lending important help in one or another phases of this project were: Bob Durant, Palyne Gaenir, Rich Krankoski, Shelia Massey, Fran Theis, Gene and Leveda Troy, Skye Turrell, and Cindy Waite, as well as my transcribers, Jamie Conrad, Lisa Worth, Jim Liddle, and Anne Myers.

My thanks also to Robert Knight for great conversation and his beautiful photos—so few of which actually made it into the book.

I also owe a debt of gratitude to my agent, Susan Gleason, to my editor at Forge, Bob Gleason, and to Bob's assistant, Eric Raab, for their enthusiasm for this project.

If I have left anyone out that deserves my thanks, I greatly apologize and assure you it was inadvertent.

No book is ever perfect, and I don't pretend for a moment to think this one is. Though I have tried to correct any I could find, there are no doubt still errors among its pages, for which I as author take sole responsibility.

A note on sources:

This book has profited greatly from the several books mentioned herein, and from the unusual access I had to three safe-drawers full of Star Gate documents that temporarily came my way during the waning months of my military career. I had to turn most of them back when I retired, but unclassified portions of them—plus notes I took—helped greatly in forming a coherent picture of the remote-viewing program as a whole. Now, with the sudden availability of 90,000 pages of Star Gate archives from the CIA, most of those documents—plus many more—are once again available to me and the public.

A few useful books for further reading:

Of books still in print as of this writing, the best place to begin is with Jim Schnabel's *Remote Viewers: The Secret History of America's Psychic Spies* (Dell, 1997).

The rest are in alphabetical order by author:

F. Holmes Atwater, *Captain of My Ship, Master of My Soul* (Hampton Roads Publishing Company, 2001).

Joseph McMoneagle, *Remote Viewing Secrets* (Hampton Roads Publishing Company, 2000).

Joseph McMoneagle, *Mind Trek* (Hampton Roads Publishing Company, 1993; 1997).

Dean Radin, Ph.D., *The Conscious Universe* (Harper San Francisco, 1997).

Charles T. Tart and Harold E. Puthoff, *Mind at Large: Institute of Electrical and Electronics Engineers Symposia on the Nature of Extrasensory Perception* (Hampton Roads Publishing Company, 1979; 2002).

Additional information plus further reading sugggestions is available at my Web site www.rviewer.com, as well as that of the International Remote Viewing Association at www.irva.org.

Foreword

Psychic warfare."

When one of my reporters, Ron McCrae, first brought these words to my attention in late 1980, I intuitively smelled a rat. The United States government was secretly spending tax dollars on something as cockeyed as psychic warfare—straight from the pages of pulp-fantasy magazines, in the same class as hyperspatial howitzers that could fire shells through a time warp or minds that could melt cannon barrels. It was clearly a misuse of money.

Ron uncovered some superficial facts that justified my first skeptical reaction. I duly reported in a series of nationally syndicated columns that the Pentagon was throwing money down a psychic rat hole. I had no inkling that I would follow this bizarre story for a decade and a half, publishing maybe a dozen columns about it over the years and eventually learning that my initial reports were wide of the mark. The United States government was indeed exploring the paranormal as a possible tool to help keep the world safe for democracy, but the tool was not psychic weaponry. It was psychic espionage.

When another reporter on my team, Dale Van Atta, took over the story, he ferreted some startling facts. The Pentagon wanted spies who, armed only with their minds, could find out what our enemies were doing in their most secret and remote places.

We discovered that the Soviets were training psychic agents, too. In fact, they were investing more time, money, and resources on psychic warfare than was our own defense department. I knew the Soviets were about to bust their budget; they were unlikely to invest in wasteful projects.

There were still other things going on that stirred our country. A source not given to lies told us of a missing Soviet reconnaissance plane, recovered by our troops after it was located in the dense African jungle by one of these "remote-viewing" psychics. Jimmy Carter finally confirmed this intelligence coup in 1995, corroborating the journalistic sleuth work we had done more than a decade earlier. We heard that our government psychics had penetrated secret Soviet bases and had picked up details unknown at the time—details later verified by U.S. reconnaissance satellites. And we learned that virtually every major federal intelligence or law enforcement agency, from the National Security Agency and the Central Intelligence Agency to the Federal Bureau of Investigation and the Drug Enforcement Administration, used the psychic spies at one time or another. As evidence filtered in, I was becoming more and more convinced.

And then a coincidence occurred that made a firm believer of even me. Though I didn't know his connections at the time, an Army officer who was one of these psychic spies met and married my managing editor, Daryl Gibson. Daryl kept the secrets of her new husband, Paul H. Smith, knowing that his job could be compromised if I mined him as a source. The most I got out of Major Smith were a few great letters home during the Persian Gulf War, which I used for their color about life in the desert when I wrote *Stormin' Norman*, the bestselling biography of General Norman Schwarzkopf. I realized that Paul could be sitting on some great stories, just because he was an intelligence officer. But I couldn't extract any sensitive information, even after Dale traveled all the way to Saudi Arabia during the war to camp out in the desert in Paul's tent near the Iraqi border.

Imagine my chagrin when, once the military's psychic-warfare program was canceled and declassified by the CIA, a source who knew all about the story I had been chasing for years emerged right from under my nose. I have learned more details since then about the nature of the remote-viewing program. My conclusion: in concept if not always in execution, it was worth the taxpayers' dollars.

The program the CIA now calls Star Gate could have been managed better. It also suffered at the hands of enemies in high places who didn't believe in it. But much of the fault lay with narrow-minded bureaucrats who lacked the imagination to see the potential that lies within the human mind. For fear

of embarrassment they tried to kill the program through neglect and depletion of resources.

Maybe I was at fault for some of that institutional angst. Because remote
viewing was controversial, and because my early columns attacked the idea
of spending defense dollars for something as arcane as "psychic spying,"
some officials were perhaps reluctant to stick with the program. Once I could
see beneath the tip of the iceberg, I changed my tune. But I, at least, learned
my lesson. The demise of Star Gate in 1995 shows that skeptics in high places
never did.

The folly of a few bureaucrats is old news; I've been reporting on such
ineptitude for years. It is the story behind Star Gate that matters now, and the
time is right for one of the insiders to tell that story in a reasoned and tem-
perate way. *Reading the Enemy's Mind* promises to be the definitive work on
the science and mystery of remote viewing, the history behind our government's involvement, and the future role this discipline will play beyond the
walls of the Pentagon.

I can tell from decades of snooping into government secrets that this
book delivers on what it promises.

JACK ANDERSON
Bethesda, Maryland

READING
THE
ENEMY'S
MIND

Army Operations Group

... a commanding
general does a
curious thing...

T he tall, lean man pacing the apron of the stage acted like he owned us,
which at that moment, he did. Major General Albert Stubblebine, III, was
the Commanding General of INSCOM, the U.S. Army Intelligence and
Security Command. And he was here in early 1983 to inspect a small corner
of his worldwide empire, the intelligence school at sleepy Fort Huachuca,
Arizona.

Stubblebine's piercing eyes were search radars probing the audience.
Wherever his gaze landed, soldiers fought the urge to squirm.

I and a few hundred of my comrades in arms were at Fort Huachuca
attending various intelligence courses for officers and NCOs. We had been
assembled at the Post Theater for an afternoon to learn at the great general's
feet, which at that moment were shod in glossy black low-quarter shoes stalking the stage at our eye level. I settled in, expecting the homilies one usually
gets from a major general on a lecture tour. And that's how it began. But it

didn't stay that way for long. As Stubblebine's lecture unfolded, it turned into a most unorthodox military pep talk.

From where I sat, half a dozen rows back, I took stock of the man. By rumor or reputation we all knew of General Stubblebine—"Bert" or "Stub" to his friends, "Stretch" behind his back to some of his fonder subordinates. This was the first time I had seen him in person and he was straight from central casting. His craggy face was set in a dour, no-nonsense grimace, his gruff voice describing new systems, new tactics, and new ideas that would propel military intelligence into the next millennium. My mind wandered away from the millennium to Lee Marvin; Stubblebine could easily have served as the actor's double. Only later did I learn that he was often referred to as "Lee Marvin's brother"—a reference that repeatedly brought scalding rebukes down upon the shoulders of anyone careless enough to mention it within earshot.

Though I no longer remember much of his speech, I do recall that he talked of changes looming on the horizon for military intelligence. In the early 1980s technology was just beginning to dramatically alter the face of the world as we knew it. Stubblebine spoke about the various "INTs" which made up his domain: SIGINT, or signals intelligence—information gleaned from the airwaves when the United States eavesdrops on foreign radio transmissions; HUMINT, or human intelligence—whispered secrets coaxed from the traditional spy lurking in the shadows; and IMINT or imagery intelligence—pictures snapped from satellites or high-flying aircraft.

He emphasized our mission as military intelligence officers; it was our job to provide commanders with the best information available, so they could fight and win on the battlefields of tomorrow. And he gave us a general's advice about how to make successful careers as intelligence officers in the Army of the twenty-first century.

I settled deeper into my seat. This was what I expected from the general who held most of the reins in the military intelligence community. Stubblebine's self-assured, down-to-earth manner was more animated than we were used to from the brass, but any of us could have predicted the main themes and topics he covered. Then he paused, just long enough to signal a change. Sensing that something out of the ordinary was about to happen, I leaned slightly forward in my chair.

"As impressive and amazing as are all the advances we are making through technology," he continued, reaching into the pockets of his dress green uniform, "they cannot compare to the power that lies within our own minds. We only have to learn to tap it." He began tossing small, glinting objects into the audience. "Now I want these back when you're through looking at them," he added nonchalantly.

"It is said," he continued, "that we only use about ten percent of our brains. What would it be like if we could access another five, ten, fifty percent? This is a frontier we are just starting to explore. Some of you now hold in your hands results of the first tentative steps of that exploration."

A low murmur began to build among the officers as the objects were examined and passed from hand to hand. In moments I held some of them in my own fingers. They were pieces of silverware, contorted into shapes that no silverware was meant to take.

Since the age of eleven I had spent my summers as hired help on farms and ranches in the West. I'd worked with tools and heavy machinery, and seen metal of all descriptions bent deliberately or by accident, both mechanically and with heat. But nowhere in my memory banks could I find anything that resembled what had been done to these eating utensils. An eerie feeling washed through me, dredging up from somewhere deep in my subconscious the German word *unheimlich*. What I was holding in my hands was *creepy*.

The tines and stems of the forks were twisted and curled in every direction. Some tines even looped around like pigs' tails. The spoons were buckled, twisted, and spun in tight spirals. My experience told me that metal mistreated like this should have cracked or broken. If great heat had produced these contortions, there would have been evidence of discoloration or fusing. But there was none.

Stubblebine was not finished. "These were bent by me and my staff. But not in any way that you've encountered before. Not by strength. Not with a blowtorch. These were bent by the power of the *mind*." He dragged out the word for emphasis, then paused to let it sink in. "It's something we can all learn to do, even any of you. And if old farts like me and my colonels can do it, I'll be interested to see what you all might accomplish someday."

Without further explanation, he ordered us to pass the silverware back to the stage. Then, suddenly, we were on our feet, standing at attention while the general left. As he disappeared, the auditorium exploded into muted pandemonium.

"What was *that* all about?" demanded one of my comrades.

"I've never seen a general do anything like it before!" snorted another, shaking his head. Others in the group were merely curious, and quizzed each other about what it might mean. From my brief look at the twisted forks and spoons, it was clear to me that unless the general was lying (unlikely), there was something bizarre going on.

Even as Stubblebine was wrapping up his speech I had been puzzling about that silverware. I vaguely remembered something I had read about a "psychic" famous for bending metal objects (it was Uri Geller, though his name wouldn't come to me then). From what I recalled, Geller had been debunked as a fraud and a charlatan, and his metal bending declared counterfeit. At the time I accepted that indictment, based on my own limited experience with the paranormal. For a friend's junior high school science project, I had tried to be psychic and failed. To me as an eighth grader, that meant ESP was probably a fiction.

In the years since Stubblebine's talk I have read or seen attempts by skeptics to debunk this form of psychokinesis, often derisively called "spoon bending." Most of these debunkers see it as a cheap parlor trick. Professional magician and die-hard skeptic James "The Amazing" Randi is fond of demonstrating a trick that he says explains away spoon bending. I have seen Randi do this and, frankly, his results bear little resemblance to what I held in my hands that day.

But no one offered further explanation, and the next morning brought a return to regular lectures and exams on topics as diverse as radio propagation theory, Soviet order of battle, and military law. The deluge of new facts shoved the experience far back into the dusty corners of my mind. There was nothing in the fading memory of Stubblebine's spoons to tell me they foreshadowed events that would change my future utterly. Or that I was soon to become intimate with whatever it was that warped Stubblebine's cutlery, and stranger things besides.

Fort George G. Meade, Maryland, met us with a curiously abandoned feeling as I and my family drove through the front gate on the last day of May, 1983. What set the mood was the empty guard shack. In our moves to a dozen other military installations over the past seven years, there was always a nattily uniformed MP to snap a salute and wave us through. This gate looked as if it hadn't seen an MP in a long while. At a post where some of the Pentagon's biggest secrets were gathered, they had left the front door wide open.

We wound along Mapes Road, which serves jointly as Maryland State Highway 198 and Fort Meade's main drag, past grassy fields and copses of pine and Eastern hardwoods. There seemed to be more parade fields and golf greens than barracks and barbed wire. To the left beyond the trees were the first clues that spy work was afoot—the buildings of the National Security Agency, topped with a jungle of satellite dishes and antennae.

Ft. Meade's sprawl had been gerrymandered by its history. Established during the First World War, the post later became the training base for more than 3.5 million men during the massive mobilization of World War II. Back then, large tracts of land were crammed with temporary wood-frame, clapboard-sided barracks, battalion headquarters, mess halls, and company day rooms housing the thousands of soldiers bound for the fields of war. But many of those buildings, nailed together for just a few years at most, were still there more than four decades after the war. I soon found out that some were even still occupied, ramshackle as they now were.

But the Army was finished with most of the old wooden structures and, a few at a time, they were being razed. As the debris was carted off and the land reseeded, large tracts of vacant real estate were left behind. This gave the place a rural, parklike feel, smack in the middle of the Baltimore-Washington corridor. I didn't know it yet, but one of those beat-up old splinter-palaces was soon to become my official home for the next seven years.

I had been assigned to the post in what amounted to a lucky fluke. Less than a year before, in the early summer of 1982, I was a lieutenant in Germany, serving as the strategic intelligence officer for the Special Forces unit stationed in the quaint little city of Bad Tölz. Snuggled at the foot of the Bavarian Alps, the town overlooked the Isar River as it rushed down from the mountains on its way to the Rhine.

My allotted three years in Germany were almost up, and I hated to leave such an idyllic posting. But the Army insisted I move on. My previous transfers, prior to attending officer candidate school, had been as an enlisted soldier, and I was always told when to be where, with little say in the matter. So on this, my first reassignment after a tour of duty as an officer, I was pleased to find that the assignments people at Military Intelligence Branch were willing to listen to my preferences. They even said I had a good chance at getting my first or second choice, as long as I didn't ask for anything too exotic.

Armed with this information, I consulted my wife Betti, who was also pleased to have a say in her fate. "What about Washington, D.C.?" she asked immediately. Betti wanted to go to graduate school for social work, and had heard that there were some top-ranked programs in the area, so D.C. seemed like a good choice.

I considered it. Many Army officers try to avoid Washington, with its stifling bureaucracy and miles of grey, institutional corridors. Eventually, most career officers end up there for at least one tour of duty. But lieutenants and captains usually try their best to avoid the seat of power so they can "stay with the troops."

It was a little different for intelligence officers, since there were many jobs in and around the District of Columbia that could boost their careers. Perhaps there was a Middle East analyst position open. I had a degree in Middle Eastern studies, had been trained as an Arabic linguist, and had ambitions of becoming a Mid-eastern foreign area specialist. So the decision seemed obvious enough.

I called my assignments officer and asked to be sent to Arlington Hall

Station in the Virginia suburbs, just down Highway 50 from the Pentagon. A former girls' boarding school, Arlington Hall was headquarters for the Army's Intelligence and Security Command, INSCOM. My assignments officer checked and reported back to me with some surprise that Arlington Hall had no openings whatsoever for lieutenants or captains, let alone anything related to the Middle East. "Call me back weekly and we'll see what turns up," he said. For two months the phone calls turned up exactly nothing. The time for a decision was fast approaching, and we were forced to consider alternatives. There was the Pentagon, but it was unlikely that a junior captain, as I would be after my imminent promotion, could find anything more interesting there than paper pushing. Nearby Fort Belvoir in Virginia was then an engineer post, and an unlikely possibility for me. I was running out of options to work in the shadow of Capitol Hill.

Then an intelligence sergeant from another unit came by my office on the top floor of Flint Kaserne for a meeting. I no longer remember his name, just how his plain olive drab fatigues contrasted sharply with the camouflaged jungle uniforms all the Special Forces troops wore. Our business finished, we lapsed into casual conversation, comparing notes and careers. I explained my assignment quandary and complained about the lack of jobs in a city otherwise crawling with soldiers.

"What about Fort Meade?" he wanted to know.

I had dismissed Meade as a possibility, thinking it was too far from Washington. Plus, the only assignment options I knew of there were at the National Security Agency, which specialized in signals intelligence. I had no interest in spending my days in a windowless concrete building full of headphone-wearing linguists as they eavesdropped on the usually boring gossip of the rest of the world. I had already had my fill of that line of work as an enlisted linguist and electronic warfare specialist. From what I'd heard, NSA jobs were mind-numbing, and officers who ended up there were "stove-piped" into signals intelligence—typecast for the life of their careers. Much of this turned out to be mistaken, but it was enough to discourage me at the time.

"Fort Meade is probably the best-kept secret in the D.C. area," my new friend told me. "It's the closest you can get to country living anywhere near the city. It's only about half an hour outside the District, and Meade itself is more like a park than a military post. It's one of the best places in the area to have a family—safe and uncrowded."

"No way do I want to work for NSA," I said.

"Oh, there are lots of other options. The 902nd MI Group for one, Ops Group, and also First Army. Other, smaller intel units are scattered around post, too." I'd only heard of the 902nd, but the others also sounded promising.

As soon as time zones between Germany and the U.S. meshed during office hours, I called Military Intelligence Branch and suggested Fort Meade.

"That's possible. I'll check. Call you back next week." But I didn't have to wait that long. The very next day the phone rang. "Hey, Lt. Smith—have I got a deal for you. Would you like to be a Mideast analyst with the 902nd MI Group? I have the requisition sitting right here on my desk."

Only weeks later we were leaving for Fort Meade, but detouring first for six months of temporary duty at Fort Huachuca for the Military Intelligence Officer Advanced Course. No doubt it was just happenstance but, looking back years later, the way I ended up at Fort Meade now seems to have a whiff of fate about it.

And now, finally, here we were at Meade. I was still destined for a Mideast-related job, but the unit assignment had changed. Instead of the 902nd MI, I was headed for something called the U.S. Army Operations Group—which everyone abbreviated as "Ops Group"—a HUMINT unit. This was where the bosses of the Army's real cloak-and-dagger spies made their home.

But before I signed in for my new job, I first had to see about finding a place for my family to live. After backtracking and wandering around the tree-lined streets, we finally came upon the post's housing office—and ran into our first problem. There was a several-month wait for a family of five with a dog.

I had a week of leave coming to me before I had to sign in to my new unit, so after some head scratching, we added our names to the waiting list, put the problem on the back burner, and headed south to visit Betti's sister and brother-in-law, Virginia and John McCaughan in Norfolk, where they had settled in for a Navy career. The McCaughan's offered a more welcoming harbor than the Fort Meade guest house, where you had to share a toilet with strangers.

John and Virginia were warm hosts, but Betti's sister had always had what I thought of at the time as quirks. We found her as entrenched as ever in what I considered paranormal "hocus-pocus." Esoteric-looking books by obscure authors such as Ruth Montgomery, Lobsang Rampa, and Jane Roberts were wedged in her bookshelves. Virginia often talked about premonitions she claimed to have had. When we were visiting six years before, she had told us of how she "knew" of the 1963 sinking of the nuclear submarine USS *Thresher* before it ever made the news. She also claimed she "knew" to the moment when her late brother Joe had his legs blown off in Vietnam. And she frequently told us about strange and arcane things she found in the various books she devoured. I was dubious, particularly when I noticed her fondness for tabloid scandal sheets. But I tried to be polite, and even pretended to listen, just to make her happy.

Abruptly, a phone call from the Fort Meade housing office cut our leisure short. "We have some quarters for you. Be here as soon as you can."

Buckner Avenue was a quiet, shady street bordered by some of the oldest permanent quarters on the post. They were two-story red-brick townhouses dating from 1950. Fortunately, ours had just been renovated, which accounted for its sudden availability. Best of all, the townhouses had full basements—the only junior officers' quarters on the entire post to have them. The third bedroom was hardly more than a closet, but with the basement we could make it work.

Our unit was second from the end. Occupying the very last row house was Fred Atwater, with his wife Joan, daughter Shelly, and sons Freddy and Jimmie. Fred was definitely not government issue. He never wore anything but civilian clothes, he never talked about his job and, though his door bore the modest placard CPT F. HOLMES ATWATER, he seldom otherwise directly admitted to being in the military. Of course we all knew he had to be, since only military personnel were allowed to live on an Army post.

Across the street lived Tom and Faye McNear, with their three children. Tom never wore a uniform either, and in fact sported a very un-military, but neatly trimmed beard. His door also declared he was a captain. When asked about his hirsute look, all he would say was, "It's my cover."

A few days after moving into our new quarters, I pulled on my dress-green uniform and walked up the steps of Nathan Hale Hall to report for my new assignment. Named after America's first famous patriotic spy, of Revolutionary War fame ("I only regret that I have but one life to lose for my country"), the hall was made of aged and imposing red brick with a drive-through archway leading to parking behind the building.

After passing through the cipher-locked door on the fourth floor, I soon learned that my immediate boss was to be Dennis Roeding, a retired Army human intelligence officer, and that I would share an office with an affably cynical coworker named Ron Kloet. My sponsor was Captain David Hoover, who shepherded me around Ops Group headquarters for the first few days while I learned the ropes.

The ropes, as it turned out, were pretty mundane. Ours was essentially a bookkeeping job. We maintained a rank of five-drawer safes standing along the walls of our dingy office. Filed inside the safes were reams of documents describing and categorizing the various questions for which our "customers" in the intelligence community needed answers. These questions were posed as "collection requirements." A collection requirement might request information about opposition leaders in the Middle East; or perhaps troop movements that could threaten U.S. interests; or even foreign tinkering with technologies that could have military uses. There were any number of topics that interested the nation's decision makers—and, therefore, the U.S. intelligence community.

In the course of snooping around in foreign countries where they were assigned, American spies would ferret out anything they could find that seemed valuable. They would then write this information into reports—IIRs, we called them, for "intelligence information reports"—which they forwarded through their secret channels.

En route, the IIRs passed through our office. These reports were the raw data of the HUMINT business. They had to be examined, analyzed, and compared with other reports, as well as with data from other intelligence sources, before the information could be determined to be useful "fact" or not. But that part was not our job.

We were only responsible for reading, then matching up each IIR with the collection requirements it most closely met. It was then passed on to whichever agency had asked for the information.

It was an essential, even vital, job, but it was empty of any of the glamor or excitement that people usually associate with espionage. Reality was very different from James Bond; I was stuck in the bureaucratic soup in which eighty percent of all intelligence work is done. Still, even if this was not the hands-on position I had been hoping for, it was at least *related* to the Middle East and would do until other opportunities, whatever they might be, came along.

Though tedious, the work itself was at first a little daunting. I have a few talents, but being a bureaucrat was never one of them. Organized, meticulous record keeping and cross-referencing was a challenge. In retrospect, it was a good apprenticeship for more complex and sometimes managerially hostile job environments in the future.

And Ops Group had an important mission. The headquarters where I worked was the main office for much of the Army's active HUMINT collection effort. Officers and civilians assigned to Ops Group were always going and coming from exotic places around the world, or sitting in on high-level meetings with counterparts from the CIA, Defense Intelligence Agency, State Department, or the other military services. Often when a phone rang, the call came from some other continent. The success or failure of U.S. spy efforts around the globe depended on the policies, guidance, and coordination we provided.

Ops Group's headquarters oversaw lower-level organizations that "handled" the case officers—government civilians and military personnel who were assigned in turn to "handle" the agents (or "assets," as they are officially known) that were our human eyes and ears in places where Americans could not easily tread. A case officer friend of mine once summed up his job by saying, "Our task is simple: we try to persuade foreigners to betray their countries." Back then, during the days of the Soviet "Evil Empire," the foreigners who "betrayed their countries" to supply us with crucial inside information often did it altruistically. They believed that helping the United States would eventually benefit their own countrymen suffering under repressive regimes. Friends of mine who are still in the HUMINT business tell me that since the fall of the Iron Curtain things have changed considerably. These days, money speaks louder than either ideology or altruism.

But there was more going on at Ops Group headquarters than I imagined. Sometime in late June or early July 1983, I again encountered General Stubblebine's spoons.

2

Tour Guide to the Twilight Zone

...forebodings of the future...

I was going through the process of learning, then forgetting, then relearning the names of the score or more new faces that came and went on a daily basis in the Ops Group headquarters. One of the names that stuck was John Nolan, a gregarious and sometimes flamboyant warrant officer. John was a fellow Mormon, so I saw him at church as well as work. He hadn't let chronic injuries from being shot down in a helicopter in Vietnam distract him from building a colorful career. A born spook, he took to his assignment at Ops Group zestfully, without explaining to me just what that assignment was. He got a kick out of a verbal cat-and-mouse game played whenever I or other rookies in the headquarters asked him what he was up to.

"If I told you, I'd have to kill you!" he'd remark with a wink. Or, "I spend a lot of time not being here." I noted some nonmilitary books that he kept around his desk—*A Course in Miracles*, *Journeys Out of the Body*, and *Frogs into*

Princes. I picked up the latter, expecting a fairy tale, and found instead a primer on neurolinguistic programming, a term completely new to me.

One day I told Ron Kloet, "I don't get the name plate on John Nolan's desk, the one that says 'Carmine J. Tizzio.' Is it a joke or something?"

"I suppose so, in a way. It's a sort of nom de guerre he uses for certain, um, *projects* he's involved in. 'Tizzio' comes from a nickname he acquired around here: 'TZO.' "

"TZO?"

"Yeah. It stands for 'Twilight Zone Officer.' But you'll have to ask *him* what it's all about. I'm not sure I ought to explain it. Or whether I even *could*."

But John was not immediately available, and I was soon distracted by other things. It didn't matter. The mystery soon started to sort itself out.

Through bits and pieces I either observed or heard around the office over the next several days, I was able to put together the outlines of an intriguing picture. It seemed that a small group of people borrowed from various parts of INSCOM had the ongoing mission of combing through all the human-potential tinkering that was going on around the country. They were looking into hypnosis, neurolinguistic programming, sleep discipline, biofeedback, Silva Mind Control, and other methods—conventional and unconventional— for boosting organizational efficiency and promoting individual growth. John was Ops Group's liaison to the mission.

The project, called "INSCOM Beyond Excellence," was chartered to evaluate all these emerging "human technologies" to see what use they might have for Army intelligence. Ops Group had been chosen as the test bed to see how or if any of these novel techniques could work in the field, using real intelligence operatives and real soldiers in practical situations. Since Nolan was mixed up in what was, by Army standards, a very strange undertaking, and since there was no official title in soldier parlance to fit what he did, and because some of the areas he dabbled in were considered more than a little over the edge, John Nolan became known as the Twilight Zone Officer, or TZO. And, of course, any spy worth his salt has a cover name. John decided "Tizzio" had the proper ring to it.

Most of what I learned wasn't strictly classified. But I came to realize that the project was still considered hush-hush; largely, I surmised, because it was so out of character for a project of this nature to exist in a no-nonsense Army.

When I finally approached Nolan with my pieced-together puzzle, he laughed and told me that I had only scratched the surface; there were things going on that I hadn't begun to imagine. Since I was getting used to the circular language and veiled innuendo that are the espionage equivalent of "marking one's territory," I took this with a grain of salt. John could see I was doubtful. "Let me show you something," he said, rummaging around in his desk.

What he came up with got my attention. "Ever seen this kind of thing before?" he said, pointing at a drawer full of bent silverware.

I prodded a couple of spoons with my forefinger. "Uh-huh. Stubblebine had some like this when he came out to speak to my MI Officer Advanced Course at Huachuca. But he didn't explain much about how they got this way."

"Well—*imagine* my surprise!" John chortled in the humor-with-a-dash-of-irony tone that I came to know well over the years. "Those were probably bent by him and his staff."

"Yes, that's what he said."

"Okay. Some of these were, too. But most of them—especially the best ones—were done by average soldiers, spouses, and their kids."

John told me more. All these bent eating utensils represented a form of psychokinesis, or mind over matter. I came to know it as "macro-PK" because the results were substantial; you could see them with the naked eye and hold them in your hands. It had a close relative, called "micro-PK," which involved mentally influencing things you *couldn't* see such as electrons, microcircuits, computer chips.

Large-scale "macro" PK, levitating a piano for example, had been reported, but John himself had not seen PK on that scale, nor was it frequently, if ever, observed in the lab. But metal bending was apparently getting to be quite common, certainly among those who hung out with Bert Stubblebine, and reportedly among many people elsewhere around the country who were unconnected with the military.

It turned out that the spoon-bending psychic, Uri Geller, wasn't the only one besides Stubblebine and his staff who claimed to bend metal objects. An engineer in California by the name of Jack Houck, whose day job was working for a major defense contractor, had turned metal bending into a sort of populist crusade. In the past few years, Houck had been hosting what he called "PK" parties, in which he would gather numbers of ordinary folks together in various settings, dump a bunch of silverware in the middle of the floor, and proceed to teach the attendees how to turn these utilitarian chunks of metal into objets d'art using only the power of their minds.[1]

In truth, there was more to it than that. Houck's methods involved a number of subtle psychological strategies, employed some guided imagery, and in the "beginner" stage allowed novices to keep the fingers of both hands on the implement they were attempting to bend.

According to Houck, normal folks have subconscious inhibitions against wantonly damaging an item that could otherwise still serve its intended function. They would be reluctant to destroy perfectly good spoons and forks. So Houck would spill the silverware out onto the floor, then kick and prod the pile with his shoe, emphasizing that these were worthless implements.

He would then have each trainee pick a utensil from the heap, grasp the ends of it with the fingers of both hands and lightly stroke a selected portion while creating a point of concentration in their minds. They were to focus intently on this point until it almost hurt to concentrate so hard. They were then to imagine passing that sensation down through arm, hand, and finally thumb or finger into the utensil. At a certain stage in the process, the trainees were taught to recognize a sensation of tackiness or warmth in the metal, which was the signal that the fork or spoon was "ready" to bend.

The technique echoed the guided imagery that innovative doctors sometimes recommend to cancer patients to mobilize the body's immune system. Houck surmised that people could thus subconsciously activate reservoirs of mental power or energy that would allow them to perform this seemingly magical feat. And he seemed to be right. His subjects twisted and contorted their cutlery with a surprising frequency, which he documented. Word of Houck's metal-bending parties spread until it reached certain ears in Washington.

As part of Stubblebine's INSCOM Beyond Excellence program, the general had created a staff agency called the Advanced Human Technology Office. Its chief was John Alexander, a lieutenant colonel with an unusual background. An infantry officer and veteran of the Vietnam War, where he served as a Green Beret, he also had earned a Ph.D. in Education from Walden University and had a strong interest in near-death experiences.

He was known in the military as the author of a journal article called "The New Mental Battlefield," an exploration of possible uses for psychic skills and other leading-edge techniques on the battlefield of the future. To the astonishment of many of the Army's brass, the article became the cover story for the normally staid *Military Review*, the official journal of Fort Leavenworth's Command and General Staff College. The Army major who edited the publication had lived through a near-death experience of his own, and as a result was open to possibilities that most of his peers would likely have rejected. He decided that Alexander's article merited top billing in the December 1980 edition of the publication.[2]

An INSCOM staff officer by 1982, Alexander had heard rumors about Houck's work. When he learned in early 1983 that Houck was coming to Washington, Alexander arranged a metal-bending party at his apartment in the Virginia suburbs. Stubblebine and other officers were among those attending, as was parapsychology researcher Andrija Puharich. Houck soon had the guests bending metal at the "kindergarten" stage. This was the elementary level that involved holding the utensil in both hands.

In an article Alexander wrote years later about the experience, he acknowledged that under those circumstances "self-delusion was very possible," but that it did "seem like the metal was softening" because of the intense mental focus of the people holding it.[3]

When Alexander's party guests finished "kindergarten," Houck moved them on to "graduate school." He told everyone to hold two forks by their bases, one in each hand. That way no one could force the metal by sheer muscle power. As Alexander tells it, he and Stubblebine were sitting near reputed psychic Anne Gehman. Both men watched as one of the forks she was holding unmistakably arched into a ninety-degree bend. Gehman had been momentarily distracted by something else going on in the room, and didn't see her own fork changing shape. "At that instant," Alexander said, "General Stubblebine and I knew for sure that the stories and reports we had heard about the potential application of psychokinesis were, in fact, true."[4]

Alexander learned how to lead the PK exercise himself, and sponsored more parties. The majority of his guests had no prior experience with anything paranormal. Yet, when their spoons began twisting spontaneously, the skeptics and agnostics began to take notice. "It was sufficient to get people very excited," Alexander wrote.

Still, he worried about the possibility of bogus "bendings," so he invited magician Doug Henning to one party to demonstrate how sleight of hand could mimic authentic PK results.

At another party, a skeptical lieutenant colonel had advanced to the "graduate" level, and was holding his two forks upright by the ends of their handles as instructed. One of the forks suddenly drooped at a right angle. As everyone in the room watched, the fork then straightened itself upright, then bent again at ninety degrees, then bent back to stop permanently at a forty-five-degree angle. The colonel was not amused.

"*Damn* I wish that hadn't happened," he said. He gingerly placed the offending fork on the table and stepped away.[5]

Houck and others wrote a number of scientific papers on metallurgical analysis of metal that had been bent. Houck began using the term "warm forming" to divorce it from the sensationalism that surrounded such terms as "PK" and "spoon bending." One paper reported the analysis of pieces of metal that had been bent using heat, mechanical force, or warm forming. Cross sections of each piece were examined microscopically to determine what if any differences were discernible between them. As expected, the sample bent by mechanical force had tiny cracks in its structure. The one that had been deformed by extreme heat showed fusing and melting of the crystalline structure. But the metal that had been bent by warm forming reportedly looked at the microscopic level as if had been manufactured that way. There were no detectable defects. Convincing photographs taken through electron microscopes illustrated the article.[6]

I didn't learn all this detail from John Nolan when he opened his desk drawer to me that day, but I heard enough to pique my curiosity. Nolan told me he was often sent on temporary duty to Munich, Germany, where INSCOM's 66th MI Group was headquartered, as well as to other places around Europe and the Far East, to check on the state of training and look for ways to use promising, unconventional methods in the field. One of his routines on these trips was to introduce soldiers to metal bending, employing the techniques he had learned from Alexander and Houck.

As mentioned above, Nolan and his bosses figured that even if psychic metal bending turned out not to have any practical use, it still might help INSCOM intelligence personnel break out of linear thought patterns and comfortable mental ruts, motivating them to think more "outside the box."

Metal bending caught on among the troops with a fervor even Nolan hadn't expected. Soldiers would bring their families to his presentations. It reached a point that when local INSCOM communities heard John Nolan was on his way for another visit, they would gather to meet him bearing their latest metallic triumphs.

He had thereby acquired plenty of twisted spoons and forks. While each one was different, there were only so many ways an eating implement could be contorted in three-dimensional space. There were many spoons and forks with handles rolled up into tight spirals; forks with tines splayed; utensils with handles curved into graceful loops; spoons with their bowls folded in half, and combinations thereof.

There were a couple of items in Nolan's collection he was especially fond of. One was a fork, the tines of which had not been bent but spiraled along their axes like decorative wrought-iron railings on a staircase. A teenager from one of the military families stationed in Germany had seized each tine by its tip and twisted it. This was not a matter of strength. It would be hard to believe that even the strongest person could do something like that merely with his fingers.

Another of his favorites was a table knife, the blade of which a different teenager had bent at a ninety-degree angle from its grip. Each half of the knife was as straight as an arrow, with none of the bowing one would expect if the feat had been accomplished by mechanical or muscle power.

Of course, what I was hearing and examining was all anecdotal. I had not yet seen it done. Still, while it might not have qualified as rigorous science, it was certainly thought-provoking. And if what I was hearing turned out to be true, the implications were obvious, even though at this point the phenomenon had not progressed beyond the parlor game stage. Little did I realize then that this metal-bending magic was but an hors d'oeuvre. The main course was yet to come.

3

Recruitment

Buckner Avenue on Fort Meade leads under tall oaks and sycamores, between two rows of identical, two-story, rust-brick townhouses where captains and lieutenants live with their families. This was Gerraghty Village, our home for the next seven years.

While I was getting acclimated to my new job at Ops Group headquarters, my family was settling into the little Gerraghty Village community. There were thirty-two families in the four sets of townhouses, more than enough to fill the street and the yards with shouting, tumbling children. My kids soon had playmates on all sides. Betti connected with a number of the mothers, and I was on friendly terms with Tom McNear, across the street, and Fred Atwater next door. Even our dog, Dusty, had a playmate in Atwaters' black lab, Ranger. The two cavorted in the wide, grassy fields that stretched out behind and to the sides of our military quarters.

Living in a neighborhood where one or both spouses worked for either the National Security Agency, Army counterintelligence, or any of a dozen other secret agencies, often made for interesting conversations. Some of the adults on the block wouldn't even admit they worked for an intelligence agency. "Uh,

I'm an employee of the federal government," was the most you could get out of them. Others could say who they worked for, but were coy about what they did. Having spent half the past decade involved in the security and intelligence field, I didn't notice these little quirks anymore; they came with the territory.

But a few things happened that went beyond what I was used to, striking me as singular. One I have already mentioned—that Army captains Fred and Tom both dressed exclusively in casual clothes, mostly jeans and open-collared shirts, and that Tom had a beard. Everyone else who was authorized civvies as "duty uniform" still had to be clean-shaven and wear at least a tie and sport coat.

During nice weather people on the block would often host informal back-yard parties. We frequently entertained with the McNears. Betti and Faye had become friends, and Tom was not only hospitable but intriguing as well. We discovered he had a complete picture-framing shop in his basement and was also an avid builder of wooden boat models. After work he taught me some of the tricks of the picture-framing trade, and Betti tried her hand at making a lobster trap for a small-scale model of a Grand Banks dory that Tom was building.

One of the McNears' parties was the setting for a minor incident that I found puzzling at the time, and significant later on. The Atwaters were also invited to the party, which included the steaming of a bushel of Maryland blue crabs in the McNear's backyard. It was to be my first taste of this Chesa-peake Bay specialty. What with the work required to salvage the little meat the creatures harbored, and the yellow-green ooze that dripped out as they were shelled, I found I didn't much care for this Maryland delicacy.

Sometime during the get-together I sidled up to Tom and, after a few pleasantries, asked point blank if his beard was necessary for his assignment. Since I was always looking for interesting future assignments, and Tom seemed to be in one, I was hoping to find out what sort of intelligence work he did.

"People aren't supposed to know I work for the Army," said Tom in response to my question, a sparkle in his eye. "With this, they never suspect a thing."

"I suppose so. But what can you tell me about what you actually do? I might like to try it myself someday."

"I'm a spy," he teased.

"So are half the people on Fort Meade." I cracked pieces of exoskeleton from the crab claw I was trying hard to eat. It dripped on my shirt.

"Sorry. If I told you, I'd have to kill you." I had heard this remark far too many times by now, but something about the way Tom said it made me laugh anyway.

"You can at least tell me if it's SIGINT, HUMINT, or IMINT," I said, referring to the three disciplines which back then categorized nearly the entire intelligence community. "*That* shouldn't give anything away!" He looked perplexed by this, as if unsure how to answer.

"Uh, actually it's none of those!" he said, finally. Now it was my turn to be perplexed. According to everything I'd learned in the Army, there *wasn't* any other category. Fred had come over during the course of the conversation, and now stood beside us. I saw Tom shoot him an amused look. I decided to try a different tack. "Okay, how about travel? Do you travel a lot?" In those days, I thought traveling around the world on government business would be great fun.

Tom thought for a moment. "Mmmm . . . you *could* say that, I suppose . . ." I wasn't sure, but I thought I heard a stifled snicker from Fred.

"Okay," I went on. "Do you travel just here in the States, or overseas as well?" No, I wasn't mistaken; Fred had snickered again.

"Well, *both* in a manner of speaking," Tom answered, and smiled a little to himself. I turned to Skip. "*You* know what he's talking about, *don't* you!"

"Fred and I work in the same office," said Tom quickly. I think he could tell I was growing a little peeved by this cat-and-mouse conversation and the humor at my expense. "Look," he said. "I'm sorry. We really can't tell you much more than that. Maybe some other time, if you have need-to-know and reason to be read-on. We work in a SAP [a special access program] which means that, because of its sensitivity, only about a hundred people in the entire country know about us." He paused for a pregnant moment. "Believe me, I'd *love* to tell you if I could."

It was clear that this part of the conversation was over. I was disconcerted. It was unusual that an Army intelligence officer could say *nothing at all* about his duties, even if only in the clipped jargon and acronyms that were our lingua franca. We went on to talk about other, safer things, but I was left wondering what Tom and Fred could be up to that involved none of the standard intelligence disciplines, but did involve travel—"*sort of.*"

A couple of weeks passed before the next puzzling encounter. It was trivial, but left me even more convinced that there was something more going on than met the eye. Tom and Fred were at my quarters and noticed a large pen-and-ink drawing I had made of a cat stalking a monarch butterfly. I'd used a stippling technique learned years before when I worked as a botanical illustrator at Brigham Young University. The drawing contained no lines; it was built with nothing but thousands of tiny ink dots applied with a fine-tipped technical drawing pen.

Tom and Fred stopped abruptly in front of the picture and examined it. I thought they must be impressed with my work. "Trackers," Tom said under his breath, and Fred nodded.

"Do you like it?" I asked, hoping to hear what this cryptic exchange had been all about.

"Uh—oh, yes!" they both said, but in a tone that didn't sound much like art appreciation. What it was instead, I couldn't quite tell. But without me having an inkling at the time, this was the incident that triggered my entree into their secret world.

Four or five days later, Tom stopped by and asked me if I was still interested in finding out what it was he did. When I said yes, he asked if I might even be interested in being evaluated for the highly secret program. I was a little less eager about this. How do you decide if you want to be evaluated for a program that you are not even allowed to know about? Tom assured me that I wouldn't have to commit to anything blindly, so I agreed.

The evaluation turned out to be a series of tests and an interview by the INSCOM staff psychologist, Lieutenant Colonel (Dr.) Dick Hartzell. Two of the tests would be familiar to most psychologists: the Meyers-Briggs Type Indicator, and the Minnesota Multiphasic Personality Inventory. Both were personality tests, designed to assess how one might deal with life situations, and relate to the world and to other people. There was also an assessment titled "Profile of Adaptation to Life," and something called the "Herrmann Participant Survey Form," which asked questions about "handedness," "energy level," and hobbies, as well as other questions to evaluate personality traits. An additional test, the INSCOM Factors Questionnaire, required the person to decide on a scale how he or she identified with certain personality characteristics described in short paragraphs.

For example, on one side of the scale might be a paragraph starting with "Socially cautious; often cool and distant in relationships with others; avoids small talk; tends to be blunt and direct in thinking and action." At the other end of the scale would be, "Socially participating; usually friendly and warmhearted; outgoing and socially relaxed." The subject had to circle a number from one to seven indicating which paragraph most closely described her or him. Wishy-washy answers in the middle of the scale were discounted, though the candidate wasn't told that. I found out later that Hartzell had designed the test to pinpoint people who were "most like" those who had been successful in using the skills needed in the mysterious program to which Tom and Fred belonged.

I had found Dr. Hartzell charming and easy to talk to, and the exercise had been interesting. Anxious to see how I had scored on the tests, I was also nagged by curiosity about just what this "special access program"—this "SAP"—was all about.

Then, one day the following week, Tom gave me a call. "You made the cut," he said in his usual laconic tone. "Friday we'll read you on, assuming you're still willing."

If you continue along Buckner Avenue past our quarters, the street doglegs once to the right, crosses the corner of a grassy field, and passes through another cluster of residences, this time the single-family houses in which the sergeants-major live. The trees here are even taller, and their branches form a canopy across the street that offers a pleasant, shady tunnel through which to escape the sun in the summer. The street ducks out from under the trees just in time to dead-end into Llewellyn Avenue, along which lie Kimborough Army Hospital and the NCO club.

Along Llewellyn and just down the street from the hospital is a short lane, which abruptly ends in grass, weeds, and crumbled asphalt among a sparse copse of oaks. The trees are all that remain since November 1996, when Army bulldozers obliterated the last trace of the two peeling old buildings that once housed INSCOM's Center Lane Program and its later incarnations.

As I turned down that lane in August 1983, it was longer, stretching perhaps 150 yards to the north, and led to what had once been a World War II training battalion's cantonment area. To the left was the old mess hall and on the right the administration building, each a single story high. Beyond them were six or eight two-story wood-frame barracks buildings, spaced evenly on either side of the lane. The barracks had been abandoned for years. Window glass was missing or in shards, and here and there an old roller blind drooped back into a weather-stained room or stirred carelessly with any random breeze. Doors where anxious recruits once stood fire watch during the graveyard hours were now hanging off their hinges or missing. The tongue-and-groove siding that clad the sagging buildings was splintered and grey with age. Those wooden skeletons imbued their surroundings with a melancholy that gnawed at me, even in the moist brilliance of a Maryland summer afternoon.

The old mess hall and administration building were still in use, if now for different purposes, and hence in better shape. They were the dirty lime green then in vogue for wooden Army buildings. I looked for the building number on the former mess hall. T-2651. This was the right place. Stepping onto the porch, I knocked on the green door, just above a five-position cipher lock. Within a few moments a short, stocky woman swung the door open.

"Hi, I'm supposed to meet Tom McNear here . . . ?" I said, a little uncertainly.

"Come *on* in," she said with a smile, emphasizing the "on," then barked over her shoulder, "Tommy, your appointment's here!" I just had time to see a row of about a dozen five-drawer safes lined up along one wall, and to glimpse, stretching along the opposite wall, a mural perhaps fifteen feet long and five feet high that depicted . . . well, that depicted outer space. This was certainly not a typical Army unit. And I thought it had felt eerie *out*side.

Tom met me a few steps over the threshold, and led me to the backmost room in the building. A handful of people at desks scattered around the long common area looked at me curiously, and I returned their glances. Some of them said hello as I passed.

I took a seat across from Tom at a long, brown wooden table that showed the scars of having been too many times through the Army's supply system. He slid a sheet of paper over to me, along the top of which was printed in capital letters: PROJECT CENTER LANE SECURITY INDOCTRINATION AND BRIEFING STATEMENT. "Here. You have to sign this nondisclosure statement and I have to read you on before I can tell you any more." I scribbled down my name and the date.

"Allll*right*." Tom said, almost exhaling the last half of the word as a transition into what came next. He reached for a sheet of paper on which some notes were typed. "I'm required to tell you that assignment to INSCOM's Project Center Lane may not be in the best interest of your military career. We do our best to make sure it has no adverse impact, but you need to be aware that it *is* an unconventional assignment choice, and if you volunteer for the program you may miss other career milestones by choosing it.

"When you are away from Fort Meade, especially while traveling on official business, you may not reveal that you are in the Army, or even associated with the Federal Government. Your family and friends can still know that you are in the military, but you may not share with anyone outside this organization, whether they have a clearance or not, and no matter what their rank, the nature of your assignment or the details of any of your work. Any questions so far?" I shook my head.

"Next, from all we've been able to tell there is no risk of physical or mental injury in our activities here. But what we do involves some unconventional technologies, and you should realize that you embark on this assignment at your own risk. Of course, if there *are* adverse consequences, you will continue to have all the medical resources of the Department of Defense at your disposal."

This point gave me pause.

"There is one other matter," Tom went on. "Because of what we do here, there is always risk that your attitudes or personality might change in some way that could affect your personal relationships. For that reason, you are allowed to tell your wife in general terms what it is you will be involved in, cautioning her of course that speaking of it further to anyone besides you could jeopardize your military career and perhaps even your safety. It goes without saying that you should never discuss details about Center Lane technology or operations with her or with anyone else who does not have a need-to-know, proper clearance, and legitimate access to this SAP." Tom stopped here and looked at me intently. "Do you still want to continue?"

If you have ever seen the movie *Men In Black,* you will have an inkling of how I felt at this point: "What's the catch?" Will Smith asks Tommy Lee Jones as Jones is introducing him to the Men In Black program. "The catch *is* . . ." responds Jones, ". . . the catch *is,* you will sever every human contact. Nobody will ever know you exist. Anywhere. Ever." Then Jones gets up and walks off, turning just before he's out of earshot to add, "I'll give you 'til sunrise to think it over." Fortunately, Center Lane security requirements were not quite as strict as this; I at least got to keep my fingerprints, my clothes, and my general identity.

Nevertheless, this amounted to more secrecy than I'd ever encountered before, even taking into account my involvement with Special Forces operations, which were some of the most sensitive around. But I'd come this far; I might as well go all the way.

"I guess so." I swallowed audibly to quell the flutter in my stomach.

"Our mission is to collect intelligence against foreign threats using . . ." and he hesitated here, as if searching for the right word. "Well . . . parapsychological phenomena. We use a paranormal skill known as 'remote viewing,' which you will be taught. We want to know if you'd be interested in joining the INSCOM Center Lane program and training to become, basically . . . a *psychic spy.*"

4

Reluctant
Warrior

...and there

is no

turning back...

Much of my life I had been a reluctant warrior. Born in Oregon, I was just turning three in 1955 when my parents moved me and my younger brothers, Kevin and Jeff, to Boulder City, Nevada. Boulder was a small town in the desert, originally built to house workers building Hoover Dam in nearby Black Canyon. All the years of my growing up, Boulder City retained the proud motto "Best Little Town by a Damsite!"

Some of my most formative experiences came during summers spent working dawn to well after dusk on ranches and farms in Wyoming and Idaho. I didn't leap eagerly at the chance for doing such grueling, if ostensibly character-building work. When I was eleven, I just happened to answer "Yes," since nothing else occurred to me when my parents proposed leaving me for a month with relatives who owned a farm on the Wyoming-Idaho border. Nearly every summer from then until I was done with college was spent fixing fences, driving tractors, milking cows, bucking hay bales, and fishing for trout in the Rockies, because that suited me better than hanging around during the hot season in a sun-baked Nevada town.

I ended up married to my first wife in haphazard, if inevitable fashion. At the end of my junior year in college, I needed a ride home from Brigham Young University. Her name was Betti, and she had just graduated from BYU. She needed someone to drive her father's stick-shift Chevy pickup loaded down with all her possessions. We discovered we both were headed to the Las Vegas area, so the solution seemed easy. I got a free ride and she got a driver. But on that trip Betti and I got much better acquainted than either of us had expected. Thanks to an intermittently clogged fuel filter, what should have been a routine eight-hour trip took an exhausting sixteen hours that often found us driving south at thirty mph on US 89 through the spectacular, if rather vacant, middle of Utah. We finally arrived at her parents' home. But after ferrying me from Las Vegas out to Boulder City in her mother's car at well after 2 A.M., Betti ended up spending the night in my parents' guest room. As she was about to drive back to Las Vegas, we found that her parents' car inexplicably had two flat tires. I swear I had nothing to do with it.

That conjunction of mishaps had repercussions that still rattle my world from time to time. Not only did we start dating seriously, but largely under Betti's influence I decided to serve a two-year mission for my church, something I had refused to consider up to that point. Those two years in Switzerland marked another watershed in my life, introducing me to languages and cultures far different from my own, and making an initial installment of mental and personal discipline that I sorely lacked.

Shortly after I returned from Switzerland in 1976, Betti and I were married—largely at her instigation, me going along because it seemed like I might as well. We spent three months poor and without serious prospects in Provo, Utah. Then she badgered me into enlisting in the Army to become a linguist. At least it was a living. And I could learn Arabic.

As a youngster I had several perennial interests. Ever since I was old enough to remember, I had been fascinated by the military. Through my elementary school years I drew pictures of tanks, planes, and warships. For a Halloween project, my kindergarten teacher insisted that I draw something with a holiday motif instead of my usual military fare. What she got was a battleship with smiling jack-o'-lanterns lining the rails. I built plastic models of military equipment, and played Army with an ardor other kids reserve for sports. At the height of the Vietnam War, I fell under the spell of the Special Forces, and was probably the only kid among the generally antiwar student body of Boulder City High School to have his own copy of Sergeant Barry Sadler's album, *Ballad of the Green Berets*.

I was also fascinated by science fiction. I devoured the old standbys—

Heinlein, Asimov, Clarke, Blish, Ellison, Bradbury, Zelazny—but Andre Norton's telepathic beasts in particular drew my attention, and I loved Zenna Henderson's stories of the People, with their psychic powers.

Sometime during the same period, with the huge popularity of James Bond, the Man from U.N.C.L.E., and other fictional secret agents I, like others of my peers, developed a hankering for the romance and adventure of espionage. I read books about spies and made stacks of drawings of fanciful secret gadgets and weapons I could imagine myself using some day.

Starting with media coverage of the 1967 Six-Day War between Israel and surrounding Arab states, I also developed a profound and long-abiding preoccupation with the Middle East, particularly the Arab-Israeli confrontation. This was natural, given my military interests, since some of the largest tank battles ever fought took place during that week-long melee, and the Six-Day War is still studied as a classic of military strategy. But this early enthusiasm for the purely military aspects eventually led to a broader interest in Hebrew and Arabic, and Mideastern politics and history that far outstripped my previous narrow adolescent focus.

I kept this fascination with the Middle East, even as I matured and my interest in the other pursuits waned. I went from dreaming of going to Annapolis or to West Point, to not wanting anything at all to do with the military by the time I graduated high school. "I won't have *any*body telling me what to do!" I snorted, whenever someone asked what happened to my dream of a military career. And though I still loved to read science fiction, the early fascination with telepathy and ESP fizzled along with the science fair project I had helped with. The experiment failed to prove that one could beat chance in guessing the patterns on Zener cards—the ones with the wavy lines and five-pointed stars. As for being involved in intelligence work, I knew *that* had been a boy's pipe dream all along.

By the time 1976 rolled around, and my new wife was peckishly trying to talk me into joining the Army as a way of feeding my family and learning Arabic (which was not then offered at BYU), my attitude was almost directly opposite where I'd been seven or eight years before. The whole notion of being in the military seemed unappetizing. I had no clue that by the time I was thirty-two *all* my youthful dreams—military, Special Forces, intelligence work, and even ESP—would come true in totally unexpected ways. The Army would be the catalyst to their fulfillment.

Eventually, my wife won, aided by our increasingly meager circumstances. In June 1976 I found myself in the recruiting facility in Salt Lake City being sworn in as a private first class, with a reporting date of August 4. My basic training was at a post I'd never heard of before, Fort Leonard Wood,

Missouri, known affectionately as "Fort Lost-in-the-Woods" since it was out in the middle of nowhere.

Basic training was an epiphany for me. It was hard, dirty, miserable, and demeaning. Paradoxically, it was also enlightening and empowering; I came to understand in a way I never had before what generations of soldiers before me had struggled through so that their fellow Americans, for better or worse, could chart their own course through history, and prosper as they went. And I met Sergeant First Class Charles Johnson, my drill sergeant, an athletic-looking African-American Vietnam vet who knew how to be tough but fair, how to accurately judge people beyond what they were on the surface, and how to teach recruits not only that integrity was more important than comfort, but that the trust between comrades could save your life.

As he intended, we all felt intimidated by Drill Sergeant Johnson. But he nicknamed me "Preacher" and, when I fired the highest score in my company on the rifle range, exclaimed, "Damn, the Preacher can *shoot!*" He sponsored me as Trainee of the Cycle for the battalion, but wasn't above making me do an inverted crawl around the encampment area when I left my M-16 unattended during a field exercise. He was a leader who cared about his men, and though he was hard as rhinoceros hide, there were what looked suspiciously like tears on Johnson's cheek the day we graduated. But maybe it was only sweat.

By the early fall I was on my way to Monterey, California, for a year's training in Arabic at the Presidio. Language training was the polar opposite of Basic. It was cerebral, laid-back, and demilitarized. We had to wear our uniforms to class and salute the occasional officer we encountered. Once in a while we'd even be assigned to a clean-up detail. But there was no KP or guard duty, so most of the time we focused on conjugating verbs, learning vocabulary, and doing homework. During the two-hour lunch breaks, I would occasionally sunbathe on the lawn next to the Presidio's gym and read Herman Hesse in German. To earn extra money (which we desperately needed in the high-cost Monterey area), I tutored other students in German and Hebrew in the evenings when I had the chance.

The year at Monterey was too swiftly over. After a few months' layover in Texas for additional training (where my daughter Mary Elizabeth was born, in December 1977), and a detour to Massachusetts to learn how to run radio-jamming equipment, I arrived at my first permanent duty station: Fort Campbell, Kentucky. My assignment was the 265th Army Security Agency (ASA) Company, which supported the 101st Airborne Division. Even as a newly minted buck sergeant, I found I spent a lot of time washing Jeeps and servicing generators and Gama-goats (ungainly all-terrain vehicles the Army eventually disposed of as too failure-prone), and virtually no time using my recently learned Arabic. It nagged at me that there *must* be more to Army life than *this*.

By the time I signed in at Fort Campbell in March 1978, I had almost two years as an enlisted soldier under my belt. It was only a few months later that Joe Evans, a friend in my linguist platoon, suggested I make the rounds with him as he went through the process of applying for Officer Candidate School. The thought of becoming an officer had never before crossed my mind, nor did it greatly appeal to me even when Joe glowingly described all the great things that went with having a commission. I believed the enlisted man's myth that officers were much worse off than enlisted because of greater responsibility and odious social commitments. But Joe begged, and my wife pouted again, so I agreed to go through the motions with him, take the tests, and fill out the paperwork. What the heck, I figured—I could always turn down the offer of a slot at OCS, even in the unlikely event I was picked.

Ironically, Joe's application was turned down and mine accepted. And there was no question by then of turning down the appointment. I left Fort Campbell in the fall of 1978 with a beat-up old car and shiny new wings on my chest, earned along with a certificate for being the Distinguished Graduate from class 52–78 of the 101st Airborne Division's famous Air Assault School, signed up for at my wife's insistence.

Officer Candidate School was just like basic training all over again, with the added distinction that it was almost twice as long, and that I was required to make decisions for myself and others over and over again, every day. Worse, I was held accountable for those decisions in ways that were more onerous than the trouble I could get into in Basic. For the first time I encountered demerits, which when added up (as they always did), could cause an officer candidate to spend monotonous hours marching back and forth across a wide tarmac parking lot with dozens of his buzz-headed peers likewise working off *their* demerits. It seemed a huge waste of time. But the tactical officers who drove us weren't worried about our time. Their aim was to teach us that even in this setting, where no one was likely to be killed or injured, our wrong decisions could have unforeseen and unpleasant consequences.

Sometime during the last third of OCS, the officer candidates receive their assignments for whichever "branch" of the Army they have been appointed to—Infantry, Engineers, Armor, Aviation, etc. Because of my language background, I was hardly surprised to get my first choice—Military Intelligence, MI for short. This happy event, however, opened the door for a further opportunity that I hadn't expected and didn't welcome.

Shortly after branch selections were announced, we were told that training slots for Airborne School there at Fort Benning were freely available to MI officers. Quotas were restricted for most other branches; it seems that enough of them were already learning to jump out of perfectly good airplanes. But too few MI officers had signed up for military parachuting, and the Army needed more.

Going through another three weeks beyond OCS of being browbeaten by cadre and doing hundreds of push-ups did not appeal to me, so I purposely avoided Lieutenant Mosser, the MI-liaison officer whose job it was to fill the airborne school quotas. But I made the mistake of mentioning the announcement to Betti. For some reason she thought I needed another set of wings to wear on my uniform, so she pestered me about checking to see whether the training slots were still open. I procrastinated, thinking that if I stalled long enough, the answer would be "no." When I finally got around to asking the question, Mosser told me she didn't know and would have to get back to me. Assuming the best, I let the thought drop from my mind.

Mosser never did "get back" to me. Instead, days before OCS graduation and my commissioning as a second lieutenant, the 50th Company first sergeant handed me orders for airborne training as soon as I was officially a lieutenant. "But I only asked whether the training slots were still open," I complained to Lieutenant Mosser. "I figured I could make a decision then!"

"Well, it's too late now," she responded. "It would look bad on your record if you turned down orders to jump school." Like it or not, I was on my way. And despite my doubts, it turned out to be a very good thing. I was right about one thing, though. It was not in any sense *fun*.

After being medically recycled once for a muscle pulled doing a few hundred push-ups during a twenty-minute "break," I finally completed airborne training, and in April 1979 my little family and I moved to Fort Huachuca, Arizona, for intelligence school. Betti was pregnant with our second child.

For six months I and my peers were taught the basics of how to be military intelligence officers, learning about Soviet military equipment and tactics, battlefield analysis, and more fundamental things, like how to don protective masks in the event of chemical attack and how to fire pistols and grenade launchers.

I enjoyed Fort Huachuca. At an altitude of 5,000 feet, with mountains rising dramatically from the western edge of the cantonment area, Huachuca summers averaged a cool ninety-five degrees, in contrast to nearby Tucson, which was always over a hundred.

Before I was really ready it was time to receive my duty assignment. I soon had orders to a tank battalion in Erlangen, Germany. Though I thought tanks were interesting, I was worried. The battalion mission involved a general defense position in the area of the Fulda Gap—the main avenue of attack for Warsaw Pact forces if World War III ever broke out. That was not what concerned me, however. The status quo had reigned for decades, the two superpowers were working on detente, and there was no reason to believe that anything would change. My real worry was that because of the battalion's mission, its soldiers spent much of the year away from home in the training areas. I was not pleased by the prospect of spending so much time apart from my family.

It was then that my parachute training unexpectedly paid off. The Special Forces unit in Bad Tölz, Germany needed a military intelligence lieutenant who was parachute-qualified. I dragged my feet at first. I wasn't sure I would be able to spend much more time at home in a Special Forces assignment than with the tank battalion. Besides, I *hated* parachute jumping. I'd had only hard landings during airborne training, and I knew that there were only two happy moments in a paratrooper's life: first, when he looked up and saw that his parachute had, indeed, opened; and second when he picked himself up off the ground and found no broken bones.

Hesitantly, I put myself on the list. There was another lieutenant ahead of me who was airborne-qualified, and also had Special Forces experience. I figured he would get the job, and I could avoid having to make the decision, while giving the appearance of being a "can-do" airborne warrior, an image we were all anxious to cultivate. My strategy failed. A few days later I was handed orders to the Special Forces Detachment (Airborne), Europe. The other lieutenant had chosen a Stateside assignment. Betti, our two-year-old daughter Mary, our new baby, James, and I were on our way to spend three years in the foothills of the Bavarian Alps where, much to my surprise, I would fulfill my early adolescent dream by wearing a green beret after all.

As with my other made-by-default decisions in the past, this one turned out to be for the best. Aside from the regular parachute jumps (which were never pleasant, despite the glorious mountainscapes that framed every exit at 1,250 feet), the tour at Bad Tölz was rewarding. It even had its exciting moments.

The first of these occurred less than a month after our arrival when, on November 4, 1979, the American embassy in Tehran, Iran, was stormed and its diplomats taken hostage. Our Special Forces troops at Bad Tölz and another airborne battalion, in Vicenza, Italy, were the closest units capable of reacting on such short notice. The Special Forces battalion was marshaled; jump-equipped aircraft were on the way. Soldiers checked their equipment and their weapons. And I received my marching orders: "Do you speak Iranian?" "Uh, I went to Arabic language school . . ." "That's close enough. You're going." I didn't even have a complete set of field gear, and they hadn't yet issued me an M-16. That was quickly remedied.

In the face of prospective combat, especially under those conditions, I remember feeling a violent clash of emotions. Thrill and adventurous excitement mixed with dread and concern for what might happen to my family if I didn't make it back. I was also an intelligence officer. Based on what I knew, it wasn't hard to figure out that the odds were very much stacked against such a hastily-thrown-together rescue operation using only two airborne battalions, thousands of miles from the nearest support base or reinforcements.

Apparently I wasn't the only one figuring those odds. Within a few hours the operation was scrapped and the unit stood down. I experienced an opposite, but equally curious emotional conflict—profound relief, coupled with regret and disappointment.

Three years passed quickly, and still it seemed too soon for my assignment in Germany to end. I had been promoted to first lieutenant and was awaiting advancement to captain, earned German jump wings, gone twice to England for Special Forces exercises, processed scores of security clearances, celebrated the birth of our third child, Christopher Carson Smith, and worked with Chief Warrant Officer Gene Lessman, at the time a gruff, burly, mustachioed counterintelligence agent in his early forties. It was one of his jobs to keep tabs on the Soviet military liaison teams (essentially legal spies authorized in West Germany by treaty at the close of World War II), and other enemy agents who poked around Special Forces business. I had no inkling that I would meet Gene a few years later under altogether different circumstances.

Still, after thirty-six months it was time to leave.

In retrospect, even my request for assignment to Fort Meade was not a decision I had made, but instead was motivated mostly by the desire to make my wife happy.

Ironically, it had yet to dawn on me that with my assignment as a Middle East desk officer at Fort Meade, my life had rather inexplicably come full circle. Like Harry Chapin's song "Taxi," where the two characters discover their youthful dreams have been fulfilled in completely unexpected ways, all *my* childhood dreams—becoming a soldier and then an intelligence officer, serving with the Special Forces, and real involvement, however peripheral, with Middle East issues, had all come true. Except one, that is. And that one, like the others, had unexpectedly just fallen in my lap.

I looked up. Tom was rubbing his short, curly beard while he watched me, waiting patiently for an answer. Maybe twenty seconds, perhaps not even that, had passed since he posed the question about whether I was willing to become a psychic spy.

I may have been reluctant many times in the past, even when my instincts told me to say yes. But not this time.

"When do I start?" I asked.

On the way out, the eyes of people at the desks met mine differently than they had on my way in.

5

SRI

"There are more things in
heaven and earth,
Horatio,
Than are dreamt
of in your philosophy."

Hamlet, Act I, Scene V

It would be another twelve years before the news would officially break of a secret paranormal espionage program. By mid-1996 thousands of print and broadcast media reports about the government remote viewing program would deluge the public. But no one would have the same breath-taken response as I did the day I learned of the government's remote viewing program. After all, the November 1995 *Nightline* program that would first reveal that the government had a stable of psychic spies would come in the midst of yet another season of *The X-Files*, a flurry of UFO "documentaries," and an already-raging flood of media coverage about the paranormal. All things considered, the public would by then have grown a bit jaded.

But in 1983, as I stood blinking in the late afternoon sun outside Building T-2651, all of this was still far in the future. For me, the revelation was stunning. I felt as if the nature of the universe had changed in an instant—as if old wives' tales scoffed at for years had suddenly turned up true. Where would it lead? I didn't know. But the sense of adventure, of having been chosen as a wizard's apprentice in some portentous quest, was palpable, and danced around me like bucket-toting broomsticks as I made my way home.

Mundane reality, however, has a way of sobering a person up. There were more immediate obstacles. I had to tell both my wife and my boss that I was about to change not only my job, but my career path as well. Neither of them was going to like it. But at least the boss would be relatively easy. Tom had assured me that Center Lane was General Bert Stubblebine's "baby." Whomever the general wanted assigned to the project, he got. And if Tom and Fred said I belonged there, it would be made so. I wasn't sure, though, how my wife would react. She didn't like me making major decisions without consulting her. I walked through our front door with a bit of trepidation.

Despite my worries, Betti took it fairly well. She was annoyed, but not as much as I expected. So I apologized, and wisely didn't tell her that even if she had objected, this life-changing decision would not have been negotiable. In the end, though, it didn't seem to matter much to her. She was engrossed in her social work master's program, and my circumstances had not changed enough to affect her schooling.

Ops Group was commanded by a taciturn, athletic-looking colonel named John Hambric. Colonel Hambric was a supporter of the remote viewing program—in fact was very much interested in anything related to what INSCOM's High Performance Task Force was uncovering. "If they think you can make a bigger contribution at Center Lane than you can here, go with my blessing," was essentially what he said upon hearing my news. I signed out of Ops Group and into Center Lane's cover organization, "Security Systems Program Division," or SSPD, on September 1, 1983.

Let me be clear here. Up until the time Tom invited me into the Center Lane Program, I had never had anything that might have been described as a "paranormal experience." In fact, I was mildly skeptical about the possibility of any sort of ESP being real, outside of the one possible exception of religion. Mormonism, to be sure, has its mystical side, though outsiders usually don't realize it. It doesn't occur to most Mormons themselves to think of things like the "whisperings of the Holy Ghost," or "personal inspiration and revelation" as being in nature mystical, much less "paranormal." While over the years I *had* experienced sudden insights and intuitions that seemed mysterious, they could, in many cases, be explained away as coincidence, and I hadn't even had much in the way of religious "paranormal" encounters.

According to Fred Atwater, my lack of "psychic" experiences wasn't a liability. In fact, in a way it was an asset. I had no bad habits or preconceptions that I would have to unlearn. But I was expected to learn some background. In preparation for my transfer into Center Lane, Fred assigned me various readings on remote viewing and parapsychology as homework. Among these was the first book ever published on remote viewing, *Mind Reach*, by Dr. Harold Puthoff and his associate, Russell Targ. From that book I gained my first hint of how this psychic spying business first began, and what it was all about. Parts of the story have been told elsewhere, but I will tell it here as well, since there are important details that have been missed, and because it is the context into which the rest of my story unfolds.

It was early 1972, and a young physicist named Harold Puthoff, fresh from postdoctoral work at Stanford University, was puzzling over some of the secrets of the universe. Puthoff's background was not typical for a theoretical physicist. He had spent a few years as a Naval intelligence officer, then transferred from the Navy to become a civilian employee at the National Security Agency. It was NSA that had sent him to Stanford to study physics, but Puthoff quickly realized that work in signals intelligence was not for him, and had resigned from the agency. He did complete his Ph.D., and went to work at SRI International—formerly the Stanford Research Institute, in Menlo Park, California.

Puthoff had been hired by SRI to do basic research in laser physics, a field in which he had made a name for himself during his graduate studies at Stanford, having written a prominent textbook in the field of quantum electronics. But now he was puzzling about yet more fundamental issues—in particular, how could physics account for life processes? Part of his speculations involved tachyons. These were elementary particles that physicists were not sure existed, but which mathematical calculations and theoretical implications seemed to predict. And if tachyons did exist, they had an interesting characteristic: they could go backwards in time. Puthoff knew that there must be some way to create a flow of these tachyons, but just what it might be he hadn't yet figured out. He suspected that if parapsychology turned out to be a real phenomenon, then some basic parapsychological effects might involve these elusive little particles. He even had support for that hypothesis from interesting research coming out of Czechoslovakia.

Then he heard about some strange experiments that might provide a clue. A New York City researcher named Cleve Backster was doing controversial work that involved hooking plants up to a polygraph ("lie detector") machine, then slicing off leaves, or burning branches, which allegedly caused a reaction in the plant that was recorded by the polygraph machine. The plants seemed to react even when a branch had been removed, then was burned or broken, some distance away. Backster concluded that there was evidence that plants could "feel" and that the reaction was not limited by distance.

Puthoff was intrigued, if still dubious. Could one set up and then detect a tachyon stream by burning a plant with a laser, while simultaneously monitoring its sister plant five miles away for a reaction? He didn't know if it would work, but thought it worth exploring. He sent a proposal to Backster, asking for comments.[1]

A few years before thoughts of tachyons began to dance in Hal Puthoff's head, a young man named Ingo Swann had begun to establish himself in the New York art scene. Born in Telluride, Colorado, Swann was educated at Westminster College in Salt Lake City in biology and art. After a stint in the Army during the Korean War era, he made his way to New York and took a job working for the United Nations to tide him over until he could get on his feet with his painting.[2]

Swann enjoyed meeting people, and was soon a fixture in some rather unusual social circles. A number of those with whom he associated were interested or even directly involved in the American Society for Psychical Research in New York. Though a self-tutored student of parapsychology and the paranormal, Swann purposely kept himself aloof from involvement in any of the ongoing experiments being conducted by such legendary parapsychologists as Karlis Osis, Gertrude Schmeidler, and Janet Mitchell. That did not, however, last long.[3]

He was finally persuaded to participate in Backster's experiments one day and seemed to have some success in creating a psychokinetic effect. Swann was soon involved in Osis's out-of-body experiments and in PK experiments for Schmeidler, attempting to mentally influence sensitive measuring devices known as thermistors, with further success. But Swann was dissatisfied in his role of passive scientific subject; he felt he could contribute something to the preliminary design of some of the research being planned, thus gaining a say in what sorts of activities he might be expected to perform. As is often the case when an outsider brings a fresh perspective to the table, a number of Swann-inspired innovations led to breakthroughs that soon had parapsychology circles abuzz. One of these was what in retrospect turns out to have been the first modern remote viewing experiment.

Swann had grown tired of the repetitive, boring "describe-what's-in-the-box" and other traditional experiments he'd been tasked with. If one could perceive things in a box in the same room, he wondered, why not see if it would work over much greater distances? But the immediate question was how such a thing could be tested.

Before long he and Janet Mitchell came up with a simple procedure that would involve a distant target and still allow immediate feedback for judging the accuracy of the perceptions. The procedure they devised also reasonably guaranteed that no alternative to ESP could help the subject (Swann) "cheat" by getting the information from some other, more conventional, source. The names of a number of cities around the country, together with the telephone numbers to their respective local weather services, were sealed inside identical opaque envelopes. At the commencement of the experiment, a disinterested third party would randomly select an envelope, Swann would be given the name of the city thus selected, and then would provide his impressions of the current weather there. It was a simple but workable pilot experiment.

On December 8, 1971 Swann reported for duty as a research subject at the offices of the ASPR. He was wired to an electroencephalograph machine—an EEG—to record his brain waves, as was common practice during other ASPR experiments. At the appropriate moment, Vera Feldman, an ASPR staffer who was otherwise unaffiliated with the research project, handed Mitchell an envelope that had been randomly chosen from the stack. Mitchell, who was in a different room from Swann, passed the target to him over the intercom: "Tucson, Arizona."[4]

"Of course, I really had no idea how to 'get' to Tucson from the rather ugly experimental room in New York," Swann said years after the event. "And when I first heard the mention of 'Tucson, Arizona,' a picture of hot desert flashed through my mind." But then, suddenly he was "there."

"Am over a wet highway," he reported. "Buildings nearby and in the distance. The wind is blowing. It's cold. And it is raining hard." He had the impression of water glistening on a highway, followed by the immediate awareness that Tucson, which gets only a few inches of rain a year, was in the middle of a torrential downpour.

"That's it?" Janet Mitchell queried.

"Yeah, that's it . . . It's raining and very cold there," Swann concluded. She dialed the Tucson weather service number. Before Swann had even gotten himself disentangled from the EEG wires, Mitchell had the feedback.

"Right now Tucson is having unexpected thunderstorms and the temperature is near freezing."

Over the course of coming weeks, a number of similar experiments were done. As things developed, it was soon clear that a label was needed for what it was that Swann was doing. After discussions between him, Osis, Schmeidler, and Mitchell, Ingo suggested the term "remote viewing," and a new discipline, a new research programme, and ultimately a new era in parapsychology was launched.

It was in this milieu that, sometime after the middle of March 1972,

Cleve Backster showed Ingo Swann the letter from Hal Puthoff. Swann had always been somewhat ambivalent about his activities in parapsychology research; he considered it a passing interest, something he would dabble in for awhile, then move on to his real life's work, which he thought would be writing and art. So he was reluctant at first to make contact with Puthoff, despite Backster's urgings.

Finally overcoming his reticence, Swann drafted a letter to Puthoff on March 30, 1972, the first step in a long-distance conversation that ended with Ingo Swann stepping off a plane at the San Francisco airport on June 4, 1972.[5]

The upshot of Swann's correspondence with Hal was the suggestion that, instead of using plants as subjects in a search for elusive tachyons, why not use human subjects who could observe and report what they experienced? Puthoff was not particularly interested in Swann's exploits in these so-called remote-viewing experiments. Instead, the physicist was much more intrigued by the psychokinetic successes Swann had demonstrated. In fact Puthoff had something special in mind to try out on his new associate, but it was to be a bit of a surprise.

On June 6, the anniversary of World War II's D-Day, Hal Puthoff ferried Ingo Swann to the Varian Physics Building, the home of Stanford University's Physics Department. There to meet them was a research associate in the Stanford High Energy Physics Lab, Dr. Arthur Hebard. Along with Hebard was a staff physicist from the Stanford Linear Accelerator, Dr. Martin Lee, and a retinue of graduate students.

Swann knew that he was going over to the campus for a psychokinesis experiment involving a magnetometer. He had done such experiments before. Magnetometers were compact pieces of equipment that fit neatly on a tabletop and measured magnetic field strengths. They had readouts that kept track of perturbations within their sensitive innards. Swann had from time to time been able to affect the machines enough to register on the readouts. He expected nothing different for this event, and was even mildly sanguine about the chance of failure in front of a bunch of stuffy academicians. If he blew the experiment, he could go home to New York and pursue his art, no longer to be bothered with this parapsychology stuff.

When everyone had clustered together in the basement of the building, the first thing Swann wanted to know was where on earth the magnetometer was. As far as he could see, there was nothing here but concrete slab, profusions of plumbing, and large, orange-painted, tubular foundation pillars. There was also a cylinder, maybe two feet in diameter, sticking up through the floor and one lone chart recorder, its slowly moving needle tracing grace-ful sine curves across a fixed sheet of chart paper.

"You're standing on it," Puthoff answered Swann's query. The machine that was to be his target was hidden under three feet of cement. This was no typical magnetometer. It had been designed to detect quarks—mysterious subatomic particles that were posited in some versions of quantum theory, but which had thus far escaped the hungry clutches of science. By the stan-dards Swann was used to, the instrument was huge. This detector was designed to be even more sensitive than most, so a passing quark, which would otherwise make only an infinitesimal mark on the physical world, might cause the needle on the chart recorder to jiggle, leaving a written sig-nature behind.

Because the machine was so sensitive, it was also heavily shielded to pre-vent it from being disturbed by irrelevant objects, events, or transient mag-netic fields moving by. It was sheathed in a special mu-metal magnetic shielding alloy and an additional layer of aluminum, surrounded by a super-conducting shield, immersed in liquid helium, and partially buried under cubic yards of concrete. The test would be to see if, through all the shielding, Swann *could* perturb it.

Swann was instantly annoyed. He had believed that he was going to per-form an experiment similar to those he'd done before. But on the face of it this was on the scale of being invited for a swim in a neighbor's pool, only to be dumped unceremoniously into the English Channel. "I was being asked to 'poke around' with a 'target' that I could not see, or even know exactly where it was in the ground beneath," Swann recalled fifteen years later.[6]

It wasn't an unreasonable experiment. But one of the topics of his and Puthoff's prior conversations was the need to thoroughly inform subjects about the experiments in which they were to take part. Now it appeared that he had been intentionally fooled, seemingly to no purpose relevant to the experiment. "Now, Ingo," Puthoff placated him. "You wanted an experiment that had no loopholes in it. Well, here it is."[7]

Swann had to admit the magnetometer presented an excellent target. Because of the shielding, it was difficult or impossible to meddle with the apparatus to produce phony results. And since Swann had no clue about the target before his introduction to it, no one could say that he had tinkered with it beforehand. Besides, this mostly skeptical group of eyewitnesses, some of whom were actually responsible for the equipment, was there to certify that any anomalous behavior of the machine could not have been physically caused by Swann or Puthoff.

Mollified, Swann agreed to have a go at it. But how, he wanted to know, was he supposed to affect something that wasn't even visible? No one had an answer. He tried mentally "probing" it a few times, but other than him claiming to sense the presence of something metal beneath the cement floor, there was no perceptible effect. Puthoff and Swann thought the onlookers seemed visibly relieved.

Normally, the magnetometer-cum-quark detector contained a small, microgram niobium ball suspended in a magnetic field. To set up the detector for the experiment, a decaying magnetic field had been induced inside it, but the hovering ball was not in use. The slow, rhythmically moving needle tracing its pattern on the chart paper recorded the gradual, orderly dissipation of the field. Any manipulation of the field or the innards of the device would show up in a waver or interruption of the neat, elegant line the needle traced. Swann made his first serious attempt.

At the point he felt as if he had made some brief connection with the mechanism of the magnetometer, the speed of the back-and-forth motion of the pen doubled. The onlookers were silent. Puthoff thought that Hebard looked surprised, and perhaps worried.

But Hebard's first suspicion was that the equipment was malfunctioning. So he suggested that it would be more convincing if the readout from the decaying field stopped altogether. Swann tried to oblige, but for perhaps five seconds nothing happened.

"Let me try to sketch it out, and that might help me focus a little better," Swann said. He started to scribble a few lines on the chart paper. By some accounts, Swann managed to produce a reasonably accurate representation of a Josephson Junction, which was an important component in the functional heart of the machine. And at the point of sketching, both Swann and Puthoff agree that the machine reacted; the pen hesitated, then it stopped. As seconds ticked by, the needle described only tiny variations at the top of a long, otherwise flat-topped line.

By this time, there was a growing chorus of whispers and mumbling from the witnesses. "Is that an effect?" Swann wanted to know. No one seemed ready to answer him. But he was asked what he had been doing while the needle reacted. Puthoff found the answer surprising. As Puthoff described later in the book *Mind Reach*, Swann "explained that he had direct vision of the apparatus inside and that apparently the act of looking at different parts resulted in producing the effects." Reportedly, Swann even correctly noted the presence of a gold alloy plate inside the machine, which the New York artist could not possibly have known was present. And as Swann described his experience, apparently calling it back to mind in the process, the machine reacted two more times, with a return to a normal pattern in between when Puthoff purposely steered the conversation away from the equipment. Each time, when Swann's attention was brought back, the chart recorder reacted.

The magnetometer had been operating for at least an hour before Puthoff and Swann had arrived, with no variation in the regularly oscillating line. So Hebard agreed to keep it running for an hour or so after their departure, to see if any further variations turned up in their absence. That would have been a sign that the perturbations were artifacts of the machine, and not human mental intervention. Lee, Puthoff, Swann, and Hebard all signed the chart paper, attesting that they were present and witnesses to the machine's strange behavior. By the time Puthoff and Swann walked out of the basement, most of the onlookers had faded away. As Swann remembered it, one even collided with an orange support pillar in his eagerness to get out. The chart recorder continued its long, slow oscillations undisturbed for the next hour or more before it was finally turned off.[8]

The event was in many ways a watershed. It was not a *conclusive* experiment, since Puthoff had not thought to arrange for concurrent monitoring by a second recording device. Though the chance was slim, there was no way to absolutely rule out the possibility that the instrument's fluctuations were the result of a faulty readout. And Arthur Hebard himself checked to see if some more mundane explanation could account for the machine's fluctuations.

"We have a helium recovery system," Hebard said when interviewed. "This container holds helium [that] goes out through a pipe and back to the compressors" in another room in the physics building. Other researchers used the system as well. "I put my hand over the recovery system, which built up a little bit of back pressure, and I noticed a large excursion of the chart recorder. So I hypothesized that . . . someone else could have been transferring helium, or there had been some glitch in the recovery pressure that could have simulated this effect.

"I'm not saying Swann didn't cause it," Hebard concluded. But given a plausible alternative explanation, the experiment was less convincing. Still, the effects had only manifested while Swann was in the room, and were correlated with some of his overt actions.[9] And, despite its rather preliminary nature, the experiment was compelling enough to attract certain unexpected attention.

Almost immediately after the event, Puthoff drafted a brief paper, describing the circumstances and results of the experiment. This paper circulated from hand to hand throughout a number of academic and research institutions around the country. As a consequence was that Puthoff was invited to speak in a few venues about the remarkable occurrence. One of these speaking engagements was at Stanford University itself. After the presentation, a tall, gangly man with bushy hair approached. He introduced himself as Russell Targ, and said he worked as a physicist for Sylvania. Puthoff had heard of Targ as someone else who was heavily involved in laser research. Targ wore thick-lensed glasses required, it turned out, partly because of a laser accident that had affected his vision, already damaged by an eye condition he'd had since childhood.

Russell Targ was not just involved in mainstream physics research. As a longtime avocation he also had an intense interest in parapsychology, and during the late 1960s had collaborated on some projects with psychologist Charles Tart, who was to become a legend in consciousness and ESP research. Though the interest they shared in exploring other forms of consciousness was the only noteworthy similarity between the two researchers, people would often confuse the names Tart and Targ over the ensuing years.

Was the Stanford Research Institute hiring people to work with Puthoff on these ESP experiments, Targ wanted to know, and if so, how could he sign up?

In fact, SRI was "hiring," but not in the typical way. Like many research organizations, newly engaged SRI associates were usually expected to bring their own funding with them, or have good prospects awaiting them in the form of outside grants or research money. Research associates who didn't pay their way at SRI by pulling in sufficient contracts to justify their positions found themselves looking for other occupations after a suitable grace period. Puthoff explained that there was no ESP research "project" as such going on.

However, after having a proposal for ESP research turned down by his employer, Sylvania, Targ had already made overtures to NASA for the same research. Both Puthoff and Targ knew Willis Harman, a prominent figure at SRI who happened to also be interested in parapsychology research. Harman agreed to lend his influence to start a project. With that, and on the strength of the possible NASA funding, Targ was brought on board in September 1972. By the time he started work, unfortunately, the NASA proposal had reached a temporary dead end. But Targ had come up with a new idea for a grant from the National Institutes of Health, which he intended to pursue at SRI. Ironically, he departed almost immediately for a few weeks in Amsterdam to attend parapsychology meetings. This left Hal holding the bag for most of the work writing up the application and justification for the NIH grant—which was ultimately rejected. Starting with Targ's return, the two were to work closely together for a decade.[10]

Puthoff and Targ made an interesting pair. Puthoff was of medium build, but Targ made him look small with his towering height of nearly six and a half feet. In many ways they complemented each other. Though Targ certainly knew much about the field, Puthoff had stronger academic credentials and was more firmly grounded in theoretical physics and science. And Puthoff's background in government bureaucracy and intelligence work was soon to prove valuable. Targ, on the other hand, brought with him a richer background in parapsychology research, and had connections with major names in that field.

In an interesting synchronicity, it turned out that both men were born in Chicago, and that their first regular jobs had been with the same employer at the same time, Sperry Gyroscope Company. Several years before they finally met, both were employed building high-powered traveling wave tubes, albeit in different locations; Targ had been in Great Neck, Long Island, and Puthoff in Gainesville, Florida. Targ had gone to Florida to consult on the project Puthoff was working on, but didn't encounter Hal at the time.[11]

Shortly after Puthoff and Targ's first meeting in June at the Stanford lecture, something even more portentous happened. Two men in dark suits knocked on Puthoff's office door. They displayed a copy of the magnetometer experiment report and asked, "Did you write this?"

They were from the CIA.

The American intelligence community was worried. It had watched for a number of years as the USSR poured millions of dollars worth of resources into what the Soviets called *psychoenergetics*, a term roughly equivalent to "parapsychology" in the West. Western researchers in the field wanted to think that *psychical* events, if they were real, could be traced back to *physical* causes, but left open the possibility "psi"—the name of the Greek letter that came to stand for the mysterious "thing" or "ability" that lay behind paranormal or psychic functioning—might yet be based on something not understandable in physical terms. Marxist philosophy, however, committed the Soviets to a strictly physical explanation for everything, even psychical events. And if all the reports flooding onto analyst desks at the CIA, DIA, and NSA were any indication, the Soviets were determined to run every detail about psychoenergetics to ground. There also were indicators that they intended to turn what they found into weaponry.

The CIA didn't know if something useful could ever be developed from ESP and psychokinesis. After all, the prevailing attitude among American scientists was that psychic functioning was nonsense. On the other hand, the Agency's analysts couldn't be sure that *nothing* would come of the Soviet research, either. The fact nagged at them that the Evil Empire never spent money, especially such large sums, on anything that didn't promise a lot of bang for the buck.

The reports coming from behind the Iron Curtain were sufficiently alarming that the CIA was on the lookout for some way of finding out just what sort of threat Soviet psychoenergetics might actually pose. Then, in June 1972, an informal report of a curious scientific experiment crossed the desk of someone at the Agency. The report detailed how a scientist at Stanford Research Institute had asked an individual to mentally interact with a quark detector in the Stanford Physics Department. The CIA was interested not only in the research, but in the researcher.

The problem the agency faced was simple: it needed a credentialed scientist or academician who could hold a security clearance, and do defense-related work in a secure facility. But this was the early 1970s, when student unrest was at its height. Not only was military-related research anathema no matter how crucial to national security it might be, but the CIA itself was thoroughly unwelcome on most campuses. It seemed unlikely that the agency could find any place in academia and outside the government to do the work needing to be done.

Then Puthoff turned up—exactly the man they were looking for to examine the ramifications of Soviet ESP. He was respected as a physicist and employed by an institution that was already involved in classified government contracts. Because of its work on nuclear weapons research, Stanford Research Institute had been divested by the university and set up as an independent research organization, to be called SRI International. Puthoff's former service as a Naval Intelligence officer at NSA was an added plus. It meant he had once been cleared for the highest levels of sensitive information, and could easily be given access again. And he understood intelligence and the intelligence community much better than most scientists. It seemed a marriage made in heaven.

It is still a mystery precisely how Puthoff's report ended up at the CIA. He thinks Targ may have inadvertently been the channel. While working at Sylvania, Russell had dealings with the CIA over technical and research issues unconnected with parapsychology. After their first encounter at the Stanford lecture, Puthoff passed Targ a copy of the magnetometer experiment write-up. The paper made its rounds at Sylvania, and may have filtered out to the CIA from there.[12]

Whatever the connection, the two CIA representatives were impressed by their discussions with Puthoff, and when they parted company with him they left a couple of thousand dollars in seed money to fly Ingo Swann back to California for further trials. On June 27, 1972, Puthoff wrote concerning the magnetometer experiment to CIA scientist Kit Green, who occupied the Life Science Desk in the agency's Office of Strategic Intelligence (OSI), starting a long-term relationship with one of the more important figures within the CIA to support the SRI remote viewing project.[13]

Sometime during the second or third week in August, CIA scientists visited SRI to observe the further evaluations they had requested. These consisted of fairly simplistic experiments involving objects hidden in various containers or in locked rooms. Swann felt that he didn't perform well for the CIA observers, and at one point even apologized to Puthoff for the poor showing. Puthoff reassured him, saying that success of individual trials was not of concern, but rather the overall trend of the research series. Looking back, Puthoff found Swann's performance more impressive than Swann did.

Targets for the experiments were usually selected by the SRI researchers. But the time came when the CIA visitors were invited to put their own choice of targets inside small boxes so no one at SRI would know what was inside. The visitors presented Swann with three sealed boxes. "Regarding two of them, I approximated the hidden contents quite well," Swann related. In the other, though, he "described something like a brown leaf, except it was on the underside of the lid and not at the bottom of the box.

"It also seemed alive," he said, "but I didn't understand how a brown leaf could be thought of as alive." The box, it turned out, "contained a living moth the [CIA] scientists had captured outside. It was reasonably large, was brown, and with its wings folded it resembled a brown leaf which nature had designed it to look like." It was found clinging underneath the lid when the box was opened.[14]

Apparently the trials were convincing. On October 1, 1972—the first day of government Fiscal Year 1973—the CIA let a small $49,909 contract to SRI for exploratory research into parapsychology. The contract was supposed to last for eight months. As it turned out, the CIA would pay SRI to conduct parapsychology research for the next three years.

The eight months was to start in January 1973. In the meantime Targ and Puthoff filled their time studying a young Israeli entertainer by the name of Uri Geller. Geller was rapidly becoming famous for psychically bending spoons, getting broken watches to run, and other startling feats of seeming paranormal powers. He also claimed to be telepathic. Geller agreed to participate over the course of six weeks in November and December 1972. With $10,000 raised by a woman named Judy Skutch and former Apollo astronaut Edgar Mitchell, the work began.

Understandably, there was much controversy about *how* Geller went about creating his seeming miracles, with skeptics convinced it was trickery, while many who had seen him in action, including a number of respected scientists, were persuaded he was for real. Space limits a full account of Uri Geller's experiments at SRI, but they can be found in more detail in Jim Schnabel's *Remote Viewers* or Targ and Puthoff's *Mind Reach*.

In the end, the SRI scientists concluded that Geller had demonstrated some very impressive effects under tightly controlled conditions. Locked in an electronically, acoustically, and visually shielded and sealed isolation room, and ostensibly using telepathy, he successfully reproduced drawings made by a variety of experimenters. These people were in some cases separated from the shielded room by a matter of feet, at other times were in a different room, and at still other times in an altogether separate building. Geller was able to reproduce significant elements of the drawings even when the experimenters were the ones sealed in the isolation room, and he was the one sequestered elsewhere.

Other experiments were done, testing whether Geller could discover, without touching them, which of a series of identical containers held a steel ball bearing, water, or some other item. He was successful in several such attempts far beyond chance. He also correctly reported the roll of dice inside a closed box eight of ten times. Many of the experiments were captured on film.

Still, though he was most famous for his psychokinesis work, Geller never successfully mentally bent or broke metal objects in the SRI laboratory under controlled conditions, though he reportedly generated many impressive and sometimes spectacular PK effects outside the lab. The SRI team reported that Geller's remote perception abilities seemed genuine, but that they had failed to obtain scientifically admissible proof of his celebrated "mind-over-matter" abilities.[15] In the end the Geller research proved almost as important for what came as a *consequence* of it as for the science of it. That consequence amounted to an invasion of skeptics.

Hard on the heels of news getting out that SRI was taking Uri Geller seriously enough to examine his purported "psychic powers," Puthoff and Targ got their first taste of the wrath of career skeptics. Leon Jaroff, science editor for *Time* magazine, heard that the two SRI researchers were to formally present the results of their Geller research at Columbia University. *Time* was famous for its skeptical attitude about anything claiming to involve the paranormal. Jaroff called Puthoff and insisted he be given the information about Geller in advance of the official announcement. Puthoff declined, saying that he didn't want to give an unfair advantage to any reporter, but invited Jaroff to attend the presentation. According to Puthoff, Jaroff said he was going ahead with a story anyway, with or without Puthoff's input. Puthoff still declined to cooperate before the official release of the research.[16] The *Time* story, entitled "The Magician and the Think Tank," duly appeared before the Columbia presentation, one-sided as promised.[17]

A second skeptical assault came from a different quarter. Professional magician and debunker of the paranormal, James "The Amazing" Randi weighed in with his own attack, published earlier but made most readily available in his 1980 book *Flim-Flam* (republished in 1982).[18] In that book, Randi made a number of accusations against the SRI research, beginning with the magnetometer experiment. Swann had not produced the effects described, Randi claimed. Then he cited a number of statements allegedly made by Dr. Hebard that altogether contradicted both Swann's and Puthoff's accounts of the event.

Randi went on to further claim that the protocols in the Geller telepathy experiments were much sloppier than the SRI scientists said they were. He noted, for example, a four-and-a-half-inch hole[19] at about waist level in the shielded room, which presumably gave Geller plenty of opportunity to physically observe the various telepathy targets. This, he said, accounted for Geller's impressive reproductions of the target drawings, requiring no paranormal link. Further, a videotape that SRI presented on March 9, 1973 at the Columbia University Physics Department Colloquium as evidence of the dice experiments was dismissed by Randi as a fraudulent reenactment of the actual, allegedly failed experiment. Randi further insisted that the tape was made *after* the cameraman it was attributed to, Zev Pressman, had left for the day, and that he, Randi, had Presssman's word on that. All this and more was presented by Randi as proof of fraud and sloppy science, which, if true, would certainly throw the SRI results into grave doubt.

The trouble was, "The Amazing" Randi's own attack was riddled with misrepresentations and false statements. It turned out (as he admitted in his own text), that he had never even so much as "set foot on the sacred grounds of SRI." That was an unfortunate oversight on his part, because if he had, he would have discovered what D. Scott Rogo, a journalist specializing in paranormal issues, later found—the "hole" in the shielded room was barely three inches in diameter, had to penetrate through a foot of shielding and insulation (creating a very narrow, tunnel-like aperture), and was actually near the floor of the cubicle, not waist-high, as Randi asserted. Geller would have had to lie flat on his stomach if he wanted to see through to the next room, and even then would have observed only a few square inches, if he could have seen beyond the thick cables that snaked through the hole and the sound-deadening caps that closed whatever space was left unblocked.[20]

Others of Randi's accusations were just as groundless. Dr. Hebard's actual description of what had gone on with the magnetometer experiment did differ somewhat from Puthoff's, but not enough to contradict the SRI version of events. And when told that Randi had quoted him as saying Puthoff had lied about some of the details of that experiment, Hebard objected vehemently.

"I don't talk that way," he told me in an interview. "I would *never* have said that Puthoff was lying."[21]

Randi's claims about the videotape turned out to be false as well. When questioned by journalist Scott Rogo, the cameraman, Zev Pressman, indignantly maintained that he was indeed present for the filming of the experiment, and that there was no reenactment. Pressman signed a legal affidavit to that effect. Further, Pressman told Rogo that he had never spoken to Randi.

There are other examples of Randi's questionable tactics, but these suffice for now. I shall only mention one more skeptical encounter here, as it sets the stage for other incidents that happened in the course of the next two decades.

Sometime midway through the Geller experiments, a project manager named George Lawrence from the Defense Advanced Research Projects Agency (DARPA) visited the lab, bringing with him two consultants, Ray Hyman (a psychology professor from the University of Oregon), and Robert Van de Castle, a psychologist from the University of Virginia. These three asked to observe the research being conducted with Uri Geller, but Puthoff and Targ declined for two good reasons. First, they often received several such requests per week, and decided long before, as a matter of policy, not to honor them, since it would be disruptive to the experiments to have a continual flow of visitors. Further, they were still not sure that Geller wasn't trying to trick them, and they didn't want to introduce the added confusion that visitors would inevitably bring to make it easier for Geller to do so.

Instead, the DARPA project manager and his colleagues were invited to interview Geller themselves and conduct their own experiments with him. As Puthoff related in *Mind Reach*, the visitors "spent an engaging couple of hours with Geller, in which they observed the informal coffee-table type of demonstration" that Geller preferred. "They tried a number of their own, and from our standpoint largely uncontrolled, experiments," which were captured on SRI videotape. The University of Virginia psychologist, Robert Van de Castle, tried one reasonably well-controlled experiment, requiring Geller to duplicate a drawing sealed inside double envelopes and kept in the psychologist's pocket, the results of which were good enough to suggest to Van de Castle that Geller was "an interesting subject for further study." Hyman and his DARPA patron, however, were unimpressed.[22]

Not long afterward, in a move that struck Targ and Puthoff as unprofessional, Hyman went public about his privileged visit to the lab to see sensitive work that had not yet been published. For Jaroff's *Time* magazine article, Hyman showed the reporter a letter describing his visit and claiming among other things that the Geller tests at SRI were done with "incredible sloppiness."

This was a remarkable accusation to make, given that the only "tests" that Hyman had seen were those he and his associates had themselves conducted. It was a foretaste of things to come from Hyman.

Over the coming decades there were to be many other brushes with skeptics, not all of them negative. Often, critics helped uncover possible weaknesses and flaws in the experimental protocols, which the SRI researchers were then able to fix. Puthoff freely admits that in the end interaction with skeptics led to better science and more reliable results.

The SRI research effort was not just a matter of testing Uri Geller and fending off skeptical attacks. In fact, these activities were but a fraction of what was to go on over the coming decades. The core effort of the research would soon focus on the novel ideas about remote viewing that Swann brought with him from the ASPR in New York, tentative as they were so far. Swann was about to do more than seven thousand psi experiments in less than eight months.[23] It was to be a grueling, but enlightening, experience.

Remote Viewing

6

"Now my suspicion
is that the universe
is not only queerer than
we suppose,
but queerer than we can
suppose."

—J. B. S. Haldane

With the proliferation since 1995 of news and opinions about remote view-ing, plenty of people think they know what remote viewing is. Plenty of them are wrong. It is popular to say that remote viewing has been around for thousands of years, but called something else. To hear some folks tell it, the Oracle of Delphi was a closet remote viewer, and that goes for tribal shamans in the Australian Outback and the storefront palm reader in the strip mall. It is popular to say that consulting a crystal ball, reading a deck of tarot cards, channeling entities from the Great Beyond, or astral projection are also remote viewing.

The first step to understanding remote viewing is to know what it *isn't*—

and it *isn't* any of those things—though it may be related to them.

Definitions of remote viewing are notoriously slippery. When research started in earnest at the Stanford Research Institute in 1973, the experimenters themselves were unclear what it was, and they had only general clues as to what it wasn't. Often, writings documenting the research avoided explicitly defining remote viewing at all, relying instead on examples of successful remote viewing trials to convey the idea. But definitions couldn't be avoided forever.

In progress reports to sponsoring agencies, Puthoff and his colleagues had to come up with a lean one-liner to describe what they were delving into. But, as is the case with most shorthand attempts to capture a complicated subject, much more was left out than was left in. One of the earliest SRI research reports defined remote viewing as: "one of a broad class of abilities of certain individuals to access, by means of mental processes, and describe information sources blocked from ordinary perception and generally accepted as secure against access."[1] In other words, remote viewers could tell you something about what was in the sealed box on the table or in the locked room next door.

Dense as this definition was, it served the purpose as far as it went. But it didn't really distinguish remote viewing from any other form of ESP behavior. The lack of precision was not accidental. One of the consequences of making something more specific is that other things are ruled out, and in this early stage the researchers didn't want to be too narrow.

Ironically, when Ingo Swann stepped off the plane in late December, 1972, to get acclimated to California before the CIA contract started in January, remote viewing wasn't even what the scientists were after.

"The purpose of the project," Swann remembers, "was for me and Hal [Puthoff] to find one psychic phenomenon that could be replicated. And it was up to me to decide which one that was going to be when it came time to offer it to the client."[2] Psychokinesis was the immediate choice. At the time, it must have seemed obvious. If PK skills could be developed and controlled, one could use them to manipulate the physical world, including the enemy's weapons. Using "mind over matter" to melt tank barrels or stop bombers in mid-flight was the stuff of comic books. Far more likely, given the subtlety of typical PK effects, was the possibility of mucking up the intricate guts of military computers, electronic equipment, or missile guidance systems.

The experiments Swann had done convinced him that PK was real. But knowing the phenomenon existed was one thing; learning to replicate it at will and to control it—*those* were the real problems.

As a target to practice PK, there was the tabletop magnetometer—more specifically, a "superconducting differential magnetometer," or "gradiometer." But Puthoff and Targ thought of some other ingenious experimental designs on which to try PK. In one of the simpler ones, the subject was asked to concentrate on a Geiger counter and try to change the background count (which was about thirty-five clicks per minute) one way or the other.[3]

Being at heart laser physicists, Puthoff and Targ also came up with a third kind of experiment, using a low-powered argon laser beam to monitor a torsion pendulum. The pendulum was suspended on a metal fiber, and sealed inside a glass bell jar. A laser beam was focused to bounce off a mirror attached to the pendulum and fall on a detector. If the experimental subject was able to mentally nudge the pendulum, the beam would be deflected, which would in turn be measured by the detector and recorded.

Unfortunately, after thousands of attempts, and some fairly potent evidence of psychokinesis, one inescapable fact emerged: it couldn't be controlled, nor could it even really be done at will. "Willed perturbation effects appear to be intrinsically spontaneous," the 1975 final report to the CIA read with typical scientific density. "It is difficult to evoke such effects 'on cue,' with the result that the phenomenon is often considered to not be under good control, and therefore not amenable to controlled experimentation."[4]

"There was lots of PK demonstrated," Swann remembers. "But it could not be replicated under conscious control." Effectively, dreams of bending tank barrels merely with brain power—or even just scrambling a few electronic circuits—remained for the time being just dreams. "We chewed up five months or more doing PK experiments," said Swann. "Then we understood . . . that the project was going to fail" because they could not come up with a way of controlling the phenomenon.[5] If they were to avoid squandering the opportunity the CIA had handed them, Puthoff and Targ would have to come up with something fast. It was May 1973, and the contract ran out in August.

Scattered among the roughly seven thousand experimental trials were a few that were not PK. Instead, they were the describe-what's-in-the-box perception experiments similar to what Swann had done over and over again at the American Society for Psychical Research in New York, and more recently for the CIA scientists. This brought to mind the so-called "remote viewing" work he had also performed at the ASPR. Besides the city-weather targets he had done well on, Swann, along with Osis, Mitchell, and Schmeidler had also pioneered what eventually became known as "outbounder" or "beacon" remote viewing.

Rather than a specific *way* of remote viewing, the "outbounder" protocol was more a means of focusing a viewer on a target. In the SRI outbounder experiments that followed, a beacon or outbounder team would be given instructions to visit a unique building, a landmark, or some other easily identifiable location, designated as the "site" or "target." Sites would be selected randomly from a pool of sealed opaque envelopes containing instructions to many locations in the Menlo Park–Palo Alto area. As the experiments progressed, the viewer was locked in various laboratory locations, among them soundproof, shielded rooms, and kept fully "blind" to the location and nature of the target. At a prearranged time the viewer would attempt to describe the location where the outbound team was standing. According to the theory, the outbounders acted as a "beacon" for the viewer to "home in" on.

The approach had not yet been tried at SRI, and Swann knew it wouldn't serve for present needs. The client, the CIA, needed something to support either covert action or its intelligence-gathering mission. PK would have been admirably suited for covert action, if it had only worked consistently. Still, remote viewing, even in its rough, preliminary form, at least showed promise for the Agency's intelligence mission. But how could it be targeted? A remote viewer could be asked to describe a secret military complex on the outskirts of Moscow, but if a beacon person had to be there, what was the point? It would be easier just to give the beacon a camera and forget the remote viewing business altogether.

Complicating the issue was that such targets would likely be nominated for remote viewing precisely because conventional intelligence means had failed. The CIA *couldn't* get an agent inside, signals intelligence had failed to turn up anything useful, and satellite photos only showed a blank roof. If there was no other way to target a remote viewer than to use an outbounder team, then remote viewing was a blind alley as well.

And then Swann had a brainstorm.

In a meeting with Puthoff, Swann, and Targ during a visit to SRI, scientist Jacques Vallee, the legendary UFO researcher, made an interesting suggestion. "All you really need is an address," Vallee observed after some discussion. Swann mulled this over for awhile.[6]

"We didn't know how to give the site location to the subject without telling them something about it," Swann told me recently when recounting the story. It was already clear that allowing the viewer to know even a little about the target before the session resulted in distorted data. "And then I had this message from beyond!" Swann said, half amused, half bemused. "That's when I had this voice in my head saying, 'try coordinates.' "[7]

Providing the location of the desired target in terms of latitude and longitude would give away almost nothing about the target. Impressions could be retrieved without a viewer's preconceptions about the site getting in the way.

But Puthoff and Targ were a hard sell. Geographic coordinates were just an arbitrary way humans had divided up the globe, they said. Latitude and longitude are not found in the natural world. Humans pretend coordinates are there by drawing lines on a globe or map, both of which are themselves only approximations of the actual world. No, Swann's fellow researchers told him, all but laughing, there was no rational way coordinates could work for targeting remote viewers.

Swann was undeterred. Who said it had to be rational? Here they were, discussing the possibility that a human could mentally detect and describe a location as far away as the other side of the globe without the aid of any of the usual five senses, and they thought the targeting mechanism had to be *rational?* That in itself seemed a little irrational.

A few days later Swann brought the subject up again. Pointing out that the experiments SRI had run so far were trivial compared to what ought to be possible, Swann noted that he "wanted to look at something more interesting than what was in the next room." Puthoff and Targ again tried to put him off. But this time Swann would have none of it. "Look . . ." he said impetuously, "let's just do a few of them for a break. It'll take half an hour at most, and then we can return to our regular experimentation."[8] Surrendering, the scientists randomly picked ten coordinates off a map in the next room. Describing only the most basic details at the sites Swann rattled off one correct response after another. A coordinate in the northern polar region elicited the response of "ice." A coordinate in the sea off the coast of the Iberian Peninsula produced the response of "Ocean. I see Spain off in the distance." Another one centered in a tropical area resulted in "Land, jungles, mountains, peninsular mountains." When they had gone through all ten coordinates, the results were encouraging enough that Puthoff decided to run Swann under better scientific controls a few days later.

Puthoff chose ten more coordinates, this time carefully selected to make the exercise harder—small lakes in the middle of broad plains, islands in otherwise empty ocean, and so on. Swann's performance on these was just as convincing as with the first set. Altogether, ten sets of ten targets each were run. The final score for the last set of ten was seven obvious "hits," two "possibles," and only one certifiable "miss." It truly looked like Swann was on to something with this idea of coordinate targeting.

The upshot of it all was a call to the CIA to send some double-blind coordinates—locations that neither the researchers (Targ and Puthoff), nor the subject (Swann) knew anything about. The CIA was quick to respond.

On May 29, 1973, Swann sat down with Puthoff and the first CIA target. No one at SRI had any clue as to what was at the end of that set of degrees, minutes, and seconds. The target couldn't have provided a better test. It was a wooded area in the hills of West Virginia, near a vacation cabin. Unknown to anyone involved in the experiment, including the person providing the coordinates, was that within walking distance of the cabin was a secret underground technical facility belonging to the National Security Agency. Even if the SRI researchers had tried to cheat by looking up the coordinates on a map they would have found nothing.[9]

"This seems to be some sort of mounds or rolling hills," Swann began. Some distance to the north he described a city, and in the target area a lot of grass. He quickly determined that in the immediate vicinity there was nothing of particular interest. "There was nothing at that coordinate," Swann recalls. "So Hal told me to look around, there must be *something* there. I looked around and found this other place, which seemed to be removed from the coordinate about half a mile."[10]

At "this place," Swann discovered manicured lawns reminding him of those around a military installation. He also reported a flagpole, structures of various descriptions, and a strong impression of something underground. In its layout, the whole site suggested to him a former Nike-Hercules missile base. He then sketched out a fairly detailed map of his impressions of where the various elements he had perceived were located. With a shrug and crossed fingers, the report was forwarded to their CIA contact. But Swann wasn't the only one to work the target. On a lark, Puthoff gave the coordinate to another man, and the results were remarkable.

On the day Puthoff was set to task Swann with the CIA coordinate, he got a call out of the blue from a fellow named Pat Price. The two men had met at a social event some time before, but Price had heard about the remote viewing work on his own and was calling up to volunteer his services. He had a long and varied job history, working at careers as different as police commissioner and mining superintendent. And he thought he had a gift. Saying nothing about its origin, Puthoff let him try the CIA coordinate, and the results were forwarded to the client along with Swann's session.

Soon, they had a reaction. "Not only was Swann's description correct in every detail," Puthoff reported in *Mind Reach*. "But even the relative distances on the map were to scale!" Of even greater interest was Price's work. According to Dr. Ken Kress, the CIA's project manager for the SRI contract:

> . . . The subjects were asked to give an immediate response of what they remotely viewed at these coordinates . . . They both talked about a military-like facility . . . a striking correlation of the two independent descriptions was noted.
>
> Pat Price, who had no military or intelligence background, provided a list of project titles associated with current and past activities including one of extreme sensitivity. Also, the code-name of the site was provided. Other information concerning the physical layout of the site was accurate.[11]

Not everything was correct in both sessions. For instance, Price provided names for personnel at the location, and these turned out not to match anyone assigned there. Still, the results of this and other attempts were impressive enough that CIA support was renewed for another two years.

Swann remembers that somewhere between thirty and sixty of these double-blind, real-world coordinates were used in remote-viewing sessions before the first CIA contract came to an end in August.[12] As promised, SRI had a replicable psychic phenomenon to offer the CIA, and it looked like it could turn out to be useful.

But the time in California had been wearing on Swann. During the eight months he had felt compelled to return periodically to his beloved Manhattan to recuperate from the stress. Now, as he climbed aboard the plane to fly back to the East Coast, he vowed it was forever. He was determined never to return to the grueling regimen of parapsychology research at SRI. "What if I come up with an offer you can't refuse?" Puthoff asked as he bid Swann farewell.

With Swann's departure, Pat Price became SRI's primary experimental subject. He had shown his mettle on a number of projects, both experimental and operational. The one that he remains most famous for is his remote viewing of the so-called PNUTS, or "Possible Nuclear Underground Test Site" target, a Soviet research and development facility outside the city of Semipalatinsk in Kazakhstan. For years afterwards, Price's results were briefed around Washington, D.C., anytime someone needed to be persuaded of remote viewing's value.

PNUTS, also known as URDF-3 (for "Unidentified Research and Development Facility-3) was for many years the center of great controversy inside the U.S. intelligence community. Based on satellite imagery and extrapolations from how the United States itself conducted clandestine tests, the CIA at first thought the facility was used for low-yield nuclear weapons testing. But soon U.S. intelligence began to suspect that something even more sinister was taking place there. Later satellite photography showed a number of approximately sixty-foot spheres being buried at the site. This contributed to other circumstantial evidence that PNUTS was actually a center for developing a powerful Soviet particle beam weapon. According to the theory, nuclear explosions were detonated inside underground steel spheres. The resultant energy would be transformed to create bursts of particle streams with billions of volts of power. In principle, it was not too different from some of the thinking behind the later U.S. "Star Wars" Strategic Defense Initiative in the 1980s. A successful particle beam program would put the Soviets far ahead of the United States in the arms race.[13]

On July 10, 1974, Puthoff and Targ received the PNUTS coordinates from one of the CIA contract monitors. Shortly after that Targ presented them to

Price. In the course of several remote viewing sessions done over the next couple of weeks, the results were astonishing. "I am lying on my back on the roof of a two- or three-story brick building," Price declared. ". . . There's the most amazing thing. There's a giant gantry crane moving back and forth over my head . . . it seems to be riding on a track with one rail on each side of the building." Within the building "on" which he found himself, he reported an assembly room where a huge "sixty-foot-diameter metal sphere" was being put together from "thick metal gores" which resembled segments of a giant orange peel. The workers were having trouble putting the gores together to form the sphere, Price reported, and needed to find some low-temperature way to keep the gores from warping during assembly. Price also reported a cluster of tall, round-topped, silo-sized compressed-gas canisters.

Price's results were soon evaluated. Highly classified satellite imagery confirmed the presence of a huge, multistory gantry crane that closely matched the sketch Price had made of the unusual structure. The crane did indeed ride on two widely separated rails, and did in fact pass over at least one two- to three-story building. Price's sketches of the gas cylinders also matched almost exactly what the satellites saw. But no sixty-foot sphere was anywhere to be seen in the material provided SRI as feedback. Spheres are not even mentioned in SRI's 1975 final report to the CIA, apparently being regarded as mere "noise" at the time. The existence of such spheres was as yet unknown to those at the CIA who were evaluating the remote viewing data.

Then, on May 2, 1977, three years after the session was done, and two years after Pat Price's death in Las Vegas of a heart attack, the respected periodical *Aviation Week & Space Technology* published an article by its military editor, Clarence Robinson. According to the article, reconnaissance satellites had produced photos of Soviet engineers digging through solid granite to bury large spheres. ". . . Huge extremely thick steel gores were manufactured" in a nearby building, the article reported. The gores were part of a large sphere measured at "about 18 meters (57.8 feet) in diameter." It was also reported that U.S. scientists analyzing the intelligence data at first "believed that there was no method the Soviets could use to weld together the steel gores of the spheres to provide a vessel strong enough to withstand" even a small nuclear explosion, "especially when the steel to be welded was extremely thick." Yet the spheres were indeed there to be seen in the current imagery. It appeared that Pat Price had a certifiable "hit" with his session on the PNUTS target.[14]

In an interesting side-note to the story, a few years after the collapse of the Soviet Union, American scientists gained access to the Semipalatinsk site.

They found there neither a place for nuclear weapons testing, nor for particle beam research. Instead, "PNUTS" was trying to build nuclear-powered rockets for spaceflight. The former-Soviet researchers wanted to know if the United States might be interested in funding a joint project to continue their work. They were amused when told the U.S. had been afraid they were trying to build a "death-ray" instead.[15]

As with other remote viewing subjects, Price struggled with accuracy in his viewings. Ken Kress, the CIA's project officer, was to say that "in general, most of Price's data were wrong or could not be evaluated . . . He did, nevertheless, produce some amazing descriptions, like buildings under construction, spherical tank sections, and the crane." All in all, though, for the CIA at least, "since there was so much bad information mixed in with the good, the overall result was not considered useful . . . ORD [Office of Research and Development] officers concluded that since there were no control experiments to compare with, the data were nothing but lucky guessing."[16]

Though this conclusion seems unflattering in light of some of Price's undeniably impressive results, it is understandable given that good intelligence analysts are trained to be skeptical of any data until they have independent confirmation. It was also just two years into the program, and many lessons about tasking, analysis, and reporting of remote viewing data were yet to be learned. In retrospect, Price's PNUTS sessions were diamonds in the rough.

Kress's guarded evaluation notwithstanding, the PNUTS work provided new insights into the nature of the remote-viewing phenomenon. In an article published twenty years later, in 1995, Targ notes that the PNUTS work tells us several new things about remote viewing. First, in its basic nature remote viewing is probably not telepathic. Price made his report on the spheres when no one else involved with the experiment had any clue they were there. He was long since dead when information about them became available. Based on words and sketches, Targ concludes that Price must have had *direct experience of the site* (emphasis in original), and could not have been reading anyone's mind. Nor could Price presumably have been precognitively seeing his own future feedback, since that did not become available until two years after his death.[17]

If it is ever proved that remote viewing success *does* involve precognitive perception of future feedback, Price's case would show something even more remarkable than remote viewing. It would be evidence that human consciousness *does* survive physical death, and that it maintains some kind of perceptual link with the physical world.

———

Price wasn't to remain the only subject to be involved in remote viewing experiments at SRI. A talented professional photographer named Hella Hammid was soon to join the ranks, as was Duane Elgin, an SRI employee, and a man named Gary Langford. Keith Harary, later a partner with Russell Targ in some commercial remote viewing projects, also participated on many occasions, beginning in the late '70s. And by 1975, after laying off for a year to write his memoir, *To Kiss Earth Good-bye*, Ingo Swann was back as well, Puthoff having made him an offer he couldn't refuse.

Through 1975, half of the SRI research effort was divided among three categories: Did people gifted in paranormal ability have common characteristics that could be identified and used to find other successful remote viewers? What neurological evidence was present when people behaved "paranormally?" What was the nature of paranormal phenomena and energy?

These were interesting questions, but the other half of the SRI effort was more intriguing—the assessment of how well remote viewing worked in practical uses. Was it effective for spying on the enemy? On that question hung the future of remote viewing, whether it would go down in history as a mere curiosity, or be a valuable tool that government agencies would pay for.

The new remote viewing recruits jumped into this real-life question with enthusiasm, first with a "technology series," which tried to determine if, and how well, instruments and machinery might be perceived by a remote viewer under double-blind conditions. Their targets included an abacus with a clock and mechanical calendar attached, a then state-of-the-art IBM Selectric typewriter, a large stand-alone Xerox photocopier machine, and a heavy-duty drill press. On the drill press, the viewers produced remarkably accurate sketches of the stool in front of the machine, the toothed shaft, and the belt drive and pulleys in the top of the machine, which weren't even visible from a normal standing position on the floor. The other targets were also successfully described. When given a black-colored computer terminal as a target, one viewer described "a box with light coming out of it . . . painted flat black and in the middle of the room." Another viewer accurately reported a computer terminal with relay racks in the background.[18]

Altogether, seven pieces of equipment were viewed double-blind by twelve remote viewers, with impressive results. Two of the viewers were visiting CIA scientists who were pressed into service. Theirs were among the best results.

The CIA contract called for a diverse range of targets, not just mechanical equipment. One experiment had viewers figuring out whether sealed envelopes contained "secret writing"—the spy trade technique of using invisible ink or other ways of disguising writing in ordinary-seeming letters. The results were encouraging, but not strong enough to be statistically significant.[19]

There was also a two-pronged attempt to devise a way of identifying good remote viewers. The first used an ESP-testing machine operating similarly to one that Charles Tart had developed. By pushing buttons, the test subject tried to precognitively choose which of four photographic slides of artwork the random-number generator inside the machine was going to light up. As soon as the viewer's choice was made, the machine made its choice. In the first round, only one of the five subjects had success beyond chance, although he was able to duplicate this feat a second time. Among those who failed to get above chance were some who had done consistently well as remote viewers. A second study done for the National Aeronautics and Space Administration with 146 subjects produced similarly poor results. As a way of uncovering remote-viewing talent, the ESP machine turned out to be a failure.[20]

The second method of pinpointing good remote viewers used both novice viewers and old hands. The "outbounder" protocol was used for these experiments, with sites around the San Francisco Bay area as targets. Results were evaluated by judges who visited the sites and tried to match them with what the viewers had described.[21]

Pat Price's part in this experiment involved nine target sites, including Stanford's Hoover Tower, a marshy nature preserve near Palo Alto, and a drive-in movie theater. When targeted on the Palo Alto municipal swimming pool complex in Rinconanda Park, Price reported a circular pool of water about 120 feet in diameter, and a rectangular pool that he thought was perhaps 60 feet by 89 feet. Also present, he thought, were a concrete-block structure, two large water tanks, and a semicircular "service yard." Price decided it must be a water purification plant, and he duly included in his sketch of the layout the sort of rotating equipment typical of such plants.

His viewing of this site turned out to be generally correct. There *were* two pools there, though Price got their dimensions wrong by just a few feet. There was a concrete structure—the pool house—and a semicircular service yard just to one side. But there seemed to be things wrong with his session as well. In his sketch he had reversed the pools, with the round one on the left instead of the right. Left-right reversals were not unusual in remote-viewing experiments; Puthoff believed that was evidence of a unique effect involving the processing of visual perceptions by the brain's hemispheres. In normal vision, input from the right visual field passes through the right optical nerve, but is then switched to the left hemisphere at a brain structure called the "optic chiasm." Input from the left visual field is switched to the right hemisphere. Our brains properly reorient the whole sight experience during processing. However, Puthoff suggests that remote-viewing visual experiences may enter the viewer's mental processes somewhere *after* the optical chiasm, and therefore the visual signals are not switched left-to-right as they would be with normal vision. Sometimes a remote viewer's brain doesn't sort this out, and the result is a left-right reversal for some parts of a target.[22] That might explain the reversed pools, but there were no water tanks at the aquatic center, and it wasn't a water purification plant.

"As can be seen from his drawing," Puthoff and Targ were to write in a paper published in the *Proceedings of the IEEE* (the journal for the Institute of Electrical and Electronics Engineers) in 1976, "he also included some elements, such as the tanks . . . that are not present at the target site." This was evidence, they thought, of "essentially correct descriptions of basic elements and patterns coupled with incomplete or erroneous analysis of function."[23]

It wasn't until 1995—twenty years after Pat Price's death—that Targ found out how well Price had really done during that session. Targ came across a Palo Alto city history document, with a picture of the property that eventually became the swimming pool complex at Rinconanda Park. For many years (until the early 1960s) the location had indeed been a water treatment plant, with two water towers placed in the area where Price had sketched them. Price had confused various elements of present and past time, and recorded them in the same remote viewing session. This led Targ to observe that "one must specify not only the target location to be observed, but the time as well" in remote-viewing tasks.[24]

The results of Price's nine trials with Bay area targets were blind-judged and ranked. The entire series resulted in seven first-place rankings, one third-place, and one sixth-place. In other words, an outside judge with no other affiliation with the experiment was able to match seven of the nine sessions to the correct targets. Since there were nine targets and nine descriptions by Price, there was only a one-in-nine likelihood of matching any one transcript to the correct target by accident. But in this experiment that happened seven times, which compounds the unlikelihood of the overall result being due to chance. The odds against this being accidental were astronomical ($p = 2.9 \times 10^{-5}$, for the statistically inclined).[25]

These results were not just a fluke. A nine-target series of remote viewing trials performed by Hella Hammid resulted in five first-place matches and four second-place matches. Again, the results were far beyond chance ($p = 5.2 \times 10^{-4}$), which statistically was not significantly different from Pat Price's run. Interestingly, Hammid was considered a "learner subject"; she didn't have the same long experience as Price, who claimed to have relied on his ESP abilities many times over the years while involved in police work. Results with two other experienced viewers, including Swann, also were impressive. But outcomes for two other beginners, while better than chance, were not statistically significant. (There were two first-place "hits" even in those series.)[26]

As a means of discriminating between those with remote viewing potential and those without, the set of experiments was a mixed bag. "Such observations indicate a hypothesis," the report concludes, "that remote viewing may be a latent and widely-distributed perceptual ability."[27] In other words, it seemed that the ability might be widespread, rather than one that just happened to turn up in a few "gifted" people.

Other important things were learned. For instance, "The primary difference between experienced subjects and naive volunteers is not that the latter never exhibit the faculty, but rather that their results are simply less reliable, more sporadic."[28] In fact, certain transcripts from the "naive" viewers were counted as some of the best individual results. What that meant was that even beginners could get solid "hits." But the more practice they had, the more often they were likely to get one of those "hits."

Another intriguing point was the role that sketching played. Frequently, verbal responses would turn out to be wrong—the result of the viewers trying to analyze and put a name on what they sensed. Many times it turned out that what viewers *sketched* was far more accurate than what they reported in words. This had important implications for the underlying psychology of remote viewing, which will be discussed later.

Some of the other important insights gained into the nature of remote viewing during this phase of the research included the following:

- Responses that *described* were far more likely to be accurate than those that involved analysis. In other words, if the target was an apple, the viewer might respond with "red, rounded, smooth, semi-soft" and be correct. But the temptation is to continue on with "It's a rubber ball!" Targ and Puthoff's 1975 report observes that "We have learned to ask our subjects simply to describe what they see as opposed to what they think they are looking at."
- Comparing responses from several viewers for the same target improved the quality of the final data. When two or more viewers were tasked to describe the same target, the judge was more likely to successfully match their descriptions to the correct target.
- Remote viewers often seemed to employ a "scanning" process. Like a honeybee flitting from flower to flower, viewers would report pieces of information from various aspects of the target. Only after many of these pieces started to fit together did a coherent idea of the target start to emerge.

- Motion at the target was usually not noticed. In fact, "moving objects often are not seen at all even when nearby static objects are correctly identified."
- In outbounder remote viewing experiments, viewers frequently described additional details beyond what the beacon team actually at the target was able to observe, which nevertheless turned out to be true of the site. Often, these details were ones that could not have been observed by the people at the site, such as closed-off areas or tops of buildings.
- Each viewer had an "individual pattern of response, like a signature." Individual viewers had a tendency to home in on certain parts of a target and avoid others, or had a preference for reporting certain kinds of data, while ignoring other kinds. One viewer might focus on architecture or terrain while another might notice more about the people present. Of course, any viewer might at any time provide any type of response data. It was just that certain viewers seemed to "specialize" in specific categories of perceptions.
- Remote viewing improves with practice. While a novice might occasionally provide excellent results, successful performances increased with practice and experience.
- Average people could be taught to remote view. In the field of parapsychology this notion was revolutionary. It turned out to have significant implications for the future.[29]

In hindsight, much progress was made and many adventures occurred over the three years the CIA funded SRI's remote-viewing program. Unfortunately, the honeymoon was about to end.

7

What They
Discovered

"This is the biggest fool
thing we've ever done!
The bomb will never go
off, and I speak as an
expert on explosives!"

–Admiral William Leahey,
talking about the atomic
bomb, in 1945

The year 1975 was not a good one for the CIA. Agency officials had been implicated in the Watergate scandal. Others had been caught spying for their political bosses on American citizens in the antiwar movement. Revelations about "mind-control" experiments and germ warfare tests on unwitting Americans brought the anger of Congress crashing down upon the agency, and led to the forming of two congressional committees to look into mischief at the CIA. The Senate committee was chaired by Senator Frank Church, who denounced the CIA as the "rogue elephant" of the intelligence community.

Representative Otis Pike led the House committee in its own highly confrontational investigation.

When the smoke cleared after a year and more of hearings and investigations, the CIA together with the rest of the intelligence community had to render obeisance not only to their usual civilian or military chains of command, but also to two new permanent congressional oversight committees. Even today these committees scrutinize intelligence-related activities to make sure they comply with federal law and, hopefully, common sense as well.

As a result of the intense political pressure brought to bear, the CIA jettisoned any questionable, marginally legal, or politically sensitive project, even if it hadn't been found out by congressional investigators. One of the victims was the fledgling remote viewing program. About halfway through 1975, SRI was informed that the CIA would no longer finance explorations into the extrasensory realm.

To be fair, there were other reasons. Almost since the beginning of the CIA's involvement in the SRI project, there was internal discord over whether remote viewing had a place as an intelligence tool, or even if it was a real phenomenon. Seemingly amazing performances such as Price's remote viewing of Semipalatinsk were looked upon with skepticism. Supporters held them up as examples of the potential remote viewing *might* have when fully developed as a skill. Naysayers pointed to the bad data that usually came along with the good and asked how one could possibly know whether a viewer was correct when answering crucial intelligence questions. Even though a few in-house CIA employees had shown some success with remote viewing, and Price himself was now working exclusively for the agency and coming up with results corroborated by other intelligence information the CIA already had or soon obtained, this ongoing debate contributed to the termination of CIA involvement after Price's sudden death in July 1975.[1]

Written opinions of detractors at the CIA were later the foundation for the Agency's 1995 official disclaimer, which said that remote viewing had been abandoned in 1975 because it didn't work. The truth was much more complicated than this. It was not that the phenomenon didn't work, but that not enough had yet been learned about how to effectively use it in operations. Saying that remote viewing didn't work because not all of it was accurate was like saying satellite reconnaissance didn't work because the majority of the take was obscured by cloud cover. But since the half-truth served the CIA's political purposes, it stands as the Agency's official position on remote viewing, in 1975 and again, twenty years later, in 1995.

Fortunately, all was not lost. Remembering that time of uncertainty, Hal Puthoff describes how his CIA contacts, still supportive of the program despite the largely political hue and cry that had risen against it, helped the SRI program survive the loss of official CIA support. "They said, 'you know we're going to have to terminate the program; *but* we still want it to go on,'" said Puthoff. "So our CIA contract monitors hand-carried us around to locate other funders."[2]

There was one attempt to work a deal with DARPA, the Defense Advanced Research Projects Agency. The CIA could transfer funds to DARPA, which would then sponsor the SRI research. That way the CIA could still support the parapsychology research effort while protecting itself from exposure. But that maneuver fell through.

Salvation emerged in the person of an Air Force civilian employee assigned to the Foreign Technology Division (FTD) at Wright-Patterson Air Force Base in Dayton, Ohio.

"It was about this time that Dale Graff contacted me from Wright-Patterson," Puthoff explained. "He just wrote me as an American citizen, not as a government representative." Graff had an interest in ESP, and had sent letters around to researchers investigating the phenomena. When he wrote Hal, he had no inkling that SRI's work had been funded by the government. "I just wrote him back," Puthoff continued. "I got millions of letters like his. But for some reason it was such a straightforward, thoughtful piece I decided to write him back." Graff soon contacted Puthoff, owning up to the fact that he was a government employee. More interesting, he said he wanted to get his own project going, and would SRI be able to be involved in some way? "Since those were days of desperation," Puthoff said, "I was of course interested."

Graff's interest in psi arose from intelligence research he was doing into ESP-related work going on behind the Iron Curtain. As a civilian analyst with a physics background, his job was to forecast new weapons and technologies that the USSR might develop in the next twenty years. One of his reports included a section on credible Soviet ESP research. Along with correspondence between Graff and Puthoff, this helped persuade the FTD's command staff to bring Puthoff and Targ in for a briefing at FTD. After the two left, Graff was invited to a closed-door meeting, where it was decided to fund the SRI effort on an exploratory basis for at least a year.[3]

The Air Force wasn't the only sponsor recruited to help during this lean time. There was a small Army contract with an organization at Aberdeen Proving Grounds in Maryland, another contract with the Navy (which was eventually canceled because some in the Navy's high command found the idea of remote viewing objectionable), and aviator Richard Bach, author of *Jonathan Livingston Seagull*, even donated around $40,000 to the cause.[4]

Publicity didn't hurt—at least, unclassified "civilian-sector" publicity. In March 1976, Puthoff and Targ wrote an article for the peer-reviewed journal *Proceedings of the IEEE,* published by the prestigious Institute of Electrical and Electronics Engineers. Titled "A Perceptual Channel for Information Transfer Over Kilometer Distances: Historical Perspective and Recent Research," it gave an overview of the history of parapsychological research, then detailed the work done with Swann, Geller, Price, and some of the others up to that point. Loaded with mathematical formulas, graphs, and charts, and illustrated with impressive remote viewing results, the twenty-five-page article sparked a huge controversy in the science community and, in fact, almost wasn't published.

At the time the editor of the journal was Robert Lucky, a leading scientist at Bell Labs. When Lucky first received the SRI paper he was hesitant. The peer reviewers returned mixed comments on whether the paper ought to see the light of day. Some of the reviewers were supportive, but one quipped, "This is the sort of thing I wouldn't believe, even if it were true!"

Puthoff and Targ went to Bell Labs to give a presentation and answer questions on their research, in the hope of persuading Lucky to publish the article. Finally, they struck a deal. Lucky could try a replication experiment at his laboratory, using the protocols and experimental design that SRI had pioneered. If the replication failed, the article would end up in the trash bin. But if it succeeded, Lucky would publish it in the journal. Using his secretary, who thought she had some psychic ability, the scientist ran a number of double-blind trials. The results were convincing enough that the article soon appeared in the publication.[5]

The *Proceedings* paper wasn't the first published in a top-ranked science journal. In 1974, accompanied by astonished complaints from the mainstream science community, the SRI researchers had published a preliminary article in the science journal *Nature,* summarizing the first eighteen months or so of their studies. Half the article focused on Geller, but Price and Hella Hammid were also mentioned.[6]

Much of the data from the *Nature* and *Proceedings of the IEEE* articles, with added detail and more human-interest material, was used in Targs and Puthoff's book *Mind Reach: Scientists Look at Psychic Ability.* Published in 1977 by Delacorte Press, the book boasted a forward by Richard Bach, and an introduction from anthropologist Margaret Mead. Surprisingly easy reading for a subject steeped in the technical jargon of the SRI Radio Physics Laboratory, the book made a strong case for what Puthoff and his colleagues were trying to do. *Mind Reach* would remain influential through several printings, until long after it was declared out of print by its publisher.

As funds started to trickle into the program, so too did a new researcher.

Dr. Ed May, a young physicist with an interest in the paranormal, applied to work with the SRI program. Feeling that increased scientific rigor would come from having another physicist on board, Ingo Swann lobbied for May's hiring. May had some previous experience in working with EEG data, and Targ and Puthoff needed someone to help analyze the huge load of data from a large experiment they were conducting. So in 1976 Ed May joined the lab, and would have an important role to play a decade later. Instead of being canceled, the SRI research moved ahead with new momentum.

One of the major research goals had always been to find out where psi phenomena came from. Because it was the most repeatable, remote viewing was the best candidate for the research. Many people tend to think of psi as being like radio signals. ESP jargon therefore included terms such as "receiver" and "sender," "signal," and "transmission." This way of thinking was natural. The kind of information obtained in SRI experiments must involve some sort of "action at a distance." But the only known means for obtaining information from distant places was via the electromagnetic spectrum—radio and television waves, electricity, or light.

So SRI set out to determine whether remote viewing needed electromagnetism to work, and if so, what part of the EM spectrum was involved. The researchers went through a process of elimination. If remote viewers could be put in situations that blocked segments of the electromagnetic spectrum, it should be possible to tell when remote viewing stopped happening, and when it started happening again. Trial and error would eventually show which frequencies in the spectrum were responsible for remote viewing, and perhaps other ESP effects.[7]

But the electromagnetic spectrum is broad in scope and certain parts of it can be very hard to block. It runs from extremely high frequencies and high energy at its top (the realm of gamma rays and X-rays) down through ultraviolet light, to visible light, then infrared, on down through the whole range of microwave and radio frequencies, to the utter bottom of the spectrum where reside radio waves known simply as "extremely low frequency," or ELF waves.

It was easy to eliminate the high end of the spectrum as a source of remote viewing signals. For high-frequency radiation to work, one had to be near its source, and still it was soon absorbed by barriers and objects it passed through. Ultraviolet and visible light could also be discounted. All one had to do to block them was to go into a windowless room and shut the door. SRI had already experimented with objects sealed in containers or locked in distant rooms, and viewers were still able to describe them. Infrared could be excluded for similar reasons.

How, though, could one get rid of the radio-frequency part of the EM spectrum, from high-frequency microwave radiation on down? After all, radio and television signals flood our homes, cars, and offices. Could one be sure that remote viewing was not caused by some weird interaction of radio waves and human physiology? It turned out that a large portion of this range could be excluded by using a Faraday-shielded room. This was a cubicle sheathed in copper mesh, with ground wires and other means for keeping various frequencies out of the room. Remote viewings were often done within this chamber, with no apparent decrease in success. But there were certain frequencies that a Faraday cage could not block—above, in the microwave range, and below in the ELF part of the spectrum.

Microwave frequencies could be eliminated as carriers of remote viewing information. Information can be carried by microwave, but only for a relatively short distance before it needs a boost, and the receiver has to be in the line of sight of the source of the microwave transmission. The signal is easily disrupted by buildings, mountains, and other obstacles. Hence the need to pepper the landscape with microwave and cell phone relay towers for modern electronic communications to work.

ELF, extremely low-frequency electromagnetic radiation, was another matter. These waves travel long distances, only gradually losing intensity. They are known for their ability to pass through shielding that would stop other forms of radiation. Indications that living organisms might be sensitive to sufficiently powerful ELF waves were also interesting from the perspective of ESP. In fact, Russian scientists were convinced of the theory that ELF was important in extrasensory perception. Some of the experiments conducted at SRI were actually replications of those of noted Soviet researcher Leonid Vasiliev. Still, the people at SRI needed to determine once and for all whether ELF really did have something to do with remote viewing. But there was a problem—since ELF passed through Faraday shielding, how could it be eliminated as a source?

There were three options, the first being distance. Though ELF waves can travel a long way, they still lose energy and carry less information at long distances. If remote viewing experiments over thousands of miles showed the same quality as those done close to the viewer, it would be strong evidence that ELF did not explain remote viewing.

The second variable was resolution—how much detail can be "seen." ELF wavelengths are very long and stretched out. Because of this, they would have a hard time in "resolving," or defining small details or small objects. For example, small objects would be virtually invisible to a radar system that used long ELF waves. If remote viewing could successfully "see" small targets, that would be good evidence against ELF as an explanation for remote viewing.

Attenuation is the third variable. Radio waves are "attenuated" when they pass through materials or objects that drain their energy. Since the copper mesh of a Faraday cage doesn't attenuate an ELF signal enough, something else had to be found that did. And given ELF's penetration power, there would have to be a lot of it.

The distance variable was fairly easily tested. Ingo Swann and Pat Price's remote-viewing sessions done for the CIA were preliminary evidence that distance didn't matter. To confirm the evidence, a series of transcontinental outbounder experiments were done. One experiment had Grant's Tomb in New York as the double-blind target. Two remote viewers in Menlo Park, California, came up with good descriptions of the site.

The next cross-country target was Washington Square in New York City, a central feature of which is a circular, sunken, amphitheaterlike structure. It is made of tiers of concentric cement rings stepping down into a basin. The viewer reported, "The first image I got . . . was of a cement depression, as if a dry fountain with a cement post in the center or inside." Further impressions were of "cement steps going into the depression, like a stadium, and the rounded edge of the top of the depression as you go up to ground level." With other details reported in the session, it was an easy match for blind-judging.[8]

Another distance trial involved Dale Graff, who had just become contract manager for the remote-viewing program. Targ and Puthoff were visiting Graff at Wright-Patterson in Dayton and Graff wanted reassurance that there really was something to this business he'd gotten himself into. Arrangements were made for Hella Hammid, who was visiting in New York, to remote view a randomly selected target. At the last minute, Graff arbitrarily chose Ohio Caverns, near Columbus.[9]

Without telling them what the target was, Graff guided Puthoff and Targ to the site and, at the appointed time, entered the vine-bedecked building that covered the mouth of the cave. They then descended the long, steep set of stairs, finally ending up about 150 feet underground in limestone passageways lit by strings of naked electric bulbs fastened to the walls. After wandering through the caverns for forty-five minutes, they left through a thick wooden door and entered a large square shaft, climbing more stairs back to the open air.

Hella described the impressions she received during the experiment. ". . . Russell and Hal . . . entering into arbor-like shaft . . . vines (wisteria) growing in arch at entrance like to a wine cellar—leading into underground world. Darker earth smelling cool moist passage . . . a very man-made steel wall—and shaft-like inverted silo going deep below the earth—brightly lit . . ."[10] Though she added details that were suggestive of an underground military facility (such elaboration was not unusual in remote viewing sessions, as I will touch on later), she got the descriptions and general nature of the site quite accurately.

There were other successful long-distance remote viewing sessions in the series, but the final one on October 31, 1976, is particularly interesting. It was a Menlo Park–to-Louisiana session, and the randomly selected, double-blind target turned out to be the New Orleans Superdome. While at the target, the outbounder dictated his impressions of the target into a tape recorder, noting that it was "a huge silvery building with a white dome . . . a circular building with metal sides." To the outbounder it looked "like nothing so much as a flying saucer." These remarks were to be provided to the viewer as feedback after the experiment was finished.

At the time of the targeting, the viewer on the West Coast (Gary Langford) drew some sketches closely resembling the target, but hesitated to give the response that first came to mind. "I don't want to tell you what I'm getting," Puthoff remembers Langford saying. "You'd just think I was crazy!" With a little urging, the viewer tentatively reported that it looked just like a big flying saucer resting in a city. Finally, the viewer decided that the target was actually "a large circular building with a white dome."

As the long-distance remote-viewing experiments wrapped up, it seemed clear that remote viewing results were not significantly affected even by long distances. The ELF hypothesis was not faring well. Noting that similar results occurred in a remote-viewing experiment conducted between Chicago and Moscow by Brenda Dunne and J. Bishaha, the SRI study concluded that distance appeared to be no barrier. The first nail was hammered into the ELF coffin.

Resolution studies came next. The smaller the target that was successfully remote viewed, the less likely that ELF was involved. But how best to present a small target? One solution was to seal small objects inside metallic film canisters. Hella Hammid was again the viewer. A person unknown to Hella and unaffiliated with the remote-viewing experiments was asked to choose ten small items and seal them inside film cans, which were then passed to a person who had no knowledge of what was inside. This person randomly numbered the containers and placed them in a safe.

When it was time to do one of the experiments, a number was randomly chosen, and that numbered canister was removed from the safe. The canister was never in the remote viewer's presence until after the experiment was finished. Instead, it was held in the custody of a beacon person kept separate from the remote viewer in a different lab room some distance away.

The results were impressive. One of the targets in the canisters was a spool of thread with a round-headed pin stuck through the strands. Hammid's response was "something thin and long . . . with a nail head at the end . . . silver colored." She drew sketches of a flanged cylinder and the unmistakable outline of a pin or small nail. For another target, the experimenter had sealed a small leather belt-buckle key ring inside the film canister. Hammid replied that she was confused.

"The strongest image I get is like a belt," she stated. But she couldn't figure out how anyone could have gotten something as large as a belt inside such a small container. Her sketches captured elements of the metallic buckle on the leather key ring.

One trial in the series produced the description of a "miniature tower . . . scalloped bottom . . . light beige." It turned out that the canister had been packed with sand and the viewer had described and sketched it as the sand would have appeared compressed inside the can, but without the can—a cylindrical tower shape, with scalloped edges where the small fluting around the can lid marked an even circle of indentations in the sand. Hammid had even sketched a raised ring around the middle of her drawing, which corresponded to a similar ridge on the can.[11]

To take the resolution experiment even further, microdots of various scenes were used. Microdots are spots of microfilm, about the size of a pinhead, containing complete, miniature images of objects or locations. If viewers could produce results from these equal in quality to those obtained from larger targets, it would be persuasive evidence against the ELF hypothesis. Again, the experiments were successful.

One of the most provocative experiments yet remained. Could ELF radiation be weakened or blocked—attenuated—enough to eliminate it as a possible channel for remote viewing? The Ohio Caverns experiment had helped. Passing through earth and rock weakened ELF waves to a degree, yet remote viewing had still worked. But there was another option available—the deep water off the California coast. A lot of seawater provided an excellent shield against ELF, if one could get deep enough. Unexpectedly, an opportunity soon presented itself.

Back in about 1971, Stephan Schwartz, the young editor of the journal *Seapower*, was unexpectedly picked to be a special assistant to Admiral Elmo Zumwalt, the Chief of Naval Operations. Schwartz's writing in favor of an all-volunteer Navy had caught Zumwalt's eye, and Schwartz spent the next three years helping to turn the Navy into an all-professional, all-volunteer force.

While still with the Navy in 1973, Schwartz came across a then-classified set of documents translating some of the work of Leonid Vasiliev, the influential Soviet scientist who was researching psychoenergetics. Vasiliev was searching for the fundamental cause of psychic behavior. He was sure that psi had a physical root, which was probably electromagnetic. Vasiliev had tried Faraday cages and other apparatus, and had Soviet psychics work from deep inside mines. As SRI would later, he managed to exclude virtually all of the electromagnetic spectrum except for the ELF range. According to the documents Schwartz read, Vasiliev decided that the only way to prove that ELF carried ESP signals was by using seawater shielding. If ESP stopped working under the ocean, then ELF was probably the culprit.

Schwartz, who had developed an interest in parapsychology, was fascinated. The Navy had been working furiously to find some way of using ELF to communicate with its ballistic-missile submarines, since no other radio frequencies worked at all when the subs were submerged—and even ELF was problematic. As a result of the Navy's interest, Schwartz had access to the latest research on the seawater shielding of ELF waves. He thought he might have a try at closing the last door in Vasiliev's research. Unfortunately, though he had the interest of Admiral Zumwalt, no one was willing to risk doing such a controversial experiment with a Navy submarine, even for a special assistant to the Chief. Schwartz's ambition went unfulfilled—at least for the time being.

Upon leaving the Pentagon, he moved to Arizona where he wrote his first book, *The Secret Vaults of Time*, about using psychics in archaeology. Then, in the fall of 1976, he got a phone call from two former Navy acquaintances, now well placed at a major ocean research institute. They had remembered Schwartz's interest in doing an undersea ESP experiment. Was he still interested in trying it? If so, they had their hands on a submarine he could use. Three thousands miles and two years away from his Navy job at the Pentagon, a submarine unexpectedly had fallen right into Stephan Schwartz's lap.[12]

It wasn't just any submarine—it was the *Taurus*, a research submersible that could dive deeper than any of the Navy's fleet subs. Schwartz's acquaintances arranged for him to have three days with the *Taurus*, which was coming down from its home in Canada for sea trials off California. The sub needed a mission, and here was one that would suffice.

Schwartz had originally thought to use his own brand of remote viewing, which he called "remote sensing." At the time, he told me, he had not heard about the SRI program, and had serendipitously developed his own approach. But in the spring of 1977 he met Ingo Swann, who introduced him to SRI's Ed May, and through them he met Hammid, Puthoff, and Targ. Once he learned the scope of the SRI experiments, he decided it might be a good idea to join forces with them. Schwartz offered Puthoff and Targ the opportunity to collaborate with him in a joint experiment using SRI remote viewers and his own submarine time. Accordingly, Schwartz was "lent" Ingo Swann and Hella Hammid to try remote viewing from hundreds of feet under the surface of the ocean, and the balance of the SRI team worked together on the rest of the experiment.

The first part of the experiment was aimed at seeing if large quantities of seawater could be "looked through" using RV. Seven remote viewers and psychics, including Swann, Hammid, and well-known psi practitioner Alan Vaughn were asked to identify the location of a shipwreck on the ocean floor off the California coast. If they came up with a location, the *Taurus* would scout it out and see if there was indeed a sunken vessel there. A location was provided, and in fact the remains of a foundered ship were discovered.

The results of the second part of the experiment were even more impressive. According to the protocol, Hammid and Swann would each take turns in the submarine for a total of four dives. At a designated depth and pre-arranged time the viewer would describe the location where Targ and Puthoff were. The location was randomly selected from a pool of six targets in the Bay area.

Schwartz decided to piggyback on the experiment to see if a message could be sent via remote viewing. If so, it might be a way of "talking" to submarines otherwise out of contact with the surface. What if each of the possible targets had a message associated with it? For example, if the target pool contained a distinctive fountain in a town square, the message that went along with it might be "surface for radio contact." If the target were a swimming pool, the message might instead be "hide under polar ice and await further instructions." This was similar to a notion of communication that Graff and Puthoff had independently been considering and they helped in developing the message/target set.

Each of the six locations in the target pool had a message attached to it. A key list of messages and their targets was sealed in an envelope to which the viewer had no access until the remote viewing was finished. At the end of the experiment, the viewer would be handed the envelope and asked to select which one of the six targets his or her remote-viewing results best described. The message on the back of whichever target was chosen would then be taken as instructions for the submarine's captain. Thus was born what became known as the ARV, or "associative remote viewing" protocol.

Hammid went first. Far out at sea the submarine submerged to a depth of 170 meters—about 550 feet beneath the surface, with the bottom of the ocean another 500 feet below. This position was calculated to offer the maximum shielding from ELF waves. The experiment was further complicated by Hammid becoming violently seasick from the tossing of the sub while it was on the surface. Nevertheless, at the appointed time, Hammid began to describe the scene where Puthoff and Targ were, 500 miles away away.

"A very tall looming object," were the first words out of her mouth. "A very, very huge tall tree and a lot of space behind them. There almost feels like there is a drop-off or a palisade or cliff behind them." She also noted that she thought Puthoff was clowning around in the tree in a very unscientific manner.[13]

Upon being handed the sealed envelope containing the six possible targets, she immediately identified the correct one—an ancient oak tree towering near the lip of a steep drop with a wide vista behind. After meeting with Puthoff and Targ later, she discovered that Puthoff had indeed been clambering boyishly around in the branches of the tree.

It was Swann's turn next. This time the submarine found a spot to sit on the ocean floor 78 meters down (about 253 feet). When it was time for the experiment, Swann reported, "Flat stone flooring, walls, small pool, reddish stone walk, large doors, walking around, an enclosed space." He then drew a rough sketch capturing the major points of what he perceived.

When presented with the sealed envelope containing a new set of six targets, Swann also immediately chose the correct one: the atrium area of a busy indoor shopping mall that did indeed have as a central feature a small pond with flagstone floors around it and a small, reddish stone path through a garden of indoor plants.

Four attempts had been planned, but the *Taurus* altered its dive schedule, so Schwartz and the SRI researchers had to be satisfied with the results they had. But those were remarkable. The degree of attenuation of ELF in seawater could be measured; in his book *Mind Race* Targ puts it at a hundredfold decrease.[14] When this information was compared with the bit-rate (the amount of data ELF waves could carry when so severely diminished) it became obvious that ELF could not be the information channel for remote viewing results. The electromagnetic spectrum was essentially eliminated as a means to explain how remote viewing, and psi in general, worked.

This had dramatic implications. Apparently there was no known physical way to shield any target on earth from the prying "eyes" of a remote viewer. But there was also a downside. If the experiments, rather than turning out negative, had proved instead that electromagnetism *could* explain remote viewing, that would have fit neatly into the prevailing scientific worldview. But since it could not, science had no way of understanding remote viewing. The result was rejection by mainstream science.

In the previous chapter I quoted a definition of remote viewing that the SRI scientists came up with early in their research. All it mainly said was that remote viewing was something that allowed people to use only their minds to perceive physical things that were hidden from the normal five senses. But now, after several more years of exploration, it was time to evaluate once again what new things had been learned about remote viewing.

In 1979 the American Association for the Advancement of Science sponsored a symposium on the current state of parapsychology. The SRI team published a paper in the Proceedings that gave an expanded definition of remote viewing, adding the concept of scale. Remote viewing enabled a person to "access and describe, by means of mental processes, remote geographical locations up to several thousand kilometers distant from their physical location," which were blocked from normal perception.

But it went further. This capacity was "developed sufficiently in several individuals to allow them to describe—often in considerable detail— geographical or technical material such as buildings, roads, natural formations, interior laboratory apparatus, and sealed targets, along with the real-time activities of persons at the target site."[15] Adding this caveat about what sorts of targets could be viewed put remote viewing well outside the scope of certain practitioners who claim to use clairvoyance to describe angelic realms; or of any tarot card readers who only give advice about such things as meeting tall, dark strangers.

Still, this did not nail things down completely. Depending on tasking, it was conceivable that a crystal-ball gazer might be able to discern information about a Soviet biological warfare facility. Or someone who normally only gave psychic readings about peoples' love lives might possibly turn up important clues on where a hostage was hidden.

In fact, Joe McMoneagle seems willing to call people "remote viewers" even if they practiced some of the more arcane psychic disciplines, just as long as they strictly followed proper experimental protocols. As Joe colorfully puts it, "If someone wants to wrap themselves in an orange sheet, hum 'Dixie' through their left nostril, while writing the information down backward in archaic Greek, that's fine. I don't know how well they might do, but as long as they do it within an approved remote viewing protocol," it might still be considered remote viewing.[16] Practicing correct protocols therefore becomes a further part of the definition of remote viewing.

Though the words often are used interchangeably, in science "protocols" are frequently different than "methods." Methods give you a recipe for how to do something. Protocols specify the *conditions* under which methods are to be used. Remote viewing protocols are nothing more than rules that must be followed if one wishes to do legitimate remote viewing. These rules are based on long-accepted standards for scientific research.

The most important of these protocols is that a remote viewer should always be "blind" to the target—never told before or during the remote viewing session what the target is. Further, in most remote viewing settings no one who comes in contact with the viewer should know what the target is. This is what is called a *double-blind* condition, where neither viewers nor anyone else in their vicinity are witting as to what the target is.

Having the viewer "blind" to the target, and insisting that others who might be be present are also blind contrasts with one common practice in the "psychic" or "intuitive" community. It is not unusual for both the psychic and those around to know far too much about the subject and the purpose of the information sought. This makes error or trickery much too easy.

Another important rule is that remote viewing targets must be verifiable; they must really exist, and there must be "ground truth" known about them. They could even be visited physically, if there was any doubt about some aspect of them.

But if there were no known "ground truth" about the target, it would be impossible to tell how accurate the remote-viewer's efforts were. Years of experiments show that a viewer's "feeling" that he or she was on the mark is nearly useless for telling whether or not the viewer actually was "on." Many times, when a viewer strongly feels that the session is highly accurate, it has actually been a bust. And, frequently, when viewers wind up a session convinced they have failed, the data they produce turns out to be very good.

If the target is impossible to verify by its nature, there is no way to tell whether *everything* the remote viewer comes up with isn't purely imaginary. Unfortunately, these days there is a strong pull in the remote viewing community from people who want to do more esoteric sorts of targets, including: UFO encounters, religious personalities or events, fantastic beasts such as the Loch Ness monster, inhabitants of other worlds, and so on.

Perhaps these things exist, perhaps they don't. But for now they are all unverifiable, and people who try to perceive them are engaging in speculation, not real remote viewing. There are those who learned the hard way about chasing these chimerical targets. But we will hear about them much later in the story.

As the SRI research progressed, it became clear that at least as far as verifiable targets, consistency, and replicability were concerned, none of the usual paranormal trappings of crystals, smoked mirrors, tarot cards, and so on were necessary. True, each of the SRI viewers had a distinctive style. Like major-league baseball pitchers, some even had favorite little rituals. Hella Hammid always wore her lucky socks while viewing, and Pat Price polished his glasses so he could "see" better. But they didn't need crystal balls or decks of cards to get results.

Bottom line: if what one does is traditionally called something else, it is probably not remote viewing. If one claims to get "psychic" information from an entity in another dimension, or if one must use a smoked mirror or crystal ball, runes or tarot cards, then it is channeling, scrying, or some form of divination, not remote viewing. These things already have names that have been used for hundreds of years. Yet there are people who want to call these very techniques remote viewing. While some who borrow the name "remote viewing" may simply be confused, others are only taking cynical advantage of a popular new term to rejuvenate their business or build their credibility.

At first blush, what I have just said seems to contradict Joe McMoneagle, who defines remote viewing as just sticking within certain science-based protocols. And perhaps it *is* contradictory. But Joe himself urges caution. "Not just anything can be called remote viewing," he declares in his book, *Remote Viewing Secrets*. "Being a remote viewer requires a lot more than is required of a psychic." In fact, "ground rules and protocols . . . [were defined] . . . so that remote viewing would *not* be viewed like any other form of paranormal functioning" (emphasis in original).[17] While from past discussions I know that Joe has a more flexible view of what can be called a remote-viewing methodology than do I, he still agrees that lines need to be drawn.

A true remote viewing method does not make hard-and-fast claims about where remote viewing impressions come from. It only traces their origins back into the viewer's own mind. All perception begins in the subconscious, whether it is vision, hearing, or remote viewing. No one knows how remote viewing impressions get into the subconscious. Remote-viewing methodologies themselves only help the viewer turn those impressions into perceptions as accurately as possible and bring them out into conscious awareness. And no esoteric instruments or elaborate metaphysical theories are needed for it to work.

As an example, one recently created offshoot of an earlier remote viewing method bills itself as "scientific." However, part of its doctrine is the belief that some remote viewing signals come from something called "subspace." Subspace is supposedly a nonphysical realm paralleling the physical one in which we live yet is allegedly just as "real." But since there is no particular reason to believe that such a thing as subspace exists, the notion of subspace as a source of remote viewing "signals" is purely metaphysical speculation. Perhaps it will turn out to be true, but there is no reason to think that it will.

Unlike other, more traditional psychic practices, RV grew up within the context of science. Mere speculation as to what "could" or "might" be true is not enough to explain where remote viewing data comes from. Remote viewing methods that toy with such fancies are in danger of stepping over the hazy line that divides real remote viewing from the excesses and frequent wishful thinking of traditional "paranormal" beliefs. I don't mean to say necessarily that these more traditional paranormal practices don't work; they likely do, at least sometimes. And they may be based on the same human perceptual ability that underlies remote viewing.

But they may instead be more like Dumbo's feather. In the animated Disney movie, a baby elephant with huge ears believes he can fly only when he is clutching in his trunk a magic feather. In the end, he discovers the feather is only a crutch, without which he can still fly perfectly well. Just like Dumbo's feather, crystal balls and tarot cards and other accessories to the paranormal may be nothing more than psychological crutches, while remote viewing may turn out to be the expression of a human perception that transcends normal physical constraints on the senses without the need for artifacts. There is more to learn before we know for sure.

Pure research experiments were not the only thing going on at SRI. The scientists still had to explore how remote viewing could be used for intelligence work. Though others were involved, Puthoff and Swann did the lion's share of the work for this part of the mission. It fit in well with Swann's motivations. He was determined to discover as much as he could about the personal experience of remote viewing, and how to get beyond that to the real data that was mixed in with the viewers' feelings and imaginings. The only way to do this was through long, laborious trial and error.

Day by day, week by week, month after month, Puthoff and Swann would work through session after session, target after target. Puthoff would provide the targets and Swann would work the sessions, keeping careful records of which procedures worked and which ones didn't. A large number of these were real operations about which some ground truth was known. None of the results of these targets are available to the public as of this writing.

But, like experiments run earlier for the CIA, some of the sites were only simulated operational targets. They were chosen to test the process so it would be more reliable when used against "live" targets. An interesting example of this was a project done against a Sylvania research and manufacturing facility in Mountain View, California. The target location included a long, two-story rectangular building with tall, thin windows up the sides and an antenna towards one end of the roof. Immediately nearby there was also a bulging, dome-shaped inflatable building that was even taller than the main building. Once given the coordinates, Swann began busily sketching the target—

first the main building—though he at first gave it arching windows. Moving on to what turned out to be the inflatable structure, he captured the rounded top of it, but gave it higher and more rigid sides. He recognized there was something unusual about it. The word "aerator" came in as a piece of data, as well as the further impression that this building kept getting "bigger and bigger."

Swann had been experimenting with capturing target sites three-dimensionally by modeling them in clay. If the viewer became kinesthetically involved with the target by shaping a model of it, this would help stifle premature conscious analysis and free up more true data about the target, he thought. The clay model created for the Sylvania target placed the various structures in proper relation to one another and correctly modeled the inflatable structure as a dome. Swann even had the rectangular main building correctly situated in relation to the other features at the site, though proportionately shorter than it actually was, and still with the wrong windows. He placed an antenna (a straightened-out paperclip) on the left side of the building instead of the right, in what was perhaps another instance of left-right reversal.

For all the minor inaccuracies, Puthoff was pleased with the results of the experiment thus far. But now he had an even more challenging move to make. He asked Swann to transfer his focus *inside* the main structure. On a new sketch, this time changing the arched windows to vertical rectangular ones, Swann drew a little pathway leading into the building, symbolic of entering the structure, and reported on what seemed most important there.

According to Puthoff, Swann described something that was "the size of a small car." There was "gas coming into it," "a lot of what looks like flames coming through holes," and it "looks like a crematorium." He sketched a large, blocky object with tubes snaking into it and an even row of little marks at the top representing his perception of "flames."[18]

It was not, as Swann's conscious mind tried to suggest, a "crematorium," at least, not exactly. It was an experimental carbon dioxide laser, oblong and boxy, about the size of a Volkswagen, with piping running into it carrying the CO_2 gas that made the laser work. In the top there was a clear, Plexiglas viewport through which, by means of a mirror, could be seen the glowing, purplish discharge that *did* look like flames as the laser was operated.

According to Puthoff, when he took Swann to the site for feedback, Ingo fumed, "How do you expect me to get this with remote viewing? I don't even know what it is when I look at it with my own eyes!"

As the two men worked through hundreds of targets, they gradually refined the process, hoping eventually to master all the important elements of remote viewing, and eliminate anything that did not contribute to its functioning and accuracy. They didn't, of course, start from scratch. The preceding years of research gave them a leg up on the project, but there was much ground yet to cover. They, in turn, were laying the groundwork for a new development, the significance of which would not be evident for years. And, outside SRI, things seemingly were progressing as well.

As Air Force sponsorship for SRI progressed, Dale Graff had assembled a few folks at Wright-Patterson, from among the military personnel at the base, to create a tiny, informal remote viewing group of his own. One, a young enlisted woman named Rosemary Smith (Graff gave her the pseudonym "Diane" in his book, *River Dreams*) showed promise as a viewer. She it was, along with Gary Langford, working out in California at SRI, who achieved the first widely publicized coup for operational remote viewing.

In March 1979 a Soviet TU-22 Blinder bomber outfitted as a reconnaissance aircraft crashed somewhere in Africa. U.S. Intelligence wanted to be the first on the scene to recover the Blinder but, unsure where within thousands of square miles it had gone down, had for two weeks been looking many miles away. Aircraft crisscrossing the region missed the plane, and satellites were unable to locate the crash site because of the dense jungle cover.[19]

In desperation, Graff's superiors called him in and asked to have Smith do her best to describe the area where the TU-22 could be found. Though she was only shown a picture of a typical Blinder and told it was down "somewhere in Africa," her description and hand-sketched map of the crash site closely matched an area where U.S. intelligence assets were not searching. As those assets were being shifted towards the indicated area, she was handed a topographic map and asked to circle the general location, and mark an X where she thought the crash was. Graff then quickly flew to California and monitored Gary Langford on the same target, this time getting no map location, but instead a very detailed description of the immediate crash scene, including a steep, jungle-covered hillside and red-colored streams running past the site.

Within two days the TU-22 had been located. It was inside the circle Smith had drawn, and within three miles of the X she had made inside the circle. The bomber had crashed into a jungle-covered hillside, on the verge of a river running red with clay from the surrounding hills. No one is quite sure how it leaked out, but the outcome of this story gained attention, including mention in a Jack Anderson column in the *Washington Post*. Years later, after the remote-viewing project was canceled, former president Jimmy Carter answered a question about remarkable occurrences during his presidency.

He had been impressed, he said, when a psychic had given a location for a missing aircraft, "and the plane was there."[20]

After this success and one other that also involved a missing aircraft, plus a number of successful experiments, Graff applied for the Director of Central Intelligence Exceptional Analyst Program, a prestigious intelligence analyst fellowship awarded by the Director of the CIA. Though Graff's proposal to study electromagnetic effects on brain processes included aspects of parapsychology research, he was still chosen to receive the important award. However, General Lew Allen, then chief of staff for the Air Force, got wind of the plan. Both Graff and Puthoff believe that General Allen, who otherwise was a highly regarded general with a distinguished career, had a bone to pick about parapsychology. He had an extensive background in nuclear physics, so perhaps his exposure to mainstream science had biased him, or maybe it was something else in his past. In any case, Graff met a staffer a few years later who confirmed the general's bias.

Aggravating the issue was General Allen's support for the MX missile that was being hotly debated in the government. He was a major proponent of the shell-game basing plan, where the cutting-edge ballistic missile would be shuttled around between shelters in America's Great Basin. According to the plan, moving a relatively small number of missiles around the desert and hiding them among perhaps twenty times that number of shelters would make it impossible for the Soviets to take out our nuclear missiles with a first strike, thus deterring Moscow from starting a war. Despite a number of major flaws in the idea, the Defense Department was pushing ahead with the idea at the urging of General Allen and others.

Unfortunately for Graff, the MX basing plan had run afoul of a study by Dr. Charles T. Tart, under the auspices of SRI, statistically demonstrating that remote viewers (assuming the Soviets had some that were competent) could significantly increase the odds of picking the right missile shelters to target. Whether or not the idea really would work in practice didn't matter. Some of the decision makers became aware that psychics might possibly be able to undermine the MX basing strategy. Neither Puthoff nor Graff could say to what extent this contributed to the demise of the MX basing plan, but they both believe it played a role.[21]

General Allen was not amused. With the remote viewing MX missile study, the publicity over the downed TU-22, and the further revelation that one of the general's own civilian employees wanted to go off and do more research on this paranormal stuff, Lew Allen drew the line. Without even notifying Graff about it, the general informed the Director of the CIA that Dale Graff's application was being withdrawn. Dale was told just before he was to board a plane for Washington, D.C., to accept the award.

Finding himself facing increasingly hostile pressure in his Air Force job, Dale Graff decided the best solution was to leave. Fortunately, another welcoming door beckoned. Though Graff worked in the Air Force's Foreign Technology Division, one of the people who saw his reports was Jack Vorona, a ranking scientist on the staff of the Defense Intelligence Agency, whose job it was to oversee the entire technical intelligence division at DIA. Vorona's civilian ranking was equivalent to a general in the military, and he wielded considerable power in the science and technical intelligence community. He was also interested in parapsychology, and was an eager consumer of Graff's reports concerning the ongoing progress of his remote viewing research. In 1981, Vorona made room for Graff on his staff, making him his action officer overseeing the SRI research, which DIA began to finance under the unclassified project nickname of Grill Flame.[22]

Another official at DIA who became involved was Jim Salyer. Selected by Vorona to be the contracting officer's technical representative, or COTR, Salyer was appointed to ensure that the SRI researchers put the government's money to proper use. At first interesting, Salyer's job soon must have become somewhat of a chore. He had to make trip after trip between his home in Virginia and the West Coast, staying for a few days to supervise execution of the contracts, then heading back. Finally, after a few years of that routine, Puthoff suggested to Vorona that Salyer move permanently to California.

Though Salyer often didn't get along well with the SRI staff, Puthoff figured that having him close would streamline relations, and it did.[23] Salyer stayed until sometime around 1989 or 1990, when he was reassigned to the East Coast. Not long after he died of cancer.

As the 1970s drew to an end, the SRI remote viewing program had been going on for nearly eight years. But the decade couldn't close without another run-in with skeptics. Ironically, this came about in an attempt to sum up the good results the program had thus far achieved. In December 1979 the Grill Flame Scientific Evaluation Committee report was released. Chaired by Manfred Gale, a senior official from Army headquarters, the committee included six scientists from both government research agencies and nongovernmental academic institutions. One committee member was the chairman of a medical school department of psychiatry; another was the head of a biostatistics and mathematics department. Others were from government research and engineering labs, while yet another was a professor at the Virginia Polytechnic Institute.[24]

After the committee scrutinized SRI's data and examined the remote viewing and psychokinesis experiments, a final report was drafted by Gale and another member of the committee, Dr. Jesse Orlansky, who had been a skeptical member of the Condon committee investigating UFO research.

Apparently, Puthoff remembers Orlansky as being a naysayer on the Gale committee. Orlansky didn't believe, for example, that biofeedback worked, though the evidence for it is largely accepted by mainstream science, and some of the others on the committee had personally been involved in successful biofeedback research.

In an interview, Puthoff told me that Orlansky ended up as one of the primary drafters of the final report, which turned out far more negative than either the SRI scientists or most of the other Gale committee members had expected. While there were some legitimate criticisms and suggestions, there were also objections written into the report that seemed to ignore some of the facts, and there were other negative comments that smacked of skeptical bias, rather than the scientific objectivity that should have prevailed. According to Puthoff, when the majority of the scientists on the review committee got a look at the report, they were dismayed. After an acrimonious meeting in which the authors of the report were verbally attacked for misrepresenting the committee's real conclusions, the incensed scientists jointly authored and signed a strong objection and rebuttal to the report as published.

Because of the controversy, the Gale report was essentially tabled and apparently not used for making decisions about the future of remote viewing research. It was, however, resurrected from time to time to provide background material for future official evaluations. Unwittingly, the committee members had set a precedent for future investigations when, more than once, a skeptical minority dramatically colored an overall positive assessment of remote viewing.[25]

The Gale report did herald a sea change for the government's involvement in remote viewing. A new kid on the block was about to steal the limelight.

8

Gondola Wish to Center Lane

... funny names hide funnier goings-on ...

Second Lieutenant Fred Holmes Atwater was perplexed. He had just taken part in a close-out briefing for officials of the Army's Missile Research and Development Command at Redstone Arsenal in Alabama. Atwater and the others with him were counterintelligence experts, specializing in OPSEC, or operations security. Their job was to snoop around Army facilities to uncover security lapses and loopholes that hostile intelligence agents could exploit to steal American secrets. Whatever they found they reported to the local commander. During the briefing the team had listed the typical problems—Soviet satellites passing overhead, the dangers of unguarded phone conversations, combinations for safes kept in a Rolodex instead of being memorized.

But the briefing had closed with an unexpected twist when one of the Missile Command's project managers pulled a book out of his briefcase. Sliding it across the table he said, "How are we supposed to protect ourselves from *this?*"

Fred Atwater turned the book around and glanced at the cover. *Mind Reach: Scientists Look at Psychic Ability*, by two scientists in California, Russell Targ and Harold E. Puthoff. Atwater looked up to confront the pregnant silence that had fallen upon the room, searching his mind for a reply. "This subject," Fred said finally, pausing as he handed the book back to its owner, "is beyond the scope of this survey. We will have to get back to you later with an answer to your question."[1]

This was not the first time Lieutenant Atwater had seen the book, nor the first time he had pondered the idea of Soviet spies using remote viewing to steal American secrets. About a year before, Fred had been a staff sergeant at the U.S. Army Intelligence Center and School at Fort Huachuca, teaching classes on OPSEC and other counterintelligence subjects to enlisted soldiers and officers at various stages in their intelligence careers. It was in that setting that he discovered and read *Mind Reach*. Fred and his friend Rob Cowart had puzzled over the book for weeks. If what was said in there was true, the two young NCOs could see nothing that would stop the *minds* of foreign agents from roaming at will through the most sensitive military bases and science laboratories in the nation. But Atwater and Cowart kept their concerns to themselves, since their colleagues at the intelligence school knew nothing of remote viewing, and were likely to be skeptical if the two sergeants tried to bring up the subject.

Fred's interest in remote viewing was temporarily derailed by a stint in Officer Candidate School (OCS). Bill Ray, his immediate supervisor, had good-naturedly needled Fred about becoming an officer. "What are you still doing here, Sergeant Atwater?" Ray would exclaim in mock astonishment each morning when they gathered for a new day at the office. "I thought you left for OCS!" Lieutenant Ray obviously thought his sergeant had what it took to be an officer. Ray's good humored badgering continued until Fred finally submitted his application for OCS at Fort Benning, Georgia. As he was literally on his way out the door for Fort Benning in 1977, Fred was called into the office of his boss, Lieutenant Colonel Webb, who liked the sergeant and had high hopes for his future. Webb said that he had friends in the assignments branch at Army personnel, and if Fred "kept his nose clean" at OCS, the colonel would get him any assignment he wanted that was appropriate for a lieutenant with Fred's background and skills.

A few months later, Atwater was back at Fort Huachuca as a freshly minted second lieutenant attending the Military Intelligence Officer Basic Course—a tiresome exercise for him, since he'd been in the intelligence field for ten years by then, and the course was meant for new officers who were just entering the Army. He had even taught some of the courses he was now forced to sit through. But there was no getting around it. As he had heard many times before, there are three ways to do things: the right way, the wrong way, and the Army way. He was stuck with the Army way.

Soon it was time to march back into Lieutenant Colonel Webb's office, salute him officer-to-officer, and ask him to make good on his promise. When Webb queried the lieutenant where he wanted to go, Fred pulled out his copy of *Mind Reach* and said, "I'm sure that somewhere in the Army, someone is looking into this. I want to go wherever that is." Webb told him to come back after he'd had a chance to check into it.

"This looks really interesting," the lieutenant colonel said the next day, handing the book back to Fred. "I can see why this could be an intelligence problem. But, Lieutenant Atwater, I have no idea who would be doing this in the government. I'll tell you what I'll do, though. You need an assignment to the Pentagon Counterintelligence Force. As a lieutenant, you'll be a team leader on the force. Their job is to check security for the whole Pentagon, which means they have access to every office in the building. It will be up to you to find this project."[2]

Fred was enthused by the idea. The orders were cut, he packed up his family, and they prepared to make the long drive from the sparse, juniper-dotted hills of southern Arizona to the humid greenery of Washington, D.C. Excited as he was about his new job, Fred dreaded the thought of trying to make ends meet on a lieutenant's pay in the high-octane economy of the nation's capital. But he never had the chance to find out what that would be like. The very day he and his family were to leave, he got a phone call. Someone had overruled Lieutenant Colonel Webb and Fred's orders had been changed. Instead of the Pentagon, he was going to a counterintelligence job at Fort George G. Meade, Maryland. Fred had lost his opportunity to prowl the halls of the building that housed the top echelons of the Army, searching for anyone who knew anything about remote viewing.

The Atwaters arrived at Fort Meade, and Fred signed into the Systems Exploitation Detachment (SED). One of SED's primary missions was to examine emerging domestic and foreign technology for potential threats to U.S. security. A related duty was to provide security advice to the Army's sensitive technology facilities. Because of the secretive nature of the unit's work, the SED office was clannish and closemouthed to outsiders.

After meeting Major Keenan, SED's commander, Fred spent a few weeks becoming acquainted with his new assignment. He was moved from one trivial job to another, getting to know the people he would work with and the jobs they did. One of the people was Staff Sergeant Mel Riley, a seasoned imagery analyst. Riley was a native of Wisconsin who, because of associations he'd had with a Chicago crime syndicate as a young adult, had nearly been rejected by the Army when he tried to enlist. But that was all behind him now. Riley had become a respected expert interpreter of satellite and aerial-intelligence photography.

Fred had no illusions about the people at SED. They were sizing him up to see if he would fit in. If he didn't, he would be hustled off to a less sensitive post. But after a few weeks of being passed around from one section to another, Major Keenan called Fred into his office and told him it was time to settle down; he had been accepted. "Take Lieutenant Colonel Skotzko's desk," Keenan said, referring to an officer who had been transferred before Fred had reported in.

One of Fred's first chores was to clean out his new desk. Skotzko had worked some projects directly for General Ed Thompson, the ACSI, or Assistant Chief of Staff for Intelligence. The ACSI was the Army's most senior intelligence staff officer, and main intelligence advisor to the Secretary of the Army. Fred didn't expect to find much of interest in the lieutenant colonel's safe; Skotzko would have parceled out any uncompleted projects to other action officers at Fort Meade or the Pentagon before he left.

The desk was as Atwater expected—a few classification stamps, stubs of pencils, the tangle of paper clips that seemed to spawn like so many bacteria in government offices. The five-drawer safe was more of the same, at least for the top four drawers. A few empty file folders rattled back and forth as Fred pulled the drawers out for inspection. But what he found in the bottom one changed the course of his life forever: inside one folder were three documents stamped "Secret." They all had to do with remote viewing.

The first document detailed the Soviet KGB's research in the paranormal. The second was a historical document covering the U.S. government's involvement in parapsychology research and remote viewing. And the third contained the names of Hal Puthoff and Russell Targ, the authors of *Mind Reach*. Under the auspices of SRI International, the two were secretly doing remote viewing research for the U.S. intelligence community.

Dazed and bemused, Fred went to Keenan and told the major what he'd found in Skotzko's safe. His boss was not surprised. One of Skotzko's assignments had been to look into remote viewing for the ACSI, since General Thompson thought there might prove to be something to it. Keenan told Fred that Sergeant Riley also had a personal interest in the subject. Then he asked Fred if he himself knew anything about remote viewing. "Yes. As a matter of fact I do!" Fred replied.

"Well," said Keenan. "Go ahead and keep the documents in your safe. You might as well be the lead man on it, now that Skotzko is gone." He directed Fred to begin a formal project, with a nickname and all.

Within a day or so, Fred had gone through the list of available code names for new INSCOM projects, and selected Gondola Wish to be the official project nickname. He had some rubber stamps made with Gondola Wish ready to slap in red ink across any official papers that he might create. Lieutenant Fred Atwater was in business. The official start for his one-man program was September 1977. Against all odds, and totally unexpectedly, Second Lieutenant Fred Holmes Atwater had not only found the desk of the person who was looking into remote viewing for the U.S. Army, he had just been ordered to *become* that person.

Now, the missile research project manager at Redstone Arsenal had handed Atwater his first project involving remote viewing. Shortly after returning to Fort Meade from the Redstone inspection, the lieutenant made his report to Major Keenan, who directed Fred to explore whether remote viewing was a threat to operations security, and if so, what could be done about it. In a matter of a few weeks Fred had obtained another classified document in which he discovered that the Defense Intelligence Agency was funding research through Puthoff and Targ's employer, Stanford Research Institute (SRI), a prestigious West Coast think tank formerly owned by Stanford University.

Fred also got in touch with Jim Salyer, the Defense Intelligent Agency's contract supervisor for the remote viewing research. Salyer told him about a civilian Air Force employee who was heavily involved in exploring the remote viewing phenomenon. The civilian's name was Dale Graff, and he was about to publish a major study documenting secret Soviet KGB-financed research into parapsychology. A quick trip to Wright-Patterson Air Force Base, where Graff was assigned, revealed that Puthoff and Targ were trying to replicate reported Soviet successes with remote viewing, to see how much of a threat it might be. Some of the results that Graff showed Atwater were compelling. There did indeed seem to be a threat.

Armed with this further information and accompanied by Jim Salyer, Fred was soon back in Keenan's office. What Atwater and Salyer had to say seemed to impress Keenan enough that he quickly agreed to the radical action that Fred proposed: INSCOM should train its own set of military remote viewers to test the actual vulnerability of sensitive facilities like Redstone Arsenal. Atwater was directed to come up with a briefing that would convince Brigadier General John A. Smith, INSCOM's deputy commander, who was in charge of the INSCOM budget, to approve funding for a pilot project to train remote viewers.

General Smith had a reputation as a man who would chew up briefers who annoyed him and send them packing before they had finished their spiels. He disliked people who couldn't cut to the chase and he had neither time nor patience for foolishness or trivia. But, despite the fearsome reputation, Smith listened intently to what Lieutenant Atwater had to say, and signed the funding approval documents. The money made possible the next step, a face-to-face meeting between Fred and the SRI International team on its home turf. As soon as preparations could be made, Fred was on his way out to Menlo Park, California, for his first of many encounters with Hal Puthoff and Russell Targ.

The visit proved to be very profitable. Back from California a couple of weeks later, the lieutenant drafted a plan for INSCOM's fledgling remote viewing effort, using SRI's input as to what desirable personality traits to look for in possible recruits. The first step was to identify who those possible candidates might be. Fred's superiors thought that someone with more rank was necessary to make the process go smoothly, so in October 1978, Major Murray "Scotty" Watt was given overall responsibility for the small unit that was to be formed. With authorization from Major General Rolya, INSCOM's commander, Fred and Major Watt surveyed INSCOM supervisors and commanders in Washington.

The two officers asked for the names of individuals who were successful in their current jobs, who were respected by their associates, and who might be willing to openly answer a few questions about psychic phenomena. Specifically, what did they think about police using psychics in criminal investigations? And might there be similar benefits for the intelligence community? Those who seemed receptive to the use of psychics would be interviewed and evaluated for possible recruitment as remote viewers.

Out of more than 2,000 people in the pool, the two officers were given the names of 117 INSCOM personnel, military and civilian, to interview. From this group they screened almost two dozen men and women who met the Puthoff/Targ criteria. Of this second cut, twelve turned out to be available for assignment to the new unit, to be known as Detachment G.

"We had basically three categories of response," Atwater recalled many years later about reaction to the survey. "Those who were 'true believers,' said, 'Oh, wow! This is wild stuff and I really believe in it!' We also had those who said, 'These psychics ought to all be arrested and kept in jail the rest of their lives because they're crazy.' And we got the middle-of-the-road group, which were the ones we actually drew from." After the initial screenings, the final selection-and-assignment process took two months, from December 1978 through January 1979.[3]

Along with new personnel, "Det G" (as it came to be called in typical Army shorthand), received a new project name as well. When Watt was assigned in October 1978, Gondola Wish was dropped and a new unclassified nickname adopted: Grill Flame. The Army Chief of Staff for Intelligence, Major General Thompson, officially decreed that the program name, embodied in Det G, would be the focal point for all Army involvement in parapsychology and remote viewing.[4]

The original idea was for Puthoff and Targ to come to Fort Meade to evaluate the twelve candidates, and choose the best three for further training. When the two scientists arrived, though, they found the group so promising that they could not reduce it to only three. Therefore, six were selected, and some of the others remained involved as part-timers, spending most of their time over the years with their regular jobs, but coming in as needed to lend a hand as additional remote viewers. Among the six were two names later to be famous in the remote viewing field—Joe McMoneagle and Mel Riley—along with two who are less well known, Hartleigh Trent and Ken Bell; plus two others who are still unknown to the public, Nancy S. and Steve H.

The plan was to send the six, one at a time, out to SRI at Menlo Park for preliminary evaluation. The best three would then return for more in-depth experience. The rotation to SRI began in April 1979.[5]

Only a few months later, on September 4, 1979, the unit had its first official operational mission. Ironically, it didn't involve the original charter of doing counterintelligence evaluation, but rather a search for a missing Navy A-6E Intruder attack jet, which had crashed somewhere in the southern Appalachians. The request came from General Thompson's office when news of the crash became known. Search and rescue aircraft had failed to locate the missing plane, though efforts were ongoing.[6]

Despite misgivings about the readiness of Det G for an operational assignment, Fred tasked one of his novice viewers, Ken Bell, who worked a single session against the target. Ken described a heavily forested area, and perceived various terrain shapes and elevations. But there was more.

"In some strange way," Atwater said years later, "if you read through Ken's transcript, he actually says: 'a mountain, a bald-knob mountain.' And the A-6E crashed into the mountain named Bald Knob." After the session ended, Watt handed Ken a large map of the Blue Ridge area of Virginia, covering thousands of square miles of terrain, and asked him to point out the location of the wreckage. Totally inexperienced in trying to correlate remote viewing results with map locations, Ken scrutinized the map in search of terrain features he had perceived during his session. Finally, in frustration, he jabbed his finger at the map. "It's here." The location he picked was within fourteen miles of where the downed aircraft was finally recovered. Allowing for the margin of error for the area that a fingertip covers on a 1:250,000-scale map, this was surprisingly close for a wild-eyed guess. Something had apparently worked.[7]

Unfortunately, the remote viewing effort turned out not to be particularly useful. Searchers found the downed aircraft before those in charge of the rescue effort received Fred's report and could act on it. For Atwater, reminiscing after his retirement, the A-6E episode epitomized from the start one of the difficulties with adapting remote viewing to operations.

"Was the RV data of value in finding the aircraft? No, because they found it before they even got our report of it being there. That doesn't deny the fact that it was an accurate remote viewing. But, 'is it of any value?' Therein lies my ten years of work [with the remote viewing unit]: can I take this unusual human phenomenon and come up with anything of practical value? In [the government's] terms 'practical value' meant useful military intelligence information."

A viewer could produce a strikingly accurate target description. But if the information thus produced was already known to the intelligence customer, or if it was new and accurate but not relevant to the problem at hand, it was usually met with a shrug of the shoulders and a "so what!" After all, military and government operators were interested in getting things done, not in proving humans are psychic. If something wasn't useful to them, nothing else about it mattered. The challenge was to do remote viewing in a way that produced results that *did* matter.

Beginning with the missing A-6E, and up through the end of 1982, Det G remote viewers were tasked with 81 projects, involving 652 operational remote viewing sessions. Many of the projects required only one or two sessions, but some needed more than a dozen, spanning several months. The granddaddy of them all was the Iranian hostage situation, against which a total of 227 sessions were done. The start date was November 23, 1979, not quite twenty days after I had my scare while in Germany during the same crisis. And the project was not formally wrapped up until the hostages were released on the day Ronald Reagan was inaugurated in January 1981. Altogether, 183 reports were sent to the client, the Joint Chiefs of Staff. The JCS sent back several evaluations and a final report, documenting Det G's performance.[8] Unfortunately, these remain classified.

Fred remembers that Det G's remote viewing efforts received a mixed grade from the Joint Chiefs. "What they said in the report was rather curious. I don't remember the exact wording, but the sense of it was that 'none of the intelligence produced for this project was particularly useful, and yours was no worse than anyone else's.' "[9]

But that didn't mean some of the data wasn't good. Feedback that the Grill Flame program received both before and after the hostages were released showed that in many cases viewers had accurately described features of the places in which the hostages had been held. And some of the other details turned out to be correct. But the same problem arose here as with the A-6E incident: ultimately, what they produced was not useful. The information had not contributed to the hostages' release, and with that as a bottom line, nothing else mattered. But there were some important benefits. After hundreds of operational sessions against the same target, the viewers and their managers learned much about what to do and what not to do for successful remote viewing operations.

One of these lessons was about target boredom. When people first hear about "psychic spies," they often form an impression that puts together the unrealistic Hollywood image of psychics with another Hollywood image of secret agents like James Bond. That creates illusions of an enigmatic hero experiencing dramatic visions of horrific events about to unfold and giving names, addresses, and photolike impressions of the villains in time to thwart their evil intentions.

Nothing could be further from reality. The very fact that mere humans can detect information and impressions through extrasensory channels that science can not yet explain is wondrous and dramatic. But the actual application of remote viewing to intelligence problems can be humdrum. Many of the remote viewing tasks during the Iranian hostage crisis were dull and repetitive. Analysts might want to know what is under each manhole cover or access door around the perimeter of the Tehran embassy compound. Or a room-by-room search of the several buildings within the compound itself might be the order of the day. And once a viewer has been through room after room, floor by floor, and found mostly desks, chairs, filing cabinets, and water coolers, one remote-viewing session starts to look like every other. Results from one session tend to "bleed" into the next, and the viewer begins to have trouble deciding if he or she is getting new data, or just overlap from previous sessions.

In the early days of scientific ESP research, "card-guessing" experiments were one of the most widely used tools to detect extrasensory activity. Subjects and researchers alike were puzzled to see how scores would fall off as the number of card-guessing trials increased. A promising subject might start out with a high percentage of hits, but after thousands of trials the scores might drop to only about chance. This became known as the "decline effect." What was going on? Boredom was a likely explanation. One can do just so many nearly identical repetitions of a task without becoming subconsciously sick of it, and shutting down one's ESP.

Fred Atwater, Scotty Watt, and the others decided that something similar must be going on with repetitive remote-viewing tasks. But what could be done? Many people today wanting to learn remote viewing for practical uses concentrate on practice targets that are laden with excitement and emotion. Such targets are often more easily detected, and are certainly more interesting to do. But to be useful operationally, a remote viewer must be able to do the boring targets as well as the exciting ones.

Partly as a result of the Iranian hostage project, Det G discovered that with experience viewers could learn to deal with the boredom. But introducing variety helped. Where possible, viewers were not tasked with the same types of targets one right after the other. Instead, they were shifted among types of targets, and even among projects. One day a viewer might be targeted against what was under a manhole cover in a Tehran street, and the next day against two or three rooms in the main embassy building. Or, instead, the viewer might work on the hostage crisis on Tuesday, and then be tasked against a biological-warfare facility at Sverdlovsk in the U.S.S.R. on Wednesday. Thursday might bring a return to Tehran, or a technical intelligence mission to collect information on the Hind-D attack helicopter the Soviets had recently fielded.

One attempt at injecting variety while focusing on a timely crisis occurred during "Desert One," the daring special operations foray into Iranian territory in an attempt to free the hostages by force. The raid ended in fiasco when mechanical problems with the helicopters halted the operation and two aircraft taxied into one another, bursting into flames on the ground.

When the Desert One operation was launched, I was involved in a Special Forces training exercise in England. We heard about it through the classified message traffic as the disaster unfolded. But my future remote-viewing colleagues were in a Best Western motel on Highway 175, just down the road from Fort Meade. Det G had been tasked to monitor the ongoing Desert One operation from start to finish using their improving remote viewing skills. It was to be an intense effort, with all the available viewers either working sessions or serving as monitors for the ones who were. Watt and Atwater had decided to move the project off-site for the duration, as a change of scene and, hopefully, as a way of enhancing the viewers' attention to the target. They had booked several rooms, and viewer-monitor teams were set up, one per room. As each session finished, the monitor would report to the command cell, consisting of Atwater and Watt. The command cell would then send them back with further taskings for the viewer. It was an exhausting, marathon-scale project. And it didn't work very well. It was not long before both viewers and monitors were frazzled, saturated, and overwhelmed.[10]

But, just as with the Iranian project as a whole, lessons were learned here too. Viewers *could* work successfully in an intense environment for a short time, doing three, four, or more sessions a day. However, after two or three days at this heavy pace, their remote viewing effectiveness dropped off. Eventually viewers stopped being effective altogether until they had enough time for rest and recovery. Though varying somewhat from one individual to another, it seemed that the long-term sustained rate for remote viewers averaged about one long session per day. One every other day was even better, but not always possible given the operational and training tempo of the unit.

The highlight of the motel experiment came when a mouse ran up Mel

Riley's pant leg while Mel was monitoring Hartleigh Trent in a session. Hartleigh preferred a pitch-black environment, so there was not a speck of light to be seen in the room. Suddenly, Mel felt something crawling up his ankle. "I didn't know what it was," he said, "until it got all four of its feet onto me." A furry, pint-sized adventurer had scampered unseen under Mel's table and clawed its way up inside his pant leg. "I sat there as still as I could, wondering what to do. I couldn't turn on the light, since that would disrupt Hartleigh's session. For the same reason, I couldn't just jump up and stomp my leg to shake the little varmint out." The venturesome rodent succeeded in scrambling halfway up Mel's calf before Mel managed to wiggle and shuffle his leg around under the table enough to expel the creature.[11]

The Iranian hostage situation may have been the most extensive project the remote viewing unit conducted over the early years of its existence, but it was hardly the only one, nor perhaps even the most interesting. Det G's viewers worked projects ranging from the status of a cement plant in a hostile country to the location of Soviet troops in Cuba. Important North Korean personalities were targeted, as well as underground facilities in Europe, chemical weapons in Afghanistan, the presence of electronic bugs in the new U.S. Embassy in Moscow, the activities of a KGB general officer, a missing U.S. helicopter, tunnels under the Korean Demilitarized Zone, and numerous buildings whose purposes were unknown to U.S. intelligence.

The agencies who levied the taskings were as varied as the projects. The CIA wanted to know about an unidentified building in East Berlin and about various people with Russian surnames. INSCOM's Threat and Analysis Center (ITAC) requested sessions be done on the notorious terrorist Carlos the Jackal, a signals intelligence site in a communist country, and an "unidentified object" on a photograph. The National Security Agency asked Det G to collect information supporting several counterintelligence projects, and the Air Force Threat Analysis Center requested information on an unidentified event that had occurred several days in the past.[12]

As with any intelligence discipline, the remote viewing unit's results were mixed. The first problem was getting feedback from real-world projects. To know how successful their efforts were, intelligence collection units rely on evaluations provided by the "customer" after the close of the project. But frequently we never learned how close we had come to the truth, how helpful we had been, or even what we had been looking for in the first place. The targets were sometimes so highly classified that substantive evaluations could not be provided. Other times, the "evals" were poorly written or incomplete. Much too often, no evaluations were ever provided at all. Once a project was complete and the necessary information obtained, the intelligence customer moved on to the next crisis or hot project, forgetting about evaluating the efforts of its intelligence provider. These are perennial problems in all intelligence disciplines, and the remote viewing unit encountered its fair share of them.

Nonetheless, Det G received many evaluations. Inevitably, some of them were negative. The CIA noted that, for a project against a downed aircraft in the Mediterranean in 1980, the unit's reports did "not appear to be accurate." In a project for the ACSI's office against a target in North Korea, the data "does not appear to have anything to do with the target area." The evaluation for the cement plant project mentioned above indicated that "overall, this task did not appear to go well." Another CIA target produced "nothing of apparent value."

There were, of course, projects for which results were partially good and partially not. Also, several projects remained unfinished for various reasons, usually stemming from cancellation or mis-tasking by the requesting agency. A number of evaluations were so highly classified that they were stored away from the unit in a Special Compartmented Intelligence Facility (SCIF).

Then there were the successful ones. The project against the Soviet troops in Cuba "provided U.S. Intelligence with the first firm evidence that the [Soviet] brigade commander had rotated [back to the Soviet Union]."[13] On another INSCOM project, "info [was] used to cue and verify other intelligence systems."[14]

A JCS project to describe some buildings in Iran produced an evaluation of "excellent." On that project, in sixteen of eighteen instances the remote viewers were able to positively identify the structures in question. In two of those sixteen instances, the activity the viewers described as being associated with the buildings was confirmed later by human intelligence gathering methods.[15]

In one CIA-initiated project, the analyst "rated the info as highly accurate and of value for operational planning. Information collected was later verified by other intelligence."[16] And on a tasking in 1980 against another Cuba target, ITAC credited Det G with the coveted "Intel First," the intelligence-community equivalent of an exclusive scoop in journalism.[17]

Of the eighty-one projects tasked to Detachment G by thirteen different agencies from 1979 through 1982, twenty-one produced positive results, six produced mixed results, another six were terminated or remained uncompleted, twelve were evaluated as negative or unsuccessful, and thirty-eight received no evaluations, or the evaluations were too classified to be forwarded to the remote viewing unit.

The actual hands-on of learning how remote viewing could be applied to operations, and then actually doing it, wasn't all that occupied the days and minds of the people at Det G. There were political and administrative issues, as well. Some of them caused as many or more headaches as trying to adapt remote viewing to practical use.

One of the first issues, and one that was to remain a thorny one for years, was the so-called "Human Use" question. In the mid-1970s the CIA, as well as other government agencies, had been called on the carpet by Congress for performing experiments on human subjects who were not told of possible risks posed by the research. In many cases, subjects didn't even know they were being experimented on. Among these was the infamous "MK Ultra" research, some of which involved dosing people with LSD without warning and without their permission. In a famous case that happened in 1953 but did not become public knowledge until 1976, one CIA experimenter secretly spiked the drink of a fellow scientist, who shortly after suffered disorientation and hallucination. A few days later, the victim threw himself from a tenth-floor window while his CIA-provided escort was napping.

Once the MK Ultra project became public, an outraged Congress passed laws making it mandatory that human research subjects be warned of any possible dangers or side effects, and that they give their willing and informed consent before being allowed to participate.

The problem with remote viewing was: did it involve experimentation on human subjects, or didn't it? Nothing invasive was being done, no foreign substances were introduced into human bodies; there were no physical intrusions that might injure or harm them. But could practicing this odd discipline possibly cause psychological or emotional harm? There was no evidence that it did, but also no way to tell if it wouldn't. So far as anyone could say, nothing unfortunate had happened to any of the people who contributed to the remote viewing research at SRI. And no adverse effects resulting from "being psychic" had been reported from several decades of parapsychology research in the civilian community, either. But that didn't mean that, given enough time or a heavy enough experimental load, some ill effects might not surface. Besides, one of the provisions of the directive that governed Human Use in the military-intelligence setting, DoD Directive 5240.1-R, required that harm to the subject's reputation be considered as well. In the notoriously conservative Army, there did seem reason to worry about that.

Still, whether being trained as a remote viewer constituted Human Use under the DoD directive was a tough call to make, and one the remote viewing unit itself was not allowed to decide. Instead, the Department of Health and Human Services guidelines (on which the DoD Human Use rules were based) required that the decision be made by a special board of experts set up for that purpose by the parent organization. The decision had gone back and forth more than once. In February 1979, the General Counsel, the Army's top lawyer, declared Grill Flame activities to constitute Human Use.[18] That determination mandated two things. The first one was easy: any person selected to become a remote viewer had to sign a statement that he or she had been fully informed of any hazards or problems that might arise from engaging in remote viewing.

The second requirement was harder. Regardless of whether all participating subjects gave their consent or not, the Secretary of the Army himself had to approve continuation of any program involving Human Use. And getting this approval could be a nightmare. Briefings and information papers had to pass through various layers of underlings before the Secretary could even be approached. The action might be shortstopped at any of those points. And even if it were to make it to the Secretary's desk, that was no guarantee it would be approved. He might opt to deny the request. Without his approval, activities involving Human Use had to be terminated. And if that happened, Detachment G and Grill Flame were doomed.

Det G was in the middle of the process in March 1979 when the Human Use determination was reversed by the Army Surgeon General's Human Use Subjects Research Review Board. Their decision that Grill Flame activities did *not* constitute Human Use trumped the Army General Counsel's ruling, just in time for the first group of remote viewer recruits to head out to California.[19] But the decision didn't *stay* trumped. On November 20, the Surgeon General's board changed its mind and decided that Grill Flame did indeed involve Human Use. It took until February 1, 1982, to get final approval from the Secretary of the Army to continue operations.[20] Meanwhile, Det G operated under interim approvals from the undersecretary of the Army who oversaw research and development programs.

During this time, other serious battles erupted. Even as Fred Atwater was taking his first steps towards creating a formal remote viewing program, General Thompson, the ACSI, was coordinating with other high-ranking Army officials to make such a project possible. Fred only found out years later about the machinations going on at some of the highest levels of the Army to support what he thought was a fairly low-level project. The consultations and negotiations took place only among those who believed the budding remote viewing effort was important. As long as things stayed within those circles, the project was relatively safe.

But because of all the briefings up and down the chain of command, the Human Use ruling forced negotiations about the Army's Grill Flame project out of their original channels and into full view of many decision makers "outside," in the larger defense community. Some of them were unsympathetic to the program. But others were enthusiastic. On January 16, 1980, Congressman Charlie Rose of North Carolina was briefed on the remote viewing program. He became one of its staunchest and longest-lasting supporters.

But then a bombshell exploded. Much of the budget for the Army's Project Grill Flame was coming from so-called P-6 funding accounts. P-6 was the designation for money earmarked for defense-related research and development programs. On March 5, 1980, William Perry, the undersecretary of Defense for Research, Development, and Acquisition who later became Secretary of Defense under President Bill Clinton, issued the infamous "Perry Memorandum," which in effect cut off access to P-6 funding for Army remote viewing. Perry decided that it was "not appropriate for Army to fund technology programs aimed at scientific demonstration of parapsychology."[21] Grill Flame's jugular vein had been unexpectedly cut.

American citizens may have the impression that the federal bureaucracy is a monolith, that every twig and branch of it knows what every other twig and branch is doing. But there are conflicts of opinion, hidden agendas, and antagonisms not only between whole agencies and branches of the government, but between individuals within the government as well.

Nothing illustrates this better than the checkered career of the remote viewing effort. Its entire history is one of bouncing from the verge of institutional extinction to ruddy health, depending on whether friend or foe had the bureaucratic upper hand. Decision makers in government agencies tend to be introverted, seeing-is-believing types who detest vagueness and don't like loose ends. In short, those able to make life-or-death decisions about projects such as Grill Flame and its descendants were too often those least likely to tolerate the open-ended nature of a remote viewing program.

Every so often, however, a bureaucracy unwittingly produces forward-thinking leaders who can accept a degree of uncertainty in a project that promises a potentially large payout. Surprisingly, for all the stodginess of the Army, such leaders emerge there from time to time. Perhaps this has something to do with the need for good military leaders who can function with innovation and flexibility in the confusion of combat. For the remote-viewing program, such leaders happened to be in place at just the right time to act as midwives in its birth, and help it survive despite the odds against it. For awhile, anyway.

Once the smoke from the Perry Memorandum cleared, decisions had to be made if the program was to survive without the P-6 research and development funding. By this time the bulk of Det G's work was foreign intelligence collection, and such projects got their money from the National Foreign Intelligence Program (NFIP). At the urging of the ACSI, General Thompson, and with INSCOM's General Rolya supporting the move, the Army leadership soon approved funding for Grill Flame to continue under the Army's share of the NFIP budget. On February 11, 1981, program management for Grill Flame was transferred down one organizational level, from the ACSI's own

office, which had direct authority over it up until then, to become the responsibility of the commanding general of the Army's Intelligence and Security
Command.[22]

More briefings followed, partly because of Human Use and other bureaucratic requirements, but also as a way of gaining friends. Congressman Rose
was briefed two more times, in April and July of 1981, followed by a briefing
in November for the new ACSI, General William Odom, who was soon to
become a leading enemy of the remote viewing program. The month previous, Det G's commander and Fred's partner in organizing the unit, "Scotty"
Watt, now a lieutenant colonel, was reassigned. His replacement was a taciturn lieutenant colonel named Robert Jachim.[23]

Spring of 1982 saw a continuation of the feverish rounds of briefings.
Members of several congressional committees, notably the House Permanent
Select Committee for Intelligence and the Senate Appropriations Committee,
were given presentations on the progress of the Army remote viewing program. In August, Lieutenant General Lincoln D. Faurer, Director of the
National Security Agency, was briefed. Within a month, Det G got the first of
nearly a dozen new taskings from NSA.

On September 29, Senator Claiborne Pell of Rhode Island was briefed by
Grill Flame representatives. Pell was a staunch supporter of remote viewing
and liked to keep tabs on what was happening in the community. But he
could do nothing for the remote viewing unit when, two days later, disaster
struck again. A congressional directive terminated National Foreign Intelligence Program funding for Army Grill Flame activities.[24] Once more, the
operational remote-viewing program's lifeline had been cut. An unconfirmed
rumor went around that someone with access to a senator on the Select Committee on Intelligence was a fundamentalist Christian who had put a bug in
his senator's ear that remote viewing was the Devil's work.

Since the remote viewers were career Army soldiers and civilians, there
was no option to fire them when the funding was cut off. Thus Det G and its
supporters had some breathing room to work out a solution. But no new
operational projects were accepted after October, though work continued on
a few that had been requested before funding was ended.

With research and development money off limits, and NFIP funding terminated, there seemed to be only one possible recourse. Major General Bert
Stubblebine, General Rolya's replacement as INSCOM's commanding general, symbolically thumbed his nose at remote-viewing's Congressional enemies. Stubblebine directed that Detachment G and Grill Flame program
activities would be funded "out of hide." INSCOM had a non-NFIP account
that could be used at Stubblebine's discretion, and that is where the remote-
viewing program would get its money. This was perfectly legal; Stubblebine

had full authority to disburse these funds to support the INSCOM mission as he saw fit, and he believed that remote viewing had great potential as an intelligence-collection tool.

On December 3, 1982, General Stubblebine officially notified the ACSI that INSCOM would fund the remote viewing program.[25] The Grill Flame project name would be retired. Henceforth its code name would be Center Lane. And instead of being Detachment G, its administrative element was renamed "Security Systems Planning Division" and placed under the Security Support Detachment of the 902nd Military Intelligence Group headquartered at Fort Meade. That meant it was not the outrider program that Det G had been, but now fell under a more conventional chain of command. And it became the pet project of Bert Stubblebine. It was about this time that Stubblebine came to Fort Huachuca with his bent forks and spoons to astonish me and my colleagues.

On the same day Center Lane was established, the unit was tasked with its first projects under the new funding stream and identity; ironically, the taskings came from the Systems Exploitation Detachment, the unit's original home.

In another twist, a month later, on January 19, 1983, Dick Delauer, Perry's replacement as undersecretary of Defense, signed a memorandum restoring the unit's access to P-6 research funding, though it was to be used only to "maintain the current INSCOM Center Lane capability."[26] In other words, research and development money could again be used to support the remote viewing program as it was, but could not be used to recruit or train more sources, or, presumably, to promote research into the phenomenon. In practice, though, it gave the unit operating funds and freed the INSCOM money to support expansion and research projects.

Some of that expansion had already begun. Work at SRI had continued apace throughout the period during which the Army remote viewing unit was being put together. Puthoff and Swann were still experimenting exhaustively with various approaches to RV to make it more reliable and more accurate. Because of the nature of the phenomenon, perfection seemed out of the question. But progress had certainly been made towards improving the process, and learning what worked and what didn't.

Shortly after General Stubblebine's assumption of command at INSCOM in 1981, things started to accelerate. One of the initiatives that resulted was the commissioning of SRI to come up with a way of training people to be remote viewers. Since the research seemed to point to the fact that many humans—perhaps all of them—had the underlying ability to remote view, if only they could understand how to go about it, it stood to reason that a training method could be developed that would allow people to be trained to do the same things that Ingo Swann or Hella Hammid or any of the other successful "natural" viewers could do.

Now the work that Swann and Puthoff had put in, coupled with all the research contributed over the years by the other SRI folks, paid off. Relying on the many lessons that had been learned over a decade of remote viewing research, a system was put together involving various stages that started a trainee-viewer from the absolute basic, simplest elements of remote viewing, and continued up through advanced performance levels. Called "coordinate remote viewing," or simply "CRV," the system was literally put together on the fly, some training modules being completed only shortly before the first students arrived for that level of training. Still, ad hoc as its development may have at first seemed, informed by years of research the method worked, and worked well. There will be more to say about CRV in coming chapters.

In July of 1982 the first two candidates for training in Ingo Swann's new coordinate remote viewing system were sent to SRI to begin training. They were Tommy McNear and Rob Cowart, Fred Atwater's old enlisted buddy with whom he had first stumbled across *Mind Reach*. Most of the first generation of viewers were gone. Ken Bell had been transferred in May of 1981, and Mel Riley was sent to Germany in August. Joe McMoneagle was increasingly having to hold down the fort, with help from Hartleigh Trent.

In the second half of 1981 and the first half of 1982, accompanied by some of the other Det G personnel, Fred, now a first lieutenant, had traveled to Arizona to screen attendees at the Military Intelligence Officers Advanced Courses for likely remote viewer candidates. At SRI, Ingo Swann and Hal Puthoff were working hard to fulfill the government contract to create an approach to remote viewing that was teachable to those who were not "naturally" psychic. The remote viewing unit was looking for two guinea pigs to serve as "prototype trainees" for the new method. Cowart had followed Atwater's lead, gone to OCS, and already completed one tour as an intelligence officer. He was back at Fort Huachuca for the Advanced Course when Fred discovered him. Cowart was not chosen simply because he was Fred's friend and had an interest in remote viewing. The entire class of officers was screened. Cowart was among those who passed the first screening, and was given the battery of personality tests designed to narrow the field to those who had the best chance of success in remote viewing. Cowart passed these with flying colors, too, and received orders for Fort Meade along with McNear, who had also scored well and accepted the assignment.[27]

With Stubblebine at INSCOM's helm, the pace of briefings was stepped up even more. The general was determined to sell the value of remote viewing to as many influential people as he could. On March 14, 1983, General John A. Wickham, vice chief of staff of the Army, was briefed; on June 13, Secretary of the Army John Marsh was filled in; and, in the biggest coup, Vice President George Bush was briefed on March 31 by Dr. Jack Vorona. Vorona headed the science and technology directorate for the Defense Intelligence Agency, and hence was in overall charge of DIA's Grill Flame effort. Vorona spent thirty minutes with Bush, who "received the briefing well," and was "interested and impressed."[28] This was not the first time Bush had been introduced to remote viewing. He had been briefed by CIA official Ken Kress at least once in the 1970s while serving as Director of Central Intelligence.[29]

The final event needed to complete Center Lane's transition to a fully-vetted INSCOM program happened on June 15, 1983, when the Secretary of the Army approved the project be established as a full SAP, a special access program.[30] This meant that outside knowledge of the program would be even more constrained than it had been up to this point. The list of people allowed to be informed of what Center Lane was actually engaged in would purposely be kept very small, hardly more than a hundred at most. People with clearances to access more conventional classified information numbered in the hundreds of thousands. Those with a "need-to-know" about Center Lane would have to be "read on," meaning they would have to sign a briefing statement that, as long as the program remained a SAP, they would not disclose anything about it to anyone else who had not also signed such a pledge. Even people who held high-level security clearances could not be told unless they had a need-to-know and had been read on.

There were differing levels to which people had access, designated as CL-1 through CL-4. CL-1 authorized basic knowledge about the unit's mission to apply remote viewing as an intelligence-collection tool, and a few other relatively superficial details. Each succeeding level of access increased the depth of information allowed. CL-4 access bequeathed the keys to the kingdom. Only those actually assigned to Center Lane, and a few other key players up the chain of command, were granted CL-4 status. The real identities of Center Lane's remote viewers and support personnel were among the facts that fell under CL-4 protection. We didn't want just anyone finding out who we were.

Being a special access program significantly increased Center Lane's security. But in the long run it contributed to the remote-viewing unit's ultimate downfall—of which more will later be said.

Three weeks after Center Lane became a special access program, SSPD's commander, Colonel Jachim, was transferred to Hawaii. Fred, now a captain, was designated "acting project manager." For the first and only time, Fred Atwater was officially in charge of the unit he had played such an important role in founding. This lasted five weeks, until August 15, 1983, when Lieutenant Colonel Brian Buzby signed in and assumed command.[31] A couple of weeks after that, I climbed aboard the roller coaster that some of the rest of them had been riding for the past five years or so. I was in for the time of my life.

9

Outbounder

...Am I really psychic,
or is this just a bad
joke...?

The green door to Building T-2561, home of the Center Lane Project, opened to reveal a decor that was at once banal and startling. A chipped enamel utility sink was on the right and a row of steel grey safes on the left. Grimy off-yellow walls gave the building's innards the squalid look of a tenement.

But, in sharp relief, on the wall opposite the door was a four foot high, twelve foot long, serenely cosmic mural. Joe McMoneagle, whom I was about to meet, had created a great swirl of galaxies, stars, and nebulae using ordinary cans of spray paint. Serving as his canvas was a fireproof panel that once had protected the walls of the old mess hall from the blistering heat of massive cookstoves. The stoves were gone, but the panel was still anchored securely to the wall. I found out just how well anchored it was when, more than a decade later, I and a remote viewer named Greg Seward failed in our effort to pry it loose from its underpinnings to save it from the coming bulldozers.

Because of its mess-hall origins, T-2561 was narrow and long—twenty feet wide and eighty feet long. Halfway down the building's open bay were five or six desks on either side, facing the front. First on the right was the secretary's desk guarding the entry to the branch chief's office, which was in a small addition tacked to the north side of the main structure.

All the furniture was worn and scarred. Funding for the remote viewing program was chronically tight, so, to equip the place, the first people assigned to the unit had gone to Fort Meade's salvage yard to rescue whatever might still be serviceable. Center Lane's desks were a hodgepodge of obsolete metal behemoths in various colors—mostly grey, but one was an interesting puce-yellow, and another a light shade of beige. Only Jeannie Betters, the administrative assistant, had a wooden desk, which she guarded fiercely.

I settled into the beige desk, uneasily noting its history. Its previous owner had been Hartleigh Trent, a Navy warrant officer who had retired and then entered the civil service for a second career. I had met Hartleigh only once, but his presence brooded over my first few weeks at Center Lane. A large, likeable man, he was suffering with cancer and died not long after I signed into the unit. Fred, Joe, Tom, and the others at Center Lane spoke fondly of Hartleigh, almost reverently. They had worked together for many months, shared adventures and new ideas, speculated about the secrets of the universe; and now Hartleigh lay dying in a nearby hospital. His coworkers maintained a rolling vigil of sorts, taking turns visiting him, trying to keep up his spirits. Fred had made Hartleigh a tape of Pachelbel's *Canon in D*, played over and over again. The soothing music seemed the only thing that could ease Hartleigh's suffering.

As I cleared out the drawers of the desk, I happened on artifacts and mementos of the person who had sat there before me. The whole experience added a somber note, yet was heartening in a strange way. If one has to die, what better setting than among people whose purpose is to explore a dimension of humanity that transcends space and time?

I was given a few days to get settled in, to do some background reading, and to get to know the others in the office. I've already mentioned Jeannie. She was short—barely five feet tall—and stout. A chain smoker and coffee guzzler with a gravelly voice to match, she brooked no nonsense. But she was also genial, and had a warm heart hiding behind her gruffness, as the families of feral cats living under our building well knew from the many bags of cat food she distributed over the years.

Fred Atwater, it turned out, was both the training and the operations officer for the unit. When I was being courted for the program, he had also been the temporary boss. The previous commander, Colonel Robert Jachim, had been transferred to Hawaii before his replacement arrived. As the senior military officer on board, Fred was designated acting branch chief. But between my selection and my release from Ops Group, the new boss had signed in.

Lieutenant Colonel Brian Buzby had a round, tolerant face and an even temper. Buzby didn't come across as an adventurer. He had been brought on board because he knew the institutional ropes within both INSCOM and the Pentagon. He knew which hallways to tread, and he knew the ins and outs of giving briefings and writing information papers—boring skills, but crucial in his new assignment as boss of an organization whose life depended on how persuasively it presented a rather bizarre story.

Charlene Cavanaugh, a new recruit like me, had arrived just a few weeks before. She was a personnel specialist, but more recently had been heavily involved as part of Bert Stubblebine's "INSCOM Beyond Excellence" task force. Charlene was to be one of my fellow trainees in the esoteric arts of remote viewing.

I had already gotten to know Tom McNear. And now I also met the unit's secretary, Nancy DeBari, a pert, attractive woman who, as a born-again Christian, gently expressed mixed emotions about being involved in a project involving psychic espionage. And I met Joe McMoneagle.

Joe was the only functioning full-time remote viewer still with the unit. Tom had been there for a year or so, but was not yet fully trained. Joe was burly, solidly built, with a bull neck and a no-nonsense attitude mediated by a humorous appreciation for the nature of our business. He had the crusty, hard-bitten, chief warrant officer's attitude that if you wanted something done right and on time, you usually had to do it yourself. By the end of my first day I knew he was a man of contrasts, inclined to voice a strong opinion on just about everything, but surprisingly attentive to opposing viewpoints.

Though he had the demeanor and carriage of one long used to soldiering, it was obvious that Joe was something else besides. I found it incongruous to hear him speak about meditation or out-of-body experiences in a tone usually reserved for ordering the emplacement of tactical radio direction-finding sets in a combat zone. It took no time at all to recognize that Joe was a collusion of old soldier and new-age explorer, which gave him a genuineness that all still recognize in him to this day, whether they agree with his opinions or not.

For the time being, that was all there was to Center Lane: seven people—eight, counting me, though I hadn't yet come to feel as if I was one of the crew.

Buzby soon figured out I had more of a flair for writing than most soldiers. I became his "word-Smith," a phrase he extravagantly overused. It was only a week or so before he had me working on my first project, a briefing for Secretary of the Army John Marsh. This was at once exhilarating and intimidating. Over at Ops Group, only days before, I had been filing reports and shuffling papers, doing some of the most menial work in the intelligence community. Suddenly, I was working on a briefing for the highest authority in the United States Army. To make things still more interesting, a version of the briefing was to be delivered the same day, October 5, 1983, to Senator Malcolm Wallop of Wyoming, who chaired the budget subcommittee for the Senate Select Committee on Intelligence, a vital figure in our financial lifeline.

So, in between my own first RV sessions, which were soon to begin, and going through background readings on remote viewing, I was also poring over the texts of previous VIP briefings and digging through the files for useful history. It was a steep learning curve, but there couldn't have been a better crash course in Center Lane's operational and political background.

But this wasn't all. The Human Use issue hadn't ended with the Secretary of the Army's 1982 approval. By the time I signed in to the unit in 1983, there were again questions whether remote viewing at Center Lane even involved formal research, much less experimentation controlled under Human Use regulations. I boned up on the issue so I could help write or edit more briefings and position papers for officials ranging from the Army General Counsel, to an officer in the Human Use Office of the Medical Research and Development Command, to INSCOM's Human Technology Review Board. In the end, the Human Use ruling stood.

Buzby must have been pleased with my work since, within a month or so of my arrival, I was holding in my hands official orders appointing me unit historian.

Many of my memories of that time are vague, mostly because the details of adjusting to a new office are always pretty much the same, whether the office deals with paper-punching or parapsychology. But one thing stands out; I was invited to sit in on one of Joe's operational remote viewings.

Normally, we fresh recruits were not exposed to any of the sessions of the more practiced hands. The thought was that, since we were due to be trained in the newly developed Ingo-methodology (as we were rapidly coming to refer to Swann's CRV), our leaders did not want us forming conclusions that we would have to unlearn later about how one did remote viewing. But they also realized that it was necessary to at least have some inkling of what the process was like. So every once in a while one or another of us would be permitted to observe or eavesdrop on an ongoing project.

By the time I signed in to the unit, Joe had become somewhat of a remote viewing legend, if only among the small group who were privy to Center Lane's secrets. He had been the viewer-of-record in a number of the RV unit's greatest coups. One particularly impressive feat was his 1980 viewing of the interior of a prototype of the then highly classified XM-1 tank, later designated the Abrams, which I was to observe performing spectacularly eight years later during Operation Desert Storm.

The XM-1 project was at the time still very secret, since there was new technology being built into the tank that the U.S. didn't want the Soviets to know about. However, rumors of our adversary's research into paranormal skills similar to remote viewing had raised concerns in a number of "black" Defense Department projects, and the XM-1 project managers wanted to see just how vulnerable their new supertank was to prying Soviet psychics.

Using a third party to disguise the source of the request, someone connected to the XM-1 gave the remote viewers a photo of an airplane hangar, with instructions to describe anything of importance inside. Parked inside the closed hangar at the time of the remote viewing session was an XM-1 tank. It had been moved there explicitly for the purposes of putting the remote viewers to the test. A good viewer would have to set aside any preconceived notions of what should be inside an airplane hangar to get at the real target.

I was not assigned to the unit when this project was completed, but later I did get to see the results Joe McMoneagle produced. He didn't just get inside the hangar; he got inside the tank. His sketches were unmistakably of a tracked armored vehicle. But of even greater interest were the sketches of the *interior* of the turret, very clearly drawn and labeled, to include general descriptions of novel laser range-finding equipment, low-visibility observation devices, and sophisticated computer equipment never before found in a main battle tank. Written feedback later given us by the project managers confirmed the accuracy of Joe's description and placement of the tank's internal equipment. Their main criticism was that in his sketch Joe had inadvertently reversed the positions of some of the equipment. Of course, the analysts didn't know that left-right reversals were an occasional eccentricity of the remote viewing process.

The XM-1 wasn't Joe's only success. In what has become his most widely known remote viewing performance, he described the contents of a massive building at a major Soviet naval base on the Baltic Sea. Some intelligence community analysts suspected that this building was being used to hide construction of the U.S.S.R.'s first aircraft carrier from the prying cameras of American satellites.

But Joe did not find an aircraft carrier hiding in there. Instead, he described the construction of a massive submarine. As Joe reckoned the dimensions, the vessel was bigger by a significant factor than any other submarine known to man. Joe described it as having a bulbous nose and an unusually broad and flattened stern, and identified a set of missile tubes that seemed to be located in *front* of the conning tower. All of this ran contrary to known submarine design standards. Joe was tasked to give an estimate of when this vessel would see the light of day. He reported that when he viewed the immense building several months in the future, it was empty.

The analysts scoffed at the data. It made no sense according to conventional wisdom. And, since the information came from such a controversial source, there was no reason why they should believe it.

But then, months later, satellite photos showed an immense submarine being fitted out alongside a quay in the Soviet naval yard. Sometime in the recent past, the Soviets had dug a channel between the harbor and the end of the construction building, and had floated the *Typhoon*, the world's largest submarine, out to its moorings. The *Typhoon* was long—about 560 feet from nose to tail—and had a flat, splayed-out stern, reminiscent of a whale's flukes. Unlike most previous NATO and Warsaw Pact subs, its conning tower (or "sail") was set far back, closer to the stern than the bow. It had a blunt, bulbous nose, and a double row of missile tubes in *front* of the conning tower, unlike U.S. submarines, whose Polaris and Trident missiles were housed in the aft portion of the vessel. Joe had been right.[1]

A few weeks after I joined Center Lane, Fred gave me a chance to see Joe McMoneagle do his stuff. Opening a drawer in his safe, Fred pulled out a folder and motioned me to follow him. We quickly walked next door, to Building T-2560. This building was clad in the identical peeling green paint as our headquarters, and had the same crisscrossing steel mesh on the windows for added security.

Fred and I entered through double metal doors and into a dingy front room. Faded burnt-orange carpet clashed with a yellow-green couch. There was a faint, musty smell which, in all the years I was there, I never managed to identify. A long, claustrophobic hallway stretched dimly before us, closed on the near end by a door with a glass window in it. Through the glass I could see a few more doors opening off this hall as it led through to the back. Fred let me into a room to the left of this hall. This was the "control room"— though it didn't control anything but the monitoring and taping equipment, which was used to record remote viewing sessions. A low shelf jutted from the wall around three sides. Stacked on this were several banks of stereo amplifiers and cassette recorders. There was a stand that held a microphone, and scattered wires, plugs, and other electronic paraphernalia.

I sat in a chair facing a bank of cassette recorders, and Fred passed me a set of headphones. "Testing, testing," Fred said into the mike in a voice that half spoke and half hummed the words. Then he switched off the mike. "Wouldn't want you chiming in at the wrong time during the session," he said. Then he walked out of the control room, crossed the hall, and entered the first door on the right, the "ERV room."

Joe had come over to T-2560 before us, and had been in the ERV room for twenty minutes already, "cooling down" on the twin bed that was in there. ERV stood for "extended remote viewing," a term coined by Fred to distinguish between the method Joe would be using that day and coordinate remote viewing, or CRV, which I and my colleagues were to learn. For a long time the story made the rounds among us that it was called "extended" because the person doing it lay "extended" on the bed in a pose of meditative relaxation. Fred later told me he named it "extended" just because it usually took longer than a typical CRV session.

The ERV process went something like this: the viewer entered the room and lay quietly, relaxing, slowing breathing and heart rate, approaching sleep. When the viewer's rhythmic breathing indicated he or she was ready, the monitor entered and sat at a small desk near the bed. He turned on a dim, red lamp so he could see to read the tasking and make notes.

Many people believe that remote viewing starts to work when extrasensory impressions bubble up from the subconscious, passing in some untraced way into the viewer's conscious awareness. The link from one mental world to the other is always tenuous, and fraught with possibilities for confusion and contamination of the information. This contamination is the infamous "mental noise" most psychics encounter—jumped-to conclusions, extraneous ideas, memories suggested by bits of half-formed impressions, vagrant thoughts, arbitrary analysis—all overlaying and usually obscuring the subtle "psychic" signal as it tries to ease its way into awareness. For remote viewing to work, some method is needed to suppress this "noisy" overlay. There will be much more about the problem of mental noise in future chapters.

In ERV we tried to suppress noise by helping the viewer maintain a hypnagogic state—the state at the edge between consciousness and sleep. This was based on the theory that the narrower the gap between one's conscious awareness and one's subconscious, the less chance there is for noise to develop. ERV requires a monitor, a second person who remains fully awake, prompting with neutral questions to avoid giving hints about the target. Such hints could derail the purpose of getting untainted information through extrasensory means. But to gather the specific data needed to answer the intelligence question du jour, it was still necessary to guide the ERV viewer to and around the target.

To direct the viewer to the target in ERV, we sometimes used an imperative sentence along the lines of "Describe the target in question." Sometimes we used geographic coordinates, a method shared with Ingo's CRV methodology. Often, ERV tasking used a photo of the target sealed inside an opaque envelope, together with the simple instruction to "Access and describe the subject of the photo inside the envelope."

This raised a novel issue. Not only did the viewer have to accomplish the amazing feat of mentally perceiving an unknown person, place, or thing perhaps thousands of miles away, but he or she must *first* access a photo inside an opaque, sealed envelope, somehow perceive its subject, and *then* describe the target in real time, not merely describe the photo. In effect, the remote viewer had to perform two different remote viewing tasks—determine what was inside the envelope, then describe the distant target for which it was a reference. Over the years we spent hours gnawing over how this could be done, and arrived at various conclusions, some of which will come to light in the course of this book. But the basic principle is still mysterious.

At this point in his remote viewing career, Joe was mostly doing extended remote viewing sessions, though he didn't know them by that name. Fred wasn't to invent the term for another year or so, by which time Joe would be gone. But on this day, Joe was flat on his back, snoring through my headphones to beat the band as Fred clipped a lapel mike to Joe's open-collared shirt. There was rustling, muttering, followed by soft breathing. Then I heard Fred speak.

"Can you hear me, Joe?" I was a bit jolted, because the headphones made it sound as if Fred was right in my ear. He must have had his own mike quite close to his lips. But I was also impressed. Fred had mastered the low, sonorous tone needed to bring a sleeping viewer back to the verge of awareness without startling him completely awake. Even *I* was soothed, and I was wide awake, sitting upright in a chair in another room.

"Mmmmm . . ." Joe responded.

"Okay," murmured Fred. "We're going to revisit the target you did during your last session. Could you describe it for me please?"

Joe cleared his throat slightly, then began to mumble, sounding, as Fred often styled it, very much like someone with a mouth full of oatmeal mush. As I listened, Joe described a compound with a white masonry wall around it, too tall to jump over. As I recall, he mentioned one or two white structures, with reddish, tiled roofs. The whole was set in a warm, humid, heavily vegetated place. His words oozed out, some so slurred as to be nearly unintelligible, but they made me think of leafy jungle, the tropics.

Joe didn't express things as succinctly as I have it here. It came in bits and pieces—descriptors, colors, textures, the feel of the place, but with the overall arrangement of the structures eventually coming clear. He mentioned the compound's layout, how building related to protecting wall, and there was some comment about security measures, the details of which I no longer remember. Fred asked Joe to continue describing the building's insides, which he had apparently begun in an earlier session. Joe proceeded room by room, voicing generalities and particulars about the layout and relation of each room to the others, as well as giving some hint of its contents. Descriptions were spotty—sometimes precise, sometimes incomplete, sometimes vague, other times remarkably specific. Overall, there seemed no consistent quality to the remote viewing information he reported. But from what I knew of difficult intelligence problems, I realized that every little tidbit would be appreciated by the customer in some intelligence agency or unit.

I remember Joe describing a man who was arrogant and powerful. The man seemed to be a major presence at this location. Perhaps he owned the property, I thought, or at least was a principal tenant; Joe didn't specify. My memory may be playing tricks on me after all these years, but I think I remember Joe describing the man as being short, perhaps Hispanic, with a pock-marked face.

The session soon drew to a close. Joe, somewhat bleary from his other-worldly state and squinting in the room lights after emerging from an hour or more in the dark, sat down to do some sketches of the facility he had viewed. His drawings matched his verbal description of a compound with one or two structures, surrounded by dense foliage. And he mapped interior partitions, locations of major items, and security points.

Joe's performance had certainly seemed impressive. Still, I had no idea what the target was, nor had I yet seen any feedback to show how well he had performed. Nor, according to the rules of the game, would I likely *ever* be privy to such evidence. Operational information was strictly sequestered from the viewers until a project was permanently closed. Even then, viewers seldom had access to results and peripheral information. We would have long since been targeted on new projects, and there was little time or interest to investigate the old ones. That was the job of the analyst and management staff.

In this case, however, I did eventually get feedback of sorts for Joe's session. In 1986 a book was published by Putnam, called *Secret Warriors: Inside the Covert Military Operations of the Reagan Era.* It was written by Steven Emerson, a senior editor for *U.S. News & World Report,* and detailed some of the abuses and mistakes made in covert U.S. operations during the early-to-mid-1980s. A number were INSCOM operations. One of them was dubbed "Operation Landbroker," set up in 1982 to investigate Panamanian president and strongman Manuel Noriega's links to weapons and drug smuggling. (At the time, INSCOM ostensibly had no clue that Noriega was being used as an occasional intelligence source by the CIA.)

As part of the operation, INSCOM agents rented a safe house near Noriega's Panama City villa, from which they were able to take photos of the compound from various angles. As Emerson tells it:

> The photos were relayed to INSCOM officials in Washington, who gave them to psychics working through a secret Army program. The

psychics studied the photos and produced a top-secret two-page report that purported to identify the layout and contents of the house, including bedrooms, kitchen, dogs, guards, and security cameras.[2]

The moment I read this passage some five years later, when I got around to reading the book, I recognized what Joe must have been working on back then, on that afternoon in the fall of 1983. No longer having access to the actual reports and session transcripts as I write this, I cannot be sure how well Joe's work corresponded to ground truth. I think he mentioned dogs, guards, and cameras in his session. But this may be false memory generated after the fact by my reading of Emerson's book.

From results of others of Joe's sessions that I was allowed to analyze in later years, and from my own and my colleagues' later experiences of this same sort, I know that it was certainly *possible* that he reported these things. The CIA has been promising since 1995 to release the bulk of the remote viewing program's documentation. Hopefully, Joe's work will be found among the archives so we can tell how close he came to the actual "facts on the ground."

Emerson's report is misleading in one respect. While photos may have been sent to Center Lane, and while the operations officer may have examined them, Joe would never have been given the opportunity to "study them" before working on the project. All the information he provided, to include the external appearance of the compound and its contents, came first through his own mind. In a recent conversation with Fred Atwater about how this all was done, I was told that Joe might "as a reward" be shown the photo after several sessions, once he had already described the target, and then, usually, only if the tasker was interested in what was *inside* the building and not at all visible in the photo.

But now I was about to get my own turn in the barrel.

"Hey, Paul. Are you ready to try a session yourself?" Fred was standing beside my desk, wearing his usual poker face under his short, sandy hair.

"Now?" I said, quite shocked. I knew it was bound to happen eventually, but I didn't feel ready.

"Nope. Tomorrow morning. Tommy and Joe will be outbounders. I'll monitor." Outbounders. I had only recently learned what that meant. The procedure we used for this at Fort Meade differed little from that employed at SRI. We had our own cache of preselected targets prepared in identical opaque envelopes, and the outbound beacon team would roll a red, ten-sided die to select an envelope at random as they left the headquarters building. The viewer would already be over in Building T-2560, "cooling down" in one of the soundproofed, windowless rooms. The outbounders would open the envelope while pausing at the stop sign at the end of lane, so they would know whether to turn left or right onto Llewellyn Avenue. They would drive to the selected target and, for fifteen to thirty minutes, try their best to interact with it in some way—look at it from various angles, run their hands over textured surfaces, listen to sounds, experience whatever could be experienced. After the outbounders returned, they would escort the viewer to the target to compare notes and see how well he or she had done as a remote viewer.

The night before my initial attempt at remote viewing passed slowly, yet too fast. The prospect of my first session loomed before me like some huge, belching locomotive, bearing down in exaggerated slow motion. To someone who has never gone through this before, it may seem curious that I should be so unsettled at the prospect of actually doing something I had so eagerly agreed to in the first place.

There were two things working together to make me feel anxious. First, there was fear of the unknown. Despite being intellectually able to dismiss such notions as silly and superstitious, one couldn't help but think of all the cultural associations "being psychic" had with other, darker rumors of the paranormal. What hidden, scary things about the universe or about one's self might be revealed in a too-successful session?

But the other, perhaps greater, fear was just the opposite—fear of failure. What happens if it *doesn't* work, I wondered? After all, everything I'd learned from the everyday world said RV couldn't be real. But even if it did work, that didn't mean it would work for me. Would I embarrass myself? Worse, would I be ignominiously cashiered from the unit as a psychic flop, fired before I had hardly begun? The next morning, at the appointed time, I found myself stalking up the splintery steps of T-2561, past the cipher lock, and into my future.

"Okay, Paul. Sit back and relax for a few moments," breathed Fred in the soothing murmur he had cultivated by years of going through this same ritual over and over. While he clipped a small mike to my shirt, he spoke into his own, laying down the date, location, and my name on the tape that would record the session for posterity. I heaved a sigh and wiggled in my chair. The few minutes dragged slowly by as I waited the requisite time for the outbounders to reach whatever their destination was. And then it was H-hour.

"We'll begin," Fred intoned. "Paul, please describe as carefully as possible the place where Tom and Joe are presently located."

Ah, Fred, where do I start? I wondered. Where could they have gone off to? There were plenty of images at hand. The Post commissary, Burba Lake, the fire station. But all these seemed more like guesses than anything "psychic." I sighed again, or maybe a couple of times.

"Remember," Fred broke in. "Describe impressions. Colors, shapes, general ideas about things." I tried again to focus, but the harder I focused, the less I seemed to get. "And remember, don't try too hard. Relax, let it happen."

Yeah, *right*. But my mind did begin to wander a little; I've never been very good at focusing on anything for extended periods without getting bored. And as my mind drifted, I began to sense vague impressions.

"Uhhnn . . . there's a room."

"Okay, good."

Good? Does that mean I'm on target? And how could he know after only one comment? But then, Fred doesn't know what the target is, any more than I do. I get it, he's just encouraging me. My performance anxiety returned full force.

"Go ahead and describe sensory elements," said Fred helpfully.

"Okay . . . well . . . the room is yellowish—well it's walls are. No, more off-white. And they're pebbly—uh, textured—little tiny pebbly bumps. And there is a window." I let my mind roam a bit. Fred kept his peace, waiting patiently for me to sort out what was coming into my head. I still doubted that it had anything to do with where Joe and Tom were, but at least for a few more minutes I could fool Fred into thinking that something constructive was going on. "Hmm. The window isn't exactly a window. It's more of a display kind of thing. There are rows of little things behind it."

"Mmmhhmmm . . ." Fred murmured encouragingly.

"And there seems to be a few tables and chairs. Reminds me of a restaurant, almost—but it's not big enough." I paused, then added reflectively, "Maybe it's a drugstore."

The sensations I'd received were fuzzy; certainly not the clear, distinct images one expects from the way psychics are portrayed in the movies or TV. All the wavy, out-of-focus perceptions that had oozed their way into the back reaches of my consciousness gradually knit themselves into a blurry impression of a smallish, yellow-white room with a counter where some sort of transactions took place. The counter inexplicably had a window in it, and there must have been other windows that let in the sun that I thought I saw.

There was also a clutch of little tea tables and spindly chairs, and people. I thought the place might have commercial aspects about it. It hardly seemed notable, certainly not the sort of thing one would pick for a remote-viewing target. But I dutifully continued to report, and Fred continued to sit stoically, acting neither excited nor disconcerted.

We were back in T-2561 by the time Tom and Joe returned, ceremonially carrying a box of donuts. Fred showed them his notes and the few sketches I had ventured. As they shuffled the handful of pages, the noncommittal looks on their faces confirmed the worst.

"Well," Joe said. "Let's give you your feedback."

We piled in the car and ate donuts as we drove north on Route 175, then turned right onto Ridge Road. Within a few minutes, Tom pulled the car onto a gravel turnout. There, blocking the eastern sun, was a huge, blue-painted, spider-legged water tower. The thing was immense, maybe 180 feet tall, and nearly as wide. It was like a giant, blue-painted mushroom; a huge, bulging dome perching on a broad central pillar, with a ring of spindly pipes arranged around the outer perimeter, apparently holding it up. It looked absolutely nothing like what I had perceived in my session. I had blown it.

We spent about ten minutes walking around the tower, trying from every angle to see if I had any elements of data in either my descriptions or sketches that might match something. I banged on the massive, metallic stem, squinted up at the bulbous tank, slalomed around between the supporting pipes, but it was hopeless. Despite the encouraging noises my comrades made, I could see that I'd been wasting my time and theirs that day. As we drove back down Route 175—them talking too much and me not enough— I sat there discouraged. I'd hoped for a miracle and been disappointed. I thought I'd learned this lesson back in junior high with the failed science fair project.

Staring out the window, I noticed something. Over on the left side of the road was a little shop, its paint a weathered white. There was something about it that caught my attention, though I wasn't quite sure why.

"Wait a minute. What's that?" I said, pointing.

"Oh, that's where we bought the donuts," Tom answered.

"Stop. Let's check it out." Tom exchanged quizzical glances with Fred, but pulled over.

As we walked through the door, I noted in front of me a counter with a display window in it through which rows of donuts peeked. On top of the counter perched a cash register. There were fluorescent lights overhead, a scattering of little two-place tables with spindly chairs, and windows through which the sun was streaming weakly. And the walls were yellow-white, with a pebbly texture. Now this is more like it, I thought.

"Sorry, it doesn't count," Fred said in response to my unasked question. I looked startled, and he noted my look. "You didn't get the target," he said. "If you don't get the target, it doesn't matter how well you get something else instead. You were supposed to describe where Tom and Joe were during the appointed time, not where they stopped for donuts."

Okay, so I didn't get the target. But I learned a valuable lesson: in this group of folks, just being psychic was no big deal. You had to be psychic about the right thing for it to make any difference at all.

10

The Monroe
Institute

... out of body
and orange
salamanders ...

In the foothills of the Blue Ridge Mountains, about a half hour's drive south from Charlottesville, Virginia, is a small tarmac road winding sharply up from the floor of the pastoral Rockfish River valley. The pavement ends abruptly at a cluster of buildings that is the Monroe Institute, a research and teaching center founded on the premise that humans are more than just their physical bodies. In fact, people come to Monroe to try to *leave* their bodies— for a little while, anyway.

The institute's creator, and its most prestigious resident until his death in 1995, was Robert A. Monroe, a gruff, poker-playing, hard-smoking former radio executive. He was an unlikely candidate to explore the possibility that human consciousness could separate from the body and go elsewhere, or elsewhen.

In the 1940s and '50s, Bob Monroe was a prominent figure in the development of commercial radio. As a result of some sleep-learning experiments in which he was involved, things began to happen to him that he couldn't explain and, for the sake of his career, dared not publicly admit. It seemed to him that at times some core aspect of himself separated from his body and soared into the unknown. This experience of separation was frequently accompanied by a buzzing or a vibration, after which he found himself visiting earthly and unearthly locations, even when he knew his body was still resting quietly at home. By 1971 he came to terms with his experiences and published a book called *Journeys out of the Body*, which became the classic work on out-of-body experiences, or OBEs.

Monroe put together a research team whose mission was to figure out how to trigger experiences similar to his. His knowledge of audio engineering led to a solution that seemed to work, at least some of the time. Nobel prize winner Dr. Roger Sperry's split-brain research at the California Institute of Technology in the 1950s and '60s showed that there was a division of labor between the two hemispheres of the human brain. Though the two halves of our brains work cooperatively, they are also specialized for certain activities. In general the so-called left brain performs linear, analytic functions, such as reading, logical reasoning, placing things in categories, arithmetic functions, etc. The "right brain" is better at pattern recognition, gestalt perception (i.e., recognizing faces, differentiating whole objects from the conglomeration of their parts), and imagery. The right brain is creative and artistic, the left brain matter-of-fact and businesslike. This division is flexible. Together, the two brain hemispheres work as partners. Some of their functions overlap or are even shared. If, through illness or injury, one hemisphere is damaged, the other sometimes is able to assume some or all of the damaged functions.

Monroe and his associates noticed that the more closely attuned and cooperative both hemispheres were, the more efficiently peoples' minds seemed to work. A further discovery showed that a *binaural beat* played into the ears of a subject could influence the brain frequencies and hence, presumably, the interaction of the two hemispheres. Anyone who has heard two notes which are almost in tune, but not quite, will remember the slight wavering quality as the sound waves from the two separate notes alternately clash and work with each other. These vibrations are caused by a physics principle called *creative* and *destructive* interference. As waves that are slightly out of sync come together, individual waves either cancel each other out, or build each other up. You can see this at the beach when waves from slightly different directions come together. Some of the waves support each other, building "superwaves" that tower over their fellows. But when the trough of one wave comes together with the crest of another, they cancel each other out, creating an unusual "flat," or apparently waveless, spot in the water.

If a tone is played in one ear, and a second tone just slightly out of phase with the first is played in the other ear, the tones "meet in the middle" and a third frequency is created. The sound doesn't actually penetrate beyond the inner ears, but the electrical signals into which the ears convert the sound are put together by a specialized brain structure which creates the electrical equivalent of a combined frequency, similar in quality to when sound waves in the air that are just out of phase with each other are run together. The vibrational "beat" created in the brain by this electrical version of constructive and destructive interference sets up a frequency pattern that can be varied by varying the tones. The brain "accepts" this artificial beat frequency as a legitimate signal, and adjusts states of consciousness to match in relatively controllable ways that are interesting, perhaps useful, but harmless. With some careful trial and error, Monroe and his technicians were able, they believed, to find the best frequencies for getting the left- and right-brain hemispheres to work together—to become synchronized. Thus Hemi-Sync (for "hemispheric synchronization") was born.

Experimenting further with his Hemi-Sync techniques, Monroe created "recipes" of binaural beat frequencies that seemed to cause selected altered states of consciousness in a human being. While the process couldn't directly cause an out-of-body experience, it was possible to set up a state of mind that was conducive for one. The institute that grew up around this technology couldn't guarantee that a person taking one of its week-long, in-residence "Gateway" workshops would end up temporarily "out of body." But many who had never managed it before *did* succeed in having an OBE, and even those who didn't almost always had an interesting and often life-enhancing experience.

Without knowing it, Monroe had been a part of the Army remote viewing effort almost from its beginnings. Starting in the late spring or early summer of 1977, before the remote viewing program was even formally begun, Fred Atwater started making visits to the institute to meet Bob Monroe. Without mentioning the unit, Fred tried to glean ideas and information from Monroe that might be useful to the new Army project.[1] For the next few years Bob was not officially told that he was providing his expertise to a government psychic espionage program, not even in September 1980, when the first Grill Flame operative attended a Gateway program at the institute. But Monroe must have wondered when, in June 1982, another Army officer attended the institute, and a third followed in November.[2]

Fred and his remote viewers weren't the only ones interested in the goings-on in the Blue Ridge. In 1983 General Stubblebine sent his High Performance Task Force folks to evaluate the Monroe program, and himself became fascinated by the institute and its offbeat founder.

When Fred gave me Bob's book, *Journeys Out of the Body*, to read, I don't recall that he told me I would be going to the Monroe Institute. Had he done so, I might have read the book from a much different perspective. As it was, I read *Journeys* with interest, finding much that resonated with my own Mormon spiritual heritage. (In fact, years later I was directed to a remark made in 1853 by early Mormon leader Brigham Young, explicitly saying that *all* humans had experiences similar to what Bob Monroe reported, but that they were usually unaware of it.) I found the whole notion of out-of-body experiences intriguing, and could see how the ability to experience such things might be useful to remote viewing. If, after all, one's awareness *could* temporarily leave one's body, then come back and report what it had discovered, all sorts of possible uses were evident.

Then, one day during that fall of 1983, I learned that I would soon be going to Virginia for the Monroe experience. There were, however, bureaucratic hoops to be jumped through. And as anyone knows who has ever been in a bureaucracy, the devil is in the details.

Unlike our predecessors, I and my fellows would not be attending a traditional Monroe Institute Gateway program, but something called a RAPT seminar instead. The acronym stood for "rapid acquisition personal training." It was purely a euphemism to disguise the real nature and intent of the program. Enamored as he was with the leading-edge ideas his task force had uncovered, General Stubblebine was anxious to expose as many of his personnel as possible to consciousness-raising encounters in the noble but, as it turned out, vain hope that he could help prepare the Army for the twenty-first century.

He intended to send not only a handful of remote viewers to Monroe, but hundreds of INSCOM staffers who had nothing to do with Center Lane. To get budget managers to approve these joyrides into the ether, Stubblebine had to make it sound as innocuous as possible. So the general persuaded the Monroe Institute to modify the standard Gateway program by adding a couple of new Hemi-Sync modules meant to help with intuitive management skills. He then billed it as a leadership course. That took care of the organizational bean counters. But there were other wickets Stubblebine had to get his ball through.

One was to justify to his immediate superiors (who knew more about what was afoot than did those further up the line), the expense and man-hours for running a few hundred INSCOM staff people, twenty at a time, through a week-long course where they spent the majority of their time flat on their backs trying to go "out of body." But Stubblebine had a solution for this problem. He claimed that the course was designed to be a screening mechanism to help identify promising remote viewing candidates for Center Lane. There were only two problems with this: our own screening mechanism already worked fine, and we didn't need any new candidates at the time.

We in Center Lane were bothered by this questionable use of our tenuous charter. We were even more bothered when we figured out another reason Stubblebine needed Center Lane as cover for sending his people through the RAPT program. He needed our hard-won Human Use certification to let his people become guinea pigs.

Once Center Lane had been shanghaied to "cover" for Stubblebine's pet program, it was inevitable that we would also get the chores of administering and justifying it as well. In late October or early November 1983, our boss Brian Buzby received a call from Stubblebine directing us to draft a memorandum with a justification in it claiming RAPT was a screening mechanism for Center Lane, and explaining why it should fit under our Human Use umbrella. With guidance from Buzby, I set about trying to make sense of a project that didn't make any sense. Buzby, I, and the others were uncomfortable with this, but as Buzby observed later in retrospect, "We rationalized it off, saying, 'You know, this isn't the best thing for the remote viewing program, but we need [Stubblebine's] support, and can't afford to lose it.' "[3] RAPT was formally approved on November 10, 1983.[4]

Because of her background in personnel management, Charlene Cavanaugh was assigned to be the action officer for the RAPT program. Throughout November 1983 we were busy filing and processing personal histories, health disclosure forms, personality assessment tests, and Human Use consent forms signed by all levels of INSCOM headquarters workers, from the colonel who was Stubblebine's chief of staff to the lowliest clerk-typist. No one was forced to participate in RAPT training. But when your commanding general suggests that he would like you to go, it is easier to volunteer than to come up with a reason why not.

This flurry of paperwork that had nothing to do with our mission caused a lot of grumbling in the Center Lane offices. It wasn't that we weren't in sympathy with Stubblebine's overall agenda. He was determined to change attitudes inside INSCOM and, hopefully, within the military itself about expanding unrealized human potential.

What might the Army be able to accomplish if soldiers could learn to access more than the ten percent of their minds that humans allegedly use? If a group of soldiers and civilians could have their consciousness "raised" by exposure to Monroe, wouldn't that be a significant start to improving the climate for such advanced ideas in the military as a whole? I don't think anyone stopped to consider what would happen if things *didn't* work out that way. To Stubblebine it seemed worth a try, and we sympathized, even if we were privately troubled by the methods. The whole RAPT project had an ominous feeling about it, and from the conversations we had, I was not the only one in the Center Lane office who had a sense of foreboding.

I was in the second group of INSCOM people to get "RAPTed," as some of us called it. On Friday, December 2, 1983, I and a score of other soldiers and Army civilians assembled behind Nathan Hale Hall at Fort Meade to board the bus to take us to the Monroe Institute. Also going along on the trip were Jeannie Betters, one of Center Lane's secretaries, and Charlene, who had been assigned to monitor the contract INSCOM had with the Monroe Institute. She had already been to a Gateway experience at the Institute a year or so before, as a member of the High Performance Task Force, so this would not be a new experience for her.

Fred had told me to look for a guy by the name of Ed Dames, who was going to be my roommate during my stay at the institute. I had never met Ed, but had heard his name mentioned once or twice. He worked at the Systems Exploitation Detachment, Fred's old unit, as an analyst specializing in biological and chemical threats, and had provided a few taskings to the remote-viewing unit in the past. He was smart, dedicated, and very enthusiastic about remote viewing. Ed had a reputation as an innovative, if unconventional, thinker, based on an imaginative solution to a particular intelligence problem (as far as I know so useful to U.S. intelligence that it remains justifiably classified to this day) for which he had received a meritorious service medal (mid-level Army award).

I soon found Ed in the group of people who were milling around awaiting the bus. He was dressed as the rest of us in civilian clothes, with sandy hair cropped short. He later admitted that he often trimmed his bangs himself, and so it looked on this occasion. Ed had penetrating eyes that often crinkled at the edges in amusement. One quickly stopped noticing the details, though, since his confidence and chutzpah soon had one wrapped up in his lively persona. He was an odd combination of single-mindedness and sardonic humor. One moment he could be gravely assuring you that the Soviets were likely to unleash vile biological weapons any minute now, and the next moment be making a rude or irreverent joke at the expense of some current military or cultural sacred cow. I liked him immediately.

We sat together on the bus and Ed did most of the talking. Back in the early 1970s Ed had been an enlisted soldier in Taiwan, working as a Morse code intercept operator for the Army Security Agency—a "ditty-bopper," in the slang of the Army intelligence community. Morse interceptors spent their days sitting at radio receivers, listening through headphones to long-wave Morse-code radio broadcasts that were the workhorse communications means for both low-tech armies and guerrilla groups trying to stay incognito. Ditty-boppers had a reputation for working long, monotonous shifts, listening to streams of dits and dahs coming through their headsets for hours, copying transcriptions of the code onto hulking old manual typewriters. They worked that way for days, stretching into months and years until finally, stark, raving mad, they would leap screaming from their chairs and hurl their typewriters through the closest available window, or so the stories went. Legend had it that there were whole psychiatric wards of ditty-boppers lounging around in strait jackets.

Ed Dames seemed to have escaped this fate by marrying a Taiwanese woman, leaving the Army after five years, and going to school at the University of California, Berkeley, majoring in chemistry, with a minor in Chinese. He graduated with high honors from Berkeley's ROTC program at a time when it was not fashionable to be involved with the military at all. He was commissioned a second lieutenant in the Military Intelligence Branch, and went off to Germany to be the tactical intelligence officer on a tank battalion commander's staff.

Ed was fond of telling horror stories about that first tour as a junior officer in a combat battalion. In addition to their normal assignments, all lower-ranking officers were required to fulfill extra duties as their names came up on a rotating duty roster. One extra duty Dames particularly disliked was Officer of the Day. ODs are nominally the commander's representative when the commander is absent, usually after duty hours and on weekends. During their shifts ODs are often required to make periodic inspections of areas where sensitive equipment is stored or mischief might get started. Often the OD must do a walk-through of the enlisted barracks, to make sure things there are in order.

This was the Army not long after Vietnam. Discipline and morale were shot, drug use and racial conflict rampant. It could be dangerous to walk through the barracks, especially if you were short in stature. It didn't even matter if you were a lieutenant and everyone else in the barracks was enlisted. According to Ed, he solved the problem in typically flamboyant fashion. Any time he had "the duty," he checked a .45 caliber M-3 "grease gun" submachine gun out of the arms room, taped two thirty-round magazines together back-to-back, and went through the barracks loaded for bear. He claims no one ever hassled him.

Another extra duty that came Ed's way was range officer when the battalion's tanks were doing their scheduled main-gun target practice. Ed tells the story that one rainy night in Germany he was standing on the fender of an M-60 tank during night gunnery practice. Other tanks were lined up beside the one on which he stood. Tank treads had churned the ground into a gooey sea of knee-deep mud. Except for the muzzle flashes, tracer rounds, and guttering aerial flares, it was pitch dark in the pouring rain.

Ed turned to step across to the next tank, when suddenly the one he was on lurched. The lieutenant lost his balance and tumbled into the two-foot gap separating the tank from its neighbor. Landing on his back between two sixty-ton steel behemoths, he found he was trapped. Because of the deep mud, he would have to roll over to get up, but the space was so narrow that any move would place him right among the road wheels and tracks of a tank. He could tell by the gunning of the engines that the tanks were about to move out. If one or the other tank were to veer even slightly when they lunged forward, he would be ground into hamburger.

"Don't move the tank!" he screamed, but his voice was drowned out between the bellowing of the engines and the firing of the main guns. "Don't move the tank!" he screamed again, squirming in the mud. And again no response.

Then, just as he was convinced he was about to be chewed into tatters, a sergeant happened to glance down between the two tanks and thought he saw something. Peering closer, he saw Ed floundering, half buried in the mud. "What the hell are you doing down there, Lieutenant?" he bellowed and, reaching down, grabbed Ed by the front of his field jacket and dragged him back aboard.

I don't remember how much of this I heard on that bus ride down to Virginia, and how much I heard later. Ed told and retold parts of his history over the coming years. But all this was quite tame compared to what was interspersed with it. Most of the four-hour bus trip Ed spent talking about space aliens and UFOs.

I had read books and articles about UFOs, and my religion taught that intelligent life existed on other worlds (but as creations of Deity, not the stuff of flying saucers or invaders from Mars). The logic of the math was persuasive; it seemed incredible and the height of arrogance to think that of literally billions, perhaps trillions of stars out there in the universe, ours would be the only one that harbored life. But I remained agnostic on the subject of UFOs. Just because there might be life on other worlds didn't necessarily mean they could, or even wanted to, visit us.

This opinion was reinforced when, on my church mission to Switzerland in the mid-1970s, I encountered a book by Erich Von Däniken showing photos of artifacts from ancient civilizations, paired with strained explanations for how these artifacts really were of extraterrestrial origin. A few months later I was shown another book featuring pictures taken by a different Swiss Ufologist, purportedly showing UFOs he had encountered. Most of the images looked like out-of-focus photographs of a wheel rim from a truck. The photos were so obviously phony that I was amazed anyone could take the fellow seriously. But to my amazement, many did.

From what I knew of UFO phenomena, there was no known confirmed physical evidence, only a large and growing number of alleged eyewitness accounts. As an intelligence officer I had learned the danger of taking eyewitnesses too seriously. A witness may be operating under any number of motivations—altruism, the need for attention, the intent to defraud, mental illness. I was also well aware of the so-called "witness effect," that several credible witnesses may observe an event, and still arrive at differing accounts of that same event. When witnesses are less credible, as their reliability goes down, so usually does the accuracy of their stories.

Of course, many times eyewitnesses can be very accurate, and that fact kept me from dismissing *all* the testimony about UFOs that had been produced over the years. There was a core group of eyewitness accounts that seemed compelling. Perhaps many, or even most UFO accounts were mistaken or purposely misleading. But it seemed to strain the limits of credibility that they *all* were.

Ed was very persuasive. He exuded confidence, seemed knowledgeable, and hinted at insider access to some of the details. I later found that what he was telling me as we rode south on Route 29 through Virginia was mostly the standard cases that were being noised around the UFO community at the time. But he seemed well versed, and he told his stories in a way that made sense and hung together. By the time we pulled up to the front of the Monroe Institute and the bus doors sprang open, he hadn't convinced me about UFOs, but he had persuaded me that I ought to take some of the reports more seriously.

The interior of the Center, as the Monroe Institute's main building was called, was warm and welcoming after the chilly sunset that greeted us on exiting the bus. Inside, all was comfortable, plush, and paneled in rustic wood to match the tree-hemmed pastures that surrounded the hilltop on which the institute sprawled. The Center had three levels; we entered at hilltop level through a hall that opened into a two-story great room. An encompassing balcony on the upper level overlooked the floor of the space below. Door after door was arrayed on both levels around the outer walls of the great room. These doors opened into our accommodations, small but comfortable rooms that contained dressers, desks, and two "CHEC" units in each.[5]

Bob Monroe loved acronyms. CHEC stood for "controlled holistic environmental chamber." A CHEC unit was a small berth, just large enough for a twin-sized air mattress. A blackout curtain could be drawn across the opening for privacy and to exclude light. These units were to be both our beds at night and our "work areas" during the day. Built into the head of the sleeping area were speakers through which wake-up music streamed every morning during the coming week. Each CHEC unit also had a set of headphones. Through these Bob Monroe's disembodied voice guided us through the various Hemi-Sync signals that moved us from one level, or Focus, to the next as our days at the institute progressed.

The signals were mixed with music or white noise on tapes that lasted for an hour or ninety minutes at a stretch, and were played through our headphones from the central electronics control booth in the lowest level of the Center. After each tape we assembled in a spacious and elegantly cheery meeting area on the lower level, draping ourselves dreamily over the soft furnishings or sprawling across the plush, white carpet. There we talked over our experiences, the imagery we might have encountered, or new insights or—and this was what everyone was most anxious to hear about—the occasional report of something that might have been an out-of-body event. These talk sessions, which resembled the encounter groups popular in psychology circles, were usually led by two experienced trainers. Our trainers were Bill Schul, a soft-spoken psychologist, and Jan Northrup, an enthusiastic woman who, at the time, it turned out, was married to John Alexander, Stubblebine's staff officer for esoteric technologies.

We had surrendered our watches on arrival and, though it was easy enough to find out what time it was, we were all happy to hand over control of our itineraries to the institute staff to manage for the next week. As a consequence, our days started about 7 A.M. when bouncy "good morning" music piped through the speakers, and we headed for the shower, followed by breakfast.

The mornings were spent alternating between our CHEC cubicles and the discussion sessions. After lunch we usually did another tape or two, then had a few hours off, during which we were encouraged to get "grounded" again by strolling through the fields or along the gravel roads spreading out from the institute.

Dinner was served sometime after sunset and, like the other two meals, had the taste of homemade about it. The institute hired local cooks who prided themselves on healthy, tasty cuisine. Evenings were reserved for lectures or thought-provoking films. One evening's program featured Bob Monroe fielding questions and talking about his experiences. On another evening we watched a film where the camera seemed to zoom close to people having a picnic in a park, then pull far away from the Earth to give one a sense of how attitudes about things can change with differing perspectives.

I already had some knowledge of Hemi-Sync, as did most new viewers in the unit. Fred had exposed me to tapes that started with Focus 3 (a state of general relaxation), and ended with Focus 10 (the so-called "mind awake, body asleep" state). As far as remote viewing was concerned, this was all the Hemi-Sync one needed. It established a sort of hypnagogic state, or mode of consciousness that was not quite asleep and not quite awake. This condition seemed helpful for ERV, whether because of the Hemi-Sync or merely by aiding relaxation; it's hard to say.

The first evening at Monroe we were given some time to settle into our rooms after dinner, but were soon called out for our first Hemi-Sync tape of the RAPT program. It took us to Focus 3. My notes from the episode mention an experience of "luminescent swirls," "warm tingle all over," and a sense of vibration and urge to "turn over without moving." All these were supposedly hallmarks of a pending OBE, but nothing further materialized.

Saturday morning took us to Focus 10 for three tapes, during which Bob's sonorous voice led us through various guided-imagery exercises. The afternoon again brought a Focus 10 tape, but during this one I had a remarkable, pronounced image of a brightly lit, arch-shaped passage, with bright, white walls and alcoves along the walls. What it meant, if anything, escaped me. But it was more vivid than anything I'd experienced under Hemi-Sync before. After dinner we did yet another Focus 10 tape.

Hearing about someone else's Hemi-Sync experience can often be about as interesting as hearing about someone else's dreams, so I will mention only the highlights. One occurred on our third day. We were up to Focus 15 by this time, and listening to what Bob Monroe called a "Free Flow" tape. Suddenly I was back in a scene from my childhood. I seemed to be near my Great-grandpa Carson's house on the western edge of Homedale, Idaho, a little town near the Oregon border. Nearby sparkled Succor Creek, the watercress along its edges as visually sharp and sensually green as if I were there again almost three decades before. Just as suddenly, I shifted from there to the smell of my Grandma Tidwell's home, felt the creaking stairs, tasted the musty odor of old books. Then I flashed through many of the prominent memories of my visits there: floating in a pond with my cousins on a raft; dangling a fishing line over the railing on the Snake River bridge; with my rubber band gun shooting Johnny Yuda off the old Sherman tank on display in the town park; sucking on frozen cherries from a bag purloined from Grandma's freezer. There was more vividness to my recollections than any other memory I can recall having. I did not have the feeling of being out of body, nor could I see how being out of body would accomplish what I had just experienced. But whatever was going on, it was more than almost-like I was there again.

On our fifth day at the institute we were to move from Focus 15 up into Focus 21. I "saw" a spectacular mix of patterns that flowed together in amorphous yet geometric forms. Suddenly it seemed in my imagination that I burst through some sort of lattice work barrier and found myself hanging motionless in empty space, facing a huge, yellow-green sun. I felt a powerful urge to keep going, but Bob Monroe's voice called me back.

Some of the tapes we did were not intended to be experiential. Instead, they involved goal-setting, "patterning" (sending oneself and "the universe" messages intended to influence future outcomes), and other exercises, some of which were undoubtedly part of the added material for RAPT.

On Thursday, December 8, with the course nearly over, we did a tape that Bob called Future 15, a Focus 15 tape during which we were to try to perceive events occurring over the next two years. Most of my impressions during this session were unexceptional; I would be living in the same house, with my kids and wife, going through the remote viewing training, and something about buying a car, all of which, unremarkably, came to be. I did have one odd image of Joe McMoneagle emerging from extensive bandages or a body cast of some sort, which I chalked up to mental symbolism of his pending retirement.

As our seven days drew to a close, we learned of plans for an unusual event. General Stubblebine was coming down to the institute for the final afternoon of our stay—and he was bringing with him a busload of folks from the INSCOM staff who had already been through RAPT or Gateway courses. All of us together were going to congregate in the white-carpeted meeting room and do a collective remote viewing exercise, an impromptu group peek into the future.

Stubblebine prefaced the exercise with an odd little speech. Though neither I nor others I've recently talked to can remember much of what he said, we all remember that it focused on an encounter with a salamander. Earlier, the general told us, he had been strolling down the lane near the institute, deep in thought, when a small orange salamander crossed his path. In the normal course of events this wouldn't have been exceptional. But to Stubblebine, in the reflective state of mind in which he found himself, it seemed an omen, a herald of truth to which he should attend. The small, mystical creature symbolized to him that he was on the right track with what he was doing in INSCOM. He told us that in a metaphorical sort of way the creature spoke to him, served as a catalyst to open a channel between his conscious mind and his intuition.[6]

Even though much of the content of what he said escapes me, I seem to remember cryptic words of encouragement and inspiration, counsel to go beyond the ordinary and seek excellence. After the brief encounter, the salamander and the general each went his separate way. At first, so symbolically did the general speak that I couldn't tell whether he meant it to be taken metaphorically, or really believed the amphibian had talked to him. But Stubblebine never intended to be taken literally, only to be encouraging, to reassure us that if we sometimes felt that we were sticking our necks out, he was already there ahead of us. Later, Ed Dames, who fancied himself a bit of a naturalist, protested that the story couldn't possibly be true, since he was sure that there were no orange salamanders in Virginia. The species was native to California. Whatever the case, this encounter between man and salamander was a curious prelude to what happened next.

We were given a few minutes to gather downstairs in the meeting area. Though the room was large, there were far more of us than the space was designed for. Folks perched on any spot that could reasonably serve as a chair. People were huddled together on the carpet, leaving only a narrow walkway clear for others to pass through the room. Some recall that there was an attempt to arrange people in a circle, lying on their backs and holding hands. We were supposed to relax, so each person was trying to lean back or recline in such a way as not to disturb his or her neighbors. The room began to look like a scene from a Fellini movie, but one where all the actors keep their clothes on.

What we were about to do was an expansion of an event the institute used as a final group exercise before sending folks home at the end of a successful Gateway week. As I recall, the original plan was to play a Hemi-Sync tape to get us all "in the mood" for precognition. But Bob decided that wouldn't work. In an open, crowded setting, there was no way to isolate left and right channels for each of us. So he went into the control booth, closed the door, and in a few moments we heard his voice over the speaker system, leading us through guided relaxation exercises. After several minutes of this, the sound of shuffled papers came distantly through the speakers. Then he spoke again.

"Will there be a terrorist attack against government facilities in the Washington, D.C., area in the next few months?" He must have been reading from a list of questions someone had given him. But the effect was jarring. After seven days of drifting without clocks in a setting designed to approach serenity and bliss, this sudden talk of terrorism was a shock. Still, we did the best we could. We had been provided paper and pen to record any impressions we received, so many of us dutifully jotted down notes, recording whatever came to mind.

"Where will the next terrorist attack take place?"

As each question was spoken, it fell like a stone on my ears. There was a pause, and then the scribbling would begin. I was quite uncomfortable by then. It had a slight touch of farce about it—a room full of military intelligence professionals, all dressed in sweat suits or other loose-fitting attire, sprawling over and around the plush furniture.

"When will the next attack take place?"

I was by no means yet an expert on remote viewing. But the procedure struck me as not likely to be successful. Wouldn't asking explicit questions start the analytic juices going, contaminating any data that someone might actually produce? I learned later that what we were doing in that basement was nothing like any form of remote viewing as it was practiced at either SRI international or in Center Lane.

There were other questions of intelligence interest; Jeannie Betters recalled some having to do with the situation in the Persian Gulf, where the Iran-Iraq war was raging. But as the session continued, it began to remind me more and more of a game I had played in high school. Everyone would recline on the floor and, like tiled words in a Scrabble game, lay our heads on each others' stomachs so we were crisscrossed all around the room. Someone would inevitably giggle, and the bouncing of the laugher's stomach would set off the next person, then the next person until, in a chain reaction, the entire room would be laughing hilariously. One difference here at the institute was that no one laughed.

The general was so obviously serious about it, and Bob Monroe's words over the intercom so sober, that we couldn't help but maintain such decorum as we had. I have to admit that by the time all was said and done, I was feeling sheepish about being involved in the event. Looking at everyone else's serious faces, though, I didn't have the nerve to admit it. Only afterward did I find out that at least some of them were feeling just like me, but didn't venture to show it under the belief that everyone else had found the experience worthwhile.

On exiting, those of us with anything to report handed in our papers. It seemed that none of our predictions or answers to questions turned out to be of any use, and if they did, we never heard about it to my recollection.[7]

In hindsight I developed more sympathy for what General Stubblebine attempted to do. Zany as the experience had seemed at points, that wouldn't have mattered if it had actually *worked*. And Stubblebine couldn't have known whether it worked until he actually had us try it.

RAPT done, we grabbed our gear, boarded the bus, and headed for home.

It was nearly Christmas. Hartleigh Trent's illness and death from cancer in October left Joe as the only fully operational remote viewer in the unit, with Tom McNear and a couple of part-timers contributing occasional sessions. During 1983, Center Lane had been involved in fifteen intelligence-collection projects, requiring fifty-seven individual sessions, quite a drop from past years, but an improvement over 1982, when funding battles had limited operations to nine projects and only twenty operational sessions. Joe worked on every one of the 1983 projects, but two other sources, identified only by number, contributed a few sessions each to some of the projects.

The U.S. embassy in Moscow, which had largely been constructed by Russian contractors, was one target. Center Lane results confirmed the existence of listening devices in the walls of the building. Several of the other projects were designated by code names, the significance of which remain obscure. But there were also targets involving two communications facilities, the U.S.S.R.'s trade mission in Madagascar, a listening device in another embassy, a biological research facility in East Berlin, and a safe house in Panama—the session Joe was working on when I was allowed to eavesdrop.[8]

After the RAPT seminar, Ed Dames returned to his regular duties at SED. Charlene and I were looking forward to the New Year as we awaited arrival of the newest member of our team. Bill Ray showed up in Fred Atwater's driveway the first week in January, unfolding his lanky frame from the front seat of a black Subaru station wagon. Out of the tailgate and every other door of the small car kids erupted. The Rays were a large, happy family.

After the stint at Fort Huachuca as Fred's superior, Bill had done a tour in Germany as chief of a counterintelligence team in Augsburg, and was just ending another Stateside tour when Fred had called him up, told him we had an opening for a captain, and sent him the screening tests. Bill had scored well enough and here he was.[9] When I first met him, something about him seemed familiar. After some questioning back and forth, we discovered the connection: Joe Evans, the fellow who had convinced me to apply for Officer Candidate School back in 1978, but who himself had so unfortunately been rejected, had gone on to be trained in counterintelligence work. I had driven up to visit Joe in Augsburg when our tours in Germany had overlapped. Bill had been Joe's commander, and I had met him there.

On Bill's first full day in the office, Ed Dames showed up again. Bill knew Ed's boss over at SED, Major George Lang, and at first he thought Ed was Lang's liaison to the RV unit. It turned out instead that Lang was offering to let Ed go through the training with us, and SED would pay his travel and lodging expenses. The idea was that Ed would remain assigned to SED, would return there between training sessions, and would go back to SED permanently after he had learned remote viewing.[10]

Brian Buzby talked over the offer with Fred and Bill. Buzby was suspicious that Lang was trying to acquire someone trained in remote viewing so SED could bypass Center Lane in the future. Fred didn't believe such a strategy could work, since one lone viewer without monitor or support staff would be nearly useless. But he still saw benefit in training Ed. Though his reasoning was later to change, when Ed's personality quirks and office behavior were better known, Fred thought at the time that once the training was finished the unit might get at least part-time use out of SED's captain. We could have the equivalent of half of a person who didn't count against our allotted personnel ceiling.

More important, even though Ed would share the same remote viewing training as the rest of us, there was no intention to use him as a viewer. He had not been selected on the same basis as had we, had not taken the same tests, nor been evaluated on the same criteria. Instead, he was meant to become a monitor/interviewer exclusively. Fred was the only experienced monitor left in the unit, and knew he would need help managing the load when there were at least three new viewers on-line, plus Tommy, who would soon become operational. Atwater reasoned that the familiarity with the remote viewing process that training with Swann would bring would help shorten Dames's learning curve in becoming a qualified RV monitor. If it worked out, they might even get Dames assigned to that job in Center Lane once his tour with SED was over.[11]

It seemed like a good idea at the time.

As a result of Atwater's lobbying on Dames's behalf, Buzby called Ingo Swann to see if a fourth person could be added to the training contract. Swann agreed, Lang's proposal was accepted, and our threesome became a foursome. So there we were, all assembled at Fort Meade awaiting our next big adventure: our first trip to California to meet Hal Puthoff and the legendary Ingo Swann, and to start learning coordinate remote viewing. The bomb ticking away inside the RAPT program was yet to explode.

II

Ingo

... we find that
"be all you can be"
is not just an Army
slogan ...

Ingo Swann and Hal Puthoff's coordinate remote viewing (CRV) method wasn't intended to make anyone "psychic," but was instead a means to exploit a perceptual channel that humans had but didn't know they had. The research seemed to show that everyone already possessed native psychic ability, but most had no idea how to tap into it. Ingo was uncomfortable with the terms "psychic," "extrasensory perception," "parapsychology," and the other jargon to describe seemingly exceptional human abilities. For him these abilities were not exceptional, nor paranormal, nor extrasensory. In fact, they were normal human mental functions that had been sidelined in a world run by scientists and skeptics.[1]

If "being psychic" was as much a human sense as hearing, seeing, smelling, tasting, and touching, then it wasn't "extra" sensory at all. Nor, was it "paranormal" or "parapsychology," when the prefix "para" means "similar to, but not the same as." And as for being "psychic?" Well, the word had come to imply a force or function beyond human ken, a power that only the gifted wield. Time-honored though this notion was, it clashed with what Ingo knew by study and experience to be true. He was careful to make plain to us from the start that whether or not there was such a thing as "being psychic," that was not what we were about. We were there to learn remote viewing.

Five of us, including Fred Atwater, who came along to observe, had gathered at the SRI International campus in Menlo Park. We came through the front door of SRI's Radio Physics Lab early on Monday, January 16, 1984, exchanging the grey Maryland winter for the brilliant sun and eucalyptus smells of California's Bay area. We checked in at the receptionist's desk, signing our cover names, and clipped security badges to our lapels. Besides myself and Fred, there were Bill Ray, Charlene Cavanaugh, and Ed Dames. As the only one not officially assigned to Center Lane, Ed would go with us during our alternating fourteen-day training cycles, but in the intervening two-week "off" periods he would return to SED for his regular duties.

We met Dr. Harold E. Puthoff first. Quiet and soft-spoken, Hal was an unusual mixture of confidence, competence, and humility. He was willing to listen to questions and ideas, and always happy to give credit to others who had contributed to the success of the SRI remote viewing program. But he also knew his stuff. The first thing he did was brief us on the background of remote viewing. Over the intervening years the exact content and details of that presentation have disappeared among my other memories. But I do remember graphs and charts, pauses for questions, and a thoughtful approach that calmed some of my uncertainties about what I had gotten myself into.

As part of our introduction to remote viewing, someone gave us a test that seemed to be an effort to produce remote-viewing results that could be scored by computer, bypassing the need for subjective human judgment. We were handed a yes-or-no checklist of details that might describe any remote viewing target: is there water at the site and is it in motion, or contained; is there a structure; what colors are important to the site? With the checklist in hand, we were given a coordinate for a target and told to record our impressions. We filled in the answer blocks, but I for one didn't feel that I had perceived *anything* but what was in the room. As far as I recall, we were never told our results. Bill Ray remembers that Ingo was very angry that such a "left-brain" approach would have been used with his students before he even had access to them. Swann was worried that the so-called first-time effect (the often exceptional results that occur in a first-time remote-viewing session) might have been spoiled for us. When I asked Ingo about it sixteen years after the fact, he couldn't recall the incident, but agreed that he would have been livid.

It was soon time for lunch, which we had in the SRI cafeteria, a few buildings over from the Radio Physics Lab. It was "dessert bar" day, and Hal thought that would be a treat for us. But the real treat was that we met Ingo for the first time. You couldn't tell from Hal's calm expression during the introductions, but I now suspect he was thinking that in a few hours we wouldn't find Ingo to be such a treat.

Ingo stood about six feet tall, and was dressed in jeans, sport jacket, and tie. He was wearing square-toed harness boots, as was his style then. A neatly clipped beard gave him an air of thoughtful composure. He had eyes that danced when something funny was said, and he spoke quietly but with animation. At first Ingo was reserved, sizing us up; planning strategies, it seemed to me. We were joined at lunch by Ed May and Jim Salyer. May was the physicist whom Ingo had helped recruit for the SRI remote viewing program eight years before, and who would eventually replace Puthoff as program director when Hal left SRI to take a position as director of the Institute for Advanced Studies in Austin, Texas. Salyer was the COTR (contracting office's technical representative) for the Defense Intelligence Agency.

Our little group had a stimulating lunchtime visit around the table, mostly on topics having nothing to do with remote viewing. The cafeteria was not cleared for classified conversations, and besides, we fledgling viewers from Fort Meade didn't know enough about the subject to make intelligent conversation. After we had licked up the last traces of ice cream and chocolate syrup, it was time to get down to work.

If I had tried to anticipate what remote viewing training might be like, this would not have been it. After the receptionist in the Radio Physics Laboratory building buzzed us through the access door, we walked down a hall, took three flights of stairs, and found ourselves in a suite of rooms outfitted specifically for remote viewing training. There were three rooms where we spent most of our time: the classroom where Ingo gave his lectures; the waiting room where we passed the time outside the remote viewing room awaiting our turns; and the remote viewing "grey room" itself, where we were expected eventually to prove ourselves.[2]

Central to the lecture room was a long table. As we walked in on that first day, we were each issued a thick dictionary. These dictionaries were to be both friend and foe during the coming year.

Training started when we took our seats at the long table, were given a stack of blank white paper for note-taking, and opened our dictionaries. Ingo tossed out words and told us to find the definitions. For example, he might say "matrix," and we would leaf quickly through the pages until we found the entry. "Read the definitions, please!" he would say, and we would each take turns reading a definition until we had read every entry under that word. Then, led by Ingo, we haggled over each, until we hit the one that he had in mind all along. We dutifully wrote down the accepted definition in our notes exactly as it appeared in the dictionary, and went on to the next word. During that first afternoon we worked through "matrix," "signal," "wave," "aperture," "signal line," and so forth.

Not until Ingo was satisfied that we understood every word he intended to use did he move on to the lecture. He wrote key points on the large board positioned near one wall as he talked, and he insisted we keep detailed notes of everything he said. If he noticed that one of us failed to jot down an item, he would glower and make some sharp remark to bring the unruly one quickly to heel.

All this note-taking was irksome for me. I had gotten through both high school and college relying on memory and taking as few notes as possible. To keep our mentor happy, I had to go against bad habits that I had practiced for years. And I admit that it hurt.

The four of us discovered that working with Ingo was definitely *not* going to be a treat. Not only were there the definitions, the lectures, and the notes, but after each lecture and all those notes he also expected us to write essays. And, by "essays," he didn't mean a haphazard collection of words such as we might have gotten away with in school. Ingo would wrap up a lecture, set us to writing, and after an hour of so of our anguish, require us to turn in our essays. He would go through them to see if we had extracted everything he deemed important from the lecture. Clucking his tongue and frowning, he would make large red marks all over them before handing them back to us. We knew then that we had missed a point, but we didn't know why, and Ingo wouldn't tell us. "I'm sure it's in your notes," he would say with a sigh and a wave of his hand, and send us off to puzzle over what the right answer might be. We would then rewrite the essay and present it to him again, to be either accepted or once more rejected.

It wasn't until the third lecture that we found out why Ingo was so adamant about note-taking and essays. His goal was to make sure the concepts he was teaching us were embedded at the very lowest level of our understanding. He wanted what we learned to be second nature, so we wouldn't even have to think about it when, in the middle of a remote viewing session, we were trying to distinguish solid information from mental "noise."

Some educators believe that the more physical senses we can involve in learning a concept or skill, the more thoroughly we absorb it, and the more easily we retain it. Ingo believed this principle implicitly. During the lecture, we heard and saw him speaking and writing on the board, thus applying two of our senses. In taking notes, we saw what we ourselves had written, and had the kinesthetic experience of forming words with our pens on the paper, adding a further sensory input. When we wrote our essays, we first had to dredge up the concepts from our memories and pick them out of our notes, bringing them fresh to mind. Then we had to organize our thoughts, and write them down on our paper, once again interacting visually and kinesthetically with the words and ideas.

This was not a new system of learning, by any means. It was the same venerable approach followed by countless teachers over the centuries, just more rigidly enforced. Unlike other academic settings, however, Ingo made sure we knew *why* we were doing it. By the time we were done, we could nearly recite the concepts in our sleep. Ingo deemed this approach to be part of the principle of "objectification," which, as we learned later, is central to successful remote viewing.

Today, nearly two decades after I first began my training with Ingo, I see many who claim to be remote viewing instructors. As far as I know, none of them uses the lecture-essay approach, rejecting the importance Ingo Swann placed in this principle. Without the rigorous note-taking students are able to learn remote viewing to some extent, but I wonder if they understand or master the skills as deeply as did those of us who learned from Ingo and used his teaching methods later at Fort Meade.

Grueling as Ingo's training was, and as much grumbling as we dared make, it was an exciting and stimulating experience. His lectures were dynamic and interactive. He carried on a dialogue with us as he talked, asking us questions, answering our questions, allowing brief tangents to explore interesting intellectual terrain. He wanted to make sure we thoroughly understood what it was we were going to do and why it worked.

Perception

Unlike many popular approaches to "being psychic," CRV methodology was not something Puthoff and Swann pulled out of a hat or glued together from random ideas that sounded nice in a lecture hall. Nor was it based on superficial feel-good ideas copied from popular speakers or books, as is often the case with many current "psychism" fads. Together, Hal, Ingo, and the others in the SRI lab had spent years researching scientific parapsychology, sense perception, psychology, neuroscience, subliminal perception, and other related fields. They had read hundreds of books and articles on these various subjects, and discussed principles with some of the original researchers who had conducted the studies. The other people Hal and Ingo worked with over the years at SRI—Russell Targ, Ed May, Pat Price, Keith Harary, Hella Hammid, and many others—had contributed in their own ways to the final product.

Deconstructing old philosophies of how people were "psychic," the SRI researchers built their theory and methodology from scratch. There was little that was superfluous or gratuitous; everything belonged. I don't claim that what they came up with could not be improved upon. They wouldn't make that claim either, particularly in light of all that has been learned about human mental and perceptual processes over the past twenty years. Improvements should certainly be possible. But the fact that what they came up with worked well then, and still does, owes much to the care and labor that went into it.

One early assumption Ingo introduced was based on his own experience: all people's perceptual abilities go beyond the "normal" five senses. Things traditionally called "extra" sensory emerge into human awareness in much the same way that normal sensory input does. If so, then "psychic" perception must follow the same rules as ordinary perception, he reasoned.

It was a radical idea to redefine remote viewing as simply normal perception. Without thinking about it first, most people would reflexively label it "psychic" behavior. This redefinition liberated remote viewing from having to make allowances for some mysterious force. Instead, RV was just a version of the same problem we solve every day in detecting, decoding, and using sensory experience from the world around us. From this approach, it doesn't *matter* where the information comes from. Information perceived through RV is like that perceived through vision, hearing, smell, or touch. Until modern science figured them out, the origins of what we receive through those senses was equally mysterious. And there are still significant parts of perceptual experience that remain mysterious to science today. In practical terms, the average guy on the street has little clue as to where or how sensory input gets into his brain. So why not treat remote viewing the same way?

This stance turned out to be very useful, not only for coming up with a practical approach to remote viewing research and applications, but for "selling" the program to skeptical government officials. The SRI team frequently had to brief various science boards and congressional oversight committees on the remote-viewing program. As Ingo remembers:

> We used perception. I made references of all the recent papers and books on perception. The oversight committees could reject anything psychic because there was no background for it. But they could not reject an effort to expand perception, because there *was* some very thorough published scientific background on *it*. We never used the word "psychic" in the Washington dog and pony shows. We had to retrain, to reeducate the people in Washington to think of it as perception. And we never had *any* problem talking to these people. They said, "Ah, well—this isn't *psychic*, then. This is *perception*."[3]

Substituting "perception" for "psychic" wasn't just a word game to try to fool scientists or congressional committees. Perception *was* the key. Ingo told me that he thought SRI had been very lucky to get him, not because he was a great "psychic" (something which he denies), but because, as an artist, he had extensively studied and then applied what he had learned about human perceptual processes. It turned out to be the key that unlocked the door.

When Ingo and Hal were working to develop remote viewing theory, they found out everything they could about the human perceptual system—how humans collect and interpret everyday sensory data. From there they drew a blueprint for a set of skills that would use that same human perceptual system to collect and interpret subconsciously perceived data. Their training discipline, coordinate remote viewing, was to be a template that overlaid known perceptual processes, allowing subliminal impressions arising from the Matrix to come to the surface and be decoded, just the same as the other senses did within their own modalities. To this day Ingo insists that making modifications to the system he and Hal created may degrade, and perhaps inhibit, remote viewing functioning.[4]

The model that was the foundation of CRV borrowed from many sources. Ingo wasn't ashamed of being a synthesist. Indeed, he was proud that one of his contributions was to discover connections and draw conclusions from existing research that no one else had noticed. His native creativity then aided him, with Puthoff's help, to bring all the relevant knowledge together. The resulting system not only made sense but—the two don't always go together—also worked. And it could be taught to people who had never had reason before to think that they would be able to do anything like this.

The sources were diverse. Norman F. Dixon's 1981 book, *Preconscious Processing*, and his 1971 work, *Subliminal Perception*, gave important clues into how our minds process perceptions and pass information between the subconscious and conscious minds. Upton Sinclair's *Mental Radio*, and Rene Warcollier's *Mind to Mind* contained important evidence about the transfer of information across space in a way that didn't involve the five senses.

Particularly important in providing a larger setting for the ideas Ingo and Hal were developing was physicist David Bohm's description of the "implicate order" in his book *Wholeness and the Implicate Order*. The "explicate" order is the interplay of energy and matter that we are used to in the outer world—trees, cars, people, planets, sunshine, and so forth. This is the realm of classical, or Newtonian, physics. The *implicate* order, by contrast, is the realm of quantum physics operating beneath the surface of the outer world of the explicate order. This implicate order is a strange domain, involving atomic and subatomic particles and their often bizarre interactions: particle-wave duality, where a subatomic entity may act like a small, solid "piece" of something while being observed, and like a wave of energy when not being observed; virtual existence, where matched particle pairs play peekaboo with reality by freely coming into and going out of existence quickly enough not to violate the principles of physics. And there was non-locality, the principle whereby influence can be exerted between particles across time and space, instantaneously and without any known intervening forces. In the process, the speed of light seems to be violated, not to mention basic notions of cause and effect. Though the evidence is still lacking, there are many who suspect non-locality will turn out to provide the explanation for remote viewing and other psi disciplines.

"The explicate and implicate order are available to human consciousness at all times," Ingo noted in one of our conversations. "People focus on the explicate order, but never focus on the implicate order. We made some very nice [charts] showing that this was the physics model that we intended to use in order to go about our research." And it sold well to the folks in Washington who were paying the bills.[5]

There were many other sources, influences, and references that figured into the development of remote viewing. Some of these will come out as this story unfolds.

Focusing on perception was all very well and good. But it left unanswered the question of what exactly it is that is perceived by remote viewing. For vision, hearing, and the other mundane senses, we have an account that seems to make sense. For vision, the story runs somewhat like this: electromagnetic radiation (visible light) is emitted by a source, such as the sun or your desk lamp. This radiation reflects off some object in your surroundings, say a red ball on the floor. The reflected radiation enters your eye, and strikes special cells in the retina on the back of your eyeball. These cells convert the radiation from one form of energy to another. This second form of energy, which involves a fairly complex electrochemical process, is passed down the optic nerve to a special region in the rear of your brain called the visual cortex. And you see a red ball.

Science has been unable to discover how these electrochemical impulses that enter the visual cortex actually end up as an image of a red ball in our minds. We just know that it works. Still, the question of *what* is perceived in vision—e.g., electromagnetic radiation—and how it is perceived is pretty well understood up to that point. The same applies to hearing, smell, taste, and touch. But there is no equivalent account for remote viewing. The *what* is still missing, though things we have learned otherwise about human perception have given us some plausible clues as to the *how*.

This is where David Bohm's implicate order comes in. If at the *micro* level humans are really quantum systems—clusters of tiny particles bouncing off and interacting with each other in ways invisible to superficial, everyday existence—then this suggests that some interconnected aspect of the quantum world may be what we encounter when we remote view. We have no inkling, though, of what that aspect might be. When I asked Ingo what he thought it was that we perceive when remote viewing, he answered that it was just "information."[6]

As he was well aware, this doesn't answer the question. Information needs a medium to support it. It may be that at the quantum level information is transferred directly through some ethereal attachment point shared by everything in the universe. Or maybe it is passed via a quantum-level, nonlocal process similar to the mysterious way in which widely separated particles can be instantaneously affected by some influence at the subatomic level. But perhaps that's not how it works at all; maybe there is no universal point of connection, and maybe non-locality is incapable of transferring the large-scale information produced in remote viewing. We only know one thing for sure about whatever the mechanism might be; that remote viewing works, and so there must be *some* source for the information.

Therein lies the major difference between remote viewing and the other five senses: we don't know what the "carrier" is. Once the information is in the mind, the story is similar to that for vision, hearing, touch, smell, and taste. But this doesn't end the account. There are still some things we can understand.

The Matrix

Every philosophical system needs a creation myth. It doesn't matter whether that philosophy is of religion, science, psychology, or remote viewing. "Myth" is often mistaken to mean something fictional. But a creation myth need not be false; it can be fully true, or a mixture of both fiction and truth.

Modern science had its roots in the fourteenth-century Renaissance. From its very beginning, science competed with religion as to which would be the authority to which the rest of the world would turn for "real" explanations of the universe. Since it "owned" the creation myth, the church had the upper hand from long before the first glimmers of the Renaissance until Charles Darwin and Alfred Wallace devised science's *own* creation myth—natural selection, together with the theory of biological evolution that grew out of it. But with the rise of Darwinism, the power struggle was turned on its head. Science replaced religion as the arbiter of truth.

Were Darwin alive today, he would see that no creation myth can survive time unscathed. Over the decades, the notion of evolution has been interpreted and reinterpreted to the point where the different versions of it are as manifold and ornate as any that surrounds the creation myth in Genesis.

Psychology, too, has its own creation myth, somewhat discredited now, which it owes to Freud and his ideas of repressed sexuality.

We four remote-viewing trainees never thought in terms of a creation myth as we sat at the table in SRI's Radio Physics lab, furiously scribbling our notes, but we were listening as Ingo spun the tale of remote viewing's own version of Genesis. It begins with the idea of a Matrix. What I am about to describe isn't a creation myth in the precise sense of Darwin or Moses. But in the way that Ingo's model gives a theory of origins and an account of how everything comes to be in the remote viewing process, it fills the same role.

The Matrix isn't really anywhere, nor is it any "when." Our dictionaries told us that a matrix was something from within which something else originates, or develops, or is formed. A womb is an example of a matrix, as is a casting mold, or the ore-bearing rock which contains flecks of gold scattered through it. A matrix can also be a bunch of crisscrossing compartments containing bits of things, and those bits can be pulled out of the matrix in various combinations to form larger objects. Parts bins in a factory, for example, would be a kind of matrix.

The computer revolution provides a further example of what a matrix is. It can be an array of interlinked coordinates, for example, the intersecting lines of a numerical table or a database, each containing an element of information which, when combined with other elements at other coordinates, can reveal patterns or groupings of information that tell complete stories. These "compartments" and "coordinates" are only made up of electrons. They do not exist in three-dimensional space the same way we do. This is very much what Ingo's Matrix is like.

One can think of this Matrix as harboring an infinity of "information points." Each of these points represents one specific object, entity, being, event, structure, etc., and contains every piece of information, past, present, or future, about the entity or object it represents. These data points exist at a set "location" within the Matrix. (I put location in quotes because, as you will see, it may not involve location in any usual sense of the word.) So, for example, let's consider the Eiffel Tower: the Eiffel Tower is a large, black, latticework metal structure in Paris. The Tower, in its parklike setting, serves as a monument, a restaurant, and a tourist attraction. Let's suppose that one of the data points in the Matrix represents the Eiffel Tower. Stored as pure information at that data point is everything having to do with the Eiffel Tower, starting from when it was first conceived, to its building diagrams, to its construction, to its current appearance, uses, and purpose, and (perhaps) its future demise.

Though the information points within the Matrix represent actual physical locations, objects, people, etc., we weren't to think of the Matrix itself and the information it contains as located in space or time. One might describe it figuratively as existing in some sort of "hyperspace" or other dimension. But wherever it "is," it hovers there, a vast repository of all the things that can be known, and which anyone with the right approach can tap.

As Ingo explained these concepts to us, Ed Dames suddenly piped up. "Why, this sounds like the Akashic Records!" Neither I, nor Bill, nor Charlene had heard the term before. We soon learned. The so-called Akashic Records turned up in the Theosophical tradition that started with Madame Helena Blavatsky in the late 1800s; the Records were also important in the beliefs of the European philosopher and esotericist Rudolf Steiner, who in the early twentieth century carried the idea into Anthroposophy, his modified version of Theosophy. The "Akashic" name comes from a Sanskrit word which refers to the all-encompassing life force that Hindus and Buddhists believe permeates all of existence. The word represents an ancient Eastern religious belief that served as the starting point for both Blavatsky's and, later, Steiner's ideas. There are variations in what different esoteric traditions believe about the Akashic Records. Most would agree, though, in thinking of them as "master records" enduring on some ethereal plane, documenting events and actions that occur in the universe.

When Ed mentioned them, Ingo was not dismissive, but he was also quick to steer us away from that interpretation. For him, the Akashic notion did not fully capture the nature of the Matrix. Like the Book of Life in the Biblical tradition, in which every act of every person is recorded to be read on Judgment Day, ideas about the Akashic Records focused more on recording human behavior and elements that pertained to reincarnation and karma.

The Matrix, on the other hand, is an archive in the fullest sense: indifferent, dispassionate, with no capacity for judging; just data, pure and simple. Yes, it catalogues human acts and events. But all other facts about the universe are to be found there, as well: information about animate and inanimate objects; about places, landscapes, substances, emotions, physical and non-physical qualities, artifacts, relations, things that are tangible and intangible, machines, history, personalities, everything. Harking back to Bohm's implicate order, the Matrix may just *be* the whole universe, perceived at a different level through senses unknown in outward, daily life. But one need not think of it this way for it to work.

It is important that the Matrix have the qualities it does. Getting information *from the Matrix* rather than from the target itself allows a remote viewer to access anything about a target site, whether it involves past, present, or (to some degree) future; inside, outside, intangible or tangible, all regardless of what the target's condition or circumstance may be at the instant of the actual remote viewing.

This implies that the source of data must be unlimited by either time or space. And since remote viewing experiments proved that the information was retrievable, that meant there had to be a way of locating only the information desired without getting a landslide of all the information available in the universe. Searchable computer databases were just becoming widely known when Hal and Ingo were brainstorming this concept. In such a database, information bits are organized by an electronic address that allows the computer to retrieve just that bit of information requested and no other. This analogy seemed to make a lot of sense. So ideas from Bohm, computers, and ancient Eastern philosophy each contributed to this new idea of a "matrix" within which all knowledge could be found. The only catch, of course, was that one had to actually be able to retrieve the information from this "matrix" for it to be useful. For this Ingo proposed something he called a "signal line."

The Signal Line

In our electron-besieged world, we are used to the idea of radio, radar, and television waves constantly flitting around us. It is only natural, then, that Ingo would seize on a radio-propagation metaphor to describe the way the Matrix and the human mind interact. Ingo told us that there was a remote viewing *signal line* that could be imprinted with selected data from the Matrix, and which could carry this data to our individual minds. As an analogy, this is much like the idea of superimposing a complex waveform onto the carrier wave of a radio broadcast. The carrier wave provides the energy necessary to transport the signal over many miles. But the information that is placed on it is in the form of many tiny variations or fluctuations in the strength or shape of the wave itself. These fluctuations are a sort of code.

Just having a coded signal is no use, of course, unless there is some way of later decoding it. In the case of our radio-wave example, one needs a radio receiver to catch the carrier wave and the coded information the wave carries. The receiver has components—antenna, transistors, capacitors, electronic filters, amplifiers, etc.—that strip the coded information off the carrier wave, then decode it so people listening to the radio can understand it. Key to the remote viewing "decoding" process is human consciousness. If the signal line is the equivalent of a radio carrier wave, then the remote viewer's consciousness is the equivalent of a radio receiver's electronic guts.

Consciousness

The next set of words we looked up in our dictionaries included "conscious," "subconscious," "limen," "unconscious," "autonomic nervous system," and so forth. Ingo's theory built upon the conventional idea of a layered human consciousness (I use "consciousness" here to mean all elements of a person's mind, whether within our immediate awareness or outside it). Our normal waking state, in which we are aware of the world around us and interact with it, we call the *conscious* state. But there is much that goes on in the human mind that is outside this conscious part, in places like the *subconscious* and *unconscious* parts of our mind.

For a long time I was confused about the difference between subconscious and unconscious. According to some dictionaries, they mean virtually the same thing, and are often even listed as synonyms. For Ingo, though, the unconscious was farther away from the waking mind, and therefore mainly inaccessible to conscious awareness. The subconscious was closer, more accessible. The remote viewing signal line terminated in the subconscious, unloading its cargo of information from the Matrix.

The dividing line between conscious awareness and conscious *unaware-ness* (i.e., the subconscious) is called the *limen,* or *liminal threshold.* Some consider the limen to be merely an interface—the "place" where conscious and subconscious "meet," like the way air and water meet at the surface of a lake. Others think of the limen as more of a barrier, resisting (but not stopping) thoughts moving from subconscious into conscious awareness. This last was the view we were urged to adopt.

Just below the level of the limen lies the upper area of the subconscious. Since it is so close to the liminal threshold, this region is often referred to as *subliminal,* rather than subconscious. Like refugees gathering in the thickets before dashing across a guarded border to freedom, impressions, perceptions, ideas, and intuitions try to make their way into conscious awareness from this subliminal frontier zone.

These "levels of consciousness," from unconscious, to subconscious, to subliminal, to limen, to conscious awareness are not specific stages, but a continuum. Except perhaps for the limen itself, there is no exact line dividing them, only matters of degree. When the signal line deposits its burden of data in the subconscious, the information mostly just stays there unless something intervenes. Since we have so little direct conscious intercourse with anything below our liminal thresholds, it is quite possible that we humans may be "on-line" with the Matrix more often than we suppose, perhaps all the time. But because the results of this contact normally stay in the subconscious, we are seldom, if ever, consciously aware of it. The goal of remote viewing is to get the subconscious to loosen its grip on some of this hoard of data so we can do something useful with it. But it must first get across the limen. Here is where the notion of "aperture" comes in.

Aperture

An aperture is a hole, space, or gap through which things may pass. In a camera, it is the opening in the lens which, when the shutter is clicked, allows light into the camera to make an image on the film. The smaller the aperture, the less light comes in and the more subdued the colors, since less "color information" strikes the film. A wider aperture gives richer colors to the picture, since it allows more light, hence more information, onto the film.

In Ingo's remote viewing theory, the aperture is the passage through which signal line information reaches the viewer's conscious awareness. Early in a remote viewing session the aperture is narrow. Information that passes through is necessarily compact and condensed. It spikes through rapidly into conscious awareness, but lasts only momentarily. As the session progresses, though, the aperture widens out, dilates. Information is unpacked, details emerge, and the "dwell time"—the amount of time the signal line stays accessible to conscious awareness—increases.

The aperture cannot really be a "hole" as the definition suggests. It makes no sense to suggest that one has a hole in one's mind. Instead, the aperture must be a certain area of permeability through the interface between the subconscious and conscious minds. One way to think of how the aperture "opens up" in remote viewing is that it gradually increases the ease with which information of different types can pass through.

The Autonomic Nervous System

There remains one further aspect of Ingo's remote viewing theory to talk about: the autonomic nervous system, or ANS. Studies beginning in the 1940s and 1950s showed something fascinating about human perception. In these experiments, words were flashed on a tachistoscope, a sort of high-speed slide projector that can display an image or a word on a screen for fractions of a second. Something shown this rapidly will not even register in the awareness of a human subject. This research demonstrated, though, that in some way the human subconscious could detect it.

When emotionally neutral words were flashed on a tachistoscope screen, they caused no apparent effect in human subjects. But if emotion-laden words flashed across the same screen, there was a noticeable reaction in the person's physiology. This impact occurred even if the word was totally unperceivable to the subject's conscious awareness. For instance, if a word with sexual or violent meaning was flashed, a galvanic skin response meter hooked to the subject showed a definite reaction, evidence that an unconscious emotional response had occurred, even though the person had not consciously "seen" the word. A polygraph, or "lie detector," works similarly, recording unconscious physical reactions; in this case, though, in response to conscious thoughts rather than subconscious ones.

What might be going on here? Without "knowing" a word had even been flashed in the first place, how could a human understand enough of the meaning of that word to have an emotional reaction to it? The evidence suggested that there was a form of cognition at the subconscious, subliminal level. Something below the threshold of awareness recognized the word and evoked an emotional response, which in turn activated the autonomic nervous system. The ANS is a network of nerves that interlink and connect all the glands, smooth muscle tissue, and automatic functions of the body. As such, it has an important role in controlling and regulating the behavior of the various involuntary mechanisms in the human body.

When a stimulus caused by an emotionally charged word activated the autonomic nervous system, the ANS then stimulated sweat glands in the skin—a typical response to emotional arousal—which altered the electrical conductivity of the skin, changing the galvanic skin response readings. It is a perfectly normal chain of cause and effect when the emotional stimulus is consciously known. But it's a bit mysterious when it isn't.

Mysterious or not, the behavior these experiments revealed suggested effects that Hal, Ingo, and their fellow remote-viewing researchers observed in the SRI laboratory. Impressions of distant targets just seemed to pop into the minds of people trying to do remote-viewings. At the same time, there seemed to be some involuntary behaviors that accompanied these impressions. One of these is what Ingo and Hal came to call *ideograms*. In a later chapter I will have more to say about ideograms, but for now it is enough to note that they are apparently inadvertent marks viewers make on their paper when first contacting the signal line at the start of a remote-viewing session.

The tachistoscope experiments showed that an external stimulus could cause a subconscious response that affected the autonomic nervous system, which in turn caused an outwardly measurable response. Ingo decided that something similar must be going on within a remote viewer. The external stimulus was not in this case an emotion-laden word displayed on a screen, but the information-bearing signal line coming from the Matrix and winding up in the viewer's subconscious, where it, in similar fashion, went on to stimulate the viewer's ANS. Ingo taught us that at the same time the signal line courses through the subconscious, it also impinges on the autonomic nervous system, which transfers the resultant impact throughout the viewer's nervous system. If the viewer had pen on paper at the time, the result was a reflexive mark—the ideogram—that represented the major aspect of the target. This major aspect was officially known as the target's "gestalt," and was the condensed, compact bundle of information that popped through the narrow aperture at the beginning of a remote viewing session. Deciphering the impressions that came along with the ideogram was what Stage 1 was all about.[7]

I have not tried to give a comprehensive explanation of CRV theory, nor in coming chapters will I try to capture the full scope of the CRV process itself. To do either one would require a full book in itself. But because of recent widespread confusion and misunderstanding about Ingo's ideas, and to help readers understand the story I have to tell, it is important to discuss both in some depth. The remote viewing theory and methodology that Ingo Swann and Hal Puthoff came up with didn't just spring into existence. They and their colleagues noticed various behaviors that regularly manifested themselves, realized that these behaviors had something important to tell them about human functioning in remote viewing, and went looking for explanations. As I will explain later, this is how ideograms were discovered and became part of RV theory.

The fact that a remote viewer could access present or past equally well, and could describe details not normally perceivable by people actually at the target (i.e., the inside of walls, the tops of tall furniture) suggested to the two researchers that there must be some sort of timeless repository of facts that could be persuaded to give up its contents when properly stimulated. This resulted in the idea of the Matrix. On the other hand, understanding of the subconscious-to-aperture-to-conscious-awareness sequence resulted from observations that the first mental contact with a target came in short bursts of compressed information, while later details became more specific and numerous, suggesting a slowing down and spreading out of the signal line flow.

People can and have come up with arguments against various aspects of the Swann/Puthoff remote viewing creation story. Perhaps, for instance, there is no vast, interactive "Matrix," but instead just the following two facts: 1) that all things are present (that is, time is an illusion and does not really exist) and 2) that at the subconscious level we are in intimate contact with everything else in our universe. Why would we need to consider anything else than this to account for remote viewing data, they ask?

Or, in another example, there have been questions raised about the role of the autonomic nervous system in CRV theory. Since the ANS apparently only interacts with glands, the smooth muscles of organs such as the heart, and other involuntary systems, without direct connection to the voluntary muscles in hand and arm, it would not be likely that the ANS *alone* could account for the formation of ideograms. The central nervous system, too, would have to be involved. This, of course, would not require a major change in CRV theory as we were taught it by Ingo Swann.

Or the signal line itself: parapsychologists have presented some strong arguments as to why a linearly propagating signal such as a radio wave or other broadcasting medium could not account for the mental transfer of information. In other words, the "transmission" model for mentally perceived data doesn't work. But to be fair to Ingo Swann, he had no intention of insisting that there was transmission involved, even though the image of an encoded signal line seemingly conjures up thoughts of radio signals projecting through space. It was just a way of thinking about what was going on that allowed people to make sense of it. In fact, that was the reason for the term "signal *line.*" It was an ordered way of receiving information that was nevertheless *different* from the normal sense of signal. And if the Matrix was indeed just an aspect of the implicate order, or if remote viewing involved some kind of nonlocality, the notion of transmission would not just be wrong—it would be meaningless.

Another whole book could be written just considering these arguments and possible responses to them. But for now, only one thought is necessary. Admittedly, Swann and Puthoff's model is hypothetical, and therefore tentative. Other than the research material used to build the theory's premises, the only evidence for the model is the fact that its concepts help achieve successful remote viewing results.

But responses or alternatives to Ingo's model are just as unproved and tentative. They have the added problem in that they tend to be ad hoc or piecemeal and not part of a consistent, systematic model. A theory cannot be fairly considered only on its parts. It must also be looked at as a whole and how that whole fits in its larger context. As far as remote viewing is concerned, there is certainly nothing better so far to replace what Ingo and Hal have proposed.

The model is not meant as a literal picture of how things "really are." Unlike other examples of creation myths—those described in the biblical Genesis, or Darwin's *Origin of Species*, or Freud's works on psychology—the remote viewing account Ingo provided is not meant to be taken as a pristine, literal statement. It is a metaphor, a model only, describing in general terms how things *must* relate for the system to work. If a Matrix the way Ingo described it to us doesn't exist, something that functions in roughly the same way has to. Even if there is no actual signal line, something that accomplishes the same purpose does exist. If it is not transmissive, the data, by whatever means provided, still must be obtained and "decoded," translated into humanly understandable terms. If one is persuaded by the evidence for remote viewing, it goes without saying that the information is there, and there must be some way of acquiring it. Ingo Swann's model gives a context for thinking about how that happens.

Unfortunately, some remote viewing instructors whose ideas and theories are derived mostly from Swann's methodology ignore the Matrix model. It doesn't fit with their own opinions; or its obvious metaphoric nature makes them think, mistakenly, that it need not be taken seriously. Others teach some derivative of CRV but leave out its creation myth, erroneously believing that it is wrong to impose a different theory on their students than what the students already believe. This assumes two things, of course: 1) that every student even *has* his own notion about how it all originates; or 2) that if he *does* have a notion about it, that his notion is even *true*. As an added benefit, of course, not bothering with the creation myth allows remote viewing courses to be shorter.

But ignoring the model comes at a cost. Even if the truth turns out to be different than how Ingo envisioned it, studying his model serves a vital function. Earlier in the book I described how Jack Houck teaches people to bend spoons with their minds. Knowing that many people are reluctant to damage perfectly useful tableware, and that this reluctance can hamper their success, Jack uses a clever psychological ploy. He dumps the implements out on the floor, prods them with his shoe, and thus assures his listeners that these articles are worthless. No one will mind if the utensils are bent and contorted into shapes that make them unusable for their original purpose. Houck is telling his audience that it's okay to function outside the boundaries of what they thought was possible. He gives them permission to succeed.

Similarly, the idea of the Matrix, the signal line, and so forth is consistent with the rest of the remote viewing method. It provides a model that makes sense. It tells those embarking on this project that what society deems to be impossible really can happen. It tells them that there is a logic behind what they are about to do: that there is a mechanism that can make remote viewing work for them. It, too, gives them permission to succeed.

12

Structure

*. . . you have to
build it if you
want them to
come . . .*

Ingo Swann exhausted us that first Monday in his classroom. And just when
we thought it was over, he insisted we each write a brief report summarizing what we had learned and how we felt about our progress that day. This
was to be the required ritual every day we trained with him. Thus, we
showed up for day two on Tuesday, knowing better what to expect in style,
but ignorant of the subject that awaited us. That turned out to be "learning
theory." Ingo thought it was important that we didn't merely *learn* remote
viewing, but that we also understood *how* we learned it. And he was right;
just knowing why we were put through the hoops seemed to make the process more effective and more tolerable.

The first guiding principle that we learned from Ingo's remote-viewing
training method was to "quit on a high." This principle sprang out of developments in sports training that had implications going far beyond the playing field. Up to that time, the traditional approach to learning a skill largely
involved rote learning. Trainers, music teachers, language instructors, and
others wanting their students to learn complex skills or behaviors ordered

long, tedious practice sessions as the best way of mastering and then excelling in a skill. Generations of students slavishly followed this counsel, and those who shirked or rebelled were warned that they were likely to fail if they ignored the exhortation to "practice, practice, practice."

Suppose a violinist is trying to learn part of a violin sonata. Under the rote approach, she begins playing through the piece, slowly at first, until she becomes somewhat familiar with it. Then the real repetitions begin. If she makes a mistake, she continues to repeat the passage until she gets it right.

Ingo's new approach would go something like this. Our violinist familiarizes herself with the music. She then works through the process, making mistakes as she goes. She attempts to correct her mistakes, and as soon as she performs the piece correctly, she stops. The idea is that by thus "quitting on a high," one's cognitive and nervous systems have the chance to incorporate or, in the word that Ingo preferred, *assimilate* the skill once it was properly executed. Research suggested that the procedure was more successful than older approaches.

Ingo explained it in this way. The brain is made up of millions of cells called *neurons*, which are linked to each other through tiny circuits, called *synapses*, that act somewhat like miniature on/off switches. When stimulated, neurons "fire" an electrical charge. Whether the relevant synapses are "on" or "off" determines which path, if any, these electrical nerve impulses travel. The details of this process are very complex, and much of how it relates to mental processes is still not understood. Enough is known, though, for Ingo's explanation to make sense.

Brain science shows that as we learn new skills, the connections between neurons grow and change so as to link together areas of the brain where the capacity to perform different parts of that skill are "stored." For simplicity's sake, let's say that there is a chain of linked neurons (and perhaps even clusters of them) that establishes the mental path necessary to play the violin sonata. The correct neurons in the violinist's brain must be linked in the right way for her to be able to perform the piece perfectly.

But this particular neuronal chain doesn't exist when the violinist first starts trying to learn the piece. Only parts of it are there, the parts she has already learned—recognition of notes and the finger and hand positions that play them, bowing the violin, and so forth. But all of these must be connected in a specific order for this piece to be learned and played. And there will be other, novel neuron groupings that will have to be constructed for particular actions unique to the playing of this particular sonata.

As the violinist works through the piece the first few times, the brain starts to make the necessary connections. But these connections can only be "programmed" by the actions of the violinist herself. Each motion, each playing of a connected set of notes, encourages neural pathways to develop in the violinist's brain. When she plays properly, the correct pathways are generated. But what happens when a mistake is made? If doing something correctly builds neural connections, wouldn't doing something incorrectly do the same thing for the wrong connections? It makes sense that practicing an error might introduce an unwanted detour on the neural chain.

Of course, our neural linkages are more robust than my discussion thus far makes it sound. There is undoubtedly a threshold of resistance that has to be crossed before pathways will alter or switch. Otherwise, we would not be able to learn or retain anything properly. But it is also easy to see how repeating a mistake may make it difficult to ingrain the right connections. Further, recent research suggests that the more a particular neural path is used, the more reinforced it becomes. In other words, like muscles, mental skills can be strengthened by repetition.

At first blush, this sounds like it supports the old approach to learning that recommends endless repetitions. There is more to it. Continual repetition may cement mistakes as readily as it reinforces accurate skills. But there is another issue. In muscle-building it is well known that one can overexercise muscles. Instead of building them up, overuse or misuse can lead to muscle damage. It is important to exercise properly, varying the routine, limiting repetitions, and taking extended breaks to allow muscle fibers broken down in the course of training to rebuild themselves. Indeed, properly used muscle fibers are rebuilt more strongly to meet the demands regular exercise makes on them.

The same idea applies by analogy to building mental "muscles." Pathways that are used more frequently become stronger. But there is a need for "assimilation"—time for the pathways to reinforce themselves after new work. Ingo believed that this rebuilding occurs in "down" time when one is not using those particular pathways. What that means is that whichever pathway was most recently used is reinforced, whether for good or ill. For Ingo, "quitting on a high" meant that when a student had an unusually good remote viewing success, or learned something new or significant by the experience, it was time to knock off for awhile.

Flushed with the victory of doing something correctly after a struggle to get there, the temptation is always strong to "try it just one more time for good measure." Ingo insisted that giving in to that urge was a bad idea, because with that one more time we might make a mistake. Then, which of the tender new neural pathways would be reinforced? We would learn through later experience that it was possible to *overtrain* in remote viewing and have the mind balk, just like an overworked muscle. Overtraining was demoralizing and mentally painful, making it virtually impossible to produce results. Each succeeding session would be worse than the last. It happened to me once during that time with Ingo, and greatly shook my confidence. The only cure was to stop trying altogether for a few days or even weeks, and gradually recover.

There is evidence for this effect in parapsychology research. Historically, psi laboratory experiments involved long repetitions of card-guessing or dice-tossing experiments. It was not unusual for an experimental subject to have great success early in the experiment. But then, after hundreds or even thousands of trials, the subject grew more and more discouraged as his scores fell off to barely chance. Though boredom might be a major culprit in this "decline effect," overtraining also may have been a contributing factor.

Associated with "quitting on a high" was an additional phenomenon that turned up in remote viewing research from the very beginning. This was something known as the "first time effect." Both Hal Puthoff and Ingo Swann emphasize that most people will likely have a success the first time or two they try remote viewing. However, once these beginning sessions are done, performance falls off and stays low for awhile until, gradually, with experience and training, the viewer's successes increase, approaching the level of the first few "brilliant" sessions.

Puthoff has a chart that graphs this remote viewing learning curve using data from many trials with many viewers. It starts high up the axis on the left, curves slightly, then falls abruptly, bottoms out, then slowly climbs again towards the right before it levels off. Hal and his colleagues at Stanford Research Institute cannily took advantage of the first time effect to challenge doubters who came to the lab asking for proof. Banking on the first time effect, Hal would challenge the questioner to try a session first. Though there wasn't always a successful first session, more than one skeptic was converted after coming up with remote viewing results that were hard to explain any other way than by admitting that it actually worked. Not until that point would Hal bring out his files showing repeated successes by other viewers that went beyond beginner's luck.

Ingo accounted for the first time effect in the same way he explained learning theory. He was convinced that the ability to perceive things remotely was as innate as any other human ability, such as walking, speech, or vision. At a person's birth there are rudimentary neural linkages in place for all these other abilities. Each neural pathway becomes strengthened with exercise. Assuming that there is a neural chain for remote viewing, then it must be dormant, as our society normally discourages people from exercising the faculty under the belief that no such thing exists.

When someone tries remote viewing for the first time, this long-dormant chain of neurons is suddenly stimulated. Since it has presumably not before been fully activated, the mind has developed few filters or impediments for it. Consequently, the first time or two remote viewing is tried are often successful. But soon the viewer's analytic processes "catch on" that something new is happening, and try to take charge. This creates "noise" in the system, which I will discuss shortly. As the noise level rapidly grows, remote viewing functioning falls off, and it is only later, once the viewer has learned more effectively how to deal with it, that performance quality starts to move back up again.

There was some support for Ingo's ideas in *Mind to Mind*, French researcher Rene Warcollier's classic treatment of long-distance mental communication. Warcollier wrote: "It may be that in the awakening of human consciousness, modes of perception existed which are called into play again in paranormal processes."[1] Warcollier thought these perceptual modes might be dormant remnants from earlier stages of human development as a species.

I don't know how much of what Ingo taught us about learning theory came directly from the science papers and books he and Hal had digested, and how much grew out of Ingo's own remote viewing experiences. But in recent years there have been additional reports that vindicate the approach. One has to do with language instruction. Recent research has shown that several ten- to fifteen-minute intervals studying a language, with breaks in between to pursue other activities, lead to faster learning and better retention than the more traditional long periods of practice.

Learning theory experts may complain that Ingo's approach is too simplistic, and that there are other complex facts about learning that should also be considered. I have no doubt that, given the nearly two decades of research that have passed since Swann developed his theory, many new things have been discovered with which his approach could be tweaked, enhanced, streamlined, or augmented. But, simplistic or not, Ingo's approach worked, and worked well.

The RV Theory lecture wrapped up with the inevitable essay. After our theory essays were blessed by Ingo, he gave us a break and a few encouraging words. When we gathered back into the lecture room, he started to tell us about structure.

Structure

Important as theory had been, structure was yet more crucial. The lecture we were about to receive would teach us the basic principles that governed the actual *process* of coordinate remote viewing. One might possibly learn how to remote view successfully without knowing the theory. But without mastering the structure of the process, it would be very difficult. A key element in remote-viewing structure uses the recording of everything that was said or perceived in a session on paper, beginning to end. Though there might be different ways one could capture structure on paper, it had to correspond in some concrete way with the structure or organization of the signal line itself.

What does it mean to say the signal line itself has structure? As I came to understand it, "structure" does not mean the signal line has a set physical pattern to it, like a suspension bridge or a tree. Near as can be told, the signal line is insubstantial, belonging for all we know to an order of existence undefinable within our external (*explicate*) frames of reference. Rather, in this case "structure" refers to the orderly way in which the signal line seems to unfold itself within the viewer's awareness—the fact that remote-viewing impressions don't arrive all at once, complex and fully formed, but only simply at first, growing increasingly complex in ever widening stages of detail.

The signal line develops as a continuum. It is like the visible-light spectrum, where violet merges into blue, blue into purple, purple to red, and so on, yet there are no distinct lines between where one color ends and the next begins. Nevertheless, there are distinct areas where red is indisputably red, and blue unarguably blue. The experience of the signal line is like this, with transition zones from one level of experiential sophistication to the next. Since we humans tend to classify things in well-defined "packages," Ingo found the best way to capture the structure of the signal line was to talk of discreet "stages" divided by specific mental events that marked the transition from a lower stage to the next higher.

Stage 1 involves the "major gestalt" of the target or site. In the previous chapter I talked about the compact, condensed signal line information that first pops through the aperture at the beginning of a CRV session. We refer to this "package" of information as the "gestalt" of a target. Imagine all the information that might pertain to a particular building, person, or geographic setting. Then imagine all that information wadded up like the innards of a baseball into one conglomeration. If all of this were to become perceivable to a viewer at once, as one compressed package, there would not be much she could say about it, except give a very general name to it, identifying its overall nature. If the target were the Eiffel Tower, the information package might contain everything there was to know about the Eiffel Tower. But all the viewer could identify in the brief glimpse offered in Stage 1 might be that the target was a "structure" or "building." But for Stage 1, this is quite enough. The task for the remainder of the session, however long it goes on, is to "unpack" as much of the rest of the data ball as possible.

In Stage 2, the signal line conveys sensory experience from the five primary physical senses: what would the viewer experience were he or she bodily present at the target site? The impressions retrieved involve raw data: colors, shades of light, smells, textures, tastes, and sounds.

The viewer proceeds through Stage 2, describing in one- or two-word sound bites what sensory qualities describe the target: "black, shiny, metallic, smooth, cold, bumpy . . ." But, gradually, the quality of information starts to change. Words relating to the dimensional qualities of the site emerge. "Tall, wide, curving, airy, crisscrossing . . ." These dimensional words—referring to the three spatial dimensions we are used to—signal the approach of Stage 3.

The dimensional aspects of a site are the core of Stage 3. By this time the aperture has opened enough to give the viewer early impressions of larger facets of the target site. Many perceptions and impressions are difficult or impossible to express verbally, and must be captured by sketching. Like a woman feeling the urge to push during the final stages of labor, the viewer often experiences an instinctive urge to sketch. After one page or several of quickly made drawings or sketches depicting target elements, the viewer moves on to Stage 4.

In Stages 4 and beyond, the signal line makes more complex data available to the viewer. Sketching is still important, but both concrete and abstract conceptual impressions such as "car," "people," "machinery," or "tourist," "foreign," "monumental," "historic," etc. become available. I shall save Stage 5 for later, as it is different in nature from the other stages. In Stage 6, the aperture opens wide to allow the viewer a full dimensional grasp of the target. Often this is captured by making a three-dimensional model of the target, using clay or other suitable material.

Ingo believes that there are further structural elements to the signal line leading to a Stage 7, or 8, and beyond.

But there is an ambiguity here. I have described the process as if it is the signal line that brings ever more detailed and complicated information to the viewer, and this is how Ingo often presented it. But that may only be a convenient fiction. Maybe there is another way to look at it. Instead of the signal line gradually increasing the complexity of information it carries to the viewer, perhaps the signal always holds the same level of data, and it is instead the viewer's mind that gradually opens to more specific detail that has been available all along. Ingo's theory accommodates either interpretation. But just as it is easier for us to talk about the Sun "coming up" in the morning and "going down" at night, when it is really the Earth that is doing all the moving, it is also more convenient to talk as if it is the signal line that is doing the work.

The formatted, written-down-on-the-paper "structure" of the remote viewing process itself is imposed upon the "structure" of the signal line, much in the way that dams, levees, diversion channels, and such are placed along an unruly river to bring it under control and make it useful. There is a slightly different nuance here, however. What is being controlled with RV structure is not the signal line itself, so much as the viewer's inner mental processes and consciousness as they interact with the signal line.

As with my discussion of theory, it is not practical to go into all the details of remote viewing structure in this book. But if you really want to understand what goes on in the Swann/Puthoff method of remote viewing, there are certain concepts and principles you shouldn't ignore. One of them is "objectification."

Objectification

Objectification, as Ingo explained during the lecture, is the process of saying out loud and writing down what is in one's mind. A thought or a wish, as long as it is kept inside one's head, has no permanence. Recent memory research, in fact, shows that the thoughts or ideas one fails to express or record are very easily and quickly forgotten. Thoughts and impressions must be "objectified"—turned into an object, rendered in some concrete form—to be taken as "real." And the most effective way of doing that in remote viewing is first by verbalizing it, then getting it all down on paper.

Objectification serves a number of purposes. First, it helps with record-keeping. By writing everything down the viewer keeps track of his perceptions, and preserves them for others to examine. Second, objectification makes easier the notoriously difficult communication between conscious and subconscious. Since all sensory input arrives in the subconscious first, before a small fraction of it is passed into conscious awareness, we talk to our subconscious every time we speak or hear, read or observe, touch or write. By saying out loud and writing down everything in a remote viewing session, we "send" this data back to our subconscious. Some parts of the remote viewing structure serve to instruct our subconscious, and by "objectifying" those things, we enlist the aid of multiple senses, in different modes, to carry the same message along several channels into our subconscious.

Objectification also serves as a psychological ploy to get the subconscious to cooperate. It "rewards" the subconscious, acknowledging that its contributions are being used and therefore "appreciated." It seems a little strange to talk this way about the subconscious, as if it were a second person within ourselves. But in many ways that is just the way it acts. In the same way that few people will long continue contributing to a marriage unless those contributions are acknowledged and appreciated, the subconscious may "shut down" if its part in the process is not acknowledged.

This acknowledgment to the subconscious serves a further function, as a sort of "feedback loop" that strengthens the connection with the signal line. As the impressions are verbally and graphically objectified, they are fed back into the subconscious as "real" data (Ingo says that objectification "gives reality" to the signal line). This sets up a "loop," much like placing a microphone in front of an amplifier. As impressions are received, objectified, then fed back to the subconscious, it is supposed to strengthen and deepen contact with the signal line, allowing ever stronger and more specific access to the data the signal line contains.

Finally, objectification also serves to "expel" mental noise. Here is where AOL, or "analytical overlay," raises its ugly head.

Mental Noise

You know all that stuff that is always swirling around in your head when you're trying not to think—all the memories, conjectures, stray thoughts, startled wonderings, confused speculations that are forever bubbling away behind the scenes in even the most disciplined minds? That is "mental noise," and it gets very much in the way whenever one tries to remote view. Many things cause mental noise. One source is called *environmental overlay*. According to Hal Puthoff, the SRI research team discovered that viewers sometimes included elements from their immediate surroundings in remote viewing sessions. Perhaps there was a picture of a sailboat on the wall or orange carpet on the floor, and the viewer would somewhere in the session report a sailboat or the color orange. These elements might, of course, happen to be at the target. But just as likely, the viewer's subconscious picked up the perceptions and passed them on uncritically to conscious awareness, thus contributing to the "noise" level.

This problem is easily dealt with. Experienced viewers often reach a point where their subconscious "learns" not to add information from the immediate surroundings. But controlling the richness of the environment helps, especially for new or less experienced viewers. Thus Ingo Swann's famous Grey Room was born.

My colleagues and I were destined to spend major parts of the next decade in a grey room at sundry locations around the country. A grey room was, literally, grey. Walls, ceiling, carpet, table, office chairs were a uniform shade of battleship grey. Track lighting in the ceiling was wired through a dimmer switch near at hand so the viewer could adjust the illumination to suit. The room was made as soundproof as possible. All in all, it was a monotonously uniform environment, but surprisingly tolerable for a confined space with no windows, a tightly fitting door, and little sensory contrast to relieve creeping claustrophobia.

Fortunately, most of the time that we were in the room as viewers we were mentally somewhere else. During a remote viewing session it was as if the walls fell away. One almost, but not quite, forgot there was a room. Remote viewing is literal realization of the old poem that ". . . stone walls do not a prison make, nor iron bars a cage. . . ."

Many times over the years I've been reminded of the grey room environment when I see or hear mention of the "blue screen" process in the movie special effects industry. Actors play out their roles in front of a featureless blue screen. Later, computer and photographic tricks make it appear as if the actors are dangling in outer space, hanging on the edge of an abyss, or standing in some exotic location, when they were really on a soundstage in Hollywood. As a remote viewer progresses through a successful session it is—metaphorically, at least—as if the grey walls are a blue screen hosting the interplay of perceptions as they flow through the viewer's thoughts.

Inclemencies are another source of mental noise. These are personal factors eating at the viewer. Perhaps the bills are due, or the viewer has a cold or a headache, or maybe a loved one is ill. Bill Ray had to cope with chronic back pain caused by a spinal fracture that occurred years earlier during a parachute jump with the 101st Airborne Division. Although these inclemencies may be serious, they are surprisingly easy to temporarily put aside just by declaring them in writing before the session. Acknowledging inclemencies is not the same as ignoring them, or procrastinating action on them. Bill didn't eliminate his back pain, but it did not distract him from his remote viewing mission either. During much of my training I was coping with marital problems, leading up to divorce. I found I could jot those worries on a sheet of paper and set them aside during a session, knowing where I could retrieve them when I was finished. To this day I can often set aside thorny problems for the short term when I need to concentrate on something else needing more immediate attention.

Analytical Overlay

Far more difficult to learn to handle than either environmental overlay or inclemencies is the great bugaboo of remote viewing: Analytical Overlay, or AOL for short. Remote viewing researchers had long noted distorted and altogether wrong data resulting from remote viewing experiments. Such dross had complicated their work of evaluating sessions and getting good data for years. Ingo found valuable ideas about mental noise being jumbled with mentally received signals in Warcollier's writings.

Sometime during his research, Hal Puthoff had also discovered Norman F. Dixon's book, *Preconscious Processing*, on subliminal mental processing, and brought it to Ingo's attention. Ingo had read Dixon's earlier book, *Subliminal Perception*, years before, but in this new one he found the same story Warcollier had told. This time, though, it was told strictly in terms of psychology, couched in scientific language, and illustrated by study after study that seemed to prove beyond much doubt that there was a whole world of perception and analysis going on underneath human conscious awareness that seldom made it out into the open.

When a person is presented with a stimulus so weak or so fleeting that it makes no impression on conscious awareness, the subconscious may nevertheless notice some details of the stimulus, and later pass them back to awareness, often in a confused way. For example, in one experiment described in Dixon's book, a picture of the Three Kings, which were three peculiar rock formations with thin necks and bulging tops standing near each other, was flashed on a screen for less than an instant, so quickly that the person watching the screen could never consciously know the photo had ever been there. Instead of three rock formations, the person later draw a picture of three people standing in relation to each other as the rocks did.[2]

The way mental noise arose in what, back then, were called subliminal perception experiments (the terminology has since changed) appeared very similar to the noise that arose in remote viewing situations. So interesting and striking were the similarities that Dixon even presented a paper on the matter at a Parapsychology Foundation conference on parapsychology and the brain, in 1978.[3]

The evidence from Warcollier, Dixon, and others whose work Ingo and Hal consulted led them to suspect that impressions from some other sensory "channel" were being dumped into the subconscious. Some of these impressions had enough energy to spike up into awareness, to be discovered and described. But combined with the data came extraneous things as well, that served to obscure or confuse the legitimate data with "noise." The "noise" observed in both subliminal perception and split-brain experiments resembled the sorts of things the SRI researchers noticed coming out of many of the remote viewing sessions in the lab. For instance, a target Hella Hammid viewed, a fenced-in pedestrian walkway over a busy street, produced a response of "a trough in the air." In another instance, a viewer made accurate sketches of a playground merry-go-round as a target, but his mental analysis caused him to verbally declare it as some sort of cupola on a building.

"It seems that raw perception . . . triggers an immediate attempt to categorize or interpret," Hal told me. "We saw that sequence over and over, where you got some flash of raw data that turned out to be correct or appropriate, immediately developing or blooming into some interpretation which was often incorrect."[4]

The outcome of all these realizations was the notion of "analytic overlay," or AOL. In remote viewing doctrine, AOL is anything extra added to signal line data as it emerges into conscious awareness. This "something added" can be interpretative, metaphorical, allegorical, comparative, analytical, or simply memories, but it is usually wrong.

Going back to our Eiffel Tower example, let's say that early in the session the viewer gets brief impressions of black, crisscrossing metallic elements. These impressions spark a memory of the steel-girder bridge the viewer had crossed the summer before while on vacation. He concludes his session with the report that the target is a large, steel bridge. The similarities between the Eiffel Tower target and the bridge are obvious, but the conclusion jumped to by the viewer is incorrect. Other AOLs have even less truth-content than the one just described. Sometimes some trivial element at the target will suggest an extended flight of fancy that bears virtually no resemblance to the actual target. In cases where the viewer "misses" and never actually makes signal line contact with the target, the resultant AOLs are devoid of any real content whatsoever.

It is because of AOL that success with typical clairvoyance and other forms of ESP is generally spotty. The practitioners have often not learned to filter out the noise. AOL is also the major problem that confronts so-called "natural" psychics, who tend to have a track record of muddled attempts punctuated by occasional brilliant successes. And it is AOL which has in the past made ESP often useless for practical applications. Both Hal and Ingo maintain that arriving at an understanding of AOL was one of the most important advances to emerge from the remote viewing research at SRI.

If we were to become any good as remote viewers, it was important for us to learn to deal with AOL. There is a lot to consider, but I will only cover it briefly here. If at all possible, preventing AOL is certainly best. The strategy is to "describe," something without "naming" it. For example, novice viewers are often tempted, when they perceive something red and round with their minds to say, "I see an apple!" They are "naming" what they *think* their perception is. But it is just as likely to be a red Christmas ornament, or a red rubber ball, or something else. It is much better to instead note the things known for sure about the perception. "There is something red, rounded, and smooth." Avoiding "naming" keeps the analytic left brain (where decisions are made about what things are) out of the act as much as possible so it cannot as easily contribute wrong answers.

Analytical overlay can also be avoided by repressing the temptation to make responses "fit." Rob Cowart, the young captain who, together with Tom McNear, became a remote viewing pioneer when taking CRV training with Ingo back in 1983, summed up what he had learned about remote viewing structure in one simple motto: "Structure! Content be damned."

Because of cancer Rob was medically retired from the Army before he could finish Ingo's training, but he went into remission and spent more than a decade with NASA before his cancer returned and took his life. But his memory will live on in that statement. It means that a viewer should always focus on doing remote viewing according to the rules and protocols, and never fret about or wonder what the target "is." Concentrating on structure means that AOL is properly handled; that data is captured and objectified; and that everything is done in proper order and put in its proper place. Doing these things faithfully helps deter the viewer from trying to "figure out" what the target is, and trying to erroneously force all the pieces to fit.

If a viewer starts to puzzle about what the target might be, the analytical part of his mind is perfectly happy to oblige by suggesting likely possibilities, which are almost always wrong. Data bits that don't seem to fit are shoved around until they do fit. Subtly, unconsciously, the viewer starts to edit incoming data, dismissing whatever doesn't fit the growing picture and even fabricating details that do fit. The result can turn out to be a hopeless mass of AOL and confusion. We were told: "Remember, 'Structure! Content be damned.'"

One final note about AOL before I move on: AOL is a fully inclusive category. There are some in the RV community who complicate things by breaking down the notion of AOL into ever smaller subcategories. "Analytical overlay" was meant to capture all the different ways one might elaborate on signal line data, whether that be through analogy, metaphor, allegory, reduction, or extrapolation. To label each of these categories of AOL as a separate kind of overlay is to encourage exactly the kind of analytic mental processes that viewers should be trying to avoid. Though on the surface Ingo Swann's remote viewing process often seems complicated, Ingo never intended it to be any more complex than it had to be. All he wanted to do was capture and manipulate the perceptual process at exactly the level of complexity necessary, and *no more*.

Stage 1

13

... into the breach at last!

Sometime in the early 1970s, Ingo Swann picked up a copy of Charles Hampden-Turner's book *Radical Man: The Process of Psycho-social Development* and came across a passage that piqued his interest. It was about the role "feedback"—or getting confirming information—plays in the development of human culture. It was not a topic that would make many hearts beat faster, but Ingo found it riveting, and it jibed with what he had been learning from psychology professor Charles Tart.[1] In the last half of the 1960s Tart had been working on trying to solve the "decline effect" in parapsychology experiments, where the scores in card-guessing and dice-rolling experiments of even stellar performers eventually fell off to no better than chance after many trials. Tart suspected that it had something to do with the lack of feedback given to the subjects. Not knowing how they were doing on an ESP test led to boredom, and made it difficult or impossible for the subjects to improve.[2]

Feedback is familiar to most people as the piercing squeal one hears when a microphone is placed in front of its amplifier. Any sound the microphone picks up is routed through the amplifier, boosted in volume, again picked up by the microphone, passed back through the amplifier, boosted again, and locked in that loop until it becomes unbearably intense. But feedback in a complex system involves information, and is far more useful than acoustic feedback. For example, information feedback is what keeps the Starship *Enterprise* going where no one has gone before. Any *Star Trek* watcher knows that the *Enterprise* has sensors everywhere, both inside and out, that tell the crew instantly what is going on in any compartment on any deck, and what is happening outside the ship for many parsecs in every direction. This allows the crew to recognize problems and react to them.

Feedback does the same thing for any other complex system, whether that system is a human being or human society. Two important things that feedback does can be applied directly to viewing: feedback helps a person "learn"; and it helps keep a system going in the right direction, whether that system is a person hiking through the wilderness, an ocean liner steaming towards Europe, or a starship trying to find its way back to the Alpha Quadrant.

How does it help the learning process? In school, a student's papers are corrected by the teacher. Things that are wrong are marked wrong , things that are right are left alone, or even praised if done particularly well. Those corrections are "feedback." If students were not told until the end of the school year what mistakes they made, or where they had gotten the wrong idea, the learning process would suffer. And if they were not told when they are doing things correctly, they wouldn't be able to give the right answers consistently.

The helmsman who fails to look at the compass after he starts his watch is as likely to end up in Africa as Europe. Being off by so much as a degree or two of heading at the start of a long ocean voyage can mean being hundreds or thousands of miles off course by the time the journey is done, so that the helmsman must continually monitor the compass. Changes in the compass reading are "feedback."

According to Hampden-Turner's book, feedback reinforces memory, while the absence of feedback decreases the quality or even suppresses the storing of memories. So important did Ingo Swann think it was that in his on-line book *Remote Viewing: The Real Story* he declared feedback to be *the* central issue [for] the development of remote viewing" in the discipline's formative years. In my conversations with him now, more than twenty years later, he continues to emphasize its importance.[3]

There are two kinds of remote-viewing feedback. The first and least controversial of these is end-of-session feedback. A remote viewer performs a session with no outside knowledge about the target. Any information about the target that surfaces during the session has to come through the viewer's mind, or not at all. When the viewer is finished with the session, he or she is handed a feedback package that includes photographs and perhaps written descriptions of the target. This feedback serves a couple of important purposes. It helps the viewer see what was right and what wrong in the data provided during the session, thus aiding the learning process. End-of-session feedback also gives closure for the session; once the target is known through the normal senses, there is no need to "be psychic" anymore, and the remote viewing process can return to dormancy until it is needed again.

A second type of remote viewing feedback is more controversial. This is *in-session* feedback, and is usually only used for training novice viewers. It consists of a limited set of comments the monitor provides in answer to the impressions the remote viewer expresses during the course of a session. The feedback the viewer is given depends on what the monitor knows about the target. If the target is the Eiffel Tower, the viewer might say "tall," to which the monitor would respond "correct." The viewer might say "cold," and the monitor might reply "can't feed back," since he doesn't know if it is cold at the Eiffel Tower at that moment. If the viewer says, "bird sounds," the monitor would likely say "probably correct." A viewer's response of "water," would get a feedback comment of "near" in return. While there is no water at the Eiffel Tower, there is water nearby. If the viewer were to say "dry and sandy," the monitor would say nothing. Ingo told us that negative feedback would detract from the remote viewing process, so he did not use words such as "wrong" or "incorrect" as feedback. He just remained silent. From my own experience with Ingo, that silence can ring louder than any words.

In-session feedback is important for several reasons. First, it keeps the viewer "on course." Few things are more discouraging to someone just starting out than to spend an excruciating hour working through a session, only to find that their perceptions went astray only a few minutes from the start, leaving fifty-five minutes of nothing but imagination. In-session feedback isn't a cure-all for this, but it certainly increases the chances that an early course correction will help keep the viewer walking the signal line tightwire.

A second, more important purpose is to help the viewer recognize immediately what it "feels like" when doing remote viewing correctly and receiving real data, as compared to when he or she does something wrong and gives an incorrect response. End-of-session feedback provides a similar learning experience, but the fledgling remote viewer is dealing with some very subtle internal impressions, which are often quite difficult to recognize even when they are still fresh in the mind. If he or she must wait to the end of the session for feedback, many of those nuances will be lost.

The five responses—"correct," "probably correct," "can't feed back," "near," and silence—are used like training wheels for a wobbly new viewer. As viewers progress and gain confidence in their abilities, in-session feedback is halted, allowing them to continue unassisted. Like a steadying parental hand for a child just learning to walk, in-session feedback helps give the viewer much-needed reassurance. In-session feedback won't eliminate failure during a remote-viewing session. But having constant "compass checks" available helps steady the viewer while he or she learns a process noted for uncertainty and imprecision.

Not surprisingly, there are objections to using in-session feedback. The most serious is that in-session feedback only serves to "lead" the viewer to the right answer by giving hints that don't come through remote viewing perception. Most of us played the "warmer/colder" game when we were children. An object is hidden somewhere in a room, and a player is guided to it through coaching comments like "you are getting *warmer*," or "you are get-ting *colder*." It is surprising how well this can work for someone savvy enough to use it effectively. Critics complain that allowing in-session feed-back is the same as giving "hotter/colder" hints, and that a clever viewer will get significant information about the target without having to "be psychic" at all. According to this view, in-session feedback hampers rather than helps the learning process. The complaint is well taken.

In defense of in-session feedback, viewers no doubt gain some informa-tion from it, but the information is trivial, confirming answers the viewer *has already provided*: "I've said that something at this target is black. The monitor has confirmed that by saying 'correct.' Therefore now I don't just *think* there is something black at the target. I'm reassured that there really is."

Of course, enough confirmed observations might allow the viewer to analytically put together some idea of what the target might be: "I know the target is black, metallic, cool, bumpy, crisscrossing, and high. Hmmm. It must be a bridge!" Despite the in-session feedback he has named the wrong target. This leads to another reason why complaints lodged against in-session feedback are overblown. In a good remote viewing session there is no way the depth and detail provided by a viewer could be accounted for by appealing to the "hot/cold" effect of feedback. For example, Ingo tells the story about author Jim Schnabel, whom he trained in 1994. Ingo gave Schna-bel the coordinates, and Schnabel immediately responded with "land and rising water." Ingo came back with "correct."

"White," said Jim.

"Correct."

"It's a hot springs!" said Jim. The target was Mammoth Hot Springs in Yellowstone; the session had lasted only thirty seconds, and Ingo had barely provided two feedback responses. I myself have done, and had students who have also done, sessions so rich in detail that it is impossible to believe that the limited in-session feedback can account for it.[4]

But even more telling than this are the sketches and three-dimensional models produced in most successful remote viewing sessions. The five mea-ger in-session feedback phrases could not begin to convey enough informa-tional content to lead a viewer to draw an elaborate and accurate sketch of the target from an angle that is not depicted in any of the feedback photos, nor build a recognizable model of the site. I quizzed Schnabel about this subject, since, as a skeptical journalist, he was sensitive to the possibility that Ingo's feedback had "led" him to the target. I had seen Schnabel's model of the Tower of the Americas (in San Antonio), as well as a number of his sketches from other sessions. "Did Ingo give you any more than his five standard feedback responses?" I asked him. He admitted Ingo had not. "How then could you possibly have gotten the detailed information necessary to make those sketches or build that model without actually remote viewing it?" Though I think he still doubts, Schnabel had to admit that Ingo's carefully limited in-session feedback could not possibly have led to what he produced.

One good example from my own experience involves a target I did at Fort Meade in the fall of 1984 with Fred Atwater as my monitor. Fred gave me the coordinates, and I at once began to get perceptions of a large, round or domed structure. In fact, the first perception-words out of my mouth before getting any feedback at all were "faceted," "domed," "shiny," "arches," "geometrical," and "broad hemispherical."

I continued along with about ten or twelve more responses, almost all of which were declared "correct," or "probably correct." In the process, I had AOLs of a large radar dome, the Taj Mahal, a geodesic dome, and the Blue Mosque in Istanbul, none of which, as per protocol, received feedback of any kind from Fred. Then I started sketching, eventually drawing a remarkable likeness of the target, which turned out to be the Hagia Sophia mosque in Istanbul. In fact, at the time I mistakenly thought that the Blue Mosque and the Hagia Sophia were the same building (they are similar in shape and construction, and located less than a mile apart), so after the session was over I accused Fred of failing to tell me that I had actually named the site.

The point here is that there was no way the "hotter/colder" effect could possibly have lead me to the accurate results I achieved after four sparse pages and a mere ten minutes or so of work. Similarly, Fred was especially careful to make sure there was no way I could have seen or learned anything about the target through ordinary means, either before or during the session. My success had to have come because of remote viewing, since there simply was no other possible explanation. This was only one of many such experiences during my training.

This issue about in-session feedback is connected to a further important matter. Unlike training sessions, most operational remote viewing sessions and virtually all laboratory remote viewing experiments require that monitors are themselves kept "blind" as to the nature of the target. When a remote viewer and his monitor are alone in a grey room, neither has a clue as to the nature of the target. This is important for various reasons which will be treated in later chapters.

In training sessions, however, the monitor usually knows what the target is. Critics often worry that having a monitor (or anyone else for that matter) in the room with the remote viewer before or during a session contaminates the process. Couldn't the viewer pick up nonverbal cues from the monitor? Couldn't the monitor, by suddenly shifting in his seat, or raising his eyebrows, or catching his breath, or emitting an inadvertent murmur give hints to the viewer?

A classic example of this sort of behavior was Clever Hans, a horse in Germany in the early 1900s who had learned to "count." Clever Hans's owner, Wilhelm von Osten, would tell the obliging horse to count to seven. Hans would dutifully thump the ground seven times with his hoof. He could in fact do this for any number, and for subtraction and addition as well. "What is four plus five?" the owner would ask, and the horse would paw the ground nine times. He was even known to give the correct answer for square roots. Everyone found this quite amazing. Skeptics could discover no tricks or cheating going on. It did indeed seem as if Clever Hans was doing arithmetic.

Hans could do math problems even when von Osten was not around and someone else asked the questions. Various tests proved that no one was purposely giving cues to Hans. It was also discovered, though, that for Hans to work his intellectual feats someone nearby had to know the right answer, and that person had to be in the horse's line of sight. Finally, an investigator came up with an explanation. Anxiously awaiting Hans's success, von Osten (or whoever was standing in for him at the time), watched Clever Han's front hooves with an air of restrained tension while the horse pawed the ground. When the correct number was reached, the owner relaxed and looked away from the hooves. It was Hans's cue to stop.[5]

From my own experience, remote viewers can and sometimes do inadvertently learn things from their monitors that contribute to session results. This effect varies from monitor to monitor. Inexperienced or careless monitors often unintentionally give away far too much through their verbal and nonverbal communications with the viewer.

In the years after we had completed our training, our erstwhile colleague Ed Dames became particularly notorious among the Fort Meade viewers for doing this on purpose. Along with our struggle to acquire the signal line, we often found ourselves struggling against Ed and his eagerness to let too much of the cat out of the bag. This was a problem even when Ed didn't know what the target was. His eager nature often led him to draw some conclusion early in the session, then try to influence the viewer's responses as the session progressed. We soon wised up to his bad habits, but it could be frustrating to have to struggle to acquire the signal line while simultaneously fending off Ed's attempts to be helpful. Some of the viewers worked with him only reluctantly, and a couple refused him as a monitor.

A monitor who recognized the pitfalls of unintentional nonverbal communication could avoid this trap, and even turn it to advantage. Ingo was a master at being blandly noncommittal in a session. Fred was also especially good at making the viewer go to the signal line, rather than to the monitor for information. He maintained the same close-mouthed, unruffled demeanor whether we were describing exquisitely accurate detail or we were way off the mark. Fred learned this over several years and thousands of sessions. He had discovered through painful trial and error that it never served either the viewer or the session well to unintentionally telegraph information to the viewer.

However, both Ingo and Fred knew (as I was to learn) that in training sessions both verbal (that is, in-session feedback) and nonverbal cues could be handy when the monitor used them in exactly the right way to promote the learning experience. Sometimes an inflection, a show of interest, or a careful choice of words can guide the novice viewer in the right direction when he becomes confused or uncertain.

I give my students an analogy for this. In 1997, when Comet Hale-Bopp was hanging in the Maryland night sky, I took my three-year-old son William out to show him the comet. Hale-Bopp was just a smudge of light, lost among the stars. Pointing and cajoling as much as I could, I failed to help poor Will find Hale-Bopp. Finally, in frustration, I put my hands on either side of his head and aimed his face exactly at the comet, and he saw it. He didn't need my further "leading" to find it, once he knew which smudge of light he was supposed to recognize.

Today, whenever I conduct remote-viewing training, I freely tell my students that I will sometimes "lead" them, if it seems necessary. I tell them that there will be times when they are on the right track and don't realize it, or when they are on the verge of straying from the signal line and a slight nudge will keep them going in the right direction. The novice learns from such hints to distinguish what correct data feels like. The right *kind* of nudge from the monitor can lead to a sudden comprehension or quicker recognition of some remote viewing principle than could a long siege of trial and error. Of course, I must reiterate: this happens only in *training*. In most operational situations both monitor and viewer should be thoroughly blind as to the identity and nature of the target.

Much of my experience and understanding of all these things came to me years later. In the meantime, I and my fellow trainees were sitting in the remote viewing suite at SRI, wrapping up Ingo's lectures on structure with anguished essay writing. Finally we were ready for the lectures on Stage 1, the last round of classroom work before we would try coordinate remote viewing session on our own.

Stage 1

Early in a remote viewing session, when the aperture is narrow, a conscious mind only briefly notices the sudden impressions that pop up into it. The viewer quickly forms an impression of the *gestalt* of the target, and little else. Gestalt is a German word for which English has no exact match. A gestalt is the total form and nature of an object or location, taken all together. It is "more than the sum of its parts," as the familiar saying has it.

Mountains, for example, are usually made of dirt, rocks, ice, snow, splashing brooks, trees, etc. If you were to have a huge pile of dirt, another pile of rocks, a heap of snow, a flock of bighorn sheep, and a pool of water in close proximity to one another, you would have all the components of a mountain, but you would not have a mountain. You would need to put the parts together in proper relation to each other—rocks and dirt mixed, snow and ice on top, trees on the sides, and animals among the trees—before you could fairly call it a mountain. That "togetherness" of all the parts, and all their relationships, is a gestalt, which we then identify by naming it with the word "mountain."

Just as there is a *mountain* gestalt, there is also a *person* gestalt; a *city* gestalt; even a *taxi cab* gestalt. There are large gestalts (mountain, ocean); there are small gestalts (praying mantis, Ping Pong ball). There are complex gestalts (steam locomotive); and simple ones (sand dunes). All but the most basic of these are usually too complicated or too specific for a remote viewer to recognize right off the bat, at the beginning of a session. The most fundamental gestalts, and the ones that are most readily identified, are these: land, water, structure, person (or living creature), and event. There are certainly others, but likely more than ninety percent of remote viewing targets wind up in one of these categories. Identifying a target's gestalt is the first task a remote viewer encounters in the Puthoff-Swann remote viewing method, and it is all there is to Stage 1. But there are a few steps that come before actually naming the gestalt. After being given the coordinate, the viewer creates an *ideogram*.

Ideograms

Over the years, Puthoff and Targ had a neat way of dealing with reporters, scientists, and government officials showing up at SRI demanding proof that remote viewing really worked. Instead of trotting out some stellar remote viewing performer, visitors were challenged to try it themselves. Many of them accepted the challenge, and a majority of them were successful. All these sessions done spontaneously by untrained people amounted to more than 140 remote viewing trials that were useful as scientific data.

In looking over the pile of transcripts from these sessions, Ingo noticed something peculiar. Both experienced and inexperienced viewers were encouraged to remote view with pen and paper in hand, to record their impressions in word and sketch during the session. But nearly every time someone launched into remote viewing, he seemed to have the urge to make a little scribble on the paper when first contacting the signal line. Ingo found something familiar about the behavior, and the scribbled results it left.

One day it suddenly dawned on him. The scribbles reminded him of a chapter in Rudolph Arnheim's classic book, *Art and Visual Perception*, which Ingo had first read when studying art at Westminster College. Arnheim had looked at the way in which young children first approached art, and what role their newly developing perceptual abilities played. When first learning to capture on paper the things around them, children made scribbles that were rather similar to those of remote viewers. It was as if the children were intuitively trying to grasp the essence of the subject they wanted to draw. Essence is closely akin to—perhaps identical with—the notion of *gestalt*. Ingo wondered if maybe these little scribbles he found in the remote viewing transcripts were an initial grasping at the major gestalt of the target.[6]

After experimenting with the concept, Hal and Ingo decided that, indeed, the scribble was a primitive representation of the target's gestalt. Seeking for a word to call it, they happened upon "ideogram," which means, basically, a graphic mark or sign of some sort that stands for an object or idea. These ideograms had an involuntary, reflexive quality about them. A viewer, when given pen and paper, almost spontaneously jotted down an ideogram as soon she heard the coordinate, unless she consciously tried *not* to create one.[7]

These reflexive marks often did not provide a recognizable shape or outline. But they still had some conceptual and experiential relation to the intended target. No two ideograms were exactly alike. They varied in form and pattern almost as infinitely as the myriad possible targets a remote viewer could be assigned to describe. Later, when Ingo began to teach the skill, if he noticed that a student was in a rut and making similar scribbles each session, Ingo made him do ideogram "drills," a conscious exercise designed to loosen up the production of the markings.

Ideograms have some interesting qualities about them. They have a motion and a feeling. Motion is not the motion of the pen itself, but rather a subtle sense of contour and direction that comes to the viewer through the signal line. The motion itself is not immediate, in the sense of being physically present. But it is nevertheless perceivable by the viewer, once he learns to be responsive to it.

By "feeling" is meant the consistency of the gestalt, not the texture. A structure or landform is usually "hard" or "solid." Water is "soft," liquid," or "fluid." Sand dunes might produce a feeling of "semisoft," while a swamp might be "semihard," or even "squishy." The "motion" and "feeling" compose what Ingo calls the "A" component of Stage 1.

The final step of Stage 1 is the "B" component. This is the place where the viewer is actually allowed to "name" the gestalt. The "B" component is the "first spontaneous analytic response to the ideogram and "A" component," but the reference to "analytic" is only meant in a limited way.

Let's say the viewer is given a coordinate, gets an ideogram, then describes the motion part of the "A" component as "wavy across" and "liquid." It is unavoidable that some analysis will lead to a declaration of "water." As Ingo's students, we were taught that this small amount of analysis was permissible in Stage 1 because it happened virtually instantaneously and then was over, before the full analytical faculties of the conscious mind could go to work on it. However, hesitating or trying to think too much at that stage almost inevitably would lead to AOL.

In recent years some remote viewing practitioners have tried to control ideograms by telling fledgling viewers that they should establish ideogram "lexicons," that is, to use only a few ideograms that are fixed symbols of specific gestalts. Under this system, a viewer might train her subconscious to produce a certain right-angled mark whenever the target is a building or other manmade structure. Water would have its own consistent mark, as would land.

This idea of a lexicon is contrary to what Ingo taught us about ideograms. Creating a fixed ideogram is like putting it in a straitjacket. It destroys the creative content. True ideograms, when left to form as they will, represent an entire bundle of impressions containing their great diversity in appearance. Restricting the forms ideograms can take and assigning set meanings to them turns them into a self-limiting alphabet with impoverished content.

The lure of this approach is understandable. Someone impatient to cut to the chase could get immediate analytical answers and avoid the chore of struggling through Stage 1 with all its uncertainties and potential for failure. The problem is that, by trying to take this shortcut, viewers put off becoming immersed in the remote viewing session. An ideogram lexicon is just as left brain in origin as is any other linguistic form. Since the core of remote viewing input emerges once the right brain becomes fully engaged, one delays the actual remote viewing process one stage longer, rather than engaging the process immediately. Like any other skill involving the need to recognize, distinguish, and identify subtle input, the only way to make remote viewing more reliable is to consistently apply the correct skills.

In execution Stage 1 is quite simple, once one masters all the subtleties of recognizing and recording the signal line. The monitor reads the coordinate to the viewer. The viewer objectifies the coordinate by repeating it aloud and writing it down on the left side of the paper. He instantly moves the pen a fraction of an inch to the right and scribbles the ideogram. Moving the pen farther to the right, he writes and says "A," then describes the motion in words—in this example, "angle up, peak, down." The feeling comes next: "hard." He quickly writes and says "B," followed by "building," or "structure." If all this is correct, the monitor responds with, "Site," acknowledging that the viewer has correctly identified the major gestalt of the target, and then shows the viewer the feedback, which in this case would be a photo of the Eiffel Tower. Often the viewer will have experienced other impressions that he has not yet learned how to express, and these will be confirmed when he sees the feedback. He will later learn how to deal with these impressions, too.

Of course, it was seldom this smooth in practice. We had AOLs to contend with, and other interruptions to the process. But Ingo had taught us how to cope with these various contingencies and, once we began practicing real remote viewing, we increasingly finished our sessions more rapidly, smoothly, and accurately. There will be some examples of these in coming pages.

As I have said, this book is not meant to be a "how to" for remote viewing, nor a full explanation of every aspect of the skill. But I have devoted several pages to explaining the theoretical background for the Puthoff-Swann remote viewing methodology for three reasons. First, I wanted to capture the true flavor of what I and my colleagues went through as we learned how to be remote viewers. Second, I thought it important to present a clear idea of what was involved in the Puthoff-Swann approach to remote viewing, and the depth of the theory and methodology underlying it.

Most of all, I wanted to show that there is more to remote viewing than just sitting down and jotting whatever comes to mind. Too many people—even some who claim to be actively involved in remote viewing—think that all they need is a simple recipe to follow and they can master it. This is the "cookie cutter" approach. Some folks come up with a list of rules specifying how they think remote viewing should be done, then try to fit everyone into them, cutting off whatever hangs over the edges. While some rules are absolutely essential, too much insistence on the rules at the expense of the principles invites trouble. In my opinion, it is necessary not just to know *what* to do, but *why* as well. Far too many folks in the RV community don't really know why they do what they do. They just copy someone else or, even worse, borrow haphazardly from this approach or that in much the same way Dr. Frankenstein assembled his monster.

Others dismiss what Hal and Ingo put together, or pay lip service to it but then go about rearranging things to suit themselves, assuming that the two remote viewing pioneers followed the same Frankenstinian process. They presume the Puthoff-Swann method was based on the usual preconceptions about "being psychic" or "mystical forces" that many other metaphysical or psychic systems depend upon.

But in order to use Hal and Ingo's approach effectively, it is essential to know why and how the system was put together. Without knowing the fundamentals, it is impossible to know properly when or how the formula can or must be bent to achieve ends and which rules should never be bent or passed over. Arbitrarily changing the rules and ignoring the underlying principles of the remote viewing structure the two so carefully put together results, not in a successful method, but in just another empty ritual.

The moment of truth had arrived for our first Stage 1 sessions. I don't think any of the four of us looked with total eagerness on the prospect of our first remote-viewing exercise. Even the hours of lecture and essay writing couldn't quell the feelings we had experienced back at Fort Meade before doing our very first outbounder remote-viewing sessions—feelings of excited anticipation, fear of failure, and dread of the unknown.

Charlene Cavenaugh (now Shufelt) recently reminded me she was scared to death while she waited for Ingo's voice to echo "Next!" out of the bowels of the remote viewing grey room. We all vividly recall the nervousness we felt, sitting there on the couch as, one by one, those going before us entered the room, closed the door, and then emerged sometime later with inscrutable expressions on their faces. Our questions of "How did it go?" or "How was it?" were answered by unsatisfactory replies of "Fine," or "Okay, I guess." We were forbidden to discuss with each other anything that went on in our individual sessions.

On that initial day Bill was the first in the room, I think. I'm sure I was last. I read a little in a book, and then lightly dozed for a few minutes, trying to relax—"cooling down," as we came to call it—while I marked time until my turn. Then I was through the door, closing it, seating myself in the chair, dimming the lights until they were just right. A stack of paper and a black Razor Point pen lay haphazardly arranged on the grey surface before me. Ingo, regarding me with an amused gleam in his eye, stroked his neatly trimmed beard, and pressed his lips together in a tight, noncommital smile.

"Well!" he finally said, exhaling. "Are we ready?" I figured that he was. I wasn't sure about myself.

I no longer remember what my first Stage 1 target was, and none of my fellows that I talked to remember theirs. But I think it was probably a mountain. It was not easy, sitting down with the expectation that I would discover and report information in real time about a distant place with which I had no obvious connection, and with no real clue how to go about establishing one. I wanted to believe that it would just happen, that my mind would suddenly light up with knowledge of flawless pedigree, easily separated from my own trivial mental wanderings, and I would be an instant success. Of course, I knew it wouldn't be that way. I fully expected total failure, and to have Ingo send me packing back to Fort Meade before the day was out.

Instead, something in between happened. I didn't blow the session entirely, nor was it a spectacular success, otherwise I would have remembered it. I do still remember the feelings of struggling with myself, and Ingo's cajoling and gruffness. I remember leaving the room afterwards still unsure if I could really do remote viewing, but excited to try it again.

Most of those first Stage 1 sessions have faded from my memory. Not until perhaps three months into the training did I start keeping a comprehensive journal to remind me of sessions I did. But I do remember one target from that first group. Ingo read me the coordinates, I executed the ideogram, and had a sudden impression of large, heaving, dark green-grey swells, foaming white at their tops, towering over me. The light at the target was dim, as if I experienced it at twilight or under a heavy overcast. A ponderous, elemental feel welled up in me. It wasn't a clear or sharp impression; in fact, it was more a "knowing" than a "seeing."

Still, I remember feeling it was there, just as sure as if I had seen it, had dragged my toes in the water, had felt the waves rolling under me. I only remember the experience, not my response. I may have said "ocean." That's at least what I wanted to say, what I should have said. But I was still an unconfident beginner; I may have just as likely declared it an AOL and continued to struggle on past it in the session. I do remember, though, that the target turned out to be a spot in the middle of the Atlantic Ocean. All that was there was water. Big, moving water.

I had much to think about on the flight home from California. What I learned from Ingo went far beyond just the first baby steps towards becoming a psychic spy. I had a whole new perspective on what made me tick. It was only one small scratch on a very large surface, but it was much more than I had even an inkling of before.

The Rusty Nail

$$14$$

... the beginning of the
end of the beginning
begins ...

Like someone who steps on a rusty nail, but doesn't yet know he has been fatally injected with lockjaw, Center Lane was dealt a deathblow during the last week of January 1984, our second week in California. And as with any budding infection, it took a little while for death to occur, a bit less than a year in this case.

The rusty nail was supplied by General Bert Stubblebine's pet project, Rapid Acquisition Personal Training, or RAPT, held at the Monroe Institute in the Blue Ridge Mountains of Virginia. A few days into the third and, as it turned out, final RAPT session at the Institute, a young officer left his CHEC unit in the middle of a Hemi-Sync tape session. To protect his privacy, I'll call him Doug Pemberton, the pseudonym Jim Schnabel used for him in *Remote Viewers*. Agitated and threatening, Pemberton approached Institute director Nancy Honeycutt, Bob Monroe's stepdaughter, who was running the office that day. Pemberton accused Nancy of not being "who she said she was," and said he knew "who she really was."[1]

Sweating profusely, Pemberton removed his shirt and began toying with a ballpoint pen, suggesting that his martial arts training made it possible for him to kill her with it. Then he accused her of working for an enemy intelligence service. Cooly, Nancy called Bill Schul, another staff member and practicing psychologist, who approached the officer and tried to calm him down. Stubblebine's office was quickly notified, and Pemberton, still behaving bizarrely and making incoherent and disconnected statements, was dispatched back to Arlington Hall Station.[2]

He was still irrational and incoherent the next day, so he was bundled off to a psychiatric ward at Walter Reed Army Hospital for several days of evaluation and treatment. Astonished to hear him babble on about Army mind readers and psychic spies, the psychiatrist assigned to his case at Walter Reed was convinced that Pemberton was delusional. INSCOM's staff psychologist, called in for consultation, was forced to tell the psychiatrist that, while the officer was indeed suffering some kind of psychotic break, the part about psychic spies was not a delusion.[3] There was no hope of completely hushing up the incident; there were too many witnesses. Remarkably, the newspapers didn't find out about it, and it was handled within INSCOM and Army channels.

Certain conclusions were bound to be drawn: Stubblebine's bizarre dabbling in occult mentalistic arts had finally sent some unwitting young soldier over the edge—or so thought many of the general's critics. It was a great stroke of luck for those who wanted the remote viewing program gone, and whispers about the incident floated around the highest levels of the Army. Center Lane's supporters either looked to damage control or ducked for cover. It didn't matter that Center Lane and remote viewing had nothing other than an administrative connection with the RAPT program. Nor did it matter that neither the Monroe Institute nor the RAPT program was really at fault. The chickens were out of the coop.

An INSCOM investigation cleared the Monroe Institute of any responsibility for the incident. It turned out that Pemberton had a history of psychological problems that no one knew about. The Institute normally conducts its own psychological screening of applicants for seminars and workshops, but the Army had assured the Institute that the necessary screening would take place prior to each participant's arrival. It was not the Monroe Institute's fault that the system had somehow been circumvented. For all other participants, Hemi-Sync had proven safe. Further, the safeguards that INSCOM had put in place *should* have prevented Pemberton from placing himself in the situation he did. But he had managed to circumvent the system.

But how could it have happened? The Monroe Institute warned that people with a history of mental problems should not participate in its seminars. So, as part of the application process for the RAPT program, each prospective attendee was required to fill out a form disclosing whether he or she had ever in the past been treated for mental illness, or suffered from mental instability. These were self-report forms—the individual was on his or her honor to report accurately and fully, which, together with a screen of medical records, was deemed sufficient to uncover any problems.

Unfortunately, as the buses were about to pull out of Arlington Hall Station for the trip down to the Institute someone realized another soldier approved to attend the RAPT session had left at the last minute on emergency leave, resulting in an unexpected vacancy. Since the soldier's place had already been paid for, the money would have to be defaulted. Learning of the vacancy, Pemberton enthusiastically volunteered to occupy the empty seat. The young officer had an interest in esoteric martial arts and the paranormal, and what little he knew of Center Lane and the Monroe Institute fascinated him. Stubblebine said no. A colonel interceded on Pemberton's behalf, but again Stubblebine said no. Finally, with minutes to go before the buses departed, a last, impassioned plea was made. The seat was empty, the contract already paid. What would be the harm of letting him go? At the eleventh hour, the general relented.[4]

There is some confusion as to whether Pemberton had filled out his medical and mental health assessment forms. Two of the principle figures involved say he got on the bus without ever submitting the paperwork. However, the INSCOM staff psychologist thought he recalled having seen some of the material before the fact. I remember that there was some trouble locating Pemberton's records after the incident, but I also remember myself and Charlene thumbing through them after they finally turned up.

As far as I have been able to reconstruct the history, it seems that most members of the INSCOM staff were asked to fill out the forms in anticipation that they might decide to volunteer for one of the RAPT programs at the Monroe Institute. So it is possible that even though he hadn't been formally invited, Pemberton filled out the assessment paperwork on his own initiative, in the hope that he might get a chance to attend a RAPT seminar, but didn't actually submit the forms through the proper channels. In any case, the fact that Pemberton had a history of treatment for some kind of psychiatric problem didn't show up on his paperwork, whether before or after the fact, and thus escaped those who might have prevented what instead came to pass.

There was some question afterwards as to why Pemberton had the high-level security clearance he did; people with a history of mental problems aren't usually granted such access. We learned later, though, that the young officer's father had once had considerable stature and influence in the intelligence community. Whether or not strings were pulled to keep Pemberton's career on track may never be known. Whatever the history, an unstable man ended up at the Monroe Institute, lying in a CHEC unit, listening to Hemi-Sync tapes while his illusions, distorted thoughts, and compulsive tendencies reinforced themselves.

Pemberton eventually recovered from his psychotic episode and went on to have a relatively successful career. When I was in another assignment in the Washington, D.C., area many years later, I ran into him. I had not met him before, but I recognized his name, and with a few well-placed questions I confirmed his identity without letting on that I knew his history. I was glad to see his career had survived the Monroe incident—even if the same could not be said for Center Lane.

Had the Army's decision-makers known how life would eventually turn out for the young officer, it wouldn't have mattered. Blood was in the water, and remote viewing's critics smelled it. As John Alexander, Stubblebine's staff officer who oversaw the RAPT program was later to remark to me, "If we had been in an armor unit in Germany and killed several soldiers in a training accident, it wouldn't have raised as big a stink as this one temporary mental lapse by a junior officer."[5]

It wasn't that the RAPT incident was particularly serious. In fact, if it weren't for the significance of the fallout that came from it, I would have preferred to have left it out of this telling altogether. But it came at a crucial time for INSCOM, for General Stubblebine, and for Center Lane. The government remote viewing program's foes had already tried to kill it several times during the preceding few years. While there was no real conspiracy directed against Stubblebine's various projects in general, nor Center Lane in particular, there was festering animosity for the program among some of the Army's senior brass. The Pemberton incident shone an unforgiving light on the strange things that Stubblebine was trying to do to bring his part of the U.S. military into the twenty-first century. As we shall see, this enmity from ranking officials was to crop up at a number of inopportune times in the future.

Over the years, the Pemberton incident became somewhat of an intelligence-community legend. I've heard assorted versions of the tale—that Pemberton came charging naked out of his CHEC unit and physically assaulted a Monroe Institute trainer, or that he was found wandering shirtless in INSCOM's war room at Arlington Hall after having scrawled "Center Lane" in large letters around the walls. Neither of these, nor several other versions of the event, turns out to be true. Unfortunately, it was the sensationalized rumors like these that often fell on the ears of those who had power over the remote-viewing program's fate.

The Big Apple

. . . one bite at a time . . .

Ingo had staged a successful revolt against the SRI establishment. Tired of spending half his life for more than a decade on airplanes flying back and forth between the East and West Coasts, he had insisted that most of our CRV training be conducted on his home turf in Manhattan. Instead of us having to traipse out to Menlo Park for two weeks at a time once a month, we would be going to Ingo at his home in New York City instead. Arrangements were made for us to stay at the Bedford—what passed for an inexpensive hotel in midtown Manhattan—and to do our training at SRI's facilities a few blocks farther uptown on Third Avenue. Rooms in the SRI suite, which was situated partway up a high-rise office building, were reconfigured as a remote viewing grey room, classroom, and waiting area.

Except for an occasional visit to SRI in California, two Mondays in a row out of almost every month for the next year the three of us living on Fort Meade (Bill Ray, Ed Dames, and myself) caught an Amtrak Metroliner at the train station near Baltimore-Washington International Airport. Charlene joined us in Baltimore.

Climbing off the train at Penn Station amid the usual Monday-morning pandemonium, we stuffed our bags into the first taxi we could flag down, and made our way up to Fortieth Street and Lexington Avenue to check into the Bedford. As soon as we had our rooms, it was a relatively short walk—a few blocks across, then uptown to the SRI offices, where we rendezvoused with Ingo. A few minutes of friendly banter allowed us time to relax, then sessions started for the week. On Friday we would catch the train back to Maryland for the weekend, since it was cheaper than keeping the hotel room, plus allowed us more time with our families. The next Monday we would repeat our trek up to Penn Station.

It was surprising how soon we began to take what we were doing for granted. True, there was always the performance anxiety before one actually went into the grey room to do a session. But the routine that we soon fell into belied the strange thing we were trying to learn. And our extended New York experience was a huge amount of fun. So much fun, in fact, that I think from time to time each of us felt a twinge of guilt that we were having it at taxpayers' expense.

What made such feelings even worse was how little "work" we actually seemed to be doing. I remember the first time that I finally manage to neatly resolve a session without the usual early confusion and misread AOLs. "See you tomorrow," Ingo said, putting the target folder away after giving me my feedback.

"Huh?" I was surprised. I had just completed a Stage 1 session that took me perhaps two minutes. I wasn't accustomed to putting in only a two-minute workday for Uncle Sam.

"Take the rest of the day off!" Ingo replied lightly. Noting my perplexity, he sighed, then adopted his lecture tone. "As I'm sure you'll *recall*, we 'quit on a high.' Now what are the occasions when we 'quit on a high'?"

"Uh . . . when we have a new cognition or breakthrough about the process, when we're feeling especially good about a session we've done, or when we have a greater than usual success," I parroted.

"And didn't you just have the best session you've had so far?"

"Uh, yes. But . . ."

"And don't you have a big, self-satisfied grin on your face because of how easy it was? You're feeling good about this session, aren't you?"

"Well . . ."

"That's at least two of the three criteria. Get out of here, and don't come back until tomorrow." I could hear Ingo chuckling as I left, and his next victim—Charlene, I think it was—entered his lair.

There weren't too many days when I only got two or three minutes of "work" in before being sent packing. And as we all advanced through the training stages the sessions got more complex and took longer. Still, we might be in the SRI offices for only half a day, or a few hours in the morning and a few in the afternoon. I think all of us were a little nonplused. To spend so little time on the job and so much on the town just wasn't the Army way.

But there was no arguing that Ingo's approach was working. Our skills as remote viewers were definitely developing. Of course, we were not just remote viewing trainees, but guinea pigs as well. Ingo was still carefully feeling his way through poorly charted terrain. He knew that quitting on a high was an important principle, but he didn't yet know how far it should be pushed. In training other CRV students later at Fort Meade, we found that much less downtime was required for the principle to succeed, and that often simply varying the routine worked just as well. What took the first of us many months to learn could be taught to a willing novice in much less time.

The unease of having so much time off was enhanced by another policy that was followed for operational viewers while back home in the Center Lane offices. To be sure, each of us had our share of administrative duties to perform. Still, these often occupied only a part of our time. Months later, with our training completed, we eventually settled into a routine where we usually worked only one operational RV session every other day, and perhaps one training session on days we weren't operational. During the occasional national crisis our operational sessions increased, but then gradually went back to a normal pace as the crisis subsided. And then, of course, there were extended periods while we trained new viewers. But at most other times we were allowed—in fact encouraged—to get involved with some other activity that was interesting to us. Our bosses preferred that these activities be beneficial to our progress as remote viewers or that in some way they generally supported the unit's or the Army's mission. But as long as we showed up for work and were available whenever called on to remote view, there were no hard-and-fast rules. The idea was that viewers functioned better when they were relaxed and not preoccupied by supervisors' deadlines or the ongoing projects that are typical of more intense military office environments.

When not writing briefings or information papers, giving lectures to new trainees or monitoring their sessions, or dealing with the occasional issues that came my way as unit security officer, I generally chose to read books on parapsychology and related subjects. I was also encouraged to enroll part-time in the Defense Intelligence College's master's program in Strategic Intelligence, and during duty hours when I wasn't viewing, I often attended classes or wrote papers on subjects such as international terrorism, the federal intelligence budgeting process, or my chosen emphasis, problems in the Middle East.

Lyn Buchanan, who was soon to be assigned to the unit, spent many hours manipulating computer programs or creating new ones. While he was at the remote viewing unit, Lyn wrote a program just for fun that automated the Army's weight control program. Lyn's computer software was widely adopted among other Army units. He received many official kudos for it. In fact, part of the programming was a software routine that automatically generated letters of appreciation addressed through the DIA hierarchy to Lyn, commending him for his fine work. The personnel office at the Defense Intelligence Analysis Center (DIAC) was always calling Lyn to come pick up another fat stack of those commendation letters.

Mel Riley, who would soon be reassigned to us after a several-year hiatus (and later another viewer, Greg Seward) engaged in hours of beadwork and other Native American crafts, while Angela Dellafiora, who was assigned to the unit in 1986, worked through an endless succession of logic problems in softbacked books she'd buy at newsstands.

One day when I was feeling guilty again, it suddenly dawned on me that, as a remote viewer, I was not a soldier or a federal employee—I was a piece of equipment. My colleagues I and were "turned on" just like any other piece of equipment, and "turned off" when not needed. There were main battle tanks, generators, radios, water-purification systems, satellite receivers, and other major pieces of equipment that were only ever used for exercises or crisis situations—running at best for a month out of the year. A machine worth many times the total salary I would ever make over my entire career might sit idle most of the time. But at those few times when it was really needed, it was worth every penny. When it wasn't running, there was always essential maintenance to be done to keep it operating in tip-top shape.

In that sense, our "leisure" activities were the equivalent of battery upkeep and regular electronics troubleshooting for equipment that was used periodically, but put on standby when not needed. While we viewers might be underutilized in comparison to the denizens of other intelligence units, being too busily engaged in minutia might actually degrade our effectiveness. With that thought in mind, my unconventional employment weighed less heavily on my shoulders.

On our very first excursion to the Big Apple, we arrived on a Tuesday instead of on the Monday schedule that would be the norm in the future. It was the twenty-first of February, 1984—I remember it as a damp, cold, blustery day. Our first order of business was to sign in to the SRI offices and receive an orientation. After the nearly three-hour train ride, this took what remained of the morning and left us looking for a place to eat lunch. That turned out to be Clancy's Bar and Grill, one of three Clancy's in the city according to Bill Ray, this one located about Thirty-ninth and Madison, nearest the SRI offices. Always happy to celebrate his Irish heritage, Bill was delighted at the choice—Clancy's reveled in its Irishness, serving such "pub grub" staples as corned beef, cabbage, and boiled potatoes for the main course.

All of us, including Ingo and (if memory serves) our commander, Lieutenant Colonel Brian Buzby, stuffed ourselves into one of the booths that lined the wall opposite the counter. Steam fogged the plate glass windows fronting the street. On the neighboring rack, our dripping coats were crammed together as tightly as were we in our booth. On the jukebox Bill punched up "The Blood-stained Bandage," a patriotic Irish anthem from the 1916 Rebellion. Over the coming year Bill was to visit this establishment often, eventually making friends with the bartender, who was always good for an occasional Guinness "on the house."

Immediately after lunch, Ingo had us doing sessions. This was the beginning of a fairly grueling several weeks of practice to develop our Stage 1 skills. It was certainly not as easy as it might have looked to an outside observer. Each session brought with it the initial angst—what if it doesn't work? I and my colleagues would take our turns sitting at one end of the grey table, with Ingo sitting opposite. Sometimes he was cheerful, sometimes glowering. Often he was only matter-of-fact or taciturn. When a session went smoothly, I quickly identified the gestalt and was finished. However, if at any time I fell out of structure or mistook an AOL for the target, there was hell to pay. But it was a quiet kind of hell.

Any time viewers discovered that they had got themselves into a blind alley, Ingo would patiently repeat the coordinate. When he felt that he had given his victim enough chances, Ingo would declare the session a miss, heave a sigh, and pull out another folder with yet another site to be viewed. I hated Ingo's sighs. It was amazing the condemnation and air of tolerant resignation he could pack into something as simple as an exhalation of breath. I think my daily all-time record with Ingo for blown Stage 1 targets was four. The others had similar stories to tell.

It wasn't that the process was *physically* demanding—or even that it was *mentally* grueling. Rather, it was emotionally draining. When I was having trouble acquiring and decoding the signal line during a training episode, it was very much like being in elementary school and chronically not getting the idea about some difficult arithmetic principle—only in this case it was one-on-one with the instructor, and an often cranky one at that. You couldn't hide behind a schoolbook or look to a classmate for hints.

I recall once when Ingo decided that my ideograms were becoming too stiff and scripted. He had me put an empty soda bottle under my wrist to act as a roller bearing when he gave me the coordinate. It didn't work very well, but he got his point across. From that point on I always tried not to consciously constrain my motions, allowing myself to create more fluid and individualized ideograms.

Day after day, week by week, we worked a succession of mountains, cities, rivers, dunes, plains, oceans, deserts, lakes, and so on. Stage 1 was divided into two phases. Phase One included targets that contained only one major gestalt within an approximately five-square-mile area. Large landforms such as mountains fit the bill here, as did large bodies of water, or sprawling cities. Phase Two included targets with more than one major gestalt—a city by the ocean, for example, or an island or, even trickier, an atoll, where there was water surrounded by land surrounded by water. Glaciers presented some viewers with the confusing impression of "hard water," which they sometimes rejected out of hand, since to an analytical mind it made no sense.

Ingo seemed to have a remote viewing site for all occasions. There were so many of them, in so much variety, that it was pointless to guess. If you were going to get it right you had no choice but to remote view. We started doing Phase Two targets in late March.

After hours, Ingo was frequently our companion and tour guide as we explored New York. For one excursion I went with him and his friend Tom Joyce to the Brooklyn Museum for the opening of a show of American watercolorists. Having majored in art for my first few years of college, I was excited to see classic works by Winslow Homer, Sanger, and even Norman Rockwell, who was otherwise best known for his work as an illustrator.

A lover of art, Ingo took us to another exhibition opening; this time that of an Israeli friend of his, Carmela Tal Baron, whom he characterized as a "visionary," or "cosmic" artist. As this was the genre in which Ingo himself worked, he was very keen to see her work. We had a number of errands to run on our way there, however. The five of us finally sidled into the Foxworth Gallery on Sixty-fifth Street wearing blue jeans and tennis shoes, while carrying a six-pack of Diet Sprite and a bag of faucets for Ingo's downstairs sink. We presented quite a contrast to the other art connoisseurs, who were mostly dressed to the nines.

I tried my best to look urbane as I made the rounds for twenty minutes while Ingo introduced me and my friends. I was quietly congratulating myself on how suavely I must be coming across when someone eased up next to me and confided that my fly was open. Fixing the problem with as much aplomb as I could muster, I was thankful that it was time for us to leave.

During that first week in New York that February, Ingo invited us to his residence for the first time. It matched his unique personality. The building had started life in the early 1900s as a wire factory. Three stories tall and faced with brown-red brick, it sat in the heart of the Bowery neighborhood, snug against the buildings on either side. A block from Cooper Union Art School, and not much farther from NYU, Ingo's neighborhood was sandwiched somewhere between Greenwich Village and the Lower East Side.

Inside, the old factory teetered on the quaint side of run-down. Welded metal stairs led up past each of three landings, passing two lower floors that Ingo had converted to apartments that he let out over the years to the likes of Broadway set designers and upscale bohemians. Ingo's apartment was on the top floor, and could be reached via the antiquated freight elevator, if you didn't choose to go clomping up the corrugated metal stairs instead.

Books were the first thing that greeted you when you entered his domain. Here was a living space that accommodated itself to the books, rather than the other way around. But there was plenty of room for curiosities as well. Where someone else might have knickknacks arranged around the room and mass-produced mountain landscapes on the walls (what my wife likes to call "sofa-sized art"), Ingo had the mounted heads of stags staring out, and an eclectic collection of religious and nineteenth-century Romantic oil paintings. Dominating the living/sleeping area was one of his own paintings, done mostly in greys and blues, depicting huge rounded boulders hovering in the air amidst crashing waves and roaring rapids. I was immediately captivated by it.

Among Ingo's furniture were pieces that must have dated from the early 1920s or 1930s, with no signs of being refurbished during all those decades. One claw-footed upholstered wooden couch sagged dangerously in the middle. The walls were paneled in dark, mellow wood, and at sunset when I looked out the large wood-framed windows at the skyline across the street, it was very much like finding myself gazing out the transom of an old-time Spanish galleon.

The ceilings, too, still reflected their Art Deco origins. They were made of greyish tin, stamped with raised floral patterns that added a distinct tactile interest to the ambience. Interesting as the apartment was, though, the real treat was to be found in the basement.

"Come, let's go down to the studio," Ingo called as he herded us into the tight confines of the freight elevator. The lift hummed loudly as it lowered us down past each floor, stopping finally below ground level. Ingo opened the elevator door with a flourish. "I want to show you *Millennium.*"

Ingo's building had a main basement, which we were now entering, plus a subbasement in which he stored his large collection of files and reference material. The main basement was at that time set up exclusively as a studio (he has since added an office area where he does most of his writing). The flooring was dark, heavily varnished boards that were cupped by years of heavy use and moist air. The walls were dingy and patched. There was the detritus of art everywhere—canvas stretchers, half-finished paintings, assorted tools and objects for reference, more dilapidated furniture. Impregnating everything were the smells of turpentine and linseed oil—fragrant odors to those who wanted to create from imagination visions for others to experience. *Millennium* was one of those visions, and it awaited us at the far end of the studio, boldly swathed in light.

It was easy to become lost in the painting. It was huge—the largest I had at the time ever seen, and only since dwarfed in my mind by an immense Bierstadt I later saw at the National Gallery in Washington. *Millennium* was a triptych—painted on three canvas panels, each taller than me, and probably half again as long as high—about twenty-seven feet long, all told.

As I took it in, I was not conscious of the timbers that anchored it from behind, so it seemed almost to float a foot or so off the floor. The side panels canted slightly inward, seeming to embrace me. A wooden bench sat at a comfortable distance from the painting, where Ingo bade us sit. He then turned out all the lights in the room but those flooding the painting and raised the volume on his stereo to play Kitaro's weighty *Silk Road Suite.*

The painting contained nothing but ocean and sky. From where we sat, I couldn't take it all in at once. Instead, when I looked forward my peripheral vision was filled by the massive waves that curled in from both edges of the panels on either side. These waves seemed to loom above us, while the ones in the foreground merely seethed and tossed. Towering thunderheads ringed the distant skies. In the middle distance, though, clouds broke and the seas began to calm. Centered in the horizon a sun blazed a golden pathway across the serene ocean towards us between a canyon of clouds blocked finally by the tossing waves that lay immediately before our eyes. Intruding into the picture were mysterious lights—pearl-like strings of iridescence, clusters of glowing orbs, with a hint of otherworldly origin about them.

Somehow it all expressed the inchoate wonder of what we had embarked upon with our remote viewing. I've since gone to see the painting many times. I once even watched anxiously as Ingo made a few last additions to it with paint and brush while tipsy from several glasses of wine. And I helped him put its final varnish coat on. But, strangely, at the time I never thought to ask him what he was trying to capture with *Millennium.*

The name suggests something Biblical, but Ingo wasn't religious in any conventional sense of the word. He had spent time among my own Mormon people in Salt Lake City. And he was deeply interested in Catholic reports of appearances of the Blessed Virgin Mary. But even this came more from a fascination with the paranormal aspects of the events than from anything religious associated with them.

For me, the painting represented both the ponderous things of the universe, and the imponderables of existence. It brought home, if only imperfectly, the inconceivable power latent in the cosmos, yet revealed hidden knowledge suffusing what we see—things beyond the manifest world which are just as marvelous and, perhaps, just as powerful.

By the third week of March—the fourth of our week-long excursions to New York, we were doing Stage 1, Phase Two targets. Then we took a five-week stretch at Fort Meade, returning on the seventh of May. I was uneasy over the long break. Would I lose my "touch," such as it was? But this crisis in confidence turned out to be unjustified. My first target site was a tropical city on a crescent bay, and I "got it" as precisely as my Stage 1 skills allowed. But the next day's target was the real confidence-builder. As I worked it, an impression of a valley and mountains emerged in my mind. Ingo sensed that some new sort of cognition was coming through, though I myself didn't recognize anything different. He called a break, feeling I needed to do some assimilating.

After the others did their sessions and we had lunch, I resumed the session at 12:30. Again, the mountain and valley emerged, along with a river and grain fields. I had, but did not objectify, the sense of buildings. Suddenly I received an impression, not quite an image, of the Snake River, and the valley at the foot of the Grand Tetons. I declared an AOL, stating "Grand Tetons," which indeed turned out to be the site.

The *National Geographic* picture Ingo had in the feedback folder was from the top of a mountain looking down on Jackson Hole, across the Snake River and to the Tetons with their lakes. Ingo was very pleased, and declared himself particularly happy with the way I had managed to stay in structure. He later commended us as "the best students" he'd had. Whether he really meant it, or whether it was just a training tactic to get the best performance out of us, I don't know. But what I was most pleased about was that the perception I had was so much different from the feedback photo itself.

Though it was clear that both the photo and my session encompassed the same target, my remote-viewing impression was from a dramatically different perspective than was the photo. This was for me the first compelling evidence that in remote viewing we weren't just remote viewing the feedback photo. Certainly, it would have been remarkable just to be able to describe a photographic image, sight unseen. But it would not have been particularly useful for real operational targets. When the goal is to discover what is going on at a location either *now* or at some time in the past when a camera wasn't present, being able to describe a photograph is of little use. The fact that I had just described the target accurately, but from a vantage point much different from what was in the photo, was very important to me.

Between our first exposure to Stage 1, Phase Two in March, and the completion of Stage 1 training, Ingo gave me at least twenty-eight more sites to remote view. One turned out to be the salt marshes at one end of the Great

Salt Lake, near the Union Pacific causeway. My remote viewing response came across as "land and water, with smells," which produced the AOL of "swamp." For another target, my impressions were of a deep, greenish-blue ocean lapping at a rocky shore with low, green vegetation. I immediately declared it to be an island. And so it was—a small, rocky island off the Irish coast covered with low, scattered vegetation. Yet another target produced impressions of water, land, "tropical" smells (humid vegetation, organic matter, etc.), buildings, city streets, cement, and storage buildings, which finally resolved down to grain elevators along a river. Though I didn't say it, I thought the river was the Mississippi, mentally placing the grain elevators near Saint Louis. My site was the Mississippi River at Cairo, Illinois. And there were, indeed, grain elevators.

That session was one of my first clear encounters with "internal editing"— a great no-no, according to Ingo. A viewer committed the crime of internal editing whenever failing to objectify—speak out and write down—*everything* perceived or thought about the target. Data that ought to be divulged is instead retained unacknowledged in the viewer's mind.

Penalties for internal editing were two-fold. If a viewer failed to objectify an AOL, the unacknowledged AOL could disrupt the entire rest of the session. On the other hand, if it was legitimate data (which was the case here) that the viewer failed to acknowledge, the data couldn't be used. If you did not speak it aloud and write it down, it was the same as if you had missed it altogether. Adding details after the fact was absolutely forbidden. "Oh, by the way—I *knew* it was the Mississippi River!" expressed after the feedback was handed over and the target made known, carried no weight with Ingo.

On one memorable site I perceived rocks, tans, browns, a very strong impression of "down," and I experienced a stomach-wrenching aerial perspective of a winding canyon with a river in the bottom. And that's exactly what it turned out to be—the spectacular Bruneau Canyon in southern Idaho, with its rushing river twisting hundreds of feet down between sheer cliffs.

Not all my sessions were successful. For a target I worked on May 10, I got an accurate ideogram and the concept of a land/water interface. I kept insisting however, that there was water on one side and land on the other, perhaps a lake, or a seashore. It wasn't until I stopped assuming that I knew what it was that I perceived a meandering, slow-moving stream flowing through a marshy area—it turned out to be a winding river in Virginia.

I wasn't the only one who was having a hard time that day. Bill took eleven pages to get his site; Charlene had to take an extended break; and Ed also took a long break, went back, and still couldn't do it. He kept describing a mental image of a wooden village at the foot of a mountain being overwhelmed by a landslide or an earthquake. He often had intimations of disaster, but none ever panned out.

Ingo finally called somebody to find out what the solar activity level was, and they reported back that it was quite high—"K-factor" of 4, on a 0–6 scale. This tied in with a working hypothesis that long-wave electromagnetic radiation in the extremely low frequency (ELF) band might interfere with certain mental functions—particularly remote viewing. I don't know if this has been decisively proved, and I have my doubts about it. But at any rate, Ingo surrendered to the inevitable and dismissed us for the day.

Any talking among ourselves about our sessions was absolutely forbidden. But from indirect references and comments, and the expressions the other three displayed when they emerged after a session, it was easy to guess that their experiences in the grey room were similar to my own—successes, failures, and some that were in between.

But we weren't always the only ones doing targets. The third week of May in 1984, Tommy McNear accompanied us to New York to continue his Stage 6 training with Ingo. When we were not doing sessions, Tom was in the grey room doing his. Ingo was so proud of Tom's performance that after one particular session our teacher broke with his usual practice and allowed us to see another student's results. The target had been Grand Coulee Dam on the Columbia River in Washington State.

An important part of Stage 6 is to make a three-dimensional model of the site using clay or other material. Tom had made a clay model of Grand Coulee Dam that impressed us all. He had the dam abutments, the long stretch of concrete blocking the river, and a rectangular structure positioned on the downstream side exactly where the power plant is at the real dam. As a final touch, Tom had hunted up a blue marker, and with it had made a series of blue, parallel lines in the middle of the structure to represent the spillway. He also scribbled blue marker behind the structure, and put a narrower band of blue leading away from what would have been the downstream side of the dam. The blue represented water, he assured us.

It was on this trip with Tommy that someone made Polaroid photos of the six of us, Ingo, Tommy, Bill, Ed, Charlene and myself, sitting in front of *Millennium*—the only time we would all have a picture taken together.

Outside of the session work, there was plenty of social interaction. Ingo would sometimes invite us down to his apartment for gourmet meals, which he rustled up under surprisingly primitive kitchen conditions. He had a hotplate, a one-basin sink, and an ancient portable broiler that he would bring up on its cart from the subbasement whenever he needed it.

We also went to movies as a group. Ingo felt they served a legitimate training purpose for two reasons. One was that they provided a valuable diversion from training, thus aiding our assimilation of the skills we had learned. Further, he felt some movies contributed to the overall atmosphere of our training, especially if they dealt with out-of-the-ordinary-world themes such as science fiction or the paranormal. Though such films might be considered escapist, it was the ambience Ingo was after. Thus, over the course of the year we went to see *Firestarter* a film adapted from one of Stephen King's books in which a young girl is being chased because of her ability to start fires with her mind. We also saw *Dreamscape*, a movie about an experiment to insert one person psychically into another person's dreams to observe and interact, sometimes with dark results. We went together to see *Star Trek III*, and were all relieved that Spock was alive again. We balanced Arnold Schwartzenegger in *The Terminator* with Mel Gibson in *The Bounty*. We entered the realm of near-death experiences with Natalie Wood in *Brainstorm* and whetted our cold-warrior zeal with *Red Dawn*.

One of our favorites, though, was *Ghostbusters*. We identified with the down-and-out parapsychologists who in the end had to save the day. While walking along Lexington Avenue a week or so afterwards, all of us even bought *Ghostbuster* T-shirts from a street vendor, and wore them now and again in a show of paranormal solidarity.

When we weren't hanging around with Ingo, we often sought each other out of an evening, swapping stories and conjectures about the universe and the odd things we were coming to discover about it. Ed Dames was always good for entertainment. He usually could be counted on for some frightening prognostication about the near future. One evening towards the end of May 1984, Ed and I ended up in Bill Ray's room in the Hotel San Carlos, where we had moved for a week when the Bedford had been booked up. Ed went on at length in the most convincing tone about UFOs and what they portended for the pending End of the World, which he was sure was imminent. Just as before, when he and I were together on the bus headed to the Monroe Institute, Ed implied without ever really saying it that he had inside knowledge of what the government wasn't divulging about UFOs and extraterrestrials. He was fond of using innuendo to inflate others' impressions of his access to insider information.

In fact, mostly fomented by Ed, we often had discussions about pending catastrophe or planet-wide doom. One of these, involving recent developments in Soviet biological and chemical warfare that Ed assured us were an immense threat, was later to cause Tommy and me no little trouble on the home front.

What with Ed's warnings, which included references to Nostradamus's poesy-framed prophecies, and the general pre-Millennial apocalyptic funk that even in the 1980s was starting to build, we all grew more and more concerned about what the future might have in store. News reports about recently discovered fault lines under New York City, together with a purported mention in Nostradamus's writings of a "new city" being destroyed during what some of the old prognosticator's interpreters thought pointed to the year 1985, had me convinced that the Big Apple was surely going to meet its doom some time in mid-decade. And it was now already 1984. When the feared disaster, as well as Ed's Doomsday scenarios failed altogether to materialize, I began to develop a hard shell of cynicism about any predictions of pending catastrophes that weren't based on concrete facts.[1]

Even with such digressions, it was an exciting and engrossing time. And, in a way, it was good to be up there in the City, away from the office. Things were brewing back there that did not bode well for our more immediate future.

16

Sharpening the Ax

> "Why, they couldn't
> hit an elephant
> at this dist..."
>
> (Last words of
> General John Sedgewick,
> Battle of Spotsylvania, 1864)

Two new recruits showed up at the Center Lane office beginning in April 1984. Sergeant first class Leonard "Lyn" Buchanan and Sergeant Dawn Lance had been discovered by General Stubblebine on one of his visits to far-flung intelligence posts in the Mediterranean and Europe. Stubblebine recruited Dawn when he found out that she was a palm-reader. Lyn caught the general's eye because of a story he'd heard that Lyn had somehow mentally caused computers to crash at the field station in Augsburg, Germany, where he was assigned. Stubblebine's logic was that, if someone was involved in something "paranormal," they must therefore be good candidates for the remote-viewing unit.

The logic did not always hold. Dawn did not work out, and after several months left the unit. This was a partial vindication of Center Lane's managers, such as Fred Atwater and Brian Buzby, who had misgivings about people who were forced on the unit without going through the assessment process. Lyn, however, turned out to be a satisfactory recruit, and brought with him valuable computer expertise which the rest of us lacked, at a time when the Army was going through a computer revolution. In that respect, Lyn took over for Joe McMoneagle, who had been the computer expert for our state-of-the-art Wang Office Information System, with its eight-inch floppies and huge platter of stacked hard disks.

At first, Lyn would spend his time in the "catch-up" phase reading the psi and remote viewing literature, and doing occasional outbounder sessions to break him in to the idea of remote viewing. The rest of us continued our training with Ingo. When we were finished, the plan was for us to train Lyn and any other recruits in the Ingo Swann CRV method we would by then hopefully have mastered.

Acquiring new people promised longevity to the unit, but we were also facing a loss. Joe was preparing to retire, and we were more than a little dismayed to see him go. He was, after all, the one with all the experience. The legendary stories we'd heard about Joe's exploits gave us a heritage, and a level of expectation to live up to. Joe began spending more and more time at the Monroe Institute for the "advanced training" that INSCOM had contracted for as a test bed to see if it would be profitable for the rest of us to improve our viewing. We saw him very seldom after that.

It was about this time that Buzby ordered me to draft the text for Joe's retirement award. It was to be a Legion of Merit, one of the highest peacetime awards a retiring soldier can be given. Such an award covers the ten-year period before the person is due to leave active duty, so I had to dig up information about Joe's time as a signals intelligence analyst and operator. But my main focus was to be his service as a remote viewer. I had to word this carefully, since mentioning psychic espionage would instantly make the award highly classified. But I was now fairly competent at stating the truth without giving anything away.

Burrowing through our files, I dredged up all the reports and taskings I could find for projects in which Joe had been involved. It made an impressive list: he had worked on projects for the Secret Service, CIA, Defense Intelligence Agency, the National Security Agency, even the Joint Chiefs of Staff. There were various Army and Air Force intelligence organizations on the list, as well.

We in the office knew how well he had done for much of this work: a brothel target associated with a Soviet spy agency (I shall say no more about this one), the *Typhoon* submarine, the XM-1 tank, the kidnaping of General James Dozier. But the unfortunate truth was that for too many of the projects worked by the remote viewing unit, including many of Joe's, there was little or no feedback to tell us whether he or his fellow viewers had done poorly or well.

Joe's award was soon approved. With that, and a boisterous farewell luncheon at a little Italian restaurant north of Laurel, Maryland, where Routes 1 and 32 crossed, Joe passed out of our lives and, we then thought, into the anonymity where we all expected one day to find ourselves. But with Joe's departure, I had the unsettling realization that Bill, Charlene, Tom, and myself were now the future of the unit. My share of that responsibility felt right then like an uneasy load to have to carry.

While we were in New York working with Ingo in the middle of May 1984—the same day as my Cairo, Illinois, target—Congressman Charlie Rose (D-NC) called Ingo at his home. We were there visiting at the time, so Ingo excused himself for a few minutes to talk to the congressman. When he returned he was excited. He had invited Congressman Rose to the coming-out party Ingo was planning for his painting, *Millennium,* and Rose was calling to give his regrets. However, the conversation had moved beyond that to Jack Anderson, the legendary muckraker who had published a number of columns in the early 1980s critical of government involvement in parapsychology.

The negative spin had been the fault of Ron McRae, a reporter on Anderson's staff who later wrote an article for *Spy* magazine about how he had bamboozled the great Jack Anderson with fabricated stories, spiced with grains of truth, about government psychic warfare.[1]

Part of Rose's message was that Anderson and Dale Van Atta, Jack's emerging heir apparent, had escaped from McRae's "antipsychic" influence and had come to believe that remote viewing might be an important national asset. They meant to do a series of favorable columns on remote viewing, asking "why so little interest was being shown towards it" by the U.S. government. Van Atta lacked accurate data on what the Soviets were up to, and had asked Rose if the congressman could provide it.

Though there was considerable information on the topic in various classified reports issued by DIA, Rose no doubt thought it was better to go instead to an unclassified source. Could Ingo help out? Ingo replied that he would anonymously supply material about the Soviet psychoenergetic research from his own research and contacts. This information could then be filtered through Rose's office to the investigative journalists. A few weeks later Ingo even showed us some of the material he had passed on. We were pleased to see Jack Anderson columns appear later in 1984 and in 1985 presenting a much more balanced image of remote viewing. There were still factual errors in the columns, but they did get some of the stories right about what remote viewing had accomplished up until then. There were to be more such columns over the years.[2]

We continued our yo-yo routine between New York City and Fort Meade through the end of May. I was given a variety of training targets that included such diverse sites as Canyonlands National Park in Utah; a meandering river in Alaska; and Tristan de Cunha, an island in the Azores. This latter target gave me the impression of "mountain," then some sense of something being "around" it; gradually I came to realize the target was "an island with a tropical feel." It was another confidence builder.

We were just about to wrap up the final week of training at the end of May when Ed had to rush home to Maryland for the birth of his son Aaron. He missed a day of training, but as effusive as he was about his new son he clearly thought it was worth the trade.

The first week of June 1984 ended our spring training cycle. In my off hours I helped Ingo do some library research for his book on appearances of the Virgin Mary. It was interesting, and my fluency with German allowed me to translate some passages for him. He was convinced that these manifestations were evidences of paranormal events. I myself was not so sure, but was willing to keep an open mind.

Ed's penchant for the apocalyptic came out once again the day after Ingo's and my trip to the library. Ed had convinced Ingo, Tom, and Joe to work remote viewing sessions against what he thought was a new Soviet weapon posing a great threat to the United States. To this day I don't know what it was, but I suspect he had in mind the so-called "Yellow Rain" that was the terror of the American biological warfare defense community for a time in the early-to-mid 1980s. The threat turned out to be nonexistent, but not until long after Ed had us all worked up about it. After doing a session and hearing Ed's impassioned description of the hazard, Tom called his wife at home and warned her that we were all going to be "annihilated" in 1986. She was suddenly agitated, and called my wife, who didn't really believe it but was annoyed that her friend had been upset. It took us a couple of days to get them settled down again.

And then we were through with the New York trips for awhile. But on June 25 we boarded a plane, bound once more for Menlo Park, California. The SRI folks at headquarters insisted that we make at least quarterly trips out there so they could check to make sure we were doing what we were supposed to. We weren't quite finished yet with Stage 1, so we did sessions the day after we arrived. The next evening we were in for a treat. Charlene, Bill, Ed, myself, and Ingo were invited to dinner at the house of one of SRI's subcontractors, Marsha Adams. Hal and Adrienne Puthoff were invited as well.

Marsha's house was beautiful. Two dawn redwoods grown from original seeds found in a centuries-old Chinese tomb graced her front yard, as well as loquat trees with their curious-tasting fruit. The house was built around a large central atrium crammed with ferns. Marsha loved crystals, and they were everywhere. She had even imported approximately one ton of amethyst crystal from a friend who owned a mine in South America. There were cut-glass crystals, too, and prisms hanging from the most unlikely places all around the place. Incongruities compounded. I discovered that she at one time had been a fly-fishing enthusiast. And I was amused by the five-foot rubber snake intertwined among the rocks near her sunken fireplace.

But it was in the back room where we were introduced to the most striking contrast. This petite brunette who had such a taste for charming, if eclectic decor was also a hard-headed scientist. She had a very sophisticated ELF (extremely low frequency) monitoring station in one of her spare bedrooms. Two microprocessors wrote data to three disk drives, one of the computers recording levels of ambient ELF activity every half hour, while its partner displayed the frequency modulation of the waves as it recorded them. A nearby printer disgorged a continuous printout of the half-hour samplings. Control and calculations were provided by an IBM PC in the living room. Thanks to the fact that ELF waves pass through unhindered by walls or structures, with all this equipment Marsha could produce a continual record of the ambient extremely-low-frequency radio activity from within her own home. Later, her data would be compared with remote-viewing experiments to see if increase or decrease in ELF levels affected the viewing quality.

Marsha was also known as the "Earthquake Lady," and her ELF readouts could be examined to see if they predicted seismic activity as well. And she maintained an Earthquake Hotline so remote viewers and other intuitive types could call in with forebodings of pending temblors. (Tom Mc-Near did that once, but I no longer recall if any earthquakes showed up after his premonition.)

Examining all this technology soon made us hungry. On the barbecue Ingo grilled prawns dressed with his own garlic butter recipe, and there was grilled chateaubriand, as well as lasagne that Adrienne brought. In those unlikely surroundings I learned a cooking secret that sticks with me to this day: corn on the cob boiled in water with a couple of teaspoons of sugar and a dollop of milk is much tastier than corn cooked in salted water, the way my Idaho relatives prepared it.

During the following weekend all of us drove up to Calistoga, where Ingo treated us to the famous baths in the viscous, smelly volcanic mud at one of the spas. Ingo's sister Murleen and her daughter joined us for dinner. It was an interesting diversion from the remote-viewing training.

I finished my Stage 1 training to Ingo's satisfaction on July 4, 1984. After the requisite essay, Ingo pronounced me ready to go on with Stage 2 as soon as the rest of us were ready. Charlene and Bill had "graduated" from Stage 1 a day or so before, but Ed was still working his way through it. The pause gave us a little time to wonder about the future. We were by then all aware that General Stubblebine was soon to leave INSCOM. We didn't know it at the time, but he had opted to retire rather than engage in a major political fight over who would get a third star and become the senior ranking Army intelligence general.[3]

His adversary was Major General William Odom. As the Army's Assistant Chief of Staff for Intelligence, Odom had replaced Ed Thompson, the general who had originally ordered the creation of an Army remote viewing program. Unlike Thompson, Odom was no fan of remote viewing, nor of any of the other leading-edge initiatives that Stubblebine had launched. In fact, the perception was widespread that he felt Stubblebine had embarrassed and perhaps damaged the Army and the intelligence community with his quirky ideas and unconventional thinking. Lieutenant Colonel Buzby, who had served under Stubblebine when the general was still a colonel commanding the 902nd Military Intelligence Group, remembers Stubblebine as a forward-looking thinker even back then, and could understand why Odom would feel uncomfortable with Stubblebine's perspectives. But now that Buzby was again working with the INSCOM commander, he had more sympathy for what Stubblebine was trying to do. He saw the sense in it, even if the rest of the Army could not.[4]

Odom, a Soviet expert, was perceived by his bosses as a smart, educated, and sagacious man. He seemed to think that dabbling in parapsychology was a waste of time and resources. And Odom fought dirty. Even though the issue had been formally investigated and resolved to the Army's satisfaction, Odom revived the fiasco of Lieutenant Pemberton's mental breakdown during RAPT training and used it to good advantage in turning the Army brass's opinions away from Stubblebine and toward himself. He also played power politics. Despite being Stubblebine's peer, Odom more than once was able to go over his head to have the INSCOM commander excluded from briefings given to senior officials by Stubblebine's own staff officers. No slouch at infighting himself, General Stubblebine could have worked to counter Odom's maneuvers with some of his own. But, in the end, the general decided that even if he won, the fight would wreak too much havoc within the Army's intelligence establishment. So he informed the chief of staff of the Army that he would retire.[5]

Not knowing of the vicious political battle that was going on, we had little reason to worry about the impending transfer of power. True, Stubblebine had been our supporter and had saved the remote viewing program from ruin more than once. When Odom got that third star he would become the senior intelligence general, but he had a job waiting for him as director of the National Security Agency and there he would have no further influence on us. We thought that any general appointed to succeed Stubblebine as the INSCOM commander would be easily persuaded by the convincing evidence we had to show for the successes remote viewing had achieved up until then. We naively thought Buzby's well-worn "Red Book" was convincing enough in its own right. It contained the sketches and words produced by Pat Price for the PNUTS briefing, Joe's *Typhoon* submarine coup, the XM-1 tank episode, some of the best of the Iranian Hostage project, and several other equally impressive samples of remote viewing successes, plus a briefing I had written for Buzby. He had been all over Washington presenting the case to Congressional staffers, generals, senior program managers, and high-ranking intelligence officials, many of whom were impressed by the evidence. Despite the apparent certainty of our continuation as a project, though, I couldn't help feeling a twinge of worry every now and again.

We returned from our second trip to Menlo Park on the weekend of July 8, just in time to scramble around rewriting and polishing up all our briefing materials. The new INSCOM commander, Brigadier General Harry Soyster had just replaced Stubblebine, and was coming up to Fort Meade, ostensibly to see if Center Lane was worth keeping around.

Soyster had started out his Army life as an artillery officer, but had changed to military intelligence midway through his career. He was close friends with the Army vice chief of staff, a four-star general named Max Thurman. Though he only wore one star on his shoulder, Soyster was on the promotion list for major general, and gained that rank shortly after assuming command of INSCOM.

The briefing for Soyster on Center Lane was set for Wednesday, July 11.[6] Instead of our usual slacks and open-collared shirts we wore coats and ties, and scurried around all morning finishing up charts and briefing texts. The general and his entourage arrived thirty minutes late at 2:30 in the afternoon, which was prompt for a general officer. Along with Soyster came Colonel Kirk, INSCOM's chief of staff, who had been in the same RAPT group at the Monroe Institute as I; Wally Del Toro, INSCOM's primary staff officer overseeing human intelligence; and Captain Mark Boyer, Soyster's aide-de-camp.

Buzby and Fred Atwater joined them in the back conference room for the briefing. We fidgeted in our chairs and pretended to find things to do.

Three hours later they emerged. Though on the surface all were smiles and handshakes, Dawn, who at the time was still with the unit, thought she sensed that things hadn't gone well. General Soyster congratulated us for doing great work, and headed out the door with his aide in tow. Soyster was "very impressed," Buzby reassured us, and thought that the program had very good people assigned to it. But the general felt he "had to make a decision" about our fate before the end of the week, when he was to leave for Europe to inspect INSCOM activities overseas.

Buzby admitted that he may have forced Soyster's hand on that decision by pointing out the various training and research contracts with SRI and others that remained to be negotiated before the end of the fiscal year if the program's momentum were to be maintained. Action needed to be taken soon, as the deadline was a little more than two months away. There was also the small matter of new personnel scheduled to be transferred to the unit at the first of the new year, specifically Mel Riley, Joe McMoneagle's protege from Gondola Wish/Grill Flame days. Buzby and Joe had gone to Europe in January to check out Lyn and Dawn, but also to see if Mel would be amenable to coming back to the unit. He was. But now Buzby didn't want him coming back home unless absolutely sure that he had a home to come to.

Del Toro and Kirk had spoken strongly on the project's behalf, and our boss was confident things *had* gone well. He was to drive down to INSCOM headquarters at Arlington Hall Station the next day to get some preliminary directives from the general. Talking with the others afterwards, I could see that we all felt relieved. Other than Dawn's vague presentiment, the outcome seemed positive. I went home for a good night's rest. So much for being psychic.

Most of Thursday passed uneventfully. We filed away the briefing materials, shuffled paperwork, Buzby left for Arlington Hall, and we twiddled our thumbs. He returned about 3 P.M. Walking through the front door, the lieutenant colonel put his briefcase in his office, and called for a meeting in the back room. As we clustered around the long conference table where, a year before, I had been invited to become an Army remote viewer, Buzby let the shoe drop.

"General Soyster has determined that the Center Lane program will probably be canceled. He said he would make his final decision tomorrow." That bombshell was followed by a moment of shocked silence. Then he went on. "He assures me that the personnel will be taken care of career-wise. If it comes to that, INSCOM will find suitable jobs for all of us. He says he just doesn't think that remote viewing is an appropriate activity for his organization to be engaged in." He paused and looked around the table. "But we do have our work cut out for us. Colonel Kirk wants us to draft a formal statement outlining the impact that cancelation of the program will have, and suggesting possible courses of action."

As late in the day as it was, we sprang to work—me shaky with disappointment. With the positive way yesterday's meeting had seemed to end up, this decision seemed to come right out of left field. It seemed arbitrary and unfair. I grew angry at what seemed to me to be a clearly foolish move. Buzby and Fred had spent three hours throwing convincing case after convincing case at the general. I had seen the evidence and I knew it was persuasive. Given what we knew about the Soviet emphasis in psychoenergetic research and applications, it was simply inconceivable that our new general could be blind to the value and importance of what we were doing. My anger served to focus my energy, spurring me on to work furiously on the documents under Buzby's guidance. When I finished the first drafts, Tom, Bill, Buzby, and I together went back over them and polished them up for the lieutenant colonel's morning trip down to INSCOM headquarters. Finishing up about 6:30 P.M., we headed home for the night. Later, Bill came over and we went for a stroll to mull over the events of the past few days.

"It will all work out," Bill assured me. But he had no suggestions as to how that might happen.

17

Stage 2

> "You are not thinking.
> You are merely being
> logical."
>
> —Niels Bohr to
> Albert Einstein

Friday the thirteenth of July, 1984. An ominous day for what was about to unfold. Arriving at the office still agitated from Thursday afternoon, I took a last look at what passed for Center Lane's obituaries—the impact statement and the memorandum of proposed courses of action—and made a few more changes Lieutenant Colonel Buzby recommended. Final copies in hand, he headed out the door and climbed into the clunky old Dodge four-door that was assigned us from the motor pool. We all sat down to wait for his return from Arlington Hall.

About mid-afternoon we heard Buzby pull up on the gravel outside. The car door slammed, there were footsteps on the porch, and the front door opened. Buzby walked in, picked out a chair, sat down, and began his tale at a maddeningly slow pace.

As my mind raced, I heard him saying, ". . . got to the Anacostia bridge and headed across town towards Arlington. Somehow, I took a wrong turn and found myself curving around in front of the Pentagon. Up ahead I saw some construction going on."

What *is* this all about, I fretted, why *doesn't* he get to the point?

"There was one of these big, diamond-shaped orange signs they put up as a warning where they've got the pavement all torn up." He waved his hands in a vague diamond shape to illustrate his story. "And . . . and, I kid you not, it said, in great big black capital letters: 'CENTER LANE CLOSED AHEAD.'" He paused to let that sink in. "It seemed like an omen."

Stunned silence. We started to laugh, then didn't know whether to keep laughing. It was black humor. But what had General Soyster actually *said*? That would make the difference between a dark laugh and blessed relief. "And when I finally got to Arlington Hall," Buzby finished, "Soyster said he had indeed decided to close Center Lane."[1]

Fate's doors had slammed shut. For what was left of that day we moped around. Things seemed even worse because we had no details about how the closing would take place. Should we clean out our desks right now? Would we be left hanging for a month until someone figured out what to do with us? Would we have any say at all in where we would end up? Some of us were nervously wondering whether we would have to uproot our families. And what about the CRV training with Ingo? The contract had already been paid and was not refundable. Would INSCOM just write the money off as a bad deal and send us packing?

As the week wore on, the picture cleared. Apparently, Soyster had never had any intention of continuing the remote viewing program. In fact, given some of the draconian changes he was making in other parts of INSCOM, it appeared that he had arrived with a set of marching orders to "clean up" the organization, eradicating from it any vestige of Stubblebine's vision. But at least we wouldn't be moving right away. The program's death rattle was to take awhile.

We discovered the following week that Soyster couldn't just arbitrarily kill Center Lane. It had been approved as an official Department of the Army program by the Secretary of the Army himself, and couldn't be terminated without the Secretary's approval, as well as that of the assistant chief of staff for intelligence, General Odom. We knew Odom would not stand in the way of the program's closure, so it was only a matter of time and formality before the Secretary agreed as well. Though the clock was ticking, we did at least have some breathing room, and Center Lane still had influential friends.

So I ended up with yet more reports and memos to write. I must have been getting the hang of it, since Buzby told me my final drafts of these had been forwarded through Soyster up to the senior Army command virtually unchanged. On July 20, Buzby met with Jack Vorona, Director of Technical Intelligence at DIA, and with Marty Hurwitz who, as Director of the General Defense Intelligence Program (GDIP) controlled a major portion of the military's intelligence budget.[2] Hurwitz was a powerful figure and a staunch supporter of the remote viewing project. Vorona was one of Hurwitz's bosses, and a patron of the remote viewing effort's research arm at SRI. Although I wasn't told at the time, Bill Ray later explained that Buzby, Vorona, and Hurwitz discussed other agencies that were secretly courting our program.

Buzby was increasingly taking Bill into his confidence. Ray was the second most senior officer in Center Lane after Buzby himself, and our boss needed Bill's help to negotiate the future of the remote viewing program. Bill was tactful and discreet, yet at the same time well stocked with common sense and hard-won experience with the Army bureaucracy. The rest of us viewers weren't aware at the time of the full ramifications of what was going on. This playing coy with us had two purposes. One was that our bosses didn't want us to be any more stressed than necessary, as there was a general belief that stress would affect our progress as viewers. The other concern was that some among our number had connections outside the unit, and Buzby didn't want loose lips to tip our hand prematurely as to what courses of action we might try.

Years after the fact Bill told me some of what went on during those rather dark days. With INSCOM's eagerness to thrust us from its fold, we found no shortage of suitors. "The CIA had expressed an interest in taking the project," Bill told me. "NSA wanted us, as did the Army Medical Research and Development Command [headquartered at Fort Detrick, on the outskirts of Frederick, Maryland]. Brian, Fred, and I drove up there and talked to the general in charge of the Command. He and his people were enthusiastic about doing scientific tests on the viewers."

Unfortunately, there were drawbacks to each of these possibilities. Bill had concerns about moving to the Medical Research and Development Command, fearing they would turn the viewers into guinea pigs, running us on various practice targets until we lost interest and accuracy. The National Security Agency, the electronic eavesdropping experts, wouldn't have made a much better home. "If we went to NSA, I saw us getting stuck perpetually testing communications security, and our accuracy would be destroyed as well," Bill recalled. And the CIA option abruptly dried up. "That was just about the time the Agency got caught mining the harbors in Nicaragua, and they felt that they could not risk a further embarrassment, so they waived any claim to taking us."[3]

Out of various high-level discussions, two alternatives emerged as the leading contenders for averting Center Lane's total annihilation. One came from Vorona. He declared himself willing to go to bat with Lieutenant General Williams, DIA's director, on a proposal that DIA absorb the project. This would expand the agency's role in the field by adding a significant remote-viewing intelligence collection capability to its already long-established research effort. It seemed like a logical home for whatever might be left of Center Lane when the smoke cleared.

The Medical Research and Development Command was the second finalist. The Command had its own intelligence division, and General Rapmund, the commander, was interested in both researching remote viewing and in using it to augment what intelligence resources he already had at his disposal. On August 1, 1984, Buzby made the first of several trips up to Fort Detrick to negotiate with Rapmund.[4]

In the midst of all this uncertainty, the time came for our next training at the SRI Radio Physics Lab in Menlo Park. The trip had already been budgeted for and, faint as they were, there were enough glimmers of light in the future that Buzby and the INSCOM chief of staff decided to let us go to start our Stage 2 training. It was not as certain whether Ed Dames would be going. As a straphanger there was less justification for him, and there was some debate back and forth about his status. It finally came down to the fact that no decision to keep him home had been made by 8 A.M. on August 6, the day we were supposed to leave, so we took him along.

Much to our surprise, the Stage 2 lecture took only a day to finish. We would have been done even sooner, but during lunch Ingo decided to take us to a thrift shop in Redwood City so he could shop for clothes. Apparently, thrift-shop wardrobes were all the rage among the New York elite, and Ingo intended to go back at the end of this training cycle dressed to the hilt. Bay area thrift shops were the place to do it. The wealth, eclectic tastes, and social conscience of the typical San Franciscan kept the shops well stocked with classy, lightly used apparel intended, no doubt, for the indigent. I'm sure the original owners had not expected that their castoffs would end up as haute couture in Manhattan society.

Stage 2 promised to be even more interesting than Stage 1 had been. The concept of it was quite simple. A viewer described what the body might feel, sense, or experience were it actually at the target location. Once a major gestalt is decoded, as we learned to do in Stage 1, Ingo told us that the "aperture" between conscious and subconscious begins to relax and widen. As a result, quick snatches of richer and more detailed impressions pop into the viewer's mind. Stage 2 involves *sensory* experiences, the kinds of impressions brought to us by our five primary physical senses: colors and qualities of light, textures, sounds, tastes, and smells.

Novices often expect remote viewing to give them fully assembled views of objects and scenes. This is a mistake. Even in real life the senses don't give us this sort of experience. All we get from our eyes are patches of color and varying intensities of light. Our ears merely give us bits of noise that change according to pitch and loudness. It is only in our brains and minds that all this panoply of light and sound is stitched together to create our perceptions of objects and scenes as *wholes*. The raw data of Stage 2 is the same raw data of the senses. In a remote viewing session the viewer does not at first "see" end-items such as "car," "people," "buildings," or "mountains." Instead, impressions include things such as red, greyish, rust-colored, tinkling, rushing, clanging, rough, glossy, jagged, salty, iodine smells, chirping, stringy, and so on. These are raw impressions that we describe almost exclusively using adjectives.

As usual, beyond this elementary concept were various additional details to Ingo's lecture; how AOL differs in Stage 2, for example, or how "S-2s," the basic sensory words one utters during a session, tend to "cluster" around each of the respective five senses. And there were the inevitable definitions to be scurried after in our dictionaries and scribbled down in our notes.

Before we knew it, Ingo was calling it a day and sending us off with our homework to the Mermaid Inn, our home away from home. We were to rack our brains for sixty basic words describing a variety of sensory experiences. I found this exercise fun, and before the night was over ended up with 124 words. The next morning Ingo went over our word lists. Even my beyond-the-call-of-duty list of 124 turned out not to be enough for him. He kept sending me back to the drawing board until my list exceeded 260 words. The exercise was not just busywork. Most people recognize many more words than they can actually use in speech and writing; their verbal descriptions are impoverished. They may, for example, recognize that the words "umber," "sepia," "ocher," and "sienna" are various shades of brown. But if shown those colors, many people could come up with only "brown" as a descriptor. Much information is lost if we can only think of one word to use in describing a large group of experiences. The same applies to other senses such as touch; when asked to describe the feel of a surface, the most we might be able to say is, "It is rough." But other words might be more accurate: "gritty," "bumpy," "pitted," "corroded."

Straining to come up with all these words and then reviewing them with Ingo greatly expanded my ability to describe the sensations I would later encounter in Stage 2. The more such "basic" sensory words I had at my immediate disposal, the less I would have to search about in my mind to find a word that expressed what sensory experience I was perceiving, and the less of an open invitation I offered to analytical overlay.

With my Stage 2 essay finished, it was time to see if the actual experience of *doing* a Stage 2 session measured up to what we had been told. My beginning attempt seemed to bear out what I had learned. I was third into the grey room for those first S-2 sessions. As I settled into the chair and adjusted the lights, I sensed the performance anxiety which I was learning to ignore. Ingo gave me the coordinate.

The line of the ideogram I scribbled had a pleasant curve to it, then sharply veered away for an inch or two. I struggled through some initial confusion before I began capturing sensory words, or S-2s: splashing, rushing, wet, damp, cascading, rocky, black, glistening, roaring, were the sorts of words I produced. I would have been hard-put to describe how I "knew" these words were right. There was some vague mental imagery involved, glimpses that were instantly there and gone of white froth plummeting into space; a sudden sensation like deep, throaty sound reverberating in my ears and against my body; an infinitesimally brief cool, tactile feel of water splashed on my skin.

I knew none of these experiences were actually *present*. Rather, they were more like brief, distant thoughts that suddenly, uncalled for, came to mind and then vanished. If someone had cross-examined me, asking if I *knew for certain* that those sensations had been there in my mind, I could not have said I was sure. Yet, somehow, they *seemed* right. I ended with "waterfall" and the impression that it was "a very pleasant place."

Jotting the ending time down at the bottom of the last page of my session transcript, I shoved it over to Ingo. He, in return, slid the feedback photo across the table to me. The target was Victoria Falls, in Africa. My ideogram had neatly captured the curving lip of the thundering waterfall, even indicating where the land broke away in a sheer drop of hundreds of feet. And all those experience-words had been exactly right. This time I really *needed* to "quit on a high."

Ingo gave me his smug cat-ate-the-canary smile.

The glow of success didn't last long. Ingo began the training the very next day by chewing out Ed Dames for "intellectualizing and philosophizing about the cosmic implications" involved in the phenomenon underlying remote viewing. Ed had been engaged in his usual seemingly compulsive ruminations about the universe, including references to UFOs and extraterrestrials, this time dragging CRV into it. He must have commented one too many times to Ingo about these theories, and our mentor had had enough.

Ingo fumed that all this speculation was messing up Ed's remote viewing performance, and that Ed had better knock it off if he wanted to keep training at SRI. Chastened, Ed went into the grey room and managed to pull off a decent Stage 2 session.

My target that morning turned out to be a desert in Namibia, and that's exactly what came through—featureless, barren, smooth, flat, rounded, and expansive, with a feeling of space and freedom. I declared it to be broad, flat plains, or desert. The next day's Stage 2 target was King's Canyon National Park in California. This time, an unusually strong visual came through— jumbled-up, rounded, cream-colored sandstone boulders, wind-weathered, with vegetation below them. The feedback photo confirmed the reality of my impressions.

I celebrated my thirty-second birthday on Monday, August 13, by learning an important remote viewing lesson. The target was Mammoth Hot Springs in Yellowstone National Park, a mass of abrupt white-and-brown travertine ledges stepping down from the crest of a low hill. The ledges were deposited by mineral-rich waters that cascade steamily down from their source. After taking the coordinate, I ended up with "brown, rough, vertical cliff overlooking a wide valley." But this didn't seem right. My Stage 2s generally felt correct, but this one wasn't coming together. I backed off and took the coordinate again, and this time received additional impressions of "steamy, brown, blue, white, hot—geysers." This was close enough, given my struggle, so Ingo ended the session.

Comparing session to target afterwards, it seemed obvious what had happened: Apparently, my point of view at the target had been next to the mineral formations that built up around the hot springs. My limited perspective fooled me into thinking I was up against a towering cliff when in reality it was the side of a travertine terrace at most only a few dozen feet off the ground. I learned that day not to trust what I *believed* about a target until I had enough data to justify it.

Even in the excitement of learning and then doing Stage 2, we couldn't completely escape what was going on back home, and the uncertainty of our fate lingered in the backs of our minds. The second day into the trip, Bill heard in a telephone call back to Fort Meade that this was to be Ed Dame's last trip. Given the tenuous circumstances, Ed's headquarters wouldn't authorize the additional travel funds. Our future was only a little less shaky; the brass had just not made a decision about us yet. Bill thought they were holding off to see what headway Jack Vorona might make with DIA's commander.

At lunch on Tuesday, August 14, Hal Puthoff had talked to Ingo about the Fort Meade project's pending cancellation. That evening, Bill, Charlene,

Ingo, and I went to dinner at a nearby steak house and talked obliquely about the problem as we picked at our food. I could tell Ingo was feeling gloomy, as well he should have. We were very much a work in progress, and I think he had hopes we would go on to vindicate the work he, Hal, and others at SRI had contributed to this new approach to human perceptual functioning.

Then, the next day, we received news that cheered us all up. Ingo, Ed, and I had gone to see the movie *Red Dawn*, about a hypothetical Soviet invasion of the United States. At the time, the movie made quite an impression on me, and the three of us discussed it animatedly on our way home. A few years earlier Ingo had written a book called *What Will Happen to You When the Soviets Take Over* which, based on how the Soviets had dealt with various groups and minorities in their own nation, extrapolated how victorious communist invasion troops might treat various social and cultural groups in the United States should they ever invade. Ed, of course, was always happy to contemplate anything apocalyptic. So we felt strongly drawn to the movie and its premise. It seemed something to worry about at the time, but now, years after the fall of the Berlin Wall, I feel a little silly to have been caught up so much in it.

After we returned from the theater, I sought Bill out. I knew he planned to call Fort Meade for further news. This time what he had to tell me was positive. Fred and Lieutenant Colonel Buzby had met once again with General Soyster. We were to be allowed to finish out the training contract through December, and it looked like Ed would continue with us.

The on-again, off-again status of Center Lane was giving us whiplash, but we were glad things were on-again, at least for now. Soyster's maneuver made political sense for him, too. He was still determined to eliminate remote viewing from INSCOM. But it was obvious that he was banking on the likelihood of passing it off to another agency, probably DIA. That would put it outside the Army, and he would have accomplished his goal while avoiding considerable trouble. Killing Center Lane outright came with its own set of consequences. Powerful supporters of the program would be displeased, and might be moved to oppose other initiatives that INSCOM, or even the Army, wanted to promote. By quietly shuffling the program off to an organization happy to run it, General Soyster had the best of both worlds. He couldn't know, of course, that this decision would come back to haunt him a few years later.

This trip to California wasn't all just remote-viewing sessions and fretting about the future. We had been invited for a dinner of baked salmon at Ingo's sister Murleen's house in a community on the south side of San Francisco Bay. Somewhere during the evening's small talk Murleen mentioned the terrible pigeon problem they were having at her office building. Apparently there were just too many of the feathery varmints living in the rafters of the buildings. An exterminator had pledged to eliminate "all but ten percent" of the birds, and promised that the pigeon survivors would certainly leave with the demise of their buddies. Poisoned grain was put out, but the mass-assassination attempt ended when a pigeon expired in midair and plummeted through the windshield of a visitor's car. It made national TV, and Charlene even recalled seeing the story on the news in Baltimore.

This reminded Ingo of a pigeon story of his own. It involved a friend of his, Princess Shirazi, who was a member by marriage of the exiled Iranian royal family. He usually referred to her as "The Princess," or just "Lucy." It seems that across the street from Lucy's New York penthouse was a Jesuit monastery with pigeon problems. The monks were catching the birds in traps and sending them off to the city incinerator for disposal. Aghast, the princess, a prominent animal lover, contacted the Jesuits and offered to take the pigeons off their hands.

A large number of the birds were captured and transferred a two-hour drive north to the princess's property in upstate New York. Released on their arrival, the pigeons reportedly strolled around for a few minutes enjoying the scenery, then took off due south for their home at the monastery.

Someone suggested that if the birds were held captive for awhile in their new surroundings in the north, they would soon feel more at home there. On that advice, the princess spent something like $900 to have a pigeon aviary built. Numbers of birds were duly transported upstate and incarcerated for several days. When finally released, they pecked at the ground once or twice, then took off to find their Jesuit friends.

The monastery was ready to go back to incineration. Lucy promised that if the monks spared the birds, she would leave the Jesuits her penthouse when she died. At this point, Ingo stepped in. He had remembered a story another friend, Lucille Kahn, had told him about a famous comedian friend of hers who had problems with pigeons hanging around and messing up the air conditioner sticking out of his apartment window. Someone had told him to put a rubber snake on the air conditioner and the pigeons would leave it alone. He tried it and it apparently worked. Unfortunately, a few nights later a violent storm blew the snake into the balcony below. The woman who lived there came out the next morning, saw the snake, and according to the comedian fell backwards into her living room, breaking her arm. She sued.

Ingo suggested that Princess Lucy get together with Lucille and work the problem out. This was not particularly easy, since he had tried to get the two together previously and they had reportedly "fought like cats." Both animal lovers, they managed to become allies for this project. But search where they would, they couldn't find any rubber snakes. Finally, they discovered an "erotic emporium" that did stock those items.

We all laughed ourselves silly at the image of the two mature ladies, Lucy and Lucille, marching into a sex shop and buying the entire stock of rubber snakes. The faux reptiles were anchored to the monastery roof so they wouldn't blow off, the Jesuits' pigeon problem was apparently solved, and Lucy became a member of the monastery's board.

On August 24, 1984, the week following our return from what turned out to be our final trip to Menlo Park, Secretary of the Army John Marsh signed the paper discontinuing Center Lane as an Army project. Barring the possibility of one or two maverick efforts being run unofficially within some unit somewhere off the radar screens of the Army brass, remote viewing was done for in the United States Army. There was a silver lining, however. The Secretary had also officially authorized negotiations to transfer the project to DIA or some other willing agency.[5] The door that we had hoped we could escape through had indeed been opened for us. While we hadn't yet actually been able to step through, we could allow ourselves to hope again.

When we continued our Stage 2 training in New York on September 4, it was in SRI's new digs on the eighth floor of the Crystal Pavilion on the corner of Fiftieth Street and Third Avenue. We had a new dress code that required coat and tie, and in that somewhat stuffy attire I worked through my first Stage 2 target of the trip—Old Faithful Geyser, another Yellowstone target. Having for a follow-on target one that is too similar to one you've recently had can be a real challenge. You tend to believe that what you are perceiving is just false impressions sparked by memories of the earlier target. But I couldn't reject impressions such as warm, smelly, white, steamy, and mounded—the latter accompanied by a quick visual impression of the mound from which the famous geyser erupts. I had "Old Faithful" on the tip of my tongue, but rejected it without uttering it, which led to great chagrin when Ingo handed across the feedback folder.

The following day included an informal lecture from Ingo on self-organizing neural nets. This expanded on what he had taught us before about how the brain adapts by building connections between brain cells to reinforce pathways used by the mental activities we perform frequently and how brain cells are reorganized to help us do new mental activities we are beginning to learn. Ingo's talk was a prelude to something he wanted to caution us about. It was important, he told us, not to "dabble" in any other psychic disciplines while we were trying to master CRV. He was concerned that trying to learn or experiment with something else would disrupt the mental structures he hoped we were forming in response to his instruction and tutoring in remote viewing. What we did *after* our full training regimen was completed was our own business.

Whether Ingo was right or not, his worries made sense to me. I remembered back to when I was trying to learn Arabic at the Army's language school in Monterey, California. A few years before enlisting to become an Arabic linguist, I had studied Hebrew for six semesters in college. In between, I had become fluent in German. To my surprise, as I worked at learning Arabic, it was the Hebrew words and structure that kept intruding, rather than the German in which I was much more proficient. After Ingo's lecture, I decided that because the Hebrew and Arabic were so closely related as languages, they must use neighboring groups of brain cells, perhaps even sharing many of the same neurons. The German didn't intrude because it was different enough not to "bleed" into my Arabic synapses. I've since learned that this view is simplistic, but in principle not so far off the mark.

But I could see how something like my Arabic-Hebrew problem might arise if, besides studying remote viewing, I tried to learn another "paranormal" art. Not only could the underlying approach perhaps differ, but there might even be a "conflict of brain cells" of sorts.

That afternoon, I had another novel remote viewing experience. I had no sooner sat down for my first Stage 2 training session of the day and pulled the stack of paper and pen over to me, than I got a brief but pronounced visual of a cluster of what could only be oil tanks.

"Uh, I have to write this down," I told Ingo. "Advanced visual of oil tank farm!" I scribbled the brief phrase down at the top of my blank sheet.

"We'll end there," Ingo said quietly.

"Huh?" I looked up, startled.

"That's the site. We'll end there." Then he started to giggle. He tossed me the folder. The target was an Iranian oil field, and right smack dab in the middle of the feedback photo was a sprawling array of oil tanks large and small. I hadn't even been given the coordinate for the target yet. It was the first time I remember having one of these AVs, or "advanced visuals." In effect, it was a sort of precognitive remote viewing, where the viewer observes some aspect of the target, or even nails it outright, before the session begins. It doesn't happen often, and can be disconcerting when it does.

Over the next few weeks we had other adventures. We all had several more Stage 2 sessions. I got trapped in my hotel room bathroom when the screw in the doorknob stripped off. We had a party on Ingo's roof to celebrate the loss of his view of the Chrysler Tower; a new high-rise was going in just down the street that would stand right in the line of sight. We helped

Ingo pick out the red velvet drapery for the canopy bed that Tom was helping him construct in his top-floor apartment. And Ingo channeled some entities for us.

Ingo had been working on what he called "analytics"—an attempt through his remote viewing structure to perceive letters and numbers. Abstract mental objects such as these are virtually unperceivable to a remote viewer, since they are left-brain, "analytic" constructs. Remote viewing is a very right-brained activity, since the right brain is specialized for, among other things, pattern recognition, but isn't optimized to "read" or recognize numbers. This had always been a problem for remote viewing. Ingo, though, was trying to come up with a way of doing it. He didn't tell us much about his approach, but he was elated about having made some kind of breakthrough.

So, after we traipsed down to the Lower East Side with him to find suitable drapery material for his bed, Ingo fixed spaghetti for us for dinner and, to celebrate his "breakthrough," dug out some of his finest wine for those among our number who drank. Later, both Tom and Charlene left to go back to the hotel, leaving Bill, Ingo, Ed, and myself. As often happened, we started discussing "cosmic" kinds of subjects. Before long, Ed was pestering Ingo with questions about a rumor he had heard concerning Ingo's alleged involvement with extraterrestrials. Both Ingo and Ed were pretty drunk by then, and as time wore on they grew even more so. Finally, as Ed continued to press him, Ingo hinted that he might be ready to reveal a few tidbits. Very much under the influence, he said he was going to do something he very seldom did. With the room dimly illuminated by fading candlelight, and me as the stone-sober witness, Ingo sat quietly for a few moments, wobbling slightly in his seat from the effects of the wine. Abruptly, he announced that he would be acting as a "go-between" for four "people" or entities who wanted to speak through him.

One of these entities would first give a lecture, after which all four would answer questions. The lecture failed to materialize, and instead "they" decided just to answer questions. Those who ventured to ask received mostly rambling and evasive answers. "Who are you?" elicited something like "one of us has gone before, one is yet to come, and one of us you have taken unto yourselves." Ingo went on then to say something about a dark-complexioned person who had been adopted into one of our families and who had something wrong with one eye. The description fit Bill's son, Robbie, quite accurately. Bill could get nothing more relevant out of Ingo, though, and our seance eventually broke up. I was pretty sure that the inebriated Ingo was just having a little fun at our expense. Little did I know that this would not be my last encounter with "channeling," and when I ran into it again, it would have nothing to do with Ingo, and it wouldn't be a joke.

18

Stage 3

. . . deck chairs on the Titanic . . .

While we were still in New York with Ingo, the dark clouds hanging over Center Lane began to part. On September 18, 1984, all the hard work of Brian Buzby, Jack Vorona, and a few other remote viewing partisans such as a lieutenant colonel in Odom's office named Jerry Fox, who nearly wrecked his career fighting for the program despite his boss's disdain for it, paid off when a Memorandum of Agreement I had helped draft was passed to General Soyster.[1] It authorized transfer of Center Lane's assets and people from the Army Intelligence and Security Command to the Defense Intelligence Agency at Bolling Air Force Base in Washington, D.C. Soyster didn't take long to sign it; the document was out of his office and on its way to General Odom, the Army's Assistant Chief of Staff for Intelligence, by September 26. Odom signed the paper on October 4, and passed it back to DIA for action.[2]

The mood in our office at Fort Meade was jubilant. We had found a new home and, since DIA was to take over management of our two old clapboard buildings, we wouldn't even have to move to get there. Just another month or two to complete the arrangements, and we would have a new taskmaster, one whom we believed would be much more benignly disposed towards remote viewing. But things didn't go quite as smoothly as we expected.

Monday, October 1, found us once again in New York. Ingo gave me a series of Stage 2 targets, including a factory complex in California, and another Yellowstone site, Morning Glory Pool. While it seemed that Yellowstone often came up in our target base, the variety of possible targets there and the richness of the sensories available made them ideal for this part of the training. The latest site presented a mix of notable sensations—sulfurous smells, heat, wetness, and vivid colors. I also had a floating tropical garden in Mexico City as a target. For this site I perceived dozens of Stage 2 sensory perceptions, mostly dealing with swampy or boggy qualities, finally detecting floral smells, which was what Ingo was waiting for. He told me I was close to finishing Stage 2. It seemed the others were close as well.

Watching television back in the hotel late that evening, I happened across the end of a *Star Trek* episode. As the final credits rolled off the screen, I was riveted by a teaser about the upcoming program. It was a TV news magazine that was to feature Russell Targ and Keith Harary, formerly of SRI. During our first expedition to Menlo Park, almost a year prior, we had learned that Russell had run afoul of Jim Salyer, DIA's contract monitor, and been forced to leave the SRI remote-viewing research program. Now here Targ was with Harary, talking on national television about psychic phenomena and the military. Someone even mentioned Grill Flame during the course of the show. Though by then the old code name for the government remote viewing program had already appeared in a Jack Anderson column, it was still classified and caused me quite a shock to hear it uttered aloud on a television in New York. It seemed that the secret project in which we were engaged was no longer quite so secret as we thought. Leaks were bound to happen, and the official response was to ignore such breaches of secrecy, rather than fan the flames of curiosity by responding or taking action against the leakers.

By the end of the third week in October all of us had finished Stage 2, and were set to begin Stage 3, the last phase of our personal training with Ingo. The training contract with SRI was due to run out and, given the political climate, further training with SRI was unlikely to be negotiated. Our training in the more advanced stages of CRV would be provided in-house by Fred Atwater and Tom McNear.

Because of the exquisitely executed sessions Tom produced, Ingo considered him to be the best out of all of us. Fred, on the other hand, had diligently monitored the progress of all of Ingo's Center Lane students, and since 1978 had kept careful notes during all the SRI briefings and technical meetings of which he had been a part. Buzby was confident Atwater and Tom together would be able to train us well.

Ingo's Stage 3 lectures began on October 23 and lasted to the twenty-fifth. Stage 3 turned out to be a natural plateau in the remote viewing process—an information-rich place to pause before going on to more complex stages. The heart of Stage 3 is sketching graphic representations of the target. If a picture really is worth a thousand words, Stage 3 can be an encyclopedia. While accurate word-pictures are impressive, there is something riveting about a line drawing, rough though it may be, that strongly resembles the overall target or some intimate detail of it.

Stage 3 emerges abruptly from Stage 2. As the viewer progresses bit by bit through the physical sensations of Stage 2, the aperture by which the remote-viewing signal line flows into awareness gradually "stretches" larger. There is a point where not just raw sensory impressions filter in, but basic dimensional concepts about the target as well. The viewer suddenly knows there is something "wide," or "long," or "tall," or "rounded," or "slanted" about the target.

By this point in the remote viewing session, there may be enough information piled into the viewer's subconscious to cause an emotional response to the target. Ingo called this "aesthetic impact," or simply "AI"—a sudden, often visceral, reaction to how the viewer feels about the target. Sometimes these aesthetic impacts can be quite pronounced. Without even being sure why, a viewer might abruptly find herself feeling uneasy, or pleasantly relaxed, or agitated, or sad, or awe-inspired (as by a stupendous vista), or even bored.

Many people have experiences similar to aesthetic impact in everyday life that have nothing to do with remote viewing. Perhaps you remember becoming suddenly and inexplicably worried or nervous walking down a street, and you couldn't quite put your finger on why. Sometimes the cause materialized when you suddenly noticed a perceived threat—a lurking figure, or a dangerous construction site. At first you had not been aware of the potential threat. But your subconscious mind, sifting through volumes of sensory input, identified a looming danger and notified you in a subtle but forceful way to watch out. This kind of intuitive, emotional experience may be a distant cousin to aesthetic impact.

An "AI" experience is often the signal that the aperture is now wide enough to allow large clusters of information through. This makes available to the viewer more complex dimensional qualities of the target. Because the viewer has a newfound ability to recognize dimensional features, sketching of parts or even the whole of the target becomes possible. These sketches may not look much at all like the target, or instead might strikingly resemble some aspect of it—or could turn out anywhere in between. If, for example, the Eiffel Tower were the target, in Stage 3 a viewer might feel an aesthetic impact of "being high up, as if I were on a tall building," and then start sketching a series of crisscrossing patterns, or a figure that tapers towards the top.

Beginners often sketch a few lines on the paper, then quit. But if a viewer persists in trying to graphically capture impressions, much detail will often be added to the first rough attempts. Perhaps concentrating on one set of intersecting lines will produce a clearer impression of two thick lines joined at their middles, with evenly spaced little bumps up and down the arms of the figure. Examination of the feedback photo at the end of the session might show a clear resemblance to the Tower's intersecting steel girders, with evenly spaced rivet heads showing along their faces.

Often a viewer captures the overall shape and proportions of the entire target. In the Eiffel Tower example, an accurate sketch might lead the viewer to recognize it and identify it as the Eiffel Tower. Less famous targets might be sketched just as accurately, but not named because the viewer doesn't recognize them.

Despite the impulse to make accurate sketches to prove that one really did "remote view the target," Ingo cautioned us that the ultimate goal of Stage 3 was not necessarily to produce a recognizable likeness of the target, but rather to free up more data. Sketching involves a *kinesthetic* process. Both intentional and unintentional movement of hand and arm muscles bring into play lower, preconscious levels of the mind. In Ingo's theory, kinesthetic involvement through sketching could carry the viewer into tighter, more intimate contact with the signal line, increasing the variety and richness of sensory and dimensional impressions.

That isn't the only benefit to sketching, however. As pen moves across paper, the viewer tries to capture internal impressions about which lines *feel* right in their shape and arrangement on the paper. It can seem as if the subconscious mind speaks through the viewer's hand, through the pen, and onto the paper—speaking not in words, but in inked gestures. Ironically, the SRI research showed that a sketch often accurately reflected important elements of the target, but when the viewer tried to verbally describe and label the sketch, left-brain analysis set in. The viewer's conscious interpretation was often wide of the truth even when the sketch itself turned out to be an accurate depiction of some aspect of the target.

One could think of the viewer as merely a device that detects and translates an incoming signal. Any detection instrument requires an output device to create a record of what is detected, whether a printer mapping the variation in a series of electronic signals or a chart recorder plotting the quaking of a fault line. By this analogy, a remote viewer's "output devices" would be his vocal cords, and a handheld pen. Written and spoken words, and the sketches (and later, three-dimensional models) are the output products. Obviously, the more skillful a remote viewer is with both words and sketching, the more accurate and trouble-free will be the "output." This is, of course, why Ingo stressed the collection of "sense" words for our Stage 2 exercise, and one reason why people with some artistic or drawing skills seem to have an edge when it comes to remote viewing. (The fact that creative arts help develop right-brain cognitive abilities also plays a role.)

I had drawn and painted since before I ever started kindergarten, had been an art major in college for three years, and had even worked as a botanical illustrator for several years. My artistic background started to prove its value in Stage 3. It was liberating to be turned loose with a pen to capture on paper those fleeting impressions and perceptions that were so hard to describe in words. Much as I had enjoyed Stage 2 with its broad spectrum of sensory impressions, entering Stage 3 was like being freed from quicksand. Deep enough into a session, I would suddenly feel the almost irresistible urge to sketch. Uttering one- or two-word sound bites, in fact, speaking itself, was no longer enough; it almost seemed a chore. I became the pen. It was probably my affection for sketching that soon brought on my first major squabble with Ingo.

My first Stage 3 session was the Aswan High Dam in Egypt. Ingo only let me go far enough to achieve aesthetic impact before ending the session. That was his only goal for the day. But there soon followed other targets: Dulles International Airport, Mount Kilimanjaro, San Juan, Puerto Rico, and Kwajalein Atoll, in the South Pacific were just a few examples.

Something strange happened in connection with the Kwajalein site. My sketch was of a radar facility near the airfield that covers much of the island. But along with the angles and framework of the radar, I also sensed the warm sunlight, languid tropical breezes, and swaying greenery. I remember feeling that it was beautiful there.

Ingo was satisfied with the session, and turned me loose for what was left of the afternoon. I walked across town to a bookstore on an errand for my wife. On a discount table I made a great find—a stack of paperback copies of Puthoff and Targ's *Mind Reach*, now out of print, for a dollar apiece.

Before I even got to the store, though, something odd happened. It was nearing the second week of November, and a cold front was blowing through, a accompanied by overcast skies and spitting snow. I walked along the gritty side streets, annoyed that I had left my jacket at the hotel. As a contrast to the scurrying flakes and blustery winds I began to think again of the Kwajalein Atoll target I had done earlier that day. Once again, I began to sense the vaguely present warmth of the sun. I had the memory of clean sand on my toes, of the palm trees and, aroma-rich breeze. Impressions of deep blue, white-capped water fell as a backdrop behind the greenery. It was like a memory, but it drew me in.

Had someone asked, I would have said that I had no illusions that it was "real," no more than if someone asked about a daydream in which I was momentarily lost. But somehow I *did* get lost in it—forgot I wasn't there. I tuned out New York; tuned out the snow, the traffic roar, the smell of exhaust, and the cold sidewalk under my shoes. More and more I embraced the sensations of a tropical island on the opposite side of the planet. And I no longer noticed my feet walking on the sidewalk, but felt instead that I was almost floating.

Then, suddenly, I came back to myself. I could sense my body starting to topple over. I staggered right, fortunately away from the approaching crowds and traffic, but towards an open freight-elevator door yawning in the sidewalk. To save myself from an undignified plunge, I put my hand on the ragged brick of a nearby building. The cold roughness against my hand helped clear my head.

As I puzzled over this odd happening on my way home, copies of *Mind Reach* tucked securely under my arm, I decided I must have experienced "bilocation." Ingo told us that bilocation occurred when a viewer is so caught up in the site, he transfers too much of his awareness there, leaving the rest of himself to manage the best it can.

Some people confuse bilocation in remote viewing with out-of-body experiences, or OBE. But a bilocation doesn't seem at all like leaving the body. If you've ever been with friends and during an idle moment slipped into a daydream and lost all track of what is going on around you, you have experienced something quite similar to bilocation. Often when people are caught up in a daydream, words spoken around them or even directed to them pass by, unnoticed. "Hey, are you *listening* to me?" a friend may need to shout to bring the daydreamer back to reality.

Bilocation happens when the viewer's attention is thoroughly captured by the sensations present at the target. For a time he is focused on the feels, looks, smells, sounds, and overall impressions being carried along on the signal line. The viewer stops "reporting back," stops speaking and writing, and seems almost to be staring off into space, as if digging deep to remember something.

Though people often think bilocation sounds like fun, it should be discouraged in remote viewing. The purpose of remote viewing is to "bring back" information about the target, and if a viewer stops describing or sketching, he is failing in his assignment. But why can't a viewer go along with the bilocation experience, then just report the information afterwards? There are two answers to this. One is that our short-term memories aren't equipped to handle all the data that can be picked up in a remote viewing session. Too much valuable data might be lost. But the second reason is that the whole point of remote viewing is to control as much as possible what is going on. Unfortunately, a bilocation is in one respect all too much like an out-of-body experience, in that the viewer loses all control over where his point of view "goes." To my knowledge there are many claims but no confirmed evidence of anyone controlling an out-of-body experience. The person just ends up wherever the vagaries of the subconscious lead. The same applies to bilocation. Once one is in the bilocation state, one surrenders all control of what is remote viewed. From our perspective as intelligence officers this was useless, and it missed the point altogether. Still, my "visit" to Kwajalein Atoll did provide grist for our conversation mill the following day.

We were wrapping up our final week in New York for November, when I received word that my wife's father had died in a Norfolk, Virginia hospital. A lifelong smoker, he had been ill with emphysema for several years. I remember how sad it was to see fiercely independent "Red" Daffer, a tall, robust jack-of-all-trades, tethered to an oxygen tank and wasting away inch by inch.

Betti had been the only member of the family who had the strength to stay with Red as he struggled for his last few breaths. As her father died, Betti experienced by proxy what could only have been a near-death experience. In some inexplicable way, she accompanied him partway through his transition from this life to the next.

Though I had studied accounts of near-death experiences to see how they might relate to remote viewing, Betti herself had been too caught up in the here and now to pay any attention, until those few poignant moments with her father.

Near-death accounts have grown common with the development of modern medicine. Many people have been brought back from clinical death thanks to miracles wrought by science. Now, since science has created this abundance of near-death reports, it feels duty-bound to explain them. I have heard objections to these accounts from scientists and other skeptics who blame them on an oxygen-starved brain generating fantasy, or an electrical spasm or a seizure in one of the brain's temporal lobes (which have to do with memory and some language skills). Still, NDEs are individually different, yet so distinctly the same that there is something compelling about the many accounts that seem to defy science. It is hardly believable that the richly coherent, emotionally laden experience can be the product of dying brain cells. Mine is a subjective reaction, but it is heavily supported by a well-documented event that took place in an Arizona hospital in 1991, recounted in *Light and Death*, a book by respected NDE researcher Dr. Michael Sabom, M.D.[3]

A thirty-five-year-old woman was about to undergo a dangerous brain operation. The weakened wall of an artery at the base of her brain was in imminent danger of bursting and killing her. Since this aneurism could not safely be removed using conventional surgery, a risky, experimental procedure appeared to be the only hope. In preparation for the operation, the woman's eyes were taped shut, her arms and legs fastened to the table, sound-deadening molded ear inserts were installed, and she was put under general anesthesia. Her head was pinned to the table by a special holding device.

Her blood was shunted through an oxygenation machine which began cooling it, stopping her heart and lungs. Body temperature was dropped to sixty degrees Fahrenheit, well below the threshold where death by hypothermia usually occurs. Then, not only was all the blood in her brain drained out, but all the blood in her *entire body*. Flat line. By any measure, she was clinically dead. The woman's vital processes, or, rather, the absence of them, were monitored throughout the procedure.

Her senses, her body, even her brain were profoundly stilled, yet she witnessed the operation, but not, apparently, from her body lying helplessly strapped and deadened on the table. Instead, she had the experience of emerging from the body and taking a position above and to the side of the action.

From that vantage point she observed, and later remembered and described without prompting, specialized pieces of medical equipment, specific conversations, and details of the actual procedure. As the surgery progressed, and she reached the outer bounds of her body's "death," she found herself going on beyond the operating room. This was the start of a classic near-death experience. She experienced a tunnel-like passageway and, bathed in bright light, soon encountered persons she knew: her grandmother, a cousin, her grandfather. They communicated with her in a way not like speaking, yet she knew what was intended. She was eventually stopped from going further and, as the doctors began to restore her blood, warm her body, and start her heart, she was urged back to her body by the relatives who had greeted her.

What can we make of this? It seems that a highly specific near-death experience occurred in the absence of *any* of the mechanisms proposed by skeptical scientists to explain it. Oxygen deprivation could not have accounted for what she reported—there was no blood supply, hence no oxygen for a good portion of an hour—meaning the woman's brain was well *beyond* being oxygen-deprived to the point of outright oxygen *starvation*. The fact that sensitive brain-monitoring equipment was unable to register even faint activity seems to put in doubt the oxygen-deprivation explanation for at least this

NDE. This latter fact seems to show that the experience could not have been sparked by a temporal lobe seizure, nor any other odd electrical activity in the brain, for that matter. There *was* no electrical activity of any sort detectable in her brain—especially in her sensory centers.

The evidence that the patient had this experience consists only of her report of it. But that she was able to provide accurate visual impressions and the content of spoken statements from a period during which she could not possibly have physically perceived these things seems strong evidence that something outside current scientific understanding occurred.

Many of her near-death perceptions bear considerable resemblance to how remote viewing is experienced, especially in the way she seems to have been able to have perceptions even without the help of the organs usually necessary for just those experiences.

My wife's "near-death" experience by proxy at her father's bedside is fairly rare, but not unheard of. In my research I have come across a smattering of other proxy experiences such as this. Remote viewing may account for what happened there in Red Daffer's hospital room. One would think that it should not be possible to vicariously experience someone else's death. One would think that dying would be the most exclusively private of acts. Yet Betti, and a few others, report an oddly convincing participation in just those intensely personal events. Perhaps close emotional or biological links with a human passing through death make something like this more possible. Maybe, on a few rare occasions, a close emotional link helps activate a pure, innate, unlearned form of the same un-sensing perception that underlies remote viewing.

When that happens, it may then be possible to experience from one's own perspective the bittersweet side of a loved one's passing over from this life to the next. If what happened between father and daughter in that hospital room back in November 1984 can tell us something more about our basic natures as humans, something science cannot yet touch, then perhaps Red's sharing of this last earthly experience with his daughter is a greater gift than either could have imagined in those last few luminous moments.

While I was gathering up our kids at Fort Meade and getting them ready for the trip to Norfolk for Red's funeral, word came through from Marty Hurwitz, head of the General Defense Intelligence Program staff, that it was a bad time to approach Congress about moving Center Lane over to the Defense Intelligence Agency. Thanks to budgetary approvals and intelligence oversight issues for which members of the House and Senate were responsible, Congress had to authorize the transfer. Unfortunately, in Hurwitz's expert judgment, the political climate was a little shaky for our advocates on the Hill, and raising the program's visibility by prematurely introducing the transfer issue could prove disastrous.

Someone would have to convince INSCOM to hold on to Center Lane's people for awhile. Instead of a full transfer, the proposal was for INSCOM to pass on to DIA only operational control of the unit for a year or so. In effect, DIA would give us our marching orders, but INSCOM would still "own" us. We had no real choice in the matter; the decision whether to take this option rested far above our lowly position in the military food chain. But we were not happy with it. In the current climate, the longer the Army had us under its thumb, the greater the chance that something could go wrong with the transfer plan and Center Lane would wither on the vine. Still, the arrangement would renew our stay of execution into the foreseeable future, and was thus far better than some of the more frightening alternatives.

This delay wasn't the only bad news. I also learned that Ingo had locked horns with Jim Salyer one time too many. At Salyer's insistence, SRI was considering dropping Ingo from its program. Since Ingo was operating as a consultant, they couldn't fire him, but that is what it amounted to. Ingo thought it looked very likely that SRI would terminate its contract with him, and not send any more his way. It seemed short-sighted; without Ingo, the SRI remote viewing program would never have gotten started in the first place. In fact, he was responsible for many of the breakthroughs that had been made. In a real way he was a goose that laid golden eggs, and thanks to Salyer they were about to have him for dinner.

The pressure was starting to tell. When we walked into the SRI office suite in New York, the first order of business was for Ed to get another dressing down from Ingo about various "crimes" committed during recent remote viewing training. For some reason, Ingo included Bill in this particular chewing out as well.

But there were also other problems. Ingo had been trying to teach us a new sketching technique he had developed within the past few weeks that he called "analytic" sketching. The idea was to write down all the dimensional impressions gleaned through the course of the session up to Stage 3. Based on the order in which the words occurred in the session, the viewer tries to make a sketch. If impressions such as "curving up, tall, wide, slanting, rounded, crisscrossing, tapering . . ." and so on were produced during the session, lines are drawn to represent the concepts, and these are juggled around in hopes of coming up with a sketch that works.

It was a very left-brain, linear approach, and I hated it. I could see where it might be useful if one stumbled into the remote viewing equivalent of writer's block and needed something to jump-start more spontaneous sketching. But I was having such good luck with the more intuitive approach Ingo had originally taught us for Stage 3 that I found this "analytic" technique not only to be a burden, but to seriously interfere with my viewing. Ingo nevertheless insisted that I use it in a number of Stage 3 training sessions, with me silently fuming as I bounced back and forth from one half-baked representation to another.

Then came the falling out. During the prior few weeks we had spent at Fort Meade, I had done a series of good Stage 3 sessions, with Fred Atwater as my monitor. Fred had asked me to take them up to New York for Ingo to see, I supposed with the aim of showing Ingo that his students were making good progress and were able to execute successful remote viewings, even outside the SRI fold. Lieutenant Colonel Buzby agreed to let me show the session transcripts to Ingo, but for reasons I never quite understood ordered me not to let him make copies of them.

I proudly drew them out of my briefcase and displayed them for my teacher. As I had hoped he was very pleased at my success. Then things took a nasty turn. Ingo said he wanted to make copies to send to Hal Puthoff for inclusion in the final SRI report on our training. I hesitated before answering. It was a painful situation to be in. The instructor I respected so much was making what seemed to me to be a reasonable request. Not only that, but it was flattering to think that my work might end up as a significant addition to the final report. On the other hand, if I agreed to let Ingo make copies, I would be disobeying the direct order of my commanding officer. I had to tell Ingo that I was forbidden to let him have copies. Ingo's face fell, and I could see he was growing angry. When he demanded to know why, I told him about Buzby's order, though I couldn't explain the why of it. In a pique, Ingo stormed out of the office, without even running Bill or Charlene on their targets for the day.

We were stunned and at a loss for what to do. I think we all understood how Ingo was feeling. Not only was he worried about the possible end of his relationship with SRI and the threat to the government remote viewing program, but he was also anticipating a medical procedure he would undergo the following week which, though relatively minor, involved surgery and recuperation, and the prospect made him anxious. But I couldn't help wondering if I had unconsciously communicated my own frustration and irritation at Ingo's sketching process as well. Whatever the case, we hoped Ingo would be better disposed tomorrow.

When we gathered the next day, December 5, Ingo had recovered his composure, and we managed to get through the day's training with no significant incidents. Everyone was walking on eggshells, feeling uneasy about the confrontation of the day before. For what turned out to be my final training target with Ingo I was given the coordinates for Devil's Tower in Wyoming.

Once again, Ingo insisted I use his new sketching methodology. I ended up with a passable sketch, though I believed by the end of the session that, had I been left to the more intuitive approach Ingo had originally taught us, my sketch would have been more accurate, and I probably would even have recognized the site as Devil's Tower. But I let the thought go.

When we each had done a session, Ingo gathered us together to say that he'd had a long talk with Jim Salyer the night before, and that Salyer had summarily told Ingo that he was through. We tried to reassure Ingo that Salyer might not have that authority. Jim Salyer worked for DIA, and was serving as that agency's contract monitor. However, Army major command was the official budgeting authority for the current SRI contracts, and Salyer was serving at their behest. He could only fire Ingo if that Army command authorized it. Still, for the moment we had to admit things didn't look particularly good. (Salyer *was*, in fact, eventually overruled.)

Ingo then asked us to pay attention for what he declared was to be his "goodbye" lecture. My notes and memory of this are a little sparse, but a couple of things came through clearly. He first told us that if we intended to use his remote-viewing system, we should use it as he had taught us or not at all. Further, altering terminology and definitions of what he had given us would be in his own words an "unacceptable change." It was clear he would brook no tinkering with the remote viewing methodology he had taught us. He well knew that people would be tempted to try to "improve upon" or "expand" on what he and Hal had developed. He also knew that such attempts would seldom be motivated by solidly grounded research findings, but usually by what the people making changes simply "thought" was best, or extrapolated from their subjective experience. This would lead, he assured us, to a form of "AOL Drive" that would hopelessly corrupt any such home-made system.

Over time I have come to realize that Ingo didn't always take his own advice. Sometimes he let his own interpretations and notions tempt him to add embellishments to the research. I have a suspicion, for instance, that analytic sketching was one of these embellishments. Nevertheless, Ingo and Hal still deserve credit for doing more than anyone else to develop and promote a remote viewing methodology that was not just effective, but transferable. No longer was the field left only to "talents" or "naturals," while the rest of unwashed humanity could merely long for a touch of the "magic." Now nearly anyone willing to take on the commitment to train and practice and work stood a good chance of becoming a successful remote viewer.

Ingo's final lecture point emphasized that "not reading the data will collapse the system." After all these years the phrase remains a little mysterious to me. Even recently, consulting with Bill and Charlene did not help to clarify it. The closest we came to Ingo's meaning was this: not learning to differentiate between signal line and noise, and then rejecting the signal as noise, would cause the remote-viewing system he taught us to fail. Many times during the coming years, we were to discover how true that was.

As we boarded the train at Penn Station one last time for the trip homeward, I found myself thinking about what a long, strange year it had been, and wondering what would come next. Not being sure that I would ever see him again, I knew that I would miss interacting with the fascinating Ingo Swann. I was unaware that our paths would continue to cross far into the future.

19

1985

... one man's limbo is another man's purgatory ...

As 1984 faded into 1985, Center Lane's operational tally reflected the turmoil of the past twelve months. There were only seven projects on the books in 1984, and the first of those was canceled by the client before any work was done (that happened occasionally, just as it did in other intelligence disciplines, usually with no explanation from the original requestor). The six remaining were evenly split between the CIA, NSA, and SED—Systems Exploitation Division, the organization to which Ed Dames belonged. These latter two projects were requested by Dames himself.[1]

Although the people assigned to Center Lane had done literally hundreds of remote viewing sessions in 1984, the majority of the sessions were for training only. A mere thirty-three had been real-world operations, and these were done almost exclusively by Joe McMoneagle before he retired. Training was essential, but it didn't help the unit's bottom line. When we viewers-in-training were ready, we hoped we could turn that around. But it didn't look like we would accomplish that anytime during 1985.

Once the Christmas 1984 holidays were over, the first order of business was to continue the training of Bill, Charlene, and me beyond Stage 3. This proceeded slower than we would have liked because of all the administrative work that had to be done. In what we took as a sort of a Christmas present but which was certainly not intended as such, General Soyster had agreed just before the holidays to put the transfer to DIA on hold and "detail" us to the agency instead. Hopefully, by the end of the coming year Congress would be in a better mood.[2]

Paperwork had to be drafted, edited, and redrafted several times to make this temporary arrangement official. During the next twelve months we also would have to create the documents that would formalize the final transfer itself, which would not occur until the opening days of 1986. The whole process was bureaucratically complex, and it frequently interrupted our remote viewing training throughout most of 1985.

Still, we launched enthusiastically into our advanced training, splitting our time between it and the tangles of red tape. We were through the Stage 4 lectures and essay-writing by the time January was half over, and I had my first Stage 4 session on January 17. With Ingo out of the picture, Fred Atwater and Tom McNear were now our teachers, drawing on what they had learned from Swann.

I instantly loved this part of remote viewing. I got to keep doing my sketching, but now also had permission to be specific in my verbal responses. Where before we would only *describe* our impressions—"an object that is smooth, red, shiny, with black round rubbery things"—we were now allowed to identify our perceptions—a red car—with fair confidence we would be right. By the time a viewer reached Stage 4, we were told, the aperture was wide enough and available data sufficient to allow cautious use of nouns and other concept-words that earlier would have been too analytical to be trusted.

For Stage 4 we were taught to create what was called a Stage 4 Matrix across the top of the session transcript paper, dividing the page into vertical columns. Appropriate impressions received during the remote viewing process could be recorded under category headings. This helped organize the data so we didn't have to remember or think too hard about it, and it also gave the left brain something to do that kept it busy sorting data instead of creating analytical overlay.

My first Stage 4 session was the Stanford Linear Accelerator, a narrow, mile-long structure with an oblong, several-story building at one end, designed for researching subatomic physics. Though during the session I had many technically related AOLs that I disposed of as I had been taught, I received many other signal line impressions relating to electrical components, electronic equipment, power, even nuclear energy. When compared with the feedback afterwards, my sketches strongly resembled various aspects of the buildings. I even drew what looked like a power transformer with insulators projecting from the top. The session ended when I produced a verbal AOL description of "particle energy beam generator" and declared the target to be a cyclotron, an atom smasher. It was an encouraging start to Stage 4.

By the time I reached my final Stage 4 training session six weeks later, I had about a dozen and a half of these targets under my belt. They weren't all successes, but many were: a science museum; a geothermal power facility; a health spa and mineral baths in Europe; and the Black Virgin of Montserrat, for which I produced a reasonably accurate sketch of the castle, a rough outline of some statuary, and impressions of a religious procession and the Virgin Mary.

The geothermal power plant site was The Geysers, in California. My viewing of it produced impressions such as:

> [L]ocated in a hilly area with . . . a definitely "California" feel . . . consists of various buildings and structures, both tall and low . . . composed of cement and stonework; rectangular. Hot, rushing, roaring, venting, bubbling water is present. Mineral smells, pipes and pipe-related apparatus, like valves are present. Hot springs and geysers are strongly suggested. The area "looks like" a battlefield.[3]

I recorded an impression of "Geothermal powerplant" on page twelve of the transcript. The feedback photo that I was shown afterwards did indeed look like a battlefield, with clouds of steam spewing from a dozen different locations across the landscape, and pipes and equipment strewn over the rolling hills.

By early March, we were finished with Stage 4 and moving into Stage 5 lectures. Tom and Fred explained to us that Stage 5 was in principle different from every other CRV stage. Stage 5 didn't involve the signal line; the viewer was "off-line," so to speak. Instead, we learned to mine the treasure trove of data that already had piled up in the subconscious during the previous four stages. Conceptually, it was simple. The remote viewing signal line carrying data into the subconscious imprinted this information on the viewer's neural circuitry during the earlier stages of the session. Concepts and impressions that did make it into our conscious awareness were often pasted-together composites of this subconscious information. A viewer may, for example, have declared "factory" as a perception in Stage 4. But what she had subconsciously perceived may have been hot, molten metal in vats, men with hard hats, loud rumbling noises, heavy equipment, and the feeling that something was being manufactured here. These subliminal perceptions were then expressed as one word, "factory." In the Stage 5 process, we novice viewers learned to extract the details still hiding in our subconscious that had registered in Stage 4 as "factory."

To illustrate, return again to the Eiffel Tower example. In Stage 1 the viewer detects that the target is a structure. Stage 2 reveals that structure to be black, metallic, cool, bumpy, hard, tall, and pointed. Stage 3 shows that it tapers to the top and is made of crisscrossing elements that have open space between them. A good Stage 4 treatment will go on to reveal that the site involves tourism, is located in a parklike setting in an urban area, is not in the United States (the notion of "French" might even crop up), and has a restaurant associated with it.

In Stage 5, the viewer might decide to see what more could be discovered about "tourism." Going through the steps for Stage 5 the viewer could then bring to her conscious mind the ideas that originally caused her to say "tourism." These could be impressions such as "camera," "sightseeing," "visitors," "souvenir," "people wearing Bermuda shorts," etc.

Obviously, there is more art than science to this process. One often has only intuition as a guide when deciding on a particular Stage 4 word to flesh out in Stage 5. And the viewer must be very careful to discriminate between legitimate impressions and other words the left brain might conjure up on its own as AOL. There are safeguards built into the Stage 5 technique, but they are not foolproof. Viewer skill and experience are still crucial factors in using this technique successfully.

The practice targets I worked during this part of the training were diverse: a broadcasting center in Moscow, the Khyber Pass between Pakistan and India, a forest fire in Oregon, the Suez Canal, a large railroad yard behind the Iron Curtain, the George Washington Bridge in New York City, the Cappadocia monasteries in Turkey.

One of my more compelling sessions was Ground Zero at Hiroshima, Japan, at the moment the atomic bomb detonated. My ideogram was a line that curled around and around and around in a roughly cloudlike shape. I didn't remember having had an ideogram like that before, and it puzzled me. My impressions were of red-and-orange colors intermingled with brown and grey. My sketches showed large, amorphous, swirling forms. I had perceptions of hot, sulfur smells.

"Site involves a swirling, roiling, billowing substance that is voluminous, extensive, and encompassing," I wrote in my session transcript. "Various temperatures are manifest here, as well as some relatively noxious chemical smells. The site seems to involve extensive fire and flames, producing smoke smells, charring, and sooty tastes." In a telling comment I went on, "No people are perceived here. Structures seem to be secondary to the site, or even irrelevant." In the end, I had an AOL of Mount St. Helens—the volcano in the American Northwest that blew its top more than thirty years after Hiroshima was devastated.

Despite such drama, I found Stage 5 less enjoyable than Stage 4. It seemed to verge on the kind of left-brain analysis that we had been warned against. While I could see the value of Stage 5—a value borne out for me in many of my training sessions—by the time Stage 6 training came around I was ready to move on.

About this time I was assigned to help my colleagues develop their drawing skills. Since sketching was an important channel for "downloading" remote-viewing information from the subconscious, the better a remote viewer could draw, the more clear and accurate the resulting data could be.

In some cases improving my fellow viewers' skills wasn't too difficult; some had previous drawing or other artistic experience. But Charlene and Bill, particularly, couldn't seem to "draw their way out of a paper bag," as Bill was proud to say. I found that my own art training wasn't much use. I had learned sketching and drawing techniques so many years before that I could not remember how I had done it. At any rate, it had taken me years to reach the skill level I was at, and I only had a relatively short time to bring my student artists up to snuff.

I turned to a book I had discovered a year or so earlier, *Drawing on the Right Side of the Brain,* by Betty Edwards. Edwards had developed an approach for teaching people to draw that, as far as I could tell, was unique at the time. Instead of the traditional rote, trial-and-error approach where students were expected to make drawing after drawing until they finally "got it right," she took advantage of the recent discoveries from the split-brain research of psychologist Roger Sperry and others about brain-hemispheric functioning.

As I mentioned in earlier chapters, much of this information had already independently made its way into remote viewing research, so I had a passing acquaintance with it. But Betty Edwards used split-brain findings to streamline the process of learning to sketch. Since it is the right hemisphere that excels at pattern and shape recognition, and plays a major role in hand-eye coordination, she developed exercises that trained people in right-hemisphere perception.

In art as in remote viewing the left brain can sometimes interfere in undesirable ways, so the book stresses drawing what you see, not what you *think* you see. In a number of ways Betty Edwards's principles for drawing paralleled what we learned from Ingo Swann about dealing with left-brain interference in remote viewing. So, besides being an easy and effective way to learn good drawing and sketching skills, *Drawing on the Right Side of the Brain* reinforced what we had already learned in our own pursuit of remote viewing.

A few afternoons a week we would meet in the conference room in the back of building T-2561 to discuss Betty Edwards's lessons. I would then assign my reluctant students exercises from the book. They griped like teenagers, but they did it. Once they had made enough progress, I began to give them trickier things to draw—a portrait of me (I couldn't get anyone else to sit still long enough to model); an oddly shaped metal widget I found lying around; I even took the label off a soft-drink bottle, tore it into long strips, and stuffed it into the bottle, then made them draw that, trying to capture the look of paper strips seen through glass.

Eventually I set Charlene and Bill and the others the task of drawing a rumpled paper bag, a feat that both of them handled much better than they possibly could have a few weeks before. They not only succeeded in drawing their way *out* of a paper bag—they were actually able to draw a passable portrait *of* one. The graduates of my impromptu course were still not perfect draftsmen, but they had learned much that was useful to them.

The point of these exercises was not to teach them how to capture difficult subjects with lines on paper. It was instead to force them to prove to themselves that by using correct principles they could draw anything. With patience, skill, and the right mind-set there was no such thing as a "hard" subject to sketch. This was the same principle we learned about remote viewing. Once we had mastered the skills, all targets were equal as far as the perceptual process was concerned.

February marked another important event in our lives as newly minted remote viewers. We worked our first official operational project—the only one the unit would run during all of 1985. On February 7 a federal Drug Enforcement Agency operative named Enrique Camarena was kidnaped from a parking lot in El Paso, Texas, as he was going to meet his wife for lunch. Camarena had spent five years working undercover in Guadalajara, Mexico, a place noted for its high level of police corruption. One or more of these crooked cops were thought to be involved in either betraying Camarena to the kidnapers, or aiding them, or both.

When it became clear not long after his disappearance that conventional means might not find him in time, someone from the DEA with some knowledge about the remote viewing program contacted our head office and asked for help. Fred Atwater found himself with the same quandary he had wrestled with once before—an emergency remote viewing project where time was of the essence, and an office full of neophyte remote viewers whose mettle had not yet been tested in the real world. But as with the missing A-6E project our predecessors had worked six years before, there didn't seem to be any other alternative, so he put us to work.

With Fred as the monitor, Bill was working the target when I arrived at the office, and I had to wait until the two of them emerged from the operations building. Years later Bill gave this account of his experience:

> I was at home, when I received Fred's telephone call. His instructions were terse: "Meet me at the office, and don't watch the news." I walked over to the office and saw Charlene's Camaro parked in front of the building. The main building was empty, so I waited. I felt that I had done well in training, but this was *real*.

Bill was feeling trepidations about working a "live" remote viewing project for the first time, and his thoughts and feelings echoed those that the rest of us were having.

> The Army was expecting me to do something which any idiot knew was impossible. I had the feeling I got before a boxing match when I used to compete. What if I made a complete fool of myself? Thinking of Ingo's voice reminding me to stick to the remote viewing structure he taught us gave my confidence a much needed boost.

He then described the experience:

> Charlene came in from the operational building looking tired and a bit drained, but gratified. I made some witty remark to show her I was calm and self-confident about working operational sites, while all the time inside my stomach two armies of butterflies were locked in a death struggle. I avoided asking her how it went, as I did not want to do anything to put more AOL in my future. Fred came in with a folder in his hand, and Charlene left for home after wishing me good luck.
>
> Fred and I went to the operations building and the session began. I do not recall all the specific details, but I remember that once I got into the session, all anxiety and doubt were gone as I focused on the remote viewing structure and on decoding the signal line. I had the feeling I nailed the target but that could be hind-sight, looking back now over fifteen years in the past. My Stage 3 sketch was one of my most detailed efforts I had ever had to that point. I drew a hacienda, an adobe-type building. There was a windmill and a dry, isolated area with mountains in the distance.[4]

When Bill finished, it was my turn. Once I was given the coordinates, I remember going forward like any other CRV session of the many I had done for training over the prior fourteen months. Ideogram, identify the gestalt; move to Stage 2 and decode the sensory elements. In Stage 3, I began sketching a two-story building, with the second floor slightly overhanging on one side. The windows were rowed across the top, but there seemed fewer of them in the first floor. I felt there was another structure just to the side, leaving a narrow passage between. There was maybe a European flavor to the setting, but only just a hint. A few trees were present but did not allay the vague impressions of a landscape that was austere, and too arid to be Europe. I remembered an odd feeling. Not one of fear, but something akin to it. I was not sure if that was something coming from inside myself, or an emotion I was getting from the target.

A few days later, the evening news brought the only feedback we ever got. Camarena and his former pilot had been found tortured and murdered. It turned out later the corrupt Guadalajara police had staged a raid on an isolated farmhouse in Guadalajara, assassinated the innocent family, and planted the bodies of Camarena and the pilot to deflect suspicions from themselves. And there, as the story unfolded on NBC, for a few seconds I saw video of the building that I had drawn in my session. My remote viewing had been accurate, but not specific enough to tip off those searching for the missing DEA agent. Even if it had been, the authorities would have found Camarena already dead, since evidence later showed he had been murdered somewhere else and moved to that place.

In the end, like the A-6E project done by our compatriots years before, our work went for naught. Our results were sent in too late, and they were not precise enough. But it was our baptism by fire, and I experienced for the first, but not the last time, the sickly shock of seeing news reports of the violent death of someone I had only a few hours before tried to find, and in some cases even made emotional contact with.

As second-in-command, Bill Ray, now patiently awaiting his promotion to major, often had to fill in when Brian Buzby was somewhere else. On one of these occasions, in early February, Bill was assigned to brief James Ambrose, the undersecretary of the Army. Bill was to be accompanied by a glowering General Odom, Stubblebine's (and remote viewing's) nemesis.

"I was of mixed emotions," Bill said when he later told me about this event. "I felt torn between the loyalty I was expected to feel for Odom, the senior intelligence general in the Army, and my loyalty to the remote viewing project and the people in it." Bill was supposed to meet with Odom at 1 P.M. to give the general an overview of what was to be briefed to the undersecretary. Odom perfunctorily waved Bill off until 2:45, expressing no interest whatsoever when Bill offered him a quick overview of the briefing's content. Bill said, "Odom and Ambrose played the 'who is most important and who will wait on whom' game, so the meeting didn't finally begin until about 3:15.

> As the two of us entered Ambrose's office, I realized that Odom was not actually in my chain of command, so I might just as well treat this as the adversarial meeting it really was. But it turned out more surreal than confrontive. It felt like I was in a Kafka short story. Odom gave a short introduction, said some semi-nice words about us [the people in Center Lane]. He emphasized that remote viewing "had not been scientifically proved," and then said it was time for the remote viewing project to move on.

Ambrose seemed to be playing the same game, assuring Bill that both Odom and Ambrose "were physicists and dealt in hard facts." This latter bit was puzzling to Bill, who was unaware of any academic background either actually had in physics. Maybe instead Ambrose had meant the word "physicalist," signifying someone who believed that everything mental could be explained by physical forces.

"Here we had a three-star general and the number-two civilian in the Army on one side, and a not-quite-promoted [to major] captain on the other. But I was the only Irishman in the room, so I figured the odds were even."

Bill had brought letters of endorsement from a number of Center Lane's clients in the intelligence community. These were from Jack Vorona at DIA; NSA's chief technologist, Dr. Scott; Deputy Director of the CIA John McMahon; and a number of letters from intelligence-collection offices within the Army. The FBI had sent a verbal endorsement along, but failed to provide anything in writing.

Bill showed these letters to Ambrose as evidence that Center Lane's intelligence product was considered a valuable asset to a number of leading figures in the community. Odom's response was that "the letters were meaningless because the agencies would write anything so they could keep access to the remote viewing project. That did not necessarily mean that remote viewing was actually valuable."

"Why would these people lie to maintain access to something that was not worth anything?" Bill responded. As the only answer, "Odom glared and Ambrose ignored the question," Bill remembers. His last remaining option was to pull out the "Red Book" and show Ambrose some of the impressive operational remote-viewing results it contained.

I showed Ambrose the [work] Joe had done on the Typhoon subma-rine. Odom explained it away as useless because they had been able to verify the submarine's existence six months later by other intelligence means, which proved there was no need for the remote viewing proj-ect. I then showed something for which we had been the sole intelli-gence source. Odom said that was invalid because they had not been able to verify it by other means. I pointed out that if the rules really were that intelligence was useless if it was later verified by other means, but also useless if it could *not* later be verified, then *no* intelligence-collection tool was worthwhile.

"I was simply *shocked*," Bill said in mock surprise, "when Ambrose decided to certify moving the project out of the Army. I do think he felt guilty, though, since he agreed to give us all the time we needed to find a new home." This granting of extra breathing room sparked another glare from Odom. It may have helped that Bill was able to show Ambrose a number of other impressive results contained in the Red Book. But at the end of forty-five minutes Bill found himself escorting Odom back to the general's office, anticipating further instructions. There weren't any.[5]

People often ask me why, if, despite its flaws, remote viewing works as well as I and my colleagues claim, does the government not use it as an intelligence-collection means any more? The reactions demonstrated in Bill's encounter with Ambrose and Odom illustrate one of the main reasons remote viewing was ultimately eliminated. It had much more to do with the attitudes of many senior leaders and managers in the military and govern-ment bureaucracies than any lack of effectiveness of remote viewing.

In his highly regarded history of the National Security Agency, *Body of Secrets*, James Bamford describes General Odom as "an arch-conservative military hard-liner," who was "stern, abrasive, and humorless." In the seven-ties Odom became a protege of Zbigniew Brzezinski, President Jimmy Carter's national security advisor, in the process earning the nickname "Zbig's Super-Hawk." Appointed to be director of NSA only a few weeks after his meeting with Bill Ray and Undersecretary Ambrose, Odom was, according to Bamford, "widely disliked at NSA and was considered by many the most ineffective director in the agency's history." At the same time he was passed over for promotion to a fourth star, the Joint Chiefs of Staff voted unanimously not to extend Odom's term of service as NSA's director.[6] In ret-rospect, Odom's attitude toward something as out of the ordinary as remote viewing should have been no surprise.

Sometime in the summer we started teaching Lyn Buchanan the principles of coordinate remote viewing. According to a note in my journal from that time, I graded Lyn's Stage 2 essay on August 30, 1985. As I remember it (and Bill Ray confirms), the task fell mostly to Fred and me, though Tom, Bill, and Charlene contributed as well. Even Ed Dames helped when he was later assigned to the unit. My most important role was to present the lectures for remote-viewing theory, structure, and stages, though I also monitored Lyn on a number of his training sessions. While Buchanan's training was progressing, we also had other things going on. One of these was mastering Stage 6.

20

Stage 6

. . . close encounters . . .

Picture Richard Dreyfuss in *Close Encounters of the Third Kind,* sculpting Devil's Tower out of a mountain of mashed potatoes. That was Stage 6— creating a physical model of a target in three dimensions, although our medium of choice was clay instead of food.

We started our lectures for Stage 6 in September with Fred Atwater and Tom McNear teaching us everything they had gleaned from Ingo Swann. Stage 6 drew on what we already knew about setting up a matrix of columns on the transcript paper to help manage the rush of data that the ever-expanding aperture brought. But, as we had progressed through learning each stage, we were developing an expanding appreciation for the dimensional qualities of the target. Now, in Stage 6, we would move beyond words and sketches to develop a three-dimensional feel for the site, which in this case could actually be *expressed* in three-dimensional space.

The point was not necessarily to make an accurate representation of the target. If the clay model turned out to look a lot like the site, that was wonderful and rewarding. But the goal was to bring the viewer into even greater kinesthetic contact with the signal line, thus freeing more and increasingly accurate information for access by conscious awareness. Ideally, the viewer ended up with both good data and an impressive model. But good data was what we were primarily after.

Even before learning Stage 6 myself I was given an assignment in the training process. I was to teach a class on sculpture to my fellow intelligence officers, a challenge that seemed even more incongruous than teaching them to sketch. Nevertheless, I hopped-to, collecting modeling clay and an assortment of sculpting tools.

On September 10, 1985, those of us learning Stage 6 gathered in the conference room to learn how to mold and carve clay into shapes and forms. It's a shame that no one thought to take a photo of us sitting around the table rolling, kneading, and poking the oily grey modeling clay into various configurations as I directed. Bill Ray thought that the Army motto of "Be all that you can be" was being pushed to new extreme.

On October 16 I had my first Stage 6 session. I was surprised with how it turned out. After I wrote down the coordinates, perceptions flooded in that eventually gelled into a number of undefinable objects in a secluded area. My sketch of one of these objects strongly resembled a low pillar or monument. Along with this information came an uncanny aesthetic impact (AI); I had a feeling about this target that I would "just as soon stay away from it." This was accompanied by a "guarded feeling." An emotion-tinged AOL came next, "like some latent danger I don't want to disturb."

The target came across as some kind of artifact that brought an ill-defined sense of power or energy with it, plus another AI of "weird feeling about this place." I soon discovered that there was a person connected with the target who was in some way affiliated with mystical things, with elements of "reverential," and "ancient." Another AI written on my session transcript is a cryptic phrase, "deep into the universe." In using Stage 5 for the word "person," I turned up "worship, honor, instruction, initiation, separated off, occultic." Going through the same process with the word "mystical" resulted in "life, death, people, philosophy, religion, society, behavior, formulae." The word "monument" yielded "commemoration, remembrance, symbology, focusing, time anchor, and centerpiece." As I recorded in my concluding summary:

> [The] site is situated in an area away by itself, is somewhat secluded, and has many rows or patterns of similar objects . . . One object is central in import, and serves as a monument, the focus of much spiritual and/or mystical interest. A sense of esoteric teaching is present, with the idea of small groups being instructed as to elements involving philosophy, religion, society, behavior, etc.—though people generally don't frequent this location. This "monument" has been set aside as a

commemoration or memorial, perhaps for a specific individual who seems in some sense to have been a mystical or spiritual "leader."

I tried to perceive phonetic sounds associated with the target, but the best I could do was "wuh" or "woo." Then I made a clay model of the central object. My sculpture had a square, solid base and it tapered towards a flat top. It was blocky and squat, but clearly geometrical in form. For some reason I scribbled the word "urn" under one of the blurry Polaroid photos taken as a record of my clay model.

At the end I looked up at Fred, who had been my monitor for the past two hours and five minutes. He had an amused expression on his face and asked me rhetorically, "Who is buried in Grant's tomb?" Then he gave me my feedback.

The target was Edgar Allan Poe's grave marker in the Westminster Burying Ground in Baltimore. The feedback picture shows it sitting on a square base, with sides that taper upward. Unlike my model, it had a slightly peaked top. The whole monument was about five or six feet tall, and bordered by neat rows of other gravestones. Later, I often passed by it on trips through Baltimore. If you look carefully when turning the corner on Green Street, you can catch a glimpse of the monument through the wrought-iron fence that surrounds the graveyard.

As the author of "The Raven," "The Pit and the Pendulum," "The Murders in the Rue Morgue," and other classics of the occult, the macabre, and the supernatural, it seemed that Poe in real life was not too far afield from my remote viewing description of him. In death, his legend has certainly grown to fit. For an early foray into Stage 6, my Poe session seemed to have been a reasonable "hit." Somehow, though, I missed the half-empty bottle of cognac and the three red roses left at the grave every year on Poe's birthday by some mysterious visitor.

Other successful Stage 6 sessions I had over the coming months included a set of reconstructed villages of Indians native to Oklahoma; the Thorne miniature rooms in the Dulin Gallery of Art in Knoxville, from which I received accurate impressions of many small, intricate artifacts dealing with American history; and Fenwick Island Lighthouse. My session summary for this latter target went as follows:

Site is an island occupied by a structure or structures, one of which is tall, cylindrical, hollow, isolated, with red, white, and silvery colors, and involves a ladder, lights, bales, wires, radiated energy (perhaps radio); environment is breezy, hazy, with bird sounds. Purpose of the structure appears to be warning or guarding. Strongly suggestive of a lighthouse concept.

My Stage 6 clay model depicted a tall, cylindrical structure with a platform around its crown. I remember not being at all surprised by the feedback of "lighthouse" when it finally came.

I was so taken with this target that on a vacation trip with my children to the Eastern Shore of Delaware, I took them to visit the lighthouse. The Fenwick Light turned out not exactly to be on an island, but surrounded by houses and trees. The original target feedback Fred had given me after my session had not included a picture, so I was glad to see that the lighthouse really did look much like my remote viewing impressions of it.

In the course of our family visit we met the Pickles, a married couple in their eighties, still going strong and full of optimism. The unofficial historians of the lighthouse, the Pickles had lived in its shadow for most of their lives. They were a wellspring of interesting details that riveted the children's interest far longer than their young attention spans usually allowed.

Being gone for two weeks out of every month that we had been assigned to Fort Meade during our training, we had not been able to settle in to any kind of a routine at the office. Now we had plenty of opportunity. We had all grown accustomed to civilian clothes, and seeing anyone in the office wearing a uniform—as Brian Buzby often did when making official calls at the Pentagon or Capitol Hill—was always a bit of a surprise.

The plainclothes thing had even led to one amusing encounter with an Army recruiter, a sergeant first class I sat next to once on the train coming home from New York. He tried to sell me on stopping by his office sometime to see if I measured up for an Army career. Since I was supposed to be traveling incognito, I tried my best to feign ignorance of such Army acronyms as "TDY" for temporary duty, which was the status I was in at the time of the encounter, or "MOS," for military occupational specialty, the label for whatever career field a soldier was trained in. When we parted company at the train station, I wondered what the sergeant would say should we accidentally bump into each other the next day at the Fort Meade Post Exchange store.

A typical day at the remote viewing unit started when we straggled in about 8 A.M. Jeannie, our secretary, was usually one of the first to arrive and dial open the heavy Sargent and Greenleaf combination padlock that secured our front door. By 8:15 we were usually all there. Lyn had the farthest to drive—about seventy miles each way from his home in rural Maryland southeast of Washington. Charlene had a commute down from Baltimore along the Baltimore-Washington Parkway. The rest of us lived almost within walking distance of the office. Bill did walk, in fact, strolling along Buckner

Avenue, wearing his trademark fedora hat and thoughtfully puffing on his ever-present pipe. Since I often had to ferry my kids to doctor appointments or babysitters before or after work, I usually drove.

For remote viewing, I had also settled into a routine of sorts. Because I had grown accustomed to "cooling down" to a Monroe Institute Hemi-Sync tape before doing sessions in the months prior to taking remote-viewing training with Ingo Swann, I had come to value those few minutes of peaceful relaxation before going into the remote viewing room to work. My well-worn pattern went something like this: about twenty minutes before my session was due to start, I would walk over to the operations building and stretch out on the bed in the ERV room. I would then drowse in the darkness while listening through headphones to music I had recorded on cassette tapes.

I preferred a mix of music. There was heavy metal (I was especially fond of the band AC/DC). But I included some country-western in the mix, as well as New Age, pop, and even some classical. The key wasn't the *style* of music; what was important was how it made me feel. I wanted something that was invigorating and energizing. At the time, I never thought it through. Just a few years ago, though, I finally realized what I was doing. I was giving myself the musical equivalent of a pregame pep talk.

When most remote viewers launch into a session, there is always the subtle angst about whether they will succeed *this* time. It doesn't matter how many outstanding sessions a viewer has done in the past, there is always the worry that *this* one will be a failure. We were, after all, being asked on a daily basis to do something that our society had drummed into us as being impossible, or even foolish. It was only natural that we should suffer from a chronic case of performance anxiety. I know I did, anyway. So even though I would say, "I'm going over to the other building to 'cool down' for my session," I wasn't really cooling down; I was gearing up. And it worked. I often still use that tactic if I'm about to launch into an especially challenging operational remote-viewing session. But these days I tell my students not to bother with "cooling down," themselves, since people can remote view perfectly well without it, and once you develop the habit, it is hard to break.

There was one other benefit to my music. It gave me a chance to sneak a little catnap, which I often sorely needed. Even with Guns n' Roses blaring in my ears, or the beat of a folksy Emmylou Harris hit keeping tempo with my pulse, I could still snooze for a few moments, taking a power nap on government time. Way too often though, I would be shocked awake.

The first time it happened, I thought I'd been visited by a ghost. It was pitch dark in the room, no one else was around, and I was zoning out on the bed, my arm lightly dangling off the edge. Suddenly I was bolt upright, my hand still tingling from a startling electrical jolt. At first I thought I had been the butt of some joke, but it was soon clear no one else was around. I was thoroughly mystified.

After a few of these incidents, I poked and prodded about the room, finally discovering the culprit. Fred had placed an ancient negative-ion generator in the room, near the head of the bed, presumably to clean the air of particles. It must have been doing a decent job of that, because the wall-length baseboard heater it stood next to had a corona of black specks embedded in the paint around where the device was standing. The little generator would apparently charge the metal, which then attracted dust particles from the air. These then fused to the paint on the heater's surface.

It explained my sudden shock. The ion generator built up a charge in its immediate vicinity. When my hand dangled too close, a spark leaped the gap and zapped me a good one. Mystery solved, I went on about my business. But just knowing the truth didn't keep me from being shocked from time to time if I got careless and forgot my ghost waiting there in the dark.

Our setting in a little copse of pine, oak, and maple trees, surrounded by open, grassy fields was relaxing and pastoral. Just over the brow of a slight hill, a small brook trickled its way to Burba Lake, where ducks, geese, and an occasional snapping turtle swam. Here among the trees we had a rude surprise in late 1984: the throaty roar of diesel engines and the screech of wood being ripped apart suddenly erupted behind our two little buildings. Rushing out, we were astonished to see bulldozers pulverizing the vacant two-story barracks buildings just a few yards away, in the old cantonment area behind our offices. It only took a few hours. The half-dozen structures were pushed into splintered piles, loaded into dump trucks, and hauled away. As the demolition progressed, I went out several times to stand at the back of Building T-2561 to watch, nervously wondering if the bulldozers might gather enough momentum to lumber over and push down our own sliver-sided buildings as well. It would be an easy enough mistake to make, and one that would not displease a number of our bosses higher up in the Army chain of command.

Being as close to nature as we were, nature often came to visit. We had many close encounters of the animal variety. A couple of workdays were turned topsy-turvy some months prior to my joining the unit when a skunk found his way under the floorboards of T-2561 and was surprised by one of the feral cats that lived there. Everyone had to crowd over into T-2560 to let the other building air out. Then there was the time that a great deal of scratching and squeaking was heard coming through the heating grates in the ceiling. It turned out a squirrel family had built a nest in the space between the ceiling and the roof joists, and the squirrel babies were engaging in mock combat.

This wasn't our only encounter with squirrels. At least once a year, usually in the fall, some hapless squirrel would try to leap from one insulator to the other on the power transformer that served our buildings and the nearby sergeants major's quarters. Sometimes the squirrel would still be touching one insulator when it reached across to the other. I remember the first time this happened. I was sitting at my computer when all of sudden there was a tremendous bang that rattled the windows. All the power went dead, instantly shutting down every piece of electrical equipment in the office. Heart beating wildly, I jumped up with the others to see if a terrorist bomb had just blown the back off our building. A quick look showed the building to be intact, so we went to explore the grounds. Under the smoking transformer we found charred bits of squirrel scattered about. This led to occasional remarks about "Rocky, the frying squirrel."

The creatures that got the most attention, though, were the cats that made their home under our buildings. Jeannie had a soft spot in her heart for animals, especially dogs and cats. My dog Dusty would occasionally get wanderlust and leap my backyard fence to come calling at the office. Even when I cautioned her not to encourage my wayward dog, Jeannie would still let Dusty in when she scratched at the door. Jeannie kept an empty coffee can to fill with water for the thirsty visitor.

Sometime in the distant past, a stray domestic cat or two had been dropped off at the edge of the road. Finding shelter under our buildings, they soon began to multiply. Over the years, there were never more than half a dozen or so, ranging from mothers to kittens. We would sometimes see them slink out of sight when we came and went. On sunny days the kittens would come out of their lair and tumble about among the fallen leaves around the footings of the building. But during cold, wet, or icy weather Jeannie and Charlene would fret about how the furry waifs were faring, huddled there under our floorboards.

Eventually, Jeannie took pity on them, and started leaving bowls of dried cat food at the side of the building. A few years later, during one particularly harsh winter, she lured some of the cats inside and left them in the building overnight, warm and cozy as guests of the United States Government. Unfortunately, cats will be cats, and Jeannie had to clean up the consequences the next morning. Her wards weren't allowed to spend the night on Uncle Sam's dime again.[1]

The highlight of the wild-cat saga was the story of a kitten named Rambo. But that happened much later and so must wait to be told.

Animal antics weren't the only amusements we enjoyed in our splintery old buildings. There were occasional practical jokes played, not just on each other, but hapless visitors as well. One I will mention here.

Among our ragged office furniture scrounged from the property disposal warehouse was a fully adjustable dentist's chair that had been declared obsolete and left gathering dust in some dark corner. Even though it weighed a couple of hundred pounds, Joe and Mel had dragged it over to our operations building. Since the chair could be adjusted to various angles and configurations, they thought that perhaps it would make a good ERV chair. The viewer could move foot, back, or head up or down, or tilt the whole ungainly thing at any angle to achieve a maximum relaxed state.

Unfortunately, it proved too unwieldy, and despite the many ways the chair could be inclined, it just wasn't that comfortable. So there it sat, a bulky, white-and-grey, metal-and-Naugahyde dentist's chair. Any time visitors toured the premises, they would always ask about the chair, and someone would have to come up with a plausible reason for why it was there. Then came a bright idea. Why not spice things up a little? Someone threw an old bedsheet over the chair and placed an old car battery on the floor next to it. They then clamped jumper cables to the battery terminals, and to the arms of the chair.

The payoff came a short time later when the fire marshal came to inspect the buildings. These inspections happened regularly, and the firefighters were intensely curious about what was going on in these two buildings. When they pulled up in their fire truck to inspect, everything on the desks was covered up, the safes were closed, and the visitors were carefully escorted around. This time was no different. The fire official plied his escort with questions about the buildings and the work that went on in them. The questions were met with the same noncommittal replies.

But then, as the inspector was walked back into the Garden Room of the operations building, there in all its glory was the wired dentist chair. Visions of the movie *Marathon Man*, in which Dustin Hoffman is tortured by a sadistic dentist, must have flashed through the hapless firefighter's mind. His eyes were suddenly big as saucers, and he hurriedly checked the charge on the extinguisher at the far end of the room, then scurried out the front door, without asking any more questions and giving the chair a wide berth.

There were transitions and near-transitions among the people in the office, or those who had once been there. The near-transition involved Joe McMoneagle. In mid-June 1985, Fred told us in the soft, measured voice he reserved both for remote viewing sessions and for momentous or solemn pronouncements, that on the seventeenth of the month Joe had suffered a near-fatal heart attack. And it had come to pass well within the two-year time window specified in the Future 15 exercise.

For Joe there was to be a triple-bypass surgery and nearly a week of playing tag with death, but eventually, after a long recuperation, he was alive. It was not until years later, when rereading my notes of my December 1983 Monroe Institute experience, that my visualization of Joe wrapped in white bandages suddenly made sense.

We also lost Buzby and Tom—not to any life-threatening crisis, but only through the normal grindings of the Army personnel machine. Tom was transferred to Fort Sam Houston in San Antonio, while Lieutenant Colonel Buzby was reassigned to Systems Exploitation Division. SED had gained a reputation of playing a little too fast and loose with the rules, and Colonel Scott, Army Operation Group's new commander, thought Buzby was just the man to clean it up. That left Bill Ray, now a full-fledged major, in charge. And Bill was up to the challenge.

On the nineteenth of October, in the middle of Stage 6 training, Charlene had a transition of her own; she married Brigadier General Jim Shufelt. Shufelt had been INSCOM's deputy commander for operations under General Stubblebine, and had also served time as Odom's assistant, which he viewed as a particularly challenging assignment. Shufelt had recently been appointed as deputy director for the Defense Intelligence Agency.

The wedding was held in Fort Meade's main chapel, a formal but pleasant red-brick building on Llewellyn Avenue just a few blocks down from the Sun Streak buildings. Charlene asked Bill and me to be ushers, and wheedled Ingo Swann into coming down from New York for the event. Even though the wedding was only a few hundred yards away from our offices, Ingo steadfastly refused to stop by and tour the headquarters of the program he had helped spawn. To my knowledge it was the only time that Ingo ever set foot on Fort Meade.[2]

21

New Home

As 1986 dawned we took stock of our circumstances. Although nothing about our decrepit offices had physically changed, it seemed that each breath came a little more freely than at any time over the prior eighteen months of uncertainty. We were out of the clutches of INSCOM, and within the friendly embrace of Dr. Jack Vorona's DT (technical and scientific intelligence directorate) within the Defense Intelligence Agency. For now, at least, we were among friends.

We also had some new faces, and some old ones, as well. Ed Dames had finally realized his dream of joining the remote-viewing program. On January 31 he was officially transferred from his old unit, Systems Exploitation Detachment (SED), to what the day before was known as Center Lane, but was now, on the same effective date as Dames's transfer, freshly rechristened as the Defense Intelligence Agency's Project Sun Streak.

As newly ordained commander of Ed's old unit, SED, Lieutenant Colonel Buzby had greased the skids to get Ed reassigned. Rather than as a viewer, Ed came to us to become a monitor and project officer, providing admin support for remote-viewing projects. He would also get to help Fred Atwater with training and operations, which for Ed was better than being left out of remote viewing altogether.

I missed the old Center Lane code name maybe, just a little. It had always reminded me of a classic Ingo Swann oil painting, *Unseen Highway*, which depicts a two-lane blacktop stretching arrow-straight into the sunset, with a highway of stars in the heavens above mirroring its course. Admittedly, the new Sun Streak moniker had a brighter and more hopeful ring to it. And street signs that said CENTER LANE CLOSED AHEAD no longer made me shudder.

Along with our connection to Jack Vorona and DIA came a closer relationship with Dale Graff who, a decade before in his analyst job with the Air Force, had rescued the SRI program from near extinction. Dale was kept busy in the intervening years not only as Jack Vorona's action officer for the ongoing remote-viewing research that DIA funded, but also as the agency's monitor of developments in parapsychology behind the Iron Curtain. With his electric hair and thick glasses giving him an intense, often distracted look, brought on by duties amounting to more than two full-time jobs, Dale visually fit the absentminded professor stereotype. But he was good-natured, if sometimes scattered. And his desk was usually even more cluttered than mine, a fact that gave me no end of satisfaction once I discovered it.

Dale was by no means a constant fixture in our Fort Meade offices. But as official go-between for Vorona, he did make fairly regular appearances. Most often, though, if we had business with him or Vorona we went to DIA headquarters in the newly opened Defense Intelligence Analysis Center, a massive, grey building on Bolling Air Force Base, just across the Anacostia River from the Washington, D.C., waterfront.

It was Dale Graff's job not only to keep tabs on us, but also to coordinate with the ongoing research effort at SRI in Menlo Park. Joe McMoneagle, now recovered from his heart attack, was a regular participant in the SRI research, which was by then directed by Ed May. In 1985 Hal Puthoff had resigned as head of the research program at SRI to accept a tempting offer to become Director of the Institute of Advanced Studies, in Austin, Texas. With a dedicated staff and a generous budget, Puthoff could pursue ground-breaking research in theoretical physics and once and for all escape the administrative headaches of working under government contract.[1]

We at Fort Meade were only occasionally reminded that the SRI effort was even still continuing. The Sun Streak viewers were kept almost completely in the dark about what was going on in California. In one respect that was good, since we could focus on our own work, which was to learn and then use remote viewing. Unfortunately, this policy of isolation later came back to haunt us.

Even if we were not quite finished with our Stage 6 training, DIA had begun to task us with operational targets—even before our official entree into the agency. The first of these taskings came our way on January 2, 1986.[2] Like so many others over the coming months and years, this operational remote-viewing project involved manmade structures. But this one was special. It turned out that we were to try to find out whether there were any Vietnam-era American POWs at certain camps in Southeast Asia.

Likely in response to rumored sightings, remote viewing missions looking for American POWs were launched as early as 1981. At least one of these involved checking an area in the former North Vietnam. The comment in the log from those early tries was that "no helpful info thus far" had been obtained, and both projects were canceled after a few inconclusive sessions.[3] The inaugural project from our new DIA bosses, however, went far beyond the scope of those earlier attempts.

The task was given to us by Brigadier General Jim Shufelt, new husband to our compatriot Charlene. Recently installed as the Defense Intelligence Agency's deputy director, the general had inherited the Prisoner-of-War/Missing-in-Action issue. One of the offices under his command was directly responsible for the POW/MIA effort. It was headed first by an Air Force colonel, who was later replaced by an Army colonel named Joe Slater. Even with an office dedicated full-time to the issue, Shufelt still found an enormous amount of his time drained away in trying to sort out the plausible reports from the many frauds and scams perpetrated by cynical people trying to reap fortune or fame from the search for missing American servicemen.

The general sought any opportunity to verify possible POW sightings, using every available intelligence discipline. Introduced to remote viewing while assigned to INSCOM, and exposed to it once again while on Odom's staff, he was now in a unique way "married" to the remote viewing project. It made sense to task the newly emerging Sun Streak program. Since it was now a DIA asset, using it would cost nothing and might provide something of value not turned up by other intelligence-gathering methods. So Shufelt had a brief meeting with Fred Atwater, then handed him off to the colonel in charge of the POW/MIA task.[4]

Atwater was faced with a problem. DIA wanted Sun Streak's viewers to find out if there actually were American POWs at any of several proposed target sites. But to make sure that viewers weren't contaminated, it would be best if all of us, including the monitors and taskers, were as blind as possible to the target. The problem was that the taskings would come from the POW/MIA office, which could tip off people at the unit what a given target was about. The viewers could be kept blind, but it would be harder to keep other key people from knowing too much. And there was a further problem. As viewers encountered one possible POW camp after another, the similarities in terrain might tip us off and our imaginations might start peopling each target, whether there really were humans there or not. A control was needed.

Atwater's solution was to ask the colonel in charge of the POW/MIA office to add decoy targets to the mix. In other words, DIA was to give us extra targets which might be similar to POW camps, but where it was known for a fact that there were no prisoners. To check our accuracy, DIA picked decoy targets about which a great deal was known. Thus, they could not only catch us if we began to see POWs where none existed, but it had the added benefit as a tool for our new master, DIA, to evaluate our work as we all moved into uncharted waters. If a viewer was clearly on the mark on a decoy target, DIA would know it and could better trust the viewer's work on the suspected POW sites.[5]

I no longer recall my experiences during this project, and probably never received any feedback on it. Since there was always the chance we might have to revisit this sort of project in the future, Atwater did not want us to know too much.

Bill Ray did, however, have fairly vivid recollections of some of the sessions he worked in support of this project—so much so that he even remembered an AOL in one of his sessions. The target he was working brought to mind the movie *The Bridge on the River Kwai*.

It was hot, humid. I got some diagrams there . . . The diagrams were of a square compound, with a stockade fence and a tower—something like you might see in a Chuck Norris movie—but all deserted, which made no sense to me, since I had no idea what the target was supposed to be . . . I was worried that it was AOL. I remember thinking, "This is kind of crazy, but it looks like a prisoner-of-war camp." A compound of some sort. There was a whole lot of feeling there; I got the feeling of being cut-off, abandoned, separated. In some of these sessions that feeling was still at the site, but there were no bodies there. There were two kinds of abandoned feelings—one from the site itself, but another from people who were no longer there, but who I could still get feelings from, abandoned feelings.[6]

The project ended after four of us had worked a total of twenty-one sessions. After examining the session data forwarded to them, the DIA analysts confirmed that we had accurately described the sites against which we had been targeted. Atwater noted:

I remember specifically talking to the analysts and getting feedback, saying "You're doing fine in terms of the remote viewing," meaning that they were getting good target descriptions . . . towers and airplanes and waterfalls and lakes and mountains that matched what was at the other end of the coordinates.[7]

But we never found any missing Americans. Analysts recognized the targets we described, but we never reported anyone who could have resembled an American POW. "The bottom line," Atwater attested, "is that we had good ground-truth verification, and never found any POWs. There were even comments from viewers like, 'There used to be some people here but they're not here now.' "

As reports of this POW-related remote viewing mission became public in later years, the fact that we had not found anyone at the sites was sometimes deemed a remote viewing "failure." But this conclusion is a result of muddy thinking of those making the observation, not the shortcomings of remote viewing. There is a big difference between getting faulty or no information, and just not finding anybody home. What we reported was that there was no one there that matched the descriptions of those for whom we were sent to look, which was in fact probably the right answer. Looked at in those terms, our POW search mission was a great success.

There were plenty of other operational remote viewing assignments during 1986. One I remember well resulted in me describing a MIRV—a multiple, independently targetable reentry vehicle—in flight.[8] A MIRV was the business end of some of the deadliest of both the Soviets' and our own nuclear-tipped intercontinental ballistic missiles. It was essentially a nose cone inside of which nestled a cluster of individual nuclear explosives. At a predetermined height over enemy terrain, the nose cone would jettison its cover and then methodically dispense up to ten thermonuclear weapons, each assigned its own individual target. A single missile with a MIRV on it could conceivably destroy ten military bases, enemy missile silos, power plants, or populated cities in a single launch.

My target was a test firing of a Soviet missile which had previously occurred, and the missile was thought to carry a MIRV. As I received the coordinate, I began sketching an ideogram that seemed to fall down the page. There was an energetic swirling around, and some odd angles. Even though at that point I had no inkling what the target was, I did know that it was manmade. I no longer recall what my initial Stage 2 sensory impressions were, but I remember my sketches better. In fact, they were accurate enough that before the end of the project I knew that I was drawing a nuclear warhead. I had sketched a cone-shaped thing that seemed to me to be removable. Inside it, I drew a cylindrical device with cup holder–shaped ports that held several smaller cylindrical objects, which had bulges or rings around parts of them. One of these I sketched as if it had been removed from its holder.

Whether my realization of the nature of the target interfered with the rest of my viewing in these sessions is hard to say. But the data that came after it still *felt* accurate. And I was caught completely off guard. It had never dawned on me that I might be given a target of this sort. Generally, the data that surprises a viewer turns out most often to be correct.

Just like many other operational targets each of us worked over the years, I got a pat on the back and "good job," but I was never given feedback on this target. Nevertheless, that session created a strong memory that I never completely forgot. A couple of years later, in reading some of the materials being reviewed in the aftermath of an inspector general's visit, I came across a brief reference to a successful session against a MIRV. Before I even saw my viewer identification number, listing me as the viewer-of-record on the project, I knew that it was mine.

Not long after this project, around March, another old friend suddenly turned up—big, boisterous Gene Lessman. I had last seen Gene in 1982 in Bad Tölz, Germany, where he was keeping an eye on the Soviet Military Liaison Mission as, authorized by treaty, it snooped around Bavaria looking for NATO secrets. Bill Ray had been friends with Gene since 1977, when they met while assigned to the counterintelligence Special Operations Detachment in Munich.

Hearing that Lessman had retired from the Army and was back in the United States, Bill set about tracking the burly, mustachioed Irishman down. Gene had a German last name from his father's side of the family, but his mother was as Irish as they come. Gene's parents had met in 1944 when his father was an American infantryman in Ireland, training for the Normandy invasion. Lessman still had family living on the Old Sod, in "English-Occupied Ireland," as Gene put it. One of these, a brother, was gunned down in his Ulster office by terrorists in the late 1980s because he believed in hiring both Protestants *and* Catholics for his construction business, based on their job skills, not on what religion they were.[9] Once, when I was visiting Gene years after the remote-viewing program's demise, he handed me as a souvenir a large, round rubber bullet that he told me had been fired into his family's yard during a disturbance.

He himself was no stranger to violence. He had served two tours with the Special Forces in Vietnam. One of those tours ended as he was about to board a helicopter for extraction after a mission. He had gone to debrief a junior Viet Cong officer who was giving information to the Americans when the soldier apparently had a change of heart and emptied his Kalashnikov rifle into both Gene Lessman and the helicopter pilot as Gene fired back with his M-16. Gene survived to fly the helicopter out using rudimentary skills the pilot had taught him, crash-landing at an airfield. The Viet Cong and the pilot died. In the field hospital afterwards, it was touch and go whether Gene himself would live. He pulled through, with the scars and vivid memories of a near-death experience to remind him of what he had been through.[10] The day he told me the story, Gene showed me the evidence by pulling up his shirt to reveal the ugly scars that marched diagonally across his torso where the enemy rounds had left their mark.

Sun Streak had a vacant personnel slot for an analyst/monitor. Gene was a competent, experienced intelligence officer, and Bill thought he would do well in the position. But Bill had another agenda as well. Gene was well-known and respected in military intelligence circles, and he was the son of a man who was himself almost a legend in those same circles. After staying with the infantry through the Korean War and being awarded a battlefield commission, Gene's father, Dale Lessman, had switched to intelligence work, and spent three decades chasing down enemy secrets for Uncle Sam. Bill thought that if word got around that Dale Lessman's son, Gene, was working with Sun Streak, it might add credibility to what we were trying to do there.[11]

Once he was on board and had been taught the ropes, Gene turned out to be an excellent monitor. One of the projects that he worked me on, which I will describe later, still sticks with me to this day.

Not only were we suddenly doing real-world operational sessions, but our targeting method had changed as well. From its very beginnings, Center Lane used the same targeting methods as had SRI. One of the most important of these was geographic coordinates—latitude and longitude expressed in degrees, minutes, and even, when precision was necessary, seconds. When a monitor spoke the geographic coordinates out loud, the viewer knew to describe what was at the intersection of the two imaginary lines on the Earth's surface.

But there were problems with this. First, critics complained that there was nothing to stop viewers from memorizing what was located at various coordinates and then just rattling off whatever they had memorized. Of course, these critics didn't stop to consider that, given the virtually infinite combinations of possible coordinates, such a feat would be even more impressive than simple remote viewing.

But the critics were almost half right. After doing enough sessions against various parts of the globe, we started to generally know when a coordinate was somewhere in the Soviet Union, or Latin America, or Asia. Surprisingly, though, instead of helping us get spectacular, if bogus, results as the critics alleged, this actually got in the way of remote viewing. For example, every time I got a coordinate in the Soviet Union I would AOL snow and ice, barren steppes, and all that, even though the target might be the warm interior of a secret building in the heart of Moscow. Using geographic coordinates tended to degrade results, not artificially enhance them.

A second problem with these sorts of coordinates was that the practice also limited targeting. Using latitude and longitude meant that we could only target things whose location we already knew. But what about targets whose whereabouts were unknown; say, a hostage, a missing H-bomb, or a crashed airplane? There were some methods for getting around this problem. A picture of a hostage, an H-bomb, or the missing aircraft could be sealed in an envelope and the viewer asked to describe the location of the subject of the photo in the sealed envelope. But photos were not always easily or immediately available. Besides, we had learned to launch a session when cued by a set of numbers, and the convenience of this was very attractive.

Largely in response to these problems, in late April 1985 we began using encrypted coordinates. It started during Buzby's regime. Fred Atwater would carry the written geographic coordinates into the branch chief's office, where we were told he or Buzby would pull out a Hewlett-Packard programmable calculator and enter the coordinates. Supposedly, the calculator was loaded with an algorithm that would "encrypt" the numbers so that their meaning was still there, but a viewer, not knowing what the encryption pattern was, would not recognize them. So, for example, "20 degrees, 34 minutes west, 48 degrees, 13 minutes north," might go into the calculator and come out "7308 2159," which would then become the target number the monitor would use to launch the viewer on the session. I, for one, was pleased by this arrangement, and felt that my viewing improved now that I wasn't always struggling to ignore the geographic coordinates.

Things went well for some time, but one day one of the viewers was assigned to monitor another viewer on an operational project. Taking the coordinate into the branch chief's office, he handed it to Bill Ray, who was by then in charge. Bill struggled with the calculator and couldn't get it to work the way it was supposed to. With a mild profanity he shoved it aside and grabbed a piece of paper instead, scribbling down whatever numbers came to mind. "Use these!" he said.

Scratching his head, the would-be monitor left the office. The session went just as well as any others. Later, the story made its way through the office grapevine, and we began to discuss the implications among ourselves. Eventually it all came out in the wash. There had never been an encryption algorithm. The Hewlett-Packard calculator was only used to generate a random number that stood for the coordinate. This came as a shock for some of us. How could we describe something, if the numbers we were given had no real connection to the target we were suppose to view? Still, we couldn't argue that we were just as successful, and often even more so, than we had been with conventional geographic coordinates.

Our astonishment was echoed by that of an intelligence analyst who had come to watch the viewing of a target he had asked us to do. From what I heard later, the conversation between the visitor and his escort went something like this:

"How do you 'send' a viewer to the right target?"

"We give him a random number which stands for the target, and then he describes what we want."

"A random number? But how on earth can assigning something completely arbitrary like that work?"

"Think about it a minute. You came here, confident that we could send a viewer to describe the interior of a secure building that no American, much less the viewer, has ever seen the inside of?"

"Right."

"And this the viewer would do mentally; no sensory connection of any kind, no visual information, no hearing, smell, anything, involved, and no technological connection either, such as TV, radio, nothing?"

"Yes."

"And to get the viewer to do this you expected us to use latitude and longitude, which do not really exist, but only stand for intersecting parallel imaginary lines that humans pretend divide up the face of the planet?"

"Uh-huh . . ."

"Then why is it harder to believe that a random number will work just as well?"

"But geographic coordinates *mean* something!"

"They only mean what we all agree they mean. There is actually no such thing as 105 degrees west, 37 degrees south. Human map-users all just agree that those numbers *stand* for a place on the surface of the Earth. We *intend* that the viewer describe what is located where those two imaginary lines cross."

"Are you saying that instead of knowing where a coordinate is on the planet, the viewer picks up on the *intention* of the tasker, the person who chooses the target?"

"That's the idea."

"I just don't get how that could . . ."

"Let me come at it in a roundabout way. In Stage 4 a good viewer can pick up on emotions of people at the target location—we call this EI, for 'emotional impact'—and can even get certain kinds of information that seems to come from people's minds. Don't worry," the escort hastened to add, noticing a sudden look of concern on the analyst's face, "it's not like we 'read' minds. But we do seem able sometimes to find out stuff that you would think could only be gotten by doing that. To be honest, we don't really *know* how it works. Some people might call it telepathy, but it's probably something else instead."

"What do you mean?"

"Maybe our minds are really what some people call 'nonlocal.' That is, we usually think of our minds filling our skulls in the same way our brains do. But maybe human minds really *aren't* confined strictly within our brains. Maybe in some way they lap over the edges and extend beyond, into the universe. This could mean that our thoughts, knowledge, ideas, and so on, once processed by the brain and the conscious mind, may end up being entered into something like Ingo Swann's Matrix. Maybe at the subconscious level there *are* no private thoughts. Any one person's thoughts could be accessed by any other person's mind."

"Now that sounds a little scary. But why do you say subconscious?"

"Well, we know that we can't 'read people's minds' consciously. At least, I can't! And yet in remote-viewing sessions we often do seem to find information relating to the thoughts of others percolating up from a viewer's subconscious. This tells me that our subconscious minds have access to things our conscious minds do not."

"Okay, I get the point, though I can't say as I'm convinced. But what does this have to do with a viewer finding a target using only a meaningless random number?"

"If what I just told you is right, then it might go something like this. The person who has the job of assigning the target—we call this person the "tasker"—decides what she wants the viewer to do. This establishes the intent. She then randomly picks some number out of a hat or gets one from a programmable calculator or whatever. This number will become the 'encrypted' coordinate. It only ever stands for *this* target. Let's say the number she picks is 8675309. She then links this number to the 'intent.' If the intent is that the viewer describe the Eiffel Tower, the full tasking might look something like this: '8675309 = describe the Eiffel Tower.' There are lots of possible ways of setting it up or phrasing the tasking, depending on the target and what we want to know about it.

"The tasker then gives *only* the number—not the tasking itself—to the monitor or whomever will pass it on to the viewer. The viewer then uses the number as the coordinate to start the session. But the tasker's intent has now also become part of the background knowledge of the Universe—this intent and the number to which it has been linked have been entered into the Matrix. Presumably, the viewer's subconscious searches the Matrix for the number and, finding it, also finds the tasking linked to it. Since this all happens at the subconscious level, however, the viewer is never consciously aware of the process. He just thinks he spontaneously starts perceiving data, which is all that matters as far as he is concerned.

"Of course," the escort concluded. "This is just speculation—a best guess. Maybe it doesn't really happen this way at all. Maybe it's just magic."[12]

In the spring of 1986 a milestone of sorts was reached, when the DIA publications office delivered about thirty copies of the freshly printed Coordinate Remote Viewing Manual. Buzby had instigated this project sometime before he left the remote-viewing unit. One day in 1985 Fred Atwater had come over to my desk, settled into the battered yellow chair I had wedged into a corner for visitors, and told me that Buzby wanted me to take the lead in writing a manual that would capture as exactly as possible the essence of what we had learned from Ingo. For perhaps half an hour we tossed around ideas about how best to approach it.

Though I would be the writer and ultimate judge of what went into the finished manual (with Fred having final approval rights), the project would be a team effort among the four of us in the office who had been trained by Ingo—Charlene, Bill, Tom, and myself. Fred provided oversight and added input. Each of us had detailed memories of Ingo's instruction, and a stack of notes from Ingo's lectures. If one of us didn't remember something clearly, the others could fill in the blanks. We were careful to make as certain as possible that nothing went into the CRV manual but the purity of the Swann-Puthoff CRV method. Even at that, one or two trivial non-Ingoisms still crept into the text. And there were a number of typos and minor omissions.

Over the course of almost a year, between training and writing briefings and responding to periodic deadlines and crises over the pending transfer to DIA, I worked on it as I found time. Referring to my notes and those of the others I would write a section, then pass them to Bill, Charlene, or Tom to read for sense and accuracy. If any changes were suggested, I compared them again to the stack of notes and checked with my fellow Ingo-trainees. If necessary, I then rewrote the disputed section in a way that best seemed to portray what Ingo had presented us.

The requirement to hew as closely as possible to the Ingo Swann method unexpectedly caused some hurt feelings in the unit. As I was in the process of writing the final portions covering the more advanced remote-viewing stages, Lyn Buchanan approached me with a handful of pages he had written for inclusion in the manual. Buchanan was in the middle of training in CRV, and had been giving a lot of thought to the methodology. He had some suggestions on how he thought the Swann-Puthoff method might be augmented or enhanced.

Although I was interested in his ideas, I could not use them. Fred and I had talked about writing another manual later that would include techniques and lessons learned in employing remote viewing operationally, but this first manual was meant to be "pure" Ingo. I learned later that for many years Lyn thought I had rejected his ideas out of hand, so I had to belatedly smooth over the misunderstanding and explain that nothing personal was meant by the rejection.

The CRV manual had a publication date on the front cover of May 1, 1986. Even before it was hot off the press, though, Fred bundled up a copy of the manuscript and mailed it off to Ingo Swann to see what he might think of it. Not long after, we received Ingo's signed reply, dated April 16, 1986:

> I've received and read through the material you sent along—and you've done me great honor in taking the time and effort to produce such a comprehensive and accurate document. I don't think I could have done this as clearly as you have and you have my deepest thanks. If nothing else, the document at least attests to the efficacy of the training method itself.[13]

The manual proved to be a valuable aid in training new remote viewer candidates who came our way over the ensuing years, and even figured in some of the controversies that erupted more than a decade after its birth. But, at the time, Ingo Swann's praise vindicated all the long work that I and my fellows had put into it.

Right on the heels of the manual's publication—on May 5—I wrote my graduation essay from Stage 6. I was now a fully operational remote viewer, if still a little wet behind the ears.

A few months after this watershed moment in my life, Sun Streak received still more new recruits. In June 1986, Master Sergeant Mel Riley was finally assigned to the unit. He was new to me, but not to remote viewing. After a tour with an Air Force aerial reconnaissance unit in Germany and a spell as a company first sergeant at Fort Stewart, Georgia, he was back at Fort Meade to continue his career as a psychic spy for the government.

Mel's return to remote viewing had been delayed for almost two years. He was originally scheduled to come back to Center Lane in 1984, but the events surrounding General Stubblebine's departure and the unit's banishment from INSCOM caused Buzby to cancel Riley's move back. It didn't seem to make sense to bring Mel back to Fort Meade if his job as a Center Lane remote viewer might be terminated only a month or so after he arrived.

Fortunately, things had changed dramatically for government remote viewing since then. Mel was quiet, friendly, and competent. I knew we would hit it off.

July 1986 brought us another new face. Her name was Angela and she had been working as a Latin-American analyst in one of INSCOM's subordinate units. Angela was of medium height, with a Mediterranean complexion and large, dark eyes, and liked to sit at her desk and work logic problems while puffing on a cigarette. She generally kept her brown hair relatively short, and she had a memorable laugh.

Angela had been "discovered" either by General Stubblebine while he was still INSCOM commander or by his chief of staff, Colonel Chuck Partridge. She was reputed to have some psychic talent, and Charlene was directed to take the steps necessary to get her assigned to the unit. It took almost two years, though, for that to happen, thanks to the uncertainties of the DIA transfer.[14] Angela was to be trained in both CRV and ERV now that she was finally on board. Though she was taught CRV, she only tried it for a little while. She did use ERV for a time, until something else happened. But that story comes later.

Meanwhile, Ed Dames was trying to find his niche at the unit. Since he was assigned as a monitor and analyst, his formal training had ended with Stage 3 when the contract with Ingo ran out at the end of 1984. But Ed still wanted to know more about the process, so he soaked up everything he could as we trained new remote viewing recruits at the unit, and carefully read the coordinate remote viewing manual when we finally completed it a couple of months later.

Ed has since claimed that he worked as a viewer during the nearly thirty-six months he was assigned to Sun Streak. However, everyone else assigned to the unit remembers that he was brought on board specifically to assist with training and monitoring, and some have denied that he ever worked as a viewer. The truth is that Ed *was* hired to be a monitor and an administrator.[15] But he did occasionally work as a viewer on crash projects or in crisis situations where virtually everyone in the office was called to perform. Altogether, the records show that of the approximately fifty operational projects that Sun Streak executed during the thirty-six months Ed was there, he was a viewer on eight—all of those during 1988, the last year he was assigned.[16]

Ed had as much to learn about being a monitor as we fledgling viewers did about remote viewing. I still shake my head at a series of training targets he gave me starting immediately after his arrival at the unit. I don't know if Ed selected all of these, or if Fred Atwater passed some of them on to try on me. Whatever the case, most of these targets were entire cities—Glencoe, Scotland; St. Paul, Minnesota; Asuncion, Paraguay; Vaduz, Liechtenstein. Except for the session on Vaduz, I did poorly on these targets. And with one exception they were badly chosen for what they were meant to be: training targets for Stages 5 and 6.

Entire cities are normally only used as Stage 1 targets, where the goal is merely to recognize the major gestalt of the site—i.e., "structure," or "city." Since the purpose of both Stages 5 and 6 is to suck as much detail as possible from the target, a city with all its myriad points of interest would present a sort of waking nightmare to the viewer. With the nearly infinite number of possible items of interest in a typical urban landscape, how could a viewer ever do anything more than arbitrarily describe a building or other feature his subconscious chooses, or get anything but an incoherent kaleidoscope of conflicting, confusing data? This is essentially what I got—a jumble of buildings and AOL.

As noted, the only exception was the Liechtenstein target, for which Ed assigned me a "+" grade (he gave me a "−" on all the others). I think I did well on this one because Vaduz is relatively compact as a city, mostly surrounded by a wall, and topped with a very distinctive castle. Unlike the other city targets, there was something notable here to be seized on in Stage 6.

Among this early group of targets Ed gave me, the only good example of a target suitable for advanced remote viewing training was Health Adventure, an interactive museum in North Carolina. Solitary and specific, it provided a neat, easily encompassed package crammed with much detail and a variety of information, which nevertheless centered around a general theme that gave a budding remote viewer experience at sorting out complex impressions enclosed in a defined space. Still, I didn't do well on this one, either, confusing some real data that I received with an AOL that refused to go away of some government or scientific building elsewhere in the world.

Culminating this series of targets on March 20 was one that, unbeknownst to me at the time, would be a harbinger of things to come: Ed targeted me on Titan, one of the moons of Saturn. As I look back through my session transcript today, I see a small amount of accurate signal line data that I received. But I also find other elements that are more troublesome. Expecting nothing extraterrestrial, my conscious awareness interpreted my perceptions in Earthly terms. I started off describing land, water, and some structures portrayed in fairly elaborate detail.

The first hint that my point of view might not be on Earth was a circular sketch of what looks very much like a planet or moon in phase. Even this I interpreted as some kind of metal object. Further along in the session, after many other details about structures, I declared the AOL of "science fiction painting," and then one of "sputnik" a page or two later. After several more pages describing technical equipment, construction work, and a host of details about persons at the site, I had a further AOL of "astronauts in their suits." Now, long after the fact, it seems to me that my subconscious was desperately trying to tell me that I wasn't in Maryland anymore.

Yet after several more pages—and a great deal of confused comments about people, technical objects, more buildings, and such—Ed gave me a movement exercise to place my point of focus high above the surface. Finally I started to pick up data that I today think was more relevant to the target: feelings of being exposed, being out in a barren area, leading to an AOL of "moon"; impressions of light and white, with a further AOL of white flash or explosion; and a sensation of being very cold. Ed gave me another directive—something about "looking up/looking down." I had an instant impression, of "something large nearby," looming in the sky. I interpreted this as being the full, harvest moon, though now I'm sure I must have been dimly perceiving the great orb of Saturn, filling Titan's bleak horizon. The session ended with an AOL of a "space vehicle falling away, irregularly shaped," and an ominous reference to "Armageddon."

After all these years, it is hard to know what to make of this session and my descriptions of structures, people, and technological devices. From later events it seemed that Ed took my results at face value, and integrated them into his changing and ever-expanding vision of how the universe must be organized and peopled.

But I myself do not trust them. Without actually going to Titan and looking, I cannot say those things I "saw" are not there. Still, the chances seem pretty slim. Not counting the occasional astronomical reference in the session, plus a few of my sketches that somewhat resemble the network of lines that space probes and telescopes have shown to be on Titan, I believe that most of what I reported was overlay of some sort—maybe placed there by my left-brain expectations, conditioned to anticipate yet another city target to match the several others I had already been given by Ed over the preceding weeks.

Whatever the case, this Titan session heralded a trend that continued into the next two years, and beyond. Besides all the operational targets I was assigned the following year, 1987, Ed was my monitor for several training sessions. Most of his choices of targets in those training sessions had to do with "anomaly" targets—UFOs, extraterrestrials, modern mysteries, or ancient artifacts, such as the Ark of the Covenant. I call these anomaly targets because they are departures from known ground truth. For most of them, there is no possible way one can ever get reliable feedback. And without good feedback, sessions like these are next to worthless as training exercises. There is no way to tell whether the viewer has provided any real data or has simply tugged something out of his imagination, or out of the tasker's mind as a result of something Ingo Swann calls "telepathic overlay." There will be more about this later.

It was sometime between the spring and late summer of that year that our government car was shot up. This wasn't as serious as it sounds, though. Apparently a bored youngster living in the sergeants major housing not far from the back door to T-2561 had acquired a new air rifle. From time to time he would amuse himself by shooting out the security light beside our back door. It was annoying to have to replace the bulb, but we could never catch the boy in the act. One evening the emboldened miscreant got ambitious. When we showed up for work the next morning, we found the headlights and taillights of our DIA-supplied Ford Citation sedan shattered, along with one of the wing windows. As I remember, there was also a BB hole at the base of the windshield. Together with Lyn, who was in charge of the vehicle's upkeep, I walked around the car tabulating the damage.

This was little more than a nuisance, but a nuisance we didn't need. At about the same time the building had been invaded by hornets, and within a day or so of the sedan incident the facility engineers were scheduled to fumigate the building with bug bombs. We would have to leave our offices early Friday afternoon and stay away all weekend. Bill Ray remembers events unfolding something like this: Bill was on the telephone with the DIA maintenance folks at Bolling Air Force Base negotiating for a replacement windshield. "What happened to the old one?" The voice on the other end wanted to know.

"It was shot out!" Bill replied. There was momentary silence on the other end.

"Shot out?" came the voice, finally.

"Yeah. They got the head- and taillights too. And a side window. But no big deal."

"Uh . . . right," the voice replied. Bill knew that the folks at Bolling thought we were into some strange things, though they weren't high enough up the bureaucratic totem pole to know exactly what. This car-shooting incident would certainly enhance our office reputation and add to their speculations.

Then the excitement level was raised yet another notch. As the engineers prepared to fumigate, someone yelled from the doorway loud enough to carry over the open phone line, "Hey, Bill, you better get out quick. They're about to set off the bombs!"[17]

In October we received Project 8609, another of the several operational tasks we performed in 1986.[18] At the time the target was very hush-hush, but the details are now declassified and available for open discussion. I'm going to tell about it here in some detail because so much information is now known about it, and because it is a good example of how we "worked" a typical project of this sort—and because I had a profound experience in trying to find out just what was going on at the mysterious top-secret Soviet research facility at Sary Shagan.

Charlene worked two sessions, Lyn worked three, and Bill worked five on this project, but for some reason I ended up tasked to do eleven of them. It turned out to be a marathon exercise to explore a group of structures of various descriptions from one end to the other.

At the time, of course, all I was given was the encrypted coordinate. Now, years later, I have discovered the tasking for Project 8609: on a draft of the final report passed on to the office that had tasked us, dated June 30, 1987, it reads "Access and describe the activities and results of activities at the Dome Section and related structures at Sary Shagan, R & D complex."

The Sary Shagan PVO Air Defense proving ground lay in a vast area centering on the city of Sary Shagan in the south-central Soviet republic of Kazakhstan. The testing facility was bordered on the east by the immense freshwater Lake Balkhash, and served as a testing range and research complex for developing a Soviet anti-ballistic missile defense. It was roughly equivalent to similar places in the United States devoted to the "Star Wars" space defense program. Clusters of imposing institutional buildings with associated technical structures such as large dish antennae, towers, test-stands, and the like dotted the landscape, interspersed with wide, empty ranges where experimental missiles and other equipments were checked out.

None of this was known by anyone involved with the actual remote viewing during the initial stages of the project. During this phase of Sun Streak's existence, viewers almost never received anything but encrypted coordinates. Monitors, too, were kept "blind" to everything but the encrypted coordinate for at least the first several sessions of a given project. From a science perspective it didn't matter whether our sessions were done under double-blind conditions or not. We weren't trying to come up with any sort of scientific "proof" about remote viewing, and therefore couldn't have cared less about having a "clean" experiment to trot out for doubters. We *were* engaged in intelligence operations, and double-blind conditions suited our purposes in that respect.

The opposite of double-blind conditions for a viewer is to be "front-loaded." Frontloading is information about the target given a viewer before she starts a session. It can be the name of the target, the nature of it, what the tasker hopes to find out—any information that might give the viewer a clue as to anything of significance about the target. Frontloading is a bad idea, since it leads to analytical overlay and distortion of the data. Maintaining double-blindness helps limit AOL, and it also serves to keep the viewer "honest." Frontloading often allows the viewer to draw inferences or conclusions about the target which are mistakenly reported as being remote viewing data. Keeping the viewer blind forces her to view, not deduce.

But there was a further important reason for maintaining double-blind conditions. If the viewer accurately reported information about which she was unwitting, but which the project manager already knew to be true about the target, it increased the likelihood that the data she then reported that was unknown to the project manager or the intelligence-community client was accurate as well. Keeping the viewer and monitor blind as long as possible provided an additional safeguard and gauge of accuracy.

However, some concessions had to be made to make remote viewing operations effective. In a more conventional spy situation, a source usually knows what it is he is looking for when he is snooping around an enemy base. With remote viewing, the viewer must be kept blind not only to what the objective is, but to the very nature of the target itself. This puts the whole process under a handicap. How can a remote viewer find the answer to the question if she doesn't even know what the question is?

Sometimes the subconscious comes to the rescue. Somehow it "knows" what is needed, and directs the viewer's attention towards the information that will answer the question. But for many complex targets something more may be needed. Perhaps even the client is unsure what he needs; perhaps he just knows from other intelligence sources that there is something going on at a location that is suspicious and needs to be explored. In those situations the viewer often provides a potpourri of details about a target, many of which are new and previously unknown, but which in the end don't matter from an intelligence perspective. At those times it can be useful if guidance can be given without contaminating the remote viewing process. This guidance can, with care, be provided through the monitor.

During some operations the monitor might receive additional information about the target, once a viewer starts reporting data that matches the sort of material the customer is looking for. For instance, the monitor might be shown overhead imagery of the target facility, indicating the specific building the customer is interested in. Or the monitor might be told to have the viewer home in on something that she has already noted in earlier sessions.

At Fort Meade, this operational information was seldom provided to the monitor until the viewer was well into a project, with at least a few sessions under her belt. Then, given this limited access to the targeting materials, the monitor was under strict instructions never to volunteer anything about the target to the viewer. Even interest in any particular target aspect was not to be shown until the viewer herself described that aspect in a session.

For example, if the target was a triangle-shaped building with radar dishes on the roof, then the monitor would not be told about this building until the viewer actually described it during the session. Before the second session the project manager might show the monitor a satellite photo of the triangle-shaped building the viewer had already described. If the customer was interested in finding out more about the radar dishes, the project manager might tell this to the monitor. But the monitor would not say anything about any of this to the viewer until she mentioned the dishes. The monitor might then ask only that the viewer describe those items in more detail. Gene Lessman had this to say about the process:

> Not only were the viewers not given "front loading," but over 75 percent of the time the monitors were also not front-loaded. Even after a session, and even after the monitor wrote up the results and submitted them, we were still not briefed back on the success or failure . . . Even on those occasions when the monitor was clued-in to the target, we were strictly prohibited from discussing successes or failures with the viewer, ever.
>
> The monitor had to be very cautious in each session to avoid intentionally or inadvertently "clueing" the viewer in the actual sessions. You can come up with "successes" by the dozens if you give the viewer the target in advance or, worse, "guide" them during the session in a way that you are in effect drawing a detailed sketch of the target and leaving it to them to fill in the colors.[19]

As I found out years later, the Sary Shagan site was somewhat star-shaped, with perhaps five or six points to the star, and lines connecting each of the points with the dome-shaped facility in the center of the design. This pattern had much in common with typical air-defense sites, where the missiles, radars, and command-and-control bunkers are laid out in a starlike configuration. Since Sary Shagan was intended as a missile research facility, this would have been no surprise. What was surprising, though, was the scope of the thing. Where an air-defense position might only be a few hundred yards in diameter, this was one was several miles across.

Gene read me the encrypted coordinates, and for a few sessions things went routinely. By this time in my remote viewing career I had developed a few little tricks and techniques that helped me sort out the data I was getting from complicated targets. For example, though the Stage 6 process usually involved sculpting a model of the target in clay, thus freeing significant information in the process, I found that I could often dispense with the clay, and "model" with hand gestures in the air the structure, device, or feature that I was exploring.

I'm sure it would have appeared strange to an outsider watching me at the table, staring unfocused into space, while tracing the outlines of some arcane piece of machinery in thin air over the table. "Air-modeling" had the disadvantage that it did not produce an actual model of the target in clay that could be photographed for a permanent record. But, often, the items that I modeled were only ancillary to the ultimate core structure of the target, and therefore not particularly important to sculpt in clay. This technique had the advantage of being fast, unmessy, and information-rich.

Similar to this technique was another I used, but this time not necessarily tracing the shape of anything. When confronted with a target with which I only had vague contact, I would, in my imagination, extend my hand and "feel" the textures, contours, and consistencies of the target. To heighten my sensory contact with it, I might imagine myself "licking" it, or even "tasting" it. All these techniques often released basic data that, if not ultimately relevant to what needed to be known about it, deepened my connection with the site, thereby allowing more complex data to flow into my subconscious to be accessed by my conscious awareness.

In the Fort Meade unit we also had mastered the technique of the *movement exercise*. An experienced remote viewer could learn to move his point of view here and there about the target—or from one target to another—in the process capturing information from different locations or vantage points. Movement exercises were especially useful in buildings with many rooms, or at facilities with lots of buildings.

Gene Lessman used movement exercises to get me from point to point at the Sary Shagan dome complex. And here I found something that puzzled him. A few sessions into this project, I came across a large, complex piece of equipment that was irregularly shaped and sported various protuberances, cabling, wires, and such, which I could "feel" as I ran imaginary hands over its outsides. There was something I didn't like about this machine. It seemed dangerous.

"Work your way around whatever this is you've found, and describe," directed Gene, who was monitoring. I tried to do so, following its contours in my mind, describing as I went. But I reached a point where I hesitated.

"I don't want to get in front of it," I said.

Hal Puthoff *(left)* and Ingo Swann striking a pose in the early years of the SRI program. Their first remote-viewing experiment sparked the CIA's interest in psychic spying. *(Courtesy of H. E. Puthoff)*

(From left to right): Hal Puthoff, Russell Targ, CIA scientist Kit Green, and Pat Price together in the mid-1970s. Price's remote viewing revealed secrets known only to the CIA and the Soviets. *(Courtesy of Russell Targ)*

Nathan Hale Hall, where
Army remote viewing began.
(Courtesy of Paul H. Smith)

The remote-viewing
operations building, T-2560.
(Courtesy of Dale Graff)

The operations building housed
remote-viewing "gray rooms."
(Courtesy of Dale Graff)

The U.S.S. *Stark* on fire and drifting
after an Iraqi attack, May 18, 1987.
(Courtesy of the U.S. Navy)

Damage to port side of U.S.S. *Stark*.
(Courtesy of the U.S. Navy)

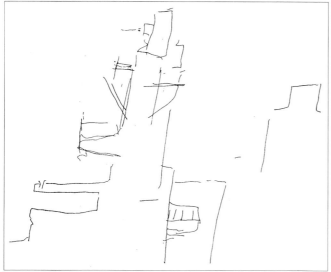

One of several sketches
from author's May 15, 1987,
remote-viewing session
describing a missile attack
on a warship. Fifty hours
later the U.S.S. *Stark* was set
ablaze by Iraqi Exocet missiles.
*(Sketch from the CIA's Star Gate
archive collection)*

Paul H. Smith and
Lieutenant Scott Hawmann
in Saudi Arabia, 1990.
Smith was sent into Iraq with the
101st Airborne Division
during Desert Storm.
(Courtesy of Paul H. Smith)

Dale Graff *(right)* talking with
Senator Claiborne Pell (D-Rhode
Island) outside the Star Gate
offices. Senator Pell came to
Fort Meade for a briefing on the
Star Gate program.
(Courtesy of Dale Graff)

Greg Seward and Dale Graff
on assignment in Key West in the
early 1990s. Data from remote
viewers led to arrests of drug
traffickers and recovery of contraband.
(Courtesy of Dale Graff)

"Why not?" Gene asked.

"It's dangerous. Something comes out of the front that is very harmful."

"What is it?"

"I don't know. Something nasty." Gene was silently thoughtful for a moment.

"Look," he finally said. "Remember, you are not 'there' physically, right? Only your point of view is there, nonphysically. Whatever is coming out of that machine cannot hurt you. You must understand. It *cannot hurt* you. Now move to the front of the thing and describe." Gene has since told me that looking at the overhead photos made him think that the target was some kind of missile silo, and he thought that I had discovered a nuclear-tipped missile. I did as instructed and moved to the "front" of the device, though still hesitantly at first, since logic doesn't always fully trump instinct. I relaxed a little when I found I really *wasn't* harmed, and discovered that whatever was coming out of the thing involved energy that was intense, focused, directed.

By this time in the session I was so far "under" in the remote viewing mode that, once I got over my fear of exposure to it, being in a stream of energy didn't seem particularly exceptional. I was interested, in a contemplative sort of way. I do remember this energy as being bright, and hot, and I seemed to feel a tugging sensation or a tingling as it passed "through" me. Once I had described this to Gene, he had other instructions.

"Okay, go down a level and describe." Though this statement was full of ambiguities—Which way is "down"? What exactly did Gene mean by "level"?—I somehow implicitly knew what he wanted. I refocused my attention on a much smaller scale. But still, all I seemed to be perceiving was hot, glowing, streaming energy.

"Go down another level," Gene instructed after I reported what I was experiencing. I complied, with the same result. We did this a couple of more times before I found a resolution that was fine enough to show a difference. I suddenly felt buffeted by tiny, unseen objects that seemed to have caused the earlier tugging or tingling.

In the years since that session I have learned something about Brownian motion, and remember at some point watching through a microscope as small, one-celled creatures jiggled about, constantly bombarded by energetic, but invisible, molecules in a drop of water. I'm sure those little paramecia felt much the way I did at this moment, being pushed and shoved by tiny things they couldn't "see." But Gene was still not satisfied. "Move down another level," he told me.

Things transformed. The buffeting stopped, and there was somehow a lighter, more relaxed ambience about the experience. I perceived something I described as "sparks." A constant stream of these ephemeral little brightnesses wafted by, past, through. Whenever I tried to focus on one, it became less of a brightness, and more of a swirl or an eddy—a tiny whirlpool of nothing that moved along, even while it spun. In my mind I reached out a hand to grasp one of these spark-eddies as it whirled by. It swirled right on "through" my imaginary hand. I could "feel" it yet not feel it, a tickle that I sensed but which wasn't precisely *tangible*. It was as if these little whirls were there, yet weren't, like little *pieces* of space streaming purposely *through* space.

I realized somehow that I was experiencing the tiniest bits of the universe. Photons, electrons, whatever—tiny charged particles of some sort streaming away. I didn't quite know what to make of the experience, nor how to describe it. I still don't, really. What I have said here only half captures the essence of what I perceived.[20]

I recognized at the time, of course, that what I tried to describe to Gene Lessman was more metaphor than "real." At the basic level at which I seemed to have found myself, one couldn't "see" things; light could only exist in its own component parts. As it turned out, what I was observing was essentially light itself. So what my mind presented to me was a representation, a model that allowed me to make sense of the experience, even if I couldn't fully express it in words. And, though I was to receive no feedback about the target until a decade and a half later in the process of researching for this book, by the end of the session there was no doubt in my mind what I had locked onto; it was some kind of functional directed-energy device. At the time, I got no other feedback than, "good job."

Now though, I think I know a little more about what it was. For years American military officials were worried that the USSR had successfully fielded a working particle beam weapon. These worries were fueled when, according to reports in 1977, a U.S. intelligence satellite flying over Sary Shagan was blinded by a burst of high energy coming from the surface of the planet. There was no question that both the Americans and Russians were in a neck-and-neck race to develop beam weapons. High-powered lasers were one approach. But the real worry from U.S. quarters was that the Soviets would develop a more fearsome particle beam. Such weapons promised great advantages. Unlike missiles or shells, a beam weapon can hit a target up to thousands of miles away virtually instantly, with no flight time having to be taken into account. What is more, unlike bullets or missiles which are effected by gravity and the vagaries of wind, beams hit exactly where they are aimed. And the awesome power such a beam could deliver, all focused on a pencil-wide spot, could be hugely destructive.

The only problem is, such beams require enormous amounts of energy to drive them. At the miles-wide, sprawling, star-shaped dome complex at Sary Shagan, remote viewing allowed us to describe nuclear generating plants at each of the points of the star, with power lines leading into the center. In remote viewing sessions Bill and I both were vectored in to describe a large hydroelectric dam, about eighteen miles away from the complex, which showed up on satellite photos. But according to the data we came up with, the dam provided power only to keep the lights and such running for the people manning the facility. The energy that powered whatever was in the center of the star came from nuclear reactors at the star's points.[21]

With the fall of the Iron Curtain, many closely guarded secrets were exposed to the light of day. Some of these were details of the high-power directed-energy developments at Sary Shagan. All that has come out so far is about lasers. The Soviets were indeed experimenting with, and using against real targets, high-energy gas-dynamic, electric discharge, and chemical lasers. Meant for anti-ballistic missile defense and satellite destruction, none of the lasers were apparently officially introduced as a weapon, though, besides the reports of blinded American satellites, there were also official protests lodged when a laser at Sary Shagan, operating at reduced power, still managed to damage some of the systems on the thirteenth Challenger space shuttle mission on August 10, 1984.[22]

Ostensibly, no successful Soviet particle beam weapons have been uncovered since the end of the Cold War. I cannot say that I would know via my remote viewing experiences the difference between a laser and a particle beam. Gene Lessman believes to this day that what I described was a particle beam, not a laser. Problems with how they propagate through the atmosphere, the immense energy demands required for even short bursts, as well as other so-far-unsolved engineering headaches have made particle beams, at least from the American side of things, an elusive prize. General belief is that the Soviet Union and today's Russia also failed to overcome these immense hurdles. But I sometimes wonder whether there is more still at Sary Shagan than has thus far emerged.

One day in early November 1986, Lyn, Bill, and I gathered in the office in our dress green uniforms, along with Lieutenant Colonel Buzby, who had returned for the occasion. It had been three years since I had worn anything but civilian clothes, and it seemed strange to be in a uniform again. Fred Atwater was there, dressed in his usual civilian attire. A few years before, the Army had moved him into a special category that had removed Atwater even further from public connection with the military. Still a captain, he nonetheless would never wear a uniform again.

As we stood there in the conference room in the back of T-2561, Buzby pinned Meritorious Service Medals on the four of us. General Soyster had signed the commendations for the medals. Perhaps it was a sop thrown us to make amends for what at the time was perceived to be a blow to our careers—being assigned as a "psychic spy." But I preferred to think of it as a nice gesture, a sort of going-away present. INSCOM had no obligation to make these awards, and could certainly have settled for something less prestigious—an Army Commendation medal, or even a mere Army Achievement Award. No doubt one of our friends still in INSCOM headquarters had recommended it, and Soyster agreed.

One of the last official acts for 1986 was the briefing in December, at the request of Senator Claiborne Pell, of the Chairman of the Senate Foreign Relations Committee, who at the time was Richard Luger.[23] Sun Streak was beginning to draw attention. Some was good, but some turned out to be unwelcome.

22

Operational!

"I've found it difficult to write them off entirely. The Scriptures say there will be such people."

—Ronald Reagan, on psychics, 1986

Our first year as adopted children of the Defense Intelligence agency, 1986, had netted us ten operational projects requiring seventy-seven viewer sessions, one-third of which had been mine.[1] On the side, we had begun the process of teaching Mel Riley coordinate remote viewing. I provided the theory lectures and Ed Dames handled the actual training sessions. Given Mel's years of remote viewing experience in the old Grill Flame days, he took to the new method with ease. Like me, though, he sometimes found Ed's choice of training targets a little unusual.

Once, Ed targeted Mel on the center of the Sun. According to Mel, there was no experience of intense heat, as one might expect—only what he called a sort of "nondescript" feeling, akin to "being atomized." And he told me recently of two instances of bilocation he experienced while working practice targets. One occurred when Ed targeted Mel several hundred years into the past.

[Ed] sent me to a place in England, called Mount St. Michael [a walled castle standing on an island a short way off the coast of Cornwall, England] . . . wound up in the middle of a battle 500 years from the present time. He had targeted me in the past . . . it was so dusty I was choking on it, and ducking . . . it was like being there in real time.

The second also involved a time shift:

The other bilocation was when he sent me to the Coliseum in Rome. I'm standing on the outside—I had no idea what the target was—and I see all these guys dressed in Roman-type clothes, kind of lined up single file, like to get into a theater or something. Then the next thing I know, I felt as if I was in the middle of a football stadium . . . everybody cheering and all that other stuff. Then all of a sudden the realization came to me . . . I'm the lion bait. It wasn't funny.[2]

Mel wasn't the only one we were training in coordinate remote viewing; Angela was also learning the ropes. She didn't find the rigor and structure of the CRV methodology particularly congenial, preferring the more relaxed "natural psychic" approach she brought with her to the unit. Gene Lessman had more success using extended remote viewing techniques with her. She seemed to take to that better.[3]

Still, operational at last and eager to show what we could do, we wrapped up 1986 and launched into 1987 with gusto, entering a busy era of remote viewing activity that in many ways was the high point of the Sun Streak period. There seemed a fervid excitement in the office air that made us feel like the whole world had opened to us at its seams, as in a way it had. We were not only maturing as remote viewers, but we were given a wide variety of assignments that allowed us to stretch and grow, which was fine with us.

And by the end of the year there were more new faces among us. The first of these was not really new. Like Mel Riley, Fernand Gauvin, our new operations officer, had a history going back to Grill Flame days. Gauvin, known to one and all as Fern, was one of those who, during the screenings in the late 1970s, had been judged to have good remote-viewing potential, but because of his assignment at the time was not able to serve full-time with the unit.

Instead, he became a "part-timer," assigned elsewhere in INSCOM, but receiving some training in remote viewing. When need and opportunity arose, these "part-timers" would come in, do a session or two, then go back to their regular jobs. Ever since I was assigned to the unit, Fern had on occasion stuck his head into the office to see how things were going. He was of French extraction, spoke the language fluently from his home life, and had the quiet, dark look of the Continent about him. I occasionally plied him with questions, learning that as a young intelligence agent in the 1950s he had served as a field officer in France. Fern had worked in human intelligence his whole career, serving at times as a case officer in the field, and at other times in administration.

Now, in late 1986, with INSCOM's Center Lane project defunct and the DIA in charge of Sun Streak, Fern had been enticed away from INSCOM. He was specifically chosen to replace Fred Atwater as the remote viewing unit's operations officer when Fred retired, a job which was originally intended for Ed Dames.[4] As time wore on, though, the plan for Ed had been rethought, and now, as Fred's retirement drew near it was decided to bring Fern in instead. Fortunately there was time for him to learn the operations-officer ropes while Fred was still with us. It was thought that Fern's long peripheral association with remote viewing, and his extensive HUMINT background, which Ed lacked, would help him more quickly master the necessary skills.

During this period, project management—the tasking, analysis, and procedural arrangements that provided support for the viewing—was handled with a rigor that kept our viewing as clean as possible and prevented sloppy practices that could have jeopardized not only our accuracy, but also our credibility. This did not, unfortunately, always hold true in the years following.

Our first 1987 project was actually forwarded to the office late in 1986. But the initial viewing didn't take place until 1987, so it bore the Sun Streak project number "8701." The task was to describe "current and projected function(s) of unusual structures at" a certain set of coordinates in the Soviet Union.[5] Satellite photos of the structures were handed to Sun Streak project managers, but most of the viewers were never shown them; before, during, or even after. The target was Dushanbe, an unusual layout of giant, puff-ball-shaped metal structures near a large building in a barren area in south-central USSR. At one time western intelligence officers believed it was another particle beam or laser facility. We know now that it was an electro-optical tracking system used by the Soviets to keep an eye on objects in space.[6] Bill Ray and I did most of the twelve sessions worked on this effort, though Lyn contributed one session and Charlene two. I have only jumbled recollections from this project, but it seems we did well. A note on some of the documentation observes that "this was a *very* successful project" (emphasis in the original).[7]

Our next mission, Project 8702 was to "identify key functions of buildings" in a city elsewhere in the Soviet Union. We were, in fact, to provide information concerning one specific building as shown in a photograph.[8] Again, viewers had no access to the pictures. Charlene Shufelt did the best on this project. She said the target was a huge structure located among a cluster of buildings situated in a barren, isolated area, and reported that a building shaped like the letter *H* was nearby. People with bright yellow visors and protective clothing worked in the target building, which itself reminded her of a huge airplane hangar with a domed roof. She found a dish antenna that could move vertically and horizontally, controlled from a console in a room inside the target building. There was some kind of intense blue light associated with the antenna. She said the area had the flavor of a nuclear launching site.

Lyn Buchanan worked two sessions against this target and, like Charlene, mentioned a "persistent bluish light" as being important. My own description of the target was similar to Charlene's, though not as detailed, and I mentioned an impression that the building had something to do with "aerospace." Although I have no feedback to be able to say how accurate our perceptions were, there were some strong correspondences between the individual impressions of the four of us who worked it (Bill Ray contributed four sessions). In the end, though, Charlene was credited as having "the best target acquisition in addressing the issue of specific interest."[9]

Similar taskings quickly followed. Project 8703 was canceled before any work was done, but in 8704 we were asked to describe the purpose of a facility located a few miles from a Soviet chemical and biological test area. The still-classified nature of the target prevents me from being more specific about its location. This project took five viewers and fifteen sessions to complete. I led with four, Charlene, Bill, and Angela each did three, with Lyn providing two.

Despite the fact that we worked completely independently of each other and blind, the correlations between our various reports were impressive. Among other details, three of us reported something green (described by me as a puffy, translucent cloud formed by an aerosol spray, by Charlene as an "emerald green light," and by Lyn as something "transparent green") that had a debilitating effect on humans. Lyn and I said it caused a burning feeling on the skin, while I noted also a "stinging sensation in the nasal passages and a watering of the eyes." Lyn and I also both said that those who knew about this phenomenon found it repulsive in some way, while Angela and I noted that the workers at the site didn't like the place, and had to be ordered to work there.

In a movement exercise to a related building, four of us described the notions of containment and people wearing protective clothing, and we all had close agreement that the building was being used to store some sort of "contaminants" or a "dangerous, manmade substance."

It usually happens in a relatively large-scale remote viewing operation like 8704 that one or two viewers will be off on a tangent. Such was the case this time with Bill, who described a group of people involved in a discussion at the target building concerning "lightweight metals and alloys." However, even Bill mentioned something useful—the presence of chickens and pigs. This might be out of place in a metallurgy lab, but would be consistent with a chemical warfare research facility, which is what all the rest of us seemed to be describing. In a considerable understatement, the report on this project noted that "there was a perceptible continuum of correlation in the information" among the viewers.[10]

Later on, in the fall, we received still more facility-type targets, such as Project 8715: "Describe nature and scope of activity at a facility at" another set of geographic coordinates, with the addendum "Describe manner in which this is accomplished"; and for project 8716: "Describe purpose of cylindrically-shaped storage structures" at a Soviet electronics plant. We also received Project 8717: "Describe purpose and features of . . . target structures at a new target site." (This project was later evaluated as having "good correlation," and given a "+" score.)[11] We had over a dozen of these "facility" targets in 1987, most of which involved secret research or technology sites in the Soviet Union.

Of course, it wasn't for us, the viewers, to answer the tasking questions that accompanied the targets; we were never even aware of them. We provided the raw data in response to the coordinates we were given. But making sense of the data was the job of a project manager—Fred Atwater or Gene Lessman. Or, sometimes, Ed Dames. It was they who had to sort out the viewers' sessions, to digest the information provided, and figure out how it went together.

This was no easy chore. Sometimes the information conflicted, while other times viewers might agree in certain details that, based on what the analyst knew about the target, seemed to be wrong. To add to the complications of sorting it all out, viewers might describe the same aspects of a target in different terms from each other, or from different perspectives. For complex targets, one viewer might know the right word for a piece of equipment or feature at a target, while another viewer with a different vocabulary might lack the necessary word and take long minutes trying to describe the concept in roundabout ways. And there was always the danger of undeclared AOL for the analyst to be wary of and try to sort out when it was encountered.

For the viewers and their monitors, these structure targets presented interesting challenges—for example, how to determine if the viewer was in the right place and at the right time to describe what the intelligence-community customer needed to know. The problem here was not peculiar to remote viewing. Suppose you, in a wide-awake state, were transported at random around the world to some nondescript laboratory. How would you begin to know what to look for, and how to make sense of what you could see or experience there? First, you would certainly see nothing special about the outside of the building. It would look much like hundreds, or possibly thousands of other buildings you had seen over the course of your travels. Once inside, you would be confronted with room after room, floor after floor, of commonplace chairs, desks, and shelves. Other rooms might be larger, with complex scientific equipment of all descriptions. How would you tell a gas mass spectrometer from a scanning electron microscope, or a materials strain-measuring gauge from some other equally obscure instrument? Perhaps someone with extensive scientific training might manage it, but the average person might be hard-pressed to sort it out.

Several of the viewers had some exposure to technical subjects, but no one could possibly be well versed in every one of the wide variety of complicated targets we encountered. With the added challenge of trying to extract the subtle impressions remote viewing presented from the subconscious, it might at first seem to be an impossible task. Working with our monitors, we had to develop some strategies that would maximize our chances for success.

First, we had to be methodical in handling the maze of buildings, rooms, corridors, and hallways encountered with some of these targets, almost creating an internal map of the facility as we traced our way through. The aerial reconnaissance photos that were sometimes provided with these sorts of taskings were very useful for this; not that the viewers would be shown the photos. The normal procedure was to give the viewer encrypted coordinates, and go through one or two sessions where both viewer and monitor were blind, while attempting to describe the outer appearance and setting of the structures in which the customer was interested. If the customer had provided corroborating materials, the project manager would then compare the viewer's descriptions to the photograph or description of the target to determine if she was in the ballpark.

If the viewer seemed to be "on," further sessions would be done, often with the monitor being given access bit by bit to the target materials as sessions progressed. For targets with several important structures near each other, such as a laboratory complex, a monitor might "walk" a viewer from one to another, until the viewer had the general lay of the land, and then more detailed work could be done.

The insides of the structures posed some of the same challenges that the outsides did. Inside there might be, for example, three floors with rooms of differing sizes and uses on each. Once directed inside, the viewer might again "walk" through each room, directed by the monitor.

A monitor might say, "Inside the structure you described as tall, grey, with few windows and an antenna on the roof, something should be perceivable." The viewer would transfer her point of view inside the building. "A room. Windows; parallel things along the walls that remind me of bookshelves," she might respond.

"Move to the next room and describe," the monitor might continue.

"A large room. Well lit. Tables. Objects. Tubes, electrical parts, papers with writing on them. Scientific. Chemical-related." After a long description that might go on for many minutes and several pages of handwritten transcript, the monitor would then encourage the viewer to move on to the next room. And so the two, acting as a team, would make their way to the heart of the structure, with the aim of discovering along the way the purpose and activities taking place there. In a sense, they were making a conceptual—and sometimes literal—map of the structure. But it was seldom a complete map. There was usually no need for that, and the configurations and relations would certainly have been distorted, given the vagaries of remote-viewing perception of dimensional relationships. At least in one respect a good remote viewer had an edge over a spy who was physically at the target; a viewer could often glean intangible facts that would not likely be discernable to someone who had sneaked into a secret facility.

I remember one case of a building where I found large reservoirs of a viscous, yellow-greenish liquid that was corrosive and nasty-smelling. All of this could have been detected by a person physically at the target. However, I also sensed that the substance was purposely intended to bring harm to people. This information would not necessarily have been available to a person at the site, unless someone there was willing to share that information. And a spy who had sneaked in would be unlikely to do something as obvious as ask. I discovered a few years later that the target turned out to be a chemical weapons factory.

This approach to canvassing targets sometimes generated a laugh. On one occasion when told to move from one room to the next, Bill Ray refused to comply.

"I can't!" he said.

"Why not?" the monitor asked.

"A wall is in the way!"

"Go through it."

"I can't."

"Sure you can. You're not really 'there'—only a little of your awareness is."

"No!" Bill continued to refuse. Instead, he looked for a door that took him out into the hall and then another door to the adjoining room. Whether the door was closed, or even locked, didn't matter. He just felt better using doors than going through walls.[12]

I never had the same inhibition. But it did make for a surprise the first time I was told to "move into the next room" during a session. I did it literally, or as literally as it can be done in remote viewing. Without thinking, I shifted my perspective from the room I was in, through the wall, and into the next space. But as I moved *through* that wall, I was astonished to find that I perceived its construction in cross section. I passed through a thin layer of paint, old crumbling fiberboard, and then firlike framing studs. This interwall space was dusty and gritty, as if a collecting place for decades of microscopic debris. On my way back out again I encountered more fiberboard, and more thin layers of flaking paint, covered by what seemed to be a layer of very ugly wallpaper.

All these perceptions came to me almost instantly—only as long as it took to traverse the short space the wall occupied. It may be that my subconscious supplied the impressions one might expect when going through a wall. But by then we had learned many times over that what surprises a viewer usually turns out to be real data. Further, if we ran into something that was different from anything we might consciously have expected or even imagined, it was usually true. Given that the experience took me completely by surprise—and that wallpaper was nothing that I would ever have imagined on purpose—I am fairly confident that the experience was real.

We had other kinds of targets besides enemy science labs. Though many of these came to us directly from DIA offices, taskings often originated from outside that agency. For several months, Dr. Jack Vorona had been chairing a regularly scheduled Remote Viewing Tasking Group for Sun Streak. Several important intelligence agencies sent representatives: the CIA often had someone present (though due to Agency politics it was usually on an informal basis); the technical intelligence director from the National Security Agency was usually there; the intelligence staffs of the Army, Navy, and Air Force sent a full colonel or the civilian equivalent; the brigadier general commanding the Army Intelligence Agency often attended, as did a representative of the Intelligence Community Staff named Cindy Hill. As Sun Streak's commander, Bill Ray was usually there, along with Dale Graff. The group met to discuss and nominate intelligence targets for us to explore. Taskings that came out of the meetings were usually funneled through Dr. Vorona's office, so our mission log showed them as coming from DIA-DT, which was the office symbol for Vorona's Directorate for Scientific and Technical Intelligence.[13]

Like our Grill Flame predecessors, we were tasked with locating tunnels being dug under the Demilitarized Zone between North and South Korea. For another mission we were asked to describe an event that had happened somewhere in the world several months previously. Showing interesting unanimity, though completely blind to the target, five of us described a sparsely inhabited, desertlike area in a Third World country where some sort of weapon was tested, resulting in the deaths or injury of a score or more of the indigenous people. Now, nearly a decade and a half after that particular project, I can only speculate that it had something to do with some new Soviet technology being tried out in Afghanistan.

Yet another assignment directed us to describe the locations of two launchers for Silkworm surface-to-surface missiles supplied to the Iranians by the Chinese. These launchers, together with their missiles, were originally discovered and identified by aerial photography. Later photography showed them missing from their original locations. Silkworms were worrisome because the eight-year Iran-Iraq war still raged, and Iran had used Silkworms before to attack ships in the Persian Gulf. American strategists feared that the missiles would be used to close the narrow straits at the mouth of the Persian Gulf, cutting off much of the world's oil supply. So when the missiles disappeared, the office tracking them asked for our help.

My first input to the problem was interesting, if indirect: upon hearing the encrypted coordinate and going through the now well-oiled CRV process, I described an object that was "linked and controlled," and associated with an "urban-located, somehow-hidden, organization that is vying in a competitive or confrontational sense with another, larger, more open organization. Having this object or device, which is heavy, metal, but still moveable when necessary, lends power or influence to those who have control of it. This advantage is lost if it becomes known where either its controllers or the device itself is located."

Here is the remote-viewing motto, "describe, don't name," taken to its logical extreme. On a first reading, the wording is spare and emotionless. Yet it captures the important dynamics between Iran and the United States, the value of the missiles (though admittedly I only mention one "object"), the fact that they were hidden, and why it was important to find them. None of this, of course, was I told prior to or during the sessions.

This time, for some reason, perhaps as an experiment, my handlers broke with tradition and at the beginning of the third session told me the "device" I had discovered was a missile, and that I was supposed to describe its location. Without knowing whose missile it was or in which country it might be, I described an oppressively hot, rundown, industrial area. Disassembled missiles were located in a large room in what appeared to be an old warehouse. It also seemed to me that the missiles would be moved in a week or so to another location in some hills not too far distant. I perceived this second location to be an old, abandoned structure with an underground component to it. I provided sketches of my impressions.

What I had described was inconclusive. Perhaps it just came out of my imagination once I had been told that missiles were involved. After all, at that time—the summer of 1987—people were fretting about missiles in the Middle East, and the Middle East was certainly consistent with my mention of an oppressively hot area.

But three other sources worked the same target, and perceived similar things. Mel described a flat plain with moderate-sized mountains in the distance. He said one location was an "aboveground dungeon" which held prisoners. Whether any prisoners were actually there was unknown. But Mel linked this location to another in foothills to the northeast. This second place was a cavern or vault dug into a hillside, hidden behind a large, sliding metal door. The cavern was empty at the time he perceived it, and he thought it had been abandoned for many years.

Lyn reported perceptions of a large complex of flat-topped buildings located in a hot, arid location. He found one "missile" in a large room, supported on a stand, being worked on by a technician. Angela used similar words to talk about the landscape and structures. She reported that the missile would shortly be moved to a new location she described as a "low tunnel."

It is hard to say whether coincidence or suggestion from possible front-loading of one or more of the other viewers contributed to the similarity of our responses. But even if all of us were told, as I was a way into the project, that we were looking for missiles, it seems unlikely that we still could have come up with elements as similar as we did.

Apparently our pooled descriptions suggested something concrete. The final report noted that "Based on an assessment of the data provided, the current storage area for the Silkworm missiles was identified at Tab B" in the report. It was also noted that we all seemed to ignore the missile launchers, and instead "concentrated on the location of the missile storage area(s) as the single most important issue in this search." This would, of course, make sense. Without missiles, a launcher is not much use.[14]

Interesting as it was, the Silkworm project seems anticlimactic when compared with a session I had worked a few months previously.

"Feel like doing an operational session today?" Ed Dames stood in front of my desk, a predator in search of prey.[15]

I eyed him dubiously. "This isn't one of your *weird* targets, is it?"

"No, not at all!" The problem with Ed was that I could never tell if he was playing it straight—doing his job as assistant trainer—or just saying whatever it took to suck me into another one of his searches for extraterrestrial life.

I scrutinized Ed's face. Protocol forbade me from asking what the session would be about. I was at his mercy.

I looked at my watch. It was 9:30 A.M. on Friday, May 15, 1987. I had time to humor him. "Sure, why not," I said.

"Okay." He smiled. "Head on over to the ops building and cool down. I'll be over in a few minutes."

I walked next door to Building 2560, entered the ERV room, and turned out the lights. Clamping my Walkman headphones over my ears, I stretched out on the bed and pushed the play button. As hard rock thundered into my ears, my mind grew active, while my muscles relaxed. This taxpayer-funded ritual was a luxury that I never took for granted—to lie motionless on a soft bed, listening to my favorite tunes, preparing myself for government work. Twenty minutes later, I heard Ed enter the building. He pushed the ERV room door open a crack to let light in—a wordless signal to me that it was time to begin. I rolled groggily off the bed and followed him down the hall to the CRV room. As usual, we took chairs at opposite ends of the table.

"Are you set?" he asked. I nodded and grunted as I wrote down my "personal inclemencies," the list of things that were bothering me and that I had to mentally set aside before we began. My wife had moved out two weeks earlier. For the time being, I was Mr. Mom to three confused kids. My car was acting up. Bills were due.

When I stopped scribbling, Ed said, "It's 1023 hours." I wrote that down. He waited until I put my pen at the usual start point on the page. "Three six nine, one four seven . . ." Ed intoned.

"Three six nine, one four seven," I repeated, writing the numbers down.

"Three one two, two zero zero," Ed finished.

"Three one two, two zero zero," I parroted. It was my coordinate for the search: 369147 312200. My hand moved reflexively, dragging the pen along, making the "ideogram," or the reflexive mark that resulted from a viewer's first contact with the psychic "signal." It formed a broken line across the page with a blip in the center where the line jogged up and then down again. I was immersed in the session.

More than a decade later, as I look at the notes from that session, they seem at the beginning routine enough. I scrawled "land," "water," "structure," and something I enigmatically called "surfaces." I saw large amounts of grey and some white. I heard a clanging sound and sniffed the faint odor of something I could only describe as sauteed "celery." There were other sensations; something greasy, cold, and wet. Nothing so far to chill the spine, yet I felt compelled to write, "forbidding, taken aback."

In another few moments I had sketched a tall structure with stair-step levels. Next to it I filled in four rows of circles, evenly spaced, which reminded me of perforated steel planking, the sheets of evenly punctured metal used to make temporary runways on soft ground. I knew that wasn't what I was seeing. It seemed more like the helicopter deck of a Navy ship.

I refined my drawing of the structure, coming up with something that spiked up, with angular projections and levels. I wrote descriptive words, and spoke them aloud to Ed. It was metal, tall, designed to be functional, not pretty. There were stanchions, extrusions, braces, and some "appurtenances" that reminded me of radars. Whatever the target was, it radiated a cold, matter-of-fact, unemotional quality. Weaponry of some sort was associated with it, though I couldn't say exactly how. And the whole thing seemed to be moving.

I glanced quickly at Ed. Was he going to assume I'd found one of his alien spaceships? No, he was clearly bored, his chin resting in his hand, his eyes staring at the tasking sheet in front of him. Whatever I was reporting didn't seem to be what he wanted. I had started by telling him I saw a land-and-water interface. Barring an alien invasion on some sandy beachhead, we were clearly not talking here about flying saucers and their little green pilots. I returned to the task at hand.

This "moving structure" was a vessel, I declared. It had something to do with waiting and watching, security and a "magnetic envelope." There was a vaguely sensed connection with antisubmarine warfare. I had the distinct impression that I was describing an American destroyer, but I dismissed that as AOL, my imagination working overtime. Whatever its type, I knew it was a warship, cruising at night a "long distance" out in a body of water bordered by large stretches of hot, flat, sandy terrain. Many of the ship's crew were asleep.

Then the session took an unusual turn.

I recorded something that I sensed occurred as a preliminary to the main event—a glare, a bright flash, and a noise I spelled out as "zzzzzzztttt." The sound came from a metal cylinder with something "like wings" on it that were short and stubby. The cylinder was "dropped and left," and turned this way and that in the air. It was "distant, then approaching." I sensed that the people on the vessel knew the object was coming at them, and I recorded their reaction: "unreal—can't believe this is going on." They milled around in confusion, unsure of what to do. They were "watching, anticipating, cowering," as the object moved somewhat erratically towards them.

And then the people and the moving cylinder "seem somehow to come together. The structure/vessel shivers, shakes, quivers." There were a "clang," a "screech," and a "metallic squeal" that set my teeth on edge. I sensed the vessel tip. There was smoke, and something falling. Dented, broken structure and parts were "tangled about." People lay amid metal debris and heat. The image came to me of hoses snaking across flat surfaces and through openings, accompanied by raised, frantic voices. The vessel was changed, I wrote. It was now "crumpled or bent."

By this time, Ed was at least paying attention. He suggested I focus more on the metal cylinder with wings. I described it as cramped, hollow, and divided into sections containing portions that were under pressure in one place, inert in another. I was confused, though; it sometimes seemed there were two of these cylinders, and then maybe only one. There was no doubt, however, that it or they were dropped from an airplane. It gave me a very strong impression of an Exocet missile in a Falklands War naval battle. More of my imagination at work, I figured, and called it AOL.

The original point of departure for the aircraft that dropped the winged cylinder was also in a hot, flat, sandy desert area just inland from the edge of the body of water in which the warship had been sailing. I somehow knew that all this was a long way from the United States.

Now I turned to the people. There were two groups, perhaps nationalities or races—those on the vessel, and a second group responsible in some way for the flying object. I tried to home in on the second group. They seemed to be wearing tan uniforms with black belts and bits of red and green. These people answered to some authority, but were lax in their conduct and professionalism; they reminded me of a militia as opposed to a professional military. Their actions were being directed from the highest possible level in their organization.

The orders originated in an austere city so far inland that face-to-face control over the actual perpetrators was not possible. The city was crowded, but sprawling, and set in a bleak landscape, surrounded by low, barren hills. The buildings were mostly square and flat-roofed, made of rough, white masonry. I sensed domestic animals in some of the streets, and noted that "it is definitely Third World," and "it makes me think of Greece with fewer trees." I had the impression that the people native to the city were argumentative, hot-tempered and, by Western standards, irrational. The thought came to me that they were speaking Arabic, but having been an Arabic linguist in the past, I dismissed that idea too, presuming once again that it was AOL.

There was a general sense of animosity towards the vessel that pervaded the actions of the people in the tan uniforms who controlled the flying object. The concept "accident," came to mind, as well as the impression that for at least someone involved with the apparent attack, it was an accident they had hoped would happen. But the effects were "far more pronounced" than they expected. Control of whatever had happened was not as professional or painstaking as it should have been. In fact, there was an aura of miscalculation about it—as my notes say, "possible damage results [were] uninten-tional." Nevertheless, there was a sense of "accidentally on purpose"—as if it were a game of "chicken" being played with the intent to intimidate without causing actual harm, meant almost as a "shot across the bow" but resulting in a miscalculation and coming "too close."

By now, Ed had had enough. What I had tuned into was not what he had been looking for and he seemed disappointed. "We'd better stop here, Paul," he said. "I guess you're just off today. But that's okay. Nobody can be on *all* the time." End-time for the session was 11:36 A.M. A little more than an hour had passed. We returned to the headquarters building, and at the end of the day went home for the weekend.

On Monday morning I got my kids off to school and was headed out the door when the phone rang. I ran back into the house to get it. "Paul, where's that session you did on Friday?" It was Fred Atwater, performing his job as operations officer.

My mind searched for an answer. I had already forgotten the session. Finally I recalled, "It's in my safe drawer."

"Well, get in here and dig it out. We want a detailed summary of it as soon as possible!"

"What's all the excitement?"

"Haven't you seen the paper yet? Go look at the front page." I retrieved that morning's *Washington Post* from the couch and unfolded it. The headline read: "Iraqi Missile Sets U.S. Frigate Ablaze, Causing Casualties."[16] Accord-ing to the story, while patrolling in the Persian Gulf shortly after 9 P.M. Bagh-dad time on Sunday, the U.S.S. *Stark* had been struck by an antiship missile fired by an Iraqi fighter-bomber.

Rushing to the office, I pored over my session transcript. It was soon clear that I had described the attack on the *Stark* in great detail, fifty hours before it actually happened. I dashed off a report and made a typed copy of the transcript (my handwriting became virtually illegible during a session). The information was quickly forwarded up the chain of command, though I have no idea how far it went.

In the aftermath of this sudden turn of events, I was briefly dumfounded, but my mental equilibrium soon returned. In the ensuing days, the more I read about the *Stark* incident, the more obvious it became how precise my description had been. A few years later I obtained a copy of the Navy's final after-action report of the tragedy, and it cleared up many of my questions, including my impression of two flying cylinders. An Iraqi Mirage F-1 fighter-bomber had fired two Exocets at the American warship from just over ten miles away. The *Stark*'s crew knew their ship was targeted by missiles only a few long seconds before the Exocets struck. Frantic warnings from lookouts came too late to avert the attack. The first missile failed to explode on impact, but punched through the ship, spreading burning fuel throughout the *Stark's* interior. However, the second Exocet did explode, demolishing large portions of the hull and superstructure. Many of the crew were asleep in their bunks, and either died there, or awoke to smoke, fire, and pandemonium. For twenty hours the *Stark's* survivors, together with teams from other U.S. Navy ships arriving on the scene, battled the inferno and tended to the casualties. Despite grim expectations, they managed to save the *Stark*, but it took months of rebuilding to get her seaworthy again. And thirty-seven American sailors died.[17]

The Iraqi jet made it safely back to its staging area at an airfield just inland from Iraq's Persian Gulf coast. From the outset, the State Department presumed the attack was inadvertent. America was, after all, unofficially friends with Iraq, and was supporting Baghdad in its war against Iran. Besides, Iraqi pilots were known as relatively poor but very enthusiastic fighter jockeys who just might make a mistake like this. Iraqi officials apologized for the regrettable error, and eventually paid reparations to the families of the dead sailors. The so-called Tanker War between Iran and Iraq had been going on for several years and, of course, accidents *do* happen.

There is an epitaph to this story. In the course of my session that Friday morning in May 1987, I reported a large aircraft with several engines orbiting and observing as the event took place. That piece of data always puzzled me. The aircraft didn't seem to be a belligerent, though after the fact I just assumed it must have been. I found my answer a decade later when I picked up the Navy's after-action report again and reread a portion that I had forgotten. Suddenly something clicked.

There had been a U.S. Air Force AWACS aircraft on loan to the Saudis, which had tracked and reported on the Iraqi Mirage jet throughout its flight. The AWACS had been providing regular updates to the *Stark* on the Iraqi jet's course. After the attack the AWACS called in two Saudi Arabian F-15s to attack the Iraqi plane, but the Saudi pilots were unable to get clearance to shoot until it was too late. With this discovery about the AWACS, the last piece fell into place.

For me the session was at once exhilarating and troubling. Were it possible for observers to look down and watch Ed and me doing our job, they would have found it tedious and forgettable. We were just two guys at opposite ends of a grey table in a grey room—one sitting with a stack of paper in front of him, muttering in a flat, sleepy voice and scribbling down isolated words and phrases, while the second guy fiddled with his pen and stole frequent glances at his watch.

Inside my head, it was an entirely different story. I was vicariously living an event that, it turned out, hadn't yet happened. A story was unfolding—compelling, intriguing, confusing, and rich in thoughts and emotions radiating from both sides in the tragedy. It wasn't for me a particularly traumatic experience, since what came from the men I was eavesdropping on was muted by the filters of space and time. As puzzled as I was about the events that I witnessed through those filters, I was still more puzzled when Ed told me I must have been "off." My impressions had *seemed* real, though from everything I knew about what was going on in the world at the time, it made no sense.

It turned out that I had done something rare not only in the annals of remote viewing, but rare for other methods of psychic prediction as well. Not only did what I perceive actually come to pass, but it was also accurate down to even small details. The colors of Iraqi uniforms, the lax professionalism and demeanor of the Iraqi military, the command relationship between pilot and superiors, even the description of Baghdad, the city where the commanding headquarters was located, were all correct for the time in which they were described.

Whenever I've told this story in the years since, I've often been asked, if we had in our hands such detailed and accurate information about an imminent and unexpected attack on a U.S. warship, why didn't we immediately report it to the Pentagon for action? I answer that it wasn't as simple as it sounds, and might not have done any good anyway.

In the first place, Ed was convinced that the session was "off." I discovered afterwards that he was trying to send me on what amounted to a wild-goose chase. It was an "open search" tasking, the intent of which was best expressed by the phrase "report on whatever the most important thing is for us to know right now." We did those open searches occasionally. But this time, Ed had something more specific in mind when he created that tasking. The "most important thing" he was looking for was tied into his fantasy about a "Supreme Galactic Council" of aliens. Despite his previous denials, he really *had* expected me to gather intelligence on UFOs or extraterrestrials.

When I didn't, he was disappointed, presumed that I had let my imagination interfere with the target, and concluded that the session was a bust. Since he was the monitor, I took him at his word, despite the seeming quality of my perceptions during the session. I was the viewer and therefore not a reliable judge of whether I was "on" or "off."

But even if we had decided the report was accurate, and tried to pass it on for action, it would have encountered a nest of dilemmas that always makes prediction difficult (and not just remote viewing prediction but even conventional, analysis-based prediction). What action can you justify based on something that hasn't happened yet, told you by a source whose reliability is doubted by the majority of typical intelligence analysts? Should every Navy ship that fit my description in every area of the world that even remotely matched my picture be put on heightened alert? If alerted thusly, should the *Stark* have fired on the Iraqi aircraft, based only on my session? Would that have altered the future by turning this into a different international incident, one that this time cast the United States as the bad guy? If the *Stark* had fired first and the dead were Iraqis, could we ever have convinced the international community that it was in self-defense? Should we shoot down a plane from a nation with which we were not at war, based solely on a report from an obscure psychic working for Uncle Sam?

In another possible outcome, the *Stark* and other ships might be ordered to go to a heightened state of alert. The attacker, upon detecting active fire control radars, would perhaps have been deterred, and thus never initiated the attack. This would have saved thirty-seven American lives and millions of dollars in damage. But our report would then have been labeled "wrong." We predicted an attack and nothing happened. The next time, like the boy who cried "Wolf!" our warnings would be ignored. A tragedy would only have been postponed, not averted.

There was yet another, bigger problem. We remote viewers usually didn't trust the sessions in which we predicted the future. More often than not, "future" sessions turned out to be wrong. Based on our previous track record, we wouldn't have been confident enough to back up our predictions with the force necessary to get the attention of someone with the power to make a difference. There are reasons for this poor showing in precognitive remote viewings, which I shall discuss more fully in the next chapter.

There were still useful lessons to be learned from the *Stark* session. One was that a remote viewer is not doomed to be a victim of telepathic overlay—the psychic impressions that come from the thoughts of others. In this case, I avoided being sidetracked by Ed's passion for UFOs. Had I picked up so-called telepathic impressions from Ed and talked about flying saucers and his mythical Supreme Galactic Council, I certainly would have been psychic. But it would have been psychic in the *wrong way* as far as useful remote viewing is concerned. A remote viewer is supposed to bring back real data from the target, not pick it from the minds of the tasker or others working on the same project.

In fact, in certain situations telepathic overlay is a real problem for remote viewers, especially when several viewers are working the same target. One viewer may perceive the actual target, while another viewer tunes into the first viewer's thoughts, rather than actual target data. If the target were, for example, a Soviet nuclear weapons plant, the first viewer might describe and sketch an elaborate device discovered inside one of the buildings. If the second viewer were on target, she could describe the same piece of equipment, but from a different perspective and include some details the first viewer overlooked.

If the second viewer instead "read the mind" of the first, then she might describe an almost identical picture. As long as the first viewer was "on target," there would be no harm done, but no new information added, either. However, if the first viewer was way off the mark, the duplicate description from the second would boost the credibility of the faulty data. Someone analyzing the two similar sessions might think the viewers had corroborated each other and nailed the target, when in reality, both had failed.

Remote viewing analysts in our unit always had to be on guard against telepathic overlay, since forwarding reports up the chain of command with false conclusions made us look unreliable and sullied the reputation—such as it was—of psychically gathered intelligence. More worrisome was the possibility that generals or admirals might use a false report from us when they pondered whether to put their troops in harm's way. The problem isn't unique to remote viewing. Every intelligence gatherer must weigh the accuracy of his information, whether it comes from the whispered words of a spy, the intercepted bits and bytes of a computer, or a psychic signal grabbed from the ether.

We were trained by Ingo Swann to "go" to the target for information rather than reading the minds of our fellow viewers, or of the taskers who picked our targets, or of the monitors who sat in on our sessions. In an effective remote viewing project, the tasker must have as few preconceptions as possible as to the nature of the target or the desired information. Otherwise, a tasker's strongly held opinions or biases may color or even run away with the impressions of the viewer. In such a case, the viewer may think she is describing the target, but is in reality reporting what is in the tasker's mind. As a result, the viewer will report precisely what the tasker expects to hear, and groundless misperceptions are enshrined as validated fact. This form of telepathic overlay came to play a significant role in events that unfolded years later, after the remote viewing project was jettisoned by the CIA.

Such was potentially the situation with the *Stark* session. Ed Dames wanted desperately for me to discover new, titillating proof of extraterrestrial life. Indeed, if he had decided in his own mind that the numbers he gave me as coordinates referred to his "Galactic Council," or some other supposed alien target, I might have been sucked into his telepathic signal. Instead he inadvertently, but fortuitously, sent me on a valid open search for "the most important thing for *us* to know about." I was subconsciously able to avoid the telepathic trap and report extremely urgent—and terrestrial—information, despite the strength of Ed's actual intent. This showed that in certain environments and with proper tasking, an experienced remote viewer *could* get beyond telepathic overlay, even when there was strong subconscious pressure towards it.

But there was another lesson to be gleaned from this incident. The *Stark* session was unusually *clean*—clean in the sense that in no way could I have been inadvertently cued through Ed's behavior or body language, or through subconsciously overhearing him discuss his goal with someone else, or by surreptitious peeking at the target folder, or any of the other myriad bluffs which skeptics and critics use to explain away remote viewing successes. I perceived a future that no tasker or monitor or kibitzer could have known about, described it in minute detail, and locked my description in a safe two days before the event took place.

As I mentioned before, it was sometimes useful for the monitors to know something about the targets for operational reasons, so they could gauge early whether a viewer was off on a tangent, or so they could recognize when a viewer was homing in on data that might help answer whatever a mission's ultimate intelligence goal might be. Of course, it was not a good idea for the monitor to know *too* much about the target, either. The more a monitor knew, the greater the risk that he or she might "lead" the viewer by providing cues verbally or nonverbally, accidentally giving target information to or creating distracting overlay for the viewer.

The end result was that our sessions were usually, but not always "pure" in the scientific sense. And although we were not scientists incubating a new vaccine, we were still sometimes criticized for not using tighter scientific protocols. It didn't seem to matter to the critics that we often produced intelligence that neither monitor, nor tasker, nor analyst, nor intelligence customer had any inkling about, yet nevertheless turned out to be accurate. We were doing our job, but sometimes the criticism rankled.

Since the *Stark* session occurred outside the rigorous confines of a lab, by the rules of science it cannot be considered scientific proof. Still, it is strong evidence for the existence of psychic phenomenon and for the credibility of remote viewing. There are enough witnesses who can attest that the session was done before the fact to establish its truth to most people's satisfaction.

I don't fancy myself to be a fortune teller. I've never before or since, over years of remote viewing, ever had a session quite like this one. The *Stark* session was a gift, plain and simple. It could just as easily have fallen into the lap of any one of my colleagues, but I was the one blessed by fortune, or by fate, which in itself is an inscrutable and humbling fact.

What the session says about national security or Iraq-U.S. relations is of only passing curiosity. What it says about the nature of time is far more compelling.

23

Transitions

"You can only see a thing
well when you know in
advance what is going to
happen."

—John Tyndall

There are two things people always want a "psychic" to do—predict the
future, and find someone or something that is missing. It wasn't any different for government remote viewers. We called these two challenges
"future" and "search." Even though they were the two things it seemed like
we were most often asked to try, they were also the two hardest things to do.
We came to expect success when we used remote viewing to describe fixed
targets, people, events, and objects in past or present time. But when it came
to future and search, all bets were off. Search was a serious problem, one that
we worked years to solve and never quite did. I will talk more about it later.

Describing future events presented other difficulties, and was also an
ongoing challenge. Stoked by media portrayals, most people have inflated
notions of how well a "psychic" should be able to predict the future. People
trying to make a living as "intuitives" sometimes make matters worse by
exaggerating their success record. They would not generate many customers

with the truth: "Twenty percent accuracy guaranteed!" By my observation, that seems to be about the best anyone can do—twenty percent, and I'm afraid even that is overoptimistic. Why so little? If one can foretell the future some of the time, shouldn't he or she be able to do it all of the time? The answer, it seems, is no.

This twenty-percent figure—which is really only a seat-of-the-pants estimate—came from many attempts by me and my cohorts, over nearly two decades, to remote view the future. We were often asked at the Fort Meade unit to predict when and where the next terrorist attack would occur; whether an upcoming missile test would be successful; when an ailing foreign leader might die; and so on. We had some successes. Joe McMoneagle correctly predicted within a few weeks when the *Typhoon* submarine would be launched after he remote viewed it hidden inside Building 402 at the Severodvinsk Shipyard in the U.S.S.R. Greg Seward, one of the last remaining viewers when the program was shut down in 1995, predicted North Korean leader Kim Il-Song's death three days before it happened on July 15, 1994. (Actually, what Greg said on July 12 was that Kim would die or become incapacitated "before October".) And of course there was my *Stark* session.

But we had notable failures predicting the future, as well—many more failures than successes. Several attempts during the early 1980s turned up projections of terrorist attacks that failed to materialize. Angela was known in the office for predicting the releases of specific hostages in Lebanon that never occurred. A project in 1989, designed specifically to see just what level of accuracy might be achieved in predicting future targets, produced barely one marginal hit out of ten tries.[1]

As a result of a previous and even more exhaustive effort in 1987, the following conclusions were drawn, extracted here from Sun Streak's 1987 annual report to Dr. Jack Vorona, Director, DIA-DT:

> An estimated 130 sessions conducted by six viewers under a Utility Assessment known as Project "P", revealed a near total inability to predict future events. Except for a few isolated, eye-catching successes, there was no evidence of consistency or reliability in the results obtained from remote viewing efforts conducted in a predictive mode. Remote viewing "the future" does not appear to be feasible or a marketable aspect of this program at this time.[2]

So why the wide discrepancy in accuracy between future targets and those in present or past time? I am convinced it is not a remote viewing failure. Instead, the culprit is the nature of time itself. First, the remote viewing evidence seems to tell us that the past is in some way "fixed"—it has already happened, and exists just the way it is. What we call the "present" is fixed in the same way.

In fact, the present *is* part of the past. After all, the "present" is just the interface where the future becomes the past—like the surface of a pond, where there is air, and then there is water, and there is no in-between. Moreover, in humans a fraction of a second in mental-processing time elapses between when the "news" that something has happened first arrives at our eyes or ears in the form of photons of light or sound waves, and when our conscious awareness *recognizes* this news. Therefore, we live a fraction of a second in the past. Everything happening around you that you think is happening *now* has already happened by the time you notice it (and this doesn't count the time it took for the sound or light to reach your senses in the first place). So for humans there really is no such thing as the present, but only the very recent past.

In a way, this makes things easier. In dealing with time we only have to worry about the past and the future. But that word "only" disguises a multitude of problems. What exactly does it mean to say that the past exists just the way it is? Does it mean that somewhere in space-time everything that has already happened is in some way frozen, and all we need do is figure out how to "go back" and look at it from any angle we want? Or does it mean that past events continue to be repeated, again and again for eternity, like some stuck record playing the same phrase over and over? I confess I don't know. All I can say is that there must be some profound difference in nature between the past and the future, because a remote viewer can describe past objects, scenes, and events much more consistently and reliably than future objects, scenes, and events.

This "fixed" path of the past is, in some ways, easy for science to swallow. Science is generally deterministic; it assumes that an event that happens "now" is completely caused by other events that happened just before it. These preceding events were in turn directly the result of other events and causes that preceded them, and so on. What happens *now* is determined by what happened a minute ago; what happened a minute ago was determined by what happened an hour ago; what happened an hour ago was determined by what happened yesterday, and so on back to the beginning of the universe.

On this principle, if we could know everything about the initial conditions of the universe, together with all the laws and principles of nature, we could predict everything that has happened or ever will happen. That would be a tall order, but doable in principle, if not in practice. Past and future would be one seamless tapestry of events, all woven inseparably together.

This makes sense, until the implications are played out: in such a deterministic universe there are no such things as accidents, and there is no such thing as free will. Everything is "programmed" by the rules of cause and effect and facts of the universe, and nothing can ever happen except what is bound to happen.

I should qualify things just a little here. This deterministic way of thinking about the universe was most firmly held in the days after Newton (from the eighteenth century on) before quantum physics became accepted in the early twentieth century. There are some random uncertainties that happen among subatomic particles and, because of this, the acceptance of the principles of quantum mechanics threw the idea of lock-step determinism into a minor tail-spin. However, some scientists argue that subatomic particles can behave just as crazily as they want at the quantum level, but that wouldn't change much at the *macro* level—the level of the "real" world—where determinism is still a powerful, perhaps irresistible force.

If the universe were truly deterministic the future should be just as easy to remote view as the past, because there would be only one possible way events could unfold. Full knowledge about the underpinnings of the universe *now* should allow an accurate picture of the universe *then*. But, as I have already pointed out, remote viewing results seem to show that this is not the case. The future behaves as if it is not deterministic, but *probabalistic*—that it is governed by a set of possibilities, and not by some already-fixed chain of events.

Some of these possibilities have greater chances of occurring, while others are less likely. But what may occur in future reality has somewhat the feel of a dice roll about it. Think of it this way: the past is like the trunk of a tree, while the future is like the branches that have yet to grow. Since they are "the future," they are only potential branches. But which way will they grow when they finally do? That is decided by what I call "decision nodes," the forks where a limb could grow one way or another, depending on what factors are realized—become "real"—at that node.

For example, I might decide to drive from my home in Austin down Loop 1 instead of along Interstate 35 on my way to the University of Texas. On Loop 1, I encounter a traffic accident that makes me late for class. Since I arrive late, I miss the announcement about a test the next time the class meets. I don't study, so I fail the test. Since I fail the test, I fail the class, don't get my degree, and end up working as a short-order cook instead of becoming a corporate CEO. If I had instead taken Interstate 35 that day, I might be head of a Fortune 500 company rather than flipping burgers.

There are, of course, other decision nodes besides which highway to take, and each could lead to a different outcome. I could have chosen to ask a classmate whether I had missed any important announcements. I might have chosen to retake the class I failed and graduated anyway. Or not. Each of these choices would lead to a somewhat different future.

Determinists would say that a complicated bunch of facts and causes linking the facts together (like how late I left the house, caused by my finishing breakfast late, caused by my sleeping in, and so on) "determined" me to take Loop 1 that day. They would say the same about each of the other decision nodes that I or anyone else face every day of our lives. But I am not a determinist. I believe that the physical world *tends* to be deterministic. But I also think that there are randomizing variables and other complexity factors, starting right at the quantum level of the universe and continuing upward to higher levels, that help make the future much more uncertain and interesting than determinists would prefer to have it.

Let's imagine the future looking somewhat like a large tree with "ghost" branches, each twig-to-be awaiting a future decision about which way it will "grow." Let's call these ghost branches "possible futures," because any one of them could become the realized timeline, but can become real only if the right decision nodes are reached, and the right branchings "chosen." Unlike a tree, the future will ultimately only have one branch that will, once realized, become the past with other potential futures sprouting notionally beyond it. Making decisions causes all the other virtual branches to never become real—to "self-prune," so to speak.

But what if we want to know which of all these branches will be realized? If you go up far enough among the "ghost branches" of our possible futures, any one of them could have much the same chance of happening as any other. Which one will be the right one; which one will be the one that ultimately becomes the past?

If a remote viewer were to do a session to determine how the future will turn out ten days hence, any one of hundreds, perhaps thousands, of these possible futures could be the right one. Each might have just as much "weight" as a future possibility as any of the others. So at the time of the session, the viewer's subconscious would be "correct" if it chose any one of them. But then, ten days later, a different "branch" turns out to be realized, because different decision nodes were activated by chance and by conscious choices of the myriad of people involved over the preceding nine days. Critics might then conclude the viewer was "wrong," since a different future actually happened than the one described. But in this case the viewer was not "wrong" in the sense we usually mean it; he just happened to view a different possible future than what was realized.

Of course, some people attempting to view the future really *are* wrong. The same rules that apply for remote viewing any other target also apply to viewing the future. If the viewer is frontloaded the chances of not just *picking* the "wrong" possible future, but actually *being* wrong go up dramatically. We all have preconceptions about what may happen in the future, and we all have wishes, some of them only half-admitted, even to ourselves, as to how it will turn out. If we are frontloaded when doing a future target, then all of that comes home to roost. It is no accident that some of the most widely hyped "remote viewing" predictions reported in the media about the future not only never happen, but turn out to have been frontloaded.

I have painted a discouraging picture about remote viewing the future. If the deck is so stacked against the viewer, why does it work at least some of the time? Because things aren't as bad as I have painted them. It turns out that not all possible futures are as "possible" as others. Some have a greater chance of occurring than do their fellows. Some major events, like earthquakes, wars, plagues, fads and fashions, outcomes of presidential elections, and so on may "lie across" several possible time lines. The heavily deterministic nature of the physical universe plays a role here. Some things are so determined by preceding causes that no quantum hiccup or fickle human choice can derail them. But none of this means the future is unalterably "fixed."

Halfway through, 1987 started to become a year of transition. Some old hands were preparing to leave. One of the first to go, at the end of June, was Bill Ray, with orders for Europe in hand. He was to go back to doing his old counterintelligence job, this time in the Netherlands. Whether or not his remote viewing experience would prove useful to him away from the rest of us and the office, he didn't know. But I think he was interested in finding out. We were going to miss Bill's fedora hat and omnipresent pipe, his optimistic outlook and jovial good sense. One thing we wouldn't miss, though, was his tendency to burst into off-key Irish songs at every opportunity.

With Bill's departure, we would be gaining a new commander to replace him. We felt the usual anxiety when a new, unfamiliar boss comes in to take over for one who was well liked. Given the nature of what we did, we were especially worried. Would the new commander be a skeptic? Or a fanatic "true-believer?" We hoped for someone in between. Both skeptics and true-believers brought their own special kinds of stresses and challenges—skeptics because they aren't willing to accept enough, and true-believers because they are willing to accept too much.

Lieutenant Colonel William Xenakis turned out to be just the right mix. He was open-minded, but cautious about taking anything just on face value. He intended to learn what he could trust about remote viewing and of what he should be careful. Bill Xenakis was not as lighthearted as Bill Ray, but he had a strong sense of humor. He didn't smoke a pipe, but we often found him with an unlit stogie clamped in his jaws. He was stockier and slightly shorter than Bill Ray, and bald. In both personality and appearance he reminded me a little of Telly Savalas, who played the gruff detective Kojak on television. Xenakis knew intelligence work, and he knew how to be an officer. He took command firmly, but gently.

Bill Ray wasn't our only loss. In July Charlene Shufelt left to take a job down at the Defense Intelligence Analysis Center, the DIAC, in her specialty, personnel management. She could have stayed longer with the remote viewing unit, but there were pressures moving her away. For one thing, the DIAC was much closer to her home in Alexandria, Virginia. She also felt that after a four-year sabbatical with the remote viewing unit, it was time to get back on her main career path.

I would miss her, probably as much as I would miss Bill. We had shared a work cubicle nearly the entire time since we were assigned in the early days of Center Lane, and I appreciated her pragmatic, relaxed attitude towards the bureaucratic storms that we had weathered together.

Charlene's replacement was a tall, slim, blue-eyed woman of Estonian descent named Gabrielle Pettingell. She had shoulder-length blond hair and, at first acquaintance, a meek, quiet attitude about her that was anything but threatening. It was also hugely misleading. Once Gabrielle—Gabi, as we came to call her—felt comfortable in her new surroundings, she became as lively and conversational as anyone in the office. She was young, only in her mid-twenties. Her youth had worked to her disadvantage a couple of years before, when she first made a bid to get into the remote viewing program.

As a young Army captain then assigned to SED, Gabi's job had been to get the goods on new Soviet and other foreign technology. And she excelled at it. One day, her supervisor, Herb, (his last name shall remain a secret because of the classified work he continues to do) had passed her some intelligence reports on certain Soviet research facilities and projects. The material he showed her seemed to hold especially intimate details about targets that she herself had been striving to get information on. She knew how rare it was to find a source who had the access necessary to report this kind of detail about highly secret locations in the U.S.S.R. How had Herb managed to get information of this quality out of the U.S. intelligence system? She was annoyed, suspecting that her mentor had been holding out on her. Herb wanted to see if she could guess the answer to that very question, so he sent her off to think about it.

Gabi stewed about it off and on for nearly a month. Then, one day when she wasn't really concentrating on the question, the answer just seemed to pop into her mind. Psychics! How else could they have gotten the specific kind of information that was contained in those reports? She knew nothing about remote viewing, nor that there was a government program, but psychics seemed the only solution that made sense. When she confronted Herb with her realization, he laughed and told her he could "neither confirm nor deny" her conclusions.

It was not long, though, before she was briefed about Sun Streak, and knew she wanted to be involved in it. Hearing that there was an open Army captain's position at the unit, she applied and interviewed for it, only to have Bill Ray decide that at twenty-four years of age she was "too young" to be moving into a position like that so early in her career.

Several months after this first disappointment, she learned that a civilian position had opened up in the unit. She credits Ed Dames—who, though assigned to Sun Streak, still kept in touch with his friends back at SED—with telling her about the job opening and greasing the skids to help get her assigned. Going on the conviction that she would get the job, she resigned her Army commission and applied as a civilian. Bill Ray was going or gone, Gabi was a year or two older with excellent credentials, and we needed someone to replace the departing Charlene; so Gabi's gamble paid off. She moved into the desk just behind mine in August 1987.[3] And, to my great relief, she couldn't care less about my cluttered work habits.

I soon found that Gabi's youthfulness was totally misleading. She was as intelligent and discerning as any two other people. I could see why she had been a success at SED, which usually went out of its way to recruit smart folks to do the challenging kind of intelligence collection and analysis the unit's mission required. Gabi had a psychology degree from the University of Florida, and had taken university physics courses while at SED to help her gain more insight into the technology she was assigned to track down. What really awed me, though, was her reading capacity. She could blast through a 300-page book in not much more than an hour, and get everything out of it that I would have gleaned at my own relatively plodding pace.

By this time I had enrolled in the Defense Intelligence College's master's program in Strategic Intelligence. The school was run by DIA, and classes were held a half hour away at the DIAC. Military personnel and government employees with the necessary background and credentials were allowed to enroll part-time, taking classes both during and after duty hours, as their schedules and supervisors allowed. In addition to the remote viewing training in which Gabi was soon embroiled, she was also interested in taking courses at the Defense Intelligence College. Before long she was writing a long paper for one of her classes on the looming threat of AIDS in Sub-Saharan Africa, and how it promised to depopulate the most productive age groups of many African nations, destabilizing the countries in the process. This was more than a decade before the topic became front-page news. Whether this was a sign that Gabi had strong precognitive talents or was just an especially insightful analyst, I can't say for sure.

Gabi's assignment and training marked a milestone of sorts for us. Training new recruits in coordinate remote viewing using the same approach Ingo Swann applied with me and my fellows took anywhere from eighteen months to two years to complete. But there was a lot of downtime with the two-weeks-on, two-weeks-off, quit-on-a-high approach that Ingo favored, which could often leave a viewer doing only one practice session a day. With Gabi we took a slightly different tack. Not that we short-changed her on the lectures or the practice. I still gave her the lectures and graded the essays, just as Ingo had done for us. Ed Dames still monitored her on scores of practice sessions over the weeks she was trained.

But we discovered working with Gabi that honoring Ingo's principle of quitting on a high didn't mean that we had to allow as much downtime from training as had been the norm. We found that taking much shorter breaks between good sessions worked just as well as taking longer ones. We also found that, while there was a need for occasional longer breaks to give the student-viewer time to assimilate the skills and experiences she had encountered, it did not need to be two weeks at a time. Sometimes just a weekend was enough.

"Quitting on a high" could also mean not necessarily "quitting," but just changing activities, doing something different. Applying what we had learned allowed us to dramatically streamline Gabi's training, while still producing a top-notch remote viewer. Within six months she was doing operational remote viewing at the Stage 4 level, and two months after that, in early 1988, she had completed Stage 6 as well. She had covered in eight months most of the same ground it had taken me more than two years to cover (factoring in some lengthy interruptions during Center Lane's cancellation trauma). For future CRV trainees, we were able to get the training time down even further, with no apparent reduction in quality.

To be fair to Ingo, when he was training me and my colleagues he was still sorting out what worked and what didn't in creating new remote viewers. It was better to take a little longer and make sure the viewer learned the process thoroughly than to do things too fast and tempt a serious case of overtraining. In later years Ingo himself streamlined things considerably, while at the same time making sure that all the proper bases were covered in the training.

Another novelty we played with in 1987 was "solo remote viewing." Up until then, we had almost always used a remote-viewing "team"—a monitor and remote viewer working together. Project 8712 was the first operational mission in which we tried dispensing with a monitor.

The mission for 8712 was to report future military activity directed against American ships and interests in and around the Persian Gulf during three specific weeks in September and the last week of October 1987. The project documentation shows that, like other "future" projects, "sporadic hits only" were obtained for the twenty-five sessions we ran.[4] With this lack of success, it was hard to gauge how well the solo process worked.

The first successful operational use of solo remote viewing was Project 8717, in which we were to describe the "purpose and features of target structures under construction at a new target site." Ten of the twenty sessions were worked solo. According to the Sun Streak annual report, "The results are encouraging; a high degree of correlation among viewers surfaced during the course of these sessions against the target."[5] A later training project designed to further evaluate how well solo worked used the historical target "Pearl Harbor event." The project documentation concluded: "Lessons learned: Solo is effective—comprised of short sessions against *a* specific question."[6]

There were some good reasons for introducing the solo technique. It allowed more of us viewers to work when we were short on monitors. It also made it easier to schedule sessions, since the project manager only had to accommodate one person's daily schedule to get any particular session done. And there were no worries about a monitor getting carried away and "leading" a viewer.

But there were problems with solo, too. Some of the earlier SRI research had shown that having a monitor often improved remote viewing results even when he, too, was blind to the target. No specific reasons were discovered for this, but there are some likely possibilities. For one, a monitor can help keep a viewer on track, that is, the monitor can gently remind the viewer to stay within the remote-viewing structure or process being used.

Having a second person in the room also seemed to give the viewer incentive to work harder and longer. Solo sessions often tended to be shorter than monitored ones. The viewers would reach a point they thought was "good enough" when working on their own. But a monitor could encourage the viewer to do more, and end up with a more information-rich session. A monitor, even when "blind" to the target, could also help a viewer better pick what direction to go with a session, what data streams to follow, what terms to elaborate on in Stage 5, or what impression received in Stage 4 to explore with a Stage 6 model.

All this points to the limitation on solo remote viewing. If a monitor can spur a viewer to work harder and get deeper into the session, then without a monitor the viewer's tasking would have to be more limited and focused to allow for the shorter attention span and less depth solo viewers tend to show. With a monitor, for example, the tasking might be to describe the function and activities of a complex of buildings in a foreign land. On the other hand, a solo viewer might be tasked only to describe the condition of a certain hostage.

As we played with all these variables we were also doing some of the most interesting projects of the year. In 1987 the U.S. Air Force was building an entirely new kind of airplane. It was nearly invisible to radar and virtually immune to many of the air defenses of prospective enemies. At the time this airplane, known popularly today as the "Stealth," was one of the Air Force's most closely held secrets. But there was worry that the Soviets knew about it. There were even indications that they were working on their own version of a stealth aircraft.

Someone in the Stealth program office wondered if Soviet remote viewers might be a threat to the project's security, so we were tasked to spy on the Stealth ourselves. How well we did would at least provide a hint as to what enemy remote viewers could discover.

"This [project] was all done against a U.S. system," Fred Atwater told me later. "It was originally meant to see from a security-assessment perspective what kind of intel data we might have lost to Soviet remote viewers—not only what the Russians could pick up on if they were remote viewing it, but could *we* pick up on the fact that there had been anything lost?"

We were tasked in several increments. "Sometimes, when we received tasking," Atwater explained, "the tasker wouldn't tell us the entire problem at first because he wanted not to give too much information up front. He wanted to trickle out information to us as he felt it was appropriate." In fact, Fred usually encouraged this approach. By giving us limited tasking in the beginning, the intelligence customer could be sure that information was not "bleeding" to the viewers and contaminating the final product.[7]

In this case, all Fred received was an encrypted coordinate for the first round. As the viewers did their sessions, it became evident that they were, for the most part, all describing an odd sort of aircraft. As he remembers:

> If I recall correctly, the first targeting was a set of coordinates, and we came back with an aircraft. And Mel's now-famous drawings. When the first drawings came back, I showed them to the outside analyst, and I said, "Well, it looks like we're looking at some kind of aircraft, but this is really weird. Please forgive the remote viewers, because sometimes they don't draw accurately." And the guy says, "No, I think this is the right aircraft you're looking at."

The analyst next gave Fred a date to use as a coordinate. Sessions worked against the date produced descriptions of an airplane crash. But that wasn't all. There were also spontaneous impressions of a person wandering around the crash site and pocketing pieces of the destroyed aircraft.

"They were very interested in that," Fred remembered, "because they were concerned about loss of pieces, worried that the Soviets had some knowledge about the structure of the skin of this thing."

What impressed Fred enough that he remembered it in detail fourteen years after the fact, was "light tubes."

> The biggest thing [I remember] was the remote viewer saying the words, "There's something here I don't understand." So I said, "Describe what it is you don't understand." "There are light tubes in this thing. There are, like, tubes of light." And I said, "Okay, fine. That doesn't mean anything to me." Later on that turned out to be extremely significant from an intelligence point of view because part of the stealthiness of the aircraft has to do with not running cables or pneumatics from the steering mechanisms to the ailerons and so forth, because that presents a radar signature. They were using a servomechanism driven by digital information over fiber optics. And that we could detect these light tubes as being part of the aircraft's mechanism—tubes carrying light inside of them—was extremely important to [the analysts].

As Fred remembers, "It wasn't until years later, on the cover of *Time* magazine when this thing came out and I saw a picture of this delta-winged aircraft, I said, 'Holy cow! This is the thing Mel drew a picture of,' when it all became evident to me."

Gene Lessman was my monitor for all five of the sessions I did on the Stealth project, and is convinced that I was the one who reported the "light tubes."[8] I don't recall that anymore myself, but I do remember some other parts of my sessions on this project. I reported three things that stick in my mind. First, I identified the skin as a composite, rather than the sheet metal that one would normally expect on an aircraft. My impressions of the surface were that it was dark, even black, and it had a matte texture to it. I knew it was some sort of composite material; I seem to remember even referring to "graphite," though I'm no longer absolutely sure. And the skin had a flexible, spongy feel to it that seemed unusual. I remember being surprised by all of this.

Second, the air intakes on the aircraft were oddly shaped. I don't know how I would have known that as I knew little of air intakes. But I definitely remember that during my session I had the thought that they were in some way unusual, and reported it. Third, the exhaust ports seemed different from any other airplane, too. I had the impression that they were hidden, which of course turned out to be true. On the B-2 Stealth bomber, both air intake and exhaust ports are specially designed both to reduce how much they reflect enemy radar and to disguise the infrared emissions of the engines.

My impressions about the skin also turned out correct. As feedback of sorts, years later I had the opportunity to examine the outside of a Stealth aircraft on display during an air show at Andrews Air Force Base. The exterior of the aircraft was black and matte in texture as I had described it. Still later I saw a television program (I believe it may have been an episode of *Nova*) where, for the first time, a reporter was allowed access to the still highly secret B-2 bomber. The program included tape footage of repairs being done to the wing of one of the B-2s. Technicians had peeled off a section of the skin, and were installing *padding* underneath it. It seemed evident that the skin was indeed a flexible composite material, and that if one were to push on it, it would be resilient and flexible, just as I had described.

I wasn't the only one who did well on this project. Mel's sketches of the aircraft were remarkable. Angela also did well. As Gene Lessman remembers, "She drew a detailed sketch—I mean, when I say a detailed sketch, that it was detailed in terms of what a viewer would draw. She drew a triangle, and then some curlycues at the end and two big boxes that turned out to be the motors, and several other components of it. Of course, she drew a flying wing. And [the analysts] came unglued about that."[9] After the fact, it seemed clear that the "curlycues" represented the jet exhaust.

The Sun Streak project management was puzzled. If this was an aircraft, where were its tail and wings? At first Gene wondered if someone in the intelligence community had assigned us some kind of UFO project. Fred Atwater didn't think so.

Altogether, four viewers worked on this project. Mel and I did five sessions each, while Angela worked four, and Lyn three. Besides the things I've already mentioned, other details showed up in the final report as a composite summary of all four viewers' findings.

> Research and development efforts for the aircraft were taking place in a hot, arid, climate, and in a location characterized by hard ground and a noticeable lack of vegetation. The "aircraft skin" was described as having a light, "plastic feel," "a soft feel," and a "textured feel." It was further described as an alloy identified spontaneously and successively as "tungsten," a "ferro-silicate," and "titanium." The aircraft skin was described by one viewer as being metallic but apparently coated with a substance that reminded one of "diamond dust." The aircraft was further perceived as being "textured" but coated smooth in a "matte" finish. It was described as dark, blackish green, shiny-smooth, remarkably clean, as if coated with epoxy or acrylic paint. Even dust did not seem to adhere to its surface.

The overall project seemed shrouded in secrecy, yet some portions . . . were generally known to the public. The configurational aspects of the wings appeared crucial to desired aircraft performance. Viewers alternately used such descriptives as a "webbed configuration," wings "shaped like a trapezoid with the narrow end attached to the fuselage," and "wing tips that are upturned and rolled up." One viewer described the presence of wings with "red tips" (edges) having the ability of "emitting energy downward." Because of the noted curvature, the wing tips seemed able to "refract" energy.

The aerodynamics involved was considered unconventional by current standards and dealt with extremes of speed, ultrafast and ultraslow. There was a sense of "droopiness," a sense of flexibility that enhanced performance and survivability. One viewer described the aircraft as being diamond-shaped, elongated much like the SR-71 or a space shuttle. The same viewer further added, "the fuselage itself provides lift, thereby reducing the amount of wing surface necessary (to provide lift)." The aircraft was virtually undetectable because of the presence of a jamming system on board. It also had the ability to "drop line of sight"; and "its systems (were) not showing at high altitudes." The aircraft flew illegally, "at night, with different numbers on the flight schedule to make it seem as if another aircraft is flying (rather than the target aircraft)."[10]

Though there are discrepancies and inconsistencies between the viewers, they do seem to be describing a Stealth aircraft. Much of the Stealth's development took place at the Air Force's facilities at Groom Lake—the notorious Area 51—located in a dry lake bed in the desert of south central Nevada. The Stealth's skin is exactly as described; it does have features for "radiating" energy, as well as for dissipating it, particularly infrared and radar waves, to make it invisible to enemy tracking systems and missiles. The bodies of the B-2 Stealth bomber, a flying wing, and the F-117 both provide lift (just as do those of the space shuttle or the SR-71 Blackbird spy plane, though both have more conventional wing designs than does the B-2), and it is easy to understand how the viewers grew confused about just how the wings and the body come together. The description of the aircraft flying at night using false registration numbers is an exact description of how it was tested to avoid attracting the notice of unauthorized people.

All things considered, our Stealth project was highly successful. Apparently the analysts who tasked us were disconcerted by that very success. They would much rather that we had failed, so they could be reassured that the Soviets might fail, too.

An apocryphal story grew out of this Stealth project. How it got started is anyone's guess. According to the story, once Fred had wrapped up the Stealth project, he reported the results to the people who had tasked us, and we went on about our other business. A week or so later, so the story goes, there was a knock on Sun Streak's front door, and in marched a couple of counterintelligence agents with orders to confiscate all our files, remote viewing transcripts and all, on the Stealth project.

"You don't have the clearances or the authorization to keep material this classified," they allegedly said, then marched out the door with anything that had to do with the project, and were never seen again. The punch line goes something like, "Feedback doesn't get any better than that!"—implying that if one's remote viewing is accurate enough to be confiscated once it is finished, it must have been really good. Though I myself couldn't specifically remember the incident, I figured it must have happened sometime when I was out of the office, so I used to tell the story every once in awhile myself.

Then I asked Fred if he could give me any details about when our Stealth files were confiscated. He looked at me for a moment with a puzzled expression and shook his head. "I know of no instance where they physically took our files from us," he said. It was my turn to be surprised. But after several minutes of discussion I was satisfied that the story was a myth. The closest Fred could remember to something like that happening was when remote viewers produced information about the design of a Chinese nuclear weapon, and Fred was told that though they had produced useful information, the feedback was too highly classified to be shown to anyone at the remote viewing unit. "But they didn't confiscate our work," Fred insisted. "They just said we can't tell you because you can't know that. And it had to do with the . . . shape of the atomic device that we discovered at [a place in China], which was very important to [our taskers] because it confirmed state of the art of the Chinese nuclear effort at that time."[11]

As far as I could discover, we never received any official feedback or evaluation on the Stealth project, but we each got unofficial feedback in our own ways. Fred got his on the cover of *Time*, and Gene remembers recognizing it in the newspaper when he read about it two years later. I got my confirmation many months after we had done our viewing on it, when the *Washington Post* ran a feature story on Stealth the following year upon its official unveiling by the Air Force. The instant I saw the article, I knew the Stealth was what I had viewed.

Not long after we finished the Stealth project, we lost Gene Lessman. After only about a year and a half with the remote viewing unit, the husky Irishman was made an offer he couldn't refuse: requested by name to become the Special Advisor on Terrorism to the commander of the Army intelligence group supporting U.S. forces in West Berlin, he was soon once more on his way to Germany.[12]

It was a prestigious assignment, and one that had more than its share of perks. Part of his job involved trips into the Eastern Sector of Berlin. He

wrote me a few letters about the fun he was having, not to mention enthusiastic news of the great deals one could get on the high-quality East German
cameras and binoculars that he came across in his travels. Gene was in Berlin
when the Wall came down in 1989. As an intelligence officer he was privy to
all the excitement going on behind the scenes leading up to the first bricks
and mortar being knocked loose from one of the greatest symbols of Iron
Curtain oppression.

But before Gene left our office to find his ringside seat to history, he
helped with one other major project. And this project might have made a difference in how certain things later turned out in the American intelligence
community, had our results been taken seriously.

24

Mole

> "Justice may be blind, but
> she has very sophisti-
> cated listening devices."
>
> —Edgar Argo

In June 1987 Dale Graff brought to the unit a mystery that had been passed to Jack Vorona's office from elsewhere in the intelligence community. There was evidence that a mole had burrowed into the heart of the Central Intelligence Agency and was leaking damaging information to the Soviet intelligence agency, the KGB. Soviet double agents who were working on the sly for American intelligence deep within the Soviet military and government were turning up dead. The CIA was baffled, not able to uncover the mole, and not even sure there was one. Someone in the intelligence community—not the CIA itself, which was unlikely to want outsiders to know what was afoot—came to us for help.

Graff handed our boss the task to "Determine the existence of a foreign intelligence mole within the CIA" and provide what information we could about it. Dale was later to tell me that he had no idea what agency requested the work. Jack Vorona had provided the tasking to him, so Vorona presumably knew. But because the CIA had not itself asked for our help, the agency that wanted us to hunt down the presumed mole was overstepping its bounds and thus preferred anonymity.[1]

So sensitive was this project at the time that it wasn't even recorded in the operations officer's log of assigned projects. The project was numbered 8710, but the log skips directly from 8709 (the Stealth project) to 8711, the Silkworm missile search problem, with no mention of 8710. Details I have about 8710 come from my own memory, the memories of other participants, and notes and verbatim copies I made of the final operational report. As will be seen, the existence of the mole became public in 1994, so the remote viewing reports I had access to are no longer sensitive, although nothing in them has been published until now. In total there were three interim reports and a final operational report. I had access to all but the first interim report. Excerpts in what follows were taken from various parts of the three remaining reports.

Our first order of business was to verify if there was a spy eating into the secret guts of the Central Intelligence Agency. Evidence and reports from that time show the CIA as unsure of how the Soviets had unmasked so many double agents, and theories other than the presence of a mole were taken seriously. But we soon found the answer.

Four of us worked on the project—Angela, Mel, Lyn, and myself. As far as I know all of us were given only encrypted coordinates, thus having no information about who or what our target may have been. In our sessions all four of us began to describe a middle-aged male "executive" or mid-level manager who seemed anxious and stressed about things he was tangled up in that were not kosher. As one of the interim reports sent to Vorona about this project put it, "The descriptions provided by these sources are uniquely similar in many aspects and tend to provide an evolving consensus on the scenario and the personalities involved."[2]

We jointly described the setting for our investigations as "a large metropolitan city located on what appeared to be the east coast of the US with major gestalts [suggestive] of the greater Washington, D.C., area." Viewers described a "modern, multi-story, office-building located among office-type structures in an area of medium to heavy traffic patterns, yet within sight of stately trees, lush vegetation, and forest-like surroundings in the near distance."[3]

According to the viewers, a "pavilion-type entryway with a patio" graced the entrance of the building, and there were "large art objects" dressing up the area. Internal security was maintained, but the measures "were not apparent to the casual observer." Any "guard posts, fences, or other controlled procedures" were not obvious, though there was an "established pass and badge system controlled and monitored in a reception area" near the building's main entry. Inside the building viewers found a structured, government bureaucracy that involved "several ongoing, secure, compartmented projects

dealing with the scientific and research and development of physical items."
Reportedly, the objects were "developed, scientifically analyzed and dispatched to other geographic areas for further testing and research."[4] We
described the organization itself as "being involved in security work, [hav-
ing] an international function and . . . highly compartmented in structure."[5]

Overall, the remote viewing sessions had painted a view fairly consistent
with the CIA's headquarters and its physical setting, other than the slant
towards building technical gadgets (which is certainly done at Langley,
though not to the degree the viewers seemed to stress).

As the sessions mounted, two main characters emerged—the middle-
aged man and "an attractive and enigmatic woman, about 30–40 years of age,
with demonstrated gift for gaining the confidence of those around her." She
was "vivacious, calculating, sinister, ambi-cultural [that is, at home in more
than one culture], clandestine, 'controlled,' socially correct and highly professional." The woman was reportedly emotionally involved with a "male
supervisor employed at the US Government facility described previously"
who apparently was the same "executive" we had found during other sessions. In fact, Mel and I both "reported distinct impressions of a close social
and perhaps even sexual association between [the] man and the woman."
Gene Lessman recently reminded me that I had described this woman as
being of Latin American origin—in fact, both he and our secretary, Jeannie
Betters, who typed up the reports, said the woman was specifically mentioned as being "Colombian."[6]

The reports continue:

> This [male] individual continued to be placed [by the remote viewers'
> reports] in a pivotal role in the general scenario and was perceived by
> all four sources as being involved in some type of clandestine activ-
> ity . . . This man was further perceived as having performed acts
> which were both secretive and in contravention to the responsibilities
> of his office and position.[7]

In one of my sessions, I even noted that this executive "illegally provided
the woman with small objects or devices taken from his place of employment. These acts were prompted by an emotional compulsion to fulfill her
wishes despite the personal risks involved." One of the project reports states
that "Three sources perceived these acts as being motivated, guided, controlled and prompted by this same woman who consistently seemed to be
influenced by forces outside her work environment." But there was more.

In one of his later sessions, Source 003 [Paul H. Smith] perceived a parallel reporting/tasking organization which was being used to manip-

ulate and control the activities of an individual believed to be the same "executive" referenced by the other sources. In this [parallel] organization, one man was perceived as a senior member. He was described as being dark-complected and power seeking. This man controlled an international network of individuals which eventually led to the woman.[8]

Our sessions pictured the "executive" as being under the sway of the woman:

Begrudgingly and with deep feelings of guilt, the "executive" has provided materials and documents to the woman at the latter's request. These materials have included documents, papers, books and "parts" (components?) further described as "small, rounded, hollow, metallic and plastic, electronic, mechanical, grey and expensive . . ."[9]

We also tried to discover surrounding facts about the situation:

Both Source 003 and Source 079 [Angela], have spent a considerable amount of time attempting to locate the area where the "Executive" type conducted his activities. To date, both sources have described an area reminiscent of the D.C. area. The Executive's home was located in the suburbs and described as a fenced or wall-lined, elegant home. He particularly valued his personal privacy and drove a grey-colored foreign luxury automobile.[10]

So what did we have thus far? We seem to have discovered a mid-level bureaucrat inside a secure, likely intelligence-related government agency in the Washington area that sounded very much like it could be the CIA. Along with the man, we had also found a woman who sounded calculating, controlling, demanding, but also accomplished, competent, attractive, and at home in more than one culture, who was manipulating the man to do secret, illegal things about which he felt deeply guilty, even while feeling compelled to do them. It seemed in fact that what he was doing was compromising secret documents and other items and materials to which he had access.

The man and the woman had a very close, perhaps even intimate relationship. The man was being controlled by a secretive, security-conscious organization that was different from—"parallel to"—the one for which he worked. The woman was reportedly part of both the man's organization and also this second, parallel organization, and used her wiles to get the "executive" to do these illegal things on behalf of the parallel organization.

This was not all we reported, however. Two other primary figures were described in the course of the project. There was an investigator who was trying to catch the executive and the woman in their illegal activities, partly by matching "locations, times, places surrounding events and people." There was also a shadowy Middle Eastern or central Asian character whose government was engaged in a protracted guerrilla war in a place closely resembling Afghanistan. This man seemed not only to be engaged in belligerent activities, but in at least one session worked by Lyn Buchanan, he and the woman were perceived to be lovers.

There was one other element present, reported I believe by Angela. Also somehow connected with the "executive" was

> a special project related to a sophisticated piece of military equipment with an integral van used to set it up on location. The project involves an object that is, "powerful, secret, new . . .", and involves complicated and expensive technologies. It produced heat, could not be used or displayed in the open and had devices to permit it to be elevated . . . The deployment or field testing of the device was imminent. More ominously however, [the remote viewing] source also perceived that this device had already been compromised that, "the people and the van will all be caught . . . ," and that ultimately, the project could be cancelled as a result of a security compromise.[11]

Our sessions also revealed less specific information about this tangled web of people and things. The final report was completed on July 30, 1987, and signed by Fern Gauvin. Not long afterwards it was given to Jack Vorona. We never heard any more about it.

Then, on February 21, 1994, seven years after our work on the CIA mole, a Central Intelligence Agency employee named Aldrich Ames and his Colombian-born wife, Rosario Casas Dupuy, were arrested on espionage charges. He was in his Jaguar on the way to CIA headquarters. She was taken into custody in their palatial, half-million-dollar home in the Washington suburb of Arlington.[12]

Ames was a bureaucrat and former spy-handler for the CIA. He was somewhat of an expert on the KGB, and over the years acted as contact for a number of important Russian sources who were passing Soviet secrets to the CIA. While on the surface loyal to the CIA, Ames was really leading a double life. In 1985 he became a Soviet spy, a mole within the Central Intelligence Agency. Before he was caught, Aldrich Ames had given away more than one hundred intelligence operations aimed at the USSR, and handed over thousands of classified documents to the KGB and the SVR, the KGB's successor after the fall of the Soviet Union.

According to Pete Earley's book about Ames, *Confessions of a Spy*, Ames compromised altogether twenty-five Soviets acting as agents for the United

States, several of whom were deep inside the KGB or its sister organizations. One of Ames's victims had been a senior general in the GRU, the Soviet military intelligence agency, and is regarded by some as having been the most important Soviet source the United States ever had. Of the twenty-five people Ames gave up to the KGB, ten were executed, including the general, who had escaped detection for twenty years and reached retirement only to be turned in by an American traitor.

By the time Ames was through, virtually every important CIA source in the Soviet hierarchy had disappeared. Ironically, many of these people spied for the U.S. not for the money, but because they thought the Soviet system was corrupt and was hurting Russia. Ames, on the other hand, spied for the KGB only for lots of cold hard cash. He had rationalized himself into believing that what he was doing caused no harm to the United States. And the people he compromised? Why, they knew the risk they were taking by spying for the United States.

Ames's wife, Rosario, was a native Colombian whom Ames had met in the early 1980s while assigned to the CIA station in Mexico City. She worked as a cultural representative for the Colombian government, and was popular in the diplomatic social scene in the Mexican capital. Ames eventually brought Rosario to the States, divorcing his first wife to marry her. Though at first they seemed to enjoy an idyllic relationship, the reality of being married to someone who only brought home a lowly public servant's paycheck eventually began to weight heavily on Rosario. The humble circumstances and frugality with which they were forced to live in Washington's high-priced economy, together with the expense of Ames's divorce from his first wife, began to wear. Rosario Ames grew increasingly dissatisfied, and Aldrich Ames became more and more distraught about the financial circumstances and his wife's unhappiness.

Though factors other than financial pressures helped lead Ames to the draconian step of spying for the KGB, money was certainly one of the strongest motivators. As stacks of KGB dollars rolled in and time wore on, the Ames's taste for luxuries and expensive purchases increased. Rosario found that money did not, after all, buy happiness, which led her to try all the harder. She became a harridan; whining, nagging, haranguing, or putting Ames down, as the mood struck her.

"She was a first-class bitch," Pete Earley quotes an FBI agent who had monitored bugs planted in the Ames's home as saying. "She definitely wore the pants in the family and she didn't do a damn thing around the house but boss him around . . . She was completely focused on herself. She was both vain and haughty and contemptuous of him."[13]

Jeanne Vertefeuille, a CIA analyst who played an important role in finally nailing Ames, thought that it was Rosario's materialism and greed that pushed Ames over the edge. "He was dominated by strong women," Vertefeuille stated. "So it was a combination of his weaknesses and Rosario's materialism that caused him to do it." Others thought both the Ameses were at fault. "Rick and Rosario used to bring out the worst in each other's personalities," Ames's sister, Nancy, remarked in an interview with Earley. "It was just the way they were sometimes."[14]

Ames, ever more pressured to please his wife, seemed increasingly motivated to continue his relationship with the KGB and, later, the SVR. To be sure, Rosario's aggrieved petulance wasn't Ames's only motivation to continue. He seemed to derive a feeling of power from spying for the other side, a sense of validation, and even a perverse sort of enjoyment in playing cat and mouse with both sides for his own profit.

Ames was eventually caught due to a number of factors, but leading them was the dogged determination of a small handful of CIA employees who would not rest until they had gotten to the bottom of why so many important CIA sources had abruptly died or disappeared. Besides Vertefeuille, this group consisted of a few other people and its implacable leader, Paul Redmond, who in late 1986 was one of the first to become convinced that the CIA had a mole. For the next eight years Redmond was one of the driving forces behind the on-again, off-again search for that mole, though his team members matched him in determination. Ames was finally caught largely because of the exhaustive efforts of a team member named Grimes, who culled mounds of reports, reimbursement vouchers, travel orders, and other paperwork to piece together Ames's overseas travel, leaves, and days off, and because of a man named Dan Payne, who followed Ames's convoluted money trail. The little group compiled lists of known KGB officers and where they had been stationed since 1985, when the mole first began to work. They also made a list of 198 names of CIA officers who could have known about any of the agents and projects that had been comprised. In the end, it all pointed to Aldrich Ames.[15]

Not all of the sources Ames gave up to the KGB were human. Some of them involved sophisticated technical means of intelligence collection. According to Earley's book, one especially important and unique technical collection project was known as ABSORB. Once ballistic missile warheads were introduced that were loaded with multiple independently targeted reentry vehicles, MIRVs, the United States had no way of determining the destructive power of a new generation of the USSR's strategic nuclear missiles. Then it was discovered that Soviet nuclear warheads were built in the western USSR and then shipped east via the Trans-Siberian Railroad to the missile silo fields. The United States was just then developing technology that could measure the number of MIRVs inside a warhead from several feet away by the slight radiation given off. An ingenious plan was worked out for rigging a railroad commercial shipping container or van with sensitive radiation detection equipment. The CIA arranged with a cooperative Japanese company to have this container transported regularly from the east coast of the USSR to the west on a Soviet freight train. The detection equipment, headed west, was sensitive and accurate enough to count the number of MIRVs in each missile warhead it passed being shipped by rail to the east. It was designed to switch itself on as minute amounts of radiation were detected, take its readings while the warhead rolled by in the opposite direction, then switch off again to await the next MIRVed warhead that passed.

The ABSORB project was highly successful for two years, helping the United States reliably evaluate the threat from Soviet nuclear-tipped missiles. But then Ames gave it away. In 1983, just as ABSORB was being readied for its first practical test, Ames was assigned a position that provided him access to files about ABSORB. The project was one of the first he leaked to the USSR after he became a turncoat two years later. In January 1986 the Soviets pulled the shipping container from its west-bound railcar, gaining a windfall in sophisticated electronics it had not seen before and extorting a half million dollars from the hapless Japanese company in exchange for not broadcasting the fact that the company had cooperated with the CIA.[16]

The rough outlines of the Ames story came out in the twenty-four sessions we did for this project. But it was too complex a problem to hope that the project would be a clean-cut vindication of remote viewing as an intelligence source. Though we got much data that was at least conceptually accurate, the view we presented was still greatly distorted in places. We made a number of mistakes, which highlight some of the problems that come with using remote viewing in certain intelligence gathering situations.

First, of course, was always the chronic threat of analytical overlay. A good example of this cropped up when Lyn and Mel both reported extensively about the shadowy Middle Eastern or central Asian figure involved in a guerrilla war who, according to them, figured importantly in the story. Lyn even described this character as a lover to the vivacious woman. Unfortunately, while there is a slight chance that such a character might have escaped detection during the investigation, it seems highly unlikely that any person of this description ever figured into the case.

Another confusion that developed was the exact role of "the woman." Besides the woman's manipulation of the man to do the devious things he did, we reported that she herself was directly involved in, and may even have been the instigator of the clandestine activity for which the "executive" was feeling such remorse. As the final project report states:

> The "Woman" often hosts or attends diplomatic-sponsored, social functions where her formal intelligence training as a spotter/assessor coupled with her impressive female charms, are used to elicit intelligence information. This spotting/assessing activity appears to be the "Woman's" primary function as a recruited asset for the US intelligence agency. She is a recognized expert in her field and her skills are in great demand.[17]

In real life, Ames's first wife, Nancy, *was* a CIA employee, but was never connected in any way with Aldrich's espionage. On the other hand, Rosario, his second wife, was a cultured, socially adept woman who loved to hobnob in diplomatic circles in her native Bogota, as well as in Mexico City and Rome, where she and Ames spent time together. Before the two developed a relationship, she was also recruited by one of Ames's coworkers to assist the CIA in Mexico City. However, this only lasted for a little while, stopping altogether once she and Aldrich Ames became a couple. There is no indication that she was ever trained as an intelligence operative, and there appears to be no evidence that she had connections with any foreign intelligence agency.

Some doubt exists that, prior to 1992, she even knew anything about the espionage Ames was committing to bring in all the cash that fueled the couple's lavish lifestyle (though she helped to cover it up once she knew of Ames's spying). Though both swear it was only in that year that she "accidentally" stumbled onto Ames's deception, some of her friends thought she probably guessed long before.[18] From the various accounts, however, it seems apparent that Rosario's demands contributed to Ames's seeking money by committing treason. Describing her as vivacious, cultured, ambi-cultural, and so on was not far off the mark; she embodied all these qualities. But in describing the "woman" in our sessions, we appear to have confused Ames's own activities with those of Rosario.

Another case where more than one actor in the Ames drama may have been combined into a composite personality involved me describing the "CIA mole" as looking somewhat like Willard Scott, the burly weather reporter for CBS Television in the 1980s. Tall and thin, Ames bears little resemblance to Scott. But a couple of the KGB operatives with whom Ames interacted bear a closer likeness to the bulky weatherman, and it is not impossible that in trying to describe the physical characteristics of the "mole," I intermingled his appearance with his partners in crime.

Why did we make the kinds of mistakes we did? In any remote-viewing project, even the most straightforward targets, such as buildings or structures, it is not unusual for various elements to be confused. Things can get jumbled up in a viewer's mind as they are shuffled between subconscious and conscious awareness. They can be perceived out of sequence, inside out, upside down, or reversed from left to right. These are fairly mundane problems, and with experience, not to mention competent monitors, taskers, and analysts, their consequences can be mitigated, though probably not altogether eliminated.

But projects like this mole case are different in important ways. Foremost is the fact that they deal so much with people's intentions. The Ames case involved several different people who had overlapping, and in some cases almost identical, intentions. A mole does not exist in a vacuum. He (or she) is but one crucial node in a larger system—a team of sorts. Without a handler and an opposing intelligence agency for which to spy, a mole by definition cannot exist.

In a problem such as this, the remote viewing focuses not on concrete things—the "tangibles," in coordinate remote viewing terminology—but on the "intangibles," the purposes, desires, goals, wants, motivations, emotions, and intentions of the people involved. Their intentions are in flux. They intertwine, wrap around each other like so many colored wires in a thick cable. Untangling those wires is tricky, and in the nebulous realm where remote viewers so often do their work, it is no wonder that the wires sometimes get crossed. Mole and handler come from different perspectives, and seek different rewards, but the goal is the same. To the extent that arriving at that goal requires melding of their intentions, one becomes much like the other. A viewer happening along, trying to unpack the relationship, may perhaps instead create a composite character, and even add overlay or interpretation to the mix.

These kinds of remote viewing circumstances also involve other intangibles, such as the roles people play. In Ames's case, there was increased cause for confusion. As Earley notes in his book, Ames himself was confused. He was astonished at times to find himself thinking and acting almost simultaneously like a dedicated CIA operative, and then, paradoxically, like a committed KGB agent. He would at one time take actions and express concerns aimed directly at protecting the security of the United States, and then, just as single-mindedly, consciously and methodically perform actions that undermined it. If the subject of a remote viewing is so conflicted, how is a viewer supposed to make logical sense of it? The fact was, we didn't do it as well as we would have liked.

The same confusion is evident in how the roles and characters of Ames's two wives seem to have been merged into one, combining further with the mental ambience of the espionage world in which Ames was fully and inextricably immersed. Whatever the reasons for our remote viewing distortions and errors, they still contributed "noise" to the subsequent analysis, making it more difficult to home in on the facts that, had they only been known, might have led to Ames being caught seven years earlier.

One final source of confusion in this project was time. While we were doing our viewing, the Ameses were serving a tour in Rome. The luxurious home in the suburbs of which we gave a brief, general description was purchased for $540,000 cash in 1989, two years after we made our report. A few other perceptions we reported seemed to better fit a time somewhat later than the period during which we were doing our viewing. It was almost as if we were subconsciously focusing on a time when Ames would be back in the States. If that was the case, then this might have been one of those few instances when "future" viewing actually turned out right, even though we weren't trying for that.

However, not all of the errors in this project report are attributable to the viewers. In writing a report, analysts themselves have to fight the temptation to try to make more sense out of the data than is necessarily justified. Most people dislike an incomplete story, one with too many loose ends and not enough conclusions. Unfortunately, in reporting operational remote-viewing results, just as in reporting other incomplete intelligence derived from other sources and methods, trying to tie up those loose ends can lead to mistaken conclusions. Some of that may have happened in Project 8710 as well. In reading through the various reports, it seemed to me that in several places the report writer might have been stretching some of the loose ends to try to tie them together. One of these was an effort to make sense of the swarthy Middle-Eastern character. It is also possible that the role of the woman grew more sinister in the report than it actually was in the session transcripts. Without the raw data, to which I did not have access, it would be impossible to tell. Though in the years since at least some of the materials were reportedly destroyed, hopefully part of the raw data will eventually become available and this case can be scrutinized in closer detail.[19]

All in all, rather than a literal, completely factual account of the CIA mole, our 1987 description of him and the circumstances in which he found himself leans more towards a caricature of the actual situation. We got a lot of the story right, but sometimes combined into one the characteristics of two or more of the people involved, and further mixed in plain old AOL. But from another perspective our work, despite its flaws, was really no more confused than much of the other information that makes its way into the U.S. intelligence community, and in fact was probably at least marginally better than much of it. That is why there are intelligence analysts, to sort through subjective errors and distortions typical of eyewitness reports, compare what is left to known fact, and come up with a picture that is as close to ground truth as possible.

We did get one part of the story right, though. In 1987 when we viewed him, Ames *did* own a grey European luxury car—a 1983 silver-grey XJ-6 Jaguar which he drove through the Alps and along the German *Autobahn* feeling, as Ames told Pete Earley for his book, "like Simon Templar, the Saint, a British agent driving in his Jaguar across Europe."

The fact of the car alone might have significantly narrowed the field of possible suspects in the CIA. How many CIA employees owned grey European luxury cars in 1987? Certainly some, but percentage-wise not that many. And how many CIA employees had a significant relationship with a Latin American woman, especially a Colombian? It is always possible that small facts such as these gleaned from our reports, coupled with the general picture we produced, when considered in light of what else the CIA may already have known, might have increased the chances of catching Ames with much of the damage he caused still undone. Unfortunately, there is no indication that anyone in a position to make a difference ever saw our data.

There is an ironic postscript to this story. As I was researching this part of the book I came across an interesting passage in Earley's *Confessions of a Spy.* In September 1984, the CIA sent Aldrich Ames to New York City to help troll for recruits among the Soviet officials attending the opening session of the United Nations that year. Without permission he brought his then-girlfriend Rosario to Manhattan to be with him for the four weeks he was supposed to stay in a CIA-rented hotel room. The hotel the agency picked was the San Carlos.[20] This was the same September we were wrapping up the last of our Stage 1 training and moving into Stage 2 with Ingo Swann. It was the same September when we were again unable to get into our usual hotel, the Bedford, and so were sent over to the Bedford's sister hotel, the San Carlos, to stay.

It turned out that we were in the same hotel, living mere feet away from the man and woman about whom we would three years later report detailed remote viewing information. Perhaps we even passed them in the lobby, maybe even said hello to them.

When I called Bill Ray to inform him of the interesting coincidence I had just discovered, he told me that, while in the San Carlos hotel bar one evening during that September, he and Brian Buzby had drinks with two CIA employees. Bill wondered if one of them might have been Ames.[21] Aldrich Ames was then a little less than a year away from committing his first treasonous acts.

25

1988

*. . . Jolly Old St. Nick—
and other figments of
our imaginations . . .*

We all were getting fed up with Ed Dames's shenanigans, and chafed at his parade of extraterrestrial targets, for which we received no real feedback at the end of our training sessions. We also grew weary of what some of us began to call his story-of-the-universe-du-jour. Ed had a habit of working a viewer on an anomaly target one day, going home and doing his own frontloaded remote viewing of the same target in the wee hours of the morning, and the next day bringing the news: "Yesterday I *thought* I knew what the role of the Supreme Galactic Council was. But I was wrong. Now I *really* know who is in charge." He would run a few more viewers on his target of choice, go home, view again into the early morning, then come in the following day with yet another version of how the universe was put together. Each version seemed to be more elaborate than the one before, sometimes even contradicting his previous story. With each new book he read, Ed's views and speculations seemed to change dramatically.

From the beginning Ed was absorbed in elaborate speculations on UFOs and extraterrestrials. Then he became enamored of *The Urantia Book*, a 2,500-page book published in 1955 that makes claims to divine revelation, and gives a complex and not always coherent account of the history and constitution of the universe. Ed's fascination segued into an interest in angels. We never knew what he would come up with next; we only knew that somehow it would figure into his tasking us in remote-viewing practice sessions. Both Bill Ray and, now, our new commander Lieutenant Colonel Xenakis had ordered Ed to lay off the anomaly targets. He would suppress the urge for a little while. But soon he couldn't stand it any more and would be back to his old tricks. This was hard for us viewers to fight because of the requirement that we be blind to the target. We often didn't know what sort of target Ed had in store for us until we were well into the session.

Ed's proclivity for exaggeration and invention didn't limit itself just to UFO targets. Under the guise of remote viewing he often speculated about future catastrophes or terrorist attacks. In the course of both operational and training sessions he tended to lead or manipulate the viewers into corroborating whatever scenario he had concocted in his head. Even our double-blind rules were no defense against this. Although Ed might be just as blind to a target as was the viewer, he often thought he knew what the target was anyway, and would start interjecting comments or hints into the session that threatened to lead the viewer on a tangent. More than one viewer had the experience of looking up during a session to see Ed, the monitor at the other end of the table, trying to remote view the target himself.

Then, one day Gabi grew frustrated when yet another of her training sessions had been "led" far too vigorously by an overzealous Ed. After a conversation with Mel an idea suddenly occurred to her for a way she could get even.

Within a few days Gabi arranged for us to gather when Ed was out of the office. Lieutenant Colonel Xenakis presided over our conspiratorial group. We each decided we would play a role, and we would studiously avoid tipping our hand to Ed so he would remain oblivious until we were ready to spring our trap. Xenakis generated a set of fake encrypted coordinates, we agreed to touch base regularly as we each contributed our piece to the scheme. Then we were ready: we were going to remote view Santa Claus.

The plan was simple. We would run this like any other remote viewing operation, only we all knew what the "target" was from the start. Dames would be given the coordinate and his marching orders by Xenakis, then would schedule us to do sessions for the project. We would each try our best to play it as if we were doing just another typical operational session. We would give answers that pointed towards Santa Claus, but they would only be in bits and pieces, one- or two-word groups, as if they were fragmentary perceptions popping in as we went through our structured remote viewing process. After each session, Dames and the viewer would each summarize the results, and Dames would then incorporate them into his growing data base for the project. In the end, he would report his findings to Xenakis.[1]

No one remembers who was first into the room. I know it wasn't me; I remember doing my session after Ed had already started to form his notion of what the target might be. Some of us reported that a person was involved who relied on stealth, operating only at night. Someone else described the activity as one might an infiltration—crossing national frontiers without official authorization, carrying packages and other items that would not be checked by customs. This cargo was stuffed into a sack carried in the back of an open conveyance.

Another viewer introduced the idea of "coming from the north," and someone else suggested that flying was involved. The perpetrator we were describing would drop down on unsuspecting American homes in the middle of the night. The fact that the event would be tied to a holiday or anniversary was said to be significant. Since I had a reputation for discovering when domestic animals were present at targets we worked, I remember introducing "draft animals" into the story line. Gabi, still in training, kept her input simple. In Stage 3 she sketched a sleigh runner. But a sleigh runner, viewed by itself, looks a lot like the landing skids of several different types of aircraft.

After every session Ed would leave the operations building yet more agitated. He knew that something serious was afoot and that we were on to it. Convinced that our viewing would unravel the plot, whatever it might be, he was always eager to launch into the next session. I still remember him, sitting intently, seriously, at the far end of the table, trying to pry more information out of me. More than once I had to stifle a snicker to keep from giving the whole game away.

Finally, Ed figured he had enough data. Based on what he had gotten from the viewers, this was the scenario he worked out: there would be a terrorist attack on the United States sometime before the end of the year. There was one main terrorist, but he was supported by a loyal cadre, many of whom were quite short, at his primary base of operations. Disguised by facial hair, this terrorist would make his assault from the north, across the Canadian border. He would avoid detection by transporting himself and his materials through the backcountry using beasts of burden, and make his final move across the border into the United States by air, using an ultralight aircraft that he assembled in Canada. It was almost Christmas, 1987.

As the final session of the Great Santa Caper wrapped up, with Mel as the viewer, Ed leaped up from his chair to bear the tale to Xenakis. But unbeknownst to Ed, Xenakis was in the control room, just a few feet down the hall. The colonel's muffled guffaw sparked the light of realization in Ed's brain. He quickly figured out he'd been "had."[2]

Ed took it good-naturedly, if a little subdued for him. He had a good sense of humor, and wasn't above playing his own practical jokes on others given a good opportunity. We all laughed, slapped each other on the back, and prepared to celebrate the holidays. Gabi even tried to do a needlepoint of Santa in an ultralight, to give Ed in fond remembrance, but she could never get it quite right. Though Ed got the joke, he still didn't get the message. It was business as usual for future remote viewing work where he was involved.

The end of 1987 brought with it a major watershed event for Sun Streak, though we didn't know it at the time. Fred Atwater, who had been with the remote viewing unit from the beginning, who had been the midwife that brought it into the world and who had shepherded it through times of trial and triumph, was leaving. After having spent ten years previously in the "real" Army, and another ten years training and guiding Army psychic spies, Fred retired to the mountains of Virginia. He had bought land on a wooded hillside near the Monroe Institute, and for the prior two years had spent nearly every weekend there clearing the land, bulldozing a road, and building a foundation and basement by hand. The project was completed when a huge crane deposited a high-end prefab house on top of the foundation walls, and the Atwaters moved in to stay. It was a beautiful, peaceful setting, and I visited him a number of times over the coming years to take a break from the franticness of the Baltimore-Washington urban corridor.

But his leaving created a huge gap among us, one that Ed Dames and Fern Gauvin together couldn't fill. With Fred's departure, Ed formally became training officer, a position he would hold for the next eleven months. But it was not much more than an honorary title in our informal hierarchy. The experienced viewers had almost as much say as Ed in how new viewers were trained and how old ones were kept in practice. But that didn't really matter, as in those days we all got along and generally worked well together as a team, despite our occasional annoyance with Ed when he would try to pull yet another UFO target on us.

Fern had officially taken over as operations officer some months before Fred left, so Fred's departure didn't change Fern's work situation. He seemed to be managing competently, along with some help from Ed, since Ed was also functioning as assistant operations officer, a position he shared with Gene Lessman until Gene left for Germany. This meant Ed worked as a project officer, managing the remote viewers and doing first-stage analysis and reporting for individual projects, while Fern had overall control of what projects were worked and by whom. Ed also received and dispensed tasking, and worked on the final reporting to DIA headquarters. He had considerable help from the experienced viewers, who later in 1988 began to be assigned as project officers on missions for which they weren't serving as viewers.

Some people mistakenly say that all Ed Dames did was keep the schedule for the operations rooms in Building T-2560. The truth is that while much of his job was administrative in nature, he had a useful role to play in the actual day-to-day remote-viewing operations. His personal interests continued to get in the way of the operational viewing, but we viewers eventually learned to describe the targets while ignoring his attempts at front-loading and his "leading" interjections.

The new year was soon upon us and more surprises were in store for 1988. The first of these came half-way through January when our boss, Lieutenant Colonel Xenakis, announced he, too, was retiring. He had come to us with over twenty years in the Army, having earned a Ph.D. in education along the way. In January he got wind of an opening at the University of Maryland, managing their education extension program, and it was too good a job to refuse. Within a matter of days he was hired by the university, submitted his retirement papers, and was gone.

Bewildered, we wondered what would happen next. How long would it take before DIA found another lieutenant colonel to be our commander? These things usually took months to arrange, and there was often at least a little overlap for the old boss to pass on some institutional knowledge to the new one. There was clearly going to be a gap this time.

The problem was solved in an unexpected way. Jack Vorona had been wanting to civilianize the commander's position anyway, and now he saw the opportunity. He did away with the lieutenant colonel position, appointed Fern Gauvin branch chief instead, and made Ed Dames the operations officer in addition to being the training officer.[3] I was a little unsure what to make of this arrangement. Fern was a great guy, if a little soft-spoken and sometimes difficult to understand. Ed, at least, was still a known quantity we had learned to deal with.

But getting rid of the Army commander brought mixed blessings. With a civilian we would not be rotating bosses every few years when an officer would be due for a transfer. This lack of upheaval could be a blessing if the civilian assigned to lead was competent, with the necessary vision to keep the remote viewing unit on track. However, each one of the succession of lieutenant colonels had brought with him just the right degree of skepticism and aloofness to keep us from becoming too full of ourselves.

Except for the special case of Bill Ray, all our commanders declined to try remote viewing themselves. They all felt that they should remain detached and objective about the process to avoid being seduced by a particular point of view, or be fooled by a line of thinking based on emotion more than objective scrutiny. These officers served to keep us honest, while presenting the appropriate objective face to officials they interacted with in their job of representing remote viewing to the outside intelligence community. It was a wise strategy, and it worked well. Not only did the previous Army commanders present the unit in a professional light, but with their pragmatic military training they also helped keep a lid on the tendency of some folks within the unit to go off the deep end with wacky ideas that cropped up from time to time.

But Fern was a viewer. He had already lost that expectation of complete objectivity. Moreover, he wasn't really an organizational man. While he had worked in and around the bureaucracy for decades, he didn't have the tough, slightly cynical mind-set of a hard-bitten Army colonel. That fact soon came home to haunt us.

During this turmoil, operational remote viewing continued. There was the standard fare of unidentified structures to be explored, and some more novel projects as well. One of these was sparked by the imminent return of Cosmos 1900, a Soviet low-orbit surveillance satellite that had lost radio contact with its control station. It was certain to crash—along with its nuclear reactor core, it was feared—sometime during the summer or fall of 1988. Countries where it might come down were gearing up disaster recovery teams in anticipation of having to clean up bits of highly radioactive reactor strewn over large areas of their real estate. Sun Streak was tasked to find out when and where Cosmos 1900 would make Earth-fall. This particular venture gives another rare glimpse at an operational remote viewing project for which there is actual feedback available from open sources. But it involved both "hard problems" of remote viewing, search and future.

Five viewers participated: Mel Riley, Lyn Buchanan, Gabrielle Pettingell, Angela Dellafiora, and—now with four operations under his belt in the role of viewer—Ed Dames. Altogether, the viewers worked ten sessions.[4] I was not involved in this project, as it took place mostly while I was on temporary duty at Fort Leavenworth for an Army training course.

Mel Riley "perceived two events occurring simultaneously yet separated by . . . about two hundred miles," according to the operational report. The most important event happened in a "cold, flat, rugged wasteland" in the northern hemisphere. Mel indicated on a map where he thought the event would occur—about 57 degrees north, 135 degrees east, putting it somewhere in the Soviet Far East. He didn't indicate a time frame for when the event might occur.

Lyn described a "structure sinking and coming to rest" sometime between August 26 and 30, and designated a map area that translated into geographic coordinates of 8 degrees north, 135 degrees east, placing it in the ocean somewhere northeast of New Guinea.

Gabi located the target at 65 degrees north, 178 degrees east, just at the farthest eastern tip of Siberia. She had the impression that the event would occur around August 1990, and described the location as a "small body of shallow, dirty, fresh water situated in an expansive, flat, open area in the Northern Hemisphere."

Ed had impressions that the target would break up into two pieces before it hit. "The larger piece comes to rest in shallow water," his part of the project report reads, "in a bleak, open, desolate, and rocky area in the Northern Hemisphere (Canada, Newfoundland, Scandinavia)." The event would occur "in late fall," sometime during October or November 1988. Ed also reported that a violent reaction, such as an explosion, would be connected with the splashdown.

Angela reported that the "payload" would come down in the Mediterranean a few miles north of Algiers, Algeria. Part of the "payload," which she called the "shell portion," was perceived to come to rest on land, also somewhere near Algiers. She declared this payload to be a "lunar vehicle," and predicted that the Soviets would recover it without incident. She went on to say that a similar "lunar" vehicle landed in Pakistan "in the recent past," and that the United States had three such lunar vehicles.

The project report's conclusion observed that "The thread of commonality in this project appears to be the splashdown in water. As anticipated, there is a wide disparity in the anticipated date of occurrence."[5]

Sure enough, Cosmos 1900 reentered the atmosphere during the first week of October 1988, broke into two pieces, and the resulting debris crashed into the ocean, but in the eastern Atlantic somewhere south of Great Britain and northwest of Africa's bulge. To everyone's great relief, a few days before taking its final dive into Earth's atmosphere, Cosmos 1900 jettisoned its nuclear reactor into a higher, stable orbit, thus saving some hapless part of the globe from potential disaster.

On reading the report, it becomes clear that there were good bits of information, but other parts were way off. Certainly, the predictive part of it was not especially useful. The closest was Ed who, depending on how one interprets his remarks, was off by as much as a month. Locating the impact zone was also a bust. Ed had the space vehicle separating into two parts, and crashing somewhere in the vicinity of Canada. Angela, too got the separation into two parts, and her account, though wrong as far as location and timing, seems at first glance remarkable because she identified the event as a crashing "lunar vehicle"—an obvious attempt to describe a space vehicle of some kind. But both Ed's and Angela's results suggest something else that might have been going on. Though I don't have the records to prove it, I suspect they may both have been working frontloaded.

For some time now, it seemed Angela had been receiving frontloading before doing sessions. I don't know if it was a regular thing, but I do have records that show several projects for which she was told in advance what the intended target was. My suspicion—and her data is consistent with the possibility—was that before she started her remote viewing she was given verbal or written tasking along the lines of "Where and when will Cosmos 1900 return to earth?" Even if she had neither read nor heard about it in the news, the "Cosmos" name itself certainly would have implied that the project had to do with a Soviet space project, and could have suggested to her a Soviet lunar vehicle. Further, if she *had* heard the news reports, it is possible that she knew of another Soviet satellite that had crashed into the Mediterranean Sea not long before. Media speculation early in the Cosmos 1900 scare had it that it would come down in late July or August, which, if she were frontloaded, could easily have influenced her choice of landing dates.

Ed was listed last in the sequence of viewers, and therefore probably did his viewing towards the end of the project, August 26. By that time the news had it that Cosmos 1900 would come down in late fall sometime, and that it would likely hit somewhere in Canada. Ed subscribed to *Science News*, a weekly magazine that carried the latest science stories, including regular updates on the status of Cosmos 1900. The fact that Ed's remote-viewing results ended up being wrong in just the same way the media reporting at the time turned out also wrong, suggests to me that he knew what the remote viewing mission was all along. We of course were aware that Ed did his own viewing at home frontloaded, and despite Ingo Swann's firm rejection of frontloaded viewing, Ed was an open advocate of the practice. He was convinced—wrongly, in my opinion—that an experienced viewer need not be blind to the target, but should easily be able to deal with AOL and preconceptions. The evidence from the Cosmos 1900 project suggests otherwise.

But even before Cosmos 1900, there were strange things afoot at Sun Streak.

It all came to a head in a weekly staff meeting sometime in the first half of February 1988, less than a month after our last military commander, Lieutenant Colonel Xenakis, suddenly retired. There were rumors noised around the office among the other viewers that Fern Gauvin and Angela were working together on some new approach to remote viewing. I didn't really pay much attention to it. People at the unit were always toying with new ideas, trying things out, experimenting with something they had heard or read about. But they knew how to do it responsibly, and understood that we didn't adopt some new technique until it had been well tested. Or, at least, so I thought.

Then we gathered for a meeting at Fern's call. Our meetings were almost always on Friday afternoon. It wasn't the best of times. The staff was anxious to be done with the week, and by Friday my usual weekday sleep-deprived schedule was catching up with me. I was hard put not to nod off during the soporific discussions about office minutiae that often ensued. Not this time, though.

After taking care of a few perfunctory administrative matters, Fern declared that he had something important to announce. He turned to Angela, who was sitting near him at the long conference table, and said that she was going to introduce us to a new remote viewing method that from now on would be used against real-world targets. What this new approach amounted to, it turned out, was channeling.

Channeling is not a new phenomenon. During an earlier age it was known as "having a familiar spirit"—contacting someone who was dead, or at least not of this world, and acting as a voice to allow the entity to speak through the channeler. Presumably, one way this worked was for these disembodied beings to take command for a short while of some of the channeler's body functions to allow the communications to take place. In the nineteenth century interest in the practice, often referred to as trance-mediumship, grew with the Spiritualist movement, but began to fade not long after the dawning of the twentieth century.

By the 1980s channeling had once again exploded in popularity. "Seth," channeled by medium Jane Roberts, and "Ramtha," reputedly a 30,000-year-old warrior incongruously brought forth in the diminutive frame of the blond J. Z. Knight, were among the ones with top billing. Other entities with names ranging from the prosaic "Michael" to the exotic "Atun-Re," along with many others, prominent and obscure, caught the public's eye and imagination.

By the time of the fateful office meeting, I already had extensive exposure to channelers, both professional and amateur, in print, on TV and video, and in person, and had done some hard thinking about the phenomenon. I had yet to be impressed by a channeler. I had not so far heard much beyond flattery and empty platitudes from any of them.

Angela's approach was in principle the same as other, more famous, channelers, but the details were a bit different. She had learned the practice on her own time and from a medium who taught out of his home in Alexandria, Virginia. When Angela worked, it wasn't so much that she was taken over by the entities, as she became involved in a conversation with them. While talking, she would scribble on a yellow legal pad with a pen. The pen would scratch back and forth across the tablet, leaving random squiggles and cross-hatchings behind. Occasionally there would be an intelligible word or phrase, left as a record of some meaningful utterance one of her spirit guides had given her.

She had several of these guides, but three made frequent appearances: "Mr. Goodman," "Dr. Einstein," and "Maurice." Whatever words and impressions they gave her, she reproduced verbally, to be recorded on tape, or by our secretary, Jeannie, who was often there to take notes. From these, reports were written and included with the data produced by the other viewers.

I can't prove that these "otherworldly" folks were not real, though I fully doubt it. But I have long since learned not to altogether reject possibilities for which one does not as yet have grounded truth. In the context of office politics it made sense at the time to act as if they existed.

I found out later that Angela's friends had cropped up much earlier in an ERV session monitored by Gene Lessman, in such a way that Gene was convinced they were real. Over the preceding sessions Angela had begun commenting to Gene when she felt that her escorts were present. The problem, it seemed to Gene, was that her perceptions of these "fellows," real or not, began to interfere with the mission. Then, at the start of one session, he put his foot down.

"I had told Angela I did not want her to use her 'buddies,'" he explained when recounting the event recently. "Then she told me that her buddies weren't happy about me telling them that. And I said, 'I don't care about that.' But then, during the session, they apparently decided to assert *their* particular will. And . . . they came at me . . . I guess *psychically* is the best way to put it. They just got in and messed with my head to the point that it actually jolted me backwards over a chair." According to Gene, Angela didn't even notice. She was deep into her session—"almost in a trance," was how Gene put it—seemingly oblivious to what was going on around her.

When I asked Gene whether he had any interaction with the "buddies" after this rather dramatic event, he replied, "No, I made a compromise with Angela, and told her to pass it along to her friends. They could have her twenty-three hours of the day, but I had her for an hour. She could deal with them. But if she was not going to deal with me under my terms, and let me have her for one hour using *my* techniques, then she was either going to have to go to another team, or I would recommend she leave the program. And it worked, at least as far as I know. Still, there was no doubt in my mind that she was calling on her friends for a couple of answers here and there."[6] Nevertheless, from that point on Gene maintained control of sessions with Angela.

What could possibly have happened to Gene to cause him to fall over a chair? He is convinced that Angela's "entities" did it. The only thing I myself can say for sure is that Gene Lessman seemed convinced that even by our standards something weird had happened to him in that room with Angela.

But here we were in what had started out to be a typical office meeting, with a bombshell in our laps. Gabi was the first to break the ice. Shouldn't any new methodology be thoroughly tested, she asked, before it was adopted as an equal partner in doing remote viewing for real-world, operational remote viewing? After all, both methods already in use at Sun Streak had been vetted through literally thousands of practice sessions by scientists and intelligence personnel alike. Efforts had been made to shake out the bugs and see what the shortcomings and strengths of CRV and ERV were before they were put to use against targets that involved national security.[7]

Fern protested that he and Angela had tested her technique on a number of targets over the past few weeks, and he was satisfied that it was just as effective as the methods we were using. That answer didn't sit well with most of the rest of us gathered around the conference table; it smacked too much of caprice. A few weeks of trials didn't match up to the years of trial and error evaluation that other methods of remote viewing had been put through. But it was my question that brought on the storm.

"Assuming for the sake of argument that this method *does* involve some kind of entities, how can we be certain of these guys' bona fides?" I asked. "How can we be sure they are who they say they are?" It was the question any good intelligence officer is supposed to ask from the very start about his sources, even if they are dead. That was all I said, but my mind was full of thoughts and concerns.

A spy-handler needs to know three things about someone who is a prospective source. First, is your source really who he says he is? The history of espionage is chock full of moles and double agents who passed themselves off as someone they were not, to the great dismay of the case officers who trusted them.

Second, what is the "placement and access" of the source—in other words, does that person work in a place that has the information you need, and does he actually have access to it? Often, a source *says* he can get the information you need, but can't really get his hands on it. Finally—and this is often the most important thing—can the source be trusted? In the murky realm of intelligence the answer is very seldom an absolute "yes." But there are ways to evaluate a source's trustworthiness in the normal world. Those methods didn't seem to be available for a source contacted through channeling. If Angela's friends were real—and I didn't admit then that I suspected they were at best merely manifestations of her subconscious—how did we know they weren't liars, pranksters, or evildoers? There was no guarantee that the entities were not just like the rest of us, with the same confused mix of truth and error floating around in their minds. Just because they existed in a different "plane" or "dimension" than the rest of us did not necessarily mean that they had any greater access to truth than anyone here. In fact, they might even be more in error about our world than are we. There was a danger that Angela's entities were being seriously overrated on their ability to deliver the goods.

I meant my questions about Angela's sources to be taken seriously, but that didn't happen. Instead, Angela left the room upset. Fern turned to glare at me, then roundly chewed us all out—even those who hadn't said a thing—for being inconsiderate and inhospitable to new ideas. It seemed evident to me at the time that not only had our boss expected us to embrace the new method as enthusiastically as had he, but from things he then said, he even wanted us to try it ourselves. He was clearly disappointed, and maybe a little hurt. We had not intended to create a ruckus, and he had not expected one. But that is how it ended up.

As I found out later, Gabi's and my misgivings were shared by nearly everyone else at the table. Still, we quickly tried to mollify Fern. Gabi and I gave our reassurances that our objections had not been personally meant, but that we only felt it would be a good idea to approach new ideas more gingerly. Some of the others cautiously agreed to try out the channeling method once they understood it better. Fern left the room calmer, but not wholly mollified.

Though for that moment I was treating Angela's theories as plausible, I still leaned towards the more likely alternative, that they were a figment of her imagination, conjured up by her subconscious to facilitate her remote viewing. This latter notion would be much less controversial, and less dangerous. Fern decided to call Angela's channeling method "written remote viewing," or WRV, because of the scribbling on the legal pad.

February was a watershed of sorts not just because of the channeling fiasco, but for another reason as well. We began the first of what was to be a marathon series of projects that spanned the next few years. Americans and other foreigners were being seized by radical Islamic terrorist groups in Lebanon and held hostage. Our government wanted to know if we could find them. The answer was yes, sort of. Ironically, the situation was not too different in principle from the Iran hostage situation, which had occupied our predecessors for many months and hundreds of sessions during the Grill Flame era.

I have mentioned the two "hard problems" for remote viewing: predicting the future, and search, or attempting to locate missing things. With search, it was no harder finding and describing the surroundings and circumstances of a missing object or person than with any other standard target. Unfortunately, describing surroundings was seldom enough. If someone wanted us to "find" a hostage kidnaped by Hezbollah terrorists in Lebanon's Beka'a Valley, we could perhaps tell them the hostage was locked up in a run-down stone building with cracked plaster ceilings, in a room with bars on the window, and peeling, yellow walls. We could tell them that the hostage was tied to a bed, and was feeling sick and depressed. We could say that the building was hemmed in by other, nearly identical buildings amidst a tangle of twisted streets filled with people speaking a language that was not English, and living under squalid conditions. We might even find out that the village itself was a group of flat-topped, masonry buildings jammed together with a few other buildings that had domes and spires, and was surrounded by rolling, rocky hills where farm animals grazed.

But this information was almost totally useless. The intelligence analysts hoping for clues that would help in a hostage rescue could guess this same information. What they needed was geographic coordinates, or a city name, or a street address. They needed to not just *find* the hostage, but *locate* him as well.

Unfortunately, remote viewing has a hard time providing numbers and names. These are analytic things that involve the left brain, and therefore invite analytical overlay when a viewer tries to discover them.

There is, after all, no inherent meaning in a street address—for example, 1005 O'Farrell Street. This is the address in Boise, Idaho, where my grandparents once lived. Why was it labeled 1005? Because it was between 1003 and 1007 and across from 1006. The numbers were chosen by city planners, but any series of digits would have worked. And what about O'Farrell? It, too, was an arbitrary choice. The street could just as easily have been named after Jones or Washington or Martin Luther King. When you get right down to it, most addresses have no intrinsic meaning, unless the street was named after a nearby geographic feature. They are devoid of descriptive content and therefore cannot with any reliability be identified by remote viewing. "Getting" addresses doesn't work, so there has to be some other way to approach Search.

In April 1988 I began attending the quarterly meetings of the Chesa-peake Chapter of the American Society of Dowsers, which met in the Homewood Friends' (Quaker) meeting hall not far from the Johns Hopkins University campus. I hoped to get some practical ideas there that might help improve our performance on search problems. The notion behind dowsing is that the physical body recognizes subconsciously when it or an implement held in the hand like a "pointer" is closing in on a hidden target. The classic example of this is the old rancher looking for underground water using a forked stick. Where the end of the stick "dips" towards the ground is where he should dig his well.

Attended by a variety of wonderful and often engagingly quirky Marylanders, the meetings were not only entertaining, but useful as well. From them I got handy tips on map-dowsing, various types of implements and how to use them, sources for additional information on dowsing, and so on. Much of the value came not from things learned there, but ideas that came to mind as a result. I even occasionally took my kids to the meetings. On one of those occasions, James dowsed for and found a dollar coin that had been stashed for a dowsing exercise in a park across the street from the meeting hall. Helpful as dowsing was, though, it still wasn't the silver-bullet solution to the search problem. Occasionally dowsing offered an astonishing success, but more frequently the results were mixed or just wrong. We struggled with the search problem for months and years, and even to this day haven't really solved it.

We had worked search problems in the past, and hostage problems as well. In fact, our first operational remote viewing as fledgling viewers had been the Camarena kidnaping in Mexico. Our first project for the Lebanese situation started on February 4, 1988, as an evaluation exercise to see what success we might have. Five of us worked a total of seven sessions against three targets: Terry Waite, the Anglican cleric who had gone to Lebanon to try to negotiate with Arab radicals for the release of hostages already held; the Ayatollah Khomeini, leader of the Iranian fundamentalist regime; and an unidentified "Middle East man of interest."[8]

A cryptic remark in the operations logbook notes something about an "Eyes response" being available, which suggests the information we developed was sent up through channels, bringing a reply from someone higher up that was designated "Eyes Only"—a secrecy classification which meant it was to be read only by specific people, and they could not copy it or take notes about its content. Without the actual response we can never be certain of our success, but the fact that such a response seems to have been received suggests that we might have hit a nerve with at least some of the data we provided.

By February 18 we were launched into the thick of it, under the project number 8808. By August 4 of the following year, 1989, 113 sessions had been worked against the following tasking: "Determine and describe physical and mental status and locations of US hostages and Terry Waite. Include Israeli hostages. [A couple of Israeli soldiers had been captured by Islamic guerrillas, and were being sought.]" We must have provided something useful, since the following note was later added to the operations log: "DB-5* indicates info related to sightings, and physical condition was 'of value.'"[9] When that August 4 assessment was made, the project was still ongoing, so no final numbers were given. I have been unable to locate any close-out reporting on the project, so it is for now hard to say how many hundreds of sessions were ultimately worked against the hostage situation.

Project 8808 was used as an umbrella for a number of subprojects having to do with the Lebanese hostage situation. There were plenty of the standard-fare remote viewing sessions done from encrypted coordinates. But there were novelties as well. On one occasion several of us were ferried down to the Defense Intelligence Analysis Center at Bolling Air Force Base outside Washington to view video footage taken of Lebanon by an Israeli unmanned reconnaissance aircraft, a UAV. The hope was that the drone might have caught pictures of something that we would recognize from our sessions, but the video triggered no response for us that I recall.

Another time at the DIAC, we were ushered into a windowless room containing a table covered by bird's-eye photographs of a Lebanese village. Obviously operating in this case frontloaded, we were asked to indicate where on the photo we sensed a hostage was being held. Working separately, most of the viewers indicated buildings in approximately the same area. Angela, though, designated a site in a large, barren, rocky patch of land on the ridge of a hill not far from a major road. There were no structures anywhere nearby, and no cover or concealment for hundreds of yards around. It would have been impossible to hide someone there, even given the scenario suggested later, that the hostage was buried in a box with an air pipe to the surface.

Subsequently, the DIA analysts passed on to us through our boss that a building the coordinate remote viewers had indicated had indeed been harboring the hostage at the time of the viewing. Of course, the data was apparently not useful, since no hostage was recovered. In a situation like this even spot-on conventionally obtained intelligence might not have helped, since often it was either logistically or militarily impossible to get forces in to mount a rescue, or the hostage had been moved before action could be taken.

*The analysis office in DIA responsible for that particular project.

It was about this time that Lyn Buchanan discovered the liabilities of being assigned to the remote viewing unit. Ever since the program's existence became public knowledge in recent years, there have been rumors that the Army purposely destroyed the careers of those assigned to the unit. This is completely untrue. But that doesn't mean careers weren't derailed. Every soldier knows that there are boxes to be checked off if one wants to be promoted. Spending a few years sidelined in a small, unconventional unit with no room for advancement within the unit did not help our promotion chances. Lyn's case is a prime example. He came to Center Lane as a sergeant first class (SFC). After a few years at Fort Meade, during which time Center Lane became Sun Streak, he was considered for promotion to master sergeant. His name was added to the promotion list, making him eligible in due course to be bumped up to the second highest enlisted grade in the Army. That promotion was expected in 1988.

Then one day Lyn got a phone call from DIA's personnel office. If you want to get promoted, he was told, you're going to have to leave the unit. To an outsider, that may look like bias, but to a soldier, it made sense. The position to which Lyn was assigned was restricted to lesser-ranking enlisted people. Our only master sergeant slot was occupied by Mel Riley, and Sun Streak didn't need any more master sergeants. Lyn had a choice: he could either transfer into a unit that had an open master sergeant's position, or he could decline the promotion. It was a tough decision, but in the end Lyn decided to stick with remote viewing.[10]

Something similar happened to me, but I didn't find out about it until the end of my career. Army officers are generally expected to have an assignment sometime during their captaincies as the commanding officer of a company-sized unit. When I was a captain, the Army was telling military intelligence officers not to worry about getting a command. "Only about 18% of all MI officers ever have the opportunity to command," I remember my officer's career branch advisor telling me. "So you don't have to worry about this. You'll almost certainly be promoted to lieutenant colonel, and have a fair chance at colonel, even without a command. All the promotion boards are receiving these instructions."

But as they say, "The Army never lies. The truth just changes." By 1995, when I was struggling through Command and General Staff College by correspondence while trying to hold down a regular Army assignment and manage a family life, MI officers' career branch had still not told me that the truth had changed. After learning I had been passed over for lieutenant colonel, I called and was told that because I hadn't had a command as a captain, and even though I had been promoted to major, I had never had a prayer of becoming a lieutenant colonel. I had not had a chance for command, because virtually the entire time I was a captain I was assigned to the remote viewing unit. Like Lyn, I could have chosen to leave the unit to further my career, but opted to stick with remote viewing. Even if I had known then how it would turn out, I would probably still have made the decision I did.

I wasn't the only one to encounter similar problems. While the commanders of the remote viewing unit usually were promoted by the ends of their careers, only one viewer ever made it to lieutenant colonel. The rest of the officers never made it past major. Fred Atwater retired as a captain, but his case was special. When he pinned on his first set of lieutenant's bars at the end of officer candidate school, he already had half his career behind him as an enlisted man. In an era when it took eleven years to reach the rank of major, Fred only had ten years left in the Army. I learned from him years later that he had in fact been on the list for major, but he chose to retire instead of accepting the promotion. He had finished his house in Virginia and wanted to live in it.

As 1988 progressed, we added more recruits to fill in the blanks left by the departure of Fred, Gene, and Lieutenant Colonel Xenakis. Since Ed and Fern took over some of the duties of those who had left us, it was decided that incoming personnel would become viewers. The first of these came to us in a nontraditional way.

Since Hal Puthoff had been enticed away from SRI in 1985 to become director of the Institute for Advanced Studies in Austin, Texas, the SRI research team had been led by Ed May. Under May's direction SRI had been looking for better ways to identify people who might make good remote viewers. They had developed a battery of double-blind remote viewing tests— nothing more than remote viewing targets to be used in assessment trials for tasking prospective candidates. These tests, though not perfect, served as some measure of a person's abilities.

One day in early 1988 Ed May, along with statistician and researcher Jessica Utts, and Jim Salyer, DIA's contract representative at SRI, showed up at the DIAC to test candidates there. Jack Vorona favored pulling folks from within DIA to fill openings at Sun Streak, over which he was ultimately in charge. He had asked SRI to screen a number of people within DIA for incipient remote viewing ability.[11]

Though Vorona had wanted to test a large number of candidates, internal DIA politics made it difficult to recruit. In the end, only a handful of people were chosen for screening. Criteria used to choose the candidates were fairly unscientific: whether candidates had expressed some interest in the paranormal; and whether they were in a position to be released by their supervisors to go to another assignment. According to Dale Graff, most of those assessed were consequently low-level employees in noncritical positions. In the end, none of them scored at the level the SRI researchers thought was sufficient to indicate remote viewing ability.

One who was screened was a twenty-something woman named Robin who worked as an administrative assistant in DIA's Freedom of Information Office. But her supervisor was willing to let her go, so in the end she came to us by default. Untrained in intelligence and unacquainted with remote viewing, she was assigned to Sun Streak with none of the usual personality screening tests, interviews, or cautious courting that had, with a few exceptions, been customary in recruiting new viewers for the remote viewing unit. "We were as surprised as any that she, or any of the [tested] group was chosen to join the unit on the basis of what we did," Ed May later informed me. "[We] were not consulted in any aspect of this decision."[12]

Ed Dames and I ran afoul of her the very first day she was assigned. I was unit recruitment officer as one of my extra duties, but had no clue we were gaining a new person until the day she showed up. It was my responsibility to have her fill out the normal assessment tests and other paperwork. I double-checked that with Fern, who told me to go ahead. I drew her aside to hand her the various tests and explain how they were to be filled out. Ed was with me, curious to meet the new employee.

She was infuriated. "I don't have to take any of your tests!" she barked. A little startled, I tried to explain that everyone who had been assigned was expected to take the personality and psychology tests to help us better understand how to approach remote viewing training with them. She refused to consider it, or even to listen to what I was trying to say. Scowling at Ed, even though he was just an innocent bystander, she stormed out of the cubicle before I could finish. Ed and I looked at each other, thoroughly bewildered. Fern soon told me that Robin would not be required to complete any of the tests.

Though Robin was often pleasant, she could also be unpredictably cranky. On the few occasions when she was really upset she could swear like a sailor and, though military folks are generally inured to cussing, it wasn't the norm in our small quarters and it was disconcerting to hear that language emanating from such a petite woman. I long clung to my first impression of her as prickly and volatile, but years after I learned there was a warm side to her. When Jeannie, the unit's secretary, was struggling with a difficult family issue, Jeannie remembers Robin as the only one in the office who regularly kept tabs on her and offered comfort and support.

Not long afterwards, Robin and Ed had another confrontation. We had been assigned to teach her CRV. I probably gave her the lectures, though I no longer remember the details. But Ed was tasked to do training sessions with her. She seemed to resent the whole process, and there was always tension in the air between Robin and Ed when they were training. Finally, one day in the middle of a session Robin burst into tears and rushed from the room. She finished her CRV training with Lyn Buchanan, but in the end gravitated toward Angela's channeling process, and eventually moving on to include tarot card readings.

We could have grown used to her idiosyncrasies if she had shown more talent for remote viewing, in whatever form she practiced it. According to those who worked directly with her, in only a few cases were her results useable. Lyn has said that when he ran a database of viewer effectiveness he discovered that, while everyone else demonstrated at least reasonably consistent remote viewing ability, Robin was able to contribute relatively little. "I remember once when she was correct in a remote viewing session," he is fond of joking. "She said 'There is blue at the target.' And there was!"

To be fair, while Robin was often much less accurate compared to the other viewers, she did occasionally contribute useful information, once giving a close approximation of the name and an accurate location for a ship in the Mediterranean carrying Libyan chemical agents. But in the end, Robin was significant to the unit not for remote viewing contributions, but for the impact she had on the ultimate fate of the remote-viewing program.

26

Bubble, Bubble,
Toil, and Trouble

*. . . misfits in
paradise . . .*

Something was amiss in the remote viewing unit. Since its founding in the late 1970s, good will had usually ruled among the psychic spies. There had been differences of opinion and disagreements, but these were usually between individuals and seldom taken personally. Professional differences were worked out in a way that seldom led to bad feelings. But now, as the summer of 1988 approached, good will was rapidly evaporating.

As nearly as I can tell, the negativity that was setting in traced its genesis to that fateful office meeting in which channeling became an accepted intelligence collection tool. Gabi's and my reaction during the meeting foreshadowed a polarization that soon developed among the people in Sun Streak. Outwardly, we tried to pretend it didn't exist. But it still smoldered.

One side coalesced around Angela and Robin, and for a little while, our secretary Jeannie. The group indirectly included Fern, who was seen as their mentor. On the other side were the other viewers, practitioners of the more established methodologies, CRV and ERV. To an outsider, it might have looked as if the office divided along methodology lines, but the picture was more complicated than that.

In an interesting way cigarettes were a contributing factor to the alliances. Jeannie, Angela, and Robin, plus Mel Riley, were the smokers in the office. In 1988, the federal government was just beginning to protect non-smokers from the hazards of secondhand smoke in the workplace. The conference room in the back of Building T-2561 became the unofficial "smoking room." Angela, Mel, and Robin's desks were back there, and Jeannie, who was posted nearest the front door to act as receptionist, would go to the conference room for smoke breaks. The three women would trade the gossip of the day while, between his remote viewing sessions, Mel sat quietly doing painstaking Native American–style beadwork. As long as Mel was in the room, their conversations were innocent enough. When he left to do a session or run errands, though, the door would be closed and their talk muted. Speculative rumors about what they might be saying fed our worries. I'm sure we were not the only professional office that experienced this phenomenon of a camaraderie developing among exiled smokers with a conversational void to fill. It didn't have to divide us, but it was a contributing factor, providing a common social connector and divider.

Those of us in the front office felt a growing us-versus-them attitude emanating from the back room. Unquestionably, our objections during the fateful channeling meeting and our failure to immediately welcome Angela's methodology were interpreted by those who did practice or support it as a personal rejection. But this interpretation was wrong. Though several of us had mixed emotions about the new practice, we were generally open-minded about new ideas—a byproduct of our line of work. Most of us thought that once a remote viewing method was shown to work, we had little reason to object to it. In the end it turned out questionable whether or not channeling, or WRV, was sufficiently effective, but at that early point the issue was still very much unresolved, and we generally chose to withhold judgment until the facts were in.

What set us off, though, were some things that came along as part of the WRV package. For one, we believed we saw a budding favoritism being shown Angela by Fern and, later, by Jack Vorona himself. As the only person in the office deemed qualified to monitor Angela's WRV sessions, Fern would spend long hours working with her over in the operations building. Not that there was anything inappropriate going on, but as Angela dominated the boss's time, it seemed to us that she began to develop a haughty attitude towards the rest of us. We thought we detected in her behavior smugness about her talents and condescension towards ours when occasion allowed.

To us, sometimes, her attitude almost seemed to verge on the absurd. Though all of us took a hand with the Lebanese hostages project, Angela worked a large percentage of the sessions. At the time Ed Dames was assigned to keep track of operational missions and their results, and I remember him commenting to several of us privately that Angela "had worked eighty sessions and had not a single hit to show for it." Given that this was a search problem, lack of success was not a crime. But it grated on us to hear Angela's sessions packaged as "hits" that we believed to be "misses." It looked to us as if marginal results were being shoehorned to fit the objectives.

In one case Angela used WRV week after week to declare that one hostage or another was about to be released by his captors in coming days. First it might be Terry Waite, then perhaps Colonel Higgins, or a week later Terry Anderson. As each predicted date came and went with no releases, she would revise the expected date and push it ahead a week or two. Then, one day weeks later, the newspapers were full of the release of one of the hostages—a European none of us recalled having heard of. Despite the fact that she had changed her predicted date numerous times, and never mentioned that particular hostage, I looked up from my desk that day to see Angela and Robin emerging from Fern's office, buzzing about Angela's "hit."

In thinking over how I should write about this unfortunate period, I puzzled about whether my attitude was merely a case of misinterpretation, or perhaps sour grapes. In other situations I have more than once discovered that I was wrong about how I had interpreted something. So I interviewed a number of my colleagues from those days, including Jeannie who, after her flirtation with the opposing camp, tried for the most part to steer clear of either group. I find that their memories track with my own.

Mel Riley, the embodiment of the live-and-let-live attitude, told me he had no personal animosity against Angela or Robin, but he was bothered by the superior airs they affected. At least four of the others have independently referred to Angela during that time as a being a "prima donna." I have noted this phenomenon among other channelers and would-be channelers whom I have either known personally or observed in action. Being the focus of intense attention seems to bring on a sort of "movie star" mentality, an almost inevitable loftiness that the "star" perhaps thinks is justly due, but which is off-putting for those watching from the sidelines.

But there was another side to the story. Years after the office closed, Angela told me that she sensed in us a lack of understanding and bias against her and her methods. She had been uneasy when others in the office, assigned to take charge of one operational project or another, thought they should be able to monitor her sessions just like anyone else's, but did not understand or respect her technique. She only trusted Fern to do that. It may be that some of our qualms came from our misinterpreting her hesitance as aloofness or as a ploy to dodge the scrutiny of her peers.

Eventually we adopted the unfortunate term "witches" in reference to the little group in the back room. Mel Riley has been blamed for first using the epithet, but I no longer remember for certain how it turned up. These events happened not long after the movie *The Witches of Eastwick* was released, and I am sure that film suggested the name.

Gender never had anything to do with it, even though that accusation is frequently used against military men who share offices and rank with women. There were strong women among the group in our outer-office clique as well, who were dismayed in the same way as we males with how things transpired. Over the years the men had respected Charlene and Gabi, as well as women before them and others who came later. If there were issues, they centered on performance or personality.

It seems astonishing that such trivial affairs so overshadowed our work in the remote viewing program, but they did. Angela and her young understudy Robin had not cornered the market on ego in our office. We all had our fair share of it. Ego seems to be an inseparable element in the frontier area of so-called psychic behavior. Perhaps there are reasons for that. It takes a lot of confidence—maybe even arrogance—to keep working day after day at something that society insists is impossible.

Whatever the case is, neither a prima donna attitude nor a clash of egos is enough to justify the alienation we felt, nor the bad feelings we harbored. There were yet more complications.

From the introduction of the WRV methodology, even untested as it was, Angela was given far more real-world operational remote viewing assignments than were the rest of us.

"For a period of about six weeks," after that fateful office meeting, Gabi remembered, "they didn't use anybody else but her on operations. We were sending out only one set of data, and that was experimental [e.g., WRV]."[1]

The numbers bear out Gabi's recollections. Over the ten months between February 1988, when WRV was introduced, and the end of that same year, the operational log shows that Angela was tasked on twenty-two projects. Lyn, Gabi and I were each assigned only nine, while Mel Riley was given eleven. (How many actual sessions for each viewer this amounted to is difficult to say, since after 1986 the operations log only breaks things down by overall project, not by session numbers.)[2] More than once, Gabi says, she stormed into Fern's office to object. "I went in and complained," she told me. "I said 'Look, you've got to use us. We're sitting here not working!'"[3]

By December 1989, the point at which twenty-two months later, the branch chief stopped making entries in the operations log, Angela had worked on a total of sixty operational projects. Robin, who only began doing operational targets later in 1988, nevertheless worked on thirty-two. Lyn and I were again tied with twenty-six each. Mel had accrued a total of thirty-four, while Gabi had worked on thirty-five projects. Ed, who departed at the end of 1988, had been the viewer on five projects during that period.[4]

To be sure, some of our numbers were low for other reasons. I took three months off from remote viewing during the summer of 1988 for a mandatory Army career course at Fort Leavenworth and some leave time. Also, Gabi, Lyn, Mel, and I had to serve as project officers on some operations and therefore couldn't work as viewers on those. Because they lacked the appropriate intelligence training, Robin and Angela were not asked to work as project officers.

This latter issue also fed our disenchantment. "What added to [the division in the office] was the fact that they were allowed to be 'prima donnas.'" Gabi noted. "They didn't have to [work as project officers], even though the rest of us had to both view and manage projects. And they were given no other additional responsibilities, whereas everybody else was kept wearing three or four hats"—such as unit fire marshal, property book officer, security officer, and so on.[5]

The various factors explain some of the disparity in numbers. But something else had to account for the fact that Angela worked on literally twice as many operations as the rest of us, and that Robin, who was a rank trainee at the start of the WRV era, ended up working as many or more projects than other viewers with years of experience.

And there was a still more serious problem. Not only were we "old-hand" remote viewers seldom tasked on operations projects during that first period, but we suspected that what data we did produce was often not even being forwarded on to the requestor. Ed, who as operations officer was privy to the reports, often commented on how it looked to him like our data was being suppressed in favor of Angela's when reports were forwarded to DIA for insertion into the intelligence system. If this was true, it was worrisome. We were all dubious of the quality of Angela's results anyway—admittedly without having much access to her's or anyone's sessions or the final reports. But what we were observing from the periphery was not reassuring, and did not bode well for our intelligence output, the very product upon which the reputation of operational remote viewing and our survival as a unit was going to be judged.

This is why I have even bothered to include so much about what, at root, was otherwise only a trivial interoffice rivalry. It seems in retrospect that this flirtation with channeling may have played a non-trivial supporting role in the ultimate fate of the remote viewing effort, because of the possible way it affected how our clients, upper-echelon commanders, and outside observers perceived the program.

Of course, we didn't know for sure that our data was being suppressed. We knew Ed was prone to exaggerate and let his view of reality filter the truth. From details I have about a number of technical targets we remote viewed, it seems that everyone's data was figured into the final reports for those projects at least. But during the period in question technical targets were a minority of the projects we worked. And they were targets that Angela neither particularly liked, nor was deemed to excel at.

I asked Jeannie for her memories of those days, whether our perceptions were true that Angela's data was generally favored over ours. Since, as secretary, Jeannie was usually responsible for putting the final touches on the reports that were sent out of the office, and since she ended up as a neutral observer during the "office wars," I thought her evaluation might be worthwhile. She confirmed Angela's status as a favored source, but she was unsure whether the data Angela produced also enjoyed preferential treatment. She seemed to think that Fern would not dare to leave out data from the other viewers.[6]

Gabi worked as project officer on dozens of operations during the years in question, and was therefore in a unique position to see how our work was being used. She came away particularly upset by the way Fern handled things. Gabi was often responsible for tasking the monitors and viewers—collecting their data, doing first-stage analysis on it, and writing the results into a draft of the final report—but she said Fern consistently refused to let her see the final reports before they were sent to DIA. As she put it:

> That was another thing that caused rancor . . . that I would be a project officer on a project, and yet would never see what went downtown. I never saw a single thing, of all the projects I managed—and I managed a lot of them. One problem was [Fern] would never let me have access to Angela's data. Even though I would work four or five regular viewers, I would never get the piece of the puzzle that Angela had, and I would never see the final product. So in essence, even though I was doing all this analysis, he would redo the analysis. I could have had three viewers who came dead on with one thing, Angela could have said something totally different, he could have gone with her, and I would never know. He wouldn't tell me. He would not show me *anything* of my project, how the final thing looked, when it went downtown. We really had some big fights about that.[7]

As far as I can tell, there was no compelling operational reason to withhold the final reports from the project officer who was responsible for compiling and analyzing our results. In fact, there are some very compelling reasons why whomever had managed a given project *should* have in fact been required to review the final report for which he or she was responsible.

According to Gabi, Fern also had the habit of "sanitizing" the feedback the office received from our customers after they had received and evaluated our results. Instead of providing the viewers with all the available feedback—a must if viewers are to improve and not become frustrated—Fern apparently usually issued only general feedback, or none at all, about the targets we had worked on for many long, grueling hours. There are good reasons to withhold feedback if an operation is likely to be tasked further. But once it is completed, there are no compelling reasons to keep feedback from the viewers.

I remember very seldom getting feedback from operations I worked during that period, so Gabi's account of it years later was not a surprise. And by late 1989 I had my own evidence that we were not seeing the full feedback. After the Department of Defense Inspector General wrote a report on Sun Streak in 1988, I was tasked to review and evaluate our results on most of the technical targets that we had remote viewed from 1986 through the first quarter of 1989—the factory complexes, research and development facilities, early warning sites, chemical warfare test ranges, and so forth. In doing this assessment, I got to see much of the feedback material withheld from the viewers at the completion of the projects. At the time it was of passing curiosity to me, but years later when Gabi told me about Fern's editing of the feedback, I began to grasp the full picture.

During this assessment in 1989, it was evident that Angela's WRV approach had often performed poorly when compared to viewers using CRV. There were a few standout projects where those results equaled the best of CRV, but for the most part her performance was much less consistent and her "noise level" much higher—in other words, too often she was just plain wrong. CRVers would at least get much of the target description correct, whether or not there was any way to judge how well the important intelligence questions had been answered. But when working frontloaded, as I discovered in those reports that she often was, Angela would frequently end up in a hopeless morass of AOL on the tech targets. On the few tech targets Robin worked, she struggled as well.

It could be argued that Angela just didn't shine on tech targets, and that her performance must have been much better on the "softer" targets to justify her being used so much more frequently than anyone else. The problem with this argument is that there was so little feedback on the "softer" targets—the hostage situations for example—to tell us whether any of us were right. When Angela was being used and the rest of us weren't, there was no way to judge whether she was better, especially that much better than the rest of us. On the few occasions feedback was available (and provided to the viewers), I recall it casting at least as favorable a light on the other methodologies as on Angela's channeling.

Adding to this was the fact that for a long stretch immediately after WRV was introduced as a methodology, Angela alone did operational sessions, while the rest of us were benched. This period mostly covered the first several of the Beirut hostage cases, for which there was no performance record whatsoever among the rest of us, against which to compare Angela's results. So there is no reason to think Angela was used and we were not simply because she was better at it. There had to be some other explanation.

It is unfortunate that for so much of this I must rely on memory. I have tried to confirm what I could, and the available information supports the picture that I have been putting together. Favoritism seems the best explanation for why Angela and Robin ended up doing so many more sessions than the rest of us. This of course begs the question—why? In a conversation I had with Dale Graff, he explained that WRV seemed to be dealing with words, names, and other analytical concepts that our customary ERV and CRV approaches to remote viewing seemed unable to address. "You can sketch all you want," Dale told me, "but you're going to still fall short of knowing the analytical stuff, the naming function."[8] Of course, CRV and ERV dealt with much more than just sketching, but admittedly it was unlikely for names and numbers to be accurately reported by those methods.

Still, it is debatable whether WRV was ever any more useful for those tasks. I suspect that its success with analytical concepts was more illusion than real. True, many more names, numbers, and other "hard" concepts were reported. The question is, were these reports *accurate*, and I think there is some reason to doubt they were. Instead, I have come to believe that channeling was favored because it was, in a sense, easier.

Fred Atwater likes to joke that, to get viewers to remote view what you want them to, you have to trick them. Though Fred's comment was meant humorously, it did hold a certain truth for both ERV and CRV. First, a project manager has to figure out how to task a viewer to get the right information to answer the "unknown"—the intelligence question. A good recent example of this was a remote viewing project to see whether Y2K—the Year 2000 computer bug—would indeed wreak havoc with society. The problem was how to tell if society would be in chaos after the dawn of the new millennium. Remote viewing Times Square in New York City at midnight would show chaos, but would that chaos come from a computer meltdown, or just one huge block party? Or what if one of us working the project in 1999 remote viewed Cincinnati in the heat of riots in the spring of 2001? That would show violence and chaos, but what was its source and how widespread was it? It would be difficult to tell using remote viewing.

On the other hand, just because a viewer found that things were peaceful in one location would be no indicator that the rest of the world wasn't falling apart. Picking the indicators to remote view could be more of a challenge than the remote viewing itself. In the case of Y2K, Fred, who headed up our experiment, decided to do it as an associative remote viewing project. The process was too complicated to explain here, but the end result was that our data predicted that Y2K had a low likelihood of causing widespread problems.

A lot of work, effort, and thought goes into a remote viewing project to make sure the right data is retrieved and as much "noise" is excluded as possible. But that can make a traditional operational remote viewing project complicated and time-consuming. At Sun Streak Fred had been both our institutional memory and our scientific conscience. Though he tried to inculcate in us his understanding of the principles, once he had retired he could no longer see to it that proper procedures were followed.

If you wanted to use CRV or ERV to find out where Terry Waite was being held hostage, viewers had to be run blind on a set of encrypted coordinates. Analysts had to try to match up what the viewers reported with known ground truth about the landmarks of the area where the hostage was most likely being held. One had to hope there was a match found that could be passed on to the authorities before the hostage was moved. There was a lot of work, hard planning, and careful thinking that went into it.

On the other hand, with a channeler all you had to do was ask the incorporeal entities, "Where is Terry Waite?" Whether these "entities" had some objective existence or instead were only constructed by the viewer's subconscious, it was much simpler to chat with the disembodied than to deal directly with the complications and vagaries of the human perceptual system. Remote viewing, especially CRV, was technical and could be a bit flighty. ERV required careful interpretation and an awareness of individual viewer idiosyncrasies. If, instead of bothering with all that, you could sit down and have a conversation with some interesting folks who just happened to be in a different reality, why not do that? Channeling didn't put a premium on long-suffering, patience, and attention to detail.

The reason not to do it, of course, was that maybe it did not work as well. Or at all. That, of course, was the unanswered question in early 1988. Yet, with that question still unresolved, the untried WRV approach was used heavily at the expense of other, more tried and true methods.

What all this boils down to is that, while we fumed over petty office politics, privately loading blame on Angela for this seemingly wayward turn in Sun Streak's course, it was perhaps more than anyone else our managers that, intentionally or not, were most at fault—if indeed anyone was.

The lynchpin in all this unrest was Fernand Gauvin, our branch chief and boss. Fern was a gentle man, and he was dedicated both to remote viewing and to his duty as an intelligence officer. But as a manager he tried to avoid confrontation, even when confrontation might be healthy, or even necessary. Because of this, he could sometimes be manipulated by someone with an agenda. And sometimes we found him hard to understand. He would launch into instructions or comments, assuming apparently that we knew what he was talking about, but the allusions he was making were either ambiguous or had to do with things about which we had no clue. It often seemed that his sentence syntax would be jumbled or not make sense. Having talked to him in later years and finding him coherent, I now wonder whether our confusion in the old days might have been due to his usual speech patterns conditioned by years of speaking French in the field, magnified by the effects of the severe stress he was under.

The stress made us all a bit paranoid. In the spring of 1988 I was directed to have a closed-circuit television and sound system installed in the CRV grey room, ostensibly to record remote-viewing sessions. That was a legitimate purpose, but we viewers sometimes felt spied upon. We would frequently hear the front door to the operations building surreptitiously open, then close. A moment or so later the red light on the video camera in the corner would come on, and we knew we were being watched without otherwise having been forewarned.

At times monitor and viewer would engage in a gripe session, either before or after our remote viewing was done. It was a way of letting off steam, which we felt ought to be private. But once the red light came on, the conversation instantly changed. This was not lost on Fern. Soon a piece of tape showed up, covering the "on" light. That of course didn't stop our sub rosa conversations. Instead, if we had something personal or private to say, one of us would peel back the tape to keep an eye on the light, then reinstall the tape once we were done.

These seemingly juvenile and petty distractions were not the only thing troubling our minds as the year wore on. In 1984 an Army-affiliated government lab, the Army Research Institute, had commissioned a study of the various "human potentials" technologies that were at the time attracting public interest. That study was finally published in 1988. To conduct the study, the Institute chose the privately run but government-chartered National Research Council, a branch of the National Academy of Sciences. The timing of the contract was probably not accidental, beginning as it did at the height of General Bert Stubblebine's interest in those very fields. A committee was created under the auspices of the NRC, and subcommittees designated to study individual areas, such as hypnosis, neurolinguistic programming, sleep-learning, the Monroe Institute's Hemi-Sync technology, stress-management techniques, and so on.

But a large section of the Institute's final book-length report was dedicated to an examination of parapsychology, especially remote viewing and psychokinesis research.[9]

This NRC study has been the most visible in a long series of investigations into remote viewing by outsiders. Now, nearly two decades later, the study is still often referred to in publications and by commentators. Unfortunately, it is also one of the most negative about remote viewing, often cited by critics who want to attack the legitimacy of remote viewing in particular, and psi phenomena in general. This would be devastating, except for the fact that the NRC study was not just biased, but seems to have been intentionally put together in a way slanted towards negative conclusions about parapsychology, while still pretending to appear objective.

When the NRC committee first met in June 1985, there were no parapsychologists included, but the parapsychology subcommittee itself boasted as its chairman one of the leading antiparapsychology skeptics—University of Oregon psychology professor Ray Hyman. Hyman was already known to SRI International researchers as one of the skeptics who, before ever first having had access to the data, had prematurely attacked SRI's examination of Uri Geller in the early 1970s. Hyman's skeptical companion in that episode, Dr. George Lawrence, was also involved in the NRC project, serving in the key role of contract monitor and coordinator between the Army Research Institute and NRC. It was Lawrence who had engineered Hyman's appointment to the committee. Another prominent skeptic, James E. Alcock, wrote the only background research paper commissioned by the NRC that focused exclusively on the subject of parapsychology.

At the time of the NRC study, both Hyman and Alcock were on the executive council of the premier skeptical organization, the Committee for the Scientific Investigation of Claims of the Paranormal (CSICOP). In March 1985, three months prior to the NRC committee's first meeting, Hyman had cosigned a CSICOP fund-raising letter that said the following:

> ". . . Belief in paranormal phenomena is still growing, and the dangers to our society are real . . . [I]n these days of government budget-cutting the Defense Department may be spending millions of tax dollars on developing 'psychic arms . . . ' Please help us in this battle against the irrational. Your contribution, in any amount, will help us grow and be better able to combat the flood of belief in the paranormal. . . ."

The first rule in conducting an objective evaluation of something is to choose an investigator who is not implacably biased against the phenomena to be studied. This rule seems to have been violated for the NRC study.

In 1985, three *years* before the NRC report was published, Hyman wrote the following in *The Skeptic's Handbook of Parapsychology* (edited by CSICOP cofounder Paul Kurtz): "The total accumulation of 130 years' worth of psychical investigation has not produced any consistent evidence for paranormality that can withstand acceptable scientific scrutiny."[10]

Thus it was no surprise when I read the following entry on page twenty-two of the 1988 NRC report: "The committee finds no scientific justification from research conducted over a period of 130 years for the existence of parapsychological phenomena." Whatever Ray Hyman's true level of objectivity may have been, it certainly appears as if he embarked on his government-funded examination of remote viewing with his mind already made up.

The NRC committee announced its findings in December 1987, and the report itself carried a 1988 copyright. While we viewers were insulated from the direct effects of the storm that followed, we heard rumblings of the excitement from a distance. Protests against the report's methodology and conclusions erupted from various quarters, notably the Parapsychology Association (PA), an organization of scientists and academics affiliated with the American Association for the Advancement of Science and dedicated to improving the quality of scientific research into parapsychology. The association published a twenty-eight-page rebuttal to the NRC's findings, pointing out among other things that the NRC committee had excluded strong, credible evidence supporting parapsychology, while accepting other, weaker analyses that opposed it. When positive evidence was cited in the NRC report, it was dismissed as being attributable to alternative explanations. No candidate alternatives were offered, however.[11]

This "alternative explanations" excuse had been used before. The Parapsychology Association rebuttal cites three instances where Hyman elsewhere tried and failed to propose plausible alternatives to explain significant parapsychological results. In one such instance cited in the PA rebuttal, Hyman admitted that in parapsychology research he was reviewing "the present database does not support any firm conclusion about the relationship between flaws and study outcome"—that is, Hyman was unable to find any faults in the experiment that could account for the significant results that were reported. Yet he persisted in rejecting the research. Hyman would again use similar words almost a decade later in another study that finally killed the government remote-viewing program—and he would yet again provide no plausible suggestions for the supposed "flaws" and "alternative explanations."

The Parapsychology Association rebuttal accused the NRC examiners of conveniently citing parts of parapsychology reports that helped their side, while ignoring parts of the very same reports that hurt their position. The worst instance of this was a study the NRC itself commissioned from highly respected Harvard social scientist, Robert Rosenthal. Rosenthal, a leading specialist in experimental methodology and meta-statistical analysis, and his coauthor, Monica Harris, had not previously been involved in parapsychology. Yet their report gave very high marks to the scientific quality of certain parapsychology experiments yielding strong evidence for psi.[12]

Seeing Rosenthal's positive evaluation, John Swet, who chaired the NRC committee, contacted Rosenthal and asked him to, in Rosenthal's own words, "suppress" the part of the Rosenthal/Harris evaluation dealing with parapsychology. Astonished at the audacity of such a request, Rosenthal refused. Despite his rejection of the request, the part of Rosenthal's paper favorable to parapsychology was neither used nor quoted in the final NRC report, although other parts of the paper not having to do with parapsychology were treated as authoritative elsewhere in NRC's report. In an interview Rosenthal told me: "I don't think they were practicing good science," referring to Hyman and the NRC investigators. Rosenthal continued:

> I don't think they were open-minded about the results that they had asked me to bring in. They had obviously made up their minds before they saw what I told them. I didn't think it was very good scientific practice to ask me to suppress results because they didn't like them. Maybe they disagreed, but I don't understand how they could have disagreed with my methodology, since it was exactly the same reading and looking for sources of bias as I applied in the other four areas that I had been asked to review.[13]

Though the NRC study did not at the time affect us viewers personally, it inflicted a festering wound that was aggravated and deepened by later events and would eventually prove fatal to the government remote viewing program.

Despite all the negativity it produced, the NRC report wasn't the worst thing perpetrated by an outside agency. Not long after release of the NRC report, the Department of Defense Inspector General's office notified our bosses that it intended to send a team to inspect the remote viewing unit. For half a day on February 16, 1988, members of the team met with Dale Graff and Jack Vorona at Bolling Air Force Base.[14] Why we were the focus of a high-level IG inspection was a mystery to those of us sequestered up at Fort Meade. We were a small, low-echelon unit with a nearly insignificant budget by Pentagon standards. In recent conversations, Dale Graff made it more clear to me. Each year the Department of Defense IG conducts high-level inspections in a different major defense component. The year before, in 1987, it had been the Army that received the IG's attention. Inspectors had found some irregularities in the procurement procedures of some of the Army's special access programs, and had decided to examine SAPs belonging to the other services and DIA as well. We happened to be one of DIA's special access programs. When the meeting on February 16 ended, apparently the IG team decided there was more to be investigated. "We'll be back," was the ominous parting message.[15]

It was about this time, early in 1988, that a new candidate for remote viewing training showed up. On a cold day in February there came a knock on the front door to T-2561. In marched Major Jared Schoonover*, an INSCOM psychologist, with a youngish-looking Army captain in tow.

"This is David Morehouse," Schoonover said, introducing the stranger to us. "Why don't you all get to know each other while I pop in to see Fern." I didn't know it at the time, but we were being set up. Morehouse wasn't left in our care simply because Schoonover needed a place to park him for a few minutes while talking to Fern. The captain wanted to work for us, badly.

Morehouse turned out to be a gregarious, friendly sort. Good-looking in a Joey Butafuco sort of way, he seemed charming and charismatic. We traded war stories as part of the military ritual of getting to know someone. The young captain had been an aide-de-camp to two generals, commanded the only independent airborne rifle company in the Army while he was stationed in Panama, and had been a Ranger company commander at Fort Stewart, Georgia. He certainly had high qualifications for an infantry officer.

Then I discovered something even more interesting. Like me, he had graduated from Brigham Young University. Captain Morehouse was a Mormon! Knowing the high ethical and moral standards expected by their religion, Mormons tend to trust one another—not always justifiably. Morehouse said that he had been looking for a new, exciting assignment. Though he was an infantry officer, he was already serving in his secondary specialty as a personnel officer in a secret operations outfit assigned to INSCOM, and to which his psychologist escort, Schoonover, had some responsibility.

It seemed fortuitous. At the time, our unit had an open slot for a remote viewer at the captain level. On the surface, at least, Dave seemed to be bright and accomplished, with an easy-going personality—all traits that would help qualify him for duty as a viewer. In my additional responsibility as recruitment officer, I told him I couldn't reveal to him what we did there, but asked if he would nonetheless be interested in taking a few tests, to see whether he might be a fit for our unit. I sent him off with a bundle of personality screen-

*Pseudonym.

ing tests, which he soon completed and returned. With much excitement I saw that he fell within the general parameters we were looking for, so I proposed to Fern we hire him. It turned out that had been the plan all along.

When Dave had walked into the office that fateful winter day, he already knew what we did there. He had heard rumors of Sun Streak's existence, discovered that Schoonover knew something about the unit; the psychologist had been read-on to the remote viewing program when he was assigned to replace Lieutenant Colonel Dick Hartzell, the former INSCOM Staff Psychologist, as the unit's psychological advisor. Morehouse pumped Schoonover for information, then wheedled the psychologist into bringing him down to our Fort Meade offices for an introduction.[16]

Schoonover, aware of trouble brewing between Dave and another officer at his unit, thought a transfer to Sun Streak might not be a bad idea, so he called Fern and got himself and his protégé invited for a visit. If Fern knew this was a job-fishing expedition, he didn't tell any of us. But he seemed happy to consider Dave.[17] Before long the deed was done, and the infantry captain was accepted into the unit. Even though he wasn't an intelligence officer, orders were being cut to assign Dave Morehouse to Sun Streak.

But because the wheels of Army Personnel turn slowly, he didn't report for duty until four months later, in June.

Before Dave arrived, the Department of Defense IG team came knocking once again on our door. The original charter for the IG inspection had centered on finances, and ours, apparently, were found to be in order. Our budget was minuscule compared to other special access programs anyway. But when the lead inspector discovered what it was that we were doing, he decided to focus special attention on us. He apparently did not like parapsychology. "The [chief inspector] involved had a very strong negative reaction just at the concept," as Dale put it. "So he took it upon himself to expose, and get to the bottom of this, and get rid of it. He just had a personal thing: 'Ah, here's one that we can get!' " Though it hadn't been the chief inspector's original charter, he decided to dig into the specifics of what we were doing.[18]

Around the middle of April one member of the team met with Dale at Dale's office in the Defense Intelligence Analysis Center. Trying to be as forthcoming as possible, Dale provided access to everything the IG representative demanded. But Dale was worried. After the February meeting with the IG team he had reviewed the records for all the projects the remote viewing unit had worked over the preceding years. What he found surprised him. Important supporting data was missing, pertaining largely to the tasking materials provided to the viewers. There were large gaps in the details as to how viewers had been tasked operationally; whether the taskings had been kept clean, or whether any frontloading had been provided; whether viewers had been given access to background information they shouldn't have had during their viewing, and so on.[19]

Dale told me the records were in such sorry shape that he ordered Ed Dames—who, as operations officer, was supposed to have kept the records updated—to work overtime to straighten things out as much as possible before the IG returned.

On the first day of May—Mayday—the IG team came to inspect. Since they had already been through all the books and files at the DIAC at Bolling Air Force Base, they wanted to come up to the Fort Meade offices to look through our safes. I say "look through," but in reality they hunkered down in the conference room at the back of T-2561 for three or four days with the door closed, and had files brought in to them as they interrogated the few allowed to be present. I don't remember that we viewers were ever even introduced to them, but I do remember that we were excluded from the proceedings in the back room. Dale Graff and Jack Vorona came from DIA for the occasion. But other than Ed Dames and Fern, no one assigned to the office was allowed beyond the conference room door.

We found this unsettling. Ed couldn't have been excluded from the meeting since he had been the unit operations officer over the several months since Fred Atwater's retirement. But we were worried what Ed might say or do when given the floor. Several of us felt that we viewers should have been included in the proceedings. We were the ones who had done the actual work, and we wanted the opportunity to testify on our own behalf. And we didn't want Ed representing our interests. We wanted to be there to administer an antidote to Dames if it became necessary. No such opportunity was granted us. And Ed, unfortunately, lived up to our fears.

It was not that he talked about remote viewing aliens and ancient mysteries. It was more the attitude he manifested in talking to the IG team. On the team were senior military and government officials—people with far more experience in military matters than Ed had. They were smart and cagey; they had to be, with a job that required them to see through subterfuge and get behind clever facades designed to misdirect and deceive those trying to find wrongdoing, malfeasance, or bad management.

Yet, according to both Fern and Dale, Ed persisted in talking down to these folks, perhaps out of defensiveness or bravado. They remember being appalled at the condescending way Ed spoke to the IG team members. The gist of Ed's message to them was this: remote viewing was far too important to be trifled with by these investigators who knew nothing of parapsychological phenomena. The lead officer, who outranked Ed by at least two full grades, merely raised an eyebrow and thanked Ed for his time. No one rebuked Dames outright, but where there had been only a gleam in their eyes, now there was fire, and they clearly smelled blood. Where they might have been less intense in their scrutiny, Ed's attitude egged them on, and they poked into every nook and cranny, looking for skeletons and smoking guns.[20]

When, at the end of the week, the IG team finally left our buildings for the last time, both Graff and Vorona were worried. The records had turned out to be sufficiently disorganized, and enough projects had been found to have "irregularities" in the eyes of the inspectors, that we could merit a scathing report. Dale's main concern was that the IG team was displeased with the amount of frontloading found in many of the sessions. They had viewed as suspect any session in which a viewer, or even the monitor, knew more about the target than an encrypted coordinate.

Within a few weeks after the IG team departed, I was off to Fort Leavenworth, Kansas, for a required Army professionalization course, the Combined Arms and Services Staff School—CAS[3], as the Army acronym had it. The course lasted from June into the first week of August. I and my roughly dozen classmates learned to function as brigade and division staff officers, played a lot of volleyball as a means of developing teamwork, and even got to tour Leavenworth's prison. One of the other captains in the group visited with a soldier he had sent there a year before for some serious infraction. Frankly, a prison full of fallen soldiers made me uneasy, and I was glad to get out of there.

An interesting sidelight of two months at Fort Leavenworth was the opportunity to meet the folks of the Leavenworth Parapsychology Study Group. This little cluster of twenty or so people met regularly to discuss esoteric topics. Though they were less students of parapsychology than they were acolytes of New Age spirituality, still they had good intentions and open minds. I gave a version of a presentation I'd put together about Rupert Sheldrake's model of "formative causation," and wondered the whole time I was interacting with the group what they would think if they knew there was a government psychic spy in their midst. I admit I itched to tell them what was going on at Fort Meade, if only so see their reaction. But I stifled it as an unworthy impulse, completed my Army course work, and at the end of the class took a month's leave.

While at Leavenworth I also had the opportunity to meet Ken Bell, who had done the first operational session at the remote-viewing unit almost ten years before. Now a lieutenant colonel, Bell was on the faculty of the Army's

Command and General Staff College. Since the remote viewing program was still a special access program, there wasn't a lot we could say aloud to each other outside a secure facility as we were. But it was still nice having the opportunity to get to meet one of the legends. When I talked to him years later, he brushed off the notion that he might be a legend of any sort. Ken wasn't one to make a fuss.

When I returned to Fort Meade after being gone most of the summer, training for Dave Morehouse was in full swing. In my absence someone else—either Gabi Pettingell or Ed—had filled in for me in giving Dave the remote viewing theory lectures.[21] I took up where they left off, and Gabi continued as his primary training monitor. Years later, in his book *Psychic Warrior*, Dave was to claim that Mel Riley was his trainer, which was a bit of an exaggeration. After Fern taught Dave the basic ropes of ERV, Mel did work some CRV and ERV sessions with him. But it was Gabi who handled the bulk of Dave's training, with some assistance from Ed and theory lectures from me.

Dave was fitting into the office well, though. His likeable personality and laid-back style beguiled most of us. Not long after reporting in to the unit, he and his wife Debbie threw a party for the office in his new house in Bowie, Maryland. That evening was full of pleasant company, good food, and the usual tale-swapping that goes on at military gatherings. This time there was quite a topper, though. At some point in the festivities Dave led a number of us into his den to show off one of his proudest souvenirs—a Kevlar combat helmet hanging on the wall with other military curios and memorabilia. The lip of the helmet was split and broken. Wedged up inside, Dave proudly showed us, was a .30 caliber bullet from an M-60 machine gun.

According to his story, a few years before his Ranger company had been sent to the Middle East to train with the Jordanian army. While Dave and the Jordanian commander were strolling around supervising a live-fire exercise, a Jordanian M-60 gunner had fired outside his sector. One of the stray rounds struck the lip of Dave's helmet and burrowed its way up between the layers of Kevlar until it stopped. The force of the impact threw Dave to the ground and, as he told us, created a whale of a headache. Checked out afterwards by the medic, he was given a clean bill of health and told he was one lucky guy. Dave quipped that if the bullet had been a half inch higher or lower his wife would have been collecting his life insurance. Later, Dave joked occasionally about the helmet incident as one of those rare brushes with fate that all of us have if we live long enough. Little did we know that the helmet would have a role to play in the future of remote viewing.

As all this was happening, the unit was working on the Lebanese hostage situation. Though Angela was still getting the bulk of the assignments, by now I and the other CRVers were working fairly often, though we were always suspicious that our work was not making it beyond the walls of the office. But starting in September 1988, another sort of target began to emerge, a kind that we would run into often in the near future. It was a search problem of a different sort. Uncle Sam wanted us to find drugs.

In the late 1980s, the war on drugs was in full swing. Increasingly, military resources were being brought to bear to try to stem the tide of illegal narcotics being smuggled into the United States. It wasn't long before someone figured out that we might be of use. Our very first project of this type was Number 8816, begun on September 15. Mel and Angela were tasked to find a suspected narcotics-smuggling vessel and its "mother ship." The logged remarks say the vessel was "found west of" a certain coastline, but that "follow-up data was in error."[22]

This meager start led to many hundreds—perhaps even thousands (the total count is uncertain)—of remote-viewing sessions directed against various narcotics-related targets over the next several years. These taskings varied from requests to describe the cargos of certain vessels to trying to find the vessels' locations, to identifying their ultimate ports of call, to locating contraband that had been cached by miscreants, to describing meetings between traffickers, and so on.

Narcotics-related targets were to be our bread and butter over the next few years, but the project that wrote the epitaph for 1988 came as a total surprise, just four days before Christmas.

Mixed Results

*. . . we win some and
lose some . . .*

On April 14, 1986, Tripoli, Libya, awoke to the concussion of American bombs raining down upon the palace of Mu'ammar Qaddafi and on military targets around Libya. President Ronald Reagan had ordered the attack, code-named Eldorado Canyon, in reprisal for Libya's alleged role in fomenting terrorist attacks against Americans in Europe and elsewhere. Just hours after the last U.S. fighter-bomber roared away from Libya's coast on the long flight back to England, we remote viewers had been put to work. We were tasked to do three things: locate a downed F-111, describe Qaddafi's current whereabouts, and search for any terrorist responses that might come over the next ten days.[1]

I remember my response to the blind tasking. Although I figured the remote viewing mission we were hastily assigned must have something to do with the Libya raid, I was in the dark as to what about the raid any of us were supposed to report. Halfway through my session I had the impression of looking up through clear, relatively shallow water from a sandy bottom. From my underwater vantage point, I seemed to be facing out into a vast ocean. Curving around behind me and to my left and right, perhaps several miles away, I felt a low, hilly shoreline, mostly tan in color. The missing F-111, it turned out, had most likely crashed into the Mediterranean Sea a few miles off the Libyan coast in shallow water.

We never reported anything useful about Qaddafi's whereabouts, and to my knowledge we never predicted that any terrorist attacks would occur in the next week and a half. That was a silly tasking, anyway, as terrorist attacks, even ones done as a reprisal, are carefully planned and may take months, or even years, before being executed.

In the Persian Gulf eighteen months later, a U.S. Navy Aegis cruiser, the *Vincennes*, shot down an Iranian Airbus, killing 290 people in a case of mistaken identity. There was no call for remote viewing, as the facts seemed clear enough.

Then came December 21, 1988, three days before Christmas, almost a year after the Airbus tragedy, and two and a half years after the Tripoli bombing. Pan Am Flight 103, a Boeing 747 carrying 259 people, most of them Americans, suddenly exploded over Lockerbie, Scotland, raining bodies and aircraft pieces down upon the roofs and fields. Eleven more people were killed on the ground by falling debris.

Within twenty-four hours of hearing news of the tragedy, the Fort Meade remote viewing team was tasked to see what could be discovered. All available viewers were pressed into service, including even Ed Dames, working for the eighth and final time as a viewer on an operational target. Included in the number was newly minted viewer Dave Morehouse, for whom this was his second or at most third project since becoming an operational viewer in September. This amounted to six of us; seven sessions were worked altogether.

As with too many of my other operational missions, I can no longer recall my results from this project. Mel Riley remembered, however, that he reported the tragedy was caused by a bomb, and that the explosive was hidden in "a boom box, or portable radio." Gabrielle Pettingell was the project officer for the Pan Am 103 mission, and she confirmed that Mel made such a report. But she also told me that, before he wandered off into various AOLs, Dave Morehouse, too, mentioned a bomb hidden in a portable radio or tape recorder.[2]

The day after Pan Am 103 went down, the major London paper *The Times* speculated on three possible causes for the disaster: catastrophic mechanical failure, collision with another aircraft, or sabotage. Sun Streak remote viewers seemed to have confirmed sabotage. It would be more than a year before official reports declared that sabotage had indeed caused the crash. Investigations by a number of government agencies proved that a suitcase containing a load of Semtex-type plastic explosive blew apart the fuselage of the jet. The explosive was hidden inside a Toshiba radio/cassette recorder.

Many of the facts surrounding the explosion aboard Pan Am 103 will never be known. The United States blames Libya for the attack, quid pro quo for the bombing of Tripoli. There are other strong suspicions that the 747 was destroyed in revenge for the accidental shoot-down of the Iranian Airbus by the *Vincennes*. Libya has now officially taken the blame, but the truth may never fully be known.[3]

Despite the fact that several departments of government were regularly using Sun Streak as an intelligence asset, our future was far from rosy. As if Ray Hyman's biased report and the IG inspection weren't enough bad news, there was yet one more shoe to drop. Ever since the military remote viewing program's founding in 1977, the three-star generals who had headed the Defense Intelligence Agency had been favorably disposed towards the remote viewing project, and, considering how minuscule Sun Streak's budget was by government standards, they had been willing to put up with the small sacrifice that the project entailed.

But that all changed in December 1988. DIA got a new director, none other than Lieutenant General Harry E. Soyster, the general who, as soon as he took charge of the Army's Intelligence and Security Command back in 1984, had immediately canceled Sun Streak's predecessor, Center Lane.

Any doubts we may have harbored of how Soyster felt about us instantly blew away when Jack Vorona and Dale Graff went to brief him on the status of Sun Streak shortly after the general arrived in the DIA Director's office in the E-ring of the Pentagon. Upon being told that DIA was still supporting a remote viewing effort, Dale Graff remembers that Soyster:

> . . . looked at us and he said, "What! You mean I was never able to get rid of that *tar baby* when it was in the Army?" And he pushed his thumb on the desk and squished it like he was squeezing a fly. It's funny now, but at the time I could have throttled the guy.[4]

Ed Dames transferred out of Sun Streak around the end of December 1988, finishing all but the last month of a standard three-year military tour. On January 10, 1989, he reported to an even more secretive unit, from which he retired on the first of October, 1991. He left our office with little fanfare. The branch chief, Fern Gauvin, was relieved to see him go and chose not to recommend him for any awards.

That didn't seem fair to me. We viewers noted Ed's departure with mixed emotions. He was personable, sincere, and enthusiastic. He could also be frustrating, with his fixation on UFOs, extraterrestrials, anomaly targets, and his penchant for putting his own eccentric spin on remote viewing tasking and results. But he had worked hard, and was certainly dedicated to the remote viewing unit and its mission. Though I sometimes think that on balance the unit would probably have been better off without him, Ed deserved at least a commendation medal. Our bosses never gave him one, but he eventually got one anyway in a rather peculiar way, which I will describe later. I don't recall there being an official going-away party for Ed, but Mel and some of the rest of us threw an informal one. Mel created an elaborate certificate for Ed that was decorated with Egyptian cartouches to which Mel had attached imaginative, humorous names for each member of the unit.

Nominally, my time with Sun Streak was up as well. Enlisted folks like Lyn Buchanan could sometimes stay in an assignment indefinitely, but officers usually had to be granted a formal extension to stay beyond three years. Though I already had almost that much time under my belt as a remote viewer by the time Center Lane became Sun Streak, the transfer of the unit from the Army to DIA was treated as an official change of station. I never actually moved anywhere, but my three-year clock started ticking all over again. Unfortunately, the alarm would sound in January 1989, just as it had for Ed.

Recognizing six months before that the deadline was approaching, Fern asked me to put in paperwork for an extension to my tour at Fort Meade. The extension request was readily approved by Captain Bisacre, career manager at Military Intelligence Branch, whom I had been authorized to tell the barest details about the remote viewing program. Bisacre was professional but pragmatic. Having him as an ally paid off again a few months later for another reason that I will soon mention. With the approval of my extension, I was stabilized in my remote viewing assignment for another eighteen months.

With all the turmoil, operational remote viewing continued apace. In 1988 we recorded 32 operational remote viewing projects, including at least 360 sessions.[5] Our 1989 operational schedule kicked off with a project in support of the new intermediate-range nuclear missile reduction treaty. We were asked to determine the locations of some of the much-feared Soviet SS-20 medium-range mobile missiles, and to see if we could find out if there were any SS-20s that had *not* been revealed by the Soviets. "Hiding" missiles would have been a clear violation of the treaty. Lyn and Angela were the viewers chosen to work the case. There reportedly was "some correlation" between their data and information coming out about the missiles. Unfortunately, one of them had also reported the presence of SS-20s in Oman and Syria—two highly improbable locations for the missiles, since the Soviets would never let these high-value weapons out of territory they did not absolutely control. As a result, the remote viewing unit's operations log notes that "credibility was questioned" because of the reported presence of the missiles in those two Middle Eastern countries.[6]

A technical target worked in early 1989 by six of us produced a comment of "poor to no correlation with known ground truth." In yet another instance, though, the task was to "describe the nature and purpose of an activity" inside a building portrayed in an overhead photograph. On this project, Mel and Angela "provided useful data" about the target.[7]

Another project for which Angela deserves real credit was Project 8916, tasked on April 24, 1989.[8] A U.S. Customs agent named Charles Frank Jordan had "gone bad" and, among other things, provided inside information to drug traffickers to help them elude interdiction efforts. Jordan had been found out and captured, but soon escaped and was on the lam. From his list of acquaintances and what was known of his habits, investigators were convinced he was loose in the Caribbean region somewhere. But search as they might, Customs, the DEA, the FBI, and the Federal Marshals couldn't find him.

Someone came up with the idea of tasking us. Again, six viewers worked on the project. What data most of us produced is still undisclosed, and with the many such projects, it is virtually impossible to remember more about it. But something is known about Angela's results, probably because she came up with an impressive and relatively unambiguous hit. As reported by Dale Graff, Angela at first placed Jordan somewhere near Lovell, Wyoming, then later said he could be found in a campground near a park in Wyoming. An Indian burial ground would also be nearby.[9]

This information was so out of line with where Jordan was thought to be, that at first the authorities were inclined to ignore it. Finally, one agent decided that it would do no harm to alert police in that part of Wyoming. Much to everyone's surprise, Charles Frank Jordan was soon apprehended as he emerged from his camping trailer in northwest Wyoming. According to the Customs official who passed on the news to Graff, an old Indian burial ground bordered the campground in which Jordan was staying. In tracing Jordan's prior movements, law enforcement officers determined that he had apparently been in the vicinity of Lovell, Wyoming, about the time Angela was doing her session. This seemed to be an instance where the channeling methodology paid off.[10]

Besides these sometimes thrilling events, our target list continued to fill up with counternarcotics type operations—detecting and reporting the locations, cargoes, and destinations of various suspected drug-smuggling ships. We almost never received feedback, whether positive or negative, on these kinds of targets. Occasionally, though, we did get a pat on the back when Dale Graff or someone else up at headquarters was able to wheedle a report out of one or another intelligence community consumer of our information.

On March 1, 1989, I had a change in status, when I was appointed as deputy project manager. Though it sounds like my new position should have brought some prestige with it, it was mostly just an administrative change. It meant I could sign official documents and was officially "in charge"—whatever that amounted to—in Fern's absence. But it brought no change in my viewing and training duties, or the other things for which I was then responsible.

About this time I also started on another task. One of the charges in the report provided by the Department of Defense Inspector General in the aftermath of their 1988 visit was that there had been an unacceptable amount of frontloading in the operational remote viewing projects conducted by Sun Streak. I was ordered by Dale Graff via Fern, our boss, to systematically evaluate as many of the science and technology-type targets we had been tasked against in the years since DIA took over the remote viewing program.[11] Dale and his boss, Jack Vorona, wanted to know as precisely as possible just how we had tasked the various projects we had been involved in over the years. They chose the science and technology target sets mainly, I suspect, because we had the best audit trail for them, and because we had gotten at least some feedback on them from the intelligence community consumers who had received our results. These targets included a total of 28 operational projects, consisting of more than 300 sessions from 1986, 1987, and 1988, and two projects from early 1989. My job was to sort out how many sessions had been done, how they had been tasked, and how good the results had been.

Mindless bean-counting was what it seemed to me at first to be, and I hated it. I had to sort through bulging folders containing tasking documents, session transcripts, and interim and final reports, looking to see how viewers were tasked, how they were monitored, and how their results stacked up against whatever ground truth was available in the folders. Quickly I discovered that not only was the task important, but onerous as the bean-counting aspects of it were, it was highly enlightening.

One of the first things I discovered, much to my annoyance, was that there was a lot of feedback we viewers could have been given after we were officially finished with several of the projects. But we never saw any of it. Feedback is the viewer's main reward, and we lived for it, positive or negative. There is no excuse not to give it to a viewer once a project is officially closed. I found photos, descriptions, and evaluation reports of our work gathering dust in these folders, and we had never seen them.

Annoying as that was, it has proved fortunate in the years since for a surprising reason. Some half-hearted believers in remote viewing have claimed that it works only in that the viewer describes the feedback—for example, a photo or map of the target that they are shown later—and not the actual target. Were this true, it would be a significant limitation on remote viewing as an operational intelligence tool; if all you could tell about a target was what someone reveals to you about it later, then you could never provide new information that the tasker doesn't already have or will eventually get. Remote viewing might still be useful, but only in cases when information that was unknown to the tasker at the time of the viewing session might come to light later and be given as feedback to the viewer.

To this day, though, I am one of the few ever to see those files of feedback material. In a number of the sessions, the other viewers produced high-quality results, including additional information not available in the feedback. That tells me they were seeing something other than their feedback. In other words, viewers can indeed obtain information about a target even though they never receive feedback as to what that target was.

Another revelation that came out of this investigation was how consistently better CRV performed compared to either ERV or the WRV channeling methodology in these sorts of projects. When I began my assessment of the records, I was filled with misgivings and worried that I would find the methodology I had been most heavily trained in might turn out to be inferior. I was prepared to accept that, but the prospect of having to adopt a different method, especially channeling, didn't fill me with much joy.

It turned out to be an empty worry. By the time I was halfway through my analysis, it was clear that in general the coordinate remote viewers produced a superior product. True, there were some awful CRV sessions in the mix, and Angela's channeling turned out some successful results on occasion. But, by and large, I remember the WRV sessions as being more prone to miss the target or filled with heavy doses of AOL. On average the ERV sessions tended to fall somewhere in between the CRV and WRV in quality.

I have struggled with whether I ought to mention these results, especially since the data on which my conclusions rest remain largely in the CIA's secret files and can't, for now, be verified. This could be seen as my attempt to discredit remote viewing methodologies that I had no interest in. But, at the time I did the study, I earnestly tried to discount my biases and be as objective as possible in my evaluations. I believe my account to be accurate and historically relevant.

There was one other discovery I made, based completely on the data and not on subjective evaluations. I discovered that there was indeed an uncomfortably high degree of frontloading in the operational sessions. But though it happened a few times with those using the CRV methodology, the largest percentage of frontloading had occurred for channeling sessions.

In all the science and technology operational sessions Angela worked between her first such target (Project 8704 in April 1987), and her last science and technology session before switching to WRV (Project 8719, in November 1987), she was tasked most of the time like the rest of us, with encrypted coordinates that conveyed no information about the intended target. These amounted to ten projects, with perhaps thirty or so sessions. Of these ten projects, she was run on three of them with some degree of frontloading.

However, when she began using the WRV/channeling methodology with the science and technology projects, the frontloading became more frequent. Contrary to our normal procedures, if the original tasking agency forwarded a photograph for analyst use or later feedback, she was often shown it at the very start of the session. She was also frequently given verbal information about the target in advance of the session. Some of the information was fairly basic; if the target was a person, she might be given the subject's name. At other times she was told something as detailed as "The target is a building located in the Soviet Union," followed by the actual questions the tasker wanted answers to. Sometimes she was both given verbal information and shown a photo.[12]

There are two problems with frontloading, one the flip-side of the other. First, advance information provided to a viewer may create insurmountable analytical overlay, as he struggles with the flood of memory, conjecture, and inference sparked by the frontloaded material. Some critics complain that frontloading allows viewers to cheat, and so disqualifies any session in which it is used. In fact, frontloading is harmful not just because it counts as cheating, but because it contaminates a session and often makes it *harder* for the viewer to be "right," rather than easier.

But there is a second, opposite problem. As I've suggested, providing the name and showing a photo of a person in advance, for example, will give the viewer a great deal of information, and allow many inferences to be drawn that might prove to be accurate. Some observer, inexperienced with the problems of frontloading, might be persuaded that the viewer is providing information via legitimate remote viewing when really it was, in a sense, just a lucky, educated guess drawn from facts deducible from the photo or the verbal guidance.

This creates a further danger. Because it *seems* to be highly accurate, this "counterfeit" information might easily mislead an observer into thinking other information the viewer produces is accurate. But this "other information" was guessed at based on the previous inference, and is more likely to turn out to be partially or fully wrong. At the very least people might be wrongly persuaded that the viewer really was "being psychic," even when that is not the case.

On the other hand, using only encrypted coordinates to "blindly" cue the viewers provides the chance early in the session to check whether the viewer is "on" or not. If, with no other cue as to the nature of a target than an encrypted coordinate, the viewer accurately provides details such as the gender, approximate age, and physical description (if the target is a person)—or physical description if the target is an object, structure, or event—then this is an added check as to whether the viewer is "on," and ready to provide accurate data about the unknowns for which answers are being sought.

After February 1988, unfortunately, Angela was only given encrypted coordinates twice. One of those times involved a project for which the intelligence customer had only provided an encrypted coordinate to the Fort Meade unit, so there was no information available for frontloading. From February 1988 on until the end of my survey, Angela worked a total of twelve more science and technology–related WRV projects, and ten of these included some sort of frontloading. Angela's protege, Robin, was shown in advance a photo of the target on two out of the four projects that she worked in this series.

By contrast, the CRV and ERV practitioners seldom received frontloading of any sort. During the same twelve projects, for example, I received frontloading once, and then only for a second session against a target, when I was shown a picture of it *after* I had already accurately described it on the basis of an encrypted coordinate. Gabrielle Pettingell received similar input once under the same conditions. Both Mel Riley and Lyn Buchanan received minimal frontloading on two occasions each.

Please keep in mind that we worked many kinds of targets, and I am talking here only of science and technology targets—the only targets for which I as yet saw hard evidence. For these science and technology targets, Angela was getting frontloading of some sort on WRV sessions 83 percent of the time. From the few times I saw her work other sorts of targets, it seemed to me this percentage was likely to extend to the many other sessions she also worked.

I'll give a typical example of this, before moving on. For Project 8814 five viewers conducted fifteen sessions to find out if SA-5 antiaircraft missiles the Soviets gave to certain Mideast nations were technically capable of "dual-use"—that is, could they be either fired into the air at aircraft or instead targeted at distant locations on the ground?[13] Four viewers—all CRVers—received only encrypted coordinates. They were expected to first discover that the remote viewing target involved missiles, then provide information that might answer the intelligence question—all without frontloading.[14]

On the other hand, before launching into her session, Angela was given the following statement: "Determine if the Soviet SA-5 missiles deployed in the Middle East—particularly Syria and Libya—serve a dual purpose."[15] Using WRV, Angela went on to say that the SA-5 was an "old-style missile" that was to be upgraded to the SA-7. However, the SA-7, already widely used by the Warsaw Pact, was actually a small, shoulder-fired, heat-seeking missile, while the SA-5, a radar-guided missile, was roughly fifty-four feet long and had to be carried around on a semitrailer. She also described the missiles—according to her there were seven in Syria and five in Libya—as being placed individually or in twos and threes near the frontiers of both countries as border defense. In reality SA-5s are deployed like other semipermanent antiaircraft missiles—a central command-and-control module, surrounded by ten to fifteen launchers. The entire facility would be located close to important military or civilian facilities that an enemy might target. Even in a dual role, SA-5s would be both ineffective and highly vulnerable as a border-defense weapon.

I don't fault Angela for "getting it wrong." All remote viewers do that from time to time. In fact, in my analysis of projects I found one in which I had to report that I "performed three sessions, but never successfully accessed [the] signal line."[16] And on the SA-5 project, the results from the other viewers were inconclusive—there was some consensus that the missiles had been upgraded, but mixed results on whether they could be used in a dual role. What is important here is how it shows the negative consequences of frontloading. Knowing the target in advance apparently caused Angela to form conclusions about SA-5s that were likely attributable to analytical thinking and not remote viewing—and even as analysis the conclusions were mistaken.

I cannot say to what extent, if any, Angela had a choice in whether to be frontloaded or not. Some of us outside the little WRV circle believed the worst of her, and thought she demanded it. However, I have since learned that on at least several occasions she objected to frontloading, but was given it anyway. This does not surprise me, since it can be very hard for a viewer to avoid frontloading if a tasker or monitor is determined to provide it.

While all this was going on, odd things seemed also to be happening with Morehouse. Looking around at what others in the office were doing between remote viewing projects, training of other viewers, and our various office duties—Mel with his Indian artifacts, me with my studies for the Defense Intelligence College, Angela with her books of logic problems—he decided he could go us one better. He started a home improvement business.

We slowly began to realize that Dave was around less and less frequently. He would often call in, say he needed to stay home with a sick child, then not show up for two or three days. Or he would tell us he had a doctor's appointment, and be absent for hours, then pull into the parking area with his construction trailer in tow. Both Mel and Lyn reported seeing the office phone number on a sign affixed to the side of Dave's van. I didn't notice that, but I think it could have been true, since I fielded at least one phone call from one of Morehouse's prospective customers. She sounded confused and surprised when I told her that, yes, a Dave Morehouse worked there, and that he did have a company called House-Tech, but that the number she had dialed was not his front office, but a government telephone.

Eventually, Jeannie the secretary started keeping track of Morehouse's absences. She told me that by the time she quit counting, she had tallied up somewhere in the neighborhood of 150 days that Dave was absent from the office.[17] Few, if any, of these absences were covered by either leave or pass. Considering that he was assigned for only twenty-four months, this represented a major gap in the unit's ability to use the remote viewing skills Morehouse had been taught. During the fourteen months from when his training was finished until December 1989, I have records showing Morehouse participating in only twenty of the sixty-one operational projects we were assigned.[18] For these twenty projects he contributed a total of *at most* thirty remote viewing sessions (as contrasted to the hundreds of sessions worked by other viewers in the office). I don't have records from January of 1990 to his reassignment out of the unit six months later, in June—but interviews with other members of the office staff as well as my own recollections indicate that his remote viewing activities were equally limited during that time.[19]

We kept waiting for Fern to do something, but he never did. Years later, I asked him why he hadn't taken action against Morehouse for his malingering. He said he was worried that *everyone* would get in trouble for their extracurricular activities if he tried to reign Dave in.[20] That seemed then, and still seems to me, to be an unnecessary fear. The rest of us managed to get the work done we were assigned. Whatever activities we engaged in beyond our work either facilitated the state of relaxation deemed ideal for a remote viewer—such as Mel Riley's patient Indian beadwork—or enhanced either DIA's or the military's mission, even if only indirectly, as did my own part-time strategic intelligence studies at DIA's Defense Intelligence College.

Part of it may have been Dave Morehouse's effusive charisma and carefully studied affability. He won people's confidence, cultivating them as friends and allies, coaxing loyalty and affection out of people, whether he had just met them or had known them for years. This helped him to be a highly successful combat-arms officer. By all accounts his troops loved him. And a good combat commander *has* to be part con artist. It is his job, after all, to convince a hundred or so otherwise normal and healthy human beings to advance in the face of possible death or mutilation to capture an objective they have only ever seen before on a map. Dave, I believe, was an expert at that. If he had stayed in combat arms instead of becoming involved in the world of intelligence and covert operations, he might indeed one day have been a general, as he has often said of himself. As it was, he entered a world where one needed certain inner resources and controls to stay on the right path, and he seems to have lacked them.

At the time, I really didn't have the wherewithal to worry much over Morehouse's shenanigans. There were lots of sessions to work, and more threats to the unit's existence to be dealt with. In my personal life, I had met Daryl Gibson, and we were dating frequently. The relationship was rendered more spicy by the fact that she was the managing editor for legendary muck-raking journalist Jack Anderson. Through his associate Dale Van Atta, Jack had uncovered and published much about the remote viewing unit—but was still hungry for more. Van Atta didn't get that "more" from me, though I was inwardly amused to think that the scoop Anderson and Van Atta sought was to be found right there in front of them.

In our viewing, we were continuing our project of trying to ferret out the locations and conditions of the American hostages in Lebanon, when one of the more unfortunate cases came our way. Back on February 17—the day after Graff's first exploratory meeting with the Department of Defense IG team—a Marine lieutenant colonel by the name of William "Rich" Higgins was kidnaped by Muslim guerrillas in Lebanon. At the time of his capture, Higgins was serving as chief of the UN truce observer group in Lebanon.

We had worked the Higgins case off and on since the kidnaping, with sessions trying to discover his plight intermingled with those targeted at Terry Waite, Terry Anderson, and other hostages in Lebanon. Then, on the thirty-first of July, we were given project 8925. It turned out that our assignment was to determine if Higgins were dead. Apparently—though I recall that I, at least, worked this session blind, so I don't think we had knowledge of it—a video had been released by Higgins's captors, the Islamic terrorist organization Hezbollah that showed someone, purportedly him, swinging with a rope around his neck, apparently dead. As a result of their sessions, those using WRV "indicat[ed] Higgins [was] alive," as the ops log has it.[21] I remember comments from the WRVers after the project was closed out that they were sure he was in good health and—the same prediction yet again—would soon be released. But that is not what I had gotten.

Sitting down at the table in the CRV grey room and taking the encrypted coordinates, I soon had a feeling of blackness, of foreboding. I seemed to perceive a masonry building in a Mediterranean-like setting, overlooking a body of water. The setting was picturesque, but that seemed beside the point in the darkness and depression that I seemed to be feeling. I had the impression that I was, once again, supposed to be looking for someone—and I seemed to find him. But, in this case, I sensed despair and dread. In the end, my conclusion was just the opposite of that provided by WRV—Higgins was dead.

And so, regrettably, he turned out to be. But I was not alone in retrieving such data. On the same day I worked my session, Mel Riley also produced strong indications that the Marine colonel (in March he had been promoted in absentia to full colonel) was dead. I remember it taking me the better part of a day to shake the funk the session had plunged me into. Higgins's body wasn't recovered until sometime in 1991, when it was dumped in a Beirut street.

Not all our work involved operational targets. In September we began a series of what turned out to be probably the only formal research remote viewing most of us had ever done at Fort Meade. Regrettably, unforseen repercussions from this work would have negative consequences a few years down the road. We Fort Meade viewers were asked to participate in an experiment being conducted by Ed May and his protégés out at SRI—but we were to do it "long distance."

In principle, it was a reasonable experiment. A series of targets would be selected on a roughly weekly basis out in California. We viewers would be given the equivalent of an encrypted coordinate to launch us on a session, and our results would then be forwarded back out to SRI for analysis. After SRI received our results, they would provide feedback to us about what the actual target had been, to bring closure to the session and informally allow us to evaluate our own work.

Sound in principle, our part of the experiment was mostly a failure in practice. The tasking note for the first of these projects I worked said the following: "This is an SRI target. Every effort has been made to replicate the conditions under which this project is being conducted at SRI. At SRI's discretion, a beacon may or may not be used during the conduct of this project."

Even if this accurately reflected the guidance of the SRI scientists (and it may not have, since it was possible the instructions had been misinterpreted by our immediate bosses), it created a problem. Not knowing whether or not there was a beacon—or not knowing who the beacon was that one was supposed to home in on—caused ambiguity in the tasking. A second problem was that, according to the standard protocol, the use of a beacon person required coordination of the time when the beacon was at the target. The viewing doesn't have to occur simultaneously with the beacon's presence at the target, but the time and date are important parts of the tasking intent. In a way it is a sort of contract or agreement between the viewer and the beacon. Not having this added further confusion.

Not knowing exactly in what mode we were supposed to view also contributed to the problem. In both training and operational viewing we had been taught to go "to" the target. I had become accustomed to winking here and there about a site, trying to capture the best angles from which to describe both verbally and in sketching whatever details I could glean. But there were suggestions that some or many of the SRI targets would be photos, and that our final score would depend on how well we described what was depicted in the photograph. Pictures are often used as targets in laboratory remote viewing because photos contain a finite amount of information from a specific perspective, which can more easily be used to control and evaluate a viewer's results—as opposed to a real-world, "on the ground" target that may have a nearly infinite variety of details, and many different ways a viewer's point of view might perceive it.

Unfortunately, to most operational remote viewers, a photograph is only a two-dimensional paper surface with colors on it. We weren't accustomed to "looking" at a photograph during a remote viewing session and describing the details in it and, in fact, in training were chastised for "remote viewing the feedback," which is what remote viewing a photo boils down to. We wanted instead to find something substantive that we could move around, get a variety of sensory experiences from—smells, textures, tastes, qualities of light, sounds, and so on. I have since learned better how to manage a photo as a target, and have had some success at it. But back then, for the most part, my fellows and I hadn't a clue. Even more disorienting was simply not *knowing* whether the target was a physical location or "only" a photograph. Looking at the target list now, years later, it is still not clear whether any of the targets were pictures, or whether they were all actual sites. Whatever the case, the instructions left us guessing on crucial elements of the project.

Still more confusion was generated by the conditions under which the viewing was done. We were not provided tasking in the way to which we had grown accustomed in our operational viewing. Instead, the SRI tasking for each week was posted for all to see on the room divider outside the branch chief's door, and we were expected to take note of the coordinates, then work the weekly experimental target whenever we found time. So in addition to our regular duties, as well as both our training and operational viewing schedules, we had to sandwich in these experimental sessions as well.

This often meant a viewer would come from the ops building drained after an hour and more of operational viewing, then have to worry about doing an additional session targeting sites out in California such as the loading dock at a shopping mall, or an airport control tower, or a paint warehouse, or the Palo Alto city dump.[22] These were not bad targets, but it was hard being enthusiastic about them after doing hours of viewings on chemical-warfare testing grounds, captive Americans in a third-world country, or trying to locate a drug smuggler's boat.

We could have probably managed this all right anyway, if we had been able to do it under our normal working conditions—on a regular schedule, monitored, and in a remote viewing room. Unfortunately, with all the operational viewing that was going on, room space was at a premium, and so were monitors. We were consequently directed to work the SRI sessions solo, and do them anywhere we could find room. It should be no surprise that, thus left to our own devices, many of the SRI sessions were done hurriedly at the end of the week, by harried viewers sitting at their desks just dashing them out before it was time to go home.

Complicating the conditions was the turnaround time. It was not unusual to work an SRI session one week, then one the next week, and still another the following week, and still not have received feedback for the first one until after the third week. It got to the point that we were often unsure which feedback went with which tasking. Again, in principle we should have been able to manage this without it affecting our viewing. But with the jumble of everything else, this just put one more obstacle in the way of good results. And it didn't help that, as far as I recall, the feedback was always verbal—a sentence or two posted on the board—and never visual.

The most unfortunate handicap, however, wasn't caused by the circumstances or environment in which we did the SRI sessions. Instead, it was our own poor morale and bad attitude towards the experiment. This had little to do with the project itself, and much more to do with the negative impressions we had formed over the years about the SRI part of the remote viewing effort. I mentioned this a few chapters ago, but it was during this experiment that it all came home to roost.

The tension between the East and West Coast remote viewing efforts had been there for a long time, and was probably the fault of both parties. A major part of the blame can probably be laid at the feet of Jim Salyer, DIA's resident contract supervisor out in Menlo Park. For the many good qualities he had, Salyer could by all accounts also be quarrelsome, arrogant, and stubborn. He was not overly pleased with having the Army involved in remote viewing, and had made no secret of that from the start. His interactions with the Fort Meade personnel were often abrasive, confrontational, and combative. Hal Puthoff's calm presence had been an important moderating influence that served to keeps things working reasonably fluidly. But when Hal left SRI in 1985 to take a prestigious job as director of the Institute for Advanced Studies in Austin, Texas, the folks at Fort Meade began to associate Salyer's attitude with the rest of the SRI contingent. This was enhanced by the fact that the new director who took Hal's place was Ed May. May didn't come across as diplomatically as had Puthoff. The leadership at Fort Meade perceived him as being focused on a single-minded pursuit of the science, and seemingly less aware of the need to establish rapport and smooth over differences.

The two camps drifted further apart, with some folks on each side tending to think of those on the other as being either a bunch of amateurs or a covey of prima donnas—which was which depended on whom you talked to. From this vantage, now years in the future, it is easy to look back and see how silly it was, and how easily it could have been fixed. More frequent and direct communication between the coasts, with more willingness to be open about how one side perceived the other could have solved the problem—or at least made it workable.

Unfortunately, both sides were somewhat victimized by a policy that was meant to help, but in fact ended up harming. Early in the game, the DIA leadership decided that isolating us at Fort Meade, away from most of what was going on in the larger intelligence community, as well as from the research part of the remote viewing effort, was important to keeping us on task and unconflicted. This policy certainly *seemed to* make sense. If we were kept blissfully unaware of the storms that periodically threatened Sun Streak's existence, our anxiety levels could be kept to a minimum, we would have fewer inclemencies to overcome when we set to viewing, and there would be fewer emotional issues to get in the way of the information we produced: in essence, fewer worries, better viewing.[23]

Like a similar policy about hiding the unit behind a screen of overclassification (which ultimately figured into the unit's demise), this policy of keeping us incommunicado turned out to be a bad idea. First, years before under INSCOM we had been somewhat exposed to administrative vicissitudes, yet the viewing had generally still gone well. During that period I, for one, was often called on to help brainstorm and write briefings in the many bureaucratic fights that erupted over Center Lane. Yet I still managed to successfully fill my remote viewing assignments (which, admittedly, at the time were more training rather than operational). It was relatively easy to shed whatever office worries filled my mind when I went over to the operations building to do my job. That same response seemed to come from everyone. Other viewers—notably Bill Ray—were involved in going out of the office to provide liaison or give briefings that helped keep the lines of communications open among agencies, yet they still managed to view competently.

But for all the good intentions that lay behind DIA's isolationist policy, we were essentially secluded from the rest of our "community," and it fostered parochialism on both sides. That attitude pervaded the way we went about our duties for the SRI experiment. I have no idea in the end how the results came out. As far as I remember, we viewers were never told how we scored in the overall analysis. It is telling, I think, that as far as I can remember none of us even seemed to care, and were only glad when we didn't have to put up with doing the sessions anymore. I did more or less keep track of how I did on the individual taskings, and remember being frustrated that I didn't do better on the experimental sessions—though not frustrated enough to make me care to figure out why.

The fallout from our poor effort didn't become apparent until after the remote viewing program was disbanded and some of it declassified by the CIA seven years later. In private, and sometimes in public, Ed May, Joe McMoneagle, and others were heard commenting on the generally poor quality of the Fort Meade viewers. I puzzled for a long time about that assessment. How could they possibly know how well we performed? They had little or no access to the thousands of operational sessions we had executed over the years since McMoneagle left the unit, in 1984. Based on the survey I had done after the Department of Defense IG inspection, plus other insights gleaned over time, I knew that housed in the safes at Fort Meade was some outstanding remote-viewing work we had done.

Then, a little while ago, I remembered that ill-fated experiment. Perhaps other research done with Fort Meade viewers after 1990 contributed to the impression left by our failed effort in 1989, but the earlier experiment was the one I know the most about. With that realization, for the first time I wished that we had done things differently when offered the chance to perform some serious research for the SRI project. We were, after all, on the same side and fighting the same battles. At the time, we just didn't think of it that way, and that was a big mistake.

Even as all of this was going on, we were still on the lookout for likely remote viewing candidates. We had two unfilled military slots and, as people transferred out or approached the ends of their tours, we needed to acquire and train new viewers. It was with that hovering in the background that I attended a lecture at a local Mormon church on the ancient Anasazi culture. The lecturer was a tall, mustached, dark-haired man named Greg Seward. The lecture was interesting. But what I found out about Greg when I went up to talk with him afterwards was even more so. It turned out he was a lieutenant in military intelligence. He had left his graduate school studies in archaeology a few years back to join the Army. What was most striking was how parallel his and my careers were. He was my age, had started out as an enlisted man, had gone to Monterey for Arabic language training, after which he had gone on to officer candidate school and been commissioned as a lieutenant in military intelligence.

But now he was assigned as the security officer for the Army Corps of Engineers headquarters in downtown Washington, D.C., and was desperately hoping to get out of the job. His commander didn't have much use for a junior lieutenant, and made it no secret that he would just as soon see Lieutenant Seward move on to greener pastures, making way for someone with more experience. I recently asked Greg to recall how he had reacted to my approaching him:

> You said that you were involved with a program that you felt that I would be interested in. Of course you couldn't tell me what it was. But it piqued my interest. Within a week or a couple of weeks . . . it was pretty short . . . I came over and you read me on. And as soon as I read the first line of the program I was hooked.

Greg was a little surprised at our humble circumstances in the dilapidated buildings, yet impressed by what he saw when he walked through the door.

> I know my first impression was, what in God's name are these people working in? It was Building 2561. And that painting of McMoneagle's—the first thing you see when you come in—it really threw you for a loop. As you [Smith] introduced me around the office, I remember trying to scope out the different cubicles to see what everybody did. But it was the perfect cover because you just had things like maps of the Middle East, or Europe or Russia, or something. No information, no indication what you folks did. I thought, you know, if the government's paying for this, this is great stuff. I think I took the [evaluation] tests, and then [Smith] took me in to meet Fern. And that was weird, because he was in that little office, wearing a cardigan sweater . . . and I thought, what am I getting myself into?[24]

Greg Seward signed in on November 2, 1989. Unfortunately, his training did not start right away. The reason is rather obscure at this late date. Greg thinks it may have been because of the operations tempo, which was very high at the time. Almost a month after signing in to the unit, Seward remembers "kind of blowing up" in a staff meeting because he was still in a holding pattern, waiting for something to happen. Afterwards, Mel took Fern aside and urged him to get things going for the new lieutenant. Soon Greg was hard at work, with Gabrielle serving as his trainer, me in my usual role as theory instructor, and Mel stepping in every once in awhile to do a practice session with him.

Mel had an instant affinity for our new recruit, based on their mutual interest in Native American lore and crafts. Though not yet as proficient as

Mel, Seward did beadwork and made replicas of Indian artifacts. Much later Greg even began making museum-quality ceremonial drums, which he worked on at home. But he did pick up the pastime of beading buckskin shirts, pipe covers, and such which, as it did with Mel, helped him relax between sessions.

But Greg wasn't the only new face that showed up at our door. Sometime around mid-1989, I got a surprise phone call from Captain Bisacre at Military Intelligence Branch. Bisacre was the assignments officer I had read on to the project when working on past personnel issues for the unit. When I answered the phone, he told me he had a favor to ask. There was a young first lieutenant, soon to become captain, who was nearing the end of a tour in Panama and needed an assignment in the Washington, D.C., area for family reasons. Her name was Linda Anderson.

Bisacre knew that we usually tried to find our own candidates to fill vacancies. But he also knew that we had an empty captain's position at our unit that hadn't been filled since Ed Dames left. He wouldn't force us to take on this new officer unless we thought she might be suitable. He wanted to know, would we be willing to at least give her a chance, see how she might do on our screening tests? After I briefed him on the call, Fern checked with the folks down at DIA headquarters then told me to go ahead. I phoned Lieutenant Anderson, then forwarded the tests to her. She knew her possible new job involved a special access program, but still had no clue as to what we did.

The tests came back, she seemed a good match, and I had been impressed with her during our phone interviews. I instructed her to go to a STU-III (a secure telephone), and I would read her on to the program. When I told her we wanted to train her to be a psychic spy, I heard her gasp, then she was silent for a moment. "Can I call you back with my answer?" she said. She wanted to think it over and get used to the idea. Her final answer was yes. To my knowledge, she was the only person ever assigned to the remote viewing program who came to us through the normal Army assignment channels.

By December 1989 Lieutenant Linda Anderson was on board, and she was soon promoted to captain in a pleasant little ceremony back in the conference room. Almost immediately we started her lectures and training sessions to turn her into a CRV remote viewer. In his first full tour as a trainer, Lyn monitored the newly promoted Captain Anderson on her training sessions. Linda found him to be excellent at the job.

Tall, blond, fit, and with a sparkling personality, she not only took to the training well and rapidly mastered the skills, but she also helped dispel some of the gloom that filled the office in those days. A natural athlete, she played on one of the Fort Meade softball teams, and was a semipro in tennis. She was also a hard worker, and always tried to see the best in people.

Linda wasn't the only bright spot in the gloom. Sun Streak was about to undergo a sea change that would go a long way towards redressing the balance against the unremitting negativeness of the NRC and DoD IG reports. What was about to happen literally extended the remote viewing program's life for several years.

28

Lawyers, Drugs, and Money . . .

> "When you have eliminated the impossible, whatever remains, however improbable, must be the truth."
>
> —Sherlock Holmes (in *The Sign of the Four*)

Our nemesis, Lieutenant General Harry Soyster, would have squashed us like a bug had he the power to do it unilaterally. But he soon realized that enough influential people were interested in Sun Streak that he couldn't dispose of us without causing a ruckus. He needed some backing, and for that he turned to the Military Intelligence Board, whose job is to look at the big picture of intelligence policy and programming, and propose recommendations for changes.

Towards the end of 1989 General Soyster called a meeting of the MIB, which he chaired as part of his job as director of the Defense Intelligence Agency. All the military services, the intelligence staffs of the major combat commands, NSA, and other defense-related agencies are represented on the MIB. Among the many items on the agenda for this meeting was what to do with Sun Streak.[1]

In preparation for the meeting, Colonel William Johnson, the staff officer charged with overseeing Army intelligence policy and operations for General Eichelberger, the Army's deputy chief of staff for intelligence (DCSINT), was assigned along with several others to do a background study on the remote viewing program.[2] He and his colleagues solicited a briefing on the project from Jack Vorona and Dale Graff. Although the two were supportive, Johnson felt their testimony relied too much on anecdotal evidence and lacked the kind of hard data he needed to best evaluate the usefulness of remote viewing. The people involved with the 1988 National Research Council report were also consulted. Unsurprisingly, they painted a dismal picture of remote viewing's effectiveness.

This preliminary study for the MIB took two months, at the end of which Johnson compiled a written report which he passed around to all his other partners in the effort for their added input. It was then forwarded to members of the MIB in preparation for the Board's December 1989 meeting. Johnson's report concluded that remote viewing was probably not operationally useful. Even though, as was also noted, the program wasn't expensive by government standards, and though the degrees of training and expertise were such that the program couldn't easily be restarted if the government later changed its mind, still Johnson felt logic and what he had learned from the NRC dictated the program should be shut down.[3]

Final discussion of the colonel's recommendation was supposed to take place during the formal MIB meeting. I was told that when time came to decide on Sun Streak's fate, there were enough dissenters that Soyster, seeing the trend, cut off the voting and said he would give remote viewing a reprieve while a proof-of-principle study was done.

Having done the research and turned in a report as directed, Johnson was satisfied that he could dust off his hands and walk away from remote viewing. The program belonged to the Defense Intelligence Agency and Johnson, as a member of the Army's intelligence staff, dwelt in a different world. But he was not to have us out of his hair so easily. His boss, Lieutenant General Eichelberger, volunteered the Army to do the operational testing and decided that, since Johnson was the budding expert, he would be the one to give it a try.[4]

First, arrangements were made for operational control of Sun Streak to be transferred from DIA to the Army, with Johnson in charge. The colonel hit the ground running and was already fully involved in the project months before the DIA director got around to signing the formal transfer of control on March 30, 1990.[5] For ten months Colonel Johnson would make every operational decision for our unit, and many administrative ones as well. This caused Dale Graff and his boss some heartburn, since Johnson didn't feel obliged to keep them informed of most of his decisions once he took control.[6]

To Johnson, this made sense. If he was going to take remote viewing for a serious test drive, he wanted a clean slate so the test was as straightforward as possible. "I had to divorce the unit from its ties to its parent organization," he told me, "and establish the test as unbiased and not influenced by any organizational influences."[7] Graff, on the other hand, felt that DIA should at least have been provided regular updates on what was being done with assets that still belonged to his agency and for which DIA was still ultimately responsible.

Of medium height, trim, and with greying hair, Colonel Johnson presented an air of quiet confidence that earned people's trust. If he said he would deliver on what he promised, that's exactly what he would do.

After wangling additional funds for Sun Streak's operational activities, Johnson got down to business. First, he had to come up with a test mission for us. But finding a niche in military intelligence as the Cold War wound down was a challenge. After some thought, Johnson decided that counternarcotics operations seemed to be the best bet, since "the intelligence process was mature and I could insert the result of the test into an ongoing intelligence system." He saw his challenge as being to take a phenomenon that was skeptically viewed by many in the intelligence community as an "unreliable and unproven intelligence tool," and show that it *could* be used in an operationally reliable way, producing useful information that "could be integrated into the intelligence cycle."[8]

Starting with a personal visit to the three-star admiral who commanded the Coast Guard, Johnson began to make the rounds to drum up support for what became a ten-month operational experiment. The colonel also approached the Joint Task Forces that were responsible for counternarcotics operations on both coasts.

Johnson's goal was to get the viewers "on the ground"—take them to the actual intelligence consumers, instead of bringing the taskings up to Fort Meade in an atmosphere insulated from users by thousands of miles and layers of bureaucracy. As Johnson put it, "They [the viewers] need to be out in the field, operational . . . We got out of Fort Meade, and down to the task force at Key West. We got [the program] known a little bit."[9] The plan was to send a subset of the viewers to Key West, Florida, where the headquarters of counternarcotics Joint Task Force 4 (JTF-4) resided, as well as out to JTF-5 in Oakland, California, for a series of operational trials. The taskings would come to us hot off the press, and the results of our work could be quickly passed to aircraft, Coast Guard cutters, Navy ships, or drug agents.

While the details of our trips were being worked out, I got the assignment to drive Colonel Johnson down to Nellysford, Virginia, to the Monroe Institute, so he could meet and confer with Fred Atwater, Joe McMoneagle, and Bob Monroe. It was mostly a fact-finding trip; Johnson didn't have in mind to bring any of these folks into the program. But he felt it was important to get a sense of how the program had begun and how it got to where it was. And just in case any useful ideas might be dropped, he was prepared to take it all in.

I was sweating a bit when I arrived at the Pentagon to pick up the colonel for the journey south. I had driven Sun Streak's government sedan down from Fort Meade, and the trip around the Beltway, across the Potomac River, and down the George Washington Parkway had been more of a nightmare than usual. I arrived at least a half hour late, and I knew that as a captain keeping a senior colonel waiting like that, I was sure to catch it. I could tell Johnson was miffed despite my apologies, but he soon calmed down as we drove south on U.S. Highway 29 through the tree-clad hills of Virginia horse-country.

I had been down this way just the previous month, during the first week of the new year, when Daryl Gibson and I made a trip to Thomas Jefferson's mansion, Monticello, with a stop first at Fred Atwater's home on a wooded hillside overlooking the Monroe Institute. In a leaky aluminum boat with one broken oar, Daryl and I, along with our dogs, had paddled out to the swimming float in the middle of the small lake at the foot of Fred's hill where I had asked her to marry me. Our wedding date was set for April 12 in the Mormon temple in Salt Lake City.

The trip south with Colonel Johnson in February was of a much different character. We were to go down and back in one day, squeezing in a tour of the Monroe Institute, a talk with Bob Monroe himself about guided visualization, and a look at Fred's lab, where he was doing research on electrical patterns in the brain and how Monroe's Hemi-Sync sound technology affected them. (Since his retirement, Fred had decided to go by his childhood nickname "Skip." But so fresh was the change that I was having a hard time thinking of him as anything other than "Fred.") Connecting every conversation that day was talk of remote viewing: what had been done in the past, and ideas for how things might be done better in the future.

After the visit to the Monroe Institute, other activities filled our days. While Johnson worked the issues of how to get us more directly involved in counternarcotics intelligence collection than we had been, we continued working other operational targets. Then, an event took place that turned out to be a watershed in the program. Colonel Johnson and his assistant, Major Dave

Hanson (who among other responsibilities was tasked with making all the operational arrangements, publishing the orders, and managing vital records), had been working feverishly behind the scenes briefing everyone from military commanders to congressional staffers, to the Secretary of the Army and the Army Chief of Staff. But on May 16 everything had fallen into place to brief four senators, William Cohen of New Hampshire (later to become Bill Clinton's second Secretary of Defense), John Glenn of Ohio, Daniel Inouye of Hawaii, and Warren Rudman of New Hampshire.[10]

We arrived somewhat before 9 A.M. and, in the company of the staffers, were ushered in to meet the senators. For awhile Johnson was sequestered with the senators, giving them a briefing while we waited nervously in an outer chamber. Then we joined them, for a demonstration of remote viewing. Our party consisted of Johnson, myself, Fern Gauvin, Gabrielle Pettingell, and Angela.

Angela went first. Johnson, who had been working to master remote viewing interviewing skills, tried to work as her monitor, but she was very nervous, had trouble with the tasking, and failed to get the target.[11] Since Gabi and I were not in the room for Angela's session, we did not know this at the time. Still, as we entered we sensed the tension. It seemed pretty obvious that failure would not bode well for Sun Streak.

We had decided before we left Fort Meade that I would monitor and Gabi would do the viewing. As we took our seats to the side and front of where the senators were sitting, I could see we were in a hearing room, which I learned later was referred to as "The Bubble." The four senators were behind a U-shaped dais, and Johnson had positioned himself and his briefing easel on one end. There was also a table there, and Gabi and I were asked to sit at opposite ends.

Senator Cohen gave us the encrypted coordinate to launch the session. Gabi was soon describing an arid, desert landscape with a prominent factory or industrial complex as a focal point. I started to sweat. I was sure she was off, since I couldn't imagine that a senator would want to test us with something as pedestrian as this.

Gabi described vile smells, and the sensation of danger and chemicals. I don't remember how much else she reported, but eventually Cohen said it was enough. Though it was hard to read their expressions, all four senators seemed interested by what had transpired. Senator Cohen held out the folded paper on which he had written the target and Colonel Johnson took it. It was Qaddafi's secret chemical weapons factory in Rabta, Libya. Gabi had nailed it.[12]

Though we at the worker-bee level were not filled in then as to why and how this meeting was important, we had been scheduled for only an hour or so of the senators' time, but ended up keeping their attention for the rest of the morning.[13] Obviously, as long as we impressed four important senators, a briefing such as this could only help. On the other hand, if we failed to impress them, it could be severely damaging. It was a calculated risk, but Johnson was willing to take it. Fortunately, it turned out that they were impressed, enough anyway that their influence later helped buy a few more years of life for the remote-viewing program.

On May 29, just thirteen days after our meeting in the Hart Office Building, we were off for our first operational trials in the field. As with any other military undertaking, our expedition had to have a name—in this case, the operations order they handed us bore the designation Azure Sea.[14] Johnson had Dave Hanson publish an "op order" for each of our deployments. It "gave a military flavor to our activities," he said and, even though there was nothing revealing in one, if ever we were questioned by uncleared people as to what we were doing, he could "just grab the op order file and let them read it. Most observers don't question op orders."[15] In our little group were Colonel Johnson, Major Hanson, Angela, Lyn, and myself. Our destination was Joint Task Force Four, or JTF-4, in Key West, Florida.

The sun-blest island seemed bustling and hospitable as our tiny commuter plane touched down that Tuesday afternoon. We had left Maryland in the middle of spring, but down here summer was in full swing. Major Hanson and I each picked up a rental car, and we chauffeured the others to our lodging. The Hotel La Concha, built in 1926, was seven stories of comfortable old rooms and a famous rooftop bar and restaurant that included at no extra cost an exquisite nighttime view of the city. Ernest Hemingway had stayed at La Concha, recording its name for posterity in his book *To Have and Have Not*, and Tennessee Williams finished his Pulitzer Prize–winning *A Streetcar Named Desire* in a room on the top floor.

We found Joint Task Force 4 to be housed in old Naval buildings on the Truman Annex of Naval Station Key West, next to what, in busier days, had been the submarine pens. Inside the intelligence and operations spaces it was cool and dim, since the windows had been covered for security reasons. Our first encounters with the JTF folks were introductory. To my surprise our main intelligence contact was Major John Koda*, an old friend from the Military Intelligence Officer Advanced Course at Fort Huachuca, Arizona. He, too, had heard General Stubblebine talk about the powers of the mind and

*Pseudonym.

handled the bent spoons that were tossed into the audience. Koda was understandably cautious, yet curious to see what, if anything, we could do.[16]

The first order of business was a demonstration session for Admiral Irwin, the Coast Guard officer who commanded the Joint Task Force. I was the guinea pig this time, and Lyn Buchanan was my monitor. One of the operations officers had picked the target. Lyn and I settled into a couple of chairs around a table in the conference room belonging to Navy captain Mike Gambacorda, the J2, or intelligence officer, for the task force. In the course of my session, I remember describing a sense of proceeding from bright sunlight into dark, through an arching-over, quonset-hut-like structure that led underground.

Though the session went on for awhile, I no longer remember much more about what I got. The target turned out to be an underground facility in Panama that the operations officer knew well. My performance seemed to impress the admiral and some of the others, though the J2 remained somewhat skeptical. Still, Gambacorda was objective enough to let us work with his people for the next several months. On Colonel Johnson's recommendation, I loaned the admiral a copy of *Mind Reach* that I had picked up in a used bookstore in Salt Lake City the month before. I never saw my book again, but from what I heard later, it was passed from hand to hand around the JTF headquarters for a number of years.

The next nine days were packed with events and operational remote viewings. To do sessions, we were given some unused rooms deeper in one of the buildings. Dusty, institutional, sparsely furnished, they nevertheless were secluded and quiet. We figured out who would use which rooms, and set to work. In the course of the operational sessions we did, I had occasion for another demonstration session.

Major Frank Kahoun was our liaison with the operations staff section for JTF-4. He was always professional in his dealings with us, and friendly, if a little reserved. But he was also a bit skeptical, unsure if he should believe there was really anything to what we claimed to be able to do. One day not long after we set up shop on Key West, Kahoun and I were alone in one of the makeshift viewing rooms. After a few minutes of discussion about how remote viewing was done, the major got around to the question he really wanted to ask.

"Would you be willing to do a demonstration session for me, right now?" I thought about it for a moment or two. I knew that I would soon be diving into a "live" remote viewing session, and I didn't usually like to do sessions too close to each other. On the other hand, Kahoun's cooperation and good will would be important to our success. I decided that it would be worthwhile to attempt an informal session, though I was nervous about it. Whenever a viewer does a demonstration session for a skeptic, the cost of failure goes up. Success is never guaranteed in any given session, so when great stakes are laid on a single session the nervousness quotient skyrockets, often driving up the chance of failure also. But sometimes risk is necessary.

"Okay," I said. "This will be a bit informal, but I'll try it. Do you have a target?"

"I do," he replied. "I wrote it down on a sheet of paper before I came in here. I've folded it put and it in one of my pockets." I explained that he should come up with an arbitrary number to serve as an encrypted coordinate. He made something up, gave me the number; I wrote it down, and launched into the session.

I remember my first impressions of a hilly, rolling landscape. Rich, green grass covered the shoulders of rounded, low hills. Little dells, equally lush, separated each ridge from its neighbor. Fog or mist hazed the distance, and bits of it wafted past. I had impressions of occasional patches of wan sunlight playing across the land. For the first few moments, I perceived the scene as pastoral and pleasant. But abruptly I realized there were people here, lots of them. They were scattered across the landscape, moving rapidly in one direction, and appeared to my mind not only to be wearing primitive clothing, but many of them to have bare legs. There were sounds of a guttural language I didn't recognize. Then it came to me that this horde of people had edged weapons, and that they were fighting each other. Reporting all this aloud, I scribbled my notes on a sheet of paper. Before I could go on, though, Major Kahoun interrupted me.

"That's good enough," he said, and tossed a square of folded paper across the table. I opened it up, spread it in front of me, and read the words he had written. "Battle of Hastings, 1066," was all it said.

Though we did plenty of operational sessions, this was not just a work trip. In fact, it was more of a courtship. Not only did we want to demonstrate what remote viewing could do for the antidrug effort, but we wanted to establish a rapport with the people behind the effort. Part of that was to get to know what the effort was. Johnson had arranged a number of special events for us that not only served to give us needed distractions from the operational viewing, but to help us get to know our colleagues in the counterdrug business. This had the added benefit of giving us a better understanding of how our work might contribute to the big picture.

We were given tours of various operations, and we went along on some operations where we wouldn't be in the way. Among the tours, we were shown around the Coast Guard cutter *Thetis*, one of the largest cutters in the fleet. We also visited a hydrofoil patrol boat, or PHM in Navy jargon. There was a squadron of six of them stationed at the Tremble Point Annex of the

Key West Naval Station. I think we toured PHM-1, the *Pegasus,* the class ship of the little fleet. It was strange to hear her crew talk of "flying" the 133-foot, 221-ton vessel, but there really isn't a better term for it. When speed was necessary the PHMs were designed to lower their hydrofoils, which were nothing more than large, broad, winglike planes attached to struts that went under the water and raised the hull of the ship a few feet up into the air, eliminating drag and allowing impressive speed for the size of the vessel. These PHMs could reach speeds of more than sixty miles per hour, even in fairly high seas. Their hydrofoil "wings" were literally flying under the surface of the water. Designed and built by Boeing, the boats incorporated parts and systems taken directly from aircraft assembly lines.

One sailor entertained us with an account of the first time some erstwhile drug smugglers encountered one of these PHMs on patrol. The smugglers were piloting a sleek cigarette boat, which they apparently thought could outrun any Navy or Coast Guard vessel that sighted them. When the smugglers spotted the hydrofoil, she was cruising on her hull, looking ungainly and no match for the speedboat. As the PHM turned towards them, the smugglers shoved the throttles full ahead, and their boat's powerful engines roared into life.

Seeing the cigarette boat racing away, the PHM's captain gave the order for "flight." As its gas turbine engines spun up to full capacity, the PHM rose on its underwater wings, and soon the apparently lumbering warship had caught up with the fleeing boat, fired a few shots across its bow, and taken the astonished smugglers into custody.

Tours were not all we had the opportunity for. There was some thought that placing us virtually "on the scene" might allow us to give almost instantaneous input as to whether a given boat or ship might be carrying contraband. With this in mind, we were taken to Boca Chica Naval Air Station on the next Key over and put on a Navy P-3 Orion reconnaissance aircraft. With four huge turboprop engines, and a long interior cabin crammed with electronics and surveillance gear, the P-3 was the largest propeller aircraft I had ever been on.

Lyn, Angela, Hanson, and I soon found ourselves flying out over the Caribbean at several hundred knots and only about two hundred feet off the water. The Naval Reserve crews that got to fly these missions clearly loved what they were doing. The task was to identify whatever surface vessels we came across, and radio in the locations and identifications of any that looked suspicious. It was quite a thrill to watch out the portholes on the side of the plane as that huge aircraft pointed a wing straight at the ocean only a hundred or so feet below and banked tightly around to get a good look at the name on the stern of a trawler or yacht. Sometimes the people on the deck would wave. Other times they would just ignore us. No matter the outcome, it was amusing, if disconcerting, to sometimes find oneself walking on the aircraft's walls when moving back and forth along the center passageway during one of these maneuvers.

We remote viewers were along to see if we got impressions about any of the boats we approached. If we felt there was contraband on board, we were supposed to note location and description. This was new for us and, try as we might, it didn't seem to work. I suspect it was because we felt too frontloaded. Here was the boat right in front of us. Was it laden with contraband or not? The pressure of making that decision within the few moments we circled the target only worsened the AOL problem, and we ended up without any clear impressions at all. It is hard to see how this might have worked very well, anyway, since most of the time there were no surface units nearby to intercept and board vessels we might have identified anyway.

Still, the trip wasn't altogether wasted. I got to ride up in the cockpit with the crew when we came in to land at Boca Chica at the end of our eight-hour patrol. The skies had been beautiful over the Bahamas. And we knew one more thing that didn't seem to work very well.

Halfway through our visit at Key West, we left on a two-day side trip. We went first to Miami, where we toured the facility where a joint team of law enforcement officers and activated National Guard troops inspected a percentage of the thousands of shipping containers that passed through Miami's port. They had a tough job, since smugglers were always coming up with new and imaginative ways to sneak narcotics into the country. In one case, we watched them probe drums of frozen guava juice with a long bar, looking for evidence. Later, customs officials at the airport showed us one can of a shipment of crab meat in which cocaine had been sealed in with the crab. They were now waiting for the owners to show up to claim the shipment. The commander of the National Guard detachment accompanied us to lunch at a Cuban restaurant in Miami Beach, and shortly thereafter put us on a plane for Nassau in the Bahamas.

We stayed at a hotel on Paradise Island. My room had a glorious view out over the yacht harbor towards Nassau. I foolishly called my new wife to tell her of the aquamarine water and rustling palm trees. She was not exactly happy for me sitting there gazing out at Paradise while she was home wrangling three newly acquired stepchildren. Ironically, at the government room rate they gave us, staying at this luxury hotel was less expensive than our lodgings in Key West. All of us wished we could continue our assignment here instead.

The next morning, we breakfasted at Dunkin' Donuts shop in Nassau. Our PX-purchased civilian clothes turned out to be poor cover. One of the other customers sitting on a bar stool across from us asked us which government agency we belonged to; the CIA, FBI, or Customs? It was a good thing that we weren't trying very hard to be clandestine; we only wanted to avoid being linked with the Army, so I guess that must have worked.

After a briefing at the U.S. embassy, we went by car to an airfield the Coast Guard was borrowing from the Bahamian government. Together with Major Dave Hanson and Colonel Johnson, Angela, Lyn, and I boarded an orange-and-white H-3 helicopter for a wave-top excursion along the Bahamian archipelago to Exuma airfield and back. Like the P-3 flight, this trip was not particularly successful in turning up smuggled narcotics. We did get a first-hand look at some of the "real estate" (mostly water) that we had no doubt been targeted against in some of our past operations, whether back at Fort Meade or those we continued to perform in between "field trips." En route, our attention was grabbed by the sight of a rusting DC-3 cargo plane. It was half-submerged in the sea, a couple of hundred yards offshore from one of the islands' airports, where it and its contraband cargo had ditched while trying to elude pursuit a year or so before.

Returning from the Key West trip ended the first separation in my and Daryl's new marriage. But it was a herald of things to come. Late in 1989, a major change had begun to loom large in my future. Military Intelligence Branch had told me that in August—at the end of my current assignment extension at Fort Meade—I would definitely be transferred out of the Washington area, and in fact would be required to fill what was euphemistically known as a "short tour." A short tour was an overseas assignment that usually lasted anywhere from thirteen months to two years, and was "unaccompanied"—that is, the soldier's family was not allowed to go to live in the area where the soldier was stationed. Korea is one common place to serve a short tour, although other places, such as Turkey and Germany, were also candidates for the soldier who had spent too much time in the States.

Upon first hearing that I would be vulnerable for a short tour, I applied to the Army contingent assigned to the United Nations peacekeeping forces in Lebanon. The fate of the kidnaped Colonel Higgins was fresh in my mind, but things seemed to be settling down over there, and an assignment to UNIFIL was only twelve months long. It would give me the opportunity to brush up on my Arabic language skills while spending time in a part of the world that I had longed to see. I was soon notified that, though I had been accepted by UNIFIL, MI Branch would not release me to perform that duty. Regular Army units were too short of military intelligence officers, I was told.

Soon I learned my destination, and it at first seemed like bad news—Panama. Not only had I no interest in a steamy, tropical climate but now, after having studied Hebrew, Arabic, and German, I was going to end up in a Spanish-speaking country. The worst of it, though, was that a "short" tour in Panama lasted for two years. It was hard for me to imagine being assigned away from my children and my new wife for that long. On the other hand, Linda Anderson and Dave Morehouse had both been stationed in Panama and assured me there were interesting things to see and do there. And, though the United States would be turning the Panama Canal over to the Panamanians a few years hence, there was still an intelligence mission to be performed in support of the counternarcotics and counterinsurgency efforts in South and Central America. I consoled myself with the knowledge that many other soldiers had put in their twenty-four months in Panama, and enjoyed it. Now it was my turn.

In those days DIA offered after-hours language training for its employees, so I signed up for a beginning Spanish class, though I felt a pull towards the intermediate Arabic course that was also offered. Daryl and I tried to plan how best to be together over the time I would be away. We thought that even without Army sponsorship she might move to Panama and rent a place near the base where I would be stationed so we could at least maintain a semblance of marriage. We were in a quandary about my children, over whom I had joint custody.

The new remote viewing initiative under Colonel Johnson earned me and my family a reprieve, however, when I was granted a further—and, according to MI Branch, emphatically final—ninety day extension so I could be used in the ongoing counter-narcotics operations. I now had until the end of November 1990, before I was scheduled to report to Panama.

But if I had managed to get some breathing room, others were leaving the unit. On June 20, only a month after the end of our first Key West expedition, we bid farewell to Mel Riley. He had reached the end of his Army career, retiring as a master sergeant, and was moving to his home state of Wisconsin. We held a fond farewell party for him at Ed Dames's house. Ed, who had become quite close to Mel, bought him a sleek, green Old Town canoe to use on the fishing lake behind Mel's new home. Greg and I gave him paddles.

Morehouse, too, departed, officially signing out on the first of June, not quite twenty-four months after having joined us—coming close to setting the record for the shortest period anyone had spent assigned to the remote viewing unit. Ed Dames had arranged a job for Dave at the same secret unit where Ed was posted. Although we generally liked Dave, none of us were really sorry to see him go. He had often not been there for us when we needed him for remote viewing operations, and it wouldn't make much difference to our workload at Sun Streak to have him transfer out of the unit. Like Ed, Dave left without an award, or any mention of one. In fact, I learned later that Fern Gauvin had expressly stated that he didn't want Dave recommended for an award because of his frequent unexcused absences.[17]

That, however, didn't stop the resourceful Dave. In his final act as a member of Sun Streak, he recommended himself, Ed, and Mel for Joint Service Commendation Medals. Mel deserved one. In fact, as a retirement award he should have been given something even higher—a Defense Meritorious Service Medal or perhaps a prestigious Legion of Merit. And Ed, too, had worked hard if a little eccentrically while assigned to the remote viewing unit, and should probably have received an award upon his departure eighteen months previously. Since any soldier may recommend another for an award for valor or service that the recommender has witnessed, Dave did nothing illegal in submitting Ed's and Mel's names for awards, though to be done by the book it should really have gone through the chain of command. However, Dave's recommendation of himself for an award was not only unethical, but turned out to be a masterful bit of cynicism, the full audacity of which was not fully apparent to me until a couple of years later when I had the opportunity to read the narratives for each of the awards.

Not surprisingly, many passages in all three awards were virtually identical. According to what Dave had written, Ed, Mel, and he each had been "the vital link to the effective integration of [the remote viewing] unit into the Defense Intelligence Agency's mission," and had been "crucial in the fusing of the units [sic] unique technology" into DIA's intelligence efforts. Also, Dave's narrative credited each one of them with having "recognized a need for a more effective unit data processing system, assisted in the design and implementation of a new system, recorded and analyzed incoming data, and insured that the system provided a substantive degree of error reduction, which enhanced the final analytical intelligence product."[18]

It was true that Ed and Mel were assigned to the unit at the time the remote viewing unit was being "integrated into the Defense Intelligence Agency's mission." But Dave didn't show up for more than two years after the integration was finished. But that was trivial. More disturbing was the "database" claim. Dave was giving the three of them credit for work actually done by Lyn Buchanan, with some guidance and participation from Ed. Mel was an innocent bystander to the deception, having no control over what Dave wrote in the award narrative.

Most glaring was the passage in the three award applications referring to actual remote viewing experience. The narrative Dave wrote for Mel reads: "[Riley's] operational and analytical skills were instrumental to the successful execution of 47 major intelligence projects which involved more than

1,000 individual collection missions" [by "collection missions" I gather he meant remote viewing sessions]. Further, "these missions were directed primarily against foreign military research and development and, most recently, global anti-drug interdiction targets." In Mel's case, the figures were not far off, if a little low as far as projects worked. According to unit records, Mel was actually a participant in at least fifty projects up through the end of 1989, and probably worked on a dozen or two more during the six months of 1990 before his retirement. If both training and operational sessions were counted, attributing 1,000 sessions to him was probably not too far off the mark.

Dave's narrative for Ed is identical to Mel's, reflecting the same 47-project figure, but attributes 800 sessions to Ed. If Dave was alluding to actual projects and sessions done as a remote viewer, then these numbers for Ed were highly inflated. As a viewer Ed worked on about eight projects, completing at most twenty sessions. But viewing wasn't his main assignment. Dave's narrative is ambiguous and could be read as referring to Ed's activities as monitor and assistant operations officer on many projects and the sessions involved in them. If that is the case, then the numbers are probably too low, given Ed's nearly thirty-six months working as project officer and monitor on the large number of projects undertaken during that time.

Most audacious were the congratulations Dave bestowed on himself. He takes credit for work on the same 47 projects, but praises himself for an astonishing 1,200 remote viewing sessions. That would amount to 200 more sessions than Mel, who was with the unit more than twice as long as Dave, and 400 more than Ed, who had been there a year longer than Dave.

Normally, such exaggerations would be relatively trivial. Few people would ever see the paperwork once the award had been granted, and the perpetrator could easily claim that it was all just a simple matter of the standard military hyperbole that inflates many an efficiency report and award recommendation. But trivial as it was, it pointed at problems of greater magnitude yet to come. And eventually both Dames and Morehouse would use these inflated military records to establish public credibility that was less deserved than what they claimed.

Less than a month after Mel retired, some of us were on the road again, under direction of an operations plan entitled "Quiet Storm I."[19] Gabrielle Pettingell, Dave Hanson, and I flew to Oakland on Monday, July 16, to be joined by Fern Gauvin and Angela. The mission this time was to establish a working relationship with the intelligence people at Joint Task Force 5, which was headquartered at Alameda Naval Air Station, a quiet little base tucked into some flat real estate on the east edge of the San Francisco Bay. Again we worked against counternarcotics targets—ships mostly—that ranged across the eastern Pacific from Hawaii to the whole West Coast of the United States. Again, we tried a helicopter flight—a long, circuit tour of the port facilities near San Francisco and along the northern side of the Bay. Other than Gabi getting some strange vibes when we overflew a cement plant, once again nothing particularly useful came out of it, though it did help to bring home to us the magnitude of the problem facing those trying to interdict narcotics entering the United States along the West Coast.

One of the highlights of this trip came on an afternoon after work when Gabi and I took a side excursion across the San Mateo bridge to Redwood City to meet Sam Taylor and his wife Gay. Sam was famous as the creator of Walt Disney's popular movies *The Absent-Minded Professor* (remade and released in 1997 as *Flubber*), and *Son of Flubber*, for both of which he wrote the screenplays, as well as the short story on which the films were based.

For more than sixty years Sam had been a prolific writer, contributing to *Colliers, The Saturday Evening Post, Reader's Digest, Esquire, Family Circle, Holiday*, and others. I knew of him mostly, though, for the books on Mormon history he had written, and because his vivacious spouse Gay and I had carried on a lively correspondence over the past couple of years about dowsing. Sam had made her an L-shaped dowsing gadget that she called "the wire." She used it to detect ripeness in produce at the supermarket and discern answers to difficult questions. Sam supported her in this, in an amused sort of way. I had originally been introduced to them through a mutual acquaintance, but our only contact until now had been by letter and telephone. We had a pleasant visit, got to see the old converted garage that for decades had served as Sam's office, and admired the beat-up manual typewriter on which he still did all his writing.

Sam was surprisingly quiet-spoken for his voluminous output in print, but when he talked his words were pithy and well chosen, and always tipped with humor. He told us a few stories of his past, mentioning his time as a reporter in Europe during World War II. Even here his modesty ruled. It was only later that I found out the full scope of his time as a writer on Eisenhower's staff, where he worked with Ernest Hemingway and Andy Rooney to cover the war as a military correspondent. During his thirty months in the job, he escaped serious injury from a B-17 crash, was almost captured by Germans, and was on the scene at the liberation of the Dachau concentration camp.

Gabi and I also enjoyed conversing with Gay about her experiences as a dowser, and learned a few things that we thought might be useful. When we left, Sam presented me with one of his custom-made "wires," little guessing that he was handing it over to a pair of government psychic spooks who would see if it could be used to support national defense. Fortunately, both

Sam and Gay outlived the secret phase of government remote viewing, so I could later tell them why we were in California that week. Characteristically, Sam was thoroughly amused.

Wednesday morning, the eighteenth of July, we left Alameda and flew to Los Angeles. For two days we worked more counternarcotics missions in Long Beach for Joint Task Force 5, and then headed home to Washington.

These trips did not mean that we stopped doing operational viewing at Fort Meade. Those who were not on temporary duty either to JTF-4 or JTF-5 continued to work projects at the office, and we travelers resumed those duties too when we returned.

As we went about our usual duties, I took time to visit an exhibit that Saudi Arabia had mounted at the Washington, D.C., Convention Center. It was quite a show, with video presentations on Saudi culture, large photo displays of Saudi Arabians in all walks of life, and large, detailed models under glass of new buildings and elaborate public works projects being planned or built by the Saudis—among them hotels, desalinization plants, port facilities, and the world's largest airport under construction—a gift from the Saudi crown prince to his father, King Fahd. Little did I know that the airport terminal would soon be my home. I came away with a green T-shirt emblazoned with the name of the Kingdom of Saudi Arabia in white Arabic script, and the prophetic English words, "Saudi Arabia, yesterday, today, and tomorrow."

On August 2, as I made plans for a short family vacation at the beach in a couple of weeks, I paid only slight attention to news reports of an Iraqi invasion of Kuwait, and media rumors that American troops might go to the defense of Saudi Arabia. My orders said I was going to Panama, so I had shoved Mideast issues to the far reaches of my mind.

I had made reservations at Fort Miles, Delaware, an Army recreation center located at the foot of an old shore-defense artillery battery (named, ironically, Camp Smith), which loomed over a quarter mile of some of the most pristine beach on the East Coast. Lewes Beach to the north and Rehoboth to the south were often standing room only during the tourist season, but the several hundreds yards of military-owned oceanfront property at Fort Miles was marvelously uncrowded. Daryl and I, along with my children, Mary, James, and Chris, arrived at Fort Miles on August 11, and I spent my thirty-eighth birthday two days later soaking up the sun, riding tandem bikes, and sight-seeing up the coast in the town of Lewes. As a birthday present Daryl gave me a pair of binoculars, which I broke in by watching dolphins splashing in the whitecaps.

We only had four days at the beach, but I took an extra day of leave after we got home and didn't report in to work until Thursday morning, the sixteenth of August. No sooner had I walked through the door than Fern delivered the news that Major Larry Wurzel, who was handling administrative issues for Colonel Johnson, had called. I was stunned to hear that my departure from Sun Streak and Fort Meade was to be "expedited"; I was being shipped out immediately. (In off-the-record conversations over the next few days with DIA personnel specialists I learned that John Berberich, who a few months before had replaced Jack Vorona as my senior rater, was actively supporting the transfer.)

I was instantly on the phone to Major Wurzel, who told me I would go first to support Third Army in Atlanta for the United States' intervention in the Kuwait crisis, which was now being called Desert Shield. Once things stabilized there, I was to be sent directly to Panama. Wurzel seemed a little confused about just exactly what these instructions involved, so the next call I made was to my branch assignments officer, Captain Bisacre, who had always tried to look out for me. With his usual cut-through-the-nonsense approach, Bisacre quickly sorted out the confusion. I was *not* going to Atlanta, nor on to Panama. I was to deploy to Saudi Arabia with the 101st Airborne Division (Air Assault), which was based at Fort Campbell, Kentucky.

Bisacre had been working with me on trying to finagle the Lebanon assignment, but had been overruled and had to issue my Panama orders. Now he said with a certain amount of pride, "Hey, look. I've worked it out so you can go to the Middle East after all!" He was right. Looming war or no, this was better for me than the Panama tour would have been. But now I wished I had earlier followed my intuitions and taken the Arabic class instead of Spanish.

I had two days to get my shots, write a will, and clear out my desk at Fort Meade. During that time Mel Riley came by the office. "Here, I want you to have this," he said, and handed me a pouch of rawhide and Native American-style beadwork. It was what Mel called "rock medicine." I had sometimes noticed him rummaging along the bed of the little creek that ran through the meadow behind our building, looking for stream-rounded pebbles, which he then encased in a leather pouch with a rawhide fringe and worked over with needle and thread, attaching complex patterns of tiny, colorful glass beads. Rock medicine was a venerable American Indian tradition. One wore it around the neck on a leather strap for protection from enemies and other hazards. The rock medicine Mel gave me was beautiful, and provided a reassuring weight under my desert camouflage fatigue shirt the whole time I was in Saudi Arabia and Iraq.

29

Desert Storm

"Sometimes I think we're
alone. Sometimes I
think we're not. In
either case, the thought
is quite staggering."

–R. Buckminster Fuller

As an enlisted person I had belonged to an intelligence unit in the 101st
Airborne, and had lived on Ft. Campbell. It was from there that I had
applied to officer candidate school. Now I was returning there, if only for a
little while, on my way to somewhere else—Operation Desert Storm. I joined
the division's aviation brigade as the new intelligence officer, or S-2.

The seven months I spent in Saudi Arabia and Iraq were not as a remote
viewer, but as a manager of more conventionally obtained intelligence. My
two closest brushes with fate were when, a week or so before the ground war
started, Joe Krupa, the brigade's assistant S-2 and I almost drove into Iraq, to
be saved only by the timely arrival of a French armored car; and when the door
I was leaning against in a flying helicopter popped open and I almost fell out.

But even though I didn't have any direct remote-viewing duties, there
was one paranormal encounter which still has me scratching my head. My

friend, Captain Kent Johnson, an Air Force liaison officer with my brigade, saw the shadow of a UFO. A couple of weeks prior to the ground invasion of Iraq, Kent was flying as an Air Force observer in an OH-58 scout helicopter with an Army pilot. They were flying at 500 feet in support of an exercise in an area with no other aircraft. As Kent described it, the two pilots simultaneously noticed a shadow moving in a straight line across the desert floor at more than 1,000 miles per hour, as they estimated.

Since there were often other aircraft around, the presence of the shadow wasn't particularly unusual. But this shadow was more than 200 yards across—"many times larger than anything known to fly," as Kent phrased it. Using techniques they had been taught, he and his compatriot scanned the heavens for any sign of the object that was casting the rapidly-approaching shadow. Nothing. "The shadow seemed to be oval in shape, with sharp, well-defined edges . . . and was traveling from southeast to northwest," Kent told me. But no matter how he looked, he never saw the craft to which the shadow belonged.

The shadow soon disappeared into the heat waves, and Kent and the Army pilot talked over what they had seen. Trying and failing to come up with a reasonable explanation, they shrugged, and went back to their mission. Then, about ten minutes later, the other pilot noticed the shadow again, this time approaching rapidly along a nearly exact reverse course from where it had gone. The two pilots again quickly scanned for a craft to go with the shadow, but found nothing. So, with typical aviator bravado, they set their little helicopter on an intercept course with the shadow. "As our tracks started to close," Kent continued, "the shadow instantly stopped dead, with no apparent deceleration." But as they neared, it abruptly returned to high speed. "There was not acceleration—just one moment it was sitting still, and the next it was moving at 800–1,000 knots" until it finally disappeared to the southeast.[1]

When Kent told me this story several days later, I think he was a little surprised that I took it matter-of-factly. He couldn't have known that I had heard other UFO stories far more incredible than his. Still, I was impressed by it. Kent is not at all the sort of person to believe in flying saucers or things that go bump in the night. He is a conservative, no-nonsense kind of guy who, before joining the Air Force, had been a police officer in Temple, Texas. I trusted his bewildered observations much more than many of the breathless stories I'd heard from others about being abducted by aliens or encounters with the Galactic Supreme Council.

Kent didn't try to speculate about this occurrence; he only reported it in his just-the-facts manner. But it was clear that he was perplexed, and bothered that he could find no common-sense solution. As he told me, he didn't know what he saw but he wasn't of the " 'I saw a UFO' mind-set," as he put it. Still, he seemed interested in further talk about it, and as our discussion progressed I sounded him out on other things, leading finally to a mention of the unclassified remote viewing at SRI. I had in mind to evaluate him as a possible candidate for Sun Streak. While still at Fort Meade, I had been engaged in discussions about reorganizing the remote viewing effort along multi-service lines. Since it belonged to DIA, a joint military organization made sense. Kent struck me as having the necessary mix of intelligence and open-mindedness, with just the right tincture of skepticism. I was no longer part of the unit, but I still wanted to do whatever I could to help it succeed, including assessing potential candidates. As I explained remote viewing in a general way, Kent seemed mildly curious, and by the time I finished giving him the run-down on how it was supposed to work, he thought he would like to see it demonstrated. I told him I had played around with it in the past, and agreed to give it a try. This is how he remembered what then transpired.

> You offered to demonstrate and asked me to envision a place, any place, and you would try to remote view it. Without giving you any clue or information about the target I had in mind, I thought about the Fine Arts building at the university I graduated from, Southwest Texas State. The building is squatly cylindrical, shaped somewhat like a tuna can, with smooth, cold red tiles, and completely surrounded by a moat full of water. Inside, I envisioned the theater where I had sat week after week in my film history class.
>
> Your description was uncanny. First you described the structure as red, round, and associated with water. Then you described the structure as cold. This comment surprised me, since it exactly captured my memories of coming out of the warm Texas sunshine into the frigid air of the theater. Finally, you described a large white rectangle that sounded like the movie screen I sat in front of every week. I was impressed.[2]

Kent and I continued occasionally to talk of these things as we shared numerous adventures in Iraq over the coming weeks. I didn't find out for several months that there was never going to be a joint-service remote viewing group at Fort Meade or anywhere else.

While in Saudi Arabia awaiting the attack into Iraq, I tried to stay in touch with my former Fort Meade colleagues. When my brigade's operations center finally got long distance phone lines and encryption equipment, I would occasionally call back to the Sun Streak office to compare notes and see if there was any useful scuttlebutt I could pick up. I learned that Dale Graff had been transferred from the Defense Intelligence Analysis Center (DIAC) at Bolling Air Force Base in the District of Columbia to replace Fern Gauvin as the new branch chief for the Fort Meade operation.

There may have been more behind this transfer than just a routine military shuffle. In late 1989, barely a year after General Soyster took over as the Defense Intelligence Agency's director, Dr. Jack Vorona lost his job as the head of the science and technology office at DIA. Vorona wasn't fired, exactly. A window-dressing job was created for him as "Chief Scientist," and he was shunted out of his influential position and into what was essentially a dead-end job. Dr. Vorona, accustomed to being in a position to make a difference, lasted less than a year before retiring. Why this change happened is not fully known, but some of it goes back to a long-term power-struggle between Vorona and Dennis Nagy, DIA's deputy director.[3]

Replacing Vorona was one of Nagy's friends, a career bureaucrat named John Berberich. Lacking Vorona's scientific credentials, Berberich was nonetheless well-versed politically and highly career-minded. Berberich was generally pleasant during the times I met him, but he seemed business-like to the point of being dismissive. It was clear that he was ambivalent about Sun Streak, and not willing to let any potential embarrassments from it stain his career. Given the political climate within DIA at the time, remote viewing promised just such embarrassment.[4]

Graff believed that Berberich transferred him to Fort Meade to stream-line the organization. Instead of a branch chief at Fort Meade sharing the management with Graff at the DIAC, the move consolidated control of the remote viewing program at Fort Meade. Graff, who was involved in a number of conventional science and technology projects, would keep his office in the DIAC where he would visit once or twice a week. He was now working the equivalent of three full-time jobs, commuting from his house on the Chesa-peake Bay.[5]

On the surface consolidation seemed to make sense. But I suspect there were ulterior motives. Sending Graff to Fort Meade increased bureaucratic efficiency. But it was also a further step towards marginalizing remote view-ing, since Graff had less time to fend off political attacks against the program. And all the fish would be in one barrel, so to speak, ripe for shooting. With General Soyster in charge, moves were afoot within DIA to wear down the unit by attrition. If such was the intention of DIA management, it didn't escape unnoticed. Here our successful presentation of remote viewing to the four senators in May 1990 may have come to the rescue.

Only a few months after Graff's transfer to Fort Meade, a letter was sent to Soyster, taking him to task for trying to undermine the remote viewing unit. Dated May 22, 1991, and signed by William F. Lackman, Jr., acting Director of the Intelligence Community Staff, the letter scolded Soyster for thwarting Congress's wishes that the program be supported and promoted.[6]

Besides budgeting research and operational funds, expressions of support from legislators (such as those who instigated Lackman's letter) extended the life of the government remote viewing effort by years in the face of determined institutional attempts to kill it off.

Besides Dale Graff's transfer to Fort Meade, other things had changed in my absence. The first was the project's code name, Sun Streak. Graff was notified by DIA's security folks shortly after his arrival that it was time for a change in name, something that was done every few years to throw off enemy agents. Graff wanted everyone to have a say in the new name, so he came into the office one day bearing a computer-generated list of code-word candidates and asked the Sun Streak crew to pick two suitable words. It wasn't easy. As Graff told me years later, "The words we had to choose from by that stage were awful. One would *never* want to go through a program calling it Cement Mixer or something like that." Still, everyone quickly agreed on the word "Star," which was on the list, but couldn't come up with a suitable second word. So Graff decided to see if he could think of an idea on his own.

> Driving home that evening I said, what's wrong with "gate"? It has a nice symbolic meaning, you know, a gateway, a portal, that kind of thing. It had a very nice symbology. So I said yeah, it's simple enough. I originally resisted it because of the Watergate [fiasco]. I came back in the next morning, and I said hey, look, the "star" part is right. But let's try "gate,"—"star gate." How about that? People looked around—I don't know how many were in there that morning—and it felt good.[7]

Graff pushed the name through the usual paperwork bottlenecks and, in a few weeks, it came back approved. Before 1990 was over Sun Streak had become Star Gate. Some people confuse the program name with the movie and television series *Stargate*, which came along a number of years later, but that was coincidence.

Along with the name change, Graff decided it was time for a change in classification status, too. Linda Anderson was assigned to handle that. Graff wanted the highly restrictive special access program (SAP) status eliminated and the unit set up as a "limited dissemination," or "LimDis" program. The change was subtle but significant. No longer would draconian guidelines have to be followed on who could be told about the unit's existence and mission. Though care still had to exercised, a wider circle of people could be informed under LimDis guidelines.

This had some important benefits. Remote viewing needed exposure to attract patrons and customers in the government. People had to know it existed and had to learn how it could be used. But so strict were the SAP guidelines, that from the early days of the project its managers were chronically hampered in attempts to recruit a wider range of customers. With more people in the know in the intelligence community, the unit could theoretically gain a larger client base, have greater opportunities for operational work, and with the added operational practice turn out increasingly better results. As it turned out, the move was probably too late in coming. The years of too much secrecy had done their damage.

Another, less fortunate change also occurred. Gabrielle Pettingell, my former remote viewing student and office mate, left the unit because John Berberich flatly denied her three months of unpaid maternity leave. Evaluating her situation, Gabi decided that with internal tensions still chronic in the unit, with the departure of me and Mel Riley, and with the obvious dislike the DIA command group had for the unit, Berberich's intransigence was just a sign of worse things to come. She found an opening at another intelligence organization that agreed to her maternity leave request and was gone. Like myself and Mel, Gabi was never replaced by another viewer. As I was to learn years later, Berberich took away Star Gate's vacant military slots and assigned them to a "higher priority activity" elsewhere in DIA. The slide of attrition was underway.

As all these other events were unfolding, Colonel Bill Johnson's effort to prove the efficacy of remote viewing had born fruit. Remote viewers from Fort Meade made additional trips to drug interdiction task forces on the East and West coasts. Despite mixed receptions—sometimes staffs and commanders reacted with interest, sometimes with skepticism or barely veiled hostility—the viewers piled up the successes. But on September 13, 1990, Gen. Soyster signed a letter terminating the ten-month effort.[8] Johnson felt that he had proved his point and his bosses wanted to move on with more pressing matters.

The end result of those months of feverish activity was a thick red binder containing the final report to the Military Intelligence Board, which had met on September 7th, documenting Colonel Johnson's assignment to see if remote viewing really worked as an operational intelligence tool. The previously skeptical Johnson concluded unhesitatingly that, in fact, it did.

There were failures, of course, but the successes were undeniable. In one instance Greg Seward correctly reported that a certain boat was loaded with contraband narcotics, and pinpointed the secret compartment. The boat was finally tracked to a dock in an East Coast port, the secret compartment was located as described, but there were only traces of drugs. The full stash soon washed up on a beach along the route the boat had taken. Fearing the Coast Guard was on to them, the crew had jettisoned their cargo.

In another instance, a viewer accurately located the rendezvous point on the high seas where one drug ship was to transfer its cargo to a smaller vessel to be smuggled onto the mainland. Based on the viewer's information, the

Coast Guard was waiting at the rendezvous point and took both vessels and millions of dollars worth of contraband into custody. To preserve the security of the operation, those in charge initially invented a story that the location had come from a tipster at a bar in a nearby seaport. But the final report dropped the cover story and credited remote viewing.

On one counter-narcotics mission before I left the unit, a joint task force received a tip that some kind of contraband was aboard a container ship that would be entering a certain port in the United States on a specific day. Container ships carried many hundreds of shipping containers the size of semi-trailers stacked from the bottom of the hold almost to the height of the superstructure. Even one ship would be a nightmare to search, and there were six of them entering the harbor that day. I ended up with the task of narrowing the search.

In the course of my session, I described a vessel and noted that indeed "contraband" was involved. I described it as white, rough, and lumpy. When the results of my session were passed to the analysts, they became excited, thinking that I had described white heroin being shipped in from the Orient. Though I had done my initial session blind, they came back to me with added details; there were six ships and I was supposed to find out on which ship and where on it the narcotics were stashed. Since the mission had now become essentially a dowsing problem, this small amount of added information was permissible. But I objected to the word "narcotics." Early on in my session I had used the word "contraband," and my monitor Gabi had continued to use that word. But the switch to "narcotics" didn't feel right, and I refused to use it.

Using a dowsing process to discover which ship carried the illicit cargo, then where it was on that ship, I located our target container forward of the superstructure, slightly to the port side, and a couple of layers down from the top. The Coast Guard stopped the huge ship and broke into the cargo at the point I indicated. They found a compartment full of white, rough, lumpy "contraband"—several tons of endangered white coral being smuggled into the United States.[9]

These and other accounts were included in the Military Intelligence Board report. Most of these stories I no longer remember, and some might still be sensitive. However, one further account is permissible here. John Koda, who had been our intermediary with Joint Task Force-4, recalled that of all the projects we remote viewed for his organization, the most dramatic was "locating the contraband buried under a large boulder on a particular beach on a specific corner of an island . . . 100 percent accurate down to an exact description of the wrapping material."[10]

In the end, our remote-viewing performance was impressive. We conducted more than a hundred projects for drug task forces on both coasts, plus other government counter-narcotics agencies. Of the two joint task forces we helped, JTF-4 provided us the most comprehensive evaluation. They sampled thirty-two projects from January 1 to August 10, 1990. Of these thirty-two, strong correlations between our findings and actual busts were found in eleven of the projects, or 34.4 percent; some correlation was found in ten, or 31.2 percent; and in another eleven (34.4 percent) no correlation was seen.[11] I remember we were personally told that on a number of occasions federal and local law-enforcement officials were able to arrest suspects and recover contraband thanks to the information we provided.

There are those who might find a 34.4 percent success rate unspectacular, and in some other field they might be right. But when it comes to intelligence operations, especially in the counter-narcotics field, our success was commendable. I was told later that of the three other intelligence disciplines that were involved, IMINT (or "imagery intelligence" involving satellite photos and reconnaissance aircraft) and SIGINT (or "signals intelligence") both scored low on the effectiveness scale. HUMINT ("human intelligence")—the purview of agents and informers—was rated at perhaps about 15 percent effectiveness.

Colonel Johnson's experiment to prove us capable had worked, and duties now called him that had nothing to do with military psychics. There were more conventional intelligence policy and programmatic issues with which he had to deal in his position on the Army intelligence staff. The countdown to Desert Storm was approaching, and there were ongoing intelligence problems with the pending war yet to be fully sorted out. With the written MIB report completed all that was left was verbal testimony to the board.

Colonel Johnson, his assistant, Major Dave Hanson, along with Major John Koda, who had been brought up from JTF-4 for the occasion, made presentations. According to Johnson, some members of the board were not thrilled to hear the success stories, and queried him as to why he hadn't done a scientific study, or included a double-blind control group. The colonel had to continually remind members of the board that such had not been his assignment. He had been directed to demonstrate whether or not remote viewing worked operationally, and he was satisfied that he had done just that.[12]

At the end of 1989 Project Sun Streak had been on the ropes. But the documented successes the remote viewing unit enjoyed under Johnson bought Project Star Gate another four-and-a-half years. It didn't hurt that Ed May, who had taken over the research side of the program from Hal Puthoff in 1985, was lobbying heavily for support among the senators and congressmen as well. But none of this could stave off the ultimate end.

After returning from the Gulf War to Fort Campbell, I spent five months over the summer of 1991 in my duties as 101st Aviation Brigade S-2. Colonel Garrett, my brigade commander, asked me to stay on. But I wanted to get back to my family, who had waited out the war in Maryland. By fall, I had found a new job in Arlington, Virginia with the Defense Intelligence Agency unrelated to remote viewing.

Though it looked like I would probably never go back to Star Gate, I stayed in touch as much as I could, usually by checking in fairly regularly with Greg Seward or Linda Anderson. On a few occasions I was asked by John Koda, now reassigned to the Pentagon, or others to give briefings about the operational use of remote viewing. And from time to time I would stop by the old office on Fort Meade to see what was going on. It was Ed Dames who gave me the opportunity to keep my hand in remote viewing during those months. Sometime in late 1989 Dames formed a commercial remote viewing company he named Psi Tech. Ed, Mel Riley, Dave Morehouse, and myself gathered to discuss forming the new company. Ultimately it was decided to create a small corporation for which Mel, Ed and Dave signed the incorporation documents.[13] Intuition had told me not to step in that deeply. I agreed that as long as no classified information was compromised and I was not put into any conflict of interest with my military duties, I would be willing to moonlight as a viewer.

Not long after, John Alexander and General Bert Stubblebine, both then retired from the military, joined the corporate board, and Lyn Buchanan was persuaded to become a part-time employee. Ed traveled to New York and convinced Ingo Swann to sign a letter authorizing Ed's use of the CRV methodology Swann and Puthoff had developed. No one thus drawn into Ed's scheme had any conscious inkling of how all this would eventually turn out.

Not long after my return from Desert Storm, Ed gave me my first Psi Tech tasking. I remember working that first session at the table in my BOQ (bachelor officer quarters) room at Fort Campbell, and faxing it back to Maryland. Because I often didn't get feedback on my Psi Tech sessions, I don't know what many of the targets were. Occasionally, though, Ed would forward news clippings, after-the-fact, or would attempt to front-load me with information when providing my tasking. Here again I resisted being front-loaded, as I had when Ed tasked me at the unit, but was less successful when working for Psi Tech. Often Ed would leave telephone messages on the answering machine with the front-loading blatantly recorded, or he would try to work it in at the opening of conversations when I wasn't on guard. It was almost as though he couldn't stop himself. For that reason I am dubious of much of my work done for Psi Tech.

Among the first projects, one had to do with investigations by the United Nations's teams inspecting Iraq for weapons of mass destruction. One of the U.N. inspectors had heard Ed on a radio program and contacted him, asking if remote viewing could find Saddam Hussein's stockpiles. Ed offered Psi Tech's resources free of charge. I produced some interesting descriptions and marked suspected locations on a hand-drawn map Ed provided. There was an Associated Press story about Ed's support to the UN team, but I never found out whether Psi Tech's data had been of any real use to the inspectors.

The Psi Tech projects to which I contributed over the years see-sawed between the ridiculous and the sublime. There were attempts to answer what made the Soviet *Phobos* Mars probe fail; what caused the devastating 1908 Tunguska explosion in Siberia; an attempt to "future engineer" a deep-space propulsion system; a re-look at ill-fated Korean Air Lines Flight 007, shot down by a Soviet fighter in 1983; an examination of how crop-circles were produced (tasked from the assumption that aliens were involved); a tasking about how a client should manage his farming and fur business.

One project, focusing on "a small object," turned out to be a search for the murder weapon in the O.J. Simpson case. There were also "missing persons" cases. One was a front-loaded project in 1995 against the Unabomber. Because I knew in advance what the target was, it was no surprise that I got impressions of a fiery explosion. But I did describe a school-like setting in what seemed to be the Chicago area that turned out to be quite similar to Ted Kaczynski's hometown and school in Evergreen Park, Illinois, a Chicago suburb. In a map dowsing, I indicated a location near Chicago. This was the area where Kaczynski's brother, who turned him in, still lived. I did the session before I or anyone else had a clue that there was a Chicago connection to the Unabomber case.

There were a number of other Psi Tech projects in which I was involved, and some in which I wasn't. Many of these Ed conducted on behalf of paying clients, but many others were performed under his own initiative, either to satisfy his curiosity or on speculation, with the hope of attracting new clients through the media attention he hoped to gain with a "hit." The Simpson case was one of these, but Psi Tech came up empty-handed. As far as I know, Psi Tech never had a single unambiguous "hit" for which it could take public credit. There were several reasons for this, and some of those will become clear as I recount the story of the "Ozone Hole."

In response to a Psi Tech tasking, I did two sessions, on March 1 and 8 of 1992. These sessions were frontloaded. In the first, Ed asked me to "follow the ozone problem out," meaning, I presumed, to do a remote viewing forecast as to how the problem of the thinning ozone layer, which was then very much in the news, would play out. I did my best to avoid the thoughts installed by the frontloading, and described in general terms the sensory experience of being in the thinning ozone. I then did a timeline exercise, in which I tried to intuit how things would unfold over the next decade or so. My answer went as follows:

> A time line exercise revealed the sense that [the radiation-shielding ozone layer] continues to thin and deteriorate until 1995 to 1996, when it then demonstrates a sudden thickening, becoming very thick to 2000, then thinning out slightly again through 2001, and continuing more or less stable through the outyears, though proceeding fairly regularly through a series of slight thickenings and thinnings.[14]

Ed's report ignored the general optimism of my data. Noting in the cover letter that "the outlook is grim," Ed's March 14, 1992 report to the client combines a worldwide outburst of volcanic activity starting as early as 1996 with ongoing, irreversible ozone depletion leading to catastrophe. He predicted that most food would have to be grown in giant climate-controlled greenhouses. One telling phrase on page three of the report is that "Die-off will occur on a global-ecological scale." Eventually, life would virtually cease to exist outside of "artificial structures" or underground shelters. Ed included much of my real-time descriptive data in the final report about the ozone depletion, but ignored my time-line results that predicted no catastrophe.[15]

He should have paid attention, because reality ended up supporting my data and discrediting his. Ever since that tasking, I have kept an eye on news reports about the ozone problem, and found my own results vindicated. A major story in the *Washington Post* on April 15, 1993—more than thirteen months after my work for Psi Tech on the ozone problem—projected a curve somewhat similar to what I had found in my session. According to the article, the depletion would peak in the mid-to-late 1990s, then prior to the year 2000 start to very gradually decrease and continue the decline until normal levels were reached sometime after 2050. There wasn't a clear "sudden thickening" of the ozone level after 2000 as I had noted, but I was close enough in my own prediction to be in the ballpark.[16]

The *Washington Post* article was just a projection, but seven years later an article in the December 4, 2000 issue of the *London Times* seemed to confirm the earlier story. It reported that unexpectedly dramatic declines in the release of ozone-depleting chemicals by industrial nations had arrested the growth of the ozone hole over the Antarctic and promised a long decline in the ozone problem over the coming decades, allowing for occasional temporary variations in the level.[17] This assessment was further reinforced by subsequent research reported in the September 18, 2002, edition of London's *Independent* newspaper.[18]

In reading through my session results and comparing them to the Psi Tech final report, I concluded that Ed favored results that were pessimistic, even apocalyptic, and carefully ignored those that contradicted that picture. This was not a new pattern for Ed. We had observed his fascination with what perhaps could be called speculative catastrophism during his three years at Fort Meade. This was but a further extension of it. It was also only an early installment of the "doom and gloom" for which he would one day become notorious.

30

Coming Apart at the Seams

"Always do right. This
will gratify some
people—and astonish
the rest."

—Mark Twain

It was painful to watch from a distance as Star Gate collapsed. No dark conspiracy brought it down, only bureaucrats with other agendas allied with pencil pushers at the upper levels of DIA who rejected the vision remote viewing offered. The changes didn't always seem significant as they happened. But some of them proved devastating in the end.

When Dale Graff arrived, he brought a change in emphasis. To the viewers, it seemed the office suddenly went from a right-brained focus to a left-brained one. Operations continued, but often in competition with more traditional desk work. One of Dale's assignments at the Defense Intelligence Analysis Center (DIAC) had been to track foreign efforts in parapsychology. That duty came with him to Fort Meade, and soon the viewers were spending time doing traditional research on parapsychology overseas—phone calls, contacts with other intelligence professionals, collecting reports. It may have been an important task, but for people uniquely trained for something else, it felt like a waste of time.

Along with Roland Travis, a mid-level DIA employee Graff brought in to serve as Star Gate's senior intelligence officer, Greg Seward and Linda Anderson were soon involved in trying to find out whether there were foreign counterparts to Star Gate. Working together, they created a 100-page report for Congress on Russian and Chinese involvement in what the Russians termed "psychoenergetics."[1]

These "foreign assessment" projects were only part of the new duties the viewers were given. Starting in 1991, Greg was assigned to help manage the contracting process between DIA and Ed May's new laboratory at Science Applications International Corporation, the think-tank to which the remote viewing research program had moved from SRI-International.

Lyn Buchanan's role of computer technician and database manager for the unit also expanded under Dale's direction. For a few years Lyn had also been managing a database of viewer performance. Unfortunately, scores were never more than rough estimates. Values for the success of any session were usually just a number between zero and five subjectively assigned by Fern Gauvin, or one of the analysts, after reading through the session transcript and comparing it to what feedback was available. Since such evaluations could not routinely be done for operational sessions due to lack of feedback, usually only training scores made it into the database.

Partly to satisfy the demands of the 1988 IG inspection, Dale wanted more emphasis on research and record keeping. With new computer equipment, Lyn's database activities expanded. Better track could be kept of sessions and projects, as well as other details about the functioning of the unit. The resulting figures gave a general idea of viewer performance, but still were never refined enough to be a clear-cut measure of how well viewers did. Despite updated electronics, viewer evaluation was still a seat-of-the-pants affair.[2]

Dale's coming had displaced Fern Gauvin from the branch chief's office. It was an awkward situation for Fern, who moved into a desk in the outer office and bided his time until his retirement in 1993. Fern was given his own domain—tasking human intelligence units to ferret out information about the dabbling of foreign governments in parapsychology. But Fern was still interested in how customers were being helped by Star Gate's intelligence product, and he had his own opinions about the way operational results should be counted. Remote viewing either answered the customer's question or it didn't. If the data provided to the customer was accurate, but still contained nothing of intelligence value, the only honest thing to do as far as Fern was concerned was to count it as a miss. On the other hand, though Dale agreed that value to the customer was important, he and Lyn also wanted an evaluation system that would measure viewer accuracy even in details that didn't matter to an intelligence user. It was a conflict between operational and scientific views. For example, if a viewer was tasked to find a lost dog, even though she described the dog and the bush where it was hiding, yet the owner couldn't find the correct bush among the hundreds of other similar bushes in the neighborhood, then the data was highly accurate but completely useless. Once, Lyn and Fern had an argument about a report to be sent to a congressional committee. Lyn's statistically driven figures showed a seventy-to-eighty percent success rate in gathering information. Fern changed it to fifteen percent, based on the actual value of the information to the customer. Lyn was incensed, but Fern maintained that he would feel the fire if he gave a too-glittering report to the committee, and the figures stood.[3]

There was another point of friction involving Fern that concerned the whole office. Over time we noticed that Fern seemed to be shredding a large number of documents. Lyn even claims to have gone so far as to jam the shredder with a screw driver to put it out of commission for a few weeks to stop Fern, though none of the rest of us remember that happening. We were worried that precious historical materials were being destroyed.[4] Years later I asked Fern about the shredding. He told me we had run out of storage space in our safes. "I had no more space," he told me. "I shredded [enough documents to make] space as we went along . . . the oldest stuff that I thought that I could spare in order to make room for the new stuff. It should not have been done, I grant that," he concluded, but it "was done on a very limited basis."[5]

In a normal government office, where it is often policy to discard documents more than a few years old this would be a perfectly reasonable approach. But this material comprised a unique and irreplaceable legacy, and I think Fern underplayed the extent of what was done. He shredded at least some operational documents of historical significance, including, apparently, the data on the CIA mole, Aldrich Ames.[6] He also shredded target folders and practice sessions viewers in the office had done on the current Pope and Mother Theresa to develop skills at targeting human subjects.[7] This happened because Fern was unsure whether it was legal to keep files on all these (it was). He felt it better to err on the side of caution, and potentially useful data was destroyed. Regrettably, instances of irresponsible shredding didn't end there, and it is certain many historically important documents disappeared forever. Fortunately, some altogether irreplaceable documents were rescued later—on a couple of occasions from the very jaws of the shredder.

One of the more profound changes Dale made upon his arrival was to mandate an end to monitored remote viewing sessions, decreeing that from that point on all sessions were to be conducted solo. One reason for this was that John Berberich had taken away all the personnel spaces for monitors; another was the theoretical possibility of telepathy between monitor and viewer skewing the results. Dale was also still gun-shy from the pounding the Department of Defense Inspector General had given us regarding alleged frontloading of monitors. Dale's solution was to ban monitors altogether, whether they were blind to the assigned target or not. He was well aware of the benefits a monitor provided, and knew that quality would suffer, but believed the resulting procedural integrity would be worth it. Dale was committed to demonstrating remote viewing's worth as an intelligence tool, but even more to the reality of the ESP phenomena. The tighter the protocols, the harder it would be for critics to fault good results.[8]

The move created a hardship for some viewers. Linda Anderson had been trained from the start to work with a monitor, and having a monitor added a small but important level of confidence to what for her often felt like a shot in the dark. When the new order went into effect, she lost that emotional support. Worse, she was never trained on how best to do a solo viewing. Linda told me she felt she never had a successful session from that point on.[9] It was only a matter of months before Linda resigned her commission for other reasons and left the Army.

In late 1991, Dale's and Greg's contracting efforts began to bear fruit. Ed May's laboratory conducted a series of experiments using Grill Flame veterans Joe McMoneagle and Ken Bell, among others and—for the first time to such an extent—the viewers at Fort Meade. One of the first of these experiments took place at the Los Alamos National Laboratory, and involved the use of a MEG—a magnetoencephalograph, a sort of electroencephalograph (EEG), with more precision as to where in the brain things might be happening.[10]

While the MEG monitored their brains, viewers tried to detect a flashing light being observed by a "sender" in a distant room. The experiment was similar to research SRI had conducted first in the 1970s with Hella Hammid and Pat Price. Since a human brain shows a certain reaction when looking at a flashing light, the MEG should be able to record the same reaction in the brain of a remote viewer perceiving a flashing light. For a target, a person would watch a video screen in a room 130 feet away from the viewer, and mentally "send" an image of a lighted grid-pattern whenever it flashed briefly on the screen.

All the Star Gate viewers—Lyn, Robin, Angela, Greg, and Linda—went to Los Alamos. Graff arranged the project in such a way that on paper it was not connected with Star Gate, and hence unclassified. This allowed Angela's twin sister, who was not a government employee, and a martial arts expert named Stephen Haynes to take part. Graff was curious to see how the latter two would fare in the experiment.[11]

In the end, the experiment showed only chance results. There were possible reasons for this, some of which Ed May listed in a subsequent report. Perhaps the video-screen target was not something that viewers could easily "see" in a remote viewing situation. Or maybe the operation of the MEG requiring the viewers to lie face down with a heavy machine hovering at the back of their heads dampened their performance. Or perhaps remote viewing input doesn't manifest itself in a way that a MEG can detect.[12] But finding out what doesn't work can be as important to scientific progress as finding out what does.

Besides the MEG experiment, others were performed, too. One included Joe McMoneagle and Ken Bell—both under contract with Ed May to act as research subjects—and Greg Seward, who came out from Fort Meade for the occasion. These three and several others participated in a lucid dreaming experiment in veteran dream-researcher Stephen La Berge's lab. A "lucid" dream is one in which the dreamer *knows* he is dreaming and can to some extent take control of what happens in the dream. At La Berge's lab and in a nearby motel, participants were handed targets in sealed, double-envelopes, and instructed that once they entered a lucid dreaming state, they were to imagine themselves opening the envelopes, and examining the photo inside. On awakening, they were to describe what they had seen.

La Berge presented the subjects with special goggles that flashed red lights when a sleeper's rapid-eye-movement sleep stage began. The lights aroused the subject's conscious awareness just enough to make him "lucid" within the dream state. La Berge did not know (or at least pretended not to know) that a government remote viewer was one of the subjects of the study. Unfortunately, the goggles gave Greg a persistent migraine and he had to drop out of the study.[13] But overall the experiment was a reasonable success since, according to the report, "rank-order analysis confirmed that robust AC [anomalous cognition, or ESP] occurred during the study."[14]

Throughout this time I stayed in touch with Star Gate. Through my grapevine I learned of the romance that had developed between viewer Robin and an important congressional staffer, Dick D'Amato, who worked for West Virginia's Senator Robert Byrd on the Senate Appropriations Committee. Since both Robin and D'Amato were unattached and had jobs in different branches of the government, there was nothing improper about their romance. But it made for headaches at DIA. Just about anything that happened administratively in the Star Gate office might eventually find its way to D'Amato's ears.[15]

More than once Dale found his own ears stinging after a phone call from his boss John Berberich wanting to know why something was said or done at the remote viewing unit that had caught D'Amato's attention. It could be helpful to have an influential Senate staffer as an advocate. But it could also make problems for decisions and policy-making when the management had to step gingerly for fear Robin would relay the news of some action or initiative to her friend on Capitol Hill. So bad was it that on one occasion in June 1993 as Dale was retiring, he made a formal complaint to the incoming branch chief about Robin making "comments of a defamatory nature" about him "to a person outside of DIA."[16]

Robin made no secret of her personal disdain for the military. This attitude may have contributed to her complaints that DIA was the wrong organization to be operating the remote viewing program and that in her opinion Star Gate really belonged with the civilian CIA. As events were to unfold, it would come to appear that her beliefs had joined hands with the D'Amato relationship to unintentionally bring about Star Gate's ruin.

This was not an especially fertile period for Star Gate. Along with the increased emphasis on research and non-remote viewing tasks, and increased administrative demands, the customer-base for Star Gate's product was eroding. Counter-narcotics taskings still came to the branch chief, but they were falling off as time went on. This was partly because the people at the two joint task forces who had learned to trust remote viewing results were reaching the end of their tours and were being reassigned. With Jack Vorona retired and his replacement uninterested in the program, with Dale Graff wrapped up in running the day-to-day operations of the office, plus his other duties, and without Colonel Bill Johnson barnstorming the Defense Department drumming up customers for Star Gate, business was getting thin.

I don't have access to the figures for operations conducted in 1991, the only year for which I don't have at least some record of what went on. I do know that besides some work for the war on drugs, remote viewers were used unsuccessfully to try to locate SCUD missile launchers in Iraq, as well as discover where Saddam Hussein might be hiding. The figures for 1992 (twenty-six projects, most of them involving single sessions) show a significant downturn from past years when taskings were brisk, and the numbers decreased still more in 1993, to only twelve. There were also four brief projects done by Joe McMoneagle, working as a contractor.[17]

Among the operational targets in 1993 were a handful that involved an attempt to locate and describe secret tunnels being built under the Korean Demilitarized Zone by the North Koreans. The U.S. Army and its South Korean counterparts had found and destroyed such tunnels in the past, and had specialized tunnel-detecting forces on regular patrol. But the tunnels were extremely hard to find, and there was hope that the remote viewers might be able to help.

I do not have the details of these projects, and wouldn't reveal them if I did, since at least some of them may still be sensitive. But DIA's chief analyst for the tunnel project personally confided to the primary viewer after ground-truth was finally uncovered that the viewer's data had been correct.[18] But the remote viewing results did not contribute to the finding of the tunnels. The reason for this was that those results never made it out of DIA. The DIA analyst told me that, try as he might, he couldn't get Berberich to take any action toward forwarding the data into the intelligence system. When Berberich left to become DIA's chief-of-staff, nothing changed.[19]

While the unit was losing steam it was also losing people. Lyn Buchanan retired from the Army at the end of 1991. And in June 1993, Dale Graff retired, capping off eighteen years of continuous involvement with the remote viewing program. Linda Anderson had her first child in April 1992, spent a month or two in the office after returning from maternity leave, and then realized she wanted much more to spend time with her new daughter than to be a remote viewer under ever worsening conditions. In August 1992, she accepted one of the early-separation incentives the Army was then granting in the aftermath of the Cold War.[20]

Greg Seward was still a member of the Star Gate team, but he had also taken one of the incentive packages, converting from Army captain to government employee, staying in the unit as a civilian. He had become very proficient in the coordinate remote viewing methodology, having honed his skills during the grueling work in support of the counter-narcotics projects. With Linda's departure, only three viewers were left, Greg, Angela, and Robin.

Graff's replacement was a retired Army officer whom I shall call by the pseudonym Andy Gillespie. Gillespie had been assigned to act as "liaison" between Berberich and the unit before Graff retired, and by varying accounts he was either sent by Berberich to keep tabs on Graff and the unit, or was someone that Berberich wanted to find a job for away from the DIAC. Through my visits to the Star Gate office and conversations with the talkative Gillespie, I came to the opinion that Berberich had not planted him as a spy, at least not with Gillespie's awareness.

Some of my former colleagues have alleged that Berberich sent Gillespie to Fort Meade with hopes that he would do fatal damage to the program simply through his inexperience. I don't know for sure if that was Berberich's intent, but it seemed to me Gillespie knew too little of remote viewing to run the unit and successfully represent it to a skeptical intelligence community. He had enthusiasm, but his lack of preparation was apparent as time wore on and it became his job to seek out customers or provide briefings to oversight agencies. As a result, the program's credibility with outsiders hit a new low.

Ed Dames and I had maintained fairly regular contact, and he continued to task me from time to time with Psi Tech targets. To my increasing irritation, he would frequently call me with news of remote viewings he had done of UFOs and space aliens. He even found outside support from a few scientists and a couple of wealthy patrons interested in the UFO phenomenon.

I worried about Ed's flights of fancy, but I grew even more anxious about his willingness to say too much about the government connection to remote viewing. In the beginnings of his commercial venture, he had been cautious in public and with his clients as to how the viewers he employed had learned their unusual skills. However, he grew increasingly bold as months passed, and began hinting to outsiders of the existence of the government program. What he revealed was unlikely in the long run to undermine national security. But Star Gate was still a classified program, and any revelations could harm it.

I grew alarmed when he started talking of a book he was working on that was to be about him and remote viewing. I recall Ed first telling me about the project when I was at his house in early 1993. At the time I hoped it was only a half-baked notion that he was mulling over, though he presented it with the same air of confidence and assurance that he used for other projects on which he was working. Ed's writing skills were adequate for Army business, but I had my doubts that he was good enough to attract a publisher. Not long after that, though, he told me that he had hooked up with a collaborator, Jim Marrs, a writer of popular nonfiction who was known most widely for *Crossfire*, a conspiracy-laced account of the John F. Kennedy assassination. Marrs was to be the author listed on Ed's book jacket, but he would base the story on what Ed told him, and Ed would be the centerpiece.

I was confused about whether the book was to be a novel or nonfiction. As Ed explained the content, it seemed more like fantasy than a realistic account. Ostensibly, this was to obscure the classified status of the unit. Soon, though, all pretense of that was brushed aside. From his remarks to me, it was clear Ed intended to tell a much distorted version of the "Star Gate" story with him as the focus. This was alarming. Too much publicity would give Star Gate's enemies plenty of reason to fold the project. I hoped that Ed wouldn't be able to pull it off, but before long the book project took on another partner: Dave Morehouse who, though still in the Army, had become Psi Tech's vice-president. The Marrs/Dames/Morehouse collaboration would be called *Psi Spies*, and was due out in late 1994, to be published by Harmony.

This would not be the first book involving a military remote viewer. In 1993 Joe McMoneagle had published his own book, *Mind Trek*.[21] In it he told about having a near-death experience while stationed in Germany, becoming interested in remote viewing, and being trained to be a viewer. Since the remote viewing program was still classified, Joe was careful to disguise the military's interest in it, never mentioning that he was involved in remote viewing on official business. I was not sure that we could expect the same discretion from Ed and Dave.

Marrs began the research, treading close to the secrets. Linda Anderson told me in April 1994 that he had phoned her at her home number that Ed had given him and, in her words, "pressed" her for information. So uncomfortable was she with his questioning that she finally refused even to speak to him.[22] A few weeks after my conversation with Linda, Ed called to tell me *Psi Spies* was finished, and would soon be published. He also mentioned he was collaborating on a book about space aliens to be written by Courtney Brown, a remote viewing student of his.[23]

But the Marrs/Dames/Morehouse book was not to be—at least any time soon. My first inkling came when Ed complained to me that Dave Morehouse was horning in too much on the project. According to Ed, Dave was colluding with Marrs to make Dave the star of the remote viewing epic, relegating Ed to a supporting role. Ingo Swann, who had been following the project from a distance, called me toward the end of May 1994 to tell me that the publication of *Psi Spies* had been delayed by the publisher until Spring 1995.[24] But that date came and went, and still no book. I began to breathe a sigh of relief. In August, Ed called me about a Psi Tech project I was contributing sessions to, and reported that the book had been put on hold by the publisher because, as Ed put it, he was suing Dave over the hijacking of the book.[25]

The book project collapsed under the weight of squabbling over who would get top billing between Dames and Morehouse—the two folks with the least experience and shortest time assigned to the remote viewing unit. In the following years, Marrs did not speak widely of the Dames-Morehouse falling-out which had undermined his book. Instead, he hinted that the CIA pressured the publisher into canceling publication.[26] Even though it wasn't true, it did create more interest for his subsequent books, including a much-reduced version of *Psi Spies* which finally saw the light of day in 2000.

There was more trouble brewing with Dave Morehouse. He had left Sun Streak in June 1990, and thanks to Ed's lobbying had been accepted into the hyper-classified program where Ed had moved at the end of 1988. Things did not work out well there for Dave, and within a few months he was moved out of that job and into a holding-position with the Army's Personnel Command, where he awaited the start-date for his Command and General Staff College (CGSC) class at Fort Leavenworth, Kansas, in September 1991.[27] He soon went off to CGSC, writing a masters thesis on non-lethal weapons which included details about remote viewing as an intelligence collection tool.[28] The school finished, Dave continued on to an assignment with the 82nd Airborne Division at Fort Bragg, North Carolina.

Beginning around April, 1994, I began hearing rumors that Dave was going to be court-martialed. I didn't have the whole story at the time, but eventually it all came out. Dave had made two mistakes involving the wife of an enlisted man who had worked as his military driver. First, he had passed on to the woman an Army-owned computer that he claimed had been his private property. When later confronted about the missing computer, Dave said he had given it to the woman to pass along to her relative only for repair, since Dave claimed he couldn't get Army technicians to do it. The woman contradicted the story. Broken or not, as far as the Army was concerned the computer had been removed from Government control and passed to an unauthorized civilian. Still, the action didn't amount to more than a misdemeanor under the Uniform Code of Military Justice, since other testimony said the computer wasn't worth much.

Unfortunately, Dave also pursued an extended affair with the driver's wife. The official 600-page military court transcript is a tale of sex and Dave's cynical manipulation of the woman. Despite having a loving wife and three kids, Dave had a wandering eye that was well-documented in the proceedings.[29] Brought up on charges of adultery, he complained that he was being persecuted. No one was ever prosecuted for that crime anymore, not even in the Army, he said.

Unhappily for Dave, he was only partly right. Affairs between soldiers of similar rank or station are often ignored. But liaisons between officers and the enlisted people over whom they have authority are treated as serious business. And it is even worse when the transgression involved the *spouse* of an enlisted person. Affairs such as that between Dave and his driver's wife significantly threaten "the good order and discipline" of the Army. Officers must often send enlisted soldiers away from home or even into life-threatening situations, and sometimes the officer that does the sending remains behind in the garrison. Soldiers have to feel they can trust their officers implicitly. Dave's court martial wasn't the first, and it was far from being the last such case to be tried by the military services. Over the next few years similar scenarios played out in which higher-ranking officers were accused of dalliances within the ranks.

I did not know the extent of Dave's problems when I received a phone message from his wife Debbie in the middle of May, 1994. When I returned her call, she confirmed the rumors I had heard that Dave was slated to be court-martialed. His hearing had been postponed and he was in the psychiatric ward of the Walter Reed Army Medical Center in Washington, D.C.[30]

A few days later, on May 21, Ingo Swann called to chastise me for being late with one of the sessions he had asked me to do, but also to update me on a number of things he was involved in. One was that he had just trained two new people, though he didn't name them (one was writer Jim Schnabel, who published the book *Remote Viewers* three years later), and had managed to take the two students from Stage One all the way through Six in just twelve days. He had to make it that short, he joked, to compete with Ed Dames, who was offering a ten-day remote viewing class.

The main reason Ingo called, though, was to tell me that the news program *60 Minutes* planned to do a show about Star Gate. Howard Rosenberg, one of the *60 Minutes* staff, had been in touch with Ingo and reported that he had already been to Walter Reed to interview Dave. Dave was even arranging to be released from the hospital for a day of leave so *60 Minutes* reporters could interview him in depth. Ingo thought there were also plans for a news crew to go to New Mexico, where Ed Dames had moved, to interview him.[31]

According to Ingo, the news program intended to do an expose of the government remote viewing program, and that Rosenberg had told him that CBS meant to chide the government for ridiculing the phenomenon in public, while operating a "black" program in secret. Ingo had told Rosenberg he would not agree to an interview about a still-classified government program.

Over the next few days, I spread word to my former colleagues and the people remaining at Star Gate. There was great concern, since exposure by a news program as widely watched and respected as *60 Minutes* could easily be the final straw for DIA's hierarchy. Air Force General James R. Clapper, who replaced General Soyster as DIA's director in 1991, had been heard complaining that every time he went to a dinner party somebody gave him the third degree about remote viewing and Ed Dames, who was eagerly giving interviews about remote viewing at conferences and to news media, sometimes hinting at government and DIA involvement.

Three days after Ingo's call, Debbie Morehouse called me again. She was worried that the *60 Minutes* production would complicate Dave's case still further. Having him show up on TV talking about government secrets would not endear him to a military court. She also asked me to visit Dave at Walter Reed. Since I was now a bishop's counselor in my local Mormon congregation, she was hoping I could give advice about how the church might be able to help her and her family in their time of crisis.[32]

Up to that point I had been reluctant to visit Dave. I figured it would be hard to gain entry to the psych ward, and I wasn't sure what frame of mind I might find him in. I also feared being "outed" to the press if I strayed too close to Dave while CBS was courting him. But I made arrangements to meet her in the afternoon of June 8 at the psyche ward, telling my boss only that I was going to visit a sick friend. Looking crisp and a little anxious, as if barely corralling a welter of emotions, Debbie greeted me with a tone of relief in her voice as I walked down the corridor to meet her.[33]

Wearing a hospital gown, Dave was in the waiting room down the hall, unshaven and with a caged look in his eyes. I made sure to tell him I was not officially representing DIA or the government in any way, but was there out of concern for Debbie and the kids. I didn't want to raise their hopes that I had some special leverage with DIA. I also confessed that I was worried about the security of Star Gate.

At the time, I was ignorant as to why Dave was in the ward. He soon admitted to the affair, calling it a stupid mistake, and complaining that it shouldn't have been an issue since both he and his paramour were separated from their spouses at the time. He said he was being unfairly persecuted by Fort Bragg's senior lawyer, the acting judge advocate general, who happened to be a woman, implying that she was turning it into some kind of feminist crusade. Dave claimed his case had been dropped on the desk of Major General William M. Steele, the commander of the 82nd Airborne Division, the day after an F-16 had crashed into a group of the division's soldiers as they prepared to board a plane for a parachute jump, killing several. According to Dave's story the general, still emotionally overwrought by the tragedy when Dave's file ended up in front of him, gave Dave two choices: resign under less-than-honorable conditions (the officer-equivalent of a dishonorable discharge) or stand court-martial. When he heard the options, Dave apparently attempted suicide, and Debbie had him committed.

The explanation for why he was still in psychiatric care was much more bizarre even than the circumstances that put him there in the first place. Within minutes after I arrived Dave was describing "evil spirits" that beset him "all the time." He said they kept talking to him, trying to get him to hurt himself or others, and described two suicide attempts.

One of the things Dave wanted me to do was to testify that remote viewing had caused the mental problems he was manifesting. He hoped that if he were diagnosed as mentally ill, traceable to a military-related cause, he would be granted a medical retirement rather than be sent to the military prison at Fort Leavenworth, Kansas. I resisted the idea, since all I could honestly say was that it *might* be possible remote viewing had affected him mentally, since there was no way to prove whether it did or didn't. Since no one *else* from the unit had ever gone crazy, it seemed unlikely that if Dave really was having mental problems, that remote viewing caused it.

Dave argued that Ed Dames's seemingly nutty ideas were evidence that remote viewing could negatively affect a person's mind. To whatever degree Ed's ideas were crazy, I responded, he already had most of them before he ever came to the remote viewing unit.

It did seem to me that a medical retirement would be the best solution for this bad situation. Dave would have some additional incentive not to spill the beans about the remote viewing project and the other classified assignments in which he had served, and his family would get to keep their benefits.

In a parting gesture, Dave made a studiously impassioned plea about leaving the Army behind, since it had "betrayed" him, and he said he wanted to try to "heal" his family, take care of his kids, redevelop his relationship with Debbie, and start a new life. When Debbie and I spoke after leaving the ward, I told her that I thought it was a convincing performance, but that it was hard to tell anymore when Dave was being sincere. Despite Dave's shortcomings, though, it was clear that Debbie still loved him, and wanted to believe. As I walked towards my car, I didn't feel like I had accomplished much that was constructive, and knew that there was more yet to come.

June 20 was Dave's first day in court. On that same day the Star Gate branch chief, Andy Gillespie, called me and said he was finally sending a memorandum on the Morehouse issue up to General Clapper, and that my name was mentioned in it, apparently as a source of information or a point of contact—though I had not passed on to Gillespie or anyone else at DIA any of what had transpired between me and the Morehouses during or after the hospital visit.[34]

There were two more hearings, one on August 26 and another on November 4. Major General Steele signed an official memorandum dated November 30, 1994 with a subject line that read "Resignation for the Good of the Service—David A. Morehouse." Since "litigating the issue of mental responsibility and discovery of highly classified information has already begun and holds the prospect of a lengthy and costly prosecution out of proportion to the nature of the charges," Steele recommended in the text of the memo "that MAJ Morehouse receive a discharge under other than honorable conditions."[35]

There was one last paragraph in the general's memorandum. If the U.S. Army Personnel Command, who had authority over the resignation proceedings, did not approve it, the trial would be back on again. Morehouse soon tendered his resignation.

All that was left hanging was the *60 Minutes* program. But after the angst and frantic phone calls, the program never aired. Rosenberg pulled the plug on the project when he couldn't get any details about the current remote viewing program. When I asked him why, he explained:

> It was virtually impossible because of the nature of the [RV] program as a 'black' program to actually find out how much of it was legitimate, how much was being financed, what the funding levels were, who the players were, how much credibility was invested in the intelligence community in the program—[finding out] all of that was impossible. No one would talk about it on the record. And [Morehouse], the principal promoter of the story and of the program, was of questionable credibility and seemed to me to have multiple agendas.[36]

Rosenberg abandoned the project, and Star Gate escaped public notoriety again, at least for the time being. I would prefer to have left out the Morehouse drama altogether, if it weren't for how it played into remote viewing's future.

31

Everything Melts into AIR

"Many of the truths
we cling to depend
greatly on our own
point of view."

—Obe Wan Kanobe in *Star Wars*

W hile the Dave Morehouse soap opera played out, other things were unfolding that would eventually make the damage he could do a moot point. It turned out that the Dames-Morehouse-Marrs book wasn't the only one afoot. I returned from a vacation to the West in August, 1994, and punched the button to retrieve my phone messages at home. On the tape was an unfamiliar voice and name—Jim Schnabel. I heard the name again the next Monday, when Skip Atwater called me from his office at the Monroe Institute. Schnabel was a freelance science writer who wanted to do a book on remote viewing. He was going to interview Skip the very next day. I called Ingo Swann, to see if he knew anything. It turned out that, to aid in his book research, Schnabel had been one of the two men who asked Ingo to train them in remote viewing a few months before. The other was an airline pilot named Bob Durant. Schnabel had already published two other books—one debunking crop circles, and one debunking alien abductions. He sounded like a skeptic on a crusade. I wondered whether it had been a good idea for Ingo to cooperate. But he seemed to think Schnabel wanted to be fair, especially since the journalist had turned out to be a pretty decent remote viewer.

I didn't hear from Schnabel again until December, which was fine with me. Unlike Skip, I was still in the military and could get in trouble for talking to a reporter about a classified program. When Schnabel finally did call, it was to ask me some questions about the *Stark* incident, where I had viewed the attack on a U.S. Navy frigate fifty hours before it actually took place. Schnabel drew me into the conversation by telling me the version of events he had heard from Ed Dames, who got many of the details wrong. I corrected some of the facts that I believed to be harmless and not classified. I dodged the rest of his questions, and eventually the conversation segued to Jim Marrs's book, *Psi Spies*, which Schnabel had heard was due out in the last part of 1995. Since I wasn't more forthcoming, he did most of the talking, hoping, I'm sure, to build my trust. He certainly knew about a lot of the people involved with the program, even folks who were not yet retired or publicly known to be connected with remote viewing. He knew about Gene Lessman, for example, though he hadn't been able to find Gene.[1]

As a further enticement, Jim told me, with the air of a confidante, that his book covered some things in the remote viewing world that even I didn't know were going on; he would tell me his secrets if I would tell him mine. With great restraint I resisted the bait, but Schnabel continued to call regularly over the next several months. I well knew that good counter-intelligence principles demanded that I just refuse to talk to him and hang up. But that didn't *feel* like the right thing to do. In the back of my mind was a sense that Schnabel was trustworthy, and that what he was up to was important. I did eventually become more open with him, though I was always careful to stick with things I knew were not sensitive or damaging either for national security or the welfare of Star Gate.

As events moved along in the remote viewing world, my personal life was progressing as well. My son William Jefferson Smith had been born on July 24, 1993, and named after his grandfather and two of his greater-grandfathers a few generations back. Five days later I was finally awarded my masters degree from the Defense Intelligence College. I'd been working on it since 1987, interrupted by a war and various intervening personal and professional crises. I also changed jobs. In September 1994 I was transferred out of DIA for good, reassigned from the intelligence collection policy office where I had spent the last three years to become chief of the Intelligence and Security Division on the operations staff for the Military District of Washington, headquartered at Fort Lesley McNair on the Washington, D.C., waterfront.

While I was occupied with all these life changes, things were going on behind the scenes for Star Gate that would soon spell major sea-changes for government remote viewing. What started it all was a line-item written into the 1994 intelligence budget mark-up language for Fiscal Year 1995. The wording ordered the Defense Intelligence Agency to surrender the Star Gate program to the Central Intelligence Agency. How this came about is uncertain, but Senator Robert Byrd was chairman of the Senate Appropriations Committee at the time, and his chief committee staffer was Dick D'Amato, Robin's boyfriend.

Robin had not hidden her disdain for the military. It rankled that she and the RV unit were subordinate to DIA, an intelligence agency run by the military. She had often spoken openly of her belief that the true home for Star Gate was with the CIA. The fact that the CIA had given remote viewing the boot twenty years before didn't seem to trouble her.

At the time, DIA's leadership might have been happy to hand over the remote viewing program, but would have preferred to ax the program outright. As later events showed, the CIA was anything but enthusiastic about the prospects of acquiring Star Gate, and certainly was not lobbying for it. That leaves the most logical account being Robin persuading D'Amato to grease the wheels for the move. The budget passed, and Congress' order to transfer Star Gate from DIA to CIA became federal law.

Fiscal Year 1995 began on October 1, 1994, which officially launched the hand-over process. Meetings between Star Gate personnel and CIA representatives took place on December 6, 1994 and February 6, 1995—the latter at the Ames Building in Rosslyn, Virginia, across the Potomac River from Washington.[2] Others followed.

While the transition process was building up steam, Star Gate moved to new digs. In early 1995 those venerable old Fort Meade fire traps, Buildings T-2561 and T-2560, were abandoned to their fate, and housekeeping was set up a mile or so away in Building 2845. The move to the new quarters was helped along when Senator Claiborne Pell came to visit decrepit T-2561 and wanted to know "where all the winos were" as he walked up the rickety steps.[3]

About the time the CIA/Star Gate transition meetings were taking place, I took my son James to the Monroe Institute to visit Skip Atwater on February 11, 1995. There were several motives for the trip. James was in the middle of a chronic teen-rebellion phase, and I hoped time in the Blue Ridge Mountains might help clear the air. But the real catalyst for the trip was a book. About two years before, I had found a hardback, first edition copy of Bob Monroe's *Journeys Out of the Body* and wanted to get it autographed.

About mid-morning we arrived at Atwater's house where it nestled among the trees, and found Skip—I was getting used to not calling him Fred—in the process of making bread. After lunch, I took James up the hill to the McMoneagle's. Joe and I discussed what he was doing at the time—an incongruous mix of construction contractor and remote-viewing consultant. We talked obliquely about the pending transfer of Star Gate, and he showed me a remote viewing session he had done for one of Ed May's experiments. The target had been the Lawrence Livermore National Laboratory, and the only targeting had come when he was shown the nameless snapshot of a man who, it later turned out, worked there. The task was to describe the location with which the man was associated. The session results (a detailed sketch has since been published in Joe's book *Remote Viewing Secrets*) were breathtaking in their precision. Joe's sketch of the layout of landmarks and structures around the laboratory complex could not have been much better had he been physically sitting there. I was encouraged that such good work was being done by the research arm of the Star Gate program. The congressionally-mandated program review should go well, I thought. Joe also told me that Dick D'Amato had visited, and that, other than a few small glitches, they had hit it off.

After we left Joe's, Skip took us on a tour of the Monroe Institute laboratory. He let James try out the special CHEC ("controlled holistic environmental chamber") unit in the lab where some of the more sophisticated Hemi-Sync sessions were done. Unlike those in the cozy dorm-style rooms of my RAPT program experience years before, this one was a large cube sitting in the middle of the laboratory floor. James climbed up the few steps, entered through the acoustically-shielded door, and stretched out on a comfortable waterbed. The unit had all the latest bells and whistles designed to enhance the Hemi-Sync experience. With the soothing environment, James was quickly sawing logs while Skip and I caught up on all the news since last we had met.

Later, James told me of an experience he seemed to have while asleep. As he slept, he says he felt somehow like he traveled up through the roof of the lab, high up over the hills, to where he could look over the entire Institute. He noticed a car moving up the road some ways away, and then suddenly he was pulled back down inside and groggily came to as Skip opened the cubicle door. James says he was still feeling disoriented as he walked with us out the front door of the lab. And there, still clicking and popping as its engine cooled down, was the car he swears he had just seen in his dream.

After dinner Skip, his stepdaughter Amelia, James, and I drove up the steeply winding gravel road to the top of the mountain where Bob Monroe's huge house perched. Bob looked old to me. He had lost weight and his face bore many more wrinkles since I last visited him in 1990 with Colonel Johnson. Though there were pauses as he searched for lost words, Bob was as lively and animated as ever. James and Amelia noted that he tended to light cigarette after cigarette and not smoke it—just hold it between his fingers and wave it around until it burned down. He told us of an idea he had for a science fiction novel he wanted to write: a man wakes up after a car accident in the body of someone else through some sort of genetic transformation involving something Bob called a "transforgene." He seemed confident that he would be working on it soon.

As 11 P.M. neared and Bob grew tired, I had him sign my copy of his book. As I handed it to him he smiled elfishly, remarking that he "hadn't seen one of these in a long time." I pointed out how that rounded out my collection. I had the very first copy of his second book, *Far Journeys*, ever to be sold and autographed, which he had signed for me almost ten years previously, in October 1985. I also had his third book, *Ultimate Journey*, which Skip had managed to get autographed for me a month before the book was officially released. Now, as Bob scribbled his name in my shelf-worn copy of *Journeys out of the Body*, I had a complete set.

James and I returned home the next day. A month later, on March 18, Skip Atwater called. "Better hold onto that book you brought down for Bob to sign." Bob Monroe was dead.

Over the next few months some of my free time was spent doing freelance remote viewing sessions for Ed Dames's Psi Tech and a few for Ingo Swann. Ingo's assignments were always intriguing. Starting in February, 1994, I had worked a couple of sessions for him on what turned out to be anomalies on the lunar surface. When Ingo later mailed me feedback, I was pleased to see that much of my data matched what Ingo and another viewer had gotten. And the data *seemed* to reveal some interesting and bizarre happenings on the Moon. I won't discuss here anything more, since it was Ingo's project and he has not given me leave to do so. The same goes for a project he had tasked me on the previous year, meant to see what remote viewing could discover about the happenings surrounding the alleged Roswell, New Mexico, UFO incident.

As the CIA prepared to absorb Star Gate, I received regular updates from my former comrades on how the transfer was proceeding. Towards the end of March, 1995, Greg Seward called to tell me the CIA had sent a memorandum stating its intent to declassify Star Gate, as well as the early CIA-sponsored research at SRI-International.[4] This didn't sound in keeping with a CIA desire to keep the program going, and should have set off warning bells.

Barely two weeks later, Greg reported an interesting synchronicity. He was on an Amtrak train going north and happened on Senator Claiborne Pell, who was one of remote viewing's strongest supporters on the Hill. Greg recognized him because Pell had been in to the Fort Meade offices several months before for a briefing. They had taken pictures of the senator standing in front of Joe McMoneagle's space mural on the office wall. Pell and Seward sat together for the rest of their journey, discussing what they could, in that unclassified setting, of developments concerning the program. Greg had a copy of the remote viewing manual in his bags and passed it to the senator as a goodwill gesture.

I made a trip over to Fort Meade in February of 1995 and tried myself to photograph Joe's mural in the now-vacant T-2561. I got the film-speed setting wrong and the slides turned out too dark to be useable. I also visited the new office a few times after that, and it became increasingly apparent that morale was falling apart. No one among what was left of the Star Gate staff had warmed to Andy Gillespie, the boss. On the few occasions I had an audience with him, he seemed too ready to gloss over or ignore problems and issues.

It was clear that remote viewing had fallen on hard times. The three remaining viewers, Greg, Angela, and Robin, had kept marginally busy during 1994, working sixty-five projects, most involving only single sessions. All these were listed as "operational" viewings, though several of them were really simulations to try to prove to a new intelligence community customer that remote viewing could be useful.[5] In most cases, Robin's viewing seemed to be no more successful than it had ever been, though Angela later told me that Robin had done much better than usual on a series of proficiency targets. And, after Graff's departure, Angela had gone back to being frontloaded to launch her sessions. Greg later told me, however, that she complained loudly about it.[6] Greg, still using the coordinate remote viewing techniques we had taught him years before, had a number of successes, but was often gloomy and down in the dumps.

Dr. Hoover*, who was acting as the CIA's liaison to the unit continued regular visits, holding closed-door meetings with Andy Gillespie, monitoring operational projects and, on at least one occasion in early March, holding

*Pseudonym.

an office meeting for the Star Gate staff. It seemed he was sizing up the office, the projects, the people, as part of the mandated program review.

All this came to a head in June 1995, when Star Gate's fortunes, which had been steadily going from bad to worse, suddenly turned very black indeed.

Star Gate's death throes began innocently enough with yet another congressionally-mandated evaluation of the remote viewing program. To do the review, the CIA hired a research firm, the American Institutes of Research, or AIR. The contract was signed in June 1995, but the review itself didn't begin until July. Two outside experts were brought in to work with the AIR staff: a widely respected statistician, Dr. Jessica Utts of the University of California at Davis, and Dr. Ray Hyman, a psychology professor at the University of Oregon. Utts had spent a year as visiting scientist at the SRI remote viewing lab, so had familiarity with the research.[7] Hyman had been a critic of remote viewing from his first visit to the SRI lab in 1972, reconfirmed by his role in the discredited National Research Council study of 1988.

The reviewers were given less than two months to examine the results of a quarter-century of research. This was an impossible task, so the volume of material was reduced in two ways: Only ten of the hundreds of remote viewing and other psi scientific experiments would be reviewed. And *none* of the thousands of remote viewing intelligence sessions prior to 1994 were to even be considered.

Utts did most of the work evaluating what research data was allowed to be looked at (fudging the rules a bit to look at legitimate data she had been forbidden to examine), and announced when she was done that "Using the standards applied to any other area of science, it is concluded that psychic functioning has been well established."[8] Hyman's part of the report was largely a repeat of similar essays he had written in the past, and could easily have been composed without even examining the data. Still, he concluded that there was an unmistakable effect which he could not account for. He could find no flaws in the experiments or mistakes in calculating the statistics.[9] Yet, in the end, Hyman rejected the evidence, recommending against remote viewing.[10]

The evaluation of the operational side of the program was just as perfunctory. Having already rejected virtually all of the operational military remote viewing data—the three to four *thousand* sessions or more that had been performed prior to 1994 by two dozen viewers—the AIR based its evaluation on approximately forty sessions conducted in 1994 and 1995 by three demoralized viewers. This means the evaluators used less than *two percent* of the data to come to the conclusion that ". . . the remote viewing phenomenon has no real value for intelligence operations . . ." and ". . . one must question whether any further applications can be justified. . . ."[11]

The AIR executive summary states that: "in no case had the information provided ever been used to guide intelligence operations. Thus, remote viewing failed to produce actionable intelligence."[12] Blatantly false though this was, it was the message the media spread widely a few months later—that remote viewing had "never" been useful for intelligence purposes.

After reading what the AIR had to say, I was sure that the CIA intended all along to destroy Star Gate. The flaws in the report were so obvious that it was hard not to believe that the Agency had given the AIR evaluators their marching orders in advance to find remote viewing worthless, and to do it in such a way as to make Congress think the assessment had been fair. There are reasons why this may have been what happened. At least two Directors of Central Intelligence who were familiar with Star Gate during its final days, Robert Gates and John Deutch, were strongly biased against remote viewing. Just two months after the AIR published its report, Gates's negative attitude about Star Gate would be very evident during a *Nightline* interview with host Ted Koppel.[13]

Deutch, while an under-secretary of Defense, had reacted dismissively to a Star Gate briefing from Dale Graff and John Berberich in 1993. Graff was told by staffers that Deutch subsequently placed the subject off limits for discussion.[14] Deutch took over the CIA in May 1995, not long before the formal transfer of Star Gate was to take place.

Budding scandal complicated the picture. Just as was the case the first time the CIA abandoned remote viewing back in 1975, the agency was once again embroiled in controversy. The CIA was being accused of complicity in the murder of the spouse of an American citizen in Latin America, in peddling drugs to inner-city youths, and in engaging in other shenanigans. Some of these allegations turned out to be false, but the CIA was nonetheless the center of a great deal of suspicion and distrust. The last thing it needed was more controversy.[15]

The evidence persuades me that, whether or not in the beginning the Agency intended to use the remote-viewing program, as time passed the CIA decided to terminate it. I would like to be more charitable and think that the CIA was discouraged by the sorry state into which the unit had fallen by 1995. Whether or not this was true, it is clear from the chronology that the decision to terminate was made even before the transfer date: The contract between the CIA and the AIR was signed in June 1995. The review began in July and was wrapped up sometime in September, with the final report published on the twenty-ninth of that month. But three months *prior* to publication—on the last day of June 1995, before the AIR review had even begun—the CIA ordered Star Gate to cease operations. The doors were locked and the stragglers were reassigned to other jobs.

Previously, there had always been some other government agency willing to step in and rescue the remote-viewing unit. This time there would be no rising of the phoenix from the ashes. After twenty-three years, literally to the month, the skeptics had won.

There are those who don't believe the program is really dead. Some people who wallow in conspiracy theories think Star Gate was sacrificed to hide a much "blacker" remote viewing operation, secreted away somewhere in the basement of the CIA. But if there was any "conspiracy," it was aimed at destroying the program, not preserving it. In the end, Star Gate's protectors—John Glenn, William Cohen, Jack Vorona, Claiborne Pell, Charlie Rose, and others—retired, or were sidelined, and remote-viewing's enemies gained the upper hand. Over time, even most of the enemies retired—Generals Odom and Soyster, CIA Directors Gates and Deutch, and numerous lesser lights. But it was too late for remote viewing in the U.S. government.

Even if some champion had wanted to revive a government remote viewing program after 1995, it would have been difficult. Dozens of worthy intelligence projects went unfunded while Bill Clinton was in the White House, thanks to his lack of attention to the military and a Republican Congress eager to reap the benefits of the "peace" dividend at the end of the cold war. Cheap as it was by government standards, a program like Star Gate would have always fallen below the funding line in those years. As I write this, the war on terror has made larger budgets available for operational intelligence and new military initiatives, but now the infrastructure is gone. Only four of the former remote viewing personnel remain in government employ, and some of them are nearing retirement. A new program would require starting from scratch, which is always the hardest thing to do with a government program.

New beginnings have their benefits—institutionalized errors and bad habits can be left behind. But starting fresh has its drawbacks as well. Valuable lessons are often left on the cutting room floor; new folks have to relearn them the hard way, wasting time and resources in the process. Most of all, the will to start a new remote viewing program seems absent from the current military and government establishment. Ours is a conventional age where the *impression* of public opinion has immense influence on decision-making. What bureaucrats *think* the public wants seems often to weigh more heavily than creativity and risk-taking in the interest of what the public *actually* wants or needs.

It is a great shame that the government has abandoned operational remote viewing. Yet an unexpected blessing came of the CIA's axing of Star Gate. Declassified, it no longer need be kept secret. Thus, a program of great, if not yet fully-realized promise, was about to be sent sprawling into the full light of the sun.

32

Remote Viewing
Hijacked!

"All you need in life
is ignorance and
confidence, and then
success is sure."

–Mark Twain

Friday, June 30, 1995. I had told my boss at Fort McNair in Washington, D.C., that I would be in late. I wanted to say good-bye. I drove over to the Star Gate building on Fort Meade and found Greg Seward packing the last of his desk's contents into a cardboard box. We talked for a few minutes, then the two of us drove over to dilapidated building T-2561, to see if we could pry Joe McMoneagle's cosmic mural from the faded yellow walls. I had brought a hammer and crowbar with me, but it was quickly obvious that if we tried to pull the painting off the wall it would break into dozens of pieces. Reluctantly, we left it for the bulldozers.

After the unit closed, Greg and Robin spent two months at CIA headquarters finishing up an assessment of foreign involvement in parapsychology. Jeannie Betters, Star Gate's secretary, who had been with the Fort Meade program longer than any other person, found a new administrative job at the National Security Agency. Angela was reassigned elsewhere in DIA doing legwork at air shows for the people who kept track of the latest in foreign military aviation technology. Robin joined her after the two-month stint at the CIA, while Greg ended up in a technical intelligence assignment. It seemed that, except for Ed Dames still making noises in his effort to commercialize remote viewing, the discipline was in danger of fading away.

But in August 1995 an article called "Tinker, Tailor, Soldier, Psi" appeared in the London *Independent* newspaper, written by Jim Schnabel to accompany a British Channel 4 television documentary called *The Real X-Files*. Though it contained errors, the article summarized more accurately than any account up until then the story of the government remote viewing program. Schnabel quoted Mel Riley, Ed Dames, and General Ed Thompson, the former Assistant Chief of Staff for Intelligence who had been the driving force behind the creation of the Army remote viewing effort. There was even an anonymous quote from me taken from a telephone conversation some months before. I was still on active duty and relieved that Schnabel had protected my identity.

At the time, both article and documentary stirred up more interest in England than they did in the States. It was a year or more before *The Real X-Files* made it across the Atlantic to be broadcast several times on the Discovery Channel. The next shoe to drop was a Jack Anderson column that appeared on November 2, 1995 in the *Washington Post*. I had not yet told my wife's former boss about my role in Star Gate, but I had made sure that Anderson's partner, Dale Van Atta, had seen Schnabel's newspaper article. I had not expected him to write another column about it, but he did, using some of Schnabel's material, plus new information gleaned from some of his old sources inside the government. Even before that, Dale Graff had forwarded me a copy of the final AIR report which, though it was unclassified and bore a September 29 publication date, had not yet been seen by the general public.

All this was just a teaser for what happened next. On November 28, ABC's Ted Koppel had a startling revelation for his *Nightline* viewing audience: The government had been using psychic spies for decades. Until then, despite occasional news items like Jack Anderson columns and partial tidbits in the newspapers, the government remote viewing connection was still largely a secret.

I had advance warning from Dale Graff and tuned in to watch *Nightline*. On the show were Dale, Joe McMoneagle, Ed May, "Norm" (a CIA agent who had tasked remote viewers often and found them useful), Jessica Utts, Ray Hyman, and former CIA Director Robert Gates.

Koppel did an admirable job walking the fence between the two sides, which wasn't just show—he seemed to have an open mind about remote viewing. Operational use of remote viewing was depicted in a positive light, with some details of the Iranian hostage project and the capture of renegade Customs agent Charles Frank Jordan highlighted. Koppel interviewed Customs official William Green, who substantiated the details of the Jordan case.

Hyman was predictably negative. Gates said he was well-informed about remote viewing but denied that it had ever been used to make or inform policy decisions—a strange sort of remark to make, as that could be said of *most* of the intelligence that is gathered, since much of what is collected is intended to support operational and tactical decision-making, not broader policy formulation. Gates also stated that after 1975 the CIA had observed remote viewing from a distance and never used it operationally again. Understandably, "Norm" was reluctant to contradict his former boss, but in his introduction he strongly implied that, indeed, the CIA had taken advantage of remote viewing operational support until at least the mid-1980s. Neither "Norm" nor Gates owned up specifically to any of the twenty-nine projects that the CIA had asked Center Lane remote viewers to perform between 1980 and 1984, nor to its participation with the Remote Viewing Working Group sponsored by Jack Vorona at DIA until at least 1987.

The fall-out from the *Nightline* program was huge. The next day the newspapers and broadcast media were full of the news. Coverage ranged from highly skeptical to cautiously interested. McMoneagle was on an ABC network broadcast called *Put to the Test*, performing well on a double-blind beacon experiment. Hundreds of reports deluged the American public from the leading television networks, newspapers, and magazines.

Later, in December 1996 and January 1997 three more Jack Anderson columns about the remote viewing program appeared, the last on January 9, giving some details of my precognitive remote viewing of the attack on the USS *Stark* in 1987. (Coincidentally, that was the last Anderson column ever carried by the *Post*. After fifty years as a staple feature in the *Washington Post*, first under Drew Pearson's byline, then under Anderson's, the column was summarily dropped.)

News about the remote viewing program caught a double wave that was to carry it much farther than anyone could then have imagined. The first of these was a blossoming public interest in the paranormal, stoked by the television series *The X-Files*. The second was the Internet. The World Wide Web was soon buzzing about this weird thing called remote viewing that the government had uncloaked.

Incensed by the AIR report's cavalier assessment of remote viewing, I took advantage of the online world in RV's defense, writing a four-part review of the AIR report using unclassified elements of three file drawers of Star Gate documents I had temporary custody of. The review was posted by a number of Web sites under the pseudonym "Mr. X," a moniker given me by writer Mike Miley when I had refused to reveal my name when supplying him information for an article he was writing for *UFO Magazine* about Ed Dames and Dames's student Courtney Brown.[1] Soon the Internet, remote viewing, and broadcast media would fuse in a way no one could have predicted. It had to do with a then relatively little-known radio personality named Art Bell, an Air Force veteran with years in broadcasting. After working in Okinawa, Alaska, and California, Bell had settled in Las Vegas as a talk radio host on a local station based in the Union Plaza Hotel. Mostly focusing on politics, his show occasionally strayed to esoteric subjects.

Meanwhile, during the early 1990s, a wealthy Las Vegas land developer named Robert Bigelow had taken an interest in paranormal things. He wanted to use some of his money to sponsor a weekly radio show that would focus on topics such as life after death, UFOs, ESP, and strange events. Bigelow had hired a former research associate from the Princeton Engineering Anomalies Research (PEAR) Lab. Her name was Angela Thompson, and Ed Dames was also courting her as a viewer for his company, Psi Tech, about the same time.[2] I was sitting at my desk in 1992 in DIA's offices in Arlington, Virginia, when I got the phone call from Ed announcing to me that he had "hired" Angela Thompson as one of Psi Tech's sources. He had high praise for her, noting her background in experimental parapsychology at the Princeton lab, and her reputed track record in remote perception and psychokinesis experiments. "That's nice," I told Ed.

I was at that same desk not quite a year later when Ed called me again in June 1993. "Hi, Paul. I'm sitting here in a restaurant in Santa Fe with Angela Thompson . . ."

"That's nice," I said.

". . . And your brother Dave!"

I paused for a moment before replying. I knew Ed wasn't above trying to pull my leg when opportunity arose. "Oh, sure!" I answered.

"No, really. Here . . ." I heard some fumbling, and then a familiar voice came on the line.

"Hello, big brother. What are you up to?" It seems that the night Angela arrived in Las Vegas to start her job with Bob Bigelow, she was invited to an informal parapsychology discussion group held in the parlor of a local man named Alan McGibbin. There she met a tall, friendly guy named Dave Smith. Within three months Angela and Dave were involved in a steady relationship that eventually led to marriage.

One day, not too long after their relationship began, Angela was talking about her work in parapsychology, and Dave mentioned that he thought his older brother Paul was doing something in that same field. That sparked a vague memory in Angela about having seen the name "Paul Smith" on a list of people who had requested articles from the PEAR Lab about their research. Later that week, Angela was talking to Ed, and asked if he knew someone named Paul Smith.

"I think I'm dating his brother David," Angela explained. Eventually Ed acknowledged that a Paul Smith contributed remote viewing sessions to Psi Tech projects.[3]

Not long after arriving in Las Vegas and starting to work for Bigelow, Angela had received the assignment to realize Bigelow's vision for the weekly radio program, and Art Bell would be the host. The show would air for two hours every Sunday night, and be called *Area 2000*. A local news reporter named George Knapp and a woman named Linda Moulton Howe—known better today as a writer and documentarist in UFO and related esoteric subjects—were hired to read news reports on the program, and Bell did the interviewing. Angela's job was to seek out news stories and recruit guests for the show. Richard Hoagland, who made a name for himself writing books and giving interviews about the "Face on Mars," was one of the early guests on the show, along with UFOlogist Bud Hopkins, and others. John Alexander, the colonel who had introduced INSCOM's General Bert Stubblebine to "spoon-bending," was Art's first guest.

Bigelow eventually ended his sponsorship, but Art Bell's little show had become so popular that Bell decided to continue it himself, syndicating it out of his double-wide trailer in the tiny, former cotton-growing town of Pahrump, Nevada, seventy miles outside of Vegas. Ironically, my former in-laws had managed the only motel in the town a decade before.

From these humble beginnings, the Art Bell show grew exponentially, eventually reaching millions of listeners every night. The show's rise coincided with the public notice and declassification of Star Gate, and it was only a short time before the two trajectories merged. On May 31, 1996, six months after Ted Koppel's *Nightline* program, Ed Dames made his first guest appearance on Bell's *Coast to Coast* late-night radio show. His subject was looming natural catastrophes that he "foresaw" using remote viewing.

Ed was in typical form, with dire warnings about the future and catastrophes he claimed were bound to happen sometime soon. Some of the details were fresh, but the apocalyptic mind-set was the same as I and my fellows in the remote viewing program had come to expect from Ed over the twelve years we had associated with him. In true form, he warned that humanity would soon have to start growing its food underground if it hoped to survive.[4]

Ed's second appearance on the show two weeks later on June 14 ended with more tales of catastrophe, but the first half was about remote viewing. In it he took credit for having brought coordinate remote viewing into the government program and for turning CRV into an operational skill as the unit operations officer. He also claimed that he had run operations at what was then Center Lane in 1984 and 1985.[5]

Of course, none of this was true, since Ed was still being trained in 1984 and had no official dealings with Center Lane in 1985. It was largely Skip Atwater who, as operations and training officer, had made CRV operationally viable for the Fort Meade unit and it had been the staffs of INSCOM and Center Lane who worked with SRI to introduce CRV into the unit. Dames knew of the unit as early as 1982, but his only real connection, until he went along with us to SRI training in 1984, was through one or two taskings he levied through Systems Exploitation Detachment (SED), the office to which he was assigned.[6]

These few projects must have been what Ed had in mind during that second Art Bell interview when he said that Joe McMoneagle "was employed by me [Dames] against a number of intelligence operations." Ed later claimed that McMoneagle "had worked for" him. The truth was that Joe probably had no clue Ed had anything to do with those few taskings. It was around this time that Ed also posted on the Internet the inflated award narrative that Dave Morehouse had drafted for him, as well as other awards (dating from outside the time he was assigned to the remote-viewing unit) and officer efficiency reports to shore up his claim of being a large cog in the military remote viewing wheel.

On the Art Bell interview Ed promoted Psi Tech, both as a commercial operation, but also as a training venue, touting his modified version of the Swann/Puthoff CRV method. He was calling his knock-off version "TRV," for "Technical" Remote Viewing. For a time, Ed was providing his students photocopies of the DIA remote-viewing manual, just outfitted with a new Psi Tech "Technical Remote Viewing" cover.

On July 19, 1996, another personality proclaiming his remote-viewing expertise debuted. This was Courtney Brown, an assistant professor of political science at Emory University who was a twenty-odd-year veteran of transcendental meditation and a graduate of Ed's nine-day TRV course three years before. Based on those thin remote-viewing credentials, Brown had set up the "Farsight Institute," where he trained groups of people to become "professional remote viewers," using what he called "Scientific Remote Viewing" or "SRV."[7]

SRV was a quirky fusion of transcendental meditation with Ed's "TRV" version of the original Swann-Puthoff methodology, adding a feature called "sub-space," a source of information that involved something roughly akin to a pseudoscience-version of a spirit world.[8] Courtney Brown's first appearance on Art Bell caused quite a stir. He talked about remote viewing Mars and finding Martians living in underground caverns in the Red Planet—but not just there. According to Brown, the Martians had founded a colony under Santa Fe Baldy, a mountain near Santa Fe, New Mexico. Supposedly fleeing the hostile environment of Mars, the Martians were trying to figure out how to move to Earth *en masse*. They weren't hostile, just desperate.

Brown's next appearance on Bell's *Coast to Coast* radio program, which by now was claiming tens of millions of listeners a night, was even more sensational. At the start of the show Art Bell announced the existence of a photograph that showed a strange object escorting the recently discovered Hale-Bopp comet as it entered the solar system. Brown excitedly announced that shortly after the photograph had been unveiled earlier that day, two teams of his trained viewers had remote viewed the object. Based on three sessions, he concluded that the object was four times the size of Earth, was part manufactured and part natural, was crewed by intelligent entities, and had been sent by the "Galactic Council" on a mission to deliver a message to humankind. Brown claimed the government knew all about it but was refusing to tell the nation.[9]

Another interview followed two weeks later. Accompanied this time by his assistant, Prudence Calabrese, who was introduced as a graduate student in physics, Brown reported that an astronomer from a "top ten" university had verified the existence of Hale-Bopp's "companion," and that he, Brown, was in possession of a number of very-high quality photographs made through a large observatory telescope. Brown passed copies of those photos to Art Bell, who posted them on his Web page. According to Brown, the unnamed astronomer even confirmed that electromagnetic signals made by intelligent beings aboard the "companion" had been received by more than one major observatory. This scientist was to hold a press conference "soon" to verify all these findings, Brown said. For now, though, he was sharing private time with his family, preparing for the publicity maelstrom.[10] In the aftermath of Brown's second interview on Bell's show, the Internet once more lit up.

Weeks passed with no press conference from the putative astronomer. Then word started circulating that the photos Courtney Brown had so credulously accepted as real were hoaxes. Within a few months, Art Bell had received evidence that the photos were fake. Brown was subjected to a rancorous on-air cross-examination by author and radio host Whitley Strieber, filling in for Bell. Whether Courtney Brown's viewers had been beguiled by frontloading, or by coaching by Brown, or by telepathic overlay, we may never know, but it was soon evident to everyone that the planetary-sized spaceship "escorting" Hale-Bopp never existed.

This was only a minor comedy of errors until thirty-nine members of the "Heaven's Gate" cult in Los Angeles committed mass suicide to catch a ride on this non-existent spaceship. Though his Hale-Bopp shenanigans played only a supporting role in the Heaven's Gate tragedy, a shocked Brown retreated from the equally shocked late-night talk-radio world to his institute in Atlanta.

Brown occasionally sent out stilted proclamations or impassioned calls-to-arms to the president or, as some of my friends reported, to the Defense Intelligence Agency, trying to rouse government action to cope with imminent catastrophe or alien visitations. None of the predicted doom materialized. Meanwhile, Prudence Calabrese abandoned Courtney Brown's ship, taking blame in a manifesto posted on the Internet for "allowing" herself to be misled, and placing the lion's share of fault on Brown's alleged lack of intellectual honesty.[11]

Exploiting the discomfiture of his competitor, Ed Dames appeared for the fifth time on the Art Bell show on January 30, 1997. Ed crowed that he had known all along that Courtney Brown's attempts at remote viewing would come to a bad end because he, Ed, had remote viewed the debacle beforehand. Brown should have known that the whole comet "companion" business was a hoax. What there was instead, Ed claimed, was a large cylinder full of "plant pathogens" being delivered by the comet. These biological agents would destroy the majority of plant life on earth—and hence the lives of eighty percent of earthlings. If folks wanted proof, they could buy Ed's newly recorded set of videotapes for home instruction in remote viewing, and they, too, could see what he saw in the future.[12]

Ed's first deadline for the dreaded event came and went without incident when the comet passed the Earth's orbit. Then he announced on subsequent interviews with Bell that the comet had merely left the cylinder in Earth's orbital path, and when our planet swept around again to that same point, *then* catastrophe would strike. That anniversary date came and went and nary a drop of plant pathogen was to be found.

I almost played an unwitting role in this fiasco. A few days before the January 30, 1997, Art Bell performance, Ed called me up and gave me a set of coordinates, ostensibly for a Psi Tech tasking. My impressions were odd. I had perceptions of a bright, white, apparently self-luminescent cloud, that seemed to be slowly roiling and swelling. This led to an AOL of volcano, which led further to impressions of devastated houses and landscapes. I declared all this latter material to be overlay—my own imagination at work, since I had been hearing of Ed's increasing doomsday prophesies. In nearly any session I worked for him I had to reject these apocalyptic thoughts that always came to mind. I reported to him the results of this session, dismissively mentioning the destruction overlays, and saying I thought my data was quite unreliable.

"No, no," he responded. "You're exactly on. I want you to do a further session, putting your pen on the self-luminescent cloud, and tell me what is in it. I need it before tonight."

What was *in* it? I was dismayed by this. One thing that had struck me about the first session was that other than being pretty, there was nothing remarkable about the cloud. Having other things to do, I didn't get around to the follow-up session for Ed, and have been thankful ever since. From the Internet buzz the next day I discovered that at the time Ed asked me to do the follow-up session, he was preparing for the interview with Art Bell that night, when he was to make his "plant pathogen" announcement.

On March 25, 1997, Lyn Buchanan, Joe McMoneagle, and I were invited onto Art Bell's show. We answered questions and tried to clear up issues that had been muddied in earlier interviews. Listener feedback was uniformly positive.[13] Bell continued to befriend remote viewing, hosting a wide spectrum of researchers and remote viewers, including McMoneagle, Ed May, Dean Radin, and others. Dames remained a popular guest, too, appearing more than thirty times in the following five years, and many times more since.

As the Brown and Dames circus played out, other sensational events in the remote viewing world were brewing. One day in June, 1996, a large manila envelope showed up in my mailbox bearing no return address and a postmark from a Washington suburb. Inside was a sizeable chunk of the transcripts from Dave Morehouse's military court hearing and a draft of his "nonfiction" book. Some loose pages bore the preliminary title, "Comes the Watcher," which various of Dave's press releases had already been touting. But on the first page of the manuscript was a new name for the book, *Psychic Warrior*.

To this day I don't know exactly where it had come from, or how the anonymous sender had acquired the manuscript, but I found it hard to stomach. Masquerading as a true story, it was heavily fictionalized, and where it approached truth Morehouse had often taken credit for the impressive deeds of others. Dave elaborated his story of getting hit in the helmet with a machine-gun bullet and turned it into a supernatural experience, replete with otherworldly beings and ethereal warnings. He played down his misdeeds at Fort Bragg, and claimed the government tried first to railroad him in court, then to kill him for wanting to spill the beans about remote viewing.

When *Psychic Warrior* appeared in print, it garnered raves and sympathy from thousands of readers and a few reviewers, earning for Morehouse interviews on television and radio, and in print. An exciting story, it was bound to stir the pulse of anyone who breezed through it from one tense moment to the next. Most readers didn't know the story it told was largely false.

Even the thing that Dave tried to portray as the root of his trouble with the military—his alleged attempt to reveal classified information by revealing the existence of the remote viewing project and all the dastardly things its people were up to—can't have been true. During the time in question I was frequently in touch with the folks at DIA. They would often fret about Ed Dames and the things he was letting slip in public. But other than the flap that arose during Dave's court-martial hearing, I don't recall that there was much worry about Morehouse also having loose lips until he started issuing press releases for *Psychic Warrior*, almost two years *after* he was drummed out of the Army—and a year after Star Gate had been cancelled.

The truth was that, though Dave knew some secrets that could damage the security of the remote viewing unit as well as two other organizations, each of which he had belonged to for only a short while, it was really Ed Dames, not Dave, who knew the most secrets. Dave Morehouse had beans to spill, but they were mostly superficial or peripheral facts that could damage the unit's security envelope, and not much else. Ed, on the other hand, had many more things he could reveal if he so chose, and for several years he was making much more noise in public than was Morehouse. Ed had even started on a book project long before Dave had, and made no secret that he was working on it. Yet Ed was never stalked, threatened, or attacked by federal agents as Dave alleges he was in *Psychic Warrior*.

After being kicked out of the Army and publishing his book, Dave went on to teach and lecture about remote viewing. Given that Gabi Pettingell and I had a major hand in teaching him how to remote view, I want to believe that he is a good trainer. Most of the people I have met who have taken his courses seem satisfied with what he provides.

The other veterans of the former military remote viewing program were aghast at the carnival Dave, Ed, and Courtney were making out of something we had given so much of our lives to. Unfortunately, all the sensationalism detracted from not just the credibility, but also the appeal of remote viewing. After being linked to Galactic Federations, subterranean Martians, and planetary-sized spaceships, finding out what remote viewing was really like, and hearing the true story of remote viewing in its relative plainness was often a letdown.

There was a bright point in that oppressively dark cloud. Over a matter of months, thousands of people from all walks of life discovered remote viewing, and many of them not only wanted to know more, but wanted to try it for themselves. Coming through the portal of Dames, Brown, or Morehouse, they may have had things to unlearn. But at least they came.

The End of the Beginning

33

> "You can tell a man's age by the amount he suffers when he hears a new idea."
>
> —Marion G. Romney

Colonel Bill Johnson insists that the government remote viewing program didn't die because it didn't work—as he ably demonstrated, it could work well when managed correctly. It died because bureaucrats went out of their way to avoid risk. This pattern is true in any bureaucracy, be it civilian or military. People seldom rise to the upper levels of a large government agency by going out on a limb. Bureaucracies reward loyal subjects who play by the rules and don't rock the boat. In a bureaucracy, equilibrium is a divine attribute. And to support remote viewing was to take a risk.

But it wasn't just risk, it was also skepticism that defeated government remote viewing. People with influence didn't *want* it to be true. I quoted one of them many chapters ago: "This is the sort of thing I wouldn't believe even if it were true." As most human behaviors go, skepticism and risk-aversion aren't that far apart. They both have to do with uneasiness when something new turns up. Both have to do with keeping things the way they are rather than the way they ought to become. Risk-aversion and skepticism are comforted by the old and alarmed by the new.

The outcry over remote viewing that erupted at the end of 1995 when the cloak of secrecy was lifted made me long to jump back into the field. Revolution was again in the air, and I wanted to be part of it. But I had to wait to get out of the Army to do it.

When I finally retired on the last day of August 1996, my future stretched out along two separate paths, and it seemed like I ought to take them both. Afterwards, I often felt like a circus rider, with one foot on the backs of each of two horses, when the horses decide to part company. One path began four months after my retirement. In January, 1997, I founded Remote Viewing Instructional Services, Inc., offering training to those who wanted to learn the same arcane skills I had been taught while stationed at Fort Meade. Many of my retiring Army-officer peers were finding uses for the more conventional skills they had picked up in the military. Some prospered in high-tech companies, while others were living comfortably as personnel directors, business managers, commercial aviators, and so on.

I looked or applied for civilian intelligence jobs in several government agencies, but my heart wasn't in it. I believed in remote viewing, believed it would yet make a difference in the world, and believed also that I could help that difference be made. So, with crossed fingers and a few words of advice from Lyn Buchanan, who had, himself, begun offering remote viewing training, I set out to teach people what at Ingo Swann's request was now being called "controlled" instead of "coordinate" remote viewing. The new business accomplished two purposes. It provided a modest income and it contributed to an increasing core of individuals who had learned remote viewing and become quiet ambassadors for it.

But teaching people remote viewing was really the second of the two paths I had chosen. The first began as I was retiring, before I even thought about opening a remote viewing training program. To my wife Daryl's dismay, I gave up searching for a steady income and registered for two semesters of undergraduate philosophy courses at the University of Maryland. I was preparing for the Ph.D. program in philosophy at the University of Texas, where I was accepted with a small fellowship for the fall of 1997. I moved my family to Austin in time for the semester to start. My remote viewing training company moved with me and helped put me through my schooling—an irony that left some of my philosophy professors shaking their heads.

Academia might seem a strange home for someone bent on advancing the paranormal. But my interests were philosophy of mind, consciousness, and the philosophy of science—all relevant to remote viewing. Whether you aim to overturn the dominant paradigm, or only want to tinker with it, two things are essential. First, you need respectable credentials. Contrary to the popular misconception, paradigms are seldom moved by outsiders with radical ideas, but rather by insiders with insight and imagination, the respect of their peers, and letters behind their names. This meant getting a real Ph.D. in a rigorous and accepted field.

Second, the military intelligence motto is "know the enemy." For years as an intelligence officer, I knew more about the Soviet military than I did my own. To help midwife a change in a paradigm you have to first know it inside and out, to understand its strengths and weaknesses, to know what should and shouldn't be changed. Fools who rush to alter things willy-nilly to suit themselves can do far more damage than calcified scholars who blindly reject new ideas.

Major paradigm-shifters of the past—Copernicus, Kepler, Galileo, Newton, Darwin, Einstein (though I by no means count myself among *them*)—all followed both of these principles. They were educated in the old paradigm, and worked within it, but recognized the outlines of the new one and were willing to dig it loose from the sediment in which it was mired.

Some of my erstwhile colleagues recognized this imperfectly. So he could have a "Dr." in front of his name, Dave Morehouse, for example, obtained a mail-order degree from La Salle University—not the prestigious La Salle in Pennsylvania, but an unaccredited "distance education" institution in Mandeville, Alabama, with no real student body nor serious campus. As I learned on ABC's *20/20*, La Salle's reputation was not helped when its president was convicted of mail fraud sometime after Dave "graduated."[1]

Others of my former colleagues and their adherents had turned instead to fables and fantasies to get attention, weaving fantastic stories about alien-human hybrids, giant solar flares dooming all life, or comets on a collision course with Earth. They "promoted" remote viewing by making it notorious, and undermined its credibility in the bargain.

A number of former military remote viewers, scientists, and friends of remote viewing became increasingly worried about the anarchy that was developing within the community. Demanding unearned recognition or credibility, people with no real credentials were posing as expert remote viewers, or were offering courses based only on what they had gleaned from books and the Internet. Some of them even pretended to be former military viewers, apparently unaware how tight that community was, and that such counterfeits were easily detected. Wild claims were being made, to be countered by yet wilder ones from opposing camps.

As a first step in bringing order to this chaos, a group of us came together in Alamogordo, New Mexico, in March, 1999, at the home of Lyn Buchanan to form a new non-profit organization. We voted to call it the International Remote Viewing Association, and among the founding delegates were: Hal Puthoff and Russell Targ, together for the first time since Targ left SRI-International in 1982; Skip Atwater, who had established the military remote viewing program more than two decades before; Colonel John Alexander, who had worked for General Bert Stubblebine in trying to exploit exceptional human performance for the benefit of the Army; Stephan Schwartz, with his long history of involvement in practical applications for remote viewing; and Angela Thompson Smith, whose willingness to work hard and her experience reaching back to the Princeton Engineering Anomalies Research lab suited her to the effort.

Lyn and I rounded out the active participants. Facilitating was David Hathcock, an interested remote viewing student who brought the whole effort together and provided the financial resources that made our convocation possible. To serve as our conscience we invited Marcello Truzzi, cofounder of the Committee for the Scientific Investigation of Claims of the Paranormal. He had parted company with CSICOP years before, saying that it had become apparent its members intended to defend their own biases with the same vigorous disregard for truth that they attributed to their paranormal-believing opponents. Truzzi's impeccable credentials both as scholar and skeptic were tempered by a highly regarded reputation for fairness and objectivity. (Sadly, as this book was being finished Marcello passed away after a long battle with cancer.)

We decided that IRVA's first mission would be to serve as a resource for credible information about remote viewing. The association also would help to develop standards of success and ethical behavior for the field, and promote sound scientific research.

The first step was support to the "Controlled Remote Viewing Conference," held immediately following IRVA's founding meeting. Hosted by Lyn Buchanan's company, P>S>I, the conference met at a resort on the Ruidoso, New Mexico, Mescalero Apache Indian reservation. In this trial effort, about seventy people attended by invitation, and it was roundly praised as a success. Lyn's generous financial backing contributed much to that success.

This first conference was not sponsored by IRVA, but members of the organization's new board of directors provided the majority of the speakers. The second conference, billed as the "Year2000 Remote Viewing Conference" and held in Mesquite, Nevada, in May of 2000, was also not an official IRVA event. Instead, a small, ad hoc committee consisting of myself as conference chair, Angela Smith, Lyn Buchanan, a student of mine named Michael O'Bannon, and one of Lyn's students, Bill Eigles, put the conference together.

This event was open to the public, and appearances by conference speakers and organizers on national talk radio and in other media helped promote it. Among the noteworthy speakers were Jessica Utts, who had defended remote viewing in the infamous CIA-sponsored American Institutes of Research study, and widely known lecturer and medical doctor Larry Dossey. As banquet speaker the conference featured the legendary psychologist and consciousness researcher Charles T. Tart. Once again, though, IRVA directors with their long-standing remote viewing experience formed the backbone of the program.

The 2001 Remote Viewing Conference, held in Las Vegas, Nevada, was the first to be officially sponsored by the International Remote Viewing Association. Highlights of this conference were presentations from noted parapsychologist Dean Radin and from Apollo astronaut Edgar Mitchell, the sixth man to walk on the moon and founder of the Institute of Noetic Sciences, which itself promotes major research into consciousness.

IRVA's next event was the 2002 Remote Viewing Conference in Austin, which celebrated three decades of remote viewing, being held thirty years almost to the week from Hal Puthoff's and Ingo Swann's first experiment together in June 1972. Ingo himself was the keynote speaker, and Hal Puthoff spoke at the Saturday evening reception. Other remote viewing luminaries who spoke were Cleve Backster, the researcher who had been the go-between in first bringing Hal and Ingo together; Dale Graff who, as an Air Force intelligence analyst, had been instrumental in saving the remote viewing program in the mid-1970s, and had been active in it until his retirement in 1993; and for the first time speaking in such a venue, my old friend and colleague Mel Riley.

With my involvement in IRVA, organizing three major conferences and helping with the fourth, managing my training company, and carrying on my studies, things in my life grew ever more complicated. But I felt all these activities were important, and worthwhile. And gradually, my two paths began to converge.

One evening, while my family and I were still living in Maryland, not long before moving to Texas, an old friend dropped in for dinner. It was John Nolan, who more than a decade earlier had filled me in on General Stubblebine's mentally-bent spoons, when I had not yet even so much as heard the words "remote viewing" spoken together. After dinner we retired to the living room to catch up with each other's lives. I sketched out for John where I wanted to go with my education and with remote viewing. He noticed that Daryl seemed a little hesitant about the direction my life was headed. She has always been the practical one in the family, and where I saw a challenging crusade she saw bills to be paid, with three children in or near college, and one still in short pants. John asked her what was on her mind.

"I guess I'm glad Paul is doing something that's important to him," she answered after a slight hesitation. "But I have to admit that I'm not yet sure why, or if, this all really matters."

That was, of course, what it all boiled down to. What was it that *really* mattered about not just my seven years as a government remote viewer, but the whole twenty-three-year history of the program? Though the outlines of an answer had been forming in my head almost from my first initiation into remote viewing, Daryl's question still gave me pause. What *did* it matter?

There were some obvious answers. For one, I and my remote viewing colleagues had learned many valuable things. We had learned that remote viewing really did work. We learned how to use it for intelligence gathering, and how to be reasonably accurate with it often enough to count. But we had also learned that it took a team to make it work very well. That contrasts sharply with the gunslinger mentality prominent among remote viewers and would-be viewers today. All the focus is on the viewer. Much like in rock 'n' roll, where everyone wants to play lead guitar, everyone wants to remote view, but only an insightful few ever think much about the monitor, tasker, or analyst. Yet, without these roles, no real operational remote viewing can be done successfully. And without that, remote viewing might as well just be another parlor game.

We learned about analytical overlay, about how our mental processes can be their own worst enemies when it comes to trying to discover unknown things about distant places and people, and we learned how to overcome AOL, at least a little bit. In doing so we came to understand ourselves just a little bit better, too.

There were negative lessons as well—and it seems we are still living them today: We learned how reluctance to change and fear of the unknown could hamper progress. We also learned that human pettiness and jealousies could dampen or destroy the sublimest of endeavors, and that very few of us are immune from these failings.

Some of those lessons-learned were making their way to wider circles of people—to the American public, whose tax dollars had originally paid for the work, and to many in the rest of the world besides. And that mattered, too. It mattered that my colleagues and I at last got to talk about what we had been through. It mattered that others could hear about what their government had done, and why. It mattered to history. Unfortunately, it also mattered that some of what we had learned and much of that history was being distorted to satisfy personal agendas or feed egos.

However, maybe none of this mattered enough to justify me gambling with my family's security, to jeopardize my future, and to risk being sprayed with the same odor as tabloid psychics, channelers of Queen Nefertiti, and UFO welcoming committees.

But there was one thing that really did matter—something we had also learned at Fort Meade as we poked our minds through basement walls of Soviet bio-warfare labs, or "looked" for hostages in Lebanon, or helped interdict drug trafficking. That was that human consciousness is *not* locked within the narrow confines of our physical bodies, that it does *not* stop at the edge of our skins, but that within certain limits a human consciousness can roam virtually at will across the face of the planet, down the hallways of time, and into at least some of the secrets of men.

That one thing is very large, indeed. Despite our experiences, and what my fellows and I have thus far been able to say about them, that one big fact about human nature is not yet understood, nor even believed within our ruling paradigm. The life-span of a paradigm is usually measured in generations. Thus, the governing paradigm of a science (or of a society) has probably been around so long that everybody takes it for granted. They think its old thoughts and follow its old rules, and can't imagine any other way of doing things. Their paradigm is transparent to them, like water is to the fish swimming in it. Take the water away and the fish flops around desperately. Most of us are inclined to kick and scream when a paradigm starts to change. As a culture we like novelty—new fashions, new tastes—just so long as things don't change too much. As a civilization, we panic at the thought of tossing out comfortable ways of thinking or doing things.

People who think new thoughts don't usually set out to change the views of an entire science, or of a society. Instead, they come up with new ideas that often are at first rejected by the Old Guard. Eventually the Old Guard is either converted or, more often, disappears from the scene. In a saying variously attributed to Max Planck, Niels Bohr, or Max Born, "Science advances funeral by funeral." So it is a little astonishing, and maybe even a little haughty, for those who do talk of intentionally "changing the paradigm," to think they could do it on purpose and all by themselves. Or even that it should be done at all.

Our current scientific model has been immensely successful in helping us understand nature and the physical world. So instead of trying to change our current paradigm willy-nilly, maybe we'll discover that the borders of our current paradigm only need instead to be widened to embrace a few things that it, for now, discounts. After all, just because remote viewing shows we can perceive things in ways physics can't explain doesn't mean physics is wrong. It may only mean that our understanding of the world is incomplete.

Skeptics fear that accepting the reality of psychic functioning will destroy science as we know it. Carl Sagan's book, *The Demon Haunted World*,[2] is full of angst about how superstition and magical thinking will take over again as it did during the Dark Ages should science give a nod to the possibility that anything "psychic" might be real. I don't think that this "takeover" is bound to happen. Paradigms don't have to be overturned. Sometimes they just need a "tune up."

As credible evidence for psi continues to mount, I am convinced that science will eventually have to take notice. I do not mean that current "normal" explanations will be able to explain the "paranormal." These "weird" things will remain weird to science as it is now construed. But, perhaps not too long from now, science will be able to expand its tent to include remote viewing as well, just as it finally managed to understand (or in some cases merely accept) other formerly weird things such as the glowing stuff known as radium, or the bizarre particle behavior called quantum non-locality.

There is, however, something standing in the way of this paradigm "change," and it isn't merely the Old Guard of the scientific and skeptical establishments. It is the "true believers" themselves, the ones who so badly want to change the paradigm, hoping that their favorite paranormal phenomena will be accepted.

I have been surprised when disbelieving, even skeptical, scientists and academics I have encountered have been willing to change their views when shown well-attested evidence. Among this number are the chairs or former chairs of two major university psychology departments (psychologists are often among the most vehement skeptics); a few physicists, chemists, and a biologist or two with Ph.D.s from respected universities; and even an occasional hard-nosed-materialist philosophy professor. I am not saying these people accept and embrace the reality of psi outright. Rather, they are willing to entertain the possibility that it might be true.

In some cases their only prior exposure to the science of parapsychology was the same tired and often discredited criticisms lodged by specialty skeptical groups such as the Committee for the Scientific Study of Claims of the Paranormal (CSICOP). In other cases their only encounters were with true believers ready to accept nearly any claim, no matter how absurd, in preference to science. When scientists find that there is a third side to the story that is not only professionally handled, but has credible results to show, they may not become instant believers, but do become willing to listen. Unfortunately, the task of bringing scientists around is made much harder by the very people who most want them to change their minds.

Just like those clinging to mainstream paradigms, there are people in the old "paranormal" paradigm who don't want to let go of obsolete beliefs, either. Instead of realizing that remote viewing and other fresh approaches to psi have the potential of developing new ways for exploring the puzzles of consciousness, these folks want to entomb these new things inside the old attitudes and beliefs with which they had grown comfortable. Many a fortune-teller or channeler has decided that remote viewing is just another name for what he or she already does. Similarly, others try to fit remote viewing into their own long-cherished metaphysical belief structures.

The trouble is, the premises of many of these belief systems contradict each other. They can't all be right and—since remote viewing seems to work despite the variety of notions many out there espouse—maybe none of them are right; maybe remote viewing fits a different model altogether. Done right, remote viewing doesn't require arcane formulas or metaphysical beliefs to work. To think that it does hearkens back to a time when many thought the planets moved because invisible angels with fluttering wings pushed them around. The fact that the belief was wrong did not stop the planets from moving. The lesson to learn from this is too often lost on those who should profit from it most: While kernels of truth may be gleaned from old beliefs and practices of "being psychic," the beliefs in and of themselves often aren't particularly helpful.

Just as was discovered with planetary motion, there is a real cause, a "bottom line," to remote viewing. But we don't yet know what that is. This has contributed immensely to the hype, sensationalism, mysticism, and confusion that has grown up around remote viewing since it became widely known to the public after 1995. With the bottom line unknown, people feel free to speculate, and present those speculations as the truth, even when they often provide only imagined evidence in support. Remote-viewing "carpet-baggers," wanna-bes, and sensation-mongers have too often brought not enlightenment, but chaos, and continue to do so. Loud clamors for attention threaten to overwhelm the struggling sparks of light.

Attempts to tie remote viewing and other legitimate psi research into old beliefs and practices make it harder for mainstream science, and mainstream society, to take it seriously. Thoughtful people who would be willing to consider psi on its merits were it presented seriously, instead find it buried under speculative and superstitious trappings. What scientist would be inclined to believe anything from someone who claims to perform remote viewing after consulting with an extraterrestrial who drops in for a visit, or from someone who maintains that crop-circles are highway markers for dimension-hopping UFOs? No doubt the field will continue to harbor such folks for years to come. But, eventually, even *their* paradigms will change. With emerging initiatives such as IRVA, and with credible, well-grounded people moving into the field, remote viewing promises to have a real future, despite the distractions.

Most things in this world have an ending. Some come in due course, others are premature and unanticipated. One of these unforeseen endings occurred in the spring of 2002 as we prepared for that year's remote viewing conference. On Saturday, June 9, Garrett Pettingell, Gabrielle's husband, called to say that Gabi had been killed in a car wreck the night before.

The shock of this still rings in my heart as I type these last few lines. Friend, advisor, fellow instructor, student, remote-viewing tasker, and analyst—she had been all these things, and now suddenly she was out of reach, out of touch. If Gabi and I learned anything from the remarkable experiences we shared during four years together at Fort Meade and another twelve beyond, separated often by space but always in touch, it was that Bob Monroe was right: We humans truly *are* more than our physical bodies—or at least more than we have presumed our bodies can be. Remote viewing and other psi phenomena show that consciousness transcends the boundaries of space and time, giving legitimate reason to think that, whatever form our awareness may take, death is no end for us.

Gabi is not *here* to see it, though she must be somewhere; neither are Pat Price, Hella Hammid, Rob Cowart, nor Hartleigh Trent—all pioneers of remote viewing who have passed on. But the remote-viewing story is really just getting started. Science itself is on a cusp, on the verge of some new change, some attempt to reconcile with its past yet break out into a future—a future that may have room in it for something as revolutionary as remote viewing.

At the end of the 1800s, at the height of the Newtonian revolution, it was fashionable to talk of the end of science, to think that science may have answered nearly all the important questions that remained. As we emerge into the twenty-first century, that same talk has been heard. But it is just as premature now as one hundred years ago. What many dedicated souls at SRI-International (and later at SAIC) and at Fort Meade and elsewhere accomplished shows that there is yet much for science to explain. There are imponderables in physics; there are mysteries in cosmology; there are unexpected marvels emerging from complexity theory; and even as we unravel the genome new puzzles appear. The mind itself has thus far resisted all attempts to decipher it. The phenomenon that lies at the root of remote viewing and its sister disciplines nestles in among all those mysteries, all those holes in human knowledge. There is still so much to learn. And thank goodness for that.

Notes

2. Tour Guide to the Twilight Zone

1. Much of the description of Jack Houck's techniques are taken from the following sources: Jack Houck, "PK Party Format and Materials Required," (March 16, 1982); and Jack Houck, "PK Party History," (December 19, 1983), both unpublished. Additional explanation was provided in interviews with John B. Alexander, cited below.
2. John B. Alexander, interview about his background and about psychokinesis, November 1, 2000.
3. John B. Alexander, "Uri's Impact on the US Army," http://www.tcom.co.uk /hpnet/jba.htm.
4. Alexander, "Uri's Impact . . ."
5. John Alexander interview about the origins of PK parties, June 28, 1998.
6. Severin Dahlin, "Remote Annealing of High Carbon Steel Parts," in *ARCHAEUS*, volume 3, (Summer 1985). General Material Genetics Institute, November 1982, p. 1; and J. B. Hasted and D. Robertson, "The Detail of Paranormal Metal-Bending," *Journal of the Society for Psychical Research*, Vol. 50, No. 779 (1979), 9–20.

5. SRI

1. Harold E. Puthoff, lecture, Austin, Texas, September 1, 2000.

2. Biographic information here is mostly from Ingo Swann interviews, October 13–15, 1999; from Chapter 3 of Swann's online book, *Remote Viewing: The Real Story* www.biomindsuperpowers.com; and from a copy of his *curriculum vitae* he provided the author in 1999.

3. Material covering Swann's introduction to and participation in the parapsychology field comes from his *Remote Viewing: The Real Story*, Chapters 4–11; and from Ingo Swann, *To Kiss Earth Goodbye* (Hawthorn Books: NY, 1975), Parts 1 & 2.

4. Except as noted, the account of the "Tucson" experiment is taken from Swann, *Remote Viewing: The Real Story*, Chapter 17.

5. Swann, *Remote Viewing: The Real Story*, Chapter 33.

6. Swann, *Remote Viewing: The Real Story*, Chapter 37, p. 2.

7. Swann, *Remote Viewing: The Real Story*, Chapter 37, p. 3.

8. Sources for the account on the magnetometer experiment at Stanford University include: Russell Targ and Harold Puthoff, *Mind Reach: Scientists Look at Psychic Ability* (Delacorte Press, 1977) 20–25; Swann, *To Kiss Earth Good-bye*, 57–60; Swann, "Real Story," Chapter 37; Puthoff interview July 29, 2000 and lecture September 1, 2000; Arthur Hebard interview, August 7, 2000; Swann interview, August 15, 2000.

9. Arthur Hebard interview, August 7, 2000.

10. Harold E. Puthoff interview, June 9, 2000.

11. Harold E. Puthoff interview, July 29, 2000 (2).

12. Harold E. Puthoff interview, July 29, 2000.

13. Ken Kress, "Parapsychology in Intelligence: A Personal Review and Conclusions," *Studies in Intelligence*, Washington DC: Central Intelligence Agency, Winter 1977. Republished with addendum in *Journal of Scientific Exploration*, Vol. 13, No. 1 (Spring 1999), 69–85; page citations refer to this publication.

14. Swann, *Remote Viewing: The Real Story*, Chapter 53, p. 3.

15. Geller experiments, Targ & Puthoff, *Mind Reach*, 135ff; R. Targ and H. E. Puthoff, "Information Transfer Under Conditions of Sensory Shielding," *Nature*, Vol. 2, No. 5476 (October 18, 1974), 602–607; H. E. Puthoff and R. Targ, "A Perceptual Channel for Information Transfer over Kilometer Distances," *Proceedings of the IEEE*, Vol. 64, No. 3 (March 1976), 329–354.

16. Harold E. Puthoff interview, February 18, 1998.

17. Jaroff, Leon, "The Magician and the Think Tank," *Time*, March 12, 1973, 110–11.

18. James Randi, *Flim-flam* (Buffalo, NY: Prometheus, 1982), 131–150.

19. Changed without explanation to 3½ inches in the 1982 edition of *Flim-flam*.

20. D. Scott Rogo, *Psychic Breakthroughs Today*, (Aquarian Press: Wellingborough, Northamptonshire, UK, 1987), pp. 216–226. In a recent conversation (January 28, 2004), Puthoff told me that both he and Targ were well aware of the problem the hole in the side of the isolation room presented for the experiments, and they took measures to prevent Geller's cheating. Some of Geller's best "hits," in fact, occurred when the target to be perceived was located in a distant room or building, far out of range of any possible view through the hole.

21. Arthur Hebard interview, August 7, 2000.
22. Targ & Puthoff, *Mind Reach*, 172–173.
23. Ingo Swann interview, August 12, 2000.

6. Remote Viewing

1. Harold E. Puthoff and Russell Targ, *Perceptual Augmentation Techniques: Part Two—Research Report*, (Stanford Research Institute: Menlo Park, CA, December 1, 1975), 1.
2. Ingo Swann interview, August 12, 2000.
3. Puthoff and Targ, *Perceptual Augmentation Techniques*, 106*ff*.
4. Puthoff and Targ, *Perceptual Augmentation Techniques*, 116.
5. Ingo Swann interview, August 12, 2000.
6. Ingo Swann interview, February 25, 2000.
7. Ingo Swann interview, August 12, 2000.
8. Targ and Puthoff, *Mind Reach*, 27–30.
9. Details on the Sugar Grove experiment are from Targ and Puthoff, *Mind Reach*, pp. 1–4, and Puthoff and Targ, *Perceptual Augmentation Techniques*, 4–7, with added information from a number of informal communications with Puthoff 1998–2004.
10. Ingo Swann interview, August 12, 2000.
11. Kress, "Parapsychology in Intelligence," 72–73.
12. Ingo Swann interview, August 12, 2000.
13. Details for the Semipalatinsk project come from Harold E. Puthoff, "CIA-Initiated Remote Viewing Program at Stanford Research Institute," *Journal of Scientific Exploration*, Vol. 10, No. 1 (Spring 1996), 63–76; Russell Targ, "Remote Viewing at Stanford Research Institute in the 1970s: A Memoir," *Journal of Scientific Exploration*, Vol. 10, No. 1 (Spring 1996), 77–88; Puthoff and Targ, *Perceptual Augmentation Techniques*, 7–12; and Kress, "Parapsychology in Intelligence," 74–78.
14. Clarence A. Robinson, Jr., "Soviets Push for Beam Weapon," *Aviation Week & Space Technology*, May 2, 1977, 16.
15. Michael Dobbs, "Deconstructing the Death Ray," *The Washington Post*, October 17, 1999, F1 & F4.
16. Kress, "Parapsychology in Intelligence," 75 & 78. For an even more skeptical evaluation of Price's Semipalatinsk project, see Daniel Stillman, *An Analysis of a Remote-viewing Experiment of URDF-3*. Central Intelligence Agency: Washington, DC, December 4, 1975, (CIA doc. No. CIA-RDP96-00791R000200240001-0).
17. Targ, "Remote Viewing at Stanford Research Institute in the 1970s: A Memoir," 87.
18. Targ and Puthoff, *Mind Reach*, 97.
19. Puthoff and Targ, *Perceptual Augmentation Techniques*, 27–34.
20. Puthoff and Targ, *Perceptual Augmentation Techniques*, 66–75.
21. Puthoff and Targ, *Perceptual Augmentation Techniques*, 35–65.
22. Harold E. Puthoff lecture, April 8, 1999.
23. Puthoff and Targ, "A Perceptual Channel for Information Transfer over Kilometer Distances," 335.

24. Targ, "Remote Viewing at Stanford Research Institute in the 1970s: A Memoir," 79.
25. Puthoff and Targ, *Perceptual Augmentation Techniques*, 40.
26. Puthoff and Targ, *Perceptual Augmentation Techniques*, 38–57.
27. Puthoff and Targ, *Perceptual Augmentation Techniques*, 58.
28. Puthoff and Targ, *Perceptual Augmentation Techniques*, 58.
29. These insights were gleaned from 58–64 of Puthoff and Targ, *Perceptual Augmentation Techniques*.

7. What They Discovered

1. Kress, "Parapsychology in Intelligence," 78.
2. Harold E. Puthoff interview, June 9, 2000.
3. Dale E. Graff interview, June 11, 1997.
4. Harold E. Puthoff interview, June 9, 2000.
5. Harold E. Puthoff lecture, January 15, 2000.
6. R. Targ and H.E. Puthoff, "Information Transfer Under Conditions of Sensory Shielding," *Nature*, Vol. 2, No. 5476 (October 18, 1974), 602–607.
7. Regarding remote viewing and the electromagnetic spectrum: Harold E. Puthoff, Russell Targ, and Edwin C. May, "Experimental Psi Research: Implications for Physics," *The Role of Consciousness in the Physical World: AAAS Selected Symposium* 57, Robert G. Jahn (ed), American Association for the Advancement of Science: Boulder, CO (1981), 37–86. Also Harold E. Puthoff lecture, April 8, 1999.
8. The Grant's Tomb and Washington Square experiments are described in Puthoff, et al, "Experimental Psi Research: Implications for Physics," 59–61.
9. The Ohio Caverns experiment is described in Puthoff, et al, "Experimental Psi Research: Implications for Physics," 61–65. Also, Dale E. Graff, *Tracks in the Psychic Wilderness* (Element Books: Boston, 1998), 26–30.
10. Puthoff, et al, "Experimental Psi Research: Implications for Physics," 63–65.
11. Puthoff, et al, "Experimental Psi Research: Implications for Physics," 68–75.
12. Stephan A. Schwartz interview, August 29, 2000. Also, Puthoff, et al, "Experimental Psi Research: Implications for Physics," 51–57; and Russell Targ and Keith Harary, *Mind Race: Understanding and Using Psychic Abilities* (Villard Books: New York, 1984), 46–50.
13. Puthoff, et al, "Experimental Psi Research: Implications for Physics," 52.
14. Targ and Harary, *Mind Race*, 50.
15. Puthoff, et al, "Experimental Psi Research: Implications for Physics," 38.
16. Joseph McMoneagle, *The Ultimate Time Machine* (Hampton Roads Publishing Co.: Charlottesville, VA, 1998), 38.
17. Joseph McMoneagle, *Remote Viewing Secrets: A Handbook* (Hampton Roads Publishing Co.: Charlottesville, VA, 2000), xi, 22–23.
18. Harold E. Puthoff lecture, September 1, 2000.
19. Dale E. Graff interview, December 26, 2001; Dale E. Graff, *River Dreams* (Element Books: Boston, 2000), 59–68.
20. "Psychic helped locate downed U.S. plane, ex-president says," Reuters, September 21, 1995.

21. Harold E. Puthoff, *Feasibility Study on the Vulnerability of the MPS System to RV Detection Techniques* (Radio Physics Laboratory, SRI-International, April 25, 1979, rev. May 2, 1979); Dale E. Graff interview, July 23, 1999.

22. Dale E. Graff interview, July 23, 1999.

23. Harold E. Puthoff interview, February 24, 2000; Dale E. Graff interview, March 12, 2001.

24. "Report of The Grill Flame Scientific Evaluation Committee," Mr. Manfred Gale, Chairman, December 1979.

25. Harold E. Puthoff interview, July 29, 2000; Dale E. Graff interviews, March 12 and May 17, 2001.

8. Gondola Wish to Center Lane

1. F. Homes Atwater interview, June 10, 1997.

2. Atwater interview, June 10, 1997.

3. F. Homes Atwater interview, July 8, 1999.

4. An 8-page printed list of chronological milestones for the Ft. Meade remote viewing unit beginning in September 1977 and ending with a hand-written entry for December 1986. The document is untitled and undated, and was provided me in the mid-1980s as an aid in drafting briefings for senior officers. Hereafter I'll refer to it as the "Chronology."

5. "Chronology," 1.

6. Operations Officer's Log. Handwritten log of operational taskings and their dispositions from the first, Project 7901, tasked Sept. 4, 1979, through Project 8944, December 27, 1989. Log was maintained by F. Holmes Atwater during his tenure, and continued by subsequent unit operations officers. The original is in my possession. Hereafter I'll refer to it as the "Operations Log."

7. F. Holmes Atwater interview, January 6, 2000.

8. "Operations Log," Project 7907.

9. Atwater interview, January 6, 2000.

10. Atwater interview, January 6, 2000.

11. Atwater interview, January 6, 2000; Melvin C. Riley interview, January 7, 2000.

12. Compiled from the first several pages of the "Operations Log."

13. "Operations Log," Project 7904.

14. "Operations Log," Project 8009.

15. "Operations Log," Project 8020.

16. "Operations Log," Project 8023.

17. "Operations Log," Project 8028.

18. "Chronology," 1.

19. "Chronology," 1.

20. "Chronology," 2.

21. "Grill Flame Activity (U)," memorandum for the Asst. Sec. Army for RD&A; Asst. Sec. Navy for Research, Engineering & Systems; and Asst. Sec. Air Force for Research, Development and Logistics, Undersecretary of Defense for Research and Engineering, signed by William J. Perry, March 5, 1980.

22. "Grill Flame (U)—Decision Memorandum," memorandum through the Vice Chief of Staff for the Army for the Undersecretary of the Army, signed by MG E.R. Thompson, ACSI, Dec. 24, 1980. "Grill Flame (U)," message, from MG E.R. Thompson, ACSI, for MG M.R. Rolya, 111800Z Feb. 81 (February 11, 1981).

23. "Chronology," 2.

24. "Chronology," 3.

25. "Grill Flame (U)," letter, IACG, signed by MG Albert N. Stubblebine III, CDR INSCOM, Dec. 3, 1982. "Termination of the Army Grill Flame (U)," memorandum for ADCSOPS-HUMINT, IAGPC-G, signed by LTC Robert J. Jachim, Grill Flame Project Manager, August 24, 1982.

26. "Grill Flame Activity (U)," memorandum for the Asst. Sec Army for RD&A; Asst. Sec Navy for Research, Engineering and Systems; Asst. Sec Air Force for Research, Development and Logistics, and Director, Def Adv Research Projects Agency, Undersecretary of Defense for Research and Engineering, signed by Dick DeLauer, January 19, 1983.

27. Atwater interview, July 8, 1999.

28. "Chronology," 4.

29. Kress, "Parapsychology in Intelligence," 80.

30. "Approval of Center Lane as a SAP," signed by John O. Marsh, Secretary of the Army, June 15, 1983.

31. "Chronology," 4–5.

9. Outbounder

1. For McMoneagle's own account of some of these sessions see his *Stargate Chronicles*, (Hampton Roads Publishing: Charlottesville, VA, 2003).

2. Steven Emerson, *Secret Warriors*, (Putnam: New York, 1988), 111.

10. The Monroe Institute

1. F. Holmes Atwater interview, February 2, 2000.

2. "Chronology," 3–4.

3. Brian Buzby interview, February 4, 2000.

4. "Chronology," 5.

5. My recollections of the RAPT experience are reinforced by notes I took during that time, as well as interviews with Charlene Cavanaugh Shufelt (February 17, 2000), and Jeannie Betters (February 17, 2000).

6. Gen. Albert N. Stubblebine (ret.) interview, March 13, 2003.

7. Jeannie Betters interview, February 17, 2000.

8. "Operations Log," 22–26.

9. William G. Ray e-mail, January 26, 2000.

10. William G. Ray interview, December 28, 2000.

11. F. Holmes Atwater interview, July 8, 1999.

11. Ingo

1. Ingo Swann interview, May 24, 1999.
2. Harold E. Puthoff interview, February 24, 2000.
3. Ingo Swann interview, February 25, 2000.
4. Ingo Swann interviews, October 13–15, 1999.
5. Swann interview, February 25, 2000.
6. Swann interview, February 25, 2000.
7. Much of the material in my discussion here and in coming chapters of the Swann/Puthoff remote viewing theory comes from the notes I took in 1984 during Swann's lectures. This same information is more formally presented in *Coordinate Remote Viewing* (Defense Intelligence Agency, May 1, 1985), available on the Internet at www.rviewer.com/CRVmanual. Additional background comes from extensive interviews with Ingo Swann (February 25, 2000; April 20, 1999, and May 24, 1999) and Harold E. Puthoff (June 9, 2000).

12. Structure

1. René Warcollier, *Mind to Mind* (Hampton Roads Publishing: Charlottesville, VA, 2001), 10. [This is a reprint of the 1948 edition, with introduction by Ingo Swann.]
2. Norman F. Dixon, *Preconscious Processing* (John Wiley & Sons: New York, 1981), 94–98.
3. Norman F. Dixon, "Subliminal Perception and Parapsychology: Points of Contact," *Brain/Mind and Parapsychology*, Betty Shapin and Lisette Coly, eds. (Parapsychology Foundation, Inc.: New York, 1979), 206–220.
4. Harold E. Puthoff interview, June 9, 2000.

13. Stage 1

1. Ingo Swann, *Remote Viewing: The Real Story*, (www.biomindsuperpowers.com) Chapter 7, p. 2.
2. Charles T. Tart, "Card guessing tests: Learning paradigm or extinction paradigm?" *Journal of the American Society for Psychical Research* 60 (1966), 46–55. And Charles T. Tart, "Toward Conscious Control of Psi Through Immediate Feedback Training: Some Considerations of Internal Processes," *Journal of the American Society for Psychical Research*, Vol. 71, (1977), 375–407.
3. Swann, *Remote Viewing: The Real Story*, Chapter 7, p. 2.
4. Ingo Swann interview, May 24, 1999.
5. Terrence Hines, *Pseudoscience and the Paranormal* (Prometheus: Amherst, NY, 1988), 83.
6. Ingo Swann interview, August 12, 2000.
7. Harold E. Puthoff interview, June 9, 2000.

14. The Rusty Nail

1. Nancy (Honeycutt) McMoneagle interview, June 26, 2000.
2. Bill Schul interview, June 28, 2000.
3. "Jared Schoonover" (pseudonym) interview, June 24, 2000.
4. Gen. Albert N. Stubblebine (USA, ret.) interview, June 26, 2000.
5. John B. Alexander interview, June 26, 2000.

15. The Big Apple

1. Most of the details about our training and time spent in New York come from the extensive journal I kept during the period.

16. Sharpening the Ax

1. Ron McRae, "Beyond Gonzo," *Spy*, (June 1992), 50–56.
2. Among the columns that appeared in the mid-1980s were: Jack Anderson and Dale Van Atta, "Psychic Spies Might Help U.S. Explore Soviets," *The Washington Post* (April 23, 1984); Jack Anderson and Dale Van Atta, " 'Voodoo Gap' Looms as Latest Weapons Crisis," *The Washington Post* (April 24, 1984); Jack Anderson and Dale Van Atta, "Pentagon, CIA Cooperating on Psychic Spying," *The Washington Post* (May 3, 1984); and Jack Anderson and Dale Van Atta, "Government Still Involved in ESP-ionage," *The Washington Post* (August 12, 1985).
3. Gen. Albert N. Stubblebine (USA, ret.) interview, August 29, 2000; John B. Alexander interview, October 4, 2000.
4. Brian Buzby interview, October 4, 2000.
5. Stubblebine interview, August 29, 2000.
6. "Chronology," 6.

17. Stage 2

1. Brian Buzby interviews, February 4, 2000 and November 22, 2000.
2. "Chronology," 7.
3. William G. Ray e-mail, September 27, 1999.
4. "Chronology," 7.
5. "Chronology," 7.

18. Stage 3

1. "Chronology," 7.
2. "Memorandum of Agreement" [Concerning transfer of personnel to DIA], DAMI-ISH, signed by LTG William E. Odum, Army Chief of Staff for Intelligence, October 4, 1984. Also, "Termination of Center Lane Operational Activities," Memorandum for Record, IAGPA-F-SD, signed by LTC Brian Buzby, Center Lane Project Manager, October 3, 1984.
3. Michael B. Sabom, MD, *Light and Death: One Doctor's Fascinating Account of Near-Death Experiences* (Zondervan, 1998).

19. 1985

1. "Operations Log," 27–28.
2. "INSCOM Center Lane Project OPCON to DIA," [Memorandum of Agreement between INSCOM and DIA], HQ USAINSCOM/DIA, signed by MG Harry E. Soyster (February 11, 1985) Commander, INSCOM, and LTG James A. Williams (March 7, 1985), Director, the Defense Intelligence Agency. Also, "Deactivation of INSCOM Center Lane Project (ICLP) as a Special Access Program (SAP)," letter, IACG, signed by MG Harry E. Soyster, Commanding General, INSCOM, March 7, 1985.
3. Descriptions of the various sessions come from the actual transcripts which I was able to archive upon leaving the remote viewing unit in 1990.
4. William G. Ray e-mail, November 25, 2000.
5. William G. Ray e-mail, September 27, 1999.
6. James Bamford, *Body of Secrets* (Doubleday: New York, 2001), 389–393.

20. Stage 6

1. Jeannie Betters interview, May 29, 2001.
2. Charlene Shufelt interviews, January 5, 1999 and October 18, 2000. William G. Ray interview, January 2, 2001.

21. New Home

1. Harold E. Puthoff interview, February 24, 2000.
2. "Operations Log," 30.
3. "Operations Log," 17.
4. BG James Shufelt (U.S. Army, Ret.) interview, January 2, 2001.
5. F. Holmes Atwater interview, January 1, 2001.
6. William G. Ray e-mail, January 2, 2001, 4.
7. Atwater interview, January 1, 2001.
8. "Operations Log," 30. [Also, "S/T Projects" (Science/Technology Projects), hand-printed list, no date, no publication data, from approximately 1989, documenting S&T targets for remote viewing operations for 1986 through mid-1989. Hereafter referred to as "S/T Projects document."]
9. Gene Lessman e-mail, August 7, 1997.
10. Gene Lessman e-mail, January 19, 1997; Gene Lessman interview, January 29, 2001.
11. William G. Ray interview, January 22, 2001.
12. This dialogue is an imaginative reconstruction based on discussions with F. Holmes Atwater during the mid-1980s, and an interview with him on January 1, 2001.
13. Ingo Swann, personal letter, April 16, 1986. Original in author's possession.
14. Charlene Shufelt interview, January 15, 2001.
15. F. Holmes Atwater interview, July 8, 1999; William G. Ray e-mail, October 23, 1999.
16. "Operations Log," 38–45.

17. William G. Ray interview, January 22, 2001.

18. "Operations Log," 32.

19. Gene Lessman e-mail, January 4, 1997

20. Gene Lessman interviews, January 29, 2001 and February 6, 2001.

21. Lessman interview, February 6, 2001.

22. Steven J. Zaloga, "Red Star Wars," *Jane's Intelligence Review* (May 1, 1997), 205; and Chapter III: Strategic Defense and Space Operations, *Soviet Military Power, 1987* (Defense Intelligence Agency: Washington, DC). Also, see extensive background information on Sary Shagan on the Federation of American Scientists' Web site at http://www.fas.org/spp/starwars/program/soviet/.

23. "Chronology," 8.

22. Operational!

1. "Operations Log," 30–32.

2. Melvin C. Riley interview, March 3, 2001.

3. Gene Lessman interview, January 29, 2001.

4. Fern Gauvin interview, September 30, 2001.

5. "Operations Log," 33.

6. See the Federation of American Scientists' Web site at: http://www.fas.org/spp/starwars/program/soviet/dushanbe.htm

7. Evaluation sheet 1-A, 8701. [This was one of dozens of unclassified evaluation sheets I completed when I was assigned in 1989 to evaluate 28 remote viewing projects against foreign science and technology targets].

8. "Operations Log," 33.

9. "Sun Streak Operational Report—Project 8702," signed Fernand Gauvin, DT-S, June 15, 1987.

10. "Sun Streak "Operational Report—Project 8704," signed Fernand Gauvin, DT-S, June 19, 1987.

11. "Operations Log," 36.

12. William G. Ray interview, January 27, 2001.

13. Dale E. Graff interview, March 12, 2001; and William G. Ray interview, April 5, 2001.

14. "Sun Streak *Interim* Operation Report #1–8711," signed Fernand Gauvin, DT-S, July 23, 1987.

15. Details of this session are from my recollection and from the original session transcript in my possession.

16. George C. Wilson and Lou Cannon, "Iraqi Missile Sets U.S. Frigate Ablaze, Causing Casualties," *The Washington Post*, May 18, 1987, A1&A23.

17. *Formal Investigation Into the Circumstances Surrounding the Attack on the USS* Stark *(FFG 31) on 17 May 1987: Volume I, Report of Investigation* (Commander, Cruiser-Destroyer Group Two: FPO Miami 34099-1262, June 12, 1987).

23. Transitions

1. "Operations Log," 49.
2. "Sun Streak—Annual Report 1987," signed by Fernand Gauvin, DT-S, January 19, 1988.
3. Gabrielle Pettingell interview, August 13, 2001.
4. "Operations Log," 35.
5. "Operations Log," 36.
6. "Operations Log," 38.
7. These and following quotes from F. Holmes Atwater interview, July 8, 1999.
8. Gene Lessman interview, March 25, 2001.
9. Gene Lessman interview, January 29, 2001.
10. "Sun Streak *Interim* Operational Report #1–8709," signed by Fernand Gauvin, DT-S, August 25, 1987.
11. F. Homes Atwater interview, July 8, 1999. [Lessman (January 29, 2001 interview) supports what Atwater says here.]
12. Gene Lessman interview, March 27, 2001.

24. Mole

1. Dale E. Graff interview, April 1, 2001.
2. "Sun Streak *Interim* Operational Report #2–8710," signed by Fernand Gauvin, DT-S, July 13, 1987.
3. "Sun Streak Operational Report–8710," signed by Fernand Gauvin, DT-S, July 30, 1987.
4. "Report," July 30, 1987.
5. "Report," July 13, 1987.
6. Jeannie Betters interviews, May 25, 2001 and May 29, 2001.
7. "Sun Streak *Interim* Operational Report #3–8710," signed by Fernand Gauvin, DT-S, July 28, 1987.
8. "Report," July 28, 1987.
9. "Report," July 28, 1987.
10. "Report," July 13, 1987.
11. "Report," July 28, 1987.
12. Most of the details of the Ames case are taken from Pete Earley, *Confessions of a Spy: The Real Story of Aldrich Ames* (Putnam: New York, 1997).
13. Earley, 341.
14. Earley, 351.
15. Earley, 293–294, 299–305.
16. Earley, 117–119, 197.
17. "Report," July 30, 1987.
18. Earley, 298–299.
19. In a recent conversation Dale Graff suggested the possibility that another mole, this one an FBI officer, may have figured into our composite of the turncoat. Robert Phillip Hanssen, who also started his treasonous career in 1985, turning in to the Soviets many of the same U.S. intelligence sources as did Ames during the same period, came closer to fitting much of the description where we were

erroneous about Ames. It is plausible to consider that, because both spies were performing similar actions with similar bad effects for the U.S. at precisely the same time, our remote viewing reports provided an account blending both of them.

20. Earley, 132.
21. William G. Ray interview, February 1, 2001.

25. 1988

1. Gabrielle Pettingell interviews, April 5, 2001, April 23, 2001.
2. Mel Riley interview, April 24, 2001; William Xenakis interview, April 20, 2001.
3. Dale E. Graff interview, March 12, 2001.
4. "Operations Log," 39.
5. "Sun Streak Operational Report—8811," signed by Fernand Gauvin, DT-S, September 13, 1988.
6. Gene Lessman interview, April 26, 2001.
7. Gabrielle Pettingell interview, April 23, 2001.
8. "Operations Log," 38.
9. "Operations Log," 39.
10. Lyn Buchanan telephone conversation, June 16, 2000.
11. Edwin C. May e-mail, May 23, 2001.
12. May e-mail, May 23, 2001.

26. Bubble, Bubble, Toil, and Trouble

1. Gabrielle Pettingell interview, May 30, 2001.
2. "Operations Log," 39–45.
3. Pettingell interview, May 30, 2001.
4. "Operations Log," 45–57.
5. Pettingell interview, May 30, 2001.
6. Jeannie Betters interview, May 29, 2001.
7. Pettingell interview, May 30, 2001.
8. Dale E. Graff interview, October 1, 2001.
9. *Enhancing Human Performance: Issues, Theories, and Techniques*, Daniel Druckman and John A. Swets, eds. (National Academy Press: Washington, DC, 1988).
10. Ray Hyman, "A Critical Historical Overview of Parapsychology," in *A Skeptic's Handbook of Parapsychology*, Paul Kurtz, ed. (Prometheus Books: Buffalo, NY, 1985), 7.
11. John A. Palmer, Charles Honorton, and Jessica Utts, *Reply to the National Research Council Study on Parapsychology* (Parapsychological Association: Research Triangle Park, NC, 1988).
12. Palmer *et al*, 11–12.
13. Robert Rosenthal interview, January 21, 2003.
14. Graff interview, October 1, 2001.
15. Dale E. Graff interview, March 12, 2001.
16. "Jared Schoonover" interview, April 27, 2000.

17. Fernand Gauvin interview, September 30, 2001.
18. Graff interview, March 12, 2001.
19. Graff interviews, March 12, 2001 and October 1, 2001.
20. Fernand Gauvin interview, September 30, 2001; and Graff interview, October 1, 2001.
21. Gabrielle Pettingell interview, August 13, 2001.
22. "Operations Log," 40.

27. Mixed Results

1. "Operations Log," 31.
2. Gabrielle Pettingell interview, August 13, 2001. Melvin C. Riley interview, September 8, 2001.
3. Rodney Wallis, *Lockerbie: The Story and the Lessons* (Praeger: Westport, CN, 2001), 27–44.
4. Dale E. Graff interview, May 17, 2001.
5. "Operations Log," 37–45.
6. "Operations Log," 46.
7. "Operations Log," 46–47.
8. "Operations Log," 50.
9. Dale Graff interview, January 24, 2003. Fern Gauvin was Angela's monitor on this project, and confirmed details in his September 30, 2001 interview with the author.
10. Testimony from Customs official William Green, ABC News *Nightline* program, November 28, 1995.
11. Dale Graff interview, October 1, 2001.
12. This and subsequent information I obtained from twenty-seven sets of evaluation sheets assessing remote viewing projects against twenty-seven foreign science and technical targets (one of the twenty-eight targets was not evaluated). The sheets evaluated each session performed by each Sun Streak remote viewer for each target. Included in the data were who monitored the session, how the session was tasked (e.g., encrypted coordinate; photo in envelope; photo, name, or target description provided as frontloading; etc.) and what details were made known to either the monitor or viewer or both prior to starting each session. Hereafter I will refer to these documents as "Evaluation Sheet," along with the year and sequence number of the sheet(s).
13. "Operations Log," 40.
14. Evaluation Sheets 1988–7A&7B.
15. Evaluation Sheets 1988–7A.
16. Evaluation Sheets 1988–8A&8B.
17. Jeannie Betters interview, February 27, 2000.
18. "Operations Log," 39–57.
19. Gabrielle Pettingell interview, August 13, 2001; Betters interview, February 27, 2000; Gregory Seward interview, March 10, 2001; Linda Anderson phone conversation, November 9, 1996; Fernand Gauvin interview, September 30, 2001.
20. Gauvin interview, September 30, 2001.

21. "Operations Log," 52.
22. Taken from the feedback notes and copies session transcripts preserved by the author from that time.
23. Dale E. Graff interview, March 12, 2001.
24. Gregory Seward interview, March 10, 2001.

28. Lawyers, Drugs, and Money . . .

1. William P. Johnson interview, June 2, 1998.
2. William P. Johnson interview, March 15, 2002.
3. William P. Johnson interview, October 24, 1998 and January 25, 2003.
4. William P. Johnson interview, November 15, 2001.
5. Memorandum March 30, 1990, Subject: "Sunstreak Program," signed by Harry E. Soyster, LTG, USA. [Transferred operational control, or OPCON, from DIA to ODCSINT, the Army's intelligence staff.] Also, Memorandum, April 27, 1990, Subject: SUN STREAK, from DT (Assistant Deputy Director for Scientific and Technical Intelligence) to OC, GC. (Doc. Number S-136/DT), signed by John T. Berbrich.
6. Dale E. Graff interview, April 1, 2001.
7. William P. Johnson e-mail, subject "Review," February 13, 2003.
8. Johnson e-mail, February 13, 2003.
9. Johnson interview, June 2, 1998.
10. Johnson interview, October 24, 1998.
11. Johnson interview, November 15, 2001.
12. Johnson interview, November 15, 2001.
13. Johnson interview, October 24, 1998.
14. Operation Order No. 001-90 (Azure Sea), Headquarters, Department of the Army, May 24, 1990.
15. Johnson e-mail, February 13, 2003.
16. Many of the details of this trip are taken from my notes and journal entries made at the time.
17. Gabrielle Pettingell interview, April 5, 2001.
18. Details are from original photocopies of the final awards, transmittal forms, and narratives in my possession.
19. Operation Order No. 004-90 (Quiet Storm I), Headquarters, Department of the Army, June 10, 1990.

29. Desert Storm

1. Kent D. Johnson e-mail, May 27, 1998.
2. K. Johnson e-mail, May 27, 1998.
3. Dale E. Graff interviews, July 23, 1999 and October 1, 2001.
4. Graff interviews, July 23, 1999 and March 12, 2001.
5. Graff interview, March 12, 2001.
6. Memorandum for LTG Harry E. Soyster, Dir DIA, "Star Gate (U)," ICS 3585-91, signed by William F. Lackman, Jr., Acting Director, Intel Community Staff, May 22, 1991.

7. Graff interview, March 12, 2001.
8. Letter, September 13, 1990, Subject Sun Streak Program, from Director, DIA, S-340/DT, signed by Harry E. Soyster, LTG, USA.
9. Gabrielle Pettingell interview, August 13, 2001.
10. "John, Koda" e-mail, December 4, 2001. [I use the "Koda" pseudonym at this source's request, as he remains involved in sensitive military operations.]
11. This information was contained on an unclassified page in the Report to the Military Intelligence Board, Project Sun Streak, Control No. SWP-HDA-005-90, ODCSINT, HQ, Department of the Army, 1990.
12. William P. Johnson interview, March 15, 2002.
13. Melvin C. Riley interview, March 16, 2002.
14. Session summary for Psi Tech session performed March 1, 1992.
15. Edward A. Dames, "Final Project Report," March 14, 1992, 3.
16. Boyce Rensberger, "After 2000, Outlook for Ozone Layer Looks Good," *The Washington Post* (April 15, 1993), A1, A18–19.
17. Mark Henderson, "Ozone Hole Will Heal, Say Scientists," *The Times*, December 4, 2000.
18. Kathy Marks, "Ozone Hole to Start Shrinking and Will Close in 50 Years, Say Scientists," *The Independent*, September 18, 2002.

30. Coming Apart at the Seams

1. Linda Anderson interview, May 12, 1998; Gregory Seward interview, March 10, 2001.
2. Dale E. Graff interview, March 17, 2002.
3. Fernand Gauvin interview, September 30, 2001.
4. Jeannie Betters interview, May 29, 2001; Seward, March 10, 2001.
5. Gauvin interview, September 30, 2001.
6. Jeannie Betters interview, May 25, 2001.
7. Melvin C. Riley interview, July 1, 2000.
8. Dale E. Graff interview, October 1, 2001; and Dale E. Graff e-mail, subject: "Attachments," March 24, 2003 (contained in attachment ps–ch#4.doc, 6).
9. Linda Anderson interview, September 25, 2001.
10. Details on these experiments come from Edwin C. May, and Wanda L.W. Luke, "Phenomenological Research and Analysis" (Cognitive Sciences Laboratory, Science Applications International Corporation, Menlo Park, CA, January 6, 1992); and Edwin C. May, Wanda L.W. Luke, and Nevin D. Lantz, "Phenomenological Research and Analysis" (draft final report), (Cognitive Sciences Laboratory, Science Applications International Corporation, Menlo Park, CA, September 23, 1992.)
11. Dale E. Graff interview, January 11, 2003.
12. May, Luke, and Lantz, September 23, 1992, 20.
13. Gregory Seward interview, December 29, 2002.
14. May, Luke, and Lantz, September 23, 1992, 8.
15. Dale E. Graff interview, May 17, 2001.
16. Memo to Robin D. from DT-S branch chief "Andy Gillespie" (pseudonym), June 24, 1993, requesting her assistance in responding to allegations made by Mr.

Dale Graff that she had made comments of a defamatory nature about him to a person outside the agency.

17. These figures come from an untitled, undated, unclassified seven-page chronological table listing all remote viewing projects done at the Star Gate project from the beginning of 1992 through the end of 1994. Hereafter I will cite this as "1992–94 Project List."

18. Gregory Seward interview, October 19. 2001.

19. Interview with DIA Korean analyst, December 12, 2001.

20. Linda Anderson interview, September 25, 2001.

21. Joseph McMoneagle, *Mind Trek* (Hampton Roads Publishing: Norfolk, VA, 1993).

22. Linda Anderson telephone conversation, April 22, 1994.

23. Ed Dames telephone conversation, May 12, 1994.

24. Ingo Swann telephone conversation, May 21, 1994.

25. Ed Dames phone call, August 17, 1995.

26. *Psi Spies* (AlienZoo Publishing: Phoenix, AZ, 2000), v–vii. [While much of this account of the Dames/Morehouse dispute comes from my own recollections and journal entries of conversations with Dames and others, Jim Marrs published his own conspiratorial version of this debacle in his book.]

27. Gabrielle Pettingell interview, April 5, 2001, and letter, April 1, 1991; William P. Johnson interview, November 15, 2001.

28. David A. Morehouse, MAJ, USA, "A New Strategic Era: A Case for Nonlethal Weapons" (U.S. Army Command and General Staff College, Fort Leavenworth, KS, 1992). [Much of the materials in this thesis were provided by John Alexander, whom Morehouse had gotten to know through Ed Dames.]

29. "Record of Trial of Major David A. Morehouse by General Court Martial," convened by the Commanding General (Major General William M. Steele), 82nd Airborne Division, dates June 20, August 26, November 4, 1994.

30. Telephone conversation with Debbie Morehouse, May 16, 1994.

31. Ingo Swann telephone conversation, May 21, 1994.

32. Debbie Morehouse telephone conversation, May 24, 1994.

33. This account and much of what follows is taken from Paul H. Smith personal journal entry, June 8, 1994.

34. "Andy Gillespie" telephone conversation, June 20, 1994.

35. Subject: "Resignation for the Good of the Service—MAJ David A. Morehouse," memorandum for the Commander, U.S. Army Personnel Command, signed by William M. Steele, Major General, Commander, 82nd Airborne Division, December 18, 1994.

36. Howard Rosenberg interview, April 18, 2002.

31. Everything Melts into AIR

1. Jim Schnabel telephone conversation, December 12, 1994.

2. Report, to Director, DIA, Subject: "Meeting with Key CIA Representatives to Brief Mission/Functions of the Star Gate Program," signed by Star Gate Branch Chief ("Gillespie"), undated.

3. Gregory Seward interview, May 4, 2000.
4. Gregory Seward telephone conversation, March 22, 1995.
5. 1992–94 Project List.
6. Gregory Seward telephone conversation, March 7, 1995, and interview February 27, 2004.
7. Jessica Utts e-mail, subject: "Re: NRC or AIR?" May 16, 1996 and interview, May 1, 2002.
8. Jessica Utts, "An Assessment of the Evidence for Psychic Functioning," in *An Evaluation of Remote Viewing: Research and Applications*, Michael D. Mumford, Andrew M. Rose, and David A. Goslin eds. (American Institutes for Research: Washington, DC, September 29, 1995), hereafter referred to as "AIR Report," 3–12.
9. Ray Hyman, "Evaluation of Progam on 'Anomalous Mental Phenomena,'" AIR Report, 3–76.
10. Ray Hyman, AIR Report, 3–45.
11. AIR Report, 4–15.
12. AIR Report, E-4.
13. On Gates's negativity: ABC *Nightline*, November 28, 1995; Dale E. Graff interview, April 1, 2001.
14. Dale Graff interviews, April 1, 2000 and March 12, 2001.
15. Douglas Waller, "Cowboys in the CIA," *Time,* April 10, 1995, 43.

32. Remote Viewing Hijacked!

1. Mike Miley, "Room With an Alien View," *UFO Magazine*, Vol. 11, No. 3, (1996).
2. Angela Thompson Smith interview, May 1, 2002.
3. Smith interview, May 1, 2002.
4. Ed Dames interview, *Coast to Coast* radio program, host Art Bell, May 31, 1996.
5. Ed Dames interview, *Coast to Coast* radio program, host Art Bell, June 14, 1996.
6. "Operations Log," 19–28.
7. Courtney Brown interview, *Coast to Coast* radio program, host Art Bell, July 19, 1996.
8. Courtney Brown, "The Scientific Remote Viewing Manual Online," (The Farsight Institute, 1996). [The latest version is at http://www.farsight.org/SRV/SRVmanualindex.html]
9. Courtney Brown interview, *Coast to Coast* radio program, host Art Bell, November 14, 1996.
10. Courtney Brown and Prudence Calabrese interview, *Coast to Coast* radio program, host Art Bell, November 28, 1996.
11. Prudence Calabrese, "My True Confessions: An Objective Eye Turned Toward the Past," February 9, 1998. "Prudence Calabrese Makes Startling 'Confession': Former Farsight RVer Cites 'Bad Science, Bad Judgment.'" CNI News, February 16, 1998.
12. Ed Dames interview, *Coast to Coast* radio program, host Art Bell, January 30, 1997.

13. Lyn Buchanan, Joe McMoneagle, and Paul H. Smith interview, *Coast to Coast* radio program, host Art Bell, March 25, 1997.

33. The End of the Beginning

1. *20/20*, American Broadcasting Corporation, December 9, 1998.
2. Carl Sagan, *The Demon-Haunted World*, Random House: New York, 1995.

Index

About
the Author

Paul H. Smith, a retired Army intelligence officer and Operation Desert Storm veteran, spent seven years in the Department of Defense's remote-viewing program, serving as operational remote viewer, theory instructor and trainer, security officer, and unit historian. Smith has a B.A. in Middle Eastern studies from Brigham Young University, an M.S. in Strategic Intelligence (Middle Eastern emphasis) from the Defense Intelligence College, and is a doctoral candidate in philosophy at the University of Texas at Austin. He is president of Remote Viewing Instructional Services, Inc. (www.rviewer.com), and vice president of the nonprofit International Remote Viewing Association.